Business Market Management (B2B)

Understanding, Creating, and Delivering Value

THIRD EDITION

James C. Anderson
Northwestern University

James A. Narus
Wake Forest University

Das Narayandas
Harvard University

D. V. R. Seshadri
Indian Institute of Management Bangalore

Pearson

Authorized adaptation from the United States edition, entitled *Business Market Management: Understanding Creating and Delivering Value, 3rd Edition,* ISBN: 9780136000884 by Anderson, James C.; Narus, James A.; Narayandas, Das; published by Pearson Education, Inc., publishing as Prentice Hall © 2009

Indian Subcontinent Adaptation

ISBN: 978-81-317-3163-5

First Impression, 2010
Twenty-Four Impression, 2022
Twenty-Fifth Impression, 2023

This edition is manufactured in India and is authorized for sale only in India, Bangladesh, Bhutan, Pakistan, Nepal, Sri Lanka and the Maldives.

Published by Pearson India Education Services Pvt. Ltd, CIN: U72200TN2005PTC057128.

Head Office: 1st Floor, Berger Tower, Plot No. C-001A/2, Sector 16B, Noida – 201301, Uttar Pradesh, India.
Registered Office: 7th Floor, SDB2, ODC 7, 8 & 9, Survey No.01 ELCOT IT/ ITES SEZ, Sholinganallur, Chennai – 600119, Tamil Nadu, India.
Website: in.pearson.com, Email: companysecretary.india@pearson.com

Printed in India at Saurabh Printers Pvt. Ltd.

To Patricia and Rosella Anderson for
their love, understanding, and support

—JCA

To Grace, Ryan, and Jeffrey Narus...
thank you for all you do.

—JAN

To Sunitha, Rohan, and Amit—my strength,
inspiration, and joy

—DN

To Prema — who believed in me through thick
and thin — thank you for your love

—DVRS

Contents

Preface

The state-of-knowledge and state-of-best-practice in business markets have advanced considerably since the publication of our second edition. The third edition of *Business Market Management* interprets and integrates these advances within the framework that our first edition established. It also strongly reflects the changes in our views of business markets and what firms need to do to prosper. Significantly contributing to these changes in our views is our new co-author, Das Narayandas, who is the James J. Hill Professor of Business Administration at the Harvard Business School. Three developments in the third edition are especially noteworthy.

We now provide detailed discussion of customer value propositions in business markets. Arguably, "value proposition" has recently become one of the most widely used terms in business marketing. Yet, our management practice research revealed that there is little specificity or agreement as to what constitutes a value proposition or what makes one persuasive. Rather than formulating customer value propositions as all benefits or all favorable points-of-difference, as our research found that most suppliers do, we advocate instead that suppliers formulate resonating focus value propositions. Further, we contend that suppliers must substantiate their value propositions, drawing on value case histories or value calculators. We have added a section on customer value propositions in Chapter 4, but we also consider them at other points in our third edition, such as Chapter 7.

The other two noteworthy developments in our third edition primarily draw on Das' insightful contributions to business marketing. We have changed the title of Chapter 8 from "Gaining Customers" to "Gaining New Business" to reflect the new concepts that we have incorporated in this edition. When it comes to selecting individual demand opportunities to serve, suppliers need to apply the discipline and deliberations that they use to inform their market selection decisions. In gaining new business, suppliers should differentiate among the various types of potential opportunities that they are typically faced with—orders and customers—and the differential consequences these potentially have on the suppliers' capabilities. Orders are predetermined and little can be done to change them. For customers, as opposed to orders, suppliers do have to create demand by first educating prospective customers, and then winning and satisfying the business generated. The resource allocation needed to win customers is typically much greater than that needed to win orders. Having identified the opportunity type, prospecting for new business begins with an assessment of fit. Here, we introduce the concept of a *value stack*. Suppliers gain insights from using a value stack to understand and construct potential value that they can create in any new business opportunity. Mapping this value stack to the customer's decision-maker stack then provides suppliers with a blueprint for organizing their selling effort to gain the initial sale. The process of gaining new business ends with the supplier validating the initial designation of the opportunity types and then realigning their efforts in case of any mismatches.

The central premise in our revised Chapter 10, which we now title "Managing Customers," is that suppliers must move beyond just focusing on select customer relationships to actively managing their entire *portfolio of customer relationships* over time. To do so, suppliers first differentiate between transactional and collaborative customers, and then develop a clear trajectory on how to cultivate and grow particular working relationships. We contrast a foot-in-the-door versus an all-at-once approach to growing customer relationships, while ensuring an equitable sharing of the value they create. Next, suppliers can use customer loyalty and the cost-to-serve customers to construct a customer portfolio matrix. Insights from this matrix enable them to execute customer migration strategies that deliver superior customer value and enhance customer profitability over time. Finally, suppliers should look ahead and periodically revisit their customer selection decisions, since their skills and capabilities are affected by the customers they choose to serve and that, in turn, affects their ability to serve other customers in the future.

Our third edition retains the framework for understanding, creating, and delivering value established in our first edition. Chapters are devoted to each of the business market processes in this framework, such as Crafting Market Strategy, Managing Market Offerings, and Managing Customers. The same four guiding principles of business market management still recur throughout the third edition:

- Regard Value as the Cornerstone
- Focus on Business Market Processes
- Stress Doing Business across Borders
- Accentuate Working Relationships and Business Networks

Our third edition continues with our second edition title of *Business Market Management* instead of *Business Marketing*. Although our book is about business marketing, our choice of title continues to reflect our recognition that marketing work processes, such as segmentation, targeting, and positioning, increasingly take place *within* business market processes such as crafting market strategy and managing market offerings. Business market processes cut across functional areas and depend upon seamless cross-functional cooperation for marketplace success. Thus, business market management requires significant participation from many functional areas, not just marketing, to decide what market segments and customer firms are of primary interest (i.e., targeting) and how to deliver superior value to them (i.e., positioning). We think that business market management better conveys this broader responsibility for the marketplace, and this perspective makes our book of greater interest not only to those in a marketing functional area, but also to those in related functional areas and general management.

To formulate, test, and refine our thinking, as well as to gather best-practice illustrations throughout our book, we continue to conduct extensive management practice research with leading Indian, European, and North American companies. We have studied and provided examples from the best practices of companies, which will resonate most strongly with our Indian readers. These leading-edge firms serve a variety of business markets, providing offerings as diverse as chemicals, bearings, air cargo service, enterprise software, and commercial banking services. This primary research enables us to generate illustrations and examples that have greater texture and richness than do examples that come from secondary sources. Because this research is conducted with firms that excel at value-based market management, the illustrations and examples that come from them provide insight into how the models, frameworks, and concepts we present can be put into practice. Reflecting this continuing commitment, our third edition contains new breakout boxes, most of which have resulted from primary management practice research. Of course, we also continue to supplement the illustrations generated from our management practice research with numerous examples from secondary sources.

The intent of our third edition remains to provide the most progressive, managerial approach to business marketing and business markets. Whether readers are students with limited experience or seasoned managers, they will find the third edition a valuable resource, containing concepts, frameworks, and best practices that will stir up and advance their thinking. We think that our third edition delivers superior value in return for the time the reader invests in it, and we believe that after reading it, you will agree.

Acknowledgments

In writing the third edition, we interpret and integrate significant developments in the state-of-knowledge and state-of-best-practice in business markets that have occurred since our second edition. Although this makes writing the third edition easier than the first or the second, we have received significant support from a number of individuals and organizations to enable us to accomplish this.

Third Edition

Many individuals and organizations have provided support to enable us to complete our third edition. Although we are grateful to them all, we single out some of them here to explicitly acknowledge their contributions.

The Institute for the Study of Business Markets (ISBM), located at Penn State University, has continued to support our research and the preparation of the third edition. Without their generous financial support, we would have been unable to produce the revision we envisioned. We are thankful to Ralph Oliva, the Executive Director of ISBM, and Gary Lilien, the Research Director of ISBM, for believing in us and our work over the years.

We thank the many managers who so graciously took time out of their overfull schedules to meet and talk with us. The best practices that these managers shared with us made an enormous contribution. In particular, we single out a number of managers for their exemplary support and assistance: Steve Dehmlow, CompositesOne; Alice Griffin, Eastman Chemical; Robb Kristopher and Debra Oler, WW Grainger; Marcel de Nooijer and Eelco van Asch, KLM Cargo; Seth Machlus, Okuma America; Harris DeLoach Jr. and Eddie Smith, Sonoco; Peeyush Gupta and Anand Sen, Tata Steel; and Clay Flynt, Volvo Trucks.

Completing a revision requires many tasks to be completed. Over the course of this revision, we have greatly benefited from the capable support and assistance of two Research Associates at the Kellogg School: Abhinav Gattani and Akshaya Gulhati.

Finally, we gratefully acknowledge a number of individuals in Amsterdam and the Netherlands, which has become our "home away from home" while conducting our management practice research in Europe. Professors Wouter van Rossum, Marc Wouters, and Finn Wynstra have significantly influenced our thinking on business market management. Fred Tromer, a retired Heineken sales executive, continues to be a gracious mentor and "gezellig" friend. We again thank the artists and their friends at Verbeelding b.v. for the evenings of thought-provoking conversation and wonderful fellowship. Gerard Gooiker and our late friend, Eddy Agelink, are a source of inspiration for us, and we are indebted to them.

From Das Narayandas: I would like to thank Professors Benson P. Shapiro and V. Kasturi Rangan for their mentorship, guidance, and support over the years in developing the concepts presented in this book. I would also like to acknowledge the contributions of several of my colleagues and coauthors, including Dean Kim B. Clark and Professors Sundar Bharadwaj, Douglas Bowman, James L. Heskett, Robert S. Kaplan, Alan MacCormack, Rowland T. Moriarty, V. G. Narayanan, John A. Quelch, V. Kasturi Rangan, W. Earl Sasser, Benson P. Shapiro, John J. Sviokla, Stefan Thomke, and Steven C. Wheelwright. I would also like to acknowledge all the financial support and resources provided by the Division of Research at Harvard Business School. Finally, I am very grateful to Barbara Trissel for all her support and efforts in helping put together the materials presented in this edition.

From D. V. R. Seshadri: I would like to acknowledge that my contributions would not have been possible without the unstinted support of Rajiv Motwani, Participant of the PGSEM Program at the Indian Institute of Management Bangalore, and Shobitha Hegde, Research Assistant. The administrative support of T. A. Krishnamurthy is gratefully acknowledged.

I would like to thank my colleagues in the Marketing Area at IIM Bangalore, in particular Mithileshwar Jha, Srinivas Prakhya, and Ramesh Kumar, for their support, trust and faith over the years, and for giving me the opportunity to teach B2B Marketing in various programs of the Institute.

Senior managers from many top Indian companies have shared their deep insights on the practice of business market management in India. I extend my sincere thanks to all of them. I would specifically like to thank Peeyush Gupta and Anand Sen of Tata Steel, Achal Raghavan, and the senior management of Aravind Eye Care System, Madurai.

At Pearson, I sincerely thank Laura Ricci for a masterful job of editing, and Amrita Dhar for extraordinary and efficient editorial support in taking this project to completion. I also thank Amarjyoti Dutta for his guidance and encouragement. The support of A. Maran, and earlier, Rajesh Shetty, is gratefully acknowledged.

James C. Anderson
James A. Narus
Das Narayandas
D. V. R. Seshadri

Research funding for this book has been graciously provided by:

About the Authors

James C. Anderson

James C. Anderson is the William L. Ford Distinguished Professor of Marketing and Wholesale Distribution, and Professor of Behavioral Science in Management at the Kellogg School of Management, Northwestern University. Professor Anderson joined the faculty of the Kellogg School in 1984 as an assistant professor of marketing. In 1987, he was named the first to hold the Kellogg School's newly-endowed William L. Ford Distinguished Chair in Marketing and Wholesale Distribution.

Professor Anderson teaches the graduate-level course in business marketing. He is a faculty member of the Executive Master's Program and teaches in a number of executive development programs at the Kellogg School. He is the program director of the Business Marketing Strategy executive program. He has consulted and provided seminars for a number of companies in North America, South America, Europe, Asia, and Australia, such as American Express, ARCADIS, bioMérieux, Orkla, ExxonMobil, FEMSA Empaque, GE, International Paper, Johnson & Johnson, 3M, Microsoft, and PPG Industries. He is Principal of James C. Anderson LLC, an international management consulting firm focusing on implementing customer value management at client firms.

Professor Anderson's research interests are in constructing persuasive value propositions in business markets, and measurement approaches for demonstrating and documenting the value of market offerings. He has written more than 40 journal articles, including five published in *Harvard Business Review*. He has written recently, along with Nirmalya Kumar and James Narus, the management practice book, *Value Merchants: Demonstrating and Documenting Superior Value in Business Markets*, published by Harvard Business School Press. He is a member of the editorial boards of the *Journal of Business-to-Business Marketing* and *Journal of Strategic Marketing*, and has served on the editorial boards of the *Journal of Applied Psychology* and *Journal of Marketing Research*. He is a Fellow of the American Psychological Association.

Professor Anderson is the Irwin Gross Distinguished ISBM Research Fellow at the Institute for the Study of Business Markets and is a member of its advisory board. He also is a visiting research professor at the School of Business, Public Administration, and Technology, University of Twente, The Netherlands. He has been a visiting research professor at Eindhoven University of Technology, the Netherlands, and at Uppsala University and Stockholm School of Economics, Sweden. He also has been vice president of the business marketing division of the American Marketing Association (AMA) and a member of the board of directors of the AMA.

Professor Anderson came to Kellogg after three years as a member of the marketing faculty of the University of Texas at Austin. Prior to that, from 1978 to 1981, he worked as a senior research psychologist in the corporate marketing research division of E.I. duPont de Nemours and Company, Inc. He earned his doctorate in Psychology from Michigan State University in 1978.

James A. Narus

James A. Narus is a Professor of Business Marketing at the Babcock Graduate School of Management, Wake Forest University in Charlotte, North Carolina, and a Distinguished Research Fellow at the Institute for the Study of Business Markets at the Pennsylvania State University. He joined the faculty of the Babcock School in 1988. Professor Narus' teaching, research, and consulting interests include value-based marketing, the management of market offerings, distribution channel design and management, and partnerships and networks within business markets.

Professor Narus routinely teaches courses on business-to-business marketing, marketing channel management, and marketing management in the Babcock School's full-time, evening, executive, and Charlotte MBA programs. His career and teaching portfolio also includes such courses as strategic account management, sales management, marketing strategy and policy, brand management, and advertising management. Over the years, Professor Narus has taught in executive development programs at Northwestern University, the Pennsylvania State University, the University of Texas at Austin, and Texas A&M University, as well as in international management seminars at the Universidad Torcuato Di Tella (Argentina), the University of Budapest (Hungary), the Copenhagen Business School (Denmark), Bordeaux School of Management (France), University College Dublin (Ireland), Dublin Institute of Technology (Ireland), Management Centre Europe (Belgium), Irish Management Institute (Ireland), and Twente University (The Netherlands).

Professor Narus has written numerous articles and research papers on business market management topics. These articles have appeared in the *Harvard Business Review, Sloan Management Review, California Management Review,* and the *Journal of Marketing,* among other journals.

Along with Professor James C. Anderson of the Kellogg Graduate School of Northwestern University and Professor Nirmalya Kumar of the London Business School, Professor Narus is co-author of the book, *Value Merchants*. Professor Narus also authored the book, *Connect with Your Suppliers: A Wholesaler-Distributor's Guide to Electronic Communications Systems,* which was published in June 2005.

Professor Narus is a member of the editorial review boards of the *Journal of Business-to-Business Marketing* and the *Journal of Marketing Channels,* as well as an ad hoc reviewer for several other publications. He is a longstanding member of the American Marketing Association. For seven years, he served as the coordinator of its Business-to-Business Marketing Special Interest Group. Professor Narus belongs to the NAPM – Carolinas and Virginia, an affiliate of the Institute for Supply Management, and is president of the Charlotte North Rotary Club.

Professor Narus has provided management consulting expertise or executive training seminars for numerous corporations including the Allen-Bradley Company, Bunge Corporation, Ciba, Corning Cable Systems, DuPont, Eastman Chemicals, Gardner-Denver Corporation, General Motors, S. C. Johnson, McKinsey & Company, Merck, Pacific Technologies, Parker-Hannifin Corporation, Rockwell Automation, and the Toronto Dominion Bank. Prior to his academic career, Professor Narus worked as a market research analyst and fellow in the corporate marketing research division of E.I. duPont de Nemours and Company, Inc. There, he conducted studies on a variety of issues related to distribution channel management. He earned his doctorate in marketing management from Syracuse University in 1981.

Das Narayandas

Das Narayandas is the James J. Hill Professor of Business Administration at the Harvard Business School. He is currently the Co-Chair of Harvard Business School (HBS) Executive Education's Program for Leadership Development. His academic credentials include a Bachelor of Technology degree in Engineering from the Indian Institute of Technology, a Post-Graduate Diploma in Management from the Indian Institute of Management, and a Ph.D. in Management from Purdue University.

Previously, Das taught the Business Marketing Strategy Elective in the MBA program at Harvard Business School (HBS) for seven years. During this time, he was elected as the Class Day faculty speaker (MBA Classes of 2001 and 2004) and has received the award for teaching excellence from the graduating HBS MBA Classes of 2000 and 2003. He was subsequently the head of the core marketing course in the required curriculum of the MBA program at HBS. He has also received the Greenhill Award that recognizes members of the HBS community who have made significant contributions to the School.

Das's background includes over six years of management experience in business marketing and sales for various multinational firms that involved field strategy development, sales and salesforce management, new product development, alliance formation, and marketing communications. Das's research interests focus on the management of customer relationships in business markets. His articles have appeared in publications that include *Harvard Business Review, Journal of Marketing, Journal of Service Research, Journal of the Academy of Marketing Science, Journal of Marketing Research,* and *Sloan Management Review.* Das has been quoted in publications such as *The Economist* and *U.S. News and World Report* among others. He is an ISBM Distinguished Research Fellow at the Institute for the Study of Business Markets and a professional affiliate of the American Marketing Association.

Das has consulted and/or developed and executed in-house training programs for such companies as Areva, Arrow Electronics, Alghanim Group, GE, Honeywell, IBM, ING, Oce, J&J, Northrop Grumman, RBS, Stryker, Merrill Lynch, Tata Group, ThyssenKrupp, Fidelity, Satyam, Liberty Mutual, 3M, Microsoft, Nortel, and Praxair in the areas of Business Marketing Strategy, Customer Management, Strategic Marketing, Pricing, Personal Selling and Sales Management.

D. V. R. SESHADRI

D. V. R. Seshadri is currently a visiting faculty member at Indian Institute of Management Bangalore in the Marketing Area. His areas of interest are business-to-business marketing, entrepreneurship, and corporate entrepreneurship. He holds a B.Tech. (Mechanical Engineering) from Indian Institute of Technology Madras, M.S. (Engineering Sciences) from University of California, and a Fellow title (Doctorate) from Indian Institute of Management Ahmedabad. He has over 15 years of industrial experience, including a five-year stint at Madras Refineries Limited.

He teaches extensively in the various long-term programs at IIM Bangalore as well as in various executive education programs for companies such as L&T, Areva, Siemens, TCS, Infosys, Murugappa Group, Tata Steel, SKF, etc. He also teaches business-to-business marketing in the PGPX Program (Executive MBA) at IIM Ahmedabad.

He has authored over a dozen articles in refereed journals, developed over 70 case studies in his areas of interest, and recently co-authored two books, *Innovation Management and Global Risk/Global Opportunity*, both with Shlomo Maital, Israel, published by Sage (India).

Section I

Introduction and Overview

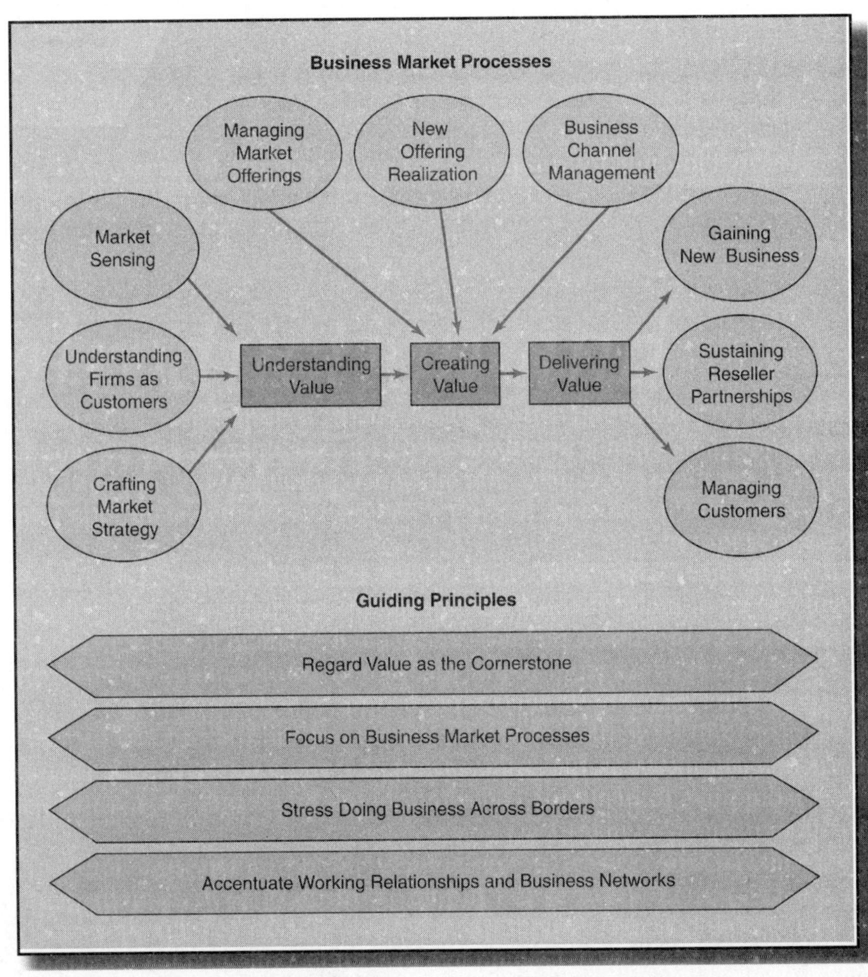

Chapter 1

Business Market Management

Guiding Principles

Overview

Much attention in recent years has been given to value and its provision to customers. However, remarkably few firms have the capability to actually assess value in practice and gain an equitable return for the value they deliver to customers. Although many supplier firm managers tout the value their market offerings provide customers, those managers have little to say when pressed for specifics on what their market offerings are actually worth to customers. One firm's stationery and business cards boast: "Delivering Superior Value with *Alpha* and *Beta* Brands."[1] Yet, when senior management was asked what actual assessments had been done to understand the value of their firm's offerings, they answered that the firm had not done any. Perhaps the firm was delivering superior value. What is more in doubt is whether the firm was receiving an equitable return, or if it was simply giving value away.

Because a large percentage of the typical firm's revenues go to pay for goods and services it acquires from suppliers, firms increasingly focus on their purchasing practices to improve profitability. Widespread quality management in production and greater availability of comparable market offerings from international sources have led firms to pressure their suppliers to reduce prices and provide discounts.[2] As a result, suppliers in many industries find that, although their sales revenues are growing, it is often at the expense of profitability. To persuade customer managers to focus on total costs rather than simply on acquisition price, suppliers must have an accurate understanding of what the customer firm values and *would* value.

For a moment, put yourself in the role of a commercial grower of millet in Haryana, where a large percentage of India's millet is grown. Millet is used both for human consumption and for animal feed. Two suppliers are offering you hybrid seeds, which are used for millet cultivation. One supplier comes to you with the proposition, "Trust us, our seeds will increase your production." The other supplier comes to you with the proposition, "We will supply you with improved seeds which will translate to INR 630 per hectare in terms of additional revenue because of their ability to prevent disease, increase crop yield, and lessen the effects of drought." Which supplier's proposition do you find most persuasive?

Business market management is the process of understanding, creating, and delivering value to targeted business markets and customers. Business market management provides a means of gaining an equitable return on the value delivered and of enhancing a supplier firm's present and future profitability. It is a progressive way of thinking about business markets and what supplier firms are attempting to accomplish in them. **Business markets** are firms, institutions, or governments that acquire goods and services either for their own use, to incorporate into the products or services that they produce, or for resale along with other products and services to other firms, institutions, or governments. By this definition, a professional painter's purchase of paint brushes from a mass merchant such as Big Bazaar would be a business market transaction, whereas a homeowner's purchase of the same paint brushes from the same mass merchant, to paint his own home, would be a consumer market transaction.

This chapter provides an overview of business market management. In doing so, it also provides an overview for this book, which is organized around nine constituent processes of business market management. Some fundamental ideas recur throughout this book. We think of these ideas as guiding principles of business market management:

- Regard value as the *cornerstone* of business market management
- Focus on business market processes
- Stress doing business across borders
- Accentuate working relationships and business networks

We sketch the business market processes and guiding principles of business market management in Figure 1.1. The figure organizes the business market processes, which constitute business market management, into three groups, based on whether they are a part of understanding, creating, or delivering value. We devote a chapter to each business market process. In the following sections of this chapter, we discuss each guiding principle.

Figure 1.1 Business Market Management

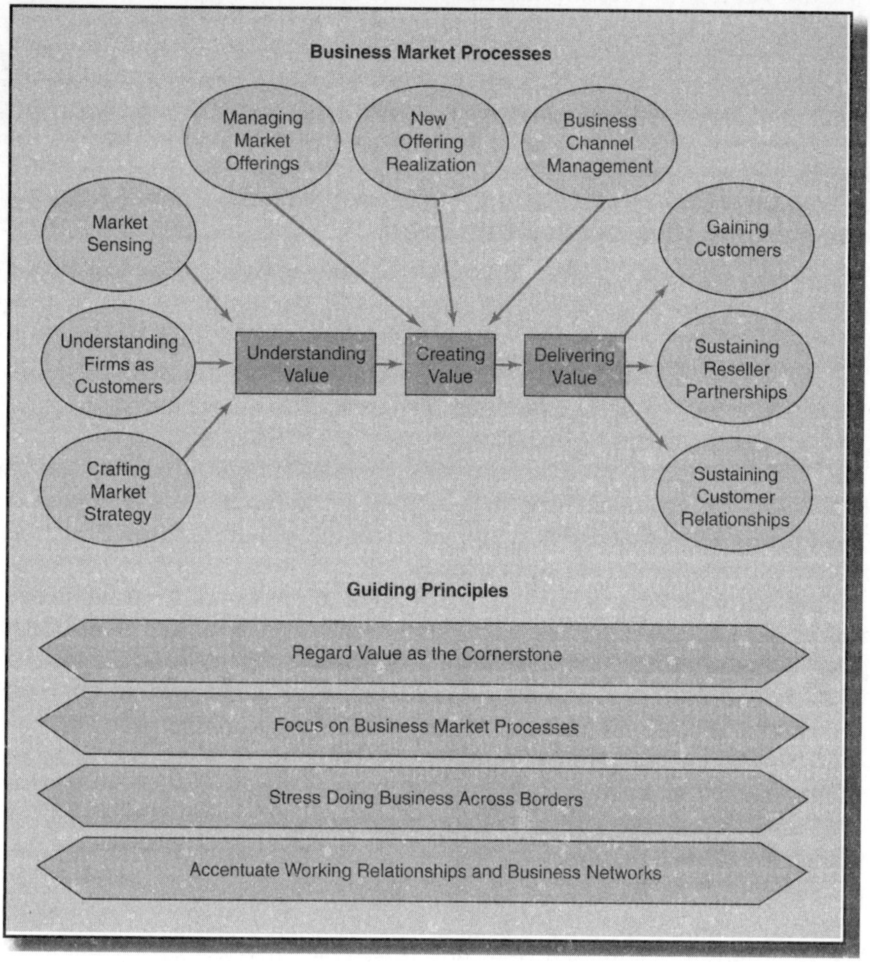

VALUE AS THE CORNERSTONE OF BUSINESS MARKET MANAGEMENT

One distinction between business markets and consumer markets is that customers in business markets predominantly focus on functionality or performance, whereas customers in consumer markets predominantly focus on aesthetics or taste. In each case, most decisions are driven predominantly, but not exclusively, by these considerations.[3] For example, it would be difficult to imagine a plant manager saying, "I bought the machine tool from Supplier X, rather than Supplier Y, because I wanted green instead of blue." However, if the plant manager judged the performance of the two machine tools in her particular application to be the same in all significant respects, then she might choose on the basis of aesthetics or taste.

We use value to express in monetary terms the functionality or performance of a market offering in a given customer application.[4] We regard value as the cornerstone of business market management because of the predominant role that functionality or performance plays in business markets. We first discuss exactly what value is in business markets, and then, how business market management crucially relies on the assessment of value.

What Is Value in Business Markets?

More formally, **value in business markets** is the worth in monetary terms of the economic, technical, service, and social benefits a customer firm receives in exchange for the price it pays for a market offering.[5] We want to elaborate on some aspects of this definition.

First, we express value in monetary terms, such as INR per kilogram, dollars per unit, euros per liter, or kroner per hour. Economists may care about "utils," but we have never met a manager who did.

Second, we can conceptually represent any market offering as a set of economic, technical, service, and social benefits a customer firm receives. By benefits, we mean *net* benefits, where any costs a customer incurs in obtaining the desired benefits, except for purchase price, are also included.[6]

Third, value is what a customer firm gets in exchange for the price it pays. Therefore, we conceptually view a market offering as having two elemental characteristics: value and price.

Finally, considerations of value take place within some context. Even when no direct, in-kind market offerings exist, there is always a competitive alternative. In business markets, one competitive alternative may be that the customer firm decides to make the product itself rather than purchase it from outside suppliers.

We can capture the essence of the concepts in our definition of value in a **fundamental value equation**:

$$(\text{Value}_f - \text{Price}_f) > (\text{Value}_a - \text{Price}_a) \qquad \textbf{(1.1)}$$

where Value_f and Price_f are the value and price of a particular firm's market offering (Offering_f), and Value_a and Price_a are the value and price of the next-best-alternative market offering (Offering_a). This equation will prove useful at a number of points in this book, such as when we consider value-based pricing in Chapter 5.

Note that we have not specified a particular perspective in our definition of value, such as the customer firm's point of view, because we regard value in business markets as a construct, similar to market share. Because it is a construct, in practice, we can only *estimate* value, just as we can only estimate market share. For example, the supplier may *overestimate* the value of a given market offering to a customer, while the customer may *underestimate* the value. The supplier may have a significantly different perception from the customer of the technical, economic, service, and social benefits that the customer firm actually receives from a market offering, or of what specific benefits are actually worth in monetary terms to the customer.

Value changes occur in two fundamental ways.[7] First, a market offering could provide the same functionality or performance while its cost to the customer changes. Remember, price is *not* considered in this cost. Thus, the technical, service, and social benefits remain constant while the economic benefits change. For example, one product has higher value than another product because it has lower conversion costs and has the same performance specifications. Second, value changes whenever the functionality or performance provided changes while cost remains the same (again, price is not a part of this cost). For example, a redesigned component part now provides longer usage until failure for the customer's customer, yet its acquisition and conversion costs to the customer remain the same. Finally, even if functionality or performance of a product is lowered, it may still meet, or even exceed, a customer's specified minimum requirement. More is better for some, but not all, customer requirements. Exceeding minimum requirements continues to deliver benefits to the customer, even though the customer deems a lesser level to be acceptable. For example, lowering the melting point of a plastic resin beyond a specified temperature requirement continues to lower the customer's energy costs and to reduce the time it takes to convert the resin into a molded plastic part.

Finally, notice that in our definition, value is the expression in monetary terms of what the customer firm receives in exchange for the price it pays for a market offering. Because make-versus-buy decisions are possible in business markets, the value provided must exceed the price paid. This difference between value and price is the **customer incentive to purchase.**[8] In this concept of value in business markets, raising or lowering the price of an offering does not change the value that offering provides to a customer firm. Rather, it changes the customer's incentive to purchase that offering.

Assessing Value in Practice

In contrast to the supplier of Alpha and Beta brands, business market management critically relies upon actual assessment of value in the marketplace. Having an accurate assessment of value provides a solid foundation for supplier firm efforts to create and deliver value to targeted market segments and customers. The recognition that the value of a given market offering can vary by market segment and by customer characteristics is a significant underpinning of business market management. Business market management strives to both understand and capitalize on this variation.

Customer firms often do not have an accurate understanding of what suppliers' market offerings are actually worth to them. Certainly, customers may understand their own requirements, but they do not necessarily know what the fulfillment of these requirements is worth to them, how differing ways of meeting these requirements affect their costs, or what changes in their requirements would be worth to them. As Irwin Gross, a business marketing expert, sagely observed:

> The vendor can't assume the customer accurately perceives or understands the value being offered. For a customer to buy a product, he or she needs to perceive only that the value exceeds the price, but not necessarily by how much.[9]

This lack of understanding requires business market managers to further develop the ability to be customer- or market-oriented in business markets. Most business market managers now understand that their firms need to translate features to benefits for their present and prospective customers. In making this translation, a supplier firm takes the customer's point of view. However, this translation is no longer adequate. Business market managers need to go beyond this point and further translate what the benefits are worth in the customer's own setting. That is, a supplier must persuasively demonstrate the value that its market offering provides to the customer. In doing so, a supplier firm not only takes the customer's viewpoint, it makes the customer firm managers' task of deciding upon a supplier easier. In an era when managers are being asked to perform a greater amount of work with fewer resources, what customer firm managers wouldn't appreciate a supplier that provides them with a more accurate understanding of what they ought to acquire? Box 1.1 elaborates on this translation.

BOX 1.1

Demonstrating and Documenting Value: Two Types of Money

Senior executives at most firms in business markets have come to realize that if they cut the cost of acquired goods and services, those savings will fall right to the bottom line as improved profitability. Thus, they establish goals for purchasing that are typically expressed as total cost reductions. These goals might be expressed as a targeted cost reduction amount, such as reducing the cost of acquired goods and services by INR 50 million in three years, as companies routinely do, or as a yearly percentage reduction, such as reducing the costs by 10%, 5%, and 5% in three consecutive years, which is also a common practice. Because purchasing management is pressed for time and may not have adequate measurement capability, the translation of these goals into purchasing practice leads to a bias. Most purchasing managers are readily able to recognize price reductions that a supplier firm offers to them, but usually do not readily see the impact of the firm's offering in terms of what this purchase might do to reduce other costs for the customer. At a deeper level, however, both of them translate into money.

The former type of money refers to cost savings that purchasing managers can readily claim, whereas the latter type of money refers to cost savings that are less apparent. Getting three bids, picking the lowest one, and then negotiating a further price concession falls into the first category. It reflects directly on the purchasing department's contribution to the goal that senior management has set. Acquiring an offering that provides a lower total cost of ownership but has a higher purchase price also earns money, but it belongs to the second category. Because of limited time and measurement capability, purchasing managers may not be able to document that they have actually received the cost savings that the supplier assured their firm. As a purchasing manager, what type of money would you prefer: the first variety which is more easily visible often through price concessions, or the second type, which requires deeper investigation to unearth?

It doesn't have to be that way. A manufacturer of controls for automating manufacturing lines has its salespeople spend time at prospective customers' worksites, gathering data on what controls would be required, what the total cost of those controls would be (not just purchase price, but all costs such as installation and training), and what the payback period would be if the customer were to purchase the controls. Salespeople pull this research together into a report that demonstrates the potential savings, which they then provide to prospective customers. Whose name appears on the cover of the report? The purchasing manager's! The supplier salesperson's name appears nowhere on the cover of the report. Now, the purchasing manager can take this report to his senior management and say, "Look, I have been doing some research in conjunction with this supplier, and this is how we can save some money." What has this supplier done? His actions have enabled the purchasing manager to convert money of the second category into money of the first category, which is more readily recognized by the purchasing manager. It also has provided a social benefit by allowing the purchasing manager to leverage his time, which is in short supply.

In Chapter 2, "Market Sensing: Generating and Using Knowledge About the Marketplace," we first present a number of methods for customer value assessment in business markets. We then present a comprehensive, practical approach for demonstrating and documenting the value of present and prospective market offerings, **customer value management**. Here, we say simply that value assessment is not always easy, but it is essential. Without a specific knowledge of the value provided, discussions with customers largely center on price. Examining our fundamental value equation supports why. Without knowledge of $Value_f$ and $Value_a$, making them absent, what's left in the equation? Knowledge of $Value_f$ and $Value_a$ also enables business market managers to persuasively counter claims that the two market offerings are equivalent.

Finally, customer firms themselves may assess the value of alternative suppliers' offerings through **value analysis**. A value analysis is conducted by a cross-functional team within the customer firm, typically with representatives from engineering, manufacturing, R&D, and purchasing. Supplier representatives may contribute to the team's analysis as well. The team assesses a market offering's attributes in terms of their functionality or performance, calculates the total costs associated with providing this specific functionality or performance, and attempts to identify lower-cost alternatives. The use of value analyses appears to be increasing, even though customer firms do not perform them often.[10]

MANAGING BUSINESS MARKET PROCESSES

Business market management is an overarching business process composed of a series of related, interdependent business market processes. A **business process** is "a collection of activities that takes one or more kinds of input and creates an output that is of value to the customer."[11] Because this definition explicitly gives creating value for customers as the purpose of a business process, it reinforces the guiding principle of value as the cornerstone of business market management.

Business market management takes a process orientation to the business unit, viewing it as a value-generating enterprise. Allaire elaborates on three different kinds of processes, each operating at a different level of the enterprise:

> At the highest level, there are **management processes**—how the CEO runs the company, how management interacts with employees, how decisions get made, and how communication takes place. Those processes set the organizational context and style of working, like "the IBM way." Then there are **business processes**, which are the focus of reengineering efforts. Business processes are large, crosscutting collections of activities, such as product design, order fulfillment, and customer service. Finally, there are **work processes**, which are the basic building blocks of business processes. Work processes are focused and operational; they are how the work actually gets done. Examples include such activities as prototype development, finished-goods warehousing, and purchasing.[12]

Therefore, in our consideration of business market processes, we must also be mindful of management processes and work processes. For example, because work processes still take place largely within functional areas or departments of a business unit, adopting a business process orientation directs greater attention to mechanisms for gaining cross-functional cooperation.[13]

In this section, we first consider shareholder value, core business processes, and the role of marketing. We then outline the specific, constituent business market processes in business market management, and articulate what the role of business marketing is within business market management.

Shareholder Value, Business Processes, and Marketing

Shareholder value is a concept that a growing number of senior executives have adopted as the ultimate criterion for evaluating business performance. Simply put, a business creates **shareholder value** when the economic returns generated from realizing its business strategy exceed the cost of capital employed to realize it. Shareholder value is reflected in the shareholder returns of dividends and appreciation in share price. Shareholder value analysis draws on estimates of a set of **value drivers**—sales growth rate, operating profit margin, income tax rate, working capital investment, fixed capital investment, cost of capital, and forecast period—to calculate the present value of forecasted cash flows and the residual value of the business after the forecast period. Although providing accurate estimates for these value drivers can challenge the expertise and forecasting capabilities of managers, and assumptions are required to estimate the residual value of a business, advocates of shareholder value stress that discounted cash flows are superior to other measures for evaluating business performance, such as earnings and return on investment.[14]

How is shareholder value related to our core concept of customer value? Al Rappaport, a pioneer and leading advocate of shareholder value, provides an insightful answer:

> Even the most persistent advocate of shareholder value understands that without customer value there can be no shareholder value. The source of a company's long-term cash flow is its satisfied customers. On the other hand, providing customer satisfaction does not automatically translate into shareholder value. Providing a comparable product at a lower cost than competitors, or providing superior value to the customer through higher quality, special features, or postsales services, are not genuine advantages if the total long-term cost, including the cost of capital, is greater than the cash generated by the sale. A business that provides more value than customers are willing to pay for is hardly competitive—and may not even be viable.[15]

Thus, translating customer value into shareholder value critically depends on a business being able to claim an equitable return on the value it delivers to customers. We contend that by persuasively demonstrating and documenting the superior value it delivers to customers, a business will be better equipped to successfully accomplish this translation.

What are the core business processes for shareholder value and customer value creation, and what contributions can marketing make to each of them?

Core Business Processes

Srivastava, Shervani, and Fahey have argued that three core business processes are essential to customer value creation, and in turn, shareholder value creation: product development management, supply chain management, and customer relationship management. **Product development management** (PDM) is the process of understanding customer requirements and preferences, anticipating how they will change, and then responsively constructing solutions to fulfill those requirements and preferences in a way that customers are willing to pay for. **Supply chain management** (SCM) is the process that "incorporates acquisition of all physical (and increasingly informational) inputs, as well as the efficiency and effectiveness with which they are transformed into customer solutions." Finally, **customer relationship management** (CRM) is the process that "addresses all aspects of identifying customers, creating customer knowledge, building customer relationships, and shaping their perceptions of the organization and its products."[16] Notice how each of these core business processes extends beyond the firm to its suppliers, customers, and other strategic partners.[17]

Contributions of Marketing

Srivastava, Shervani, and Fahey contend that infusing each of these core business processes with marketing capability is crucial to the creation of customer value and that marketing activities can positively affect the cash flows that underlie shareholder value. A marketing perspective can bring about a shift in each core business process:

- The change to a market-driven PDM process entails shifting from an emphasis on designing the most technically superior product to creating a solution that enables customers to experience the maximum value and benefit from its use.
- The change to a market-driven SCM process entails shifting from a focus on obtaining the functionally best inputs at the cheapest possible prices to designing, managing, and integrating the firm's own supply chain with that of both suppliers and customers.
- The change to a market-driven CRM process entails shifting from a modus operandi that views customer relationships as solely the means to sell, deliver, and service a product to one that regards them as means to learn about customers' needs and wants and how best to create, satisfy, and sustain them.[18]

Marketing's contribution to making these core business processes more market-driven has positive effects on the cash flows for a business. Marketing can contribute to the acceleration of cash flows through involving customers earlier in the PDM process, focusing new offering realization efforts to reduce the time to market; and through persuasively demonstrating and documenting the new offering's value, gaining earlier adoption from targeted customers. Marketing can contribute to the enhancement of cash flows by creating value-based sales tools that enable the sales force to capture a greater portion of the superior value delivered. Through superior demonstration and documentation of the value customers receive, marketing can assist customer purchasing managers in turning the second category of money referred to in Box 1.1 into the first category of money and, at the same time, not have to give as much value away in the form of incentive to purchase. Marketing can contribute to reducing the volatility and vulnerability of cash flows through superior monitoring of competitors, accurately gauging their resources, capabilities, and intentions, so as to minimize marketplace surprises that undercut forecast sales and profits of the business's market offerings. Finally, marketing can contribute to the residual value of the business through increasing the number of profitable customers and creating customer expectations that the business will continue to deliver superior value because of its superior anticipation of changing customer requirements and preferences.[19]

Business Market Management and Business Marketing

We have purposely chosen *Business Market Management* (*B2B*) rather than *Business Marketing* for the title of our book. Why? Isn't this a book about business marketing? Yes, it is a book about business marketing, but we recognize that the nature of marketing practice in business markets is changing.[20] A growing requirement for marketplace success is that marketing work processes, such as segmentation, targeting, and positioning, take place *within* business market processes such as market sensing and managing the market offering. Business market processes cut across functional areas and depend upon seamless cross-functional cooperation for marketplace success. Therefore, business market management requires significant participation from many functional areas, not just marketing, to decide what market segments and customer firms are of primary interest (i.e., targeting) and how to deliver superior value to them (i.e., positioning).[21] We think that business market management better conveys this broader responsibility for the marketplace, and this perspective makes our book of greater interest not only to those in a marketing functional area, but also to those in related functional areas and general management. What are the constituent business market processes of business market management, and what role does business marketing play?

Business Market Processes

As we mentioned earlier and depict in Figure 1.1, the business market processes that constitute business market management can be organized into three groups, based on whether they are a part of understanding, creating, or delivering value. Because a number of market initiatives are underway at any given time, the firm will be engaged in most or all of these business market processes concurrently.

Market sensing, understanding firms as customers, and crafting market strategy are the component business market processes for understanding value. **Market sensing** is the process of generating knowledge about the marketplace that individuals in the firm use to inform and guide their decision making. It is a market-driven process of learning about present and prospective customers and competitors, as well as other actors that affect them and the firm, such as resellers and regulatory agencies. The substantive facets of market sensing are defining the market, monitoring competition, assessing customer value, and gaining customer feedback. **Understanding firms as customers** is the process of learning how companies rely on a network of suppliers to add value to their offerings, integrate purchasing activities with those of other functional areas and outside firms, and make purchase decisions. **Crafting market strategy** is the process of studying how to exploit a firm's resources to achieve short-term and long-term marketplace success, deciding upon a course of action, and flexibly updating it as learning occurs during implementation. We discuss these business market processes in Chapters 2, 3, and 4, respectively.

Managing market offerings, new offering realization, and business channel management are the component business market processes of creating value. **Managing market offerings** is the process of putting products, services, programs, and systems together in ways that create the greatest value for targeted market segments and customer firms. **New offering realization** is the process of developing new core products or services, augmenting them to construct market offerings, and bringing them to market. Realization encompasses all of the activities a firm does to transform an idea into a market offering that it commercializes. **Business channel management** is the process of designing a set of marketing and distribution arrangements that create superior customer value for targeted market segments and customers, and executing those arrangements either directly through supplier firm sales forces and logistics systems or indirectly through resellers and third-party service providers. We devote Chapters 5, 6, and 7, respectively, to these business market processes.

The component business market processes for each of the first two sets come together for the firm to understand and create value, respectively. In contrast, the firm delivers value in three distinct ways. We indicate this in Figure 1.1 by the direction of the arrows linking the business market processes to the metaprocesses of understanding, creating, and delivering value.

Gaining new business, sustaining reseller partnerships, and managing customers are the business market processes for delivering value. **Gaining new business** is the process of differentiating business opportunities, prospecting for new business, assessing the fit with supplier offerings and priorities, gaining the initial order, and fulfilling it to the customer's complete satisfaction. **Sustaining reseller partnerships** is the process of a supplier and its resellers fulfilling commitments they have made to deliver value to customer firms, strengthening this delivered value, and working progressively together to continue to fulfill changing marketplace requirements. **Managing customers** is the process of differentiating transactional and collaborative customers, delivering offerings that fulfill the respective requirements and preferences of a portfolio of customers in a superior way, and getting a fair return in exchange. We discuss these business market processes in Chapters 8, 9, and 10, respectively.

Business Marketing

In the philosophy and practice of business market management, what is the role of business marketing? The essential undertaking of **business marketing** remains what it has been conceptually for many years: Understand what the customer does, and would, value. Management guru Peter Drucker voiced this point in 1980: "The true meaning of marketing [is] knowing what is value for the customer."[22] What is changing slowly is the practice of business marketing, with emerging recognition of what advances in marketing work processes and marketing relationships are needed to realize and profit from this understanding of value.

The marketing work process of customer value assessment is crucial to understanding value. Neglected or absent in most firms in business markets, customer value assessment is a work process in need of the greatest advancement. Customer value assessment can be a business marketing capability that gives a firm a marketplace advantage over its competitors. In conducting value assessments and building customer value models, a firm not only gains detailed knowledge of what customers value, but also has some capacity to shape how customers view their own requirements. Further, by gaining an understanding of what the customer would value, now or in the foreseeable future, business marketers significantly affect their own firm's business market processes, such as managing market offerings and new offering realization.

Segmentation, targeting, and positioning are the fundamental building blocks of business marketing, and having value as the cornerstone of business market management affects each of these work processes. Value-based segmentation moves beyond the conventional bases of partitioning markets, such as product market or size of customer firm, to examine product application, customer capabilities, and usage situation as potential ways for the supplier firm to further segment the market and gain some leverage. Value-based targeting compels the supplier to decide which market segments and customer firms have requirements that most closely match what the supplier does relatively well (i.e., its distinctive competencies and capabilities).[23]

Value-based positioning orients and updates each of the "four Ps":

- ***Product.*** Business marketers construct flexible market offerings that consist of naked solutions—only those product and service elements that *all* segment members value—wrapped with options that *some*, but not all, segment members value. In this way, the supplier's offerings are responsive to the residual variation in customer requirements and preferences that remains, no matter how finely the market is segmented.
- ***Pricing.*** Pricing is based on what a market offering is worth to the customer, rather than its cost to the supplier or simply matching a competitor's price.
- ***Promotion.*** Marketing communications are more focused, tailored to varying requirements for gaining customers or sustaining relationships with customers and resellers, and shape and reinforce the supplier's value proposition to each constituency.
- ***Place.*** Business marketers design distribution channels that are customer-driven. They also provide channel offerings that build marketplace equity, and implement cooperative channel arrangements that are adaptive to customer requirements, which sometimes can change from order to order.

Business marketers, along with the sales force, have had primary responsibility in the past for managing marketplace relationships—with present and prospective customers, with the firm's resellers, and with the firm's competitors.

With the emphasis on relationships and networks in business market management, the role of business marketing in managing relationships expands significantly. As suppliers engage in closer, more collaborative relationships with selected customers and resellers, business marketers need to strengthen their relationship management knowledge and skills, particularly in the areas of communication and negotiations. Business marketers also increasingly need to employ these in defining and refining areas of collaboration and competition with competitors.[24]

In addition to strengthening external relationships, business market management demands that business marketers strengthen their internal relationships with other functional areas. Business marketing should act as the catalyst in helping other functional areas understand how the firm generates value in its market offerings and how this value varies across defined market segments and customer characteristics. To do this, business marketers need to continually communicate what they are learning from the marketplace and, wherever possible, to involve managers from other functional areas in learning firsthand. Customer visits, observation of focus group discussions with customers, and participation in reseller advisory councils are ways for managers in other functional areas to deepen and broaden their understanding. McKenna nicely articulates the growing demands on marketers in contributing to and managing relationships: "The marketer must be the integrator, both internally—synthesizing technological capability with market needs—and externally—bringing the customer into the company as a participant in the development and adaptation of goods and services."[25]

Doing Business Across Borders

Because business markets are predominantly concerned about functionality and performance, business market management stresses doing business across international borders. Customers in country markets in the Americas, Asia, and Europe are seeking essentially the same functionality and performance from business market offerings in such industries as machine tools, computer software, chemicals, and management consulting. In contrast, because aesthetics and tastes tend to vary, often dramatically, across country markets, firms in consumer markets have greater difficulty doing business across borders. Consider, for example, the difficulty the U.S.-based Kelloggs initially had in launching its breakfast cereal in India.[26] Relative to offerings for consumer markets, offerings for business markets require much less adaptation for suppliers to sell them across borders.

A number of developments help suppliers of business market offerings in doing business across borders. The ongoing reduction and elimination of trade barriers and tariffs is leveling the playing field for foreign suppliers to compete with domestic suppliers in their home-country markets. Innovation in logistics and transportation, such as containerization of cargo and use of intermodal transportation, enable firms to reach foreign markets more efficiently and cheaply. Advances in communication technologies, ranging from telecommunications to Internet commerce, continue to erode the barrier of geographical distance between suppliers and prospective customers in other country markets.[27]

These changes make it easier for firms to do business across borders, but firms also have strategic reasons to stress doing business across borders. Foreign markets provide firms with a means for profitable growth, because they can leverage comparative advantages that they have developed in their home-country markets. This source of growth is preferable to pursuing business from prospective customers in the home market that have requirements and preferences different from what the firm does well.[28] Another strategic reason is that the experience and learning firms gain in doing business across borders better prepare them to withstand foreign competition in their home-country markets.

Some readers may believe that doing business across borders is something that only large firms in business markets can do successfully. As the accompanying Box 1.2 on India's automotive component manufacturing companies illustrates, medium and small firms can be worldwide market-share leaders. A number of medium and small firms in Inida are significantly increasing their sales abroad, often with the assistance of local, state, and national government agencies.[29]

The Government of India and many state governments in the country have programs to assist small and medium-sized businesses in doing business in other countries. As a start, embassy officials distribute company literature to various contacts. India Commercial Service personnel, posted at the embassies and missions in various countries help arrange meetings with key executives at targeted companies, and sometimes even accompany representatives of Inida firms as advisers and interpreters of both language and business customs for a low fee. Technological advancements such as video conference, Internet, etc., save time and expense involved in traveling abroad. Internet-enabled e-market places provide forums for Indian suppliers seeking business in international markets, and link suppliers to qualified customers and potential business partners around the world.[30]

Regardless of their size, firms in business markets do face some additional considerations in doing business across borders. In this section, we discuss language and culture, cross-border negotiation and dispute resolution, and currency exchange and payment risk.

Language and Culture

Doing business across borders does not always mean that the language and culture of managers from the supplier and customer firms will be different, just as doing business within the same country does not always mean that the culture and language will be the same. For example, Argentina and Uruguay have essentially the same culture and language, and both countries are members of the Mercosur free trade area, which further facilitates doing business across their border.[31] Yet, within India, there are different languages and sub-cultures. For instance, the business cultures in Delhi, Mumbai, Chennai, and Kolkata are very different. In Gujarat, a lot of business is conducted on the basis of relationships: millions of rupees are transacted based simply on verbal commitments. Most often, though, the language and culture of managers from supplier firms and customer firms located in different countries will be different.

BOX 1.2
Indian SME Automotive Component Manufacturers Take on the World

In India, the small and medium enterprise (SME) sector is a vital employment, output and export generator, and a fertile ground for fostering entrepreneurship. India has over 500 medium sized and over 10,000 small manufacturers in the auto component industry, which supply components to major Indian and MNC auto manufacturers in India, besides registering robust growth in the export business. Many of these companies are family owned or closely held, and managed by their owners.

The critical factors in the success of these companies are as follows:

1. *Large and growing Indian middle class.* This has resulted in robust growth of the Indian auto industry, resulting in many large Indian and MNC companies aggressively entering into manufacturing. The industry has grown in various clusters around Manesar in the North, Pune in the West, Chennai in the South, Jamshedpur–Kolkata in the East, and Indore in Central India. Each of the major automobile manufacturers in these clusters sought to obtain 80% or more of their component requirements from SME vendors within a 50 kilometer radius of their companies. As a result, investment is flowing into the component industry, and large numbers of SME auto component manufacturers are being developed.

2. *High demand, local raw materials, low labor costs, high productivity, and intense competition.* The combination of these creates a vibrant auto component industry. The large growth within the auto industry, coupled with intense competition among the players, forced SMEs to adopt globally benchmarked quality processes. It also necessitated that they grow rapidly to derive economies of scale and consequent cost competitiveness on a global scale. This enabled SMEs to successfully foray into international markets after catering to the demands of their respective proximate auto customers. The fierce competition among global auto companies in the developed countries incentivized them to look for cheaper, yet high-quality supply sources, resulting in a warm reception to the advances of the Indian component manufacturers. These manufacturers have graduated over the years from supplying components in the international after-markets to supplying to global original equipment manufacturers (OEMs) in developed countries, meeting exacting quality, delivery, and cost specifications.

3. *Governmental focus and consequent support.* Recognizing the central role automakers had played in the growth of the economy through direct and secondary benefits, the Government of India outlined a 2006–2016 10-year mission plan to further develop the auto industry, including the auto components industry, into a global hub. The government extended support in various forms to the SME auto component manufacturers, by providing access to credit through banks, creating necessary infrastructure, accelerating the creation of necessary ecosystems such as research and development facilities, education facilities oriented to this industry, testing laboratories, and so on.

Jorn Madslien, "Indian Auto Firms Eye Global Markets," 18 April 2007, *news.bbc.co.uk/2/hi/business/6548451.stm*; "The Automotive Mission Plan 2016," 31 January 2007, *http://www.dhi.nic.in/Final_AMP_Report.pdf*; "Export Performance of Small and Medium Enterprises in India," October 2005, *http://www.eximbankindia.com/Research_Brief-Sep-05.pdf*.

A first step in doing business across borders is to determine what language to use. English is regarded as the language of international business, because it is the most frequently used.[32] The language that businesspeople are most likely to know other than their native language is English. Even in circumstances where managers from one country do know the language of their counterparts' country, they may prefer to speak English. French and German managers, for example, may conduct business discussions in English, because it does not give either side an advantage.

Alternatives to using English are to use the language of one of the parties, use another language that both parties are willing to use, or rely on interpreters. When the supplier and customer managers do not have a common language that they are comfortable using for business discussions, one or both parties need to employ interpreters. Use of interpreters, however, can lengthen the time needed for the business discussions, change the "atmosphere" of the discussions, increase the costs of the discussions, or increase the chances for misunderstandings.[33] Nevertheless, doing business through interpreters is sometimes the only viable alternative.

The meaning that managers attach to the words and actions of their counterparts in a business discussion depends in part on the culture of the managers. Culture is an abstract and imprecise concept; it broadly refers to the bundle of characteristics that uniquely define members of a particular group. A particular group's distinctive language, its social customs, the specific artifacts and art forms it produces, and the legal and economic structures that govern it collectively convey its culture. Culture also comprises a set of assumptions, values, beliefs, and norms that are socially instilled in members of the group, which serve as a guide to appropriate behavior and to understanding the words and actions of others.[34]

It is difficult to say how much influence culture has on doing business across borders in business markets. Broad definitions of culture tend to neglect the influences of ideology and personality, which cut across national cultures. Ideology refers to an organized set of values and beliefs that individuals hold about how life should be lived and the means for accomplishing this lifestyle. Personality refers to the traits or behavioral predispositions, such as extroversion or introversion, that a person manifests to a greater or lesser extent and which collectively define that person's character. Commonalities and differences in ideology and personality may exert greater influence on how managers from different countries relate to one another than do their national cultures.[35] In its review of cultural explanations, *The Economist* concluded, "Culture is so imprecise and changeable a phenomenon that it explains less than most people realize. . . . And within the overall mix of what influences people's behavior, culture's role may well be declining, rather than rising, squeezed between the greedy expansion of the government on one side, and globalization on the other."[36]

Still, business market managers must be perceptive about any cultural influences, so they can tailor the social elements of a market offering to enhance its value to managers in firms within that culture. A useful start is for the managers to think through the influence of their own culture on their behavior and their assumptions about how to behave. Before doing business across borders, managers should also gain some understanding of the culture of their business counterparts. Managers should especially learn about the characteristic ways of doing business in that culture, such as the meaning and timing of business entertainment, and how to show respect. The managers also should seek to understand the company culture of their business counterparts and how this reinforces or contradicts the country culture.[37] Finally, although managers need to be culturally aware, they need to regard their business counterparts first as individuals and resist cultural stereotyping.

Cross-Border Negotiation and Dispute Resolution

When supplier firms consider doing business across borders, they need to decide how flexible they will be with the policies and practices they use to conduct business in their home-country market. That is, to what extent are they willing to negotiate ways of doing business across borders that are different from how they do business in the home-country market? Also, to what extent are they willing to negotiate ways of doing business that vary across different foreign country markets? A supplier firm's willingness to negotiate depends on a number of considerations, such as the profitability of the business to be gained, the perceived benefits of a relationship with the prospective customer firm, and any anticipated consequences of the negotiated deal on the supplier's business in other country markets.

Cross-Border Negotiations

Cross-border negotiations can differ from domestic negotiations in eight critical respects: (1) culture, (2) unfamiliar and uncomfortable settings, (3) the influence of ideology, (4) greater or lesser involvement of government in business, (5) defining which country's laws govern the business transaction, (6) instability and sudden change in the foreign market, (7) dispute resolution, and (8) foreign currencies.[38] The culture of each negotiator or, often, negotiations team affects their interests and priorities as well as the strategies that they will employ in the negotiation. The complementarity between the interests and priorities of each negotiator will enable them to trade them off in ways that generate value-creating or integrative agreements. The strategies of each negotiator will affect the interaction patterns in the negotiation, which can facilitate or hinder reaching an integrative agreement. The negotiation strategies that each side pursues also will be shaped by its expectations of who on the other side is involved in the negotiation, what roles they play, what the informal influences are, and what process the other side engages in to reach an accord, such as top-down, consensus, and multistage coalition building.[39]

Although supplier managers might prefer to negotiate with the prospective customer firm within their own country, the supplier often has to travel to the customer's country, which may impose difficulties. The customer's country may lack the amenities to which the business traveler is accustomed. The time difference from the home country may be significant, leading to jet lag. Outside the actual negotiations, communicating with local people in their own language or the traveler's native language (or some combination) may be a struggle. The physical surroundings and climate may be dramatically different. Also, the support services readily available at home may be difficult to find or otherwise problematic. These potential difficulties contribute to the psychological and economic costs of doing business across borders and lessen the chance of successfully negotiating an equitable deal.

Supplier managers may find they have significant ideological differences with their counterparts in cross-border negotiations. Private investment, profit, and individual rights are three principal areas where ideological differences may arise.[40]

Whenever possible, managers should downplay ideological differences and seek ways to accommodate the prospective customer, which may require imagination and pursuing creative alternatives. For example, a principle codified under *Sharia*, Islam's holy law, is the prohibition of interest payments on loans. To respect this principle, a foreign supplier working with a bank may employ the Islamic financial instrument of *murabaha*, or markup, where "instead of lending to a customer which buys goods with the money lent and pays interest on the loan, the financial institution buys the goods and sells them to the company at a higher price at a later date."[41]

Governments in country markets vary significantly in the extent to which they control or actively participate in commercial activities. Thus, government officials may simply need to be apprised of ongoing business discussions, their approval of any business deal may be required, or they may even be the main participants in the cross-border negotiations. Separate from the extent of government control is the issue of which country's laws—the supplier firm's or the customer firm's—or a third (neutral) country's laws will govern the business transaction. "Virtually all international business contracts contain a clause stating that the law of a particular country, to the exclusion of all other laws, will apply to a transaction and to any disputes that may arise between the parties."[42] The taxes applicable under each country's laws can be a determining factor in this decision.

Firms routinely use country risk assessments to understand and manage their exposure in doing business in a particular country, and they often factor this evaluation into the pricing for negotiated deals as risk premiums.[43] The India-based Dabhol Power Company (DPC), with a capacity of about 2000 MW and investment of about $3 billion (at the time, roughly INR 100,000 million), was set up to supply electric power, primarily to the state of Maharashtra. General Electric was to supply the key equipment (turbines), Bechtel was to build the plant, and Enron was to manage the company. Phase-I, with a capacity of 740 MW, was expected to use naphtha as fuel; Phase-II was expected to use LNG (liquefied natural gas) as fuel after constructing the necessary LNG-handling infrastructure and to result in ramping up capacity to maximum target levels. Construction for Phase-I started in 1992 and was completed two years behind schedule. In 1996, with the formation of a new state government by the Shiv Sena/BJP combine, the LNG project got into deep trouble. The change of government led to a complete reopening of the project, and several major lapses were identified, including a lack of competitive bidding and transparency, and potential environmental damage. The capital cost of INR 44.9 million per MW was considered too high. The power purchase agreement (PPA) was also deemed severely flawed for allowing the price of power purchased by the Maharashtra State Electricity Board (MSEB) from DPC to be linked to the price of fuel and to the INR/U.S. dollar exchange rate, both of which were seen to be outside the realm of state governmental control. Moreover, the new government observed that, rather than anticipating a decrease in the price of power as had been their previous experience, the PPA, in fact, had provided for price escalation. To quote from a report of the chief minister of the new government in Maharashtra, "This contract is anti-Maharashtra. It smacks of lack of self respect and is irrational. Accepting it in its present form is like betraying the people of Maharashtra. This agreement is no agreement at all." The contract was essentially canceled. Afterwards, until 2001, Enron struggled in vain to salvage the project. It is a different matter that a few years after this action, Enron itself became bankrupt, and the project continued to drift.[44]

Cross-Border Dispute Resolution

A crucial issue to negotiate before doing business across borders is how to resolve any disputes that may arise. International commercial arbitration as a preagreed dispute resolution mechanism not only avoids the greater costs of litigation, it also provides additional motivation to the two parties to work out disagreements themselves. "Most international contracts today contain a clause that should a dispute arise between the parties (even if one of the parties is a government or state corporation), they will not go to court, but will refer the matter to an arbitrator or arbitrators, usually located in a third country, to hear the matter and make a decision."[45] Whenever possible, the two parties should specify a particular arbitration institution, such as the International Chamber of Commerce, the American Arbitration Association, or the London Court of Arbitration, to which they will submit any disputes. Firms can gain enforcement of arbitration decisions by these institutions in the courts of countries that have signed the treaty: the United Nations Convention on the Recognition and Enforcement of Foreign Arbitral Awards.[46]

Finally, in the next section, we consider how firms doing business across borders resolve the problem of foreign currencies.

Currency Exchange and Payment Risk

When a firm in one country wants to do business with a firm in another country, one term that the two firms must specify is the currency for the transaction: the supplier firm's country currency, the customer firm's country currency, or some third country's currency (e.g., Indian Rupees, U.S. dollars, Japanese yen). Depending on the currency chosen, one or both firms will need foreign currency exchange service.[47] Further, if either firm perceives significant risk in doing business with the other, a letter of credit may be required to enable the transaction to take place. A **letter of credit** (LC) is an irrevocable commitment that the customer firm's bank issues specifying the conditions under which payment for the transaction will be made to the supplier firm (e.g., when the bank is presented with an acceptable bill of lading and packing list for the products). Finally, when the supplier also believes that significant risk is associated with the issuing bank, it may require its bank or some other bank to **confirm** the letter of credit, which is an irrevocable guarantee by the confirming bank that payment will be made when the specified conditions have been satisfactorily met.

Foreign currency exchange, letters of credit and their confirmations, and other services that enable firms to do business across borders are provided by the correspondent banking units (CBUs) of commercial banks. These CBUs are responsible for managing a set of relationships with banks in other countries, referred to as correspondent banks, that provide agreed-upon banking services (e.g., confirming letters of credit) to one another. Without these correspondent banking relationships, it would be virtually impossible for companies to conduct any cross-border trade. Correspondent banks provide account and trade services to each other that facilitate the efficient movement of payments across borders and provide protection to both the sellers and buyers doing business across borders. ABN-AMRO (AA), the large Dutch bank, provides an instructive example of how correspondent banking works.

AA has branch offices in about 50 countries, yet it does business in more than 100 countries. The Correspondent Banking Group (CBG), with its head office in

Amsterdam, has correspondent bankers in 40 countries in which AA has branch offices. In countries where it has no local branch, AA relies on its correspondent banks. In countries where AA has a local branch, some competition naturally occurs between the branch network and the correspondent banks for the same business (e.g., payment traffic, LCs), and this is especially so for the 40 branches where there is a local correspondent banker. In these circumstances, AA CBG has to strike a delicate balance between directing business to its correspondent banks and targeting corporate customers to take direct through the AA (branch) network. Sustaining cooperative relations with the correspondent banks is essential because the local AA branch is dependent on domestic banks for funding and, often, foreign exchange clearing.

Not only do correspondent banking units do business across borders themselves; more important, they enable their corporate clients to do so.

Working Relationships and Business Networks

A firm's success in business markets depends directly on its working relationships. The working relationships themselves are embedded in business networks comprised of connected relationships. These relationships and business networks enable firms to attain outcomes, such as profitability and marketplace success, that they could not achieve acting alone. Hence, the final guiding principle of business market management is that firms should accentuate working relationships and business networks.

Working relationships and business networks are complex phenomena that exist at multiple levels. We can think about them at the level of the individuals who participate in them as part of their work activities. We can also think about them at the level of the functional areas or subunits that relate to one another, such as the relationship between marketing and manufacturing within a business unit. At this level, the relationships may be within the same firm or across firms, as in the relationship between marketing in a supplier firm and purchasing in a customer firm. Finally, we can think about them at the business unit level, where the actors are firms engaged in working relationships, such as a customer firm and supplier firm working relationship; a distributor firm and manufacturer firm working partnership; or a customer firm, distributor firm, and manufacturer firm business network.

In this section, we first consider work teams, which capture working relationships and work networks of individuals. We then move to working relationships between firms in business markets. We end by broadening our consideration to the embedded context in which working relationships occur: business networks.

Work Teams

Work teams have become the primary mechanism for accomplishing working relationship goals within and across functional areas, other business units, and firms. A **work team**, or simply a **team**, "is a small number of people with complementary skills who are committed to a common purpose, set of performance goals, and approach for which they hold themselves mutually accountable."[48] Katzenbach and Smith distinguish teams from other forms of working groups in terms of performance results:

> A working group's performance is a function of what its members do as individuals. A team's performance includes both individual results and what we call "collective work-products." A collective work-product is what two or more members must work on together, such as interviews, surveys, or experiments. Whatever it is, a collective work-product reflects the joint, real contribution of team members.[49]

Significantly, teams create value in their collective work-products that could not be produced outside of the team setting.

How do teams accomplish this? Through synergy, which comes from the Greek word *synergos*, which means working together. Yet, creating value through synergy requires that the individuals on the team possess the blend of skills needed to achieve the team's purpose.[50] Three broad categories of skill requirements are technical or functional expertise, problem-solving and decision-making skills, and interpersonal skills. Somewhat paradoxically, the last category may be the most critical skill set and the most difficult to find. "Common understanding and purpose cannot arise without effective communication and constructive conflict, which in turn depend on interpersonal skills. These include risk taking, helpful criticism, objectivity, active listening, giving the benefit of the doubt, and recognizing the interests and achievements of others."[51] Senior management should not overlook the process aspects of teamwork, with the corresponding need to train individuals on how to work together as a team and develop their interpersonal skills.

Many firms have trouble with teams.[52] What are the characteristics of effective teams that will help business market managers steer clear of potential troubles? Aravind Eye Care System (AECS), based in Madurai, India, a world leader in providing eye care, has found that there are several characteristics, which we outline in Box 1.3. Individuals coalesce into a team through the process of translating *a clear, elevating goal* into specific performance goals for which they are mutually accountable (*a results-driven structure*). A *collaborative environment* is crucial for the team to produce collective work-products. Trouble occurs when team members are not able to "check their egos at the door," or attempt to advance their own (or their functional area's) agenda over the team agenda. Further, any violation of team members' trust in one another produces a diminishing return of trust: After a disappointment, trust can be rebuilt, but never to its prior level. A final problem occurs when team members talk past one another ("You're talking so loudly I can't hear you!").

Notice in Box 1.3 that there are two broad levels used at AECS to foster teamwork: organizational cultural aspects relating to people and attitudes, and process-related aspects concerning organizational design. Taken together, they are complementary and mutually reinforcing. Firms may need to change existing measurement and compensation systems to accurately measure and reward team-based performance. Some management thinkers, though, do not support monetary compensation specifically tied to team performance.[53] Reflecting the necessary but not sufficient character of monetary compensation, a senior manager wryly observed, "It's not the money, it's the money!" Finally, a key aspect of *principled leadership* is the "180 feedback" that Baxter managers get anonymously from their direct reports once a year. This feedback

BOX 1.3
Characteristics of Effective Teams at Aravind Eye Care System (AECS)

On the organizational cultural aspects

- There is a clear mission statement, "Eliminate needless blindness," reflected in both strategies and day-to-day operations.
- At the time of hiring new recruits to the organization, the orientation program clarifies how the new employee's role contributes to this overarching purpose—even in the case of a janitor. This is further explored and reinforced periodically on occasions like "mission day."
- Operational tasks and decisions are guided by the philosophy of "patient-centered care." At all times, every member of the staff is encouraged to do what is best for the patients, even if it interferes with the staff's direct duties. For instance, if a patient looks lost, any passing staff is expected to ensure that he or she is guided to the appropriate point of care.
- During staff selection, overarching importance is given to "cultural fit" rather than "competence" in order to ensure harmony and teamwork. Competencies are easier to develop than the right orientation and work ethics.
- On the compensation front, AECS has stayed away from productivity-linked or revenue-linked formulas. Organizational harmony cannot be achieved if rewards are skewed and accrue to certain people simply by virtue of the nature of work they are performing. Likewise, there may be other works in the organization that need to be done, but may not warrant rewards or fit neatly into formalized reward mechanisms. Not all contributions to an organization's overall efficiency can be put into a productivity matrix. For instance, an ophthalmologist may appear unproductive when judged by the number of operations he/she performs, but he/she may be effective nonetheless as a mentor or advisor. Skewed and ill-conceived reward systems, while seeking to reward some individual performers, could end up perpetuating inequities. At AECS, such rewards systems are therefore avoided.

On the process side

- The workflow is highly standardized both on the clinical and on the administrative side.
- The details are well understood and transparent. Fees for each patient category are fixed and well known to all concerned staff. Consequently, it is possible for billing to be handled at the lowest administrative level.
- The staff is well trained to handle all aspects of their respective jobs.
- Emphasis is given to good documentation, such as keeping meticulous records of which tests have been done and what the next steps are, in the context of patient care.
- There is a high level of staff involvement in handling complaints, suggestions, and process improvements.
- The layout and process flow are designed to facilitate linear flow to cater to high patient volume.
- Resources are continually balanced to minimize waste and underutilization.
- Task assignments are planned in advance and clearly communicated. For instance, all concerned staff attached to surgical wards would know their respective surgery postings a week ahead of time.
- There is a strong emphasis on discipline, especially punctuality. Most tasks require multiple people; for example, surgery cannot start till the whole surgical team and the patient are present. This aspect underscores the need for punctuality.
- Meticulous planning is done the previous day to ensure adequate staffing, supplies, etc., for the tasks to be done on the next day. This helps avoid any confusion about the roles and tasks of each employee.

Discussions with R. D. Thulasiraj, Executive Director, Aravind Eye Care System, 2009.

BOX 1.4
AECS Reinforces Teamwork to Better Serve Hospital Customers

Multiple aspects in the workings of Aravind Eye Care System (AECS) have been designed to foster teamwork. Top managers believe that teamwork is the key to achieving the highest levels of excellence. This can be seen from the fact that Aravind Hospital, which is part of AECS, has achieved the highest levels of productivity, highest quality, and lowest cost, among all eye care providers in the world.

The result of such extraordinary teamwork in Aravind is that a typical eye surgeon performs over 2,500 cataract operations per year, against an Indian national average of 250. An eye surgeon at Aravind is responsible for performing cataract eye surgeries for patients on two operating tables. To make this a reality, a team of four nurses assists the doctor on each operating table. With their extensive support, the surgeon is able to perform the specialized 10-minute cataract surgery on one patient who has been earlier prepared by a team of nurses. Once the specialist procedure is completed by the surgeon, the nurses complete the remaining procedures, wheel the patient out, and bring the next prepared and waiting patient for operation on the same operating table.

In the intervening time, the doctor turns around to the adjacent table and completes his/her 10-minute procedure on another patient, who has been kept ready by that table's set of four nurses. The eye surgeon continues in this manner, alternating between the two operating tables, for six hours each day.

For the system to function smoothly, exemplary teamwork is vital on the part of all nurses and surgeons as well as other support staff involved in patient registration, housekeeping, etc. The systems are geared to handle very high volumes, typically over 1,000 patients per day across their five hospitals in Tamil Nadu.

Discussions with R. D. Thulasiraj, Executive Director, Aravind Eye Care System, 2009.

is critical for managers to understand how they are perceived and what interpersonal skills they need to develop further.

Box 1.4 describes a program AECS used to promote and reinforce teamwork in delivering health care.

Working Relationships

All customer and supplier firms that do business together have some sort of working relationship. After all, people in business markets do not buy from people they do not know. Most firms have a policy that purchases can be made only from approved vendors, where some effort has been made to understand the quality and reliability of the vendor's offering. Moreover, a working relationship between a customer firm and a supplier firm can range along a continuum:

> Purely **transactional relationships**, where the customer and the supplier focus upon the timely exchange of basic products for highly competitive prices, anchor one end. Purely **collaborative relationships**, or partnerships, anchor the other end. This latter kind of relationship comes about through **partnering**, which is a process where a customer firm and supplier firm form strong and extensive social, economic, service, and technical ties over

time, with the intent of lowering total costs and/or increasing value, thereby achieving mutual benefit.[54]

The working relationship between a customer firm and supplier firm depends upon their mutual interest in working together. Because the relationship takes place within some industry context, it will depend in part on marketplace norms, which vary by industry. We discuss a supplier firm's relationship strategy and implementation at length in Chapter 10, "Managing Customers." Here, we want to discuss what prospective partner firms need to agree upon when they begin a collaborative relationship and the development of such relationships.

Collaborative Relationship Agreements

A collaborative relationship between two firms is a kind of **strategic alliance**, which is simply a commercial agreement between two (or more) parties to work together in some mutually defined ways.[55] Because of the natural misunderstandings that can occur in communication between firms, we recommend that this agreement be written. Although the detail, length, and formality of alliance or partnering agreements vary widely in practice, we recommend that firms specify three basic considerations: **"gives & gets," time horizon**, and a **preagreed dispute-resolution mechanism**.

"Gives" capture the specific investments and resources each firm contributes, such as knowledge, personnel, fixed assets, and money, whereas "gets" capture the specific gains each firm receives, such as greater expertise, enhanced capabilities, or additional profits. The challenge for each firm is to understand and evaluate the gives and gets from its own perspective *and* from the perspective of the prospective partner firm. There are often disconnects: What one firm believes it is giving to its partner firm is significantly different from what the partner perceives that it is getting. Beyond this, "gives" have a cost associated with them, whereas "gets" have a value associated with them. Therefore, each firm also needs to discover gives that it can provide that would have more value to the prospective partner than that partner's perception of the cost of the gives that it is being asked to provide.

Each firm should comprehensively list both its gives & gets and those of its partner. Exchanging these lists allows the firms to discover any discrepancies that exist in perception of the gives & gets. They can then negotiate changes to attain equity, so each partner firm perceives that the value of what it is getting is greater than the cost of what it is giving. After agreement is reached on an equitable set of gives & gets, the partner firms need to specify a process for handling unanticipated changes in the gives & gets as well as unforeseen gives & gets that may arise. Gives & gets provide a mechanism for defining the scope of the cooperation between firms, the specific resources and activities each firm will contribute, and the specific outcomes of the cooperation that the firms anticipate.

Time horizon specifies the period of time the firms agree to work together. When the time for collaboration is lengthy, intermediate partnership reviews may also be specified, most likely corresponding to scheduled completion of defined milestones that chart progress in the collaboration. At the end of the time horizon, the firms agree to mutually review the relationship and determine their willingness to continue in the collaborative relationship.

A preagreed dispute resolution mechanism specifies how the two firms will handle any disagreements they cannot resolve themselves. Options include negotiation, mediation, and arbitration, and two or more dispute resolution procedures may be used in sequence.[56] It is crucial that the firms specify a mechanism at the outset of the collaboration. One of our sayings is, "It's hard to dance smoothly when your pants are on fire!" In fact, two marketing scholars from Australia offered business dancing as an intriguing metaphor for collaborative relationships.[57] Firms with a preagreed dispute resolution mechanism find that they not only avoid costly litigation, but are also motivated to find a way to work out disagreements themselves. Thus, it not only lowers the cost of conflict, it fosters productive resolution of the conflict that does occur.

Collaborative Relationship Development

Most firms in business markets now realize that to prosper they must have close, collaborative relationships with selected suppliers, customers, and value-added resellers.[58] A crucial question then is: How do collaborative relationships develop over time? We contend that the participating firms in a relationship experience and manage that development as a series of **exchange episodes**.

Relationship development begins with a partner selection stage. Even when two firms have been doing business together on a transactional basis, they will need an initial exchange episode where the defined purpose becomes more collaborative. Often, this episode takes the form of a pilot program in which each firm gains a better understanding of what collaborative exchange between them might mean. For example, a supplier firm and customer firm might experiment with single-sourcing at one plant in the customer's manufacturing network.

Each exchange episode is composed of four sequentially related events, which are "critical incidents when parties engage in actions related to the development of their relationship."[59] The events are defining purpose, setting relationship boundaries, creating value (and claiming value), and evaluating exchange outcomes. Through information sharing and negotiation, the two firms mutually define the nature of their collaboration as well as establish its limits. Creating value through joint action (that could not be created by each firm acting independently) is the primary reason for collaborative relationships. Expectation of future collaboration, where working together will enable the creation of more value, has a strong influence on each firm's willingness to share the created value. Each firm evaluates its outcomes from the exchange episode against its expectations and against outcomes it perceives it could have obtained from collaborating with others instead.

At the conclusion of each exchange episode, each firm decides whether to continue the relationship at the same level, to broaden it, or to curtail it. The collaboration may be broadened through expanded scale or scope. As the collaborative relationship progresses, the two firms may be engaged in a number of concurrent exchange episodes, with overlapping beginnings and endings, and some with no apparent common coordination.

We regard each of these exchange episodes as a business strand of the collaborative relationship between the two firms. The same actors within each firm may engage in several overlapping exchange episodes, and distinctly different groups of other actors may engage in different exchange episodes. More likely is a mixture of common and distinct actors engaged across the set of exchange episodes occurring at a given point in time. In our view, the numerous business strands become "interwoven" through conscious coordination (mutual strategy) by the partner firms and repeated social interaction between the actors.

The partner firms continuing to engage in collaborative exchange episodes together constitute a relationship maintenance stage. In addition to renewing sequentially related exchange episodes, such as a single-source, just-in-time supply arrangement, the partner firms may initiate other exchange episodes that broaden the collaborative relationship. Conversely, when an exchange episode comes to an end, the partner firms may mutually decide not to renew this strand of collaborative exchange. It may be that this strand has reached its natural conclusion between the partners, such as in a customer's material substitution where the supplier does not have capability in the new material. Alternatively, because of changing self-interest, one or the other partner firm may unilaterally decide to terminate this strand of collaborative exchange (in extreme circumstances, it may occur even partway through an exchange episode).

Ongoing collaborative relationships may be broadened in some respects, curtailed in others. In this way, relationship maintenance is a more overarching, organic stage that captures the ebb and flow in the collaboration between the customer and supplier firms over time. Rather than being a separate stage, we consider relationship dissolution as simply the ultimate conclusion (or termination) of the relationship maintenance stage.

Business Networks

As firms build a number of close, collaborative relationships, or alliances, the inevitable next step is understanding how to better interrelate the set of relationships. A **business network** is a set of two or more connected business relationships. *Connected* means the extent to which "exchange in one relation is contingent upon exchange (or non-exchange) in the other relation."[60] Moreover, two connected relationships of interest can themselves be both directly and indirectly connected with other relationships that have some bearing on them, as part of a larger business network. As illustrated in Figure 1.2, a focal relationship is connected to several different relationships that either the supplier or the customer has, some of which are with the same third parties.[61]

Figure 1.2 Connected Relations for Firms in a Dyadic Relationship

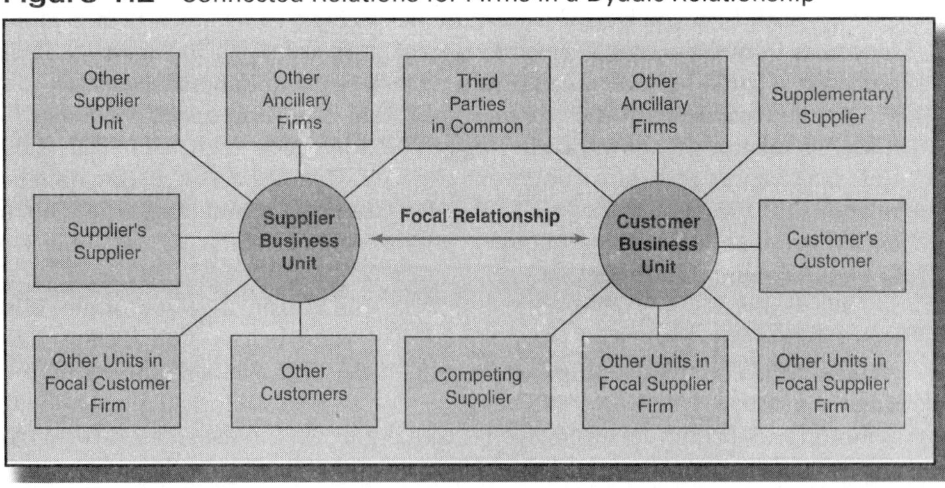

Source: James C. Anderson, Håkan Håkansson, and Jan Johanson, "Dyadic Relationships Within a Business Network Context," *Journal of Marketing* (October 1994), 3.

A type of business network of particular interest to business market managers is the **alliance network**, which is a clique of interrelated and coordinated business relationships.[62] Firms engage in alliance networks to create new markets, to bring together resources that are beyond any two firms, to gain consensus on a "dominant design" that will speed the adoption of an innovation, and to spread risk across a greater number of firms. We begin with a case study of building and managing an alliance network. This study of India's Light Combat Aircraft (LCA) business network, which we present in Box 1.5 both motivates our discussion of analyzing business networks and serves as a source of examples.

BOX 1.5

Building India's Light Combat Aircraft through the Alliance Network

In the early 1980s, the Indian Air Force was in need of its 4.5th and 5th generation aircrafts. Its 2nd generation aircraft and MiG-21 fighter aircraft, mainstays of the Indian Air Force at the time, were aging quickly. The government's Ministry of Defense Long-Term Equipment Plan of 1981 forecasted that India would be 40% short of its fighter aircraft targets by 1995. The light combat aircraft (LCA) program was India's initiative to manufacture the 5th generation fighter aircrafts indigenously.

Accordingly, in 1983, the Defense Research and Development Organization (DRDO) obtained permission to develop LCAs—lightweight, multirole, tailless, compound delta wing, supersonic, and single-engine jet fighters. An important objective was to catalyze the advance of the Indian aerospace industry and possibly open doors for the future export of this sophisticated fighter aircraft.

The year 1984 saw the establishment of the Aeronautical Development Agency (ADA) to manage the LCA program. ADA, part of the DRDO, is a consortium of over 100 defense laboratories, industrial organizations, and academic institutions. The project was to be carried out in two phases: Phase-I, at a cost of INR 21.9 billion, would develop the design, construct and test two technology demonstrator aircrafts (TD1 & 2), construct a structural test specimen, construct two prototype vehicles (PV1 & 2), and create any necessary infrastructure. Phase-II, with a total cost of INR 23 billion, would include the construction of three more PVs: PV-3, the production variant; PV-4, the naval variant, and PV-5, a trainer; along with other associated facilities. ADA was responsible for the design and development of the LCA's avionics suite and its integration with the flight controls, environmental controls, aircraft utilities systems management, stores management system, etc., besides having overall project management responsibility.

Hindustan Aeronautics Ltd. (HAL), established in 1964, is a government-owned, high-level aerospace research and production facility primarily focused to meet the country's defense requirements. It has several successful R&D programs to its credit. HAL was the lead partner and principal contractor in the LCA project, and was charged with managing several aspects including the communication suite, air-to-air and air-to-ground data links, the friend or foe interrogator, the gas turbine starter unit, and the multi-mode radar, which was to be a joint effort of HAL and the Electronics and Radar Development Establishment (LRDE). In its role as the principal contractor, HAL was responsible for LCA design, systems integration, airframe manufacturing, aircraft final assembly, flight testing, and service support.

(continued)

BOX 1.5
Continued

The project definition (PD) phase was performed from October 1987 to September 1988. Based on its extensive expertise in aviation, France's Dassault Aviation was invited to review the PD phase and provide advice.

The combat vehicle adopted the state-of-the-art fly-by-wire (FBW) technology. Because of its technological sophistication, developed countries that had this technology were unwilling to provide FBW technology for the LCA project. Consequently, the necessary control laws for FBW controls were developed by India's National Control Law team (CLAW), formed by the National Aeronautics Ltd. and supported by the Aeronautical Development Establishment (ADE). As the control laws were progressively incorporated to build the flight control system software, from 1993 to 1996, they were tested on the British Aerospace simulators in the U.K. and at Lockheed Martin simulators in the United States. After India's second successful nuclear test in 1998, developed countries suddenly withdrew all support for the LCA project. CLAW was successfully tested on Minibird and Ironbird test rigs at ADE and HAL, respectively.

HAL's Hyderabad division and LRDE, Bangalore, were selected to jointly lead the development of multi-mode radar. DRDO's Centre for Airborne Studies was responsible for testing this radar. By 2006, owing to time and budget problems, ADA began to look at alternative off-the-shelf solutions and subsequently agreed to a bid offered by Israel's Elta.

The Gas Turbine Research Establishment was charged with providing the GTX-35VS Kaveri after-burning turbofan, the aircraft's main propulsion system. This was a latest-technology engine that would give effective thrust and conserve fuel by aiding proper combustion. In 2006, after the embargo was lifted on the supply of sensitive technology to India, a $105 million contract (at the time, INR 4.725 billion) was awarded to General Electric for supply of 17 F404-GE-IN20 turbofan engines to be used in initial batches of the LCA. This order was further augmented in 2007 to include 24 F404-GE-IN20 after-burning engines. Due to the problems encountered with Kaveri, the French aircraft engine company Snecma was invited to provide technical assistance. In May 2009, expecting further delays, ADA began evaluating the purchase of 100 more powerful engines from either EuroJet or General Electric.

A large number of other Indian organizations were involved in the design and development of various other sub-systems of the aircraft. Its head-up display was developed by the Indian government–owned Central Scientific Instruments Organization in Chandigarh. Liquid crystal multifunction displays were developed by Bharat Electronics Ltd., another public sector company. The landing-gear materials were sourced from Mishra Dhatu Nigam Ltd., Hyderabad, with Bharat Forge involved in building certain sub-assemblies. India's Nuclear Fuel Complex led the team that developed the titanium half-alloy tubes needed for the hydraulic power transmission. The Defence Avionics Research Establishment developed an indigenous Full Authority Digital Engine Control. The DRDO's Central Vehicle Research and Development Establishment designed and developed the mounted accessory gearbox and power take-off shaft for the LCA.

For a country with little track record in advanced aerospace systems, ADA's LCA project was audacious in its vision. Only three of the 35 major avionics components and line-replaceable units are foreign in origin. The rest are indigenously developed by a wide range of organizations falling under the ADA umbrella. Even within imported systems, there is a drive to progressively increase the Indian content. Two critical technologies—the development and manufacture of advanced carbon-fiber composites structures and skins

BOX 1.5
Continued

and a modern "glass cockpit"—were developed completely within India. Additionally, ADA's Autolay integrated automated software system for the design and development of 3-D laminated composite elements has resulted in a profitable spin-off: It has been licensed to both Airbus and Infosys.

The maiden flight of the LCA prototype successfully took place in 2001. The first batch of 20 LCA fighter aircraft are expected to be inducted by the Indian Air Force in 2010, with the first LCA squadron based in Tamil Nadu in South India. At the end of the day, was the LCA project worthwhile? Consider the ultimate price tag for the Indian Air Force: The LCA will cost about INR 1.1 billion, compared to the price tag of the Swedish JAS-39 *Gripen* (INR 1.5 billion, equivalent to $34 million) or the French *Rafale* (INR 2.7 billion, equivalent to $61 million). Most importantly, the LCA project has boosted India's general aerospace capabilities while increasing the national confidence level and raising its esteem in the international community.

"Light Combat Aircraft Test-Flown Successfully," *http://www.drdo.org/products/lca.htm*; "Tejas Light Combat Supersonic Fighter, India," *http://www.airforce-technology.com/projects/tejas/*; "Hindustan (HAL) Tejas / Light Combat Aircraft (LCA) Light Multi-Role Fighter," *http://www.aerospaceweb.org/aircraft/fighter/lca/*; B. Harry, "Radiance of the Tejas," *Vayu Aerospace Review* 1 (2005) , *http://www.bharat-rakshak.com/IAF/Aircraft/Current/611-LCA-Links.html*; "NFC Develops Titanium Product for LCA, GSLV," *The Hindu Business Line*, *http://www.blonnet.com/2006/06/09/stories/2006060904140900.htm*.

Business Network Characteristics

The LCA business network aptly illustrates three characteristics increasingly found in business networks, particularly alliance networks. First, it is organized around developing and realizing an envisioned market opportunity. The relationships depicted in the LCA business network are connected to other relationships not depicted, just as other non-depicted relationships between the depicted firms are organized around other market opportunities. As an example, Dessault Aviation, France is a major subcontractor on the French Rafale fighter, which competes against the Lockheed Martin F-16 fighter in world markets. From a business market management perspective, a meaningful way to delimit a network is around a defined market opportunity.

Second, the relationships between firms may not be simple ones, but **multiplex relations**, where the firms are potentially suppliers, customers, and competitors to one another for the same market opportunity. For example, BAE Systems is one of the partners in several other fighter aircraft programs such as the Typhoon Eurofighter program, which could be viewed as a competitor to the LCA. Third, business networks are increasingly international in composition, unlike business networks such as the Japanese *keiretsu* or the Korean *chaebol*, which are domestic business networks.[63]

Analyzing Business Networks

We can analyze business networks using a model with three components: actors, activities, and resources.[64] **Actors** are firms, such as customers and suppliers, or other organizations, such as regulatory agencies, that perform activities and control resources. Actors perform **activities** such as transactions (e.g., order management cycle) and create value through transforming resources. **Resources** refer to anything that actors explicitly value, such as technical know-how, equipment, personnel, or capital, which they can use to generate greater value for themselves and others. Even though a firm may possess a given resource, for strategic purposes, it may instead look to other firms to collaboratively develop the resource.

Three pivotal concepts help us analyze business networks: network horizon, network context, and network identity. Let's analyze each in terms of actors, activities, and resources. **Network horizon** refers to how extended an actor's view of the network is. It depends on the actor's experience as well as on the structural network features, such as the connectedness of relationships. A firm may engage banks, consultants, or export management companies as "scouts" to extend its network horizon. For example, Standard Chartered, the British merchant bank, ran a series of ads touting its international networking capability in China, where it can provide its clients with "market studies, introductions, and joint-venture assistance."[65]

The part of the network within the horizon is the actor's **network context**. The network context is structured in terms of the three earlier components: the actors, who they are and how they are related to each other; the activities, what activities are performed and the ways in which they are linked together; and the resources, what resources are used and the pattern of adaptation between them. The contexts are partially shared by the network actors, at least by those close to each other. Yet, because of differential knowledge and experience, every actor has a different network context. Consider, for example, how the network context for Boeing, which has a commercial aircraft unit as well its military aircraft unit, would be different from that for Lockheed Martin, which does not have a commercial aircraft unit.

In this ambiguous, complex, and fluid configuration of firms that constitute a network, in which the relations between firms have such importance, the actors develop **network identities**. Such an identity refers to how the firms see themselves in the network and how they are seen by other network actors. Network identity captures the uniqueness of each firm in its set of relationships. As such, it is time dependent and context related. For example, India-based Bharat Forge made such an impression on some of the foriegn sub-contractors with its work on the LCA project that it could conceivably get future orders for other aircraft projects. Network identity communicates a certain orientation toward others, such as being positively connected, having a multiplex relationship, or having no relationship. It conveys a certain competence in terms of an actor's perceived capability to perform certain activities, and it has a certain power content.

For business networks to possess advantages beyond the sum of the involved dyadic relationships, consideration must take place within those relationships about their connectedness with other relationships. A firm needs to consider how generalizable or incompatible a relationship with its partner firm will be judged to be by other actors in the network. Through a relationship, a firm can signal other actors about its availability and willingness to have relationships with them.

BOX 1.6
ABN-AMRO Correspondent Banking Group

Decentralizing the Network

Some years ago, the Correspondent Banking Group (CBG) of ABN-AMRO (AA), the large Dutch bank, moved to decentralize its correspondent banking relationships from the head office to the bank's own network of local branches. Prior to this change, AA CBG Amsterdam had responsibility for managing correspondent banking relationships with 4,300 banks. These responsibilities included providing product coverage (e.g., credit lines, trade services) for services sold to these banks, as well as conducting due diligence on credit limits that AA extended to 3,000 of the correspondent banks.

Clearly, the situation was unworkable. Simply too many bank customers needed the attention of too few CBG relationship managers. Relationship managers were geographically too far away from their correspondent bank customers, which led to communication barriers and prevented building close relationships. As a result, client contact was too infrequent. To find a better way to conduct business, AA senior management looked to where in the AA (branch) network correspondent banking was exemplary. The United States seemed to be working well, so they sought to understand why it was working there and what could be generalized to other parts of the network.

To change the network, AA senior management tapped Wolf Platzer for the role of network **architect**. Platzer was running the correspondent banking unit for European American Bank, an AA U.S. subsidiary. In this assignment, he had become aware that AA was missing out on opportunities for its correspondent banking business because of infrequent contact with bank customers and uncoordinated business development efforts of the local AA CBG units. Platzer began to work out policies and procedures that were more flexible to accommodate the needs of AA's correspondent bank customers and, in turn, their corporate clients that were doing business across borders. The more efficient these correspondent relationships could become (e.g., lower processing cost and higher execution speed), the more the banks' corporate clients could benefit as well. His vision was of a correspondent banking unit network comprising a head office correspondent banking unit, regional correspondent banking units, and local correspondent banking units, each with defined primary and support responsibilities.

In this decentralized network, three senior relationship managers occupy the role of **caretaker**: one responsible for the Americas, one for Asia, and one for Europe, the Middle East, and Africa. These managers have the functional responsibility for correspondent banking in their sectors. Hans Duijn, Senior Vice President and Head of Correspondent Banking at the time, acted as the **lead operator** for the decentralized network. Business cases were made by AA branch managers for adding a local correspondent banking unit, or Duijn approached a country manager or regional manager, wanting more correspondent banking presence there. Duijn expected to be consulted on all correspondent banking appointments made at the local AA branch, and the head office was sometimes asked to do some "head-hunting."

Implementation of the network change was done in a practical way, as the capabilities of the local and regional CB units improved (e.g., building regional infrastructure in terms of technology and creation of a regional credit committee). Funding for the needed training and development came out of several pockets, depending on the resource needed: products, marketing materials, or training.

Conversely, having a relationship can make a firm repulsive to other actors, even though the firm may desire a relationship with them. For example, Mitsubishi has been reluctant to engage in collaborative relations with Daimler-Benz because Mitsubishi has a strong supplier relationship with Boeing, whereas Daimler-Benz is part of the Airbus consortium, an ardent rival to Boeing.[66] A firm needs to consider how complementary and irreconcilable the activities it undertakes with its partner firm are with its activities in other connected relationships. Finally, a firm needs to consider how transferable resources developed with its partner firm are to other connected relationships and how particular they are to that single relationship. For example, some of the technical know-how that Bharat Forge develops in its participation in the LCA alliance network may be transferable to new supply relationships with aircraft companies such as Airbus, Boeing or Embraer in the future.

A final aspect of analyzing and managing business networks is network roles. Snow, Miles, and Coleman argue that in constructing business networks, certain managers operate as brokers, creatively marshaling resources that other actors control.[67] They sketch out three broker roles that significantly contribute to the success of business networks: the architect, who facilitates the building of specific networks, yet seldom has a complete grasp or understanding of the network that ultimately emerges; the lead operator, who formally connects specific actors into an ongoing network; and the caretaker, who focuses on activities that enhance network performance and needs to have a broader network horizon. These network roles may be more apparent in some business networks, such as alliance networks, than in others. In Box 1.6, the decentralization of the ABN-AMRO Correspondent Banking Group provides an illustration of these network roles in practice.

SUMMARY

This chapter provided an overview of business market management. In so doing, it also provided an overview for this book, which is organized around the constituent processes of business market management. Four fundamental ideas that recur throughout this book are the guiding principles of business market management: (1) regard value as the cornerstone of business market management; (2) focus on business market processes; (3) stress doing business across borders; and (4) accentuate working relationships and business networks.

Value is the monetary worth of all a market offering provides to a customer firm. Although value in business markets is a construct, business market management relies upon assessment of value in the marketplace. Translating customer value into shareholder value depends on a business being able to claim an equitable return on the value it delivers to customers. We contend that through persuasively demonstrating and documenting the superior value it delivers to customers, a business will be better equipped to successfully accomplish this translation.

Business market management is a business process that is itself composed of a series of related, interdependent business processes. Each of these business market processes is the subject of a chapter in this book. The essential undertaking of business marketing remains what it has conceptually been for many years:

Understand what the customer does, and would, value.

Because business markets are predominantly concerned about functionality and performance, their offerings are valued similarly across borders more than is the case for consumer market offerings, where aesthetics and taste predominate. Nonetheless, business market managers doing business across borders will likely have to resolve complications arising from language and culture, cross-border negotiation and dispute resolution, and currency exchange and payment risk.

Finally, a firm's marketplace success in business markets is directly dependent upon its working relationships and, because these relationships are connected to other relationships of interest, its business networks. Thus, business market managers must be adept at analyzing, understanding, building, and playing an active part in work teams, working relationships, and business networks.

ENDNOTES

1. To disguise the firm's identity, we have not used its actual brand names.
2. Howard Gleckman, with Gary McWilliams, "Ask and It Shall Be Discounted," *Business Week*, 6 (October 1997): 116, 118.
3. Of course, we recognize in stating a generality that exceptions do occur, such as when a firm purchases art for display on the walls of its corporate headquarters or when a consumer purchases power tools for home repairs.
4. By **market offering**, we mean the core product or service that a supplier offers, augmented with its supplementary services, programs, and systems. We define market offering in greater detail in Chapter 5. Although usage varies across business markets, functionality most often refers to what specifically the core product or service does, such as a white pigment providing whitening, brightening, and opacifying when it is added to a coating. Performance most often more broadly refers to all that a market offering provides to a customer firm and includes consideration of the costs a customer incurs in obtaining the functionality.
5. James C. Anderson, Dipak Jain, and Pradeep Chintagunta, "Customer Value Assessment in Business Markets: A State-of-Practice Study," *Journal of Business-to-Business Marketing*, 1, no. 1 (1993): 3–29.
6. For a recent conceptualization and empirical assessment of benefits and sacrifices as determinants of customer value, see: Ajay Menon, Christian Homburg, and Nikolas Beutin, "Understanding Customer Value in Business-to-Business Relationships," *Journal of Business-to-Business Marketing*, 12, no. 2 (2005): 1–38. Menon, Homburg, and Beutin consider price as part of customer value, which differs from our conceptualization. For a recent critical review of alternate conceptualizations of customer value, see: James C. Anderson, "From understanding to managing customer value in business markets," in *Rethinking Marketing: Developing a New Understanding of Markets*, Håkan Håkansson, Debbie Harrison, and Alexandra Waluszewski, eds. (Chichester, England: John Wiley & Sons, Ltd., 2004), 137–159.
7. Lawrence D. Miles, *Techniques of Value Analysis and Engineering*, 3rd ed. (Washington, DC: Lawrence D. Miles Value Foundation, 1989).
8. Economists refer to this difference as "consumer surplus" (cf. Robert S. Pindyck and David L. Rubinfeld, *Microeconomics* [New York: Macmillan, 1989]). This expression is doubly inapt in business markets because our focus is on customers, not consumers, and in our context, this difference is not a "surplus," but an absolutely necessary inducement for customers to purchase a supplier's offering.
9. Irwin Gross, "C-ing Customer Value," *Marketplace: The ISBM Review* (Spring 1992): 4.

10. Miles, *Techniques of Value Analysis*; Lawrence Miles, "Value Analysis: Buying Is a Spirited Game," *Purchasing World* (September 1984): 46; Hamid Noori and Russell Radford, *Production and Operations Management: Total Quality and Responsiveness* (New York: McGraw-Hill, 1995). Value analysis is sometimes referred to as value engineering; see Louis De Rose, *Value Selling* (Chicago: Amacom, American Management Association, 1989).
11. Michael Hammer and James Champy, *Reengineering the Corporation* (New York: Harper Business Press, 1993), p. 35.
12. David A. Garvin, "Leveraging Processes for Strategic Advantage: A Roundtable with Xerox's Allaire, USAA's Herres, SmithKline Beecham's Leschly, and Pepsi's Weatherup," *Harvard Business Review* (September–October 1995): 89 [emphases added].
13. Recognizing the difficulty businesses have in redesigning business processes successfully, Hammer has recently provided a framework of process enablers and enterprise capabilities to evaluate and guide business process transformation. See: Michael Hammer, "The Process Audit," *Harvard Business Review* (April 2007): 111–123.
14. In this section, we draw on the classic source: Alfred Rappaport, *Creating Shareholder Value*, rev. ed. (New York: The Free Press, 1998). For Rappaport's recent thinking on governance principles for shareholder value creation, see: Alfred Rappaport, "10 Ways to Create Shareholder Value," *Harvard Business Review* (September 2006): 66–77. For an extended treatment of the implications for shareholder value on marketing, see: Peter Doyle, *Value-Based Marketing: Marketing Strategies for Corporate Growth and Shareholder Value* (Chichester, England: Wiley, 2000).
15. Rappaport, *Creating Shareholder Value*, p. 8.
16. Rajendra K. Srivastava, Tasadduq A. Shervani, and Liam Fahey, "Marketing, Business Processes, and Shareholder Value: An Organizationally Embedded View of Marketing Activities and the Discipline of Marketing," *Journal of Marketing* (special issue 1999): 168–179. Both quotes are taken from p. 169.
17. Michael Hammer, "The Superefficient Company," *Harvard Business Review* (September 2001): 82–91.
18. Srivastava, Shervani, and Fahey, "Marketing, Business Processes." The three quotes are taken from pp. 170 and 172.
19. Srivastava, Shervani, and Fahey, "Marketing, Business Processes;" and Rajendra K. Srivastava, Tasadduq A. Shervani, and Liam Fahey, "Market-Based Assets and Shareholder Value: A Framework for Analysis," *Journal of Marketing* (January 1998): 2–18.
20. For an extended treatment of the changing marketing concept and its implementation, see a pair of articles by Frederick E. Webster, Jr.: "Defining the New Marketing Concept," *Marketing Management*, 2, no. 4 (1994): 22–31; and "Executing the New Marketing Concept," *Marketing Management*, 3, no. 1 (1994): 9–16.
21. Benson P. Shapiro, "What the Hell Is 'Market Oriented'?" *Harvard Business Review* (November–December 1988): 119–125.
22. Peter F. Drucker, "Learning from Foreign Management," *The Wall Street Journal*, 4 June 1980, 24.
23. Webster, "Defining the New Marketing Concept"; Webster, "Executing the New Marketing Concept"; and Gary Hamel and C. K. Prahalad, "Strategy as Stretch and Leverage," *Harvard Business Review* (March–April 1993): 75–84.
24. Max H. Bazerman and Margaret A. Neale, *Negotiating Rationally* (New York: The Free Press, 1992); Max H. Bazerman and Margaret A. Neale, "Negotiating Rationally," *Business Week Advance Executive Brief*, vol. 1 (New York: McGraw-Hill, 1992), 1–22; Adam M. Brandenburger and Barry J. Nalebuff, "The Right Game: Use Game Theory to Shape Strategy," *Harvard Business Review* (July–August 1995): 57–71; and Gary Hamel, Yves L. Doz, and C. K. Prahalad, "Collaborate with Your Competitors—And Win," *Harvard*

Business Review (January–February 1989): 133–139.
25. Regis McKenna, "Marketing Is Everything," *Harvard Business Review* (January–February 1991): 65–79.
26. Bhanu Pande, "Crunch Time for Kelloggs," *Business Standard*, November 5, 2001, available in: *www.magindia.com/manarch/news/man4100.html*
27. "Trade Winds," *The Economist*, 8 November 1997, 85–86; "Delivering the Goods," *The Economist*, 15 November 1997, 85–86; "When Trade and Security Clash," *The Economist*, 6 April 2002, 59–62. For an example of how Japan Airlines is using the Internet to attract new, foreign sources of supply, see "Webbed Flight," *The Economist*, 8 February 1997, 66.
28. For further discussion of the strategic advantages of pursuing growth in foreign markets, see Michael Porter, "What Is Strategy?" *Harvard Business Review* (November–December 1996): 61–78.
29. Details are available in various reports by agencies such as Centre for Monitoring Indian Economy (CMIE), Federation of Indian Chambers of Commerce and Industry (FICCI), and Confederation of Indian Industry (CII).
30. Latest Market Development Assistance – Guidelines Of Ministry of Commerce, Government of India at: *www.embindia.org/eng/documentos/LatestMarketDevelopmentAssistance.doc;* For an example of the assistance provided by Indian Embassies to Indian companies, see: A brief note on working of Commercial Wing, Activities undertaken by Mission/Post to promote trade & investment, available at: *www.cgidubai.com/index.php/trade_commerce/a_brief_note_on_working_of_commercial_wing;* visit for example, India's largest B2B Marketplace at: *www.tradeindia.com.*
31. "The Grand Illusion," *The Economist*, 26 November 1994, 17; and "Downhill from Here," *The Economist*, 29 July 2006, 36.
32. "Sharp Tongues: The Nordics' Pragmatic Choice Is English," *The Economist*, 14 June 2003, 9; "Cultural Explanations: The Man in the Baghdad Café," *The Economist*, 9 November 1996, 23–26; Jeswald W. Salacuse, *Making Global Deals* (New York: Times Books, 1991).
33. Salacuse, *Making Global Deals*.
34. Jean-Claude Usunier, *Marketing Across Cultures*, 2nd ed. (London: Prentice Hall Europe, 1996); "Cultural Explanations," *The Economist*.
35. Jack D. Wood, "Culture Is Not Enough," in *Mastering Management*, George Bickerstaffe, ed. (London: Pitman Publishing, 1997), 414–418.
36. "Cultural Explanations," *The Economist*, 23, 26.
37. Geert Hoftstede, "The Interaction Between National and Organizational Value Systems," *Journal of Management Studies* (July 1985): 347–357. As mentioned earlier, the country may be multicultural, in which case the specific cultural group of the business counterparts needs to be understood.
38. Adapted from Salacuse, *Making Global Deals*, 7.
39. Jeanne M. Brett, *Negotiating Globally* (San Francisco: Jossey-Bass, 2001); James K. Sebenius, "The Hidden Challenge of Cross-Border Negotiations," *Harvard Business Review* (March 2002): 76–85.
40. Salacuse, *Making Global Deals*.
41. Nigel Wilkins, *The Correspondent Banking Handbook* (London: Euromoney Books, 1993), 28. See also "Islamic Banking: Forced Devotion," *The Economist*, 17 February 2001, 76–77; and "Islamic Finance: West Meets East," *The Economist*, 25 October 2003, 69.
42. Salacuse, *Making Global Deals*, 122.
43. "Business in Difficult Places: Risky Returns," *The Economist*, 20 May 2000, 85–88; "The Worm That Never Dies," *The Economist*, 2 March 2002, 12; "The Short Arm of the Law," *The Economist*, 2 March 2002, 63–65; and "Everything for a Price," *World Press Review*, October 2001, 6–15.
44. Tony Allison, "Enron's Eight Year Power Struggle in India," *Asia Times Online*, 18 January 2001, *www.atimes.com/reports/CA13Ai01.html;* "The Enron Corporation: Corporate Complicity in Human Rights Violations," *www.hrw.org/reports/1999/enron*.

45. Salacuse, *Making Global Deals*, 128.
46. Salacuse, *Making Global Deals*. See also "Happy Endings Not Guaranteed," *Business Week*, 20 November 2002, 69–73.
47. We limit our discussion to the more common occurrences of currency exchange and payment risk in doing business across borders. Firms may employ hedging to protect themselves against large foreign currency exchange fluctuations; see, for example, Stephen D. Makar and Stephen P. Huffman, "Foreign Currency Risk Management Practices in U.S. Multinationals," *Journal of Applied Business Research* (Spring 1997): 73–86. Foreign currencies that are nonconvertible provide additional problems to resolve; see, for example, Ben Craig, "Competing Currencies: Back to the Future?" *Economic Commentary* (Federal Reserve Bank of Cleveland), 15 October 1996; and "World Wire: Prague, Russia Set Up Barter," *The Wall Street Journal*, 21 March 1991, A15.
48. Jon R. Katzenbach and Douglas K. Smith, "The Discipline of Teams," *Harvard Business Review* (March–April 1993): 112.
49. Katzenbach and Smith, "The Discipline of Teams," 112.
50. Some management thinkers recommend that senior managers acquire knowledge of the informal networks of relationships that individuals have across functions and divisions and factor this into decisions about team composition. See David Krackhardt and Jeffrey R. Hanson, "Informal Networks: The Company Behind the Chart," *Harvard Business Review* (July–August 1993): 104–111.
51. Katzenbach and Smith, "The Discipline of Teams," 115.
52. "The Trouble with Teams," *The Economist*, 14 January 1995, 69. For a recent article on the challenges of managing multicultural teams, which is a more frequent occurrence, and strategies for dealing with these challenges, see: Jeanne Brett, Kristin Behfar, and Mary C. Kern, "Managing Multicultural Teams," *Harvard Business Review*, November 2006, 84–91.
53. Christopher Meyer, "How the Right Measures Help Teams Excel," *Harvard Business Review* (May–June 1994): 95–103; Alfie Kohn, "Why Incentive Plans Cannot Work," *Harvard Business Review* (September–October 1993): 54–56, 58, 60, 62–63; "Rethinking Rewards," *Harvard Business Review* (November–December 1993): 37–39, 42–45, 48–49; and "Just Desserts," *The Economist*, 29 January 1994, 69.
54. James C. Anderson and James A. Narus, "Partnering as a Focused Market Strategy," *California Management Review* (Spring 1991): 95–113.
55. For a review on alliance management, see Robert E. Spekman, Theodore M. Forbes III, Lynn A. Isabella, and Thomas C. MacAvoy, "Alliance Management: A View from the Past and a Look to the Future," *Marketing Science Institute Working Paper*, Report No. 95-119 (December 1995): 1–32.
56. Jeanne M. Brett, Stephen B. Goldberg, and William L. Ury, "Managing Conflict: The Strategy of Dispute Systems Design," *Business Week Advance Executive Brief*, vol. 6 (New York: McGraw-Hill, 1994), 1–26; see also Todd B. Carver and Albert A. Vondra, "Alternative Dispute Resolution: Why It Doesn't Work and Why It Does," *Harvard Business Review* (May–June 1994): 120–130.
57. Ian F. Wilkinson and Louise C. Young, "Business Dancing: The Nature and Role of Interfirm Relationships in Business Strategy," *Asia-Australia Marketing Journal*, 2, no. 1 (1994): 67–79.
58. This section draws heavily on James C. Anderson, "Relationships in Business Markets: Exchange Episodes, Value Creation, and Their Empirical Assessment," *Journal of the Academy of Marketing Science* (Fall 1995): 346–350. See also David T. Wilson, "An Integrated Model of Buyer-Seller Relationships," *Journal of the Academy of Marketing Science* (Fall 1995): 335–345.
59. Peter Smith Ring and Andrew Van de Ven, "Developmental Processes of Cooperative Interorganizational Relationships,"

Academy of Management Review (January 1994): 112.

60. Karen S. Cook and Richard M. Emerson, "Power, Equity, Commitment in Exchange Networks," *American Sociological Review* (October 1978): 725. For consideration of how customer and supplier firms create value through their commitment to business network relationships, coordinating their activities with those of their business partners in connected relationships, see Desirée Blankenburg Holm, Kent Eriksson, and Jan Johanson, "Creating Value Through Mutual Commitment to Business Network Relationships," *Strategic Management Journal*, 20 (1999): 467–486.
61. Alajoutsijärvi, Möller, and Rosenbröijer have defined this set of connected relationships with the focal relationship as the *focal business net* to delineate it from the broader business network in which these relationships are embedded. See Kimmo Alajoutsijärvi, Kristian Möller, and Carl-Johan Rosenbröijer, "Relevance of Focal Nets in Understanding the Dynamics of Business Relationships," *Journal of Business-to-Business Marketing*, 6, no. 3 (1999): 3–35.
62. Ranjay Gulati, "Social Structure and Alliance Formation Patterns: A Longitudinal Analysis," *Administrative Science Quarterly* (December 1995): 619–652; and Benjamin Gomes-Casseres, "Group Versus Group: How Alliance Networks Compete," *Harvard Business Review* (July–August 1994): 62–66, 70, 72–74.
63. Kenichi Ohmae, "The Global Logic of Strategic Alliances," *Harvard Business Review* (March–April 1989): 143–154.
64. This section draws upon James C. Anderson, Håkan Håkansson, and Jan Johanson, "Dyadic Relationships Within a Business Network Context," *Journal of Marketing* (October 1994): 1–15.
65. "International Networking," Standard Chartered Advertisement, *The Economist*, 23 April 1994, 1–2.
66. Steven Brull and Brandon Mitchener, "The Alliance Demands Patience: Five Years On, Daimler and Mitsubishi Are Still Talking," *International Herald Tribune*, 15 December 1993, 11, 15.
67. Charles C. Snow, Raymond E. Miles, and Henry J. Coleman, Jr., "Managing 21st Century Network Organizations," *Organizational Dynamics* (Winter 1992): 5–19.

Section

Understanding Value

Business Market Processes

Managing Market Offerings

New Offering Realization

Business Channel Management

Market Sensing

Understanding Firms as Customers

Crafting Market Strategy

Understanding Value

Creating Value

Delivering Value

Gaining New Business

Sustaining Reseller Partnerships

Managing Customers

Guiding Principles

Regard Value as the Cornerstone

Focus on Business Market Processes

Stress Doing Business Across Borders

Accentuate Working Relationships and Business Networks

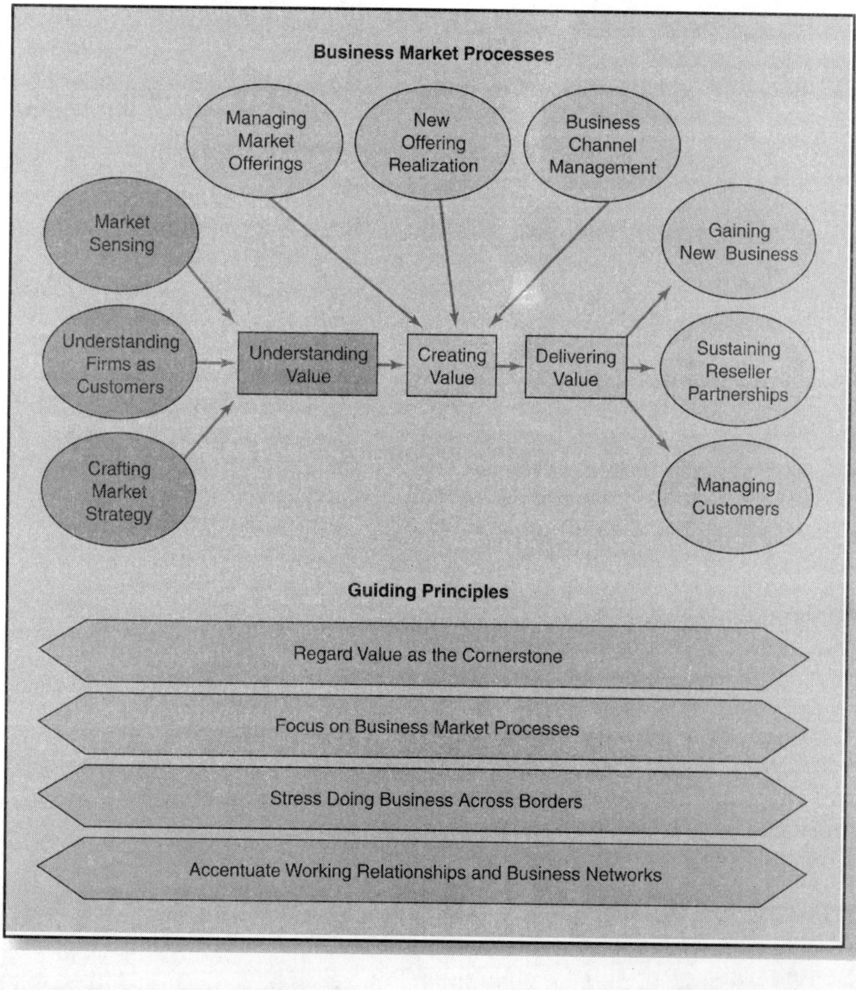

Chapter 2

Market Sensing

Generating and Using Knowledge About the Market

Overview

Market-driven firms are distinguished by an ability to sense events and trends in their markets ahead of their competitors. They can anticipate more accurately the responses to actions designed to retain or attract customers, improve channel relations, or thwart competitors. They can act on information in a timely, coherent manner because the assumptions about the market are broadly shared. This anticipatory capability is based on superiority in each step of the process. It is achieved through open-minded inquiry, synergistic information distribution, mutually informed interpretations, and accessible memories.[1]

Day calls this distinctive capability of market-driven organizations *market sensing*. He has also sketched out a market sensing process, which is shown in Figure 2.1. Market sensing can provide a firm with an edge over its competitors, yet most firms do not recognize this. We have never seen a business that was in trouble because it had too much knowledge about its market, yet we routinely encounter businesses in trouble because they have faulty or inadequate knowledge about their markets.

Market sensing is the process of generating knowledge about the market that individuals in the business, such as

Figure 2.1 Market Sensing: Process for Learning About Markets

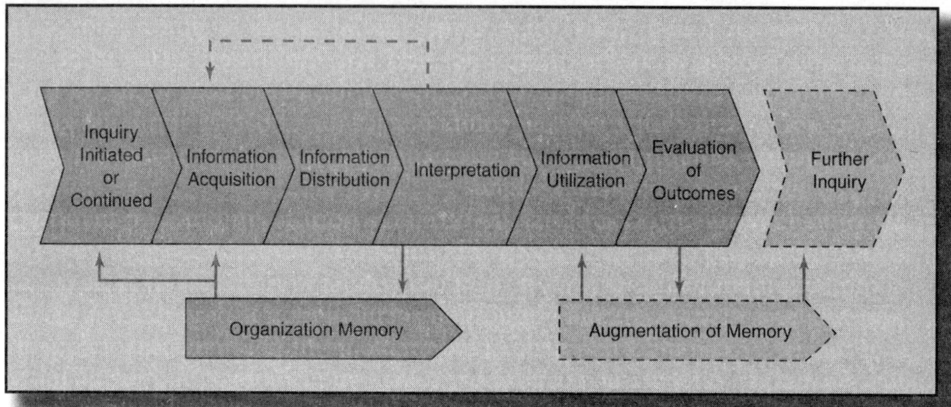

Source: George S. Day, "The Capabilities of Market-Driven Organizations," *Journal of Marketing* (October 1994): 43.

business market managers, salespersons, or senior executives, use to inform and guide their decision making. Market sensing is a market-driven process of learning about present and prospective customers and competitors, as well as about other actors that affect them and the business, such as resellers and regulatory agencies. Market sensing enables business market managers and others in the business to formulate, test, revise, update, and refine their **market views**, which are simplified representations of the marketplace and how it works. Market sensing greatly contributes to the value of these mental models by providing a way to test assumptions about customers, competitors, and the firm's own resources and capabilities that often are largely implicit. It also advances decision rules and heuristics that supplier managers use to interpret and act upon changes in the marketplace.[2]

This chapter is organized around four substantive facets of market sensing: defining the market, monitoring competition, assessing customer value, and gaining customer feedback. To attain a distinctive capability in market sensing, the firm should strive to be superior to its competitors in each of these facets, particularly in assessing value, because value is the cornerstone of business market management. Figure 2.2 provides an overview not only of these substantive facets of market sensing but also of the chapter. Before we discuss each substantive facet, though, let's briefly consider some requirements for market sensing as a business market management process.

Market sensing encompasses market research, which is a crucial business marketing process for generating knowledge about the market, but it is broader than that. Marketplace knowledge is generated in other ways; for example, when supplier engineers have discussions with customer engineers about customer development projects at an

Figure 2.2 Substantive Facets of Market Sensing

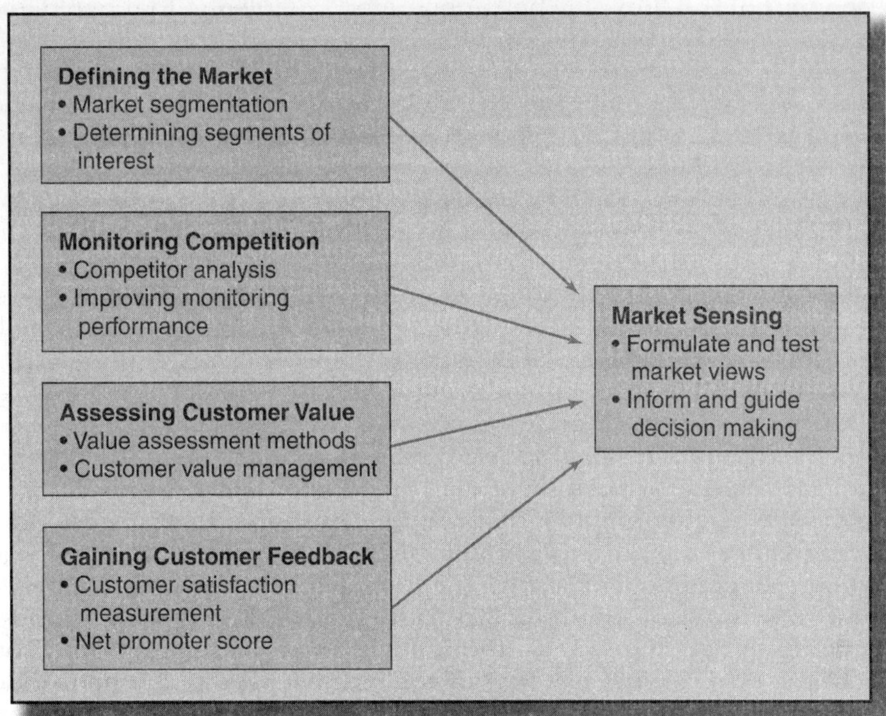

industry or professional association meeting, or when manufacturing managers talk with equipment suppliers about new equipment and learn that competitors have purchased it. Moreover, use of the generated knowledge by individuals in the firm to inform and guide their decision making is a crucial part of market sensing. Thus, the generated knowledge must be accessible and individuals must be willing to use it.[3]

The generated knowledge may be tacit, where the individuals possessing it have difficulty expressing it or putting it in an explicit form that others can use. Seasoned salespeople may develop routines and practices, such as subtle variations in their sales presentations that enhance their performance, but which they may not be able to readily articulate. Based on trial-and-error learning, production workers may make subtle, minor adjustments to the component materials "recipe" or to equipment to make products that perform better in particular customer applications. Individuals can use metaphors, analogies, and conceptual models as tools to transform their tacit knowledge to explicit knowledge that is valuable to others in the firm. Knowledgeable individuals also can transfer their tacit and explicit knowledge to others by serving as coaches, allowing those others to acquire the knowledge through guided practice, observation, problem solving, or experimentation, providing them with feedback.[4]

Firms have great difficulty realizing what they *do* know. Individuals in one part of the firm may have generated knowledge that could inform and guide the decision making of individuals in another part of the firm, yet each is unaware of this knowledge and its availability. It is a challenge for a firm to pull together all it knows about the market and to make this knowledge available to relevant individuals in a meaningful way. Firms traditionally have used reports, plans, written policies and procedures, and manuals to provide a collective or **organization memory**. Progressive firms increasingly employ sophisticated information technology to create relational databases, link disparate databases, and provide decision-support tools, such as expert systems and decision calculus models. In an ever-changing marketplace, it is essential for firms to refresh, update, and assess the continued accuracy of the information in the organization's memory.[5]

An old saying in German business is "If Siemens only knew what Siemens knows." This paradoxical saying captures the difficulties that large, multinational firms, such as the conglomerate Siemens, have in knowledge management. **Knowledge management** refers to the processes and supporting systems that enable a firm to gather know-how, best practices, and learning that potentially have value elsewhere in the firm, convert them into a form that can be readily found and understood, and then make them accessible for reuse more broadly within the firm. To make progress against this saying, Siemens made a substantial investment in a "sharenet," which is an intranet system on which knowledge is posted for use throughout the firm. In preparing its bid for a high-speed data network linking Kuala Lumpur with its new airport, Siemens Malaysia found itself lacking some necessary know-how. A search on the sharenet revealed that Siemens was already working on a similar project in Denmark. Adapting what had been done there to its own setting, Siemens Malaysia was able to leverage this knowledge gained from Denmark to win an order for a pilot project.[6]

Even when it is accessible, generated knowledge about the market has little value if individuals are not willing to use it. A user's trust in the individual who generates the market knowledge, or market research, significantly predicts willingness to use the market research. The user's perception of the researcher's integrity and willingness to reduce research uncertainty (through the provision of explanations for research results) are significant antecedents of the user's trust in the research provider.[7] Further, a complementary blend of formal and informal communications between providers and users in different functional areas significantly contributes to the users' perceptions of the quality of the market intelligence. In turn, this perception of quality significantly affects their use of that market intelligence. Formal dissemination of market intelligence itself is a significant, direct antecedent of its use. "Although informal communications may provide greater openness and clarification opportunities, formal communications tend to be more credible and verifiable, thereby encouraging the use of intelligence, particularly if it is contrary to receivers' prior beliefs."[8]

More broadly, individuals' willingness to use knowledge management systems depends on their perception that doing so provides worthwhile assistance to them, which depends, in part, on the process the firm pursues to make contributions to its knowledge database. Customer service representatives at Xerox share insights they gain when fixing Xerox machines through a process that ensures that what finally makes it into their Web-based, knowledge management system, known as the Eureka database, is relevant, accurate, and easily understood. Reps submit suggestions or tips to local experts, who work together with the rep to screen and refine them. Tips that pass this initial screen are submitted to a centralized review process, where the relevant business unit screens the tips, eliminates redundancies, and further refines the tips, contributing any deeper technical expertise needed. Tips that ultimately are placed in the Eureka database have the contributing rep's name attached to them, providing social recognition. Interestingly, in the pilot program to design this system, Xerox found that the reps preferred this social recognition to financial incentives for contributing tips, which they felt might subvert the process.[9]

Defining the Market

In **defining the market**, business market managers choose descriptors that characterize and delimit a market, with the intent of pinpointing groups of firms that are of greater interest to the supplier firm. The descriptors chosen significantly affect the way a firm views a market, what its prospects are, and the courses of action it subsequently pursues. Market segmentation and determining market segments of interest are fundamental to defining the market.

Market Segmentation

"If you're not thinking segments, you're not thinking."[10] Levitt made this provocative observation a number of years ago, and it is even more true now, as markets have become more diverse and dynamic. **Market segmentation** is the process of partitioning a market into groupings of firms that have relatively similar requirements and preferences for market offerings within each grouping, and relatively different requirements and preferences between groupings. When segmenting markets, business market managers look for descriptors that capture significant differences in requirements and preferences for market offerings or how prospective customers will respond to marketing initiatives. Different descriptors can provide dramatically different views of the market and provide insights to gain competitive advantage.

Significantly, irrespective of which descriptors a firm chooses, any market segmentation requires empirical support to validate the market view it suggests. Otherwise, the firm may overlook some subtle, yet critical, distinctions that exist. As an example, a manufacturer of downhole drills initially grouped strip mines and quarries together into a single segment, thinking they were similar. Strip mines and quarries both use downhole drills to create blastholes in which workers place explosives to blow the "face" off the production wall to extract material such as iron ore or limestone. The manufacturer developed a new downhole drill that was capable of drilling significantly more feet per hour, which would provide users with time savings and lower cost. In its subsequent market research, the manufacturer discovered that a faster drill would provide significantly greater value in strip mines than it would in quarries. An additional step in the quarries' production process was the cause of this difference. Unlike strip mines, quarries perform a crushing operation on the extracted material. It turns out that the crushing equipment that reduces the blasted rock to a smaller, more uniform size creates a "bottleneck" in the typical quarry's production process. One blast each day extracts enough material to keep the crushing equipment running at full capacity. In contrast, a faster drill that shortens the drill-blast-clear cycle significantly improves a strip mine's productivity.

Business market managers use a variety of ways, or bases, to segment markets. Often, they rely on several bases in conjunction to further segment or subsegment markets. We first discuss conventional bases of segmentation, then more progressive bases of segmentation. Whatever bases of segmentation business market managers decide on, they should apply the following four criteria to judge validity of their proposed segmentation scheme:[11]

1. ***Measurable:*** Can the size, growth, and market potential of a segment be measured?
2. ***Profitable:*** How profitable is the marketing effort likely to be? What is the payoff from each segment?
3. ***Accessible:*** Can segments be identified and reached successfully?
4. ***Actionable:*** Can effective marketing and sales programs be formulated for attracting and serving the segments?

Conventional Bases of Segmentation

Industry, customer size, customer behavior, and geography are customary ways of segmenting business markets. Finding **industries** that use (or might use) a supplier firm's market offering is a first step in segmentation. In North America, business market managers often use the North American Industry Classification System (NAICS) codes, which succeeded the U.S. Standard Industrial Classification (SIC) codes, to segment an industry.[12] Other countries too have their own basis of classifying industries. As an example of the successively finer industry classifications that four-digit versus six-digit NAICS codes provide, ship and boat building has the four-digit code of 3366, whereas boat building itself has the six-digit code of 336612. One problem that business market managers find with using NAICS codes is that the classification may still not be precise enough for their needs. For instance, a supplier of fiberglass resin for structural applications such as boat hulls would find the 336612 code insufficient, in that it also includes manufacturers of boats with aluminum hulls, which are not potential customers.

Business market managers segment by **customer size** when they believe that firm size is a strong proxy for customer demand for their firm's market offerings.

Specific measures of customer size, which often come from secondary sources, are total sales, number of employees, and number of locations (e.g., plants). **Customer behavior** captures a number of actions that firms take. Doing business with the supplier is a basic one, resulting in four segments: firms that are purchasing the supplier's market offering for the first time; firms that have purchased the supplier's market offering previously and currently are purchasing it; firms that have not purchased the supplier's market offering; and firms that have previously purchased the supplier's market offering, but no longer are purchasing it. Business market managers may further segment present customers' purchase behavior based on their extent of usage of a market offering—light, medium, or heavy.

Finally, business market managers segment by **geography** when they believe that customer location has a significant effect on doing business. Many firms implicitly use a basic geographic segmentation: the home-country market versus "the rest of the world." Most of these firms do business only in their home-country market. When the home-country market is large, firms may segment further and pursue business only on a local or regional basis.

Progressive Bases of Segmentation

Many business market managers are finding that the conventional bases of segmentation no longer have the vitality that they once had. Even though they may provide a useful start, they are not enough to pinpoint groups of customers with sufficiently similar requirements and preferences. To gain a more detailed understanding of how customer requirements and preferences vary, business market managers use more progressive bases of segmentation, such as application, customer capabilities and business priorities, usage situation, and customer profitability.

Business market managers segment by **application** because firms that use the supplier's core product or service in the same way or for the same purpose tend to derive value from it similarly. As an example, Glen Raven Mills, a manufacturer of acrylic woven fabrics, found two different applications for its products within the marine market: outside the boat as boat covers and canopies, and inside the boat as seat covers.[13] Customers had distinct requirements and preferences for each application. Another often-occurring application segmentation is between sales to original equipment manufacturers (OEMs) and replacement (aftermarket) sales for maintenance, repair, and operating (MRO) applications. For example, SKF India, a Swedish bearings manufacturer, supplies its products both to automobile manufacturers (OEMs) and to after-markets, as spares.

Customer capabilities can be a worthwhile basis of segmentation when customers vary significantly in what competencies they possess and what knowledge and skills they want suppliers to provide. Many firms now focus on their core competencies and strategic capabilities and rely on outside firms to provide the rest.[14] Some customer firms, for example, may possess technical know-how and problem-solving capability, while others do not and expect their suppliers to provide these aspects. **Customer business priorities** strongly influence which capabilities customer firms seek to possess as sources of competitive advantage, and they also provide a progressive basis of segmentation themselves. In Box 2.1, we describe how major Indian IT software vendors seek to grow their businesses with

BOX 2.1

Segmentation Concepts Adopted by Large IT Service Providers to Grow Their Business with a Large Multi-national Customer Firm

On September 1, 2005, ABN AMRO Bank announced the outsourcing of its IT (Information Technology) operations to five IT vendors: Tata Consultancy Services (TCS), Accenture, Patni, IBM, and Infosys Technologies. The total deal was valued at 1.8 billion Euros ($2.2 billion) over a five-year period.

ABN AMRO is a Netherlands-based bank, which commenced business in 1824. It has over four million retail clients, about 370,000 business clients, and total assets in excess of 203 billion Euros. It operates in multiple countries across the world.

ABN AMRO had chosen Accenture, IBM, Infosys, Patni, and TCS as its preferred vendors for IT application development. These vendors were mandated to develop new applications across all business units of the bank. Altogether, the Indian IT vendors were assured of 500 million Euros over the five-year period.

By consolidating its back office through such a large outsourcing deal, the bank figured it could save $300 million annually, starting in 2007. It would also free up its own human resources to develop innovative new products and boost revenues, valued at $23 billion in 2004.

The "preferred vendor" statuses accorded to these five IT service provider firms came with certain service expectations. If these were not met, penalty clauses would be triggered against the defaulting vendors. The vendors were expected to fully support the transition of the suite of applications from the various business units of ABN AMRO. A governance structure between ABN AMRO and the vendors was put in place to support the application transition.

For most of the Indian vendors, ABN AMRO is one of their largest accounts, with the potential to grow even larger. As part of periodic account planning, the service providers review their quarterly performance and evaluate the potential to cross-sell additional services to ABN AMRO. Given the potential and the performance expectations from a client as large as ABN AMRO, the reviews are usually scheduled with the CEO and/or the business unit head of the service provider.

Such accounts are usually categorized by the Indian IT service providers as "priority accounts" and hence receive senior management focus when it comes to addressing critical resource requirements. All stops are pulled out to make the right resources available for the customer. This is done for several reasons: to prevent competitors from gaining entry into the account; to prevent penalty clauses from being triggered due to inability to service the customer firm's request as a preferred vendor and leverage opportunities to cross-sell new services and intellectual property (IP).

Such large accounts offer significant avenues for continued growth of business, as the IT service provider can continue to access other groups within the customer firm for more business. One way that a typical IT service provider would segment a large customer like ABN AMRO would be based on its geographic presence or by the industry groups that it serves, such as business units within the bank, which serve customer firms in the manufacturing or service sectors. Typically, each of the business units of the bank provides funding for its respective IT projects from its own budgets.

While planning for the growth of the customer account, the IT service provider adopts strategies to penetrate different parts of the customer firm, viz., the different business

BOX 2.1
Continued

units, for more business, by positioning its service capability or intellectual property to obtain further business opportunities in its favor vis-à-vis the competition. Each of these business units of the customer firm has its own differing priorities, and decisions to award contracts to IT service providers are often made at the level of the business unit itself.

For instance, while a vendor like TCS may leverage its significant experience in Latin America to penetrate the Latin American business unit of the bank, another vendor like Infosys would leverage its deep expertise in investment banking to penetrate the Asset Management business unit. In this manner, each vendor seeks to maximize the fit between its capabilities and the priorities of the specific business unit of the customer firm. The vendor thus seeks to tap into its large pool of resources to effectively address the priorities of each of the customer firm's business units. In this manner, all the major Indian IT vendors were able to sell additional services such as testing & validation, enterprise solutions, domain solutions, technology offerings, etc., to different parts of ABN AMRO. These vendors also pursued growth opportunities to position their intellectual property in order to penetrate new business units of the bank, enbling the IT service providers to penetrate new global markets and generate higher profitability.

Contributed by C. Venkatesh Vilapakam, Participant, EPGP Program, Indian Institute of Management Bangalore.

a large customer firm, by segmenting the customer firm's business units based on each business unit's respective business priorities.

Customers may use a core product or service in the same application, but may have markedly different requirements and preferences for it across **usage situations**. For example, truck fleet owners have different time and price sensitivities for truck parts that they purchase for scheduled maintenance versus those for emergency repairs of roadside breakdowns. Another instance of usage situation segmentation is a distributor that segmented its customers based on the number of lines on the order: Customers that were using the distributor for "fill-in" orders paid a higher price than "full-order" customers.

Segmentation based on customer behavior has advanced from simple purchase behavior to more sophisticated analyses of doing business with customers. Progressive business market managers, as an example, segment on **contribution to profitability**; that is, how much profit does the supplier earn from doing business with a particular customer? They use measures such as the cost to serve a customer and the customer's willingness to pay for offerings to gain estimates of contribution to profitability. On the horizon for firms in business markets is gaining estimates of customer equity, which assesses the expected profits from doing business with a customer for as long as the relationship lasts.[15] Cisco provides an outstanding example of a firm that segments its market on the value of customers to Cisco *and* the value of Cisco's offerings to customers, which we recount in Box 2.2.

BOX 2.2
Cisco Segments on the Value of Customers and the Value of its TelePresence™ Offerings

Organizations today face an array of business challenges, including an increased need for interaction between different stakeholders, the rising costs and stresses of travel, the need to make faster decisions, and the desire to be ecologically responsible. While many of today's visual communication solutions are adequate for ordinary collaboration sessions, Cisco TelePresence™ promises a lifelike experience that mimics an in-person interactive session among people spread across different countries. Since TelePresence allows participants to meet for many hours at a time without experiencing "meeting fatigue," it can be used to replace physical meetings and are the normal mode for groups of people located in different cities to transact business. TelePresence helps people meet, share content, create high-quality video recordings and events, consult with experts, and deliver powerful personalized services, all using the power of the network for an immersive in-person experience.

Although TelePresence can serve many organizations in many markets, certain industries have much more potential to harness the value delivered by it. These organizations can gain significant competitive advantage from deploying the technology aggressively. Cisco plans to first target organizations in the following industries. This is based on a very systematic approach to segment the market.

IT/ITES (IT-enabled services) industry. The constant need for travel, geographically dispersed teams, and a collaborative style of working make the IT (information technology)/ITES (IT-enabled services) segment a leading area for potential sales of TelePresence. For many global organizations which have a regional office in India, such as IBM Global Services, Amdocs, etc., TelePresence can serve as one of the most critical links to collaborate with their respective global head offices. Likewise for the big Indian IT firms, it can provide a powerful mode for linking to their dispersed development teams across the country as well as client-facing teams spread across the world. It can also provide a powerful vehicle for client interactions.

Internet Service Providers (ISPs). ISPs such as VSNL and BSNL could act as strategic partners to TelePresence vendors. They can bundle bandwidth along with a TelePresence suite to sell one-stop solutions to end users.

Professional Education Colleges. Leading Indian educational institutes are setting up new international campuses. TelePresence opens the possibility of bringing the advantages of physical classrooms to distance learning spread across multiple geographies.

Pharmaceutical industry. Firms in the pharmaceutical industry can benefit from TelePresence in research and development and sales training, both of which are critical to the sustenance and growth of their businesses. Collaboration between scientists in laboratories spread across the world with patients in clinical settings, doctors and other health care professionals, regulators and their corporate counterparts, legal and compliance groups and sales and marketing teams can happen at very early stages of new product development (NPD), without incurring large travel-related costs, that would incur in the case of physical meetings. This kind of collaboration is quite necessary to make NPD launches successful in the pharmaceutical industry.

Health Care Industry. TelePresence allows medical specialists located in big cities such as Bengaluru or Mumbai to practice

BOX 2.2
Continued

tele-medicine, offering expert medical consultation to patients located in far-flung and impoverished towns and villages in the remote hinterlands of the country as well as in the other parts of the world. Remote locations such as Ajjipura in Chamrajnagar District of Karnataka usually do not have the necessary medical infrastructure for treatment. However, the need for proper diagnosis of patients suffering from chronic ailments is acute and immediate; only after such diagnosis can the patient be directed to the right treatment in an appropriate municipal hospital in a nearby town or in the bigger cities. Narayana Hrudayalaya, based in Bengaluru, Karnataka, and Aravind Eye Hospital, based in Madurai, Tamil Nadu, have been practicing tele-medicine for the last few years using satellite technology. In this manner, the resources of specialist medical professionals as well as physical infrastructural resources can be more fully utilized, while providing immense relief to patients. TelePresence has a huge potential to alleviate human suffering of such patients who otherwise have no access to high-quality health care.

Professional Services. Consultants, lawyers, etc., all know that client relationships are vital to their success. They are also frequently located far from their most important clients, as well as from partners and co-workers with whom they need to collaborate. Professional services are often high-value businesses in which clients expect and require a high level of care. Replacing an in-person meeting with a low-quality virtual collaboration session will not meet clients' requirements. TelePresence can deliver a high-end experience that allows all participants to connect on a visceral and emotional level and thus engage in high-quality interactions. In businesses like professional services, this difference could make the difference between success and failure.

The above segments have been arrived at by Cisco as a consequence of a systematic approach to segment the market. Because TelePresence systems require significant time and resource investments, as well as the right room and design elements, companies should be judicious about their deployment. It is important to deploy the technology at the most effective location for key persons to access as needed. At the same time, security and network issues must be addressed. The decision to deploy a TelePresence system should be based on the value it presents to the customer firm at a particular location.

By qualifying the basic industry-specific segmentation criteria with additional parameters such as roles and location, more insight into the requirements of the customer can be obtained. In this manner, Cisco places itself in a better position to serve its customers. Each resulting segment will be actionable, unique, and substantial. It will enable Cisco to support efficient, customer-focused customer acquisition, retention, and growth, since through such segmentation, the company explicitly seeks customers who value the company's offering and thereby gets customers who are of value to Cisco from a revenue and profitability perspective. Gaining insights into such segmentation of the market as described above requires working closely of cross-functional teams within Cisco, encompassing various functions including market development, market research, market information systems, product management, and sales. All the effort to arrive at the

(*continued*)

BOX 2.2
Continued

appropriate segmentation is based on a clear understanding of why a prospective customer would purchase Cisco's TelePresence over competitive offerings from other suppliers. A two-stage segmentation approach enables Cisco to zero in on relevant segments for its TelePresence offering: the first step is to segment customers or prospects on their present or potential value to Cisco. Having addressed this, the next step is to subsegment on the attractiveness or perceived value of Cisco's TelePresence offering to customers or prospects.

Contributed by Amit Aggarwal, Pawan A. Hardikar, Sandeep Datta, Sidharth Bhardwaj, D. S. S. D. P. Sreenivas, Participants, EPGP Program, Indian Institute of Management Bangalore. *Sources:* Cisco Web site *http://www.cisco.com/en/US/netsol/ns669/networking_solutions_solution_segment_home.html*; "Audio Video Conferencing: Reason to Rejoice, Voice & Data," "Polycom Again Recognised For Leadership In India's Voice And Video Communications Market," *http://www.indiaprwire.com/pressrelease/information-technology/2009090733193.htm.*

Finally, progressive business market managers update geographic segmentation to take advantage of doing business across borders. They segment firms based on those firms' requirements and preferences, where this segmentation is across country markets. Segments with relatively similar requirements and preferences may actually be composed of customers located in several country markets. In this way, suppliers can standardize by providing the same market offering in a number of country markets, and customize by providing more than one offering in each country market.[16]

Determining Market Segments of Interest

Whatever market-segmentation approach business market managers pursue, as part of their research they need to assess which markets—and segments within them—are of greater interest to the firm. This approach enables the firm to pinpoint which groups of customers it should pursue, and as importantly, what groups it should not. As Chuck Lillis, former CEO of US WEST Media Group, once observed perceptively: "I will know when our businesses are doing a good job of market segmentation when they can articulate who we should *not* sell to."[17] Gaining an understanding of market segments of interest occurs in two related steps: (1) obtaining estimates of each defined market segment's size and growth, and (2) assessing its sales and profit potential.[18]

Market Segment Size and Growth

Business market managers would like to know how many prospective customers are in each segment, how much of the defined offering category they will purchase, and how each of these factors will change over time. Two concepts that provide these figures are market potential and total market demand. **Market potential** "identifies the maximum units of a defined product or service capable of being purchased within a designated geographic area, during a designated time period, when supported by a realistic level of marketing activity." In contrast, **total market demand**, which tends to have a shorter time focus, is a prediction of the actual number of units that will be purchased.[19]

Business market managers can use three approaches for estimating the market potential for a segment: the buildup method, the chain ratio method, and the index method. The buildup method is simply taking market potential estimates from subsegments, using available secondary research or conducting primary research, and combining them to reach an estimate for the segment. The chain ratio method starts with a large number of prospective customers as identified by the business market manager, perhaps from using NAICS codes or equivalent industry classification codes available in the country. This number is then multiplied by a series of percentages (ratios) that correspond to the assumptions made, such as the percentage of potential customers that use a certain technology, to arrive at a final estimate. The index method ties the estimate to a single factor affecting the market, such as the number of new housing starts, or to multiple factors, which the business market manager might obtain from an econometric forecasting service. By their nature, these approaches cannot provide precise estimates, and their accuracy is heavily dependent on the validity of the assumptions that a business market manager makes.[20]

Business market managers would like to know which market segments will have the largest growth in total market demand over some time horizon of interest, such as the next year, three years, or five years. Barnett describes the four basic steps needed in any forecast of total market demand:[21]

1. Define the market.
2. Divide total industry demand into its main components.
3. Forecast the drivers of demand in each segment and project how they are likely to change.
4. Conduct sensitivity analyses to understand the most critical assumptions and to gauge risks to the baseline forecast.

At the outset, the business market manager should define the market broadly, such as by the basic functionality that prospective customers are seeking. The second step is market segmentation, using the progressive bases of application, customer capabilities, and usage situation. The drivers of demand most often are macroeconomic variables and industry-specific developments, which the business market manager might ask a number of industry experts to predict. Finally, rather than putting these numbers together to produce a single estimate of future demand, business market managers should construct several scenarios. Each scenario is built around a set of internally consistent assumptions, with the set of scenarios spanning a set of plausible outcomes.[22]

Naturally, forecasting market potential or total market demand for new categories of market offerings or for embryonic markets is especially challenging. As an example, consider Univac, which pioneered commercial computers:

> In 1950 Univac's market research predicted that by the year 2000 there would be one thousand computers in use. Its initial forecast called for sales of about a dozen large mainframes to the Census Bureau, Bell

Laboratories, the Atomic Energy Commission, and similar large-scale users. . . . The forecast failed because it was based on the mistaken assumption that the market for computers was for advanced scientific purposes. Univac did not foresee the extensive, but mundane, business applications to which those wonderful machines were mostly put. IBM's success was due to its focus on business customers rather than scientists.[23]

In these situations, business market managers should use multiple methods to produce a combined forecast, which likely will be more accurate than the forecast from any single method. They need to be aware of their assumptions and challenge each one. An assessment of the value of an innovation relative to existing alternatives should be a crucial input to any forecast. How does the innovation provide superior functionality or performance over existing alternatives, or how does it provide equivalent functionality or performance at a lower price? Finally, business market managers might build scenarios to produce a set of plausible demand estimates.[24]

Sales and Profit Potential

Business market managers also would like to know what the potential is for their firms' market offerings in each market segment. **Sales potential** "identifies what one particular firm could sell if it applied maximum marketing effort."[25] In contrast, a **sales forecast**, which tends to have a shorter time focus, is a prediction of the actual number of units that a firm will sell with defined commitments of marketing and sales resources.

Supplier firms often use sales force composites or regression analyses to estimate sales potential and a sales forecast for each market segment.[26] With a sales force composite, the business market manager asks each salesperson to predict how much of each market offering he or she will sell, and then combines the predictions to produce the firm's overall sales potential or sales forecast. With regression analysis, the manager uses past years' sales, often along with particular macroeconomic variables and industry drivers, to predict future years' sales. The sales forecast and predicted total market demand, taken together, provide a prediction of the supplier's market share for each segment.

For market segments that the firm presently serves, business market managers should strongly consider building up their sales and profit forecasts from estimates of their **share of each customer's business**.[27] At the broadest level, a supplier's share would be defined as the percentage it supplies of the customer's total purchase requirements for all product offerings that the supplier would be able to supply. In short, what percentage of the total business that a supplier and customer could potentially do together are they doing?

Knowing the share of total customer requirements supplied, though, provides no understanding of where the most profitable prospects for growth are. To determine the best prospects for profitable growth with customers, which may come from discovering possibilities of doing more business in a different way, a supplier needs a more fine-gauged understanding of its shares of each customer's business. Understanding the share of the customer's business for each product category supplied provides a more insightful picture. When the customer has multiple locations, further insight comes from understanding how the supplier's business is spread across locations. Thus, if a customer has 10 plants in its manufacturing network, what percentage of each plant's purchase requirements does each of the supplier's offerings account for? A supplier can find that the percentage of a given offering it supplies can vary dramatically across customer locations, from being single source to supplying nothing at all. The cost to serve a customer and the customer's own total cost of ownership can each vary significantly, depending on how the same amount of supplier business is spread across locations.

Most firms rely upon their sales forces to gather the data to estimate shares of customers' business. To gain initial acceptance and sustain the data gathering effort over time, supplier management must have persuasive answers to the questions "Why should the sales force cooperate in this task?" and "Why should the customers cooperate in this task?" Each must clearly understand why it is beneficial to them to participate. Indiamart.com, the leading online B2B marketplace for Indian business market products and services, focuses its market serving efforts to maximize the share of its customers' business, as described in Box 2.3.

BOX 2.3

IndiaMART Looks at its Share of its Customers' Business

IndiaMART.com is a B2B marketplace that helps buyers and sellers transact by offering a reliable common online platform. It is an online directory of Indian exporters and manufacturers who are focused on business markets and is based on the Yellow Pages concept. In addition to online listing, it provides B2B marketplace services such as banner advertising, premium listings, portal sponsorship, online tenders and offers both buyers and sellers a seal of authenticity that is the basis for development of trusting business relationships between buyers and sellers.

IndiaMART has targeted supplier firms from the Indian small and medium business (SMB) segment. It offers its services to these firms, which need to take their products to the global B2B marketplace, but lack the required visibility and capability to reach these markets on their own. Having provided the visibility of its member supplier firms to potential markets for free, IndiaMART works with these firms to develop their capabilities such as creating an effective Web presence or conducting auctions, to help them accelerate their revenue growth. In this way, IndiaMART has crafted a value-based strategy of "operational excellence," carefully implemented by the company's founder since its inception.

Consequently, IndiaMART provides a compelling value proposition to its customer firms. Even a single modest transaction of INR 0.1 million enabled by IndiaMART for the supplier firm can cover the expenses incurred for creating a Web site, posting the offer for sale, etc. All this costs the customer

(continued)

BOX 2.3
Continued

firm only INR 19,000—a mere two percent of an average transaction value—which compares very favorably with other means of reaching far-flung markets. Trust from the perspective of the foreign buyer is enhanced by IndiaMART's validation of the exporter firm's authenticity.

IndiaMART had the first mover advantage, having created the first Indian online directory for small and medium businesses to access global business markets. The company focused on customer's share of business rather than market share. For buyers, IndiaMART adds value in inbound logistics (procurement) by improving the ability of buyers to buy raw materials/products efficiently. Likewise, for sellers, IndiaMART improves outbound logistics and sales. Over a period of time, IndiaMART has focused on adding value in each of the primary activities of its customers, who include both business market buyers and sellers who are enrolled with the company's online platform. Its focus is on customer benefits rather than the features that it provides.

Based on superior market sensing, IndiaMART identified a huge gap in the Indian SMB segment, where competent and high-quality sellers were seeking global markets but did not have ready access to them. Likewise, foreign buyers were seeking high-quality but cost-effective offerings that they could procure through a trustworthy mechanism, which again they hitherto had no access to. By bringing the sellers and buyers together on a common platform, leveraging the Internet, IndiaMART created a winning value proposition for both parties. This was done through an end-to-end offering, by working with sellers for enhancing their levels of technology usage, providing procurement logistics services, marketing services, and avenues for sales and related services. IndiaMART is able to increase the share of its customer's business by providing superior value and encouraging overall development and growth. By clearly articulating why its offering is beneficial to its customers, IndiaMART is able to obtain the cooperation of both its sales force and customers, as it grows its business by gathering accurate data about the marketplace and leveraging the consequent insights it gains from this effort.

Contributed by Ramkumar Kaleeswaran, Participant, PGSEM Program, Indian Institute of Management Bangalore. *Sources:* "What is IndiaMART.com?," *http://www.indiaMART.com/help/about-indiaMART.html*; "IndiaMART.com Reverses Indian Media Trend," *http://www.indiaMART.com/press-section/releases/indian-media-trend.html.*

Business market managers typically derive profit potential and predicted profit from the sales potential and sales forecast by making additional assumptions. As an example, the business market manager might multiply the sales forecast in units by the past year's contribution margin to provide the predicted gross profit dollars for each market segment. More sophisticated analyses take into account more subtle differences in customers and market segments, such as the cost to serve or the willingness to pay for augmenting services.

Monitoring Competition

Business market management is the process of understanding, creating, and delivering value to targeted market segments and customers. Business market managers have a goal of gaining knowledge about present and prospective customer requirements and preferences as their principal concern. However, because customer judgments about the value of the firm's market offerings take place within the context of market offerings from other firms, business market managers also need knowledge about their competitors. They use knowledge about competitors in crafting their own firm's market strategy, anticipating competitors' reactions to it, and deciding what reactions to make in response to competitors' actions in the market.

How do business market managers determine which set of firms to monitor? They look at the other market offerings that present and prospective customers consider as alternatives to their firms' market offerings. The firms providing them are their competitors. Much the same is done for market segments that the firm is considering entering: What firms currently are supplying market offerings that are most closely related to the firm's anticipated market offering? It is more difficult to determine which firms to monitor that *may* become competitors. These firms are not currently doing business in a market segment of interest, but may be entering it in the near future. In these instances, business market managers rely on their research-and-development colleagues to monitor advances in technologies from outside the industry that have the potential, with further innovation, to provide entry for firms employing the new technology in their market offerings.[28] Business market managers especially need to monitor merger and acquisition activity in related industries that could produce business units that are formidable, potential competitors.

Although firms typically spend most, if not all, of their monitoring resources on present competitors, business history suggests that firms should devote a greater proportion to potential and new competitors. IBM has a high-level scouting capability that it calls "Crow's Nest," where a team responsible for scanning specific topics at the periphery passes on to senior management insights it generates about potential competitive threats or opportunities. As another example, GE used a "destroyyourownbusiness.com" initiative to challenge business units to apply Internet business models to destroy their current businesses. In doing this, managers had to examine the implications for their businesses, which enabled them to better spot potential competitive threats as well as opportunities.[29]

We next discuss a framework for competitor analysis. Business market managers can use this framework to synthesize a comprehensive understanding of each of their competitors. We then suggest some ways to improve monitoring performance.

A Framework for Competitor Analysis

Porter provided a good framework for competitor analysis.[30] This framework consists of four diagnostic components: future goals, assumptions, current strategy, and capabilities. Pulling together knowledge of these areas provides a comprehensive understanding of each competitor.

Future Goals

Understanding what a competitor wants to accomplish in the market provides insight into what actions it will take and how it will react to the firm's actions. Competitors have financial goals, such as increasing profitability or reducing the cost of sales. They also have market performance goals, such as growing market share or increasing the percentage of sales from recently introduced products. Goals exist at the corporate level and the business unit level as well. Gaining an understanding of the compensation plans of senior management, business market managers, and the sales force often will reveal these goals. Learning that a competitor is embarking on a companywide or business-unit-wide training program can signal a shift in its goals, such as when DuPont Company educated its workforce on being market oriented.[31]

Assumptions

Understanding what assumptions a competitor makes about itself, other firms in the industry, and in its market view are critical for predicting what it will do. Significantly, the competitor itself may not be explicitly aware of some of its assumptions. Identifying biases or blind spots of a competitor's managers suggest areas a firm can exploit. **Blind spots** "are areas where a competitor will either not see the significance of events (such as a strategic move) at all, will perceive them incorrectly, or will perceive them only very slowly."[32]

Marketplace success may cause senior management to have blind spots. Perhaps because of its great success with VAX minicomputers using proprietary systems, the former Digital Equipment Corporation (DEC) was slow to comprehend the industry's movement to open systems. Even though DEC founder and former CEO Kenneth Olsen was regarded as a visionary, he did not adjust well to an evolving business environment. In retrospect, for example, he stated, "You can be sure our plan was perfect; it's just that the assumptions were wrong."[33]

Current Strategy

A competitor's current market strategy guides its actions in the marketplace, as well as suggesting its likely reaction to the firm's actions. The firm should understand a competitor's market strategy in terms of its three basic components: the competitor's selected target markets, the competitor's positioning of its market offerings, and the marketing mix that it is implementing in support of its market strategy.[34] The firm usually has little difficulty understanding what segments a competitor is targeting. Finding out what industry and trade publications a competitor has selected for advertising and studying the content of its ads should indicate which market segments it is pursuing. A firm's sales force can also learn what sales force promotions a competitor is running. To learn about the positioning of a competitor's market offerings, a firm can study the content of the competitor's ads and the editorial statements it makes about its offerings, obtain its sales literature, visit its Web site on the Internet, and visit its booth at trade shows.

The firm should also have little difficulty gaining knowledge about a competitor's marketing mix, with pricing perhaps being the exception. In gaining an understanding of a competitor's target markets and positioning, the firm will already have studied the competitor's promotion element of the marketing mix. Whenever possible, the firm should purchase and analyze a competitor's market offering to better understand its product element. The firm should learn from its sales force which channels of distribution a competitor is using, especially any new channels. Gaining an accurate understanding of a competitor's pricing is often difficult because of problems in determining comparability.[35]

Capabilities

To gauge its strengths and weaknesses relative to a competitor, the firm needs to know the core competencies and strategic capabilities of that competitor. Specifically, the firm should investigate a competitor's capability to conceive and design, produce, market, finance, and manage. In the process, the firm also should examine a competitor's recent history to estimate how well that competitor is able to adapt to change and how quickly it is able to respond to actions of its competitors.[36]

Finally, the firm needs to gauge a competitor's strength of will or commitment to compete in each market segment.[37] What significance does each of the competitor's market offerings and segments hold for it? For market offerings or market segments that the competitor regards as crucial, it will make strong retaliations to the firm's marketing actions. At times, a competitor's commitment may be emotionally driven, so that what it does is not rational in terms of overall or long-term profitability. As an example, senior executives may have sentimental attachments to particular offerings or market segments that launched them to success in their careers with the firm.

Improving Monitoring Performance

With some persistence, creativity, consistency of effort, and a reasonable investment of resources, managers can gain sufficient knowledge about competitors to inform and guide their decision making. However, monitoring competitors in many firms falls short, with the firms having a sketchy understanding of their competitors. How can firms improve their monitoring performance? They need to have competitor intelligence systems in place, and they need to practice seeking out disconfirming as well as confirming evidence in building knowledge about competitors.

Competitor Intelligence Systems

To improve monitoring performance, firms need to implement an organized approach for seeking, gathering, analyzing, and interpreting competitor data, and for disseminating the resulting information to guide decisions. An outstanding framework for accomplishing these tasks is the Fuld Intelligence Pyramid™ constructed by Fuld & Company, a leading firm in competitive intelligence consulting. We reproduce this framework in Figure 2.3. Let's consider how businesses would use this framework to strengthen their competitive intelligence.[38]

As preparation prior to working through the Intelligence Pyramid, businesses must decide which competitive issues are critical to address and frame them in a set of questions whose answers are sought. In a business culture where time is increasingly a scarce resource, focus is essential to motivate and direct the assistance of those working throughout the business. The competitive questions for which answers are sought should be accompanied by compelling rationales for what is needed and why, to gain the needed support. The business also should provide social recognition, which may be preferable to monetary rewards, to individuals providing critical competitor information. As an example, the general manager of a bearings distributor gave up his parking spot, which was right next to the building entrance, and awarded it each month to the salesperson who contributed the most valuable piece of competitive information.

Figure 2.3 The Intelligence Pyramid

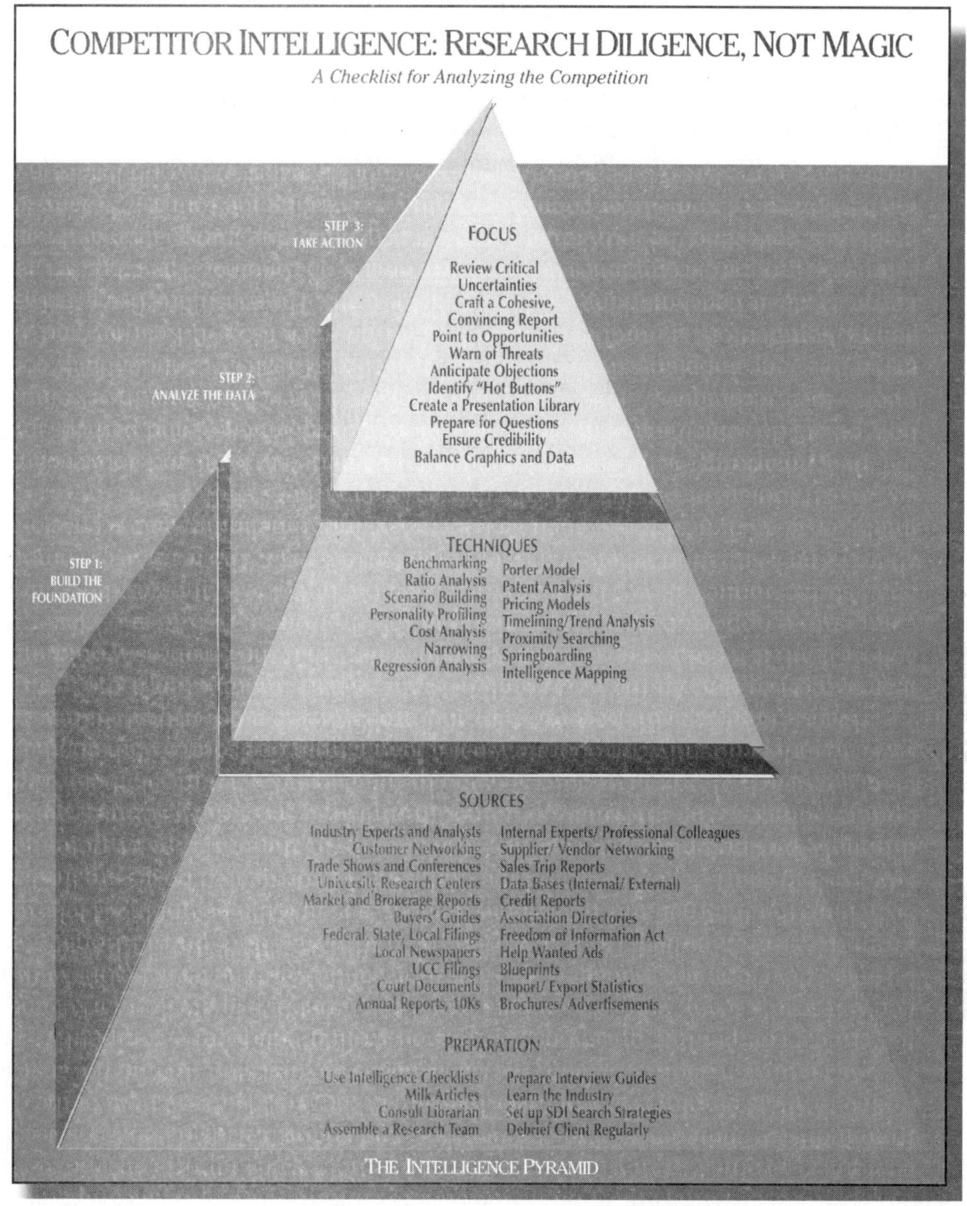

The managers with primary responsibility for competitive intelligence function as catalysts for the whole process. To use a circus metaphor, they act as "ringmasters," directing and sequencing the activities going on around them. For example, they should contact others in the business who will be attending a trade show to alert them to seek out critical competitor information. After (or even during) the show, the manager contacts the attendees again to debrief them on what has been learned.

Progressive businesses also use group productivity software in conjunction with internal computer networks (intranets) to create competitor intelligence systems that are readily accessible and useful. Ceregen, the biotechnology unit of Monsanto Company, uses Lotus Notes on its intranet to continuously update competitor (and customer) profiles from public news sources, field sales reports, attendees' notes from industry conferences and conventions, and so forth. This database is accessible online to all its employees, wherever they are in the world, at any time of the day.[39]

As Figure 2.3 depicts, *building the foundation* is the first step. To find the answers to the critical competitive questions, the business often will form a competitive intelligence research team, whose members may be competitive analysts, market analysts, business development managers, or sales representatives. The team begins with background research culled from a variety of traditional and untraditional sources. Searching the Internet and traditional databases is just the beginning. Help-wanted advertising, court documents, and the underside of corrugated boxes are the less traditional—but potentially revealing—documents in the universe of potential secondary sources. The information gained from these secondary sources guides the team's research to primary sources—who to contact and what to ask them. The team seeks to independently corroborate what it learns from one source with another.

Analyze the data is the second step, and probably the most critical. Rarely can the team expect to find all the data it might want. What's more, even if the team could collect it all, it would take so much time to collect that the business would miss the competitive opportunity it was seeking in the first place. Astute and clever use of analysis techniques allows the team to make more out of less. It gives the team a perspective on a situation where it has less than perfect data. The team uses competitive intelligence analytical tools, such as benchmarking, timelining, and scenario analysis, to extrapolate or predict a rival's moves or a market's shift.

Benchmarking "is the art of finding out, in a perfectly legal and aboveboard way, how others do something better than you do so you can imitate—and perhaps improve upon—their techniques." Progressive firms engage in benchmarking their competitors (as well as noncompetitors that represent best practice). To satisfy confidentiality concerns among competitors, a number of consulting firms, such as A. T. Kearney and Towers Perrin, facilitate benchmarking efforts among the firms. The consulting firms first assist in setting up groups of companies that will benchmark one another. They then act as intermediaries, collecting the individual company benchmarking information and reporting the best practices to member companies without revealing the sources.[40] Many leading firms, such as the Isreal-based Teva, a pharmaceuticals major and world leader in Active Pharma Ingredients (APIs), with significant operations in India, routinely send teams of senior managers from various geographies of their global operations, to countries such as India and China, to benchmark their practices against leading companies in the pharmaceutical industry as well as in other industries such as IT, steel, and automotive.

Timelining is a technique to predict how the very near future will unfold, by drawing on knowledge of the steps inherent in some process and how long it typically takes to perform each one. Experts within a business, supplemented perhaps by outside consultants, can lay out the milestones to track the progress of a competitor in activities such as opening a new plant or introducing a new product to the market. Timelining enables a business to make the most of incomplete data to generate a fairly accurate understanding of its competitors' moves.

Take action is the third step, corresponding to the highest level and pinnacle of the pyramid, which is *focus*. Here, the team pulls together all it has learned from the analysis, reducing all the charts and interview transcriptions and all the observations to a few pithy conclusions that create opportunities through decision. Businesses at this level benefit from these early warnings to give their managements opportunities to stay ahead of the market and the competition. An essential characteristic of the focus level is acting on these generated insights expediently, while few other businesses know about them.

Seek Disconfirming as Well as Confirming Evidence

Individuals who have primary responsibility for monitoring competitors have dual tasks to perform in generating accurate knowledge about competitors. They seek *convergence* of data from more than one source to increase their confidence in its meaning about a competitor. For example, they might confirm a salesperson's report of competitor price cutting of a market offering by seeking other instances where this has happened. Market research from an outside firm might be used to further improve confidence in an inference made about a competitor's price cutting.

At the same time, though, the monitor has the task of seeking out *disconfirming* evidence. Continuing with the example, how many instances can be cited where the competitor did *not* cut the price of the market offering? A common bias in managerial decision making is seeking out confirming evidence to support an inference, while not seeking out disconfirming evidence that would invalidate the inference. Individuals who have primary responsibility for monitoring competitors need to be mindful of this potential bias and must pursue both kinds of information to provide the most accurate knowledge about competitors. A recommended means of generating contradictory evidence is to assign the role of "devil's inquisitor" to someone on the management team. Rather than arguing against the commonly held position, as a "devil's advocate" would do, this individual instead asks questions to challenge the prevailing point of view, pushing the others to look for disconfirming evidence outside their bounds of awareness.[41]

ASSESSING CUSTOMER VALUE

"Everything is worth what its purchaser will pay for it."

—Publilius Syrus, first century, B.C.

Although this maxim is old, actually assessing what some present or potential market offering is worth to present or prospective customers remains a challenging task for business market managers. Because assessing value in monetary terms initially appears to be such a daunting task, most firms in business markets do not even try to do it. Yet, the small but growing number of progressive firms that excel at customer value assessment find that the more value assessments they do, the easier the assessments become. That is, through experience and learning, they develop this business marketing capability. They also uniformly find that value assessment provides them with superior knowledge about the market that they are able to convert to superior market performance.

As stated in Chapter 1, customer firms often do not have an accurate understanding of what suppliers' market offerings actually are worth to them. Even some government customers are realizing this inadequacy and are looking to potential suppliers to show them how they can add value or reduce the total cost of government.[42] As part of their proposals, though, governments increasingly want suppliers to guarantee results, something that suppliers cannot do knowledgeably without value assessment. Moreover, irrespective of whether the customer is in the public or private sector, value assessment provides better understanding of the customer's business to both the customer and the supplier. Without value assessment, business market managers make decisions based on a sketchy and often inaccurate understanding of not only how alternative suppliers' differing ways of meeting the customer's requirements affect its costs, but also what changes in the customer's requirements would be worth.

We first discuss a number of methods that firms in business markets have used to assess value. We then present customer value management, which is a comprehensive, practical approach for demonstrating and documenting the value of present and prospective market offerings in business markets.

Value Assessment Methods[43]

Value assessment is the work process of obtaining an estimate of the worth in monetary terms of some present or proposed market offering or elements of it. Business market managers have employed a number of methods to provide estimates of value. These methods vary significantly in the extent to which they rely upon customer perceptions of worth versus supplier assessment of the functionality or performance of an offering and its worth (i.e., gathering empirical data).

Internal Engineering Assessment

With this method, scientists or engineers within the supplier's own firm conduct laboratory tests on a product to provide an estimate of its value. Application of this method depends on detailed knowledge of the customer's usage system. As an example, if the supplier's product is a component part of the customer's product, the supplier needs to have a detailed understanding of the customer's production process and how the supplier's market offering affects all other costs incurred in making that product. To provide a value estimate, the supplier typically makes some assumptions about the way in which results from lab tests will generalize to the customer's actual use of the product.

Field Value-in-Use Assessment

With this method, supplier personnel (or their consultants) conduct interviews and often gather data at customer firm(s) to provide a comprehensive listing of benefit and cost elements associated with usage of the supplier's market offering compared with the incumbent or next-best-alternative offering. Making explicit assumptions, they assign monetary amounts to these elements to provide an overall value estimate of its market offering in that application. In contrast with internal engineering assessment, field value-in-use assessment requires considerable customer firm cooperation and active participation to arrive at an estimate of customer value.

Supplier firms sometimes do process mapping in field value-in-use assessment to be certain that they have captured all of an offering's benefit and cost elements. Grainger Consulting Services (GCS), a unit of the industrial supply distributor W. W. Grainger, has used process mapping to study the total costs a client incurs in acquiring MRO items. In numerous engagements, GCS mapped out processes such as inventory replenishment and unplanned purchases, as well as subprocesses, such as issuing a purchase order and MRO credit card payment. GCS charts the activity flows in a process using Post-it® notes on a large sheet of paper, where the functional areas are the rows and the detailed steps in the process are the columns. GCS also gains estimates of the time it takes to perform each step and the total compensation costs of individuals performing the step. After the process has been delineated adequately, GCS transfers the data to spreadsheet software to portray the process in a compact way and to calculate its costs. Armed with this knowledge, Grainger can show the customer how its distribution system can lower the customer's total acquisition costs by greatly reducing the number of emergency purchases and lowering the cost per purchase order for the remaining ones.

Indirect Survey Questions

Participants in a field research study act as informants for their firms and answer questions on how one or more changes in a presently used market offering would affect certain aspects of their firm's operations. From these answers, typically combined in some way with other known information, supplier analysts can derive estimates of the worth in monetary terms of each change in the market offering. This method enables a supplier firm to fill critical gaps in its knowledge of the customer firm's usage system as it relates to the supplier's market offering. Note that a critical assumption of this method is that the customer has an accurate perception of the effects of the studied changes upon its usage system.

Focus Group Value Assessment

Within a focus group setting, participants are shown potential product offerings or product concepts and then asked what the value of these offerings or concepts would be to their firms. This method is a qualitative approach to gaining a better understanding of the perceptions and reactions of participants. In doing so, the research analyst also generates estimates of value. The participants typically are knowledgeable individuals within customer firms that are targets for the studied market offering, although a supplier firm also may be interested in the reactions of industry consultants or pundits.

A telecommunications firm employed focus group value assessment to understand the worth of a number of advanced intelligent network (AI-Net) services, such as single-number reach. Single-number reach is provided from a central office switch and seeks out an individual a caller is trying to reach at a sequence of different telephone numbers the individual has previously programmed. Single-number reach also provides the option of voice mail. (The recipient of the call has the option of putting the caller into voice mail without the caller ever knowing the recipient was reached.) As an initial target market segment, the firm conducted focus groups with itinerant, Generation-X professionals, some of whom had six telephone numbers on their business cards!

At the beginning of each focus group, the moderator demonstrated the single-number reach service, using a specially arranged prototype. The moderator then asked focus group participants to write down their first impressions of the service and how much they would be willing to pay per month for the service. The participants then engaged in a discussion of the service, how they would most likely use it, and so on. At the conclusion of the approximately hour-long discussion, the moderator asked the participants to write down their interest in the service, using a 10-point scale, and again, how much they would be willing to pay per month for the service.

Although the firm was interested in the actual monetary amounts given at the beginning and at the end, it was more interested in any pattern of differences between the specified amounts. An ominous pattern would be significant declines from the initial amounts to the ending amounts, indicating that the participants were initially intrigued with the service, but upon further consideration, concluded that the service would actually provide them little value. No significant change between the initial amounts and ending amounts would be a preferable pattern, provided the specified amounts were sufficiently large for the service to be profitable. The final pattern, significant increases from the initial amounts to the ending amounts, would indicate that when the participants thought about the service, they came to recognize its greater value to them. This pattern would suggest the crucial role of business marketing communications in conveying the value of using the service to prospective customers.

Direct Survey Questions

In a field research survey, participants are given a description of a potential market offering or product concept, and then are asked what its value would be to their firms. Participants might be asked, "What would your firm be willing to pay for this offering?" Participants may be unwilling to answer candidly, or they may not know enough about their own usage systems and the offering's effect on them to answer accurately. The extent to which either of these occurs will affect the validity of the value estimate. A series of follow-up questions would be asked to gain an understanding of how parts of an offering contribute to its overall perceived value.

Conjoint Analysis

Conjoint analysis is a family of methods for statistically transforming a research participant's judgments about potential market offerings into estimates of the value the participant places on those offerings' constituent attributes and the alternative levels of those attributes.[44] We limit our consideration to the most commonly used conjoint analysis method: the full-profile approach employing ordinary least squares (OLS) estimation. In a field personal interview or a combination telephone-mail-telephone research methodology, research participants are asked to evaluate a set of potential market offerings. Each offering typically appears on a separate card, which lists the set of attributes the supplier is studying, along with the specific level of each attribute that the offering possesses. For example, in a conjoint study of titanium dioxide, a white pigment used as a primary component in coatings, the supplier studied four attributes: dispersability, gloss, hiding power/tinting strength, and price. The attribute of dispersability, for example, had two levels: 10 minutes and 30 minutes time required to attain 7 Hegman fineness units in a Cowles high-speed disperser.[45] The levels of the attributes the supplier is studying are systematically varied within the set of offerings.

Participants provide a purchase preference rating for each offering. The research analyst then uses OLS regression analysis to decompose the ratings into estimated **part-worths** or values for each level of each attribute. The range of these part-worths for each attribute provides an estimate of the relative value of the attributes themselves. Price should be included as an attribute in the design so that the part-worths can be scaled in monetary terms.

Benchmarks

In a field research survey, participants are given a description of a market offering, typically the present industry standard, that serves as a **benchmark offering**. They then are asked how much more their firm would be willing to pay for selected additions (or increases) in attributes or features to this benchmark offering. Likewise, they might be asked how much less their firm would expect to pay for selected reductions in attributes or features from the benchmark offering. The benchmark method trades off some of the methodological rigor and breadth of value estimates that conjoint analysis provides in favor of lower cost and ease of use.

Compositional Approach

The compositional approach is also sometimes called the **self-explicated approach** because research participants are asked to directly express the value they place on each of a number of attributes and their selected levels. As an example, participants might be asked to provide the value in Indian Rupees per unit for each of three alternative levels of a particular attribute, where all other attributes of the market offering were the same (held constant). When this assessment is done for each attribute, the values given for the attribute levels then can be added to provide estimates of the value of various market offerings to the participant's firm. Although the composition approach has the strength of being relatively easy to use, it does have some potential shortcomings, such as finding that the sum of the values for the component attribute levels is greater than the value the participant actually places on the offering as a whole.

Some research in marketing, though, has found that a self-explicated approach that places some constraints on how research participants generate their estimates provides a surprisingly good prediction of actual choice.[46] This approach has three steps in gathering participant perceptions. First, the research participants indicate any attribute levels that are totally unacceptable; that is, they would reject any potential offering containing that attribute level, no matter how attractive the other attribute levels of the offering might be. Second, for the remaining levels, the participants designate the most-preferred and least-preferred levels of each attribute as 10 and 0, respectively, and then indicate a value within this range for any other levels on each attribute. Finally, the participants designate the attribute where the change from the least-preferred to the most-preferred level is most valuable as 10, and then rates the other attributes relative to it from 0 to 10.

Practitioners have also made advances in the use of constrained, self-explicated approaches. Business & Market Research Ltd., an English market research firm specializing in business market research, developed an approach that is relatively easy for research participants to complete, yet also provides estimates of value in monetary terms. Business & Market Research's approach appears in Box 2.4.[47]

BOX 2.4
Measuring Customer Value at Business & Market Research Ltd.

Business & Market Research Ltd. (B&MR) has conducted many studies to understand what end-users perceive as the total market offering and how they value the different components. This is a particularly important exercise in markets such as electricity, where customers perceive the core products of alternative suppliers to be almost identical. The winners in these markets are those who augment their core products with the right combination of added-value components, such as special tariffs, superior service backup, and easily understood billing.

To optimize the bundle of attributes that is added to the core product, B&MR must isolate the value that customers attach to each attribute. Having established the relative worth of an attribute, B&MR must then determine at what level it should be delivered. B&MR's constrained, self-explicated approach uses initial exploratory research to develop a *Customer Service Grid.* This grid lists all the attributes that augment the generic core product. For each attribute, a scale from poor to good is defined using the customers' own language. A limited example is shown here, although in reality B&MR typically might have 20 to 30 different attributes, with up to eight levels for each.

The numeric points in the grid correspond to the approximate relative costs of providing the service levels, thereby conveying to the research participant that the costs for providing the different levels of the different services can vary greatly. B&MR determines these relative costs of provision in consultation with senior management at

CUSTOMER SERVICE GRID

ATTRIBUTES	LEVEL OF DELIVERY				
Speed of answering the phone	Is often not answered and I call back 0	Is answered in at least 10 rings 3	Is answered in 7–10 rings 6	Is answered in 4 rings 8	Is answered in 3 rings 12
Availability of contact person	Never anyone available and I leave messages 0	Somebody available, though not a named contact 5	Named contact usually available and if not, calls back same day 15	Named contact always available 25	
Knowledge of contact person	Person I contact can only answer a few questions and I have to contact someone else for the rest 0	Person I contact can answer most questions and I have to contact someone else for the rest 10	Person I contact can answer most questions, and if necessary, will contact someone else to get me the answer 15	Person I contact can answer all questions 25	

(continued)

BOX 2.4
Continued

the client firm. Thus, in the example, to always have a named contact available is five times more expensive than simply having somebody available. Note that each basic level of service delivery starts at zero, because the client is concerned about the additional costs of adding to its basic product.

Once B&MR has developed the customer service grid, it can use it in a number of ways to understand value. Participants might be asked to indicate where a current provider was across all attributes, and then be given a certain number of points to spend (typically 30 to 50 across 20 or more attributes) and asked how they would spend them to improve the offering. B&MR calculates for each project the specific number of points that participants are given to spend, based on the total points on the grid and the client's inclination to make changes (i.e., they want to make wholesale changes, or small-scale improvements). Essentially, the number must be high enough so that participants can afford the most expensive improvement if they want it, yet it must be low enough so that they cannot afford to improve the offering to the best possible level on each line. Thus, the participants have to make choices, revealing the levels of service for each attribute that they value most, given those levels' costs. Once all data are gathered, B&MR can model them to identify the optimum service offering (i.e., which would appeal to the most respondents) and examine the impact of not meeting certain criteria (i.e., underspecifying the offer). Finally, with a sufficiently large sample, B&MR's approach will normally identify segments that value different overall products, with an indication of the relative price differential between them.

B&MR has used this approach in many different markets. In both financial services and public utilities, it has helped clients define meaningful customer service standards that give customers what they value. In mature industrial markets, it has identified the optimum market offering. Getting the add-ons right in these markets is particularly important because core products can be identical (e.g., chemicals) and service enhancements (e.g., on-site technical backup) very expensive.

Importance Ratings

In a field research survey, participants are given a set of attributes of a market offering and then are asked to rate them on importance to their firm. The participants also are asked to rate each of a number of supplier firms with respect to their performance on each of the attributes. Multiplying each supplier's performance rating on each attribute by that attribute's importance rating and summing them across attributes produces a competitor analysis of the relative value each supplier's market offering provides. A significant shortcoming of importance ratings as a method of customer value assessment is that they do not provide an estimate of the worth in monetary terms of the market offering or its elements. Importance ratings also do not provide an estimate of a customer firm's relative value for a change in the level of performance on one attribute versus another.[48]

Customer Value Management[49]

Customer value management is a progressive, practical approach that, in its essence, has two basic goals:

- Deliver superior value to targeted market segments and customer firms.
- Get an equitable return on the value delivered.

Customer value management relies upon *customer value assessment* to gain an understanding of customer requirements and preferences, and what it is worth in monetary terms to fulfill them. Although firms may be able to accomplish the first goal without any formal assessment of customer value, it is unlikely that they will be able to accomplish the second goal without it. Simply put, to gain an equitable or fair return on the value their offerings deliver, suppliers must be able to persuasively demonstrate and document the superior value they provide customers relative to the next-best alternative for those customers. As we recount in Box 2.5, when suppliers do not spend the time and money on customer value management, they are unaware of how much *not* doing it is costing them.

BOX 2.5
Can Suppliers Afford *Not* to Build Customer Value Models?

An electronics engineer was leading his firm's development effort for a next-generation, electronic control device, which was projected to have a total cost of about INR 350. An important component of this device was a power factor correction (PFC) integrated circuit (IC). This engineer had narrowed down the potential suppliers for these PFC ICs to two: Supplier A, which was quoting a price of INR 22.50 per IC, and Supplier B, which was quoting a price of INR 17.50 per IC. The firm anticipated purchasing 5 million of these PFC ICs for the new control devices.

This electronics engineer happened to be enrolled in a part-time, evening MBA program where he was taking a graduate course in business marketing. Having learned in this course that customer firms should focus on total value of ownership rather than simply purchase price, he decided to build a customer value model, to fulfill part of his course requirements and to determine which of the two suppliers would provide the greater value to his firm.

Pulling together the data and building the customer value model, the engineer estimated that Supplier A's offering was worth INR 7.95 more per PFC IC than Supplier B's. Two value elements emerged as the most critical points of difference between the two suppliers. Supplier A provided *earlier access to product samples*, which significantly shortened the time to market for the new devices. Because of the competitive nature of the customer firm's own market, getting to market earlier with new devices affected both the revenue and profit it earned. Supplier A also provided superior *technical engineering support*, which provided design expertise and was a supplementary engineering resource that the customer firm would otherwise have to supply itself. There also were other points of difference that were of lesser monetary value.

Drawing on the customer value model results, the engineer's recommendation to purchasing was that, even though Supplier A's price was INR 5.00 more expensive than

(*continued*)

BOX 2.5
Continued

Supplier B's, the firm should purchase the PCF ICs from Supplier A because of the superior value that its offering provided. In delivering this report to the purchasing manager who was supporting his development project, the engineer related the outcome of his research to the purchasing manager. "That's interesting to learn," replied the purchasing manager with a smile. "But I think that you will be interested to learn that in the meantime, I have negotiated a price reduction with Supplier A from INR 22.50 to INR 17.50 per IC!"

Think for a moment about what occurred. By not standing firm on its price in the negotiation, how much incremental profit had Supplier A just given away? INR 25 million—on one transaction with one customer. Yet Supplier A's salesperson is not the culprit here. His firm is. Supplier A had done no customer value research, built no customer value models, and constructed no value-based sales tools to enable the salesperson to persuasively demonstrate and document the superior value of his offering relative to Supplier B's.

Interestingly, as part of his research, the engineer interviewed the salespersons from Supplier A and Supplier B, and asked each of them what they thought the source of their offering's superior value was relative to the other. The salesperson from Supplier A did not name either of the two value elements that provided the greatest differential value. Apparently, he was unaware of the extent of the differences between his offering and Supplier B's on these elements or what these differences were worth to that customer. Instead, he stated that he believed that his offering was worth more, attributing it to his dedicated and superior servicing of the account. His superior service was worth something: INR 0.10 per IC in the engineer's customer value model!

Perhaps sensing that this superior service was not worth the INR 5.00 price difference between quotes, when push came to shove, Supplier A's salesperson reduced the price to match Supplier B's lower price. Now, even with a value-based sales tool that enabled him to persuasively demonstrate his offering's superior value, as part of the give-and-take of negotiation, he might have reduced the price somewhat and perhaps even split the price difference with the purchasing manager. Even in this latter scenario, though, Supplier A still would have retained INR 12.5 million in incremental profit.

This case study brings to life a choice that most often remains implicit for suppliers and, as such, one that they cannot fully know the consequences of implicitly making. They can spend the time and money upfront to persuasively demonstrate and document the superior value that their offerings deliver and capture a more equitable portion of this delivered value. Or, they can choose not to, and give value away unknowingly as price concessions, just as Supplier A did in this case study. Either way, suppliers are going to pay. As this case study amply reveals, can suppliers afford *not* to build customer value models?

An essential undertaking in customer value management is building **customer value models**, which are data-driven estimates of what a present or prospective market offering is worth in monetary terms to targeted customers relative to the next-best-alternative offering for those customers. Some suppliers have built what they regard as customer value models, but which have the character of being "data light" and "assumption heavy." Quite naturally, customers are skeptical of such models, claiming that they do not accurately reflect their businesses. In contrast, customer value management stresses building customer value models that are "data heavy" and "assumption light." Wherever possible, suppliers gather data to minimize the number of assumptions made and to ensure that the assumptions that are made are reasonable.

Customer value management is a process that can be viewed as five phases: (1) translating business issues into projects, (2) customer value workshop, (3) customer value research, (4) constructing a business case for change, and (5) value realization.

Translating Business Issues into Projects

In the initial phase, senior managers think through significant issues that the business is facing, where greater knowledge of customer value would enable them to make more profitable decisions. Customer value management has been used to inform and guide a variety of management decisions, such as which potential product developments and modifications to make; which augmenting services, programs, and systems to offer as standard or for-fee options; setting pricing strategy and tactics; and which market segment(s) to target. Because customer value management costs both time and money, with time becoming a scarcer resource, it should be applied to business issues that are significant for the business unit.

To give a broader experience and understanding of customer value management and what its potential is, we counsel firms to engage in a pilot program where they tackle three to five business issues. A project is defined for each issue, where decisions are made about the scope of the project, the definition of success, and the team leader and composition of the team that will carry out the customer value research to address the issue.

For customer value research projects to succeed, the active support of senior management is crucial. Most often, a senior manager serves as the sponsor or champion of each team, which should be decided before the start of the projects. Even though senior managers should communicate to the teams the importance of the pilot program to the business, they make a more visible statement through how they spend their own time. Making the commitment to attend at least the opening morning of the customer value workshop, monitor the progress of their team, and attend the presentation day for the business cases sends a strong signal to the teams.

Customer Value Workshop

The teams come together for a Customer Value Workshop, which is a two- or three-day session where they gain the requisite knowledge and skills to build customer value models and plan and launch their projects. During this workshop, they practice building customer value models using one or more case studies written for that purpose. In breakout sessions, each team begins to define the value elements for their project, determine the next-best alternative to their market offering, decide which customers to invite to participate in the customer value research, and create their work plans for accomplishing the project.

Each team begins by listing all the value elements for the market offering under consideration. Value elements define in a comprehensive and elemental way how the offering reduces customer costs or adds value to what the customer is trying to accomplish, and they capture the technical, economic, service, and social benefits that customers receive from the offering. A fundamental consideration here is to be *comprehensive* and *elemental*. Leaving out elements—particularly if they are unfavorable for the supplier's market offering relative to the next-best-alternative offering—compromises the effort and undermines its credibility with customers that detect the missing elements. By being as elemental as possible, the supplier firm is able to more accurately gauge the differences in functionality and performance its offering provides relative to the next-best alternative. Customer managers may find it easier to answer broadly stated questions, such as the cost of an hour of downtime in the customer's plant. However, their answers often will leave out effects on the customer's business, producing less valid estimates of worth.

Teams are advised to write out this list of the value elements, which can be lengthy, in relatively quick fashion, drawing on their collective experience. Each team next hypothesizes what kinds of customers would receive the greatest value from the offering and what kinds of customers would receive the least value. Team members determine what customer characteristics, such as application or customer capabilities, best capture these hypothesized differences in value received and could be used to segment (or further segment) the market. The team uses these customer descriptors to define two market (sub)segments that would be of most interest to study in the customer value research.

Each team next considers what would be the next-best-alternative offering in the minds of customers in each segment. The team selects the next-best-alternative offering and the firm providing it for each segment (the next-best-alternative offering may vary between selected segments, and on rare occasions, teams may choose to study two next-best-alternative offerings within a segment). The team then revisits its list of value elements, with this next-best alternative in mind.[50]

Although firms are doing many wonderful things for their customers, the reality in most business markets is that so, too, are the competitors supplying the next-best-alternative offering doing many wonderful things. So, to focus the customer value research and make it more manageable, we take advantage of a rearrangement of the fundamental value equation from Chapter 1:

$$(\text{Value}_f - \text{Price}_f) > (\text{Value}_a - \text{Price}_a) \quad \textbf{(2.1)}$$

$$(\text{Value}_f - \text{Value}_a) > (\text{Price}_f - \text{Price}_a) \quad \textbf{(2.2)}$$

$$\Delta\ \text{Value}_{f,\,a} > (\text{Price}_f - \text{Price}_a) \quad \textbf{(2.3)}$$

where Value_f and Price_f are the value and price of the focal firm's market offering (Offering_f), Value_a and Price_a are the value and price of the next-best-alternative market offering (Offering_a), and Δ denotes the difference in value between Offering_f and Offering_a. Thus, what really matters is not the value of each offering but the *difference* in value between the two offerings compared to the *difference* in their prices.

For each value element on its list, the team decides whether there is a difference on its offering's functionality or performance on that element relative to the next-best alternative. Teams are encouraged to be candid in their appraisals. If the team is honest with itself, out of a lengthy list, the team typically will decide that only a handful of value elements are differences between offerings. Most of these differences will be in favor of the team's offering, yet some will be differences favoring the next-best-alternative offering. Value elements on which the team believes that there are no differences between the two offerings are termed **points of parity**. Value elements on which the team believes that there are differences are termed **points of difference**.

The team constructs an initial **value word equation** for each point of difference, which expresses in words and simple mathematical operators (e.g., +, ÷) how to assess the differences in functionality and performance on the element and what those differences are worth in monetary terms. Accompanying each value word equation are the assumptions that the team makes about the value element and how its monetary value can be assessed. It is crucial to be *explicit* in all assumptions made.

The teams focus their customer value research on the points of difference, setting the points of parity aside.[51] In initial meetings to invite customers to participate in the customer value research, team members relate the list of value elements and which elements they regard as points of parity and points of difference. Team members then share the initial value word equations for the hypothesized points of difference. If the team has been honest with itself, the customers will largely agree with them. Inevitably, though, on some value elements they will disagree with the team's assessment. For example, the customer might regard a point of parity as a point of difference favoring the next-best alternative. Value elements on which disagreements occur are termed **points of contention**. Such disagreements should not be regarded as bad because they provide further motivation to the customers to participate in research and gather data to resolve the point of contention. We elaborate on points of difference, points of contention, and word equations in Box 2.6.

BOX 2.6
Points of Difference, Points of Contention, and Word Equations

Customer value research focuses on the points of difference and points of contention between the studied market offering and the next-best-alternative offering. Together, these capture the prospective differences in value between offerings and what they are worth in monetary terms. The intent of the supplier is to demonstrate and document these differences so that customer managers can easily grasp them, understand precisely how the supplier has assessed them, and find the results persuasive. To assist in accomplishing this task, we have created the concept of value word equations.

A value word equation expresses in words and simple mathematical operators (e.g., +, ÷) precisely how to assess the differences in functionality and performance between the studied offerings for a value element and how those differences are converted into worth in monetary terms. One is constructed for each point of difference and point of contention, where the value element, expressed as either cost savings or incremental profit, is on the left side of the equals sign and the components defining the differences in functionality or performance and what these are worth are on the right side. Value word equations counter two rampant problems in business markets. The first is "value claims," where suppliers argue that their offerings deliver cost savings or added value relative to the next-best alternative, but when pressed for detail, can provide few, if any, specifics of exactly how this occurs except, perhaps, for unverifiable stories having the character of "fishing tales." The second rampant problem is "spreadsheet mania": the construction of overly complicated, difficult-to-understand spreadsheets by technically-minded individuals who want to show-off their Excel® modeling skills. The result is densely packed, number-laden spreadsheets with minimal-to-nonexistent explanations of

(*continued*)

BOX 2.6
Continued

what the numbers mean. When questioned about their contents, even their creators sometimes have difficulty reconstructing what is meant.

In contrast, customer value research teams first construct a value word equation for each point of difference and point of contention. These value word equations make clear to the teams and the customers participating in the research what data need to be gathered and how those data will be combined to provide value estimates. After the data have been gathered, in presentations of the results, each value word equation first is presented. Then, the data are substituted in each equation to calculate the estimate in monetary terms for each value element. These results are then collected in a value summary, which we refer to as the customer value model. As an example, a point of difference between two large-format document reproduction systems (denoted as B and next-best-alternative A) was the number of paper jams a customer would experience each day. Because the copies these systems produce could be 1 meter wide by 15 meters long (e.g., a process flow diagram for a dairy), when the customer had a paper jam, it was quite a paper jam! The word equation for this point of difference was expressed as:

$$\text{Paper Jam Cost Savings}_{B,A} = [(\text{paper jams per day} \times \text{minutes to fix jam})_A - (\text{paper jams per day} \times \text{minutes to fix jam})_B] / 60 \text{ minutes per hour} \times \text{operator wages per hour} \times \text{annual work days}$$

Substituting in the gathered data, an estimate for this value element then was calculated as:

$$\text{Paper Jam Cost Savings}_{B,A} = [(3 \times 10)_A - (1 \times 10)_B] / 60 \times \text{INR } 318.20 \times 240 = \text{INR } 25{,}456.00$$

Thus, the estimate for this value element was INR 25,456.00 annually for system B relative to system A.

Accompanying each value word equation are the assumptions that the team is making about the value element and how its monetary value is assessed. In all customer value research, some assumptions will be needed to complete the analysis. The assumptions might be about the functionality or performance the market offering actually provides in the customer's specific setting, particularly for aspects that are extraordinarily difficult or costly to measure. Alternatively, assumptions might be made in assigning worth in monetary terms to measured differences in performance an offering provides in the customer's setting. Continuing with the example, an explicit assumption made was that if operator hours could be reduced, the Engineering Department would reassign the operator to other value-adding tasks.

It is crucial that the supplier be *explicit* in the assumptions it makes. When a customer firm catches the supplier in one or more implicit assumptions, particularly ones that are dubious, it has a devastating effect on the credibility of the whole analysis. In contrast, when all assumptions are made explicit, customer management simply can disagree with them. When disagreement happens, the astute supplier invites customer managers to share the rationales underlying their alternative assumptions. Depending on how plausible their rationales seem, the supplier can either adopt the alternative assumptions for the analysis or suggest that the supplier and customer engage in some joint research to mutually discover the most appropriate assumptions for the customer's specific setting.

Customer Value Research

The customer value research that each team conducts proceeds in three steps: (1) gaining initial customer cooperation, (2) gathering the data, and (3) analyzing the data. These steps are considered next.

Prior to contacting any present or prospective customers to participate in the research, the team has some tasks to perform. First, it must decide on present or prospective customers that are of most interest to have as research participants in each subsegment. Although the number of research participants sought will depend on the market, typically the team seeks the participation of six to eight customers from each subsegment. The team next thinks through why the customers should cooperate in the research. In our experience, customers cooperate in customer value research for one or more of four basic kinds of reasons: a low-cost resource to better understand their business, an opportunity to benchmark, earlier access to some new product or service, or the desire for a lower price.

The team next considers what managers at the customer firm the team would like to meet with. It contacts the salesperson responsible for each customer that the team wants to participate in the research, explains the purpose of research, and gains the salesperson's support. The salesperson provides names and contact information for managers to invite for the initial meeting.

In the initial meeting, the team members explain the purpose of the research and what the customer can expect to gain from participation. They discuss the hypothesized points of parity and points of difference, gain customer agreement, and discover any points of contention. They then reach agreement on value word equations that capture each point of difference and point of contention. Revisiting the points of difference and points of contention, they discuss what sources of data that the customer presently generates or would be able to generate to provide an estimate of each point of difference and point of contention. They discuss timing and resource requirements for data collection. Finally, they discuss what sources of data outside the customer firm (e.g., industry association studies) might be worthwhile to pursue.

In doing the research, wherever possible, the team prefers to gather data rather than simply rely on customer perception. If the customer volunteers to generate or collect the data, the team should inquire into the method that will be used. Wherever possible, team members should offer to work with the customer to generate or gather these data.

The team needs to be creative, using other sources where desirable or necessary. Independent industry consultants or knowledgeable personnel within the supplier firm can be sources of initial estimates. In some instances, retired customer personnel may be a resource. Where the provision of a service element mitigates a risk the customer would otherwise have, supplier firms sometimes employ actuarial consultants to estimate what the cost of that risk would be. QUALCOMM drew upon American Trucking Association research studies to provide ranges for some of the elements in its value model for its OmniTRACS® mobile communication system.[52]

When the data have been gathered, the team analyzes them to estimate what each value element that is a point of difference or a point of contention is worth in monetary terms. It also calculates the mean and the variance (or standard deviation) for each. It then conducts comparisons between the two studied subsegments to understand how the estimate for each value element varies across the two. The team next collects these value element results in a value summary—the customer value model. The team should be certain to list any assumptions made in assigning monetary amounts to each element.

To gain a deeper understanding of the results, the team performs sensitivity analyses, using the information on the variances around each element. It considers what characteristics might drive the variation in value and whether that variation warrants a new segmentation approach. It identifies which customers are the most attractive prospects.

The team finally considers the **value placeholders**, which are value elements that the team believes are worth something to customers but either are too difficult to obtain data for or are social elements. Relying on customer perception, what is each qualitatively worth? How might proxy estimates be obtained? When no other source than customer perception is available, framing the worth of the element in the customer's mind is critical. What seems reasonable? Although QUALCOMM assigns no monetary amounts to some less tangible elements, it still includes them in its analysis as value placeholders. In this way, QUALCOMM conveys that it believes those elements are worth something to the customer and leaves open the possibility that some specific amount might be ascertained in the future.

Constructing a Business Case for Change

Based on the knowledge of value that the team gains from its research, what does it recommend that the business do differently? The business case for change should address:

1. What specific actions does the team recommend based on its customer value research?
2. What resources would be needed to accomplish the recommended changes in doing business?
3. What are the specific concerns in implementing the business case?
4. What milestones can be specified to chart the progress in accomplishing the change?
5. What would be the profitability impact if the business case for change were approved?

These business cases are presented to senior managers who have served as project sponsors and the top management of the business unit. The business case should be viewed as a prospective commitment: If senior management provides the requested resources, the business will deliver the specified results, especially the estimated incremental profitability.

Value Realization

The period following the presentations of business cases for change to senior management is a critical phase for realizing the value, and incremental profitability, identified in the business cases. Value-based sales tools need to be created and training devised to give the sales force practical experience using them. Supporting changes in performance review and compensation may be needed. A method of feedback should be put in place to document the value that customers actually experience relative to what was promised to them. Finally, a system for tracking the incremental profitability actually realized should be put in place.

Suppliers not only use customer value models to inform and guide their own decision making, they also use them to create value-based sales tools that better enable their sales forces to persuasively convey the superior value their firms' offerings provide. These tools tend to take one of two forms: value case histories and value assessment as a value-adding, consultative selling tool. **Value case histories** are written accounts that document the cost savings or added value a customer firm actually received from its use of a supplier's market offering. Sonoco Products Company's Protective Packaging Division (SPPD), for example, audits actual cost savings that implementation of its total packaging solution proposals produce. At the end of the first year, SPPD constructs a cost-of-use case study and reports the findings to customer management. SPPD maintains a database of these cost-of-use case studies, which SPPD salespersons draw on when making proposals to other prospects. These case studies persuasively convey the cost savings that the prospects themselves would likely realize.

Value assessment itself can become a value-adding service that suppliers offer as part of a consultative selling approach. They develop customer value assessment tools, which we term **value calculators**, as spreadsheet software applications that salespeople or value specialists conduct on laptop computers to demonstrate the value that customers would receive from their offerings. Although these value calculators are typically quite user-friendly, they may require input data that the customer does not have readily available. To facilitate gathering the required input, the supplier may develop a worksheet that pulls together the necessary input data.

BT Lifters, a Division of BT Products AB (which is a member of Toyota Industries Corporation), based in Sweden, created *BT Virtual Warehouse*, which is a logistics planning system, to help customers make a significant difference in the profitability of their businesses through lowering the total cost of the handling process. BT Lifters uses *Virtual Warehouse* when a customer is contemplating a change in materials handling or is adding a new facility. The data necessary as input for using *Virtual Warehouse* require some competence on the customer's part. Some customers know the required data well, others do not. BT Lifter's most senior salespeople serve as internal materials handling champions for the customers and work with them in using *Virtual Warehouse* and doing the analysis. They even will provide "hands-on" data collection as needed at the customer's facility.

Although some customers use logistics consultants to help them in facilities planning, the advantage of working with BT Lifters and using *Virtual Warehouse* is that it provides a combination of planning the warehouse and specification of the kind and number of trucks needed to optimize warehouse performance. A case example illustrates this advantage. Birkenstock, a German manufacturer of health shoes, decided to build a new warehouse in Asbach, Germany. An in-house consultant responsible for the procurement process for this new warehouse had made a layout that indicated three lift trucks would be necessary to handle the pallet movements per hour. By using *Virtual Warehouse*, BT Lifters was able to demonstrate how an alternative layout in conjunction with its high-performance trucks required only two trucks—one fewer truck and also one fewer operator. According to BT Lifter's management, without *Virtual Warehouse*, they would never have been able to find this new solution and see the detailed performance results for their trucks. In addition, they believed that they would not have been able to convince Birkenstock management that their solution was correct without the *Virtual Warehouse* assessment.

Suppliers that practice customer value management understand that they must not only demonstrate the value that their offerings would deliver to customers; they must also document the cost savings and incremental profits their offerings actually deliver to customers purchasing them. Thus, they work with customers to define the measures on which they will track the cost savings or incremental profit produced, and then after a suitable period of time, work with customer managers to document what the actual results have been. They use these tools, which we term **value documenters**, to further refine their customer value models, create value case histories, enable the customer managers to obtain cost savings for which they will get credit and enhance the credibility of the demonstrated value of their offerings, because customer managers know that the supplier is willing to return to document the actual value received. Network India Ltd's (a disguised name) practice of customer value management with a large central government organization provides an outstanding case of the significant benefits to each firm, which we relate in Box 2.7.

BOX 2.7
Customer Value Management Benefits Networks India Ltd. (NIL) and Its Customers

Networks India Ltd. (NIL, name changed to preserve confidentiality) is a large telecom equipment manufacturing company which manufactures state-of-the-art digital EPABX (Electronic Private Automatic Branch Exchange). For the EPABX, NIL had technical collaboration with a major Japanese telecom company for technology transfer as well as for manufacturing of the product in India. NIL enjoyed a huge market share in India in the 1980s and 1990s and was among the top two EPABX suppliers in the country. NIL primarily operates in business markets, supplying private digital exchanges to private and government organizations. Customers range from small organizations which require only 40 to 50 office extensions to large government organizations like Defence, Railways, ONGC, or NTPC, which may require up to several thousand lines.

NIL's core product is a modular EPABX used to switch and connect intra-building calls. Its modular nature allows NIL to augment the core product's capacity and functionality by adding on required hardware modules and software features. Along with the appropriately configured product, the firm packages a number of additional services.

For example, a wide variety of models catering to different customers with different capacity requirements are available. NIL supplies EPABX with different line configurations ranging from 24 to 10,000 subscriber lines. The core technology is the same, but the capacity of the core product is enhanced for configurations with larger number of subscriber lines.

NIL's most prominent customer to date has been a large central government organization with heavy requirements for effective intra-office communications. By nature, the customer had a wide variety of requirements and very detailed specifications. Moreover, the customer's specifications were very stringent with regard to verifying the validity of the product. The buyer personnel typically remained unconvinced until all features were demonstrated to their satisfaction. Moreover, when investing in new products or technologies, the customer organization wanted a whole team of their operating personnel to be trained on each aspect of the product. They also mandated good documentation on the product, its maintenance, and thorough transfer of knowledge regarding

BOX 2.7
Continued

the activation of all the features of the system.

The customer organization was looking to upgrade their telephone exchange system at its Mumbai office. To begin with, NIL did a good job in understanding the key demands of the customer. Once NIL understood the requirements, it offered an appropriate Telecom package of the configured EPABX (core product), along with specific augmented services.

Prior to the implementation of NIL's system, the customer organization had several telephone exchanges installed at different locations which supported various kinds of old, rarely used telecom signaling technologies. Consequently, the customer required an EPABX using the latest digital technology but which could also support all older signaling technologies to interface with the old switches existing in the network. NIL was able to offer this facility by adding the right signaling modules to the core product.

The customer required only 5,500 lines but wanted the ability to upgrade to up to 10,000 lines in the future. The NIL switch was one of the few technologies that could offer this capacity. Moreover, being modular, the system's capacity could be enhanced in incremental steps as per future requirements.

To control its operations around the clock, communication was critical to the customer organization. Consequently, even a minute of down time in the exchange was unacceptable. NIL digital switches provided a full hot-standby feature where the entire control system would be duplicated so that the standby unit could concurrently take over in case of failure of the active control unit.

With their previous Mumbai exchange system, the maintenance staff of the organization used to manually test the health of each subscriber line either periodically or based on complaints received. This required a lot of effort and was not very efficient. As part of its offering, NIL offered a new system: a line tester equipment (LTE) which could quickly run a health check on a range of lines, generate reports, and help to troubleshoot line conditions when problems were reported.

Customers required that its entire team of technical staff be trained on the new technology before purchasing and installing the system. NIL offered an elaborate training program with a dedicated technical services team. It also offered a full pre-delivery customer inspection at the factory premises including detailed product feature demonstrations. The customer also required a very strong after-sales support team from its vendor. NIL had the largest sales and support team across India.

This fit between customer's needs and the capabilities of NIL and its product resulted in NIL winning the contract in the face of stiff competition. This was possible through superior market sensing and customer value management by NIL. Both the vendor and the customer were happy with the outcome. Over a period of time, NIL was able to win many more contracts from other offices of the customer organization and became the predominant supplier to the customer for digital switches. The continued business that NIL received from the customer organization was based on demonstration of value that the customer firm got by using NIL's EPABX system. This demonstration in the form of a value models was provided by NIL to the customer organization to convince the customer about the superiority of NIL's offering.

Contributed by Nikhil Popli, Niloy Das, Unus Ebrahim, Vishal Sharma, Vivek Gupta, Participants, EPGP Program, Indian Institute of Management Bangalore.

GAINING CUSTOMER FEEDBACK

Gaining knowledge of how well the supplier firm has met its customers' requirements and preferences is a crucial facet of market sensing. Based upon its knowledge of what targeted market segments and customer firms value and would value, the supplier constructs its market offerings. In marketing these offerings, the supplier, in essence, makes a promise that its offerings will satisfy the customer's requirements and preferences. Gaining customer feedback enables the firm to learn how well it has fulfilled its promises to customers. Customer feedback can tell the supplier where its offerings provided the functionality and performance customers expected, and where they did not. Thus, customer feedback provides the supplier with a chance to remedy problems that occur and to retain a customer's business. It also gives the supplier an early warning of changing customer requirements and preferences.

Although many supplier firms draw no distinctions and simply seek feedback from present customers, they can benefit from gaining customer feedback from three distinct kinds of customers. New customers provide valuable feedback on the initial experiences a firm has in doing business with the supplier and knowledge about converting new customers to established customers. Established customers provide essential feedback on how well the supplier sustains its relationships with customers and how the supplier's share of the customer's total purchase requirements is likely to change. Finally, customers that recently have stopped doing business with the supplier provide critical feedback on how the offering fell short of what was promised, the adequacy of the supplier's service recovery processes, and potential problems in the supplier's targeting and customer selection strategies.[53]

We first consider two related kinds of customer feedback: customer satisfaction measurement and customer value analysis. We end with considering the most recent customer feedback measure, derived from what its promoters tout as "the ultimate question": Net Promoter Score.

Customer Satisfaction Measurement

Customer satisfaction measurement experienced the kind of fervent adoption by the business community in the 1990s that Total Quality Management (TQM) received in the 1980s. Although the fervor for customer satisfaction measurement appears to be dwindling in recent years, most firms in business markets still are using customer satisfaction measurement in some form to monitor how well they are doing with their customers. A number of firms still even have customer satisfaction ratings linked to compensation for salespeople and others within the firm.

We first discuss a superior approach to customer satisfaction measurement and then consider some issues in what customer satisfaction results mean for the supplier.

American Customer Satisfaction Index (ACSI)

Fornell and his colleagues have provided the most comprehensive and methodologically rigorous approach to customer satisfaction measurement.[54] They recognize that no matter how carefully a researcher crafts a measure of customer satisfaction, in addition to assessing customer satisfaction, it also will likely measure other factors not of interest, as well as contain random measurement error. To overcome this problem,

Figure 2.4 The American Customer Satisfaction Index

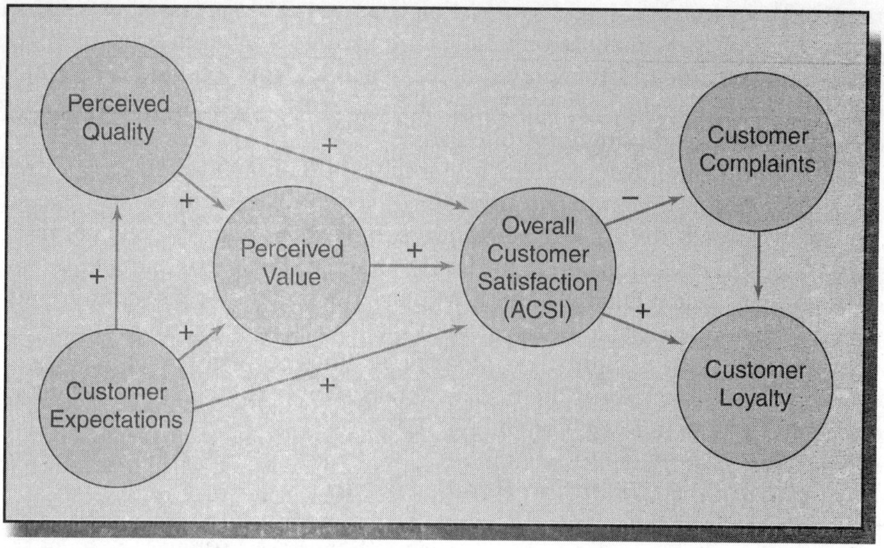

Source: Claes Fornell, Michael D. Johnson, Eugene W. Anderson, Jaesung Cha, and Barbara Everitt Bryant, "The American Customer Satisfaction Index: Nature, Purpose, and Findings," *Journal of Marketing* (October 1994): 8.

Fornell and his colleagues use multiple measures of customer satisfaction, which enables them to converge on the underlying concept of interest. They also embed the concept of customer satisfaction in a model that specifies its critical antecedents and consequences. They then use a sophisticated statistical analysis, partial least squares, to estimate the relationships between the measures and their intended underlying concepts, such as customer satisfaction, and the relationships among the concepts themselves, such as the relationship between customer satisfaction and customer loyalty. This approach produces results that demonstrate greater reliability and validity and provides supplier firms with a broader understanding of customer satisfaction.

We reproduce the American Customer Satisfaction Index (ACSI) model in Figure 2.4. **Overall customer satisfaction** "represents a cumulative evaluation of a firm's market offering, rather than a person's evaluation of a specific transaction."[55] The three measures of overall customer satisfaction include an overall satisfaction measure, a measure of the extent to which an offering's performance falls short or exceeds expectations, and a measure of the offering's performance relative to the customer's ideal product or service in the category. Customer expectations, perceived quality, and perceived value are antecedents of overall customer satisfaction. Note that customer expectations affect customer satisfaction not only directly, but also indirectly through their effects on perceived quality and perceived value. Customer complaints and customer loyalty are consequences of overall customer satisfaction. Two measures define customer loyalty: a rating of repurchase likelihood and a composite measure that assesses how increases in price and decreases in price would change the customer's purchase decision. Notice that the effect of customer complaints on customer loyalty is not specified in advance because it depends on whether a supplier resolves complaints in a way that either builds or damages customer loyalty.

The ACSI model builds on earlier work that Fornell did in Sweden, where he constructed a national customer satisfaction "barometer" to assess how well Swedish industry was doing. Fornell and his colleagues started similar indices in other countries besides Sweden and the United States, such as New Zealand. Their model of overall customer satisfaction can be applied to study customers at the level of a nation, an industry, or a single supplier firm.

At the level of the firm, Anderson, Fornell, and Lehman found that overall customer satisfaction is a significant predictor of economic returns to the firm, such as return on investment (ROI). Further, Anderson, Fornell, and Mazvancheryl found a significant positive relationship at the level of the firm between customer satisfaction and shareholder value. Finally, Fornell, Mithas, Morgeson, and Krishnan found a significant positive relationship at the level of the firm between firm customer satisfaction and market value of equity (i.e., stock price times number of outstanding shares) and that it is possible to beat the market consistently with lower systematic risk by investing in firms that do well on the ACSI.[56]

What Customer Satisfaction Results Mean

Even with reliable and valid measurement of customer satisfaction, supplier firm management still needs to understand what the results mean. What does the difference between customers that are satisfied and customers that are completely satisfied—the difference between a "4" and a "5" response on a five-point customer satisfaction measure—mean for the firm? Jones and Sasser researched the relationship between customer satisfaction and loyalty, studying 30 firms in five industries that include both consumer and business markets.[57] By **customer loyalty**, they mean:

> Broadly speaking, customer loyalty is the feeling of attachment to or affection for a company's people, products, or services. These feelings manifest themselves in many forms of customer behavior. The ultimate measure of loyalty, of course, is share of purchases in the category.[58]

Note that Jones and Sasser's ultimate measure of customer loyalty is the same as the earlier concept, **supplier's share of customer's business**: that is, the percent of a customer's total purchase requirement for a market offering that the supplier obtains. In their research, though, Jones and Sasser used an intention to repurchase measure as a proxy for customer loyalty. Their results show that the relationship between customer satisfaction and repurchase intention is not a simple, linear relationship, but one where completely satisfied customers are loyal to a much greater extent. A case example from Xerox that they report illustrates this finding: Totally satisfied customers were six times more likely to repurchase Xerox products over the next 18 months than were satisfied customers.

Recent research suggests that suppliers should not mistake customer tenure (i.e., the length of time the supplier has done business with a customer) with customer loyalty. Just because customers have been doing business with a supplier for a long time does not mean that they will be less costly to serve, that they will pay more for the supplier's offerings, or that they will engage in positive word-of-mouth communication about the supplier with others—all actions ascribed to loyal customers. Instead, suppliers are advised to assess customer loyalty by the extent of their customers' agreement with statements such as, "This supplier has earned my loyalty."[59]

Value is an essential antecedent of customer satisfaction and loyalty. Jones and Sasser observe: "Even in markets with relatively little competition, providing customers with outstanding value may be the only reliable way to achieve sustained customer satisfaction and loyalty."[60] Perceived value is an antecedent of overall customer satisfaction in the ACSI model, too. Understanding the pivotal role that value plays, a senior executive at DuPont Company once commented: "I am not out to delight my customers. . . . I just want to become indispensable to them, so that they can't live without me."[61]

The preceding quote alludes to what a number of suppliers state that they are pursuing—**customer delight**, which means to exceed rather than simply meet customer requirements and preferences. For example, one supplier's expressed goal is 100% customer delight. Businesses should rethink their unqualified pursuit of this goal, though. First, increasing performance levels is most often more costly, so supplier management must understand customers' willingness to pay for this performance and how much it will reduce profitability. Second, exceeding expectations tends to raise customers' expectation levels, so suppliers should pursue customer delight only to accomplish some strategic purpose, such as collaborative relationships with customers that afford the supplier a superior means of learning about changing market requirements. Lacking this purpose, completely satisfying customer requirements and preferences is sufficient.

Finally, suppliers should recognize that they may not be able to delight or even completely satisfy certain customers. It may well be that the supplier's market offering cannot deliver superior value against that customer's specific requirements and preferences, and to do so would be extraordinarily difficult or costly. This realization underscores the critical nature of selection strategies in determining which market segments and customers to serve, as well as the need to recognize mistakes in account selection.[62]

Customer Value Analysis

Gale proposed customer value analysis to remedy two shortcomings that he sees in customer satisfaction measurement programs.[63] Often, these programs do not survey noncustomers that are purchasing the offerings of competitors. They also do not provide a market assessment for supplier firms of how well they are doing relative to their competitors. Even though a supplier's performance is improving and customers report that they are satisfied, if a competitor's performance is improving faster, the "satisfied" customers will eventually defect.

Gale recommends that suppliers construct a **market-perceived quality profile** to pull together customer (and noncustomer) feedback.[64] Renee Karson, Director of Customer Value Measurement at US WEST Communications, provided a hypothetical illustration shown in Table 2.1.[65] Research participants first allocated 100 points across a set of attributes important in their purchase decisions (quality drivers), such as voice reliability, to reflect their relative importance. They then rated the performance of each service provider on each quality attribute, using an 11-point rating, where 0 is poor, 5 is acceptable, and 10 is outstanding. Multiplying each provider's average perceived quality on each attribute by the average importance weight, summing these products, and dividing by 100 produced the customer satisfaction score for the supplier firm and its

TABLE 2.1 A Hypothetical Illustration of a Market-Perceived Quality Profile for US WEST Communications: Small Business Customer Segment

Overall Quality Drivers					
Category	Importance	US WEST Score	Primary Competitor Score	US WEST Ratio	Best In Class
Voice Reliability	30.0	9.0	9.0	1.00	Company A
Repair Service	20.0	8.0	8.5	.94	Company B
Data Reliability	20.0	8.0	7.0	1.14	US WEST
Account Relationship	10.0	7.2	8.5	.85	Company C
Installation Service	10.0	7.0	7.5	.93	Company C
Billing Service	10.0	6.8	6.5	1.05	Company A
Customer Satisfaction Score:		8.0	8.1		
Market Perceived Quality Ratio:				99.9	

Source: Renee Karson, formerly Director Customer Value Measurement, Market Intelligence and Decision Support, US WEST Communications.

competitors. From the illustration in Table 2.1, we see that US WEST had a customer satisfaction score of 8.0, while its primary competitor had a score of 8.1. Dividing the supplier firm's average score on each attribute by that of a primary competitor (or the average of all other competitors), multiplying each ratio by its associated importance weight, and then summing produced a **market-perceived quality ratio**. In the illustration, US WEST fell slightly below its primary competitor with a ratio of 99.9.

As part of its customer value measurement program, US WEST augmented the market-perceived quality profiles with additional analyses. Research participants provided an overall price rating, an overall quality rating, and a value score ("Thinking about both quality and price, how would you rate US WEST on what you get for what you pay?"). To understand the relative contribution of quality and price to perceptions of value, US WEST regressed the overall value score on the overall quality and overall price measures. US WEST also measured nine specific price attributes, such as installation charges, which enabled it to regress the overall price rating on the specific price attributes to statistically determine the relative contributions of each to overall perceptions of price. Customer value measurement as practiced at US WEST provided an ongoing assessment to alert business units to emerging opportunities or threats. It can lead to "spin-off" market research studies that could provide value assessments expressed in monetary terms, using approaches such as conjoint analysis.

Net Promoter Score

An article in the *Harvard Business Review* entitled "The One Number You Need to Grow" and a subsequent book with the title *The Ultimate Question: Driving Good Profits and True Growth* have created a stir in gaining customer feedback. Fred Reichheld, a well-known author and consultant in customer loyalty, contends in them that businesses should scrap their customer satisfaction surveys and replace them with a single question and number for superior outcomes. The question is: "How likely is it that you would recommend [company X] to a friend or colleague?" Research participants respond on a 11-point scale, where 10 means "extremely likely," five means "neutral," and zero means "not at all likely." The number is the *Net Promoter Score* (NPS), which is derived from the answers to this willingness-to-recommend question. Reichheld asserts that research relating the answers to this question to customer actions of referral and repurchase revealed three logical clusters. *Promoters* are customers who give a "9" or "10" rating, *passives* are customers who are passively satisfied and give a "7" or "8" rating, and *detractors* are customers who give a "0" to "6" rating. Reichheld then defines the net promoter score as the percentage of promoters minus the percentage of detractors.[66]

Reichheld claims that businesses cannot build an effective customer-feedback system from present customer satisfaction survey methods and practices. He elaborates on the shortcomings of satisfaction surveys, organized under 10 reasons. "In the best tradition of late-night comedy, here are the top ten reasons that satisfaction surveys are a joke":[67]

#10: Too many surveys, too many questions
#9: The wrong customers respond
#8: Employees don't know how to take corrective action
#7: Too many surveys are marketing campaigns in disguise
#6: Survey scores don't link to economics
#5: Plain-vanilla solutions can't meet companies' unique needs
#4: There are no generally accepted standards
#3: Surveys confuse transactions with relationships
#2: Satisfaction surveys dissatisfy customers
#1: Gaming and manipulation wreck their credibility

Among these criticisms, #6 may be the most disturbing to senior management. Reichheld argues: "Our research indicates that satisfaction lacks a consistently demonstrable connection to actual customer behavior and growth."[68]

A number of firms serving business markets, such as GE, American Express, and Intuit, have adopted this net-promoter approach. When GE adopts something, such as the Six Sigma quality system, it tends to have a strong influence on what other firms in business markets do. Predictably, GE even has tied its managers' compensation to net promoter scores, with 20% of their bonuses now dependent on them.[69]

Before businesses adopt the net-promoter approach to customer feedback, we advise them to carefully examine the claims made for it and issues in implementing it to generate insights for improvement. Although characterizing customers as promoters, passives, or detractors is conceptually appealing, we question how the scale ratings are assigned to these three categories. Particularly troubling is the assignment of customers giving a rating of "6" to detractors, as a "6" is above "5," which is neutral, and thus would be a mildly positive rating. Therefore, it would seem consistent to assign customers giving a rating of "6" to the passively satisfied customer category, passives.

Another concern about the net-promoter approach is that the same improvement in NPS can come in two different ways: moving detractors to passives, or moving passives to promoters. Reichheld expresses the managerial charge as: "'We need more promoters and fewer detractors in order to grow.' The goal is clear-cut, actionable, and motivating."[70] Contrary to his assertion, the goal is not so clear-cut: Should the manager focus on moving detractors to passives or focus on moving passives to promoters? How to accomplish either one also is not apparent from estimating a simple NPS number. Reichheld may recognize himself the lack of direction in a simple NPS number because, in his book, he subsegments promoters, passives, and detractors by high or low profitability to put forward *three* priorities for improvement. Businesses may or may not agree with Reichheld's set or ordering of priorities, but we recommend that they pursue a similar subsegmentation of promoters, passives, and detractors based on customer profitability and then define their own priority of actions to improve NPS. Doing so, though, likely would mean monitoring the percentage changes in promoters, passives, and detractors, and rewarding managers on them (perhaps further subsegmented on profitability), rather than simply on the change in NPS.

When a firm has a number of business units, we advise management to tailor the question to the specific business unit or, perhaps, even a particular market offering. Thus, "How likely is it that you would recommend [business unit X/market offering X] to a friend or colleague?" While Reichheld advocates that businesses ask the ultimate question and very little else, even he concedes that a business may want to have a follow-up question or two for diagnostic purposes. To make the net-promoter approach truly actionable, we strongly concur with this. He offers two questions: "What is the primary reason for the score that you just gave us?" or for any rating below "10": "What is the most important improvement that would make you rate us closer to ten?" He also suggests, whenever possible, offer to customers who have given a poor rating the chance to have an employee contact them to try to resolve their problem, although doing so would seem to contradict his advice of maintaining the confidentiality of individual customer responses.[71]

While the net-promoter approach appears to be gaining support within the business community, it has attracted criticism, primarily from marketing academics and consultants working in customer satisfaction measurement. They point out that, contrary to the contention of Reichheld, the significant positive relationship of customer satisfaction to desirable financial outcomes for businesses has been established in numerous studies. We earlier reviewed some of these articles by Fornell and his colleagues, which established the significant positive relationship of customer satisfaction, as measured by ACSI, with return on investment, shareholder value, and market value equity. Further, customer satisfaction has been found to have a significant positive relationship with share of customer's business. Unlike the research to which Reichheld refers, these articles have gone through a rigorous peer review process, where knowledgeable reviewers scrutinize the research, analyses, and results to verify that they support the authors' findings and conclusions. This quote from Claes Fornell perhaps best captures the sentiment of these critics: "Clearly, it's attractive to have something simple. But to have something simplistic that points you in the wrong direction is not recommended, either." Businesses may indeed want to adopt the net-promoter approach, but as with any customer feedback approach, they should work through exactly what it will provide them and then validate the relationships between customer feedback on the measure and the market and financial outcomes that they are seeking.[72]

SUMMARY

Market sensing is the process of generating knowledge about the marketplace that individuals in the firm use to inform and guide their decision making. It is a market-driven process of learning about present and prospective customers and competitors, as well as other actors that affect the firm, such as resellers and regulatory agencies. Market sensing enables business market managers and other relevant individuals to formulate, test, revise, update, and refine their market views, which are simplified representations of the marketplace and how it works. We organized this chapter around four substantive facets of market sensing: defining the market, monitoring competition, assessing customer value, and gaining customer feedback.

In defining the market, business market managers choose descriptors that characterize and delimit a market, with the intent of pinpointing groups of firms that are of greater interest to the supplier firm. Market segmentation and determining market segments of interest are fundamental to defining the market. Market segmentation is the process of partitioning a market into groupings of firms that have relatively similar requirements and preferences for market offerings. Business market managers gain an understanding of which market segments are of greater interest by obtaining estimates of each defined market segment's size and growth, and its sales and profit potential.

Because customer judgments about the value of the firm's market offerings take place within the context of market offerings of other firms, business market managers also need knowledge about their competitors. We discussed Porter's framework for competitor analysis, which consists of four diagnostic components: future goals, assumptions, current strategy, and capabilities. To improve monitoring performance, supplier firms must have competitor intelligence systems, such as the Fuld Intelligence Pyramid™, and seek disconfirming as well as confirming evidence about competitors.

Customer value assessment is the work process of obtaining an estimate of the worth in monetary terms of some present or proposed market offering, or elements of it. Business market managers have employed nine methods to provide estimates of value. Customer value management is a comprehensive, practical approach for demonstrating and documenting the worth in monetary terms of what a supplier is doing, or could do, for defined market segments and customer firms. An essential undertaking in customer value management is building customer value models, which are data-driven estimates of what a present or prospective market offering is worth in monetary terms to targeted customers relative to the next-best-alternative offering for those customers.

Gaining knowledge of how well the supplier firm has met its customers' requirements and preferences is a crucial facet of market sensing. Gaining customer feedback tells the firm how well it has fulfilled its promises to customers and provides the supplier with a chance to remedy problems and retain a customer. We considered two related kinds of customer feedback: customer satisfaction measurement and customer value analysis. We ended with considering the most recent customer feedback measure, derived from what its promoters tout as "the ultimate question": Net Promoter Score.

ENDNOTES

1. George S. Day, "The Capabilities of Market-Driven Organizations," *Journal of Marketing* (October 1994): 44.
2. George S. Day, "The Capabilities of Market-Driven Organizations," 37–52; George S. Day, "Learning About Markets," *Marketing Science Institute Report No. 91–117* (June 1991): 1–23; Berend Wierenga and Gerrit H. van Bruggen, "The Integration of Marketing Problem-Solving Modes and Marketing Management Support Systems," *Journal of Marketing*

(July 1997): 21–37; and Gerald Zaltman, "Rethinking Market Research: Putting People Back In," *Journal of Marketing Research* (November 1997): 424–437.

3. Simply put, *data* are codified observations; *information* is data that have been interpreted or put into context using some decision framework; *intelligence* results from making judgments or inferences about the meaning of the information; and *knowledge* is intelligence about which there is greater certainty and acceptance. For more discussion of data, information, intelligence, and knowledge and how they can be considered as an ordered progression in their worth to the firm, see Vincent P. Barabba and Gerald Zaltman, *Hearing the Voice of the Market* (Boston, MA: Harvard Business School Press, 1991), pp. 45–46 and Chapter 6.
4. Dorothy Leonard and Walter Swap, "Deep Smarts," *Harvard Business Review* (September 2004): 88–97; Zaltman, "Rethinking Market Research"; and Ikujiro Nonaka, "The Knowledge-Creating Company," *Harvard Business Review* (November–December 1991): 2–9.
5. Day, "Learning About Markets"; and Wierenga and van Bruggen, "The Integration of Marketing Problem-Solving Modes." It is crucial that a firm periodically test the validity of the knowledge in its organization memory, such as recorded insights drawn from past analyses, and heuristics about the meaning of marketplace relationships.
6. "Electronic Glue," *The Economist*, 2 June 2001, 77–78. The quote is from p. 77.
7. Christine Moorman, Rohit Deshpandé, and Gerald Zaltman, "Factors Affecting Trust in Market Research Relationships," *Journal of Marketing* (January 1993): 81–101.
8. Elliot Maltz and Ajay Kohli, "Market Intelligence Dissemination Across Functional Boundaries," *Journal of Marketing Research* (February 1996): 57–58.
9. John Seely Brown and Paul Duguid, "Balancing Act: How to Capture Knowledge Without Killing It," *Harvard Business Review* (May–June 2000): 73–80.
10. Theodore Levitt, *The Marketing Imagination* (New York: The Free Press, 1983), p. 128.
11. Thomas S. Robertson and Howard Barich, "A Successful Approach to Segmenting Industrial Markets," *Planning Review* (November–December 1992): 6 [emphasis in original].
12. NAICS codes can be obtained at *http://www.naics.com*. This Web site also matches the NAICS codes to their corresponding old SIC codes.
13. James C. Anderson and James A. Narus, "Partnering as a Focused Market Strategy," *California Management Review* (Spring 1991): 95–113.
14. C. K. Prahalad and Gary Hamel, "The Core Competence of the Corporation," *Harvard Business Review* (May–June 1990): 79–91; and George Stalk, Philip Evans, and Lawrence E. Schulman, "Competing on Capabilities: The New Rules of Corporate Strategy," *Harvard Business Review* (March–April 1992): 57–69.
15. Das Narayandas, "Note on Customer Management," *Harvard Business School Note* 9-502-073 (Boston, MA: Harvard Business School Publishing, 2002); Robert S. Kaplan and V. G. Narayanan, "Measuring and Managing Customer Profitability," *Journal of Cost Management* (September–October 2001): 5–15; and Robert C. Blattberg, Gary Getz, and Jacquelyn S. Thomas, *Customer Equity* (Boston, MA: Harvard Business School Press, 2001).
16. Imad B. Baalbaki and Naresh K. Malhotra, "Marketing Management Bases for International Market Segmentation: An Alternate Look at the Standardization/Customization Debate," *International Marketing Review*, 10, no. 1 (1993): 19–44. Finally, for a worthwhile resource on segmentation in business markets, see Grahame, Dowling, Gary L. Lilien, Arvind Rangaswamy, and Robert J. Thomas, *Harvesting Customer Value: Understanding and Applying Customer Value Based Segmentation* (2003), available at: *http://www.marketingIQ.com.*
17. Roger J. Best, *Market-Based Management: Strategies for Growing Customer Value and Profitability*, 3rd ed. (Upper Saddle River, NJ: Prentice Hall, 2004), p. 120 [emphasis in original].

18. When market segments correspond to different country markets, country risk can be an additional factor that supplier firms assess in determining which segments are of interest. See, for example, "Business in Difficult Places: Risky Returns," *The Economist*, 20 May 2000, 85–88.
19. George J. Kress and John Snyder, *Forecasting and Market Analysis Techniques: A Practical Approach* (Westport, CT: Quorum Books, 1994); and F. William Barnett, "Four Steps to Forecast Total Market Demand," *Harvard Business Review* (July–August 1988): 28. The quote is drawn from Kress and Snyder, *Forecasting and Market Analysis Techniques: A Practical Approach*, p. 224.
20. Kress and Snyder. See the discussion in Chapter 13.
21. Barnett, "Four Steps to Forecast Total Market Demand," p. 28.
22. Kress and Snyder. We discuss constructing scenarios in Chapter 4.
23. Steven P. Schnaars, *Megamistakes: Forecasting and the Myth of Rapid Technological Change* (New York: The Free Press, 1989), pp. 134–135.
24. Kress and Snyder. See the discussion in Chapters 10 and 11. See also: Paul Saffo, "Six Rules for Effective Forecasting," *Harvard Business Review* (July–August 2007): 122–131.
25. Kress and Snyder, p. 219.
26. Kress and Snyder, p. 219.
27. James C. Anderson and James A. Narus, "Selectively Pursuing More of Your Customer's Business," *MIT Sloan Management Review* (Spring 2003): 42–49.
28. We discuss this further in Chapter 6, as part of creating market-oriented realization.
29. George S. Day and Paul J. H. Schoemaker, "Scanning the Periphery," *Harvard Business Review* (November 2005): 135–148; Schnaars, "Megamistakes."
30. Michael E. Porter, *Competitive Strategy* (New York: The Free Press, 1980). We draw on Chapter 3 of *Competitive Strategy* for this section, and adapt it where necessary to the business market management context. Professor Porter also makes the point that the firm should apply this framework to study *itself*, as a means to better understand what conclusions competitors are likely to draw about the firm.
31. Donald R. Lehmann and Russell S. Winer, *Analysis for Marketing Planning*, 5th ed. (Burr Ridge, IL: McGraw Hill/Irwin, 2001).
32. Porter, *Competitive Strategy*, p. 59.
33. Kenneth Labich, "Why Companies Fail," *Fortune*, 14 November 1994, 60. Digital Equipment Corporation was acquired in June 1998 by Compaq Computer Corporation, which merged with Hewlett-Packard Company in May 2002.
34. Lehman and Winer, "Analysis for Marketing Planning." We discuss positioning in business markets in Chapter 4.
35. Michael V. Marn and Robert L. Rosiello, "Managing Price, Gaining Profit," *Harvard Business Review* (September–October 1992): 84–94.
36. Prahalad and Hamel, "Core Competence"; Stalk, Evans, and Schulman, "Competing on Capabilities"; and Lehman and Winer, "Analysis for Marketing Planning."
37. Lehman and Winer, "Analysis for Marketing Planning."
38. We are grateful to Leonard Fuld, founder and president of Fuld & Company, for his generous assistance with this section. For further information on competitive intelligence, see Leonard M. Fuld, *The Secret Language of Competitive Intelligence*. (New York: Crown Business, 2006); and Stephen D. Solomon, "Spies Like You," *Fortune Small Business* (June 2001): 76–82.
39. Thomas A. Stewart, with David C. Kaufman, "Getting Real About Brainpower," *Fortune* (27 November 1995): 201–203.
40. Jeremy Main, "How to Steal the Best Ideas Around," *Fortune* (19 October 1992): 102–106. The quote on benchmarking is drawn from p. 102.
41. Max H. Bazerman and Dolly Chugh, "Decisions Without Blinders," *Harvard Business Review* (January 2006): 88–97; Max H. Bazerman, *Judgment in Managerial Decision Making*, 6th ed. (New York: John Wiley & Sons, 2006).
42. Stephen Goldsmith, "Can Business Really Do Business with Government," *Harvard Business Review* (May–June 1997): 110–121.

43. This section draws heavily from James C. Anderson, Dipak C. Jain, and Pradeep K. Chintagunta, "Customer Value Assessment in Business Markets: A State-of-Practice Study," *Journal of Business-to-Business Marketing*, 1, no. 1 (1993): 3–29.
44. For a basic exposition of conjoint analysis, see Chapter 21 of Naresh K. Maholtra, *Marketing Research: An Applied Orientation*, 3rd ed. (Upper Saddle River, NJ: Prentice Hall, 1999). For a discussion of recent advances, see J. Douglas Carroll and Paul E. Green, "Psychometric Methods in Marketing Research: Part I, Conjoint Analysis," *Journal of Marketing Research* (November 1995): 385–391. For discussions of the practical considerations in applying conjoint analysis, see Joseph Curry, "After the Basics," *Marketing Research* (Spring 1997): 6–11; and Susan Auty, "Using Conjoint Analysis in Industrial Marketing," *Industrial Marketing Management* (June 1995): 191–206.
45. Notice the amount of technical detail that is provided to ensure that the supplier and the participants have the same understanding of what exactly the attribute levels are and what they mean.
46. V. Srinivasan and Chan Su Park, "Surprising Robustness of the Self-Explicated Approach to Customer Preference Measurement," *Journal of Marketing Research* (May 1997): 286–291.
47. In February 2002, Business & Market Research, Ltd. was acquired by Wirthlin Worldwide and took the name Wirthlin Europe. In September 2004, Wirthlin Worldwide was acquired by Harris Interactive. See: *http://www.dti.gov.uk/files/file11478.pdf* and *http://www.harrisinteractive.com/news/allnewsbydate.asp?NewsID=842*, respectively.
48. David B. Montgomery, "Conjoint Calibration in the Customer/Competitor Interface in Industrial Markets," in *Industrial Marketing: A German-American Perspective*, eds. K. Backhaus and D. Wilson (Berlin: Springer-Verlag, Inc., 1986), pp. 297–319.
49. This section draws heavily from James C. Anderson, *Customer Value Management* (Wilmette, IL: James C. Anderson LLC, 2007). For more on customer value management, see: James C. Anderson, Nirmalya Kumar, and James A. Narus, *Value Merchants: Demonstrating and Documenting Superior Value in Business Markets* (Boston: Harvard Business School Press, 2007).
50. Some businesses have relatively little insight into how their offerings differ from those of competitors or into potential changes that they might make in their offerings that customers would value. In these situations, scouting research is worthwhile, most often using the "Day in the Life of the Customer" qualitative approach. See: Anderson, Kumar, and Narus, *Value Merchants*, Chapter 3; and Francis J. Gouillart and Frederick D. Sturdivant, "Spend a Day in the Life of Your Customers," *Harvard Business Review* (January–February 1994): 116–125.
51. Once in a while, a team might pursue a point of parity that represents a *nuisance* to customers. Nuisances are points of parity where, if a supplier could make a difference, it would have a significant effect on the value the customers receive and it also would deliver a social benefit of ending or reducing the "pain" customers experience.
52. We discuss the OmniTRACS mobile communication system and how QUALCOMM conducts value assessments for it in Box 8.5.
53. Frederick F. Reichheld, "Learning from Customer Defections," *Harvard Business Review* (March–April 1996): 56–69.
54. Claes Fornell, "A National Customer Satisfaction Barometer: The Swedish Experience," *Journal of Marketing* (January 1992): 6–21; Eugene W. Anderson, Claes Fornell, and Donald R. Lehman, "Customer Satisfaction, Market Share, and Profitability: Findings from Sweden," *Journal of Marketing* (July 1994): 53–66; and Claes Fornell, Michael D. Johnson, Eugene W. Anderson, Jaesung Cha, and Barbara Everitt Bryant, "The American Customer Satisfaction Index: Nature, Purpose, and Findings," *Journal of Marketing* (October 1996): 7–18.

55. Fornell et al., "The American Customer Satisfaction Index," p. 8.
56. Claes Fornell, Sunil Mithas, Forrest V. Morgeson III, and M.S. Krishnan, "Customer Satisfaction and Stock Prices: High Returns, Low Risk," *Journal of Marketing* (January 2006): 3–14; Eugene Anderson, Claes Fornell, and Sanal K. Mazvancheryl, "Customer Satisfaction and Shareholder Value," *Journal of Marketing* (October 2004): 172–185; and Anderson et al., "Customer Satisfaction, Market Share, and Profitability."
57. Thomas O. Jones and W. Earl Sasser, Jr., "Why Satisfied Customers Defect," *Harvard Business Review* (November–December 1995): 88–99.
58. Jones and Sasser, p. 94.
59. Frederick F. Reichheld, "Lead for Loyalty," *Harvard Business Review* (July–August 2001): 76–84; Werner Reinartz and V. Kumar, "The Mismanagement of Customer Loyalty," *Harvard Business Review* (July 2002): 86–94; and "Letters to the Editor: The Mismanagement of Customer Loyalty," *Harvard Business Review* (November 2002): 125–129. The Loyalty Acid Test for customers and employees can be found at *http://www.loyaltyrules.com.* Recent research has found that business unit employee satisfaction-loyalty shows a substantial relationship with customer satisfaction-loyalty and business unit profitability. See: James K. Harter, Frank L. Schmidt, and Theodore L. Hayes, "Business-Unit-Level Relationship Between Employee Satisfaction, Employee Engagement, and Business Outcomes: A Meta-Analysis," *Journal of Applied Psychology* (April 2002): 268–279.
60. Jones and Sasser, "Why Satisfied Customers Defect," p. 90 [emphasis in original omitted].
61. Joseph Weber, with Linda Bernier and Edith Updike, "For DuPont, Christmas in April," *Business Week,* 24 April 1995, 130.
62. For more on cautions in customer satisfaction, see Dawn Iacobucci, Kent Grayson, and Amy Ostrom, "Customer Satisfaction Fables," *Sloan Management Review* (Summer 1994): 93–96; Jones and Sasser, "Why Satisfied Customers Defect"; and Wilton Woods, "After All You've Done for Your Customers, Why Are They Still NOT HAPPY?" *Fortune* (11 December 1995): 178–180, 182.
63. Bradley T. Gale with Robert Chapman Wood, *Managing Customer Value* (New York: The Free Press, 1994); and Bradley T. Gale, *How Much Is Your Product* Really *Worth?* (Boston, MA: Bradley T. Gale, 2002). For an approach that uses customer value analysis in conjunction with a measure of customer loyalty to derive a loyalty index that captures the nature of the satisfaction-loyalty relationship, see Madhav Srinivasan, "New Insights into Switching Behavior," *Marketing Research: A Magazine of Management & Applications* (Fall 1996): 27–33.
64. A potential problem with grouping data from customers and noncustomers together is that they may have significantly different perceptions of the importance of different attributes in a market offering and the alternative suppliers' performances on them. Because of this potential discrepancy, we would recommend first performing the analyses separately to assess any differences before combining the two subsamples in a single analysis.
65. Renee Karson headed a customer value measurement group at US WEST. In her group were six Customer Value Managers who worked closely with the market/business units to identify, define, monitor, and analyze customer value perceptions of US WEST and its competitors. US WEST did not follow Gale's exact approach in practice. Instead, it tailored the approach to its specific needs for understanding its industry. US WEST merged with Qwest Communications International in 2000, where Karson now is Senior Director of Marketing.
66. Frederick F. Reichheld, "The One Number You Need to Grow," *Harvard Business Review* (December 2003): 46–54; and Frederick F. Reichheld, *The Ultimate*

Question: Driving Good Profits and True Growth (Boston: Harvard Business School Press, 2006).

67. Reichheld, *The Ultimate Question*, p. 78, with elaboration of the top 10 reasons on pp. 78–93.
68. Reichheld, "The One Number You Need to Grow," p. 49.
69. Kathryn Kranhold, "Client-Satisfaction Tool Takes Root," *The Wall Street Journal*, July 10, 2006, B3; and Jena McGregor, "Would You Recommend Us?" *Business Week*, January 30, 2006.
70. Reichheld, "The One Number You Need to Grow," p. 54.
71. Reichheld, *The Ultimate Question*, p. 96.
72. Timothy L. Keiningham, Terry G. Vavra, Lerzan Aksoy, and Henri Wallard, *Loyalty Myths: Hyped Strategies That Will Put You Out of Business—and Proven Tactics That Really Work* (Hoboken, NJ: John Wiley & Sons, 2005); *http://www.loyaltymyths.com;* Bruce Cooil, Timothy L. Keiningham, Lerzan Aksoy, and Michael Hsu, "A Longitudinal Analysis of Customer Satisfaction and Share of Wallet: Investigating the Moderating Effect of Customer Characteristics," *Journal of Marketing* (January 2007): 67–83; and Timothy L. Keiningham, Bruce Cooil, Tor Wallin Andreassen, and Lerzan Aksoy, "A Longitudinal Examination of Net Promoter and Firm Revenue Growth," *Journal of Marketing* (July 2007): 39–51. The quote from Claes Fornell is from: McGregor, "Would You Recommend Us?" p. 95.

Chapter 3

Understanding Firms as Customers

Overview

A detailed understanding of customer requirements, preferences, and purchasing processes enables supplier managers to know where their resources and capabilities have the greatest potential to create and deliver customer value. Supplier managers use this knowledge to guide decisions about which market segments and customer firms to target. Moreover, these insights serve as a beacon, directing a supplier firm's market offering management and new offering realization activities. On a more tactical level, detailed understanding of firms as customers allows a supplier to focus efforts on those customer managers who matter the most in a purchase decision, to tailor its information to the preferences of those managers, and to persuasively demonstrate why the supplier's market offerings deliver superior customer value.

Understanding firms as customers is the process of learning how companies rely on a network of suppliers to add value to their offerings, integrate purchasing activities with those of other functional areas and outside firms, and make purchase decisions. In this chapter, we examine each aspect of the process. We begin by discussing how progressive firms reconfigure the task of securing external resources—from executing transactions to managing supply. We introduce three purchasing orientations—buying, procurement, and supply management—and investigate their defining themes, concepts, and practices.

Figure 3.1 Understanding Firms as Customers

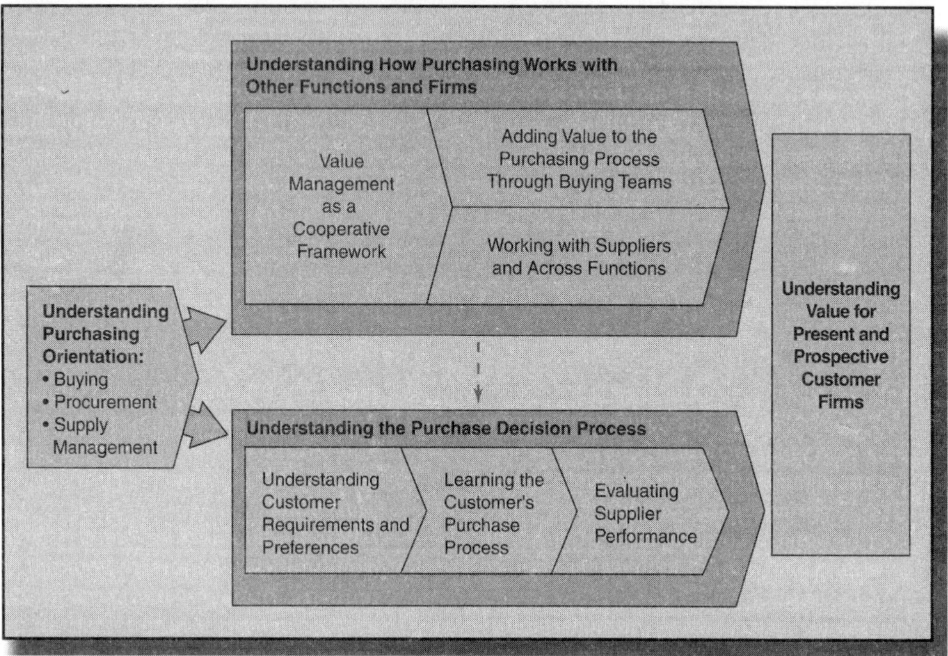

Next, we explore such initiatives as cross-functional buying teams and early supplier involvement programs that progressive firms increasingly employ to make more productive use of their resources. Finally, we describe how companies make actual resource acquisition decisions. Among the major issues we address are how business market managers gain a better understanding of customer firm requirements and purchase decision processes, and how customer firms evaluate supplier performance. We depict the process of understanding firms as customers in Figure 3.1

Understanding Purchasing Orientation

Broadly speaking, **purchasing** is the process of acquiring resources and capabilities for the firm from outside providers. **Purchasing orientation**, on the other hand, is the philosophy that guides managers who make purchasing-related decisions and delineates their domain and span of influence. Seasoned business market managers know that all customer firms do not share the same purchasing orientation. They are aware that shrewd customer firms may even embrace several at once, deliberately matching each orientation with a specific category of acquired products or services. When business market managers understand a customer firm's purchasing orientation, they can more knowledgeably decide such things as whether to serve the account,

Figure 3.2 Purchasing Orientations and the Value Network

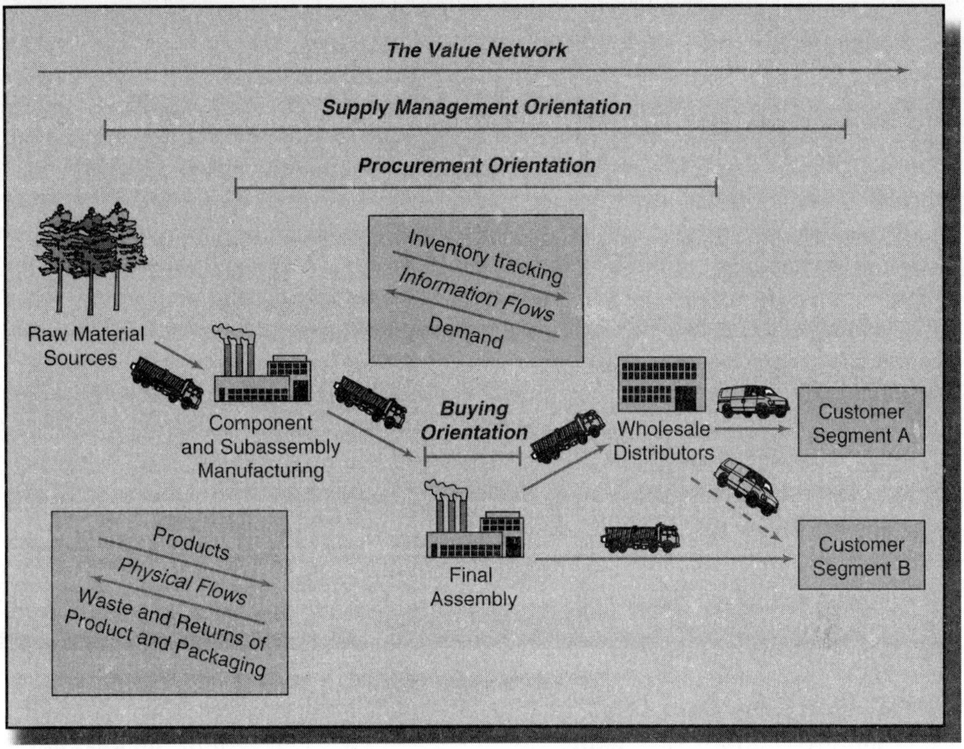

Source: Adapted from a chart by Professor Sunil Chopra, J. L. Kellogg Graduate School of Management, Northwestern University, 1999.

how to adapt the market offering to better meet the customer firm's requirements and preferences, and how to craft persuasive sales presentations.

In practice, customer firms commonly select from three purchasing orientations—buying, procurement, or supply management.[1] Figure 3.2 illustrates the scope of the three purchasing orientations from the perspective of a customer firm, a final assembly manufacturer. The icons and arrows represent the **value network**, or set of organizations that perform portions of business processes designed to create economic, technical, service, and social benefits, and then equitably share those resulting benefits. The diagram indicates that as the manufacturer's purchasing orientation progresses from buying to procurement to supply management, the domain and span of influence of purchasing broadens.[2]

Our fundamental value equation 1.1 from Chapter 1 helps distinguish the thrusts of the three orientations. With a buying orientation, a customer manager's efforts focus solely on minimizing the price paid in a given transaction commonly for a single product or service. Breaking down value in the equation into benefits minus any costs incurred to achieve them shows the intent of procurement and supply management. With a procurement orientation, a customer manager strives to reduce the total costs of ownership of an offering, which is often composed of a bundle of products and/or services or a total solution. With a supply management orientation, a customer manager seeks to obtain the greatest value relative to price from a close working relationship with a supplier.

The Buying Orientation

It is essential that business market managers recognize which prospective customer firms have a buying orientation, because these firms afford managers the fewest degrees of freedom for creating and sharing value. As shown in Figure 3.2, buying is the most narrowly focused purchasing orientation. **Buying** concerns executing discrete transactions, often for a single item at a time, with suppliers. A buying organization's prime objective is to reduce its annual **total spend** or the monetary amount of acquisitions in a given year. Buyers maintain arm's-length, often adversarial relationships with vendors. Buying practices are tactical and short-term in nature. Under this orientation, buyers often have little if any input concerning what to acquire, in what quantity, and when. Firms commonly reward buyers for reducing prices paid to suppliers and for lowering the total spend from the previous year.

The central pursuits of the buying orientation are:

- Obtain the best deal in terms of price, quality, and availability from suppliers.
- Maximize power over suppliers.
- Avoid risk wherever possible.

Obtaining the Best Deal

When given a purchase request by another functional group, the buyer searches potential vendors for the best combination of price, quality, and availability. The buyer treats quality and availability as "order qualifiers" when evaluating competitive offerings. That is, they are necessary for a supplier to be considered but not sufficient to gain the order. Initially, buyers use price as an order qualifier, too. As Ross points out, customer firms rarely consider a vendor's offering unless its price falls within the acceptable price band for that product or service class. A price band represents the range of acceptable prices around the average price paid for a product or service. In many industries, the price band is ±3% of this average. Under a buying orientation, the customer firm then usually selects the lowest-price vendor offering. Thus, price is the sole "order winner."[3]

How do buyers get the best deal? To understand these dynamics fully, let's assess buying as a form of distributive negotiations. In **distributive negotiations**, the customer and supplier assume that the "value pie" is fixed in size. Both firms see the situation as win-lose with one gaining more pie only at the expense of the other. Customer and supplier haggle over one thing—price. To gain the best price, both firms resort to gamesmanship and persuasion, while withholding critical information.

To bolster their negotiating position and lower the minimum price the supplier is willing to accept, buyers draw on two tools—price analysis and supplier cost analysis. In a price analysis, the buyer compares a seller's price proposal (bid) to the prices charged (or bid) by other possible vendors. Technological innovations, such as shared information systems and the comparison agents on the Internet, bring greater price transparency, making it far easier for buyers to conduct price analyses. Armed with price comparison data, the buyer is obviously in a better position to demand price concessions.[4]

Supplier cost analysis entails a review of actual or estimated cost data for a potential vendor. To conduct a supplier cost analysis, the buyer obtains all information possible on supplier costs directly from supplier personnel. Then, industrial engineers from the buyer's firm estimate the remaining supplier costs using published data on materials usage, labor rates, and equipment utilization. The buyer then adds on a "reasonable" profit margin to arrive at a "fair" price, which is demanded during negotiations. Typically, buyers use the supplier's overall corporate profit margin gleaned from annual reports as an estimate of reasonable profit. Of course, such analyses are based upon two pivotal assumptions. First, they presume that a buyer has a better understanding of efficient production processes. Second, they assume that the overall corporate profit margin accurately reflects the profit margin on the offering that the customer purchases and that the customer has the right to determine what constitutes a "reasonable" profit margin for the supplier firm.[5]

Maximizing Power over Suppliers

Power is the ability of one firm to get another firm to undertake actions it wouldn't undertake on its own. In a given transaction, the firm that has the power advantage or leverage can force the weaker firm to make price concessions. Thus, if the customer firm has the power advantage, it can secure a lower price from the supplier.[6]

How can a customer firm gain power over suppliers? When buyers do act to gain power, they often turn to two related tactics—commoditization and multisourcing. Through **commoditization**, buyers eliminate or downplay any points of difference between the value elements of competing offerings. For example, a buyer might contend that one supplier's technical support services are equivalent to another supplier's service. In essence, the buyer tries to equalize and remove $Value_f$ and $Value_a$ from the fundamental value equation 1.1, leaving competing vendors with reducing price as their only means for gaining an advantage and thus the sale. Through **multisourcing**, the customer firm requests price quotations from and places orders with a number of suppliers, playing one off against the other. To get more business, each supplier cuts price, triggering a downward price spiral.

As corollaries to multisourcing, buyers avoid sole-sourcing and single-sourcing because they would make the customer firm too dependent on one supplier. Buyer concern may be somewhat justified because of the possibilities of catastrophic events such as labor strikes, raw materials shortages, and plant explosions. In a **sole-sourcing** situation, only one supplier produces a needed product or service. Examples might include rare raw materials, patented product innovations, and new technologies. To avoid sole-sourcing, the buyer postpones acquisition of an offering until competitors emerge. In a **single-sourcing** situation, the buyer purchases the firm's total requirement from one vendor even though alternatives exist. Historically, buyers refrain from this practice "to keep vendors honest."

Critically, buyers are careful not to "squeeze" suppliers too much on price. If the customer firm does not allow a supplier a measure of profit, the supplier might go out of business or stop producing the needed offering. This event would reduce the number of potential suppliers, increasing the power of the remaining suppliers and ultimately, prices. Thus, buyers engage in an intricate "dance" with suppliers, relentlessly seeking price reductions yet stopping short of bankrupting them.

Avoiding Risk

Most managers try to minimize their exposure to risk, but buyers have a penchant for avoiding risk altogether. They use two tactics for avoiding risk—follow established procedures and rely on proven vendors. Research has demonstrated that buyers tend to use time-honored decision rules or heuristics when buying products and services such as the following. Seek quotes from at least three competing vendors. Divide an order among several suppliers with the greatest share going to the lowest bidder. Consider new vendors only if their bid is 10% less than that of lowest-priced incumbent supplier.[7]

Buyers also seek to avoid risk by relying on proven vendors. Often, buyers even give these preferred suppliers breaks during the purchasing process. For example, buyers frequently afford incumbent suppliers the right to "meet or release," which means that whenever an incumbent supplier's bid is significantly higher than that of a new supplier, the buyer allows the incumbent to revise its quotation downward. The buyer accepts the new supplier's bid only if the incumbent refuses to lower its bid. Importantly, the buyer does not extend the same courtesy to new suppliers.

Developments in Buying

It is important to emphasize that the practice of buying is evolving. An increasingly popular practice is that of **target pricing**. This approach is commonly used in the Japanese automobile industry. Target pricing works as follows. Through market research, buyers determine the target price for their product or service among their firm's customers. For instance, they might conclude that a given car model must sell for INR 1 million. Next, managers divide the car into systems and estimate what portion of the car's price should come from each system. They "drill" downward to subsystems and eventually to parts. Thus, buyers might conclude that in order to market a INR 1 million car, they cannot pay more than INR 1,000 for a door handle. When entering into negotiations with prospective suppliers, buyers demand a INR 1,000 or less door handle.[8]

Another trend in buying is **global sourcing**. As the world becomes smaller because of breakthroughs in communication and transportation, buyers are increasingly able to take advantage of international marketplaces. Moreover, international suppliers often feature reduced prices, increased quality, and new technologies. Most important, buyers use global sourcing to broaden the customer firm's portfolio of suppliers, and in turn, enhance the firm's purchasing power. While the extent of global sourcing has exploded, there has been some retrenchment in buying practices due to added risk. Buyers increasingly must deal with materials contamination, suspect product quality, and unreliable deliveries from international vendors. Their response has been to reconsider domestic suppliers and willingly pay higher prices, at least for a portion of their total spend, in order to secure higher quality and predictable deliveries.[9]

Electronic networks, including the public Internet and private extranets, now enable customer firms to simultaneously reap the price reduction benefits of multisourcing and global sourcing through **e-sourcing** or online purchasing. Among the e-sourcing tools that buyers have begun to use in earnest are comparison agents, online reverse auctions, and eRFQs. Comparison agents or "shopping bots" are software programs that enable a firm to search the Internet for suppliers of specific products or services, rank order those vendors from lowest price to highest, and place orders with the lowest-priced supplier. A firm can rely on internal comparison agent software or contract for the services of a third-party application service provider. Comparison agents are most useful for buying widely available, standardized, or branded commodity items.[10]

In an online reverse auction, two or more suppliers bid against one another electronically to secure an order from a customer firm. Participants place bids anonymously in a Dutch auction format (i.e., descending monetary amounts), with the lowest bidder most often winning the entire order (i.e., if the lowest bidder does not meet specifications, the customer firm may select another bidder). Depending on the nature of the products and services being exchanged and bidding rules, an online auction can last from five minutes to several hours.

Although online reverse auction service and software providers claim that price savings commonly range between 10% and 50%, managers at GXS (formerly GE Global eXchange Services), which conducted more than 32,000 auction events from 2000 through early 2002, are more sanguine, citing average price savings between 7% and 9%. Some customer firms publicly tout millions of rupees in total price savings from online reverse auctions. Others privately lament that such savings have come at the expense of product quality, timely delivery, support service, and long-term collaboration with trusted suppliers. Research suggests that online reverse auctions are most beneficial to buyers when securing low-tech commodities, used equipment, and surplus or distressed merchandise.[11]

For a fee or commission on a transaction, a customer firm can post an electronic request for quotation (eRFQ) on a third party moderated Web site (e.g., GXS) or on a business-to-business (B2B) exchange (e.g., Covisint, ChemConnect, Exostar). Suppliers from around the world can then electronically submit quotes for the order. In a sealed bid format, the customer firm automatically selects the lowest bidder. In an eRFQ plus negotiations process, customer managers identify the lowest bidder and then follow up with direct contacts to negotiate an even lower price.[12]

Purchasing experts cite overspecification as a major cause of needlessly high-priced goods and services. An overspecified offering contains "bells and whistles" that are not needed to meet a customer's requirements in a given application. Through **defeaturing** or **cooperative pricing**, customer and supplier managers work together to identify superfluous features, attributes, and performance specifications that can be eliminated or relaxed in exchange for lower price. For example, a customer firm may trade longer lead times, fewer product variations, fewer delivery locations, or less technical support for reduced prices. Importantly, defeaturing can yield win-win outcomes in that the customer gains the offering it truly requires at a lower price, while the supplier sustains a reasonable profit margin.[13]

The Procurement Orientation

Although the buying orientation still remains predominant, progressive customer firms have adapted their thinking, often in response to two related observations. They realize that for the typical firm, the costs of goods and services purchased account for about 60% of net sales and that a INR 1 reduction in total costs has the same impact on net profits as a INR 6 increase in revenues. The INR 1 reduction drops right to the bottom line, whereas only INR 1 of every INR 6 in revenue typically does. With so much at stake, a customer firm cannot afford to make shortsighted, strategic acquisition decisions. For the supplier firm, this insight makes all the difference in the world, in that they can work closely with the customer firm to create and share additional value.[14]

As diagrammed in Figure 3.2, **procurement** entails broadening the domain and span of influence of purchasing. The firm doggedly pursues quality improvements and cost reductions through the integration of procurement activities such as order processing with such other functions as materials handling, logistics, and physical distribution, and through more cooperative relationships with suppliers. The procurement group becomes strategic in its thinking and proactive in its efforts. Its highly trained professionals evolve from buyers into managers of external resources. Increasingly, they focus on acquiring total solutions or offerings comprised not only of products and services but also technology and knowledge.[15]

With a procurement orientation, a firm seeks to increase its productivity through the following:

- Improving quality
- Reducing total cost of ownership
- Cooperating with suppliers

Improving Quality

Firms that adopt a procurement orientation are deeply committed to producing high-quality offerings. Instead of relying on abstract notions of goodness or aesthetics, these firms define **quality** as "conformance to specifications that result in a product which meets customers' expectations." **Specifications**, in turn, describe the offering that the firm is seeking. In contrast to buyers, procurement managers are actively involved in writing specifications as participants in, or even as the leaders of, cross-functional teams. Written specifications come in several forms. Functional specifications delineate what an offering does, technical or materials specifications describe the physical properties of the acquired product, process specifications describe how the offering is to be produced, and performance specifications tell what outputs the customer firm will get from using the offering.[16]

The advantage to defining quality in this manner is that procurement managers can readily measure it by comparing an offering's specifications to company requirements. The consistently closer the offering is to customer requirements, the higher the quality. Procurement managers classify products and services that fail to meet company requirements as **underspecified** and those that provide far more features than necessary as **overspecified**. Under a procurement orientation, the purchasing manager seeks "perfect" quality in the form of offerings that precisely meet company requirements.

To achieve higher quality, procurement-oriented firms practice Total Quality Management (TQM). The International Organization for Standardization (ISO) describes TQM as "a management approach to an organization centered on quality, based on the participation of all its members and aiming at long-term success through customer satisfaction, and benefits to the members of the organization and society." TQM alters procurement thinking and practices. Procurement managers realize that they must work closely with other functional areas to better define the firm's product and service requirements and to coordinate the acquisition and flow of these products and services throughout the organization. And they understand that they are responsible for sustaining the quality of acquired goods.[17]

Reducing Total Cost of Ownership

Procurement managers apply strategic cost management, making purchasing decisions based on the goal of minimizing total cost of ownership rather than just reducing supplier prices. We define the **total cost of ownership (TCO)** as the sum of purchase price plus all expenses incurred during the productive lifetime of a product or service minus its salvage or resale price. Such expenses fall into three categories: acquisition, conversion, and disposal.[18]

Acquisition costs are those associated with securing an offering and include search costs, processing orders, and delivery charges. W. W. Grainger dramatizes these costs and proposes a solution for unplanned purchases in an advertisement in Figure 3.3 Firms incur conversion costs when using an offering. They include warehousing and handling, inventory storage, materials processing, installation and maintenance, repair, and operating supply costs, as well as the cost of poor quality. Corrective actions that a customer must take in response to quality problems also are a part of conversion costs. Disposal costs encompass recycling, environmental protection, and waste management expenses.

To estimate these costs, procurement managers regularly perform TCO analyses. **TCO analysis** applies activity-based costing (ABC) concepts and methods to quantify all expenses related to the use of a product or service apart from price. "Although TCO and ABC both are costing systems, TCO is focused on a firm's interfaces with suppliers to support decisions related to sourcing strategy, while internal activities are the scope of ABC systems." In contrast to customer value assessment, which we describe in Chapter 2, TCO analysis focuses on expenditures and does not consider revenue-generating opportunities an offering might afford.[19]

Through a TCO analysis, procurement managers identify the firm's major **cost drivers** or those factors that influence the nature and level of a major expenditure category. They summarize findings in the form of a TCO model on an interactive spreadsheet. With a TCO model, procurement managers can readily evaluate numerous sourcing scenarios, quantifying trade-offs among cost drivers and developing comprehensive sourcing strategies in order to reduce and avoid unnecessary costs.

By using a comprehensive TCO model, they avoid the so-called "seesaw effect" that blindsides managers who only consider price or a single cost when making a purchasing decision. The seesaw effect characterizes situations where an action intended to lower one cost unintentionally causes other costs to rise. The net result is to negate potential cost savings or to even increase overall costs. For

Figure 3.3

Source: Advertisement courtesy of W.W. Grainger, Inc.

example, in the recent rush to acquire customer relationship management (CRM) systems, firms that based their decisions solely on the purchase price of basic CRM software or on the opportunity to reduce customer data collection costs reportedly were dumbfounded months later to discover that they had to spend four to six times more for necessary auxiliary software, hire consultants to write customized programs to link it to legacy systems, and wait 6–18 months for the system to be fully operational.[20]

TCO analyses often reveal opportunities to eliminate costs. For example, research has demonstrated that acquisition costs often exceeded the price of an item, particularly in the case of unplanned purchases of maintenance, repair, and operating (MRO) supplies. This realization prompted companies to seek new ways to reduce these costs. One simple yet effective solution is the use of corporate purchasing cards. A **corporate purchasing card** is a company credit card with predefined spending limits issued to authorized personnel for the acquisition of MRO items, personal computers and related equipment, and office supplies. By streamlining costly and timely paperwork associated with purchase approvals, a corporate credit card saves time and money. Research shows that purchasing cards have reduced average transaction costs from $91 per order to less than $15 while cutting order fulfillment time from an average of 9.1 days to virtually zero.[21]

TCO analyses also demonstrated that the key long-term benefit from e-sourcing comes in the form of cost rather than price savings. Researchers discovered, for example, that firms gain spectacular price savings the first time they use a reverse auction for an item. As they run additional auctions for that item, firms observe that price savings decrease and bottom out and that prices may actually increase as the number of participating suppliers falls. At the same time, they find that cost savings related to better specifications and standardized requests for quotation (RFQs), more accurate requirement forecasting, reduced safety inventories, the elimination of manual and paper-based order processing, and global sourcing remain stable or even grow. This potential prompted leading reverse auction suppliers such as Ariba and GXS to offer a greater variety of cost savings services.[22]

In order to achieve TCO reductions, procurement managers strive to integrate their efforts with other functions in their own firms, such as manufacturing, materials handling, and logistics. They increasingly rely on enterprise resource planning (ERP) systems. **ERP systems** are server- or Internet-based software applications that warehouse, manage, and report cross-functional accounting, financial, inventory and order processing, payroll transactions, and data from a centralized location.[23]

Serving as the foundation "back office" data processing software, ERP systems often host major "front office" applications including supply chain management (e.g., e-sourcing, order tracking), enterprise relationship management (i.e., personnel files), customer relationship management, and partner relationship management (i.e., channels and strategic alliance data) software. In recent years, ERP systems incorporated materials requirement planning (MRP I) and manufacturing resource planning (MRP II) software designed to determine the quantity and timing requirements of materials used in the manufacturing operation and provide the user with simulation capability to analyze alternative production scenarios.

Cooperating with Suppliers

With a procurement orientation, managers must draw upon resources of suppliers to gain significant quality improvements and cost reductions. For example, they may call upon a supplier to codesign products. To lower delivery and inventory costs, they may integrate their logistics function with those of suppliers. For these kinds of things to happen, age-old adversarial relationships must give way to those where there is greater cooperation.

Through cooperative relationships with suppliers, customer firm managers attempt to expand the value pie for both firms. This effort requires a new form of bargaining—integrative negotiation. **Integrative negotiation** is based upon the assumption that resources can be expanded to benefit both parties. The process entails identifying shared interests and goals, freely exchanging information, emphasizing commonalities and minimizing differences between parties, and seeking creative and nonobvious solutions that meet the goals of both sides. Agreement is accomplished by first prioritizing the interests of both sides and then trading off less important interests for critical interests so that both firms achieve their primary goals. For example, a major paint company wanted to gain 100% share of a customer firm's annual requirement for coatings. The customer firm wanted to reduce the total cost of coating the parts it produced by 10%. Rather than haggling over price per liter of coating, the customer firm agreed to give the vendor 100% of its requirement if the vendor could meet the customer's cost savings goal.[24]

Customer managers actively work with suppliers to improve the quality in two important ways. The first is standardization of requirements. Dobler and Burt define **standardization** as "the process of establishing agreement on uniform identifications for definite characteristics of quality, design, performance, quantity, service, and so on." Standardization applies not only to physical characteristics but also to operating practices, procedures, and systems. Progressive firms require their suppliers to meet international standards, such as ISO 9000, before they are approved as potential vendors. In a second approach, procurement managers help suppliers establish their own quality assurance programs. Quality assurance entails methods and procedures for production, such as statistical process control, product testing, defect prevention, and process inspections.[25]

Another way to cooperate is target costing. **Target costing** differs fundamentally from target pricing in that its focus is on reducing TCO, not simply price. Customer managers begin by setting a target price for their product. Then they determine a target cost that would enable the firm to profitably market the product at that price. Let's use the automobile example again and say that company managers conclude that a target price of INR 1 million is desirable and that the total costs for a given model cannot exceed INR 900,000. At this point, they evaluate the TCO of various systems, subsystems, and components that comprise the automobile. Customer managers conclude that the TCO the firm can incur on one door handle including price and installation costs is INR 2,000 and ask the door handle supplier to provide a solution that does not exceed that amount. Here, the supplier has the flexibility to respond in two different ways. The supplier can lower the price of a door handle appropriately so that it meets the INR 2,000 target cost. Alternatively, the supplier can propose creative cost reduction programs to achieve the INR 2,000 target. As contrasted with target pricing, target costing requires customer and supplier to work together, sharing technical, process, and cost information.

The Supply Management Orientation

Firms migrate to a supply management orientation when managers realize that the fate of their organization is inextricably linked to other companies in the value network depicted in Figure 3.2. Moreover, they recognize that they are not just acquiring a product or solution from a supplier, they are building a long-term relationship. Thus, **supply management** entails the integration and coordination of purchasing with other functions within the organization as well as with other firms in the value network, such as customers, customers' customers, resellers, suppliers, and suppliers' suppliers. Under supply management, the business market manager views purchasing "not just as a department, but as a series of value-adding activities." Supply managers, highly trained middle- and upper-level managers, become so involved with strategic planning and dealing with key suppliers that they may no longer do any buying![26]

Supply management has four central tenets:

- Focus all of the firm's efforts on delivering value to end users.
- Craft a sourcing strategy around the firm's core competencies and resources.
- Build a supply network that efficiently completes required business processes.
- Sustain highly collaborative relationships with select supplier and subsupplier firms.[27]

Focus on End-Users

Traditional corporate strategy seeks demand largely through technology push—sell what you can make. Reflecting this strategy, buying and procurement strive to meet the specifications of manufacturing and the forecasts of sales. Advocates of supply management turn this thinking on its head. Relying upon demand pull—make what you can sell—supply management proactively directs the entire supply network to meet the requirements of end-users. Their primary goal is to efficiently deliver the greatest value possible to end-users.

To better understand the end-user, supply managers participate in market research projects, customer advisory councils, and personnel exchange programs. Taking a supply network perspective, managers learn about the worth of their firm's market offering not only to immediate customers but also to their customers' customers. They relay value assessment results to their own product and service development group and to key suppliers, suggesting changes in respective offerings. Once market offerings have been redesigned, supply managers then use market research findings to help reengineer business processes across the entire supply network to deliver superior value to end users.[28]

Craft a Sourcing Strategy

Supply managers act as catalysts in formulating and administering a **sourcing strategy**. The overall process has several steps, depicted in Figure 3.4. First, senior management, with the assistance of supply managers, identifies the core competencies of the firm. Although the concept is widely used in management circles, many firms have difficulty articulating their own core competencies. Quinn and Hilmer describe core competencies as skills or knowledge, not products or functions. They are flexible, long-term platforms capable of adaptation or evolution. Core competencies are limited in number. They provide unique sources of value network leverage in areas where the company can dominate. Finally, they are important to customers in the long run. In Chapter 4, we describe and provide examples of core competencies.[29]

Figure 3.4 The Strategic Sourcing Process

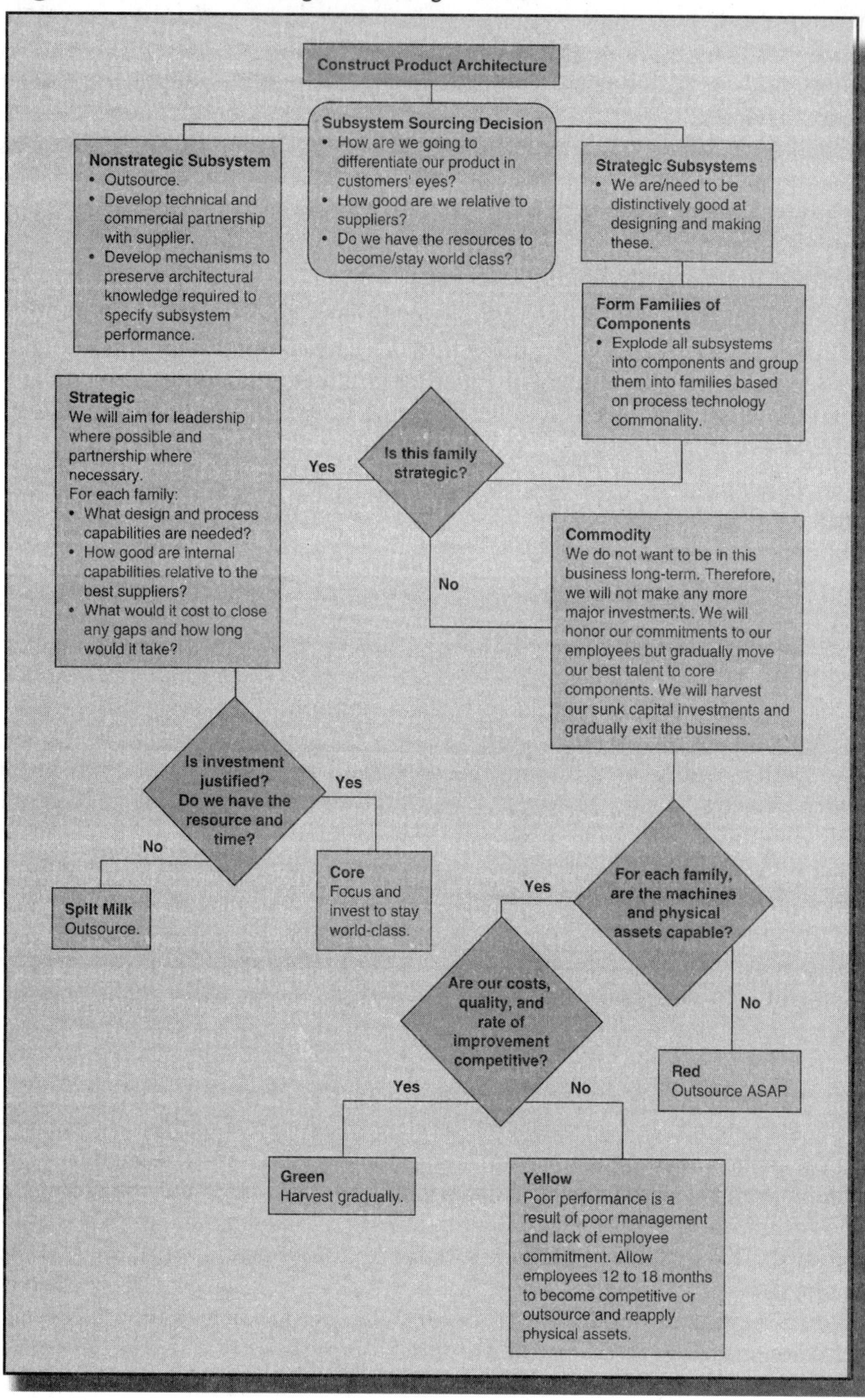

Source: Ravi Venkatesan, "Strategic Outsourcing: To Make or Not to Make," *Harvard Business Review* (November–December 1992): 103.

Second, managers divide the firm's products and services into systems, subsystems, and components. Next, they categorize systems, or subsystems if systems are too broad, as strategic or nonstrategic. Wherever feasible, firms outsource nonstrategic systems or subsystems—those that involve mature technologies and have many qualified vendors.

Companies also outsource strategic systems or subsystems whose internal design and production capabilities have eroded to the point of noncompetitiveness. Firms gain outsourcing results not only on a transactional basis but also through a variety of long-term partnering arrangements, such as codevelopment, technology licensing, and joint ventures. The firm then makes a concerted effort to improve production processes for marginally competitive strategic systems and subsystems. After a prespecified time period, managers reevaluate these systems and subsystems. If they remain marginally competitive, they are also outsourced.

Finally, the firm insources, or produces itself, the remaining strategic systems and subsystems. Why? The company has superior expertise and stands to gain a high rate of improvement and major technological advancements from their continued production.

Build a Supply Network

Managers establish a vision for a supply network and set goals using the concept of the lean enterprise. According to Womack and Jones,

> The **lean enterprise** is a group of individuals, functions, and legally separate but operationally synchronized companies. The notion of the value stream defines the lean enterprise. The lean group's mission is collectively to analyze and focus a value stream so that it does everything involved in supplying a good or service (from development and production to sales and maintenance) in a way that provides maximum value to the customer.[30]

Under the lean enterprise concept, purchasing becomes a center of expertise within the firm. Supply managers rotate jobs, working within the supply management group on strategic purchasing tasks and on cross-functional teams completing broader company tasks. Based upon experiences on teams or assignments in other divisions, supply managers identify problems the firm faces in purchasing policies, procedures, and practices. When they return to a functional area assignment, they locate the best purchasing practices within the firm, conduct research, and benchmark other industries to find state-of-the-art solutions. The purchasing department becomes a repository for knowledge of best practice. When assigned to new cross-functional teams, supply managers disseminate their findings to colleagues across the company.

In a lean enterprise, firms rely on a network of direct suppliers and a larger number of second- and third-tier suppliers, share critical information across functions within and between firms, practice just-in-time management, and participate in codesign projects. In Box 3.1, we demonstrate how Maruti manages a supply network. To build an operational supply network, managers rely upon the techniques of business process engineering to specify value-adding activities, identify partner firms, and chart the flows of activities across firms in the form of a supply network model.[31]

A **supply network model** traces the value-adding steps needed to produce a desired market offering from the ultimate customer backward through a variety of

BOX 3.1
Maruti's Supply Management Network

As the flagship Japanese venture in India to manufacture automobiles, Maruti Suzuki Ltd. (Maruti) is credited with setting up India's first vendor base for manufacturing passenger cars in northern India, in the mid-80s. Before Maruti's arrival, setting up a dedicated vendor network base was not common in India. A good number of vendors who used to supply to Suzuki in Japan followed it to India and established operations by forming joint ventures with Indian companies.

Given the nature of the car industry, Maruti and the suppliers focused on long-term relationships. Such contracts accounted for over 70 percent of the total contracts that Maruti had with suppliers. Maruti and Suzuki themselves contributed equity in cases of 13 such supplier companies where the required investment was high and the component was technologically sophisticated. This vendor base proved to be a competitive advantage for Maruti when Suzuki included it as a part of its worldwide procurement plan to source components for its facilities all over the world. Maruti has about 400 suppliers of which 248 are located in close proximity to its plants. Some of the major suppliers include Asahi India Glass, Bharat Seats, Climate Systems India, Denso India, Mark Exhaust Systems, and Sona Koyo Steering Systems.

Many small firms in India were willing to supply to Maruti but were far behind in technological capability. Consequently, Maruti and Suzuki had to invest considerable time and resources in their development. The solution was to provide vendors with large-scale technology transfers and consistent technical assistance. To achieve this objective, Suzuki arranged many joint ventures between Suzuki's suppliers in Japan and Indian suppliers.

Maruti also helped its suppliers with funding arrangements. It took equity positions in several supplier firms. For those firms that needed to import machinery from Japan, Maruti provided assistance to procure this machinery.

As lean production is one of the key practices for Japanese manufacturers, Maruti encouraged its suppliers to locate their plants close to its Gurgaon plant, near Delhi, in north India. Initially, this put the suppliers at a disadvantage because they were required to make location-specific investments. From the perspective of the suppliers, it was a high-risk proposition because Gurgoan is completely land locked and far from any ports. These lacunas were compensated by Maruti's willingness to forge long-term relationships. Over time, Gurgaon itself became an attractive business hub, catalyzed largely by the presence of Maruti and its supplier network.

Maruti continuously pushed its vendors to improve on quality, pricing, and other operational parameters. It even pushed some of its suppliers to achieve just-in-time (JIT) delivery levels comparable to those achieved by Japanese suppliers in the 1980s. Most importantly, Maruti did not appropriate the full value of these improvements all by itself. Several components makers achieved world-class quality and productivity levels, and, in the process, have become leading exporters. Examples include Pune-based Kalyani Brakes, which set up manufacturing facilities close to Maruti at Manesar near Gurgaon.

Consistent with its philosophy towards suppliers, Maruti has taken various steps to improve the ongoing supply management process. In 2004, Maruti Udyog Limited, in collaboration with its suppliers, set up the Maruti Centre for Excellence (MACE) to provide consultancy and training support to its suppliers and sales network. MACE enabled this network to achieve world-class standards in terms of quality, costs, service, and technology orientation.

BOX 3.1
Continued

MACE is a "not-for-profit" society to which Maruti has contributed modest seed funding to help get started. This organization works closely with Maruti's vendors and other partners to implement world-class practices such as total quality management (TQM), total productive maintenance (TPM), and team-oriented problem solving (TOPS) techniques.

The goal of MACE is to develop the core competencies of each of Maruti's suppliers to come up to world-class standards. Many of Maruti's dealers and suppliers have ISO 9000 certification. Some leading suppliers have also implemented TPM, TQM, and lean management practices with the help of reputed international consultants.

The strategy behind helping its vendors including its Tier-II vendors rise to world-class standards was that Maruti, with its expansion of manufacturing capacities, needed a sustained supply of quality components at reasonable prices. It was therefore imperative to encourage Tier-II vendors to fill the likely gap in the quality auto components supply chain that cannot be bridged by Tier-I vendors alone. To achieve a competitive edge, Maruti took proactive steps to directly reach out to Tier-II suppliers to improve their quality and cost efficiency.

Recently, Maruti Suzuki upgraded some of its suppliers to sole global suppliers for Suzuki Ltd., its parent organization. Some of them included Delphi in Bengaluru and Kalyani Brakes. This provides a big incentive for vendors to improve their quality and cost efficiency. From Maruti's perspective, promoting Indian suppliers is a good policy. Maruti has made considerable investments in upgrading the level of its suppliers to world-class quality. Through this intervention, Maruti has made many of them into its global suppliers; it has thus been able to leverage cost efficiency, quality, and delivery capabilities of these vendors in its international markets. Maruti treats its suppliers as long-term partners in development. Consequently, it is able to generate value not only for itself but also for its suppliers.

Contributed by Induj Charu, Participant, PGP Program, Indian Institute of Management Bangalore.
Sources: Murali Patibandla, *Evolution of Markets and Institutions: A Study of an Emerging Economy* (London: Routledge, 2009); "Maruti MACE Will Now Tutor Tier-II Vendors," *Deccan Herald*, 3 August 2007; "Maruti Serenades Vendors," *Hindustan Times*, 28 July 2007; "Maruti's One Gram, One Component Idea," *http://www.cartradeindia.com/car-bike-news/maruti-s-one-gram,-one-component-idea-110328.html.*

first-, second-, and third-tier suppliers.[32] Numerous supply network models are documented and illustrated in the operations research literature. The models determine the optimal number of members, ideal amounts and locations of inventory, and delivery routing.[33]

For example, when securing predictable quantities of MRO items, supply managers commonly design a **make-to-stock model** featuring manufacturers that produce standardized products to demand forecasts, lengthy distribution channels, and local dealers that provide one-stop shopping, local delivery, and credit services. When acquiring personal computers (PCs) in a large one-time transaction, supply managers might select a **build-to-order model**, directly purchasing the PCs from a vendor such as Dell Computers. A build-to-order model utilizes mass customization and flexible manufacturing, features rapid delivery, and encourages substitution of new technology in product designs.

In the case of essential spare parts, supply managers might choose a **continuous replenishment model** or **efficient customer response (ECR) system**. In an ECR system, a single vendor manages a customer's entire plant inventories, immediately replacing out-of-stock items through an electronic data interchange (EDI) based logics network. To obtain access to next-generation technology, supply managers might recommend a **design-to-build model** whereby customer and supplier R&D personnel jointly develop a new product. In turn, the supplier would produce the one-of-a-kind product in a single batch.[34]

Sustain Highly Collaborative Relationships with Select Suppliers

Supply managers learn to collaborate with key suppliers in even more creative ways. For example, in Box 3.2 we describe how ITC Ltd. worked with its major

BOX 3.2
ITC's e-Choupal Program

ITC Ltd.'s e-Choupal is one of the best examples in India of how a company can leverage a social environment to optimize a previously underperforming part of the value chain, and, in the process, accommodate stakeholders to the benefit of all. ITC Ltd. is a diversified business conglomerate with presence in cigarettes, hotels, agri-business, etc. and is one of India's most valuable corporations.

Soybean farmers had been living in the dark ages with no access to market demand data, no awareness of best practices, low-quality infrastructure, low-quality input (seeds, pesticides), limited weather information, and no transparency of product pricing in either local or international markets. As a consequence, there was widespread exploitation by various middlemen when farmers took their produce to *mandis* (local commodity markets) that were located far away from their villages. Farmers were forced to sell their crop for prices far below the going rate.

The division at ITC that managed the soya business had a mandate to significantly increase its revenue. This was not possible until the inefficiencies in the value chain were removed. ITC came up with a brilliant plan of using the existing social infrastructure to bring about a transformational change in the way soybean is bought and sold.

Computers were set up at *choupals* (village meeting places for informal assembly) which enabled farmers to get information about demand, pricing, best practices, weather forecasts, and anything else they needed. The e-Choupals, as they were called, were storehouses of tacit knowledge, and this was captured and shared among farmers in an organized way.

ITC opened up its hubs (e-Choupals), which were at the same or lesser distance than the *mandi*. Farmers now had the option of going to the *mandi* or to the ITC hub to sell their produce. The farmers could partake of all the benefits of the e-Choupal, such as access to information, and still decide to sell their produce at the *mandis* if they wished. However, they were guaranteed to get a fair deal on both pricing and quantity at the ITC hub. In a marketplace hitherto characterized by rampant

BOX 3.2
Continued

cheating of the farmers by middlemen, both on pricing and quantity (through inaccurate weighing of the produce), this was a refreshing change. The middlemen also benefited from the process since they were incentivized to set up the e-Choupals and to help ITC in the buying and selling process.

There was another piece of the puzzle, which further strengthened the relationship between farmers and ITC. The e-Choupals were shopping centers where farmers could buy herbicides, sowing seeds, lanterns, fertilizers, and soybean oil at fair prices. They could also be used as marketing channels for insurance, seeds, fertilizers, agro-chemicals, and credit. The traditional *choupals* operated on the basis of trust, and this was carried over to ITC's e-Choupals; trust and choice were cardinal principles in the new system.

Through its e-Choupal initiative, ITC transitioned the purchasing orientation of the soybean farming industry from buying orientation to supply management orientation, by forming lasting relationships with all stakeholders and providing them a compelling value proposition.

Contributed by Rajiv Motwani, Participant, PGSEM Program, Indian Institute of Management Bangalore.
Sources: Ali Farhoomand, Saurabh Bhatnagar, "ITC e-Choupal: Corporate Social Responsibility in Rural India," 30 June 2008.

suppliers to form lasting relationships and provide a compelling value proposition for all stakeholders through the e-Choupal program. Other firms create password-protected extranets to permit supplier firms to exchange proprietary data and collaborate on joint cost-reduction or in new offering realization programs.

With a supply management orientation, customer and supplier firms strive to equitably share delivered value. Increasingly, they employ value-in-use and value-in-use price as yardsticks for evaluating the superior value of the supplier's offering and for agreeing upon a fair price. **Value-in-use** (VIU) represents the difference in value minus the difference in price that a supplier's offering (Offering_f) provides a customer firm relative to a competitive offering (Offering_a).[35] Using our fundamental value equation 1.1, we calculate it as follows:

$$\text{VIU}_{fa} = (\text{Value}_f - \text{Value}_a) - (\text{Price}_f - \text{Price}_a) \quad \textbf{(3.1)}$$

Value-in-use price (VIU price) or the indifference price is the monetary amount at which the customer has no preference between the supplier's offering (Offering_f) and the next-best-alternative supplier's offering (Offering_a). Supply managers, as well as business market managers, calculate the VIU price because it approximates the maximum price a customer firm should pay for a market offering and thus can serve as a critical upper bound in price negotiations.[36] Algebraically manipulating the fundamental value equation 1.1, we state the VIU price of Offering_f relative to Offering_a as follows.

$$\text{VIU Price}_f = \text{Price}_a + (\text{Value}_f - \text{Value}_a) \quad \textbf{(3.2)}$$

Figure 3.5 Purchasing Portfolio Matrix

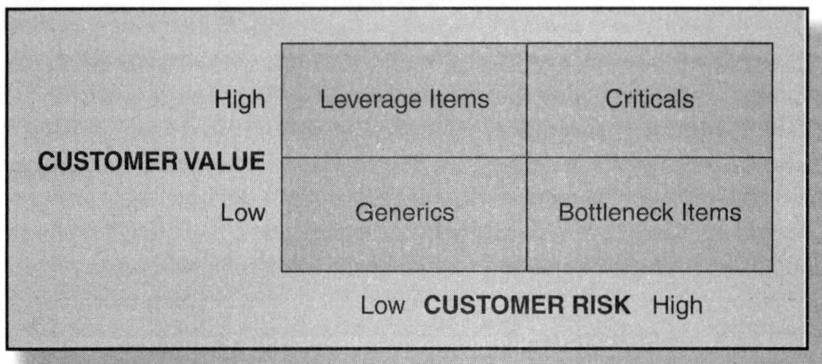

Apply Purchasing Portfolio Management

Noting that firms purchased a wide variety of products and services, consultant Peter Kraljic argued in a now-classic article that a company may have to adopt multiple sourcing strategies, build unique supply networks, and sustain diverse relationships with suppliers as a function of the supply situations it faces. Kraljic proposed that a firm's purchasing approaches could be summarized and managed via a **purchasing portfolio** or **supplier segmentation model**. Popular among scholars and managers in Europe, the Kraljic approach spawned variations that take a commodity perspective in focusing on the nature of products and services being acquired.[37]

In Figure 3.5, we synthesize the various versions of the Kraljic-inspired models. The rows capture the customer value and the columns the customer risk associated with purchasing and using a given offering. Following value assessments and risk analyses, supply managers categorize acquired offerings as either **generics** (e.g., MRO items), **leverage items** (e.g., raw materials), **bottleneck items** (e.g., essential spare parts), or **criticals** (e.g., new technology). Then they pursue two overall goals: (1) add value through functionality-cost management, service, effective administration, and the sourcing and integration of innovation; and (2) reduce risk through quality, availability, assurance, agile responsiveness, and sourcing activities. Kraljic and others recommend distinctive tactics to accomplish these ends for each of the four offering groups.

As with other portfolio approaches, academics and consultants urge supply managers to strive for advantage and balance by taking steps to move offerings across the matrix into more beneficial categories. Professor Arjan van Weele articulates one of the most elaborate approaches. He argues that the customer firm's ultimate objective should be to shift as many offerings to the leverage grouping as is possible. Why? Because in leverage circumstance, the customer firm governs the relationship and garners the greatest share of value created.[38]

To cultivate a greater number of leverage items, van Weele urges supply managers to initiate a variety of actions. At some point in time, most firms require criticals and must forge strategic partnerships with important vendors. In these alliances, the customer firm seeks to lower the cost of performance through such things as early supplier involvement, codevelopment, and codesign programs. Long term, van Weele counsels supply managers to reduce dependence on these vendors by standardizing and simplifying specifications and cultivating alternate suppliers. When successful, managers transform these criticals into leverage items. In the case of bottleneck items, supply managers must seek to lower the costs of operations. As with criticals, supply managers can relocate them to the leverage category through standardization and simplification. Alternatively they can attempt to convert them into generics by keeping emergency stocks on hand, hedging, Internet buying, relaxing standards, modularization, and/or pooling requirements.

For generics, van Weele urges customer firms to pursue lower acquisition costs. Customers do so by reducing the number of buys and by consolidating orders through techniques such as blanket or systems contracts, facilities management, and outsourcing. When successful, customer managers change them into leverage items. Last, in the ideal case of leverage items, van Weele recommends that customer firms enhance their purchasing power by reducing the number of suppliers and then using that superior power to secure lower prices and force suppliers to assist in lowering the customer firm's conversion costs.

Putting Knowledge of Purchasing Orientation to Use

Business market managers gain significant insights from understanding a customer firm's purchasing orientation. Knowing whether a firm embraces buying, procurement, supply management, or several orientations simultaneously says a great deal about how a supplier will be able to create and deliver value to that customer. For example, a customer firm with a buying orientation largely constrains a supplier to focus on reducing its own costs and passing the reduction along to the customer in the form of lower price. Although the supplier may understand how a higher-priced material would lower the customer's conversion costs, the supplier may be unable to persuade the customer even to consider making changes in its production process. Instead, the buyer simply tells the supplier to "Quote the spec" if it wants to do business.

Certainly, an understanding of a firm's purchasing orientation ought to significantly affect a supplier's customer selection strategy. Depending on how they create and deliver value, suppliers might focus on firms that are seeking the lowest purchase price, the lowest total cost, or the greatest value. For example, an offshore supplier with lower labor costs, but no in-country inventory or technical support, may focus on selling container loads to firms with a buying orientation.

Looking internally at their own firms, business market managers recognize that they too are customers. A better understanding of how their firm's purchasing strategies and activities contribute to or hinder the completion of business processes helps business market managers pinpoint ways to improve their organization's ability to create and deliver value to the marketplace. In Box 3.3, we provide an example of purchasing orientation as practiced by IBM India.

BOX 3.3
Purchasing Orientation at IBM

IBM has been well known through most of its recent history as the world's largest computer company and systems integrator. With about 400,000 employees worldwide, IBM is the largest information technology company in the world and among the most profitable. The company has scientists, engineers, consultants, and sales professionals in over 170 countries.

IBM internally is organized under six major businesses or brands: systems and technology; global technology services; software; global financing; global business services; and sales and distribution and research.

These businesses operate as almost-independent entities, and each forms a fairly large internal capital market. IBM has often been described as having a sales-centric or sales-oriented business culture. All other functions or activities are driven towards meeting sales targets or winning in the marketplace.

IBM re-entered India during the 1990s in a partnership with the Tata group (TISL), going on to establish its own entity (IBM India Private Limited). Post-2000, IBM witnessed rapid growth and has become one of the largest multinational presences in India. All six businesses have their footprint in India. Not only does IBM India cater to the domestic market, but also acts as the most significant global delivery center for IBM across all geographies.

Within IBM, the responsibility for developing and transforming procurement, logistics, engineering, and manufacturing is owned by the Global Supply organization. This organization comprises over 9,000 regular employees and encompasses Global Procurement (General and Services, Production, Materials and Supply Assurance, Procurement Engineering, and Client Services Procurement), Global Logistics, Services Parts Operations, Manufacturing Engineering, and Manufacturing. The entire organization is managed via an integrated end-to-end governance model and management system with focus on efficient and effective supply operations. With responsibility for INR 222,180 crores in expenditures, including clients' spending, on a wide range of items that include office supplies, travel services, and raw materials, Global Supply supports the needs of every part of IBM throughout the world in a centralized and globally integrated manner.

The Global Procurement division of Global Supply is responsible for buying products such as computer parts and services like travel at the lowest possible prices. Previously, IBM manufactured most of the parts and products that it sold. This has changed over time. Today, IBM relies on suppliers to provide the quality and dependability necessary to meet its commitments to the customer. Hence, selecting the best suppliers and leveraging the amount spent are very important to the continued growth of IBM's business.

Apart from catering to the internal needs of the organization, Global Procurement is also involved in offering integrated procurement solutions to external customers. Technically, the organization offers to take over the entire procurement function of customers and run it on their behalf.

Purchasing or procurement activities at IBM India are integrated and aligned under Global Supply organization and are no different from the company's global procurement processes. In fact, IBM India plays a key role in implementing standard procurement processes in IBM, across all geographies.

A fair-value determination analysis provides a fair indication of IBM's purchasing orientation. The organization uses two analytical techniques to determine fair value:

BOX 3.3
Continued

1. *Price comparison:* Comparing the proposed price to valid industry or IBM pricing for the same or similar product or service.
2. *Cost build-up:* Comparing the proposed price to a price calculated by building up the costs of the various components (i.e., material costs, process steps, labor rates, freight, etc.)

Though the process is titled, "fair-value determination," the associated techniques do not include value calculation and only aim at obtaining goods and services at the minimum possible price. Furthermore, the source selection techniques used by IBM are focused on price comparisons between competing suppliers rather than looking at "total cost of ownership" or "total value." In its dealings with suppliers, the huge size and reach of IBM allow it to garner a lion's share of value in its favor. The purchasing processes and techniques adopted by IBM suggest that in most of its purchases, the primary orientation of the company is to obtain products and services at the lowest purchase price.

Contributed by Anuj Sahu, Pranav Prajapati, Rakesh Bhansali, Sudheendra H. Sreedharamurthy, Tariqhusain Shaikh, Participants, EPGP Program, Indian Institute of Management Bangalore. *Sources:* "Global Procurement, IBM," *http://www-03.ibm.com/procurement/proweb.nsf/ContentDocsByTitle/United+States~Global+ Procurement.*

Understanding How Purchasing Works with Other Functions and Firms

We next examine how purchasing provides greater value to end-users by working closely with other functions as well as other firms. We begin by discussing value management, which provides a comprehensive framework for cross-functional and interfirm cooperative activities. Then we examine the buying team as the major tool for cross-functional coordination. In the process, we discuss the roles of buying team members, the various buying situations teams confront, and team tasks. We conclude the section by showing how purchasing expertise can add value in the new offering realization or existing offering modification processes.

Value Management as a Cooperative Framework[39]

Value management (VM) entails the systematic use of value techniques as a general problem-solving method in business, research, and administration. Value management is practiced at all levels of the organization. At the strategic level, all executives learn to "manage by value." That is, they systematically and routinely take into account the concepts of function and performance when making important decisions. At the tactical level, all personnel focus on the "management of value" by completing projects designed to sustain or enhance the value of their market offerings.

Value management allows a firm to better focus and efficiently sustain its operations, to gain a clearer understanding of the needs and priorities of its customers, and to deliver optimal value to the customer with trade-offs between performance and cost.

The pioneering work of Lawrence Miles at General Electric during the 1960s on the techniques of value analysis (VA) provides the foundation for value management.[40] **Value analysis** (or value engineering) is a method of value assessment that customer firms use to evaluate supplier offerings. A consortium led by the French Association of Value Analysis (AFAV) and the Association of German Engineers (VDI Zentrum Wertanalyse) explored, developed, and articulated the value management approach for the European Union.

The consortium began with VA, which is project focused, and "exploded it" outward, deliberately making value management more strategic in its thrust. Thus, the consortium first urges firms to adopt a customer-value philosophy and a set of action guidelines. Central among these, as is the case with our approach, is the goal of achieving optimal value, which is the best possible ratio of quality to total cost delivered to customer firms. Three of the four guiding principles of business market management—value is the cornerstone of business management, focus on business processes, and place emphasis on working relationships and business networks—closely correspond to those of VM.

After adopting a value management philosophy, a company then sets into place a value management system (VMS). The VMS is composed of an operating structure, management, and methods that are responsive to the external environment. Often the operating structure takes the form of cross-functional teams, task forces, and councils. Once in place, the VMS undertakes two sets of actions. As contrasted with traditional VA efforts, the VMS completes strategic and far-ranging corporate initiatives referred to as management tasks, which emphasize such diverse activities as strategic planning, new product realization, new plant design, and product positioning. At the same time, managers conduct highly focused and more traditional VM projects. For example, a value team might search for ways to reduce the TCO of a critical component in one of the firm's market offerings.

To complete specific VMS tasks, managers use a variety of traditional operations management tools, including business process reengineering and quality-function deployment. The consortium also created additional VMS methods. When confronted with a task, a cross-functional team chooses the method or combination of methods that are best suited to the problem at hand.

Adding Value to the Purchasing Process Through Buying Teams

The **buying team** or buying center "refers to all those members of an organization who become involved in the buying process for a particular product or service." Business market managers must consider three aspects of buying teams: member roles, buying situations, and tasks.[41]

Team Member Roles

Roles are the responsibilities of buying team members. The job title of the manager who performs these roles will likely vary from one organization to the next. Let's examine a simple buying team task—hiring a service vendor to repair a piece of equipment. The initiator is the person within the firm who realizes the acquisition of a product or service can solve or avoid a problem. For example, a production worker watches a piece of equipment erratically produce defective parts and concludes that it needs to be repaired. The worker-initiator alerts the shop manager to the problem. The manager then contacts purchasing. The gatekeeper controls the flow of information in and out of a firm and provides vendor personnel with access to key personnel. Thus, the purchasing manager forwards a list of certified vendors to the shop manager for consideration.

The influencer guides the selection process by expressing preferences or recommending vendors or offerings. For instance, the production worker prefers and lobbies for a particular service contractor because its technicians are easier to work with and more personable. The decider has ultimate responsibility for determining which product or service will be purchased and for choosing the supplier. In our example, the shop manager selects the service contractor and is therefore the decider.

The buyer is the individual who negotiates with the vendor and formally executes the purchase or acquisition. Thus, the purchasing manager issues a formal work order and arranges a service contractor call. Finally, the user is the individual who employs the acquired product or service. In our example, the production worker returns to the job following the repair of the equipment.

With a VM philosophy, the buying team operates beyond the transaction—team members attempt to add value to the process. In our example, team members practice the Japanese method of kaizen or continuous improvement. As the contractor repairs the equipment, the production worker ponders, "How can I use the equipment more effectively to avoid breakdowns?" The purchasing manager seeks out and evaluates information on more reliable equipment and on alternative service vendors. The shop manager, in turn, examines the equipment in the context of overall production flow and proposes a preventive maintenance schedule and the redesign of parts of the manufacturing process. Last, the purchasing manager reduces costs by shifting to a long-term service contract.

Successful business market managers gain a deep understanding of the distribution and performance of buying roles within each customer firm. They use this knowledge to craft and disseminate customized promotional messages, as well as to gather intelligence. To begin with, they learn whether the buying team is a nominal group in which members operate independently, or a formal group in which members meet face-to-face to make decisions. In our example, the buying team is a nominal group because members do not work together. Next, managers identify key players within a customer firm who perform these roles. These role assignments vary from firm to firm and within firms over time. For instance, a classic mistake for a sales representative is to call on a purchasing manager over a period of months, only to then learn that the shop manager ultimately makes the purchase decision.

Last, business market managers must learn whether all members of the buying team are aware of the total value of the supplier's offering. In certain instances, individual members are aware of only the specific value elements that benefit their particular functional areas of the customer firm. In this case, one of the major promotional tasks confronting the business market manager will be to inform each buying team member how the offering benefits all other functional areas and the customer firm as a whole. In doing so, supplier managers not only increase the potency of their value proposition but also the likelihood they can gain a price premium.[42]

Buying Situations

Business market managers also study customer firm buying situations. The distribution and performance of team roles is often a function of purchase situations. Scholars have identified three recurring purchase situations: straight rebuy, modified rebuy, and new task. These three situations represent a "newness" continuum of the purchasing tasks customers encounter. We characterize the three purchase situations by the customer's knowledge of its functional and technical specifications. In a new task buying situation, the firm confronts a novel requirement. Managers do not know what the functional or technical specifications of the offering should be. With a VM philosophy, if the new task requires innovation, the firm charters a cross-functional team that uses techniques such as process reengineering to create "lean" procedures for purchasing the item.[43]

In a modified rebuy, the customer firm has had experience securing the product or service, but managers need to reevaluate alternatives. Perhaps, for instance, users are dissatisfied with the current supplier or product. Alternatively, managers know the functional specs but are uncertain as to what the technical specifications should be. To solve the problem, the firm assembles a quality circle to suggest a new product, vendor, or substitute materials.

In a straight rebuy situation, the company has considerable buying experience and requires little or no new information about the offering. Functional and technical specifications are well documented, and the buyer only needs to learn price and availability. As a solution, the firm reorders the item from a preferred vendor. With VM philosophy, the buying team also explores how the reorder process might be simplified, such as with an automated inventory replenishment system.

Buying Team Tasks

Today, buying teams perform both strategic and tactical tasks. Commodity procurement strategy (CPS) teams develop a comprehensive strategy for the acquisition of entire product or service categories, assemble and cultivate a supplier base for the category, and identify suppliers that can solve difficult technical problems related to the category. For example, Hewlett-Packard (HP) created CPS teams for each major category of its products and services. Team members come from R&D, manufacturing, quality assurance and control, and purchasing. They evaluate suppliers on the basis of such things as technology, quality, cost, responsiveness, and delivery. They also determine which supplier gets what proportion of HP's business, and they negotiate long-term supply contracts with these vendors.

Companies deploy a variety of buying teams to address tactical issues. Supplier certification teams help selected suppliers reach desired levels of quality, reduce costs, improve service, and increase delivery reliability. Specification teams select and then write appropriate functional, technical, and process specifications for goods and services to be acquired. Supplier performance evaluation teams monitor their activity and performance data and rate vendors.

Working with Suppliers and Across Functions

Business market managers integrate purchasing activities with those of suppliers and other functions to develop supply resources, improve existing offerings, and contribute to new offering realization.[44]

Developing Supply Resources

Managers in diverse functional areas can assist with the performance of purchasing activities in several key ways. Based on their contacts and experience, they can help purchasing managers find and qualify new suppliers from around the world. Technical people from operations and R&D can work side by side with suppliers to improve vendor's capabilities. Often, customer firms even make financial investments in supplier firms to ensure the flow of materials and new technologies. Last, technical service personnel can provide consulting and training to strengthen supplier service.

Improving Existing Offerings

Progressive customer firms collaborate with suppliers to improve existing offerings. They conduct joint value or TCO assessments to find process improvements and materials substitutions. They determine the most economic lot-sizing for supplier production and establish long-term contracts for dedicated production lines to meet specific customer firm requirements. And, they rethink and reallocate tasks from supplier firm to customer firm, or vice versa. The following example from General Motors (GM) demonstrates how such a collaborative approach can streamline inbound logistics and materials handling and benefit both supplier and customer firms.

To improve its performance and lower costs, GM revamped the inbound logistics and materials handling of parts to its 26 assembly plants across the United States, Canada, and Mexico. Previously, decentralized purchasing, transportation, materials handling, and production personnel at each plant independently handled parts for their respective operations. This practice led to inefficiencies, backlogs, and cost overruns. GM called in long-time supplier Penske Logistics to set up and operate a system to manage the inbound logistics and materials handling operations for each of GM's 26 plants. Now, Penske or subcontractors ship all parts directly to a Penske warehouse in Cleveland, where they are sorted by GM plant and then shipped out in a timely fashion via truck or air.

Counterintuitively, GM's outsourcing strategy has not resulted in layoffs and has improved the status of both purchasing and materials handling personnel. Relieved of the burdens and headaches associated with the management of inbound parts, these groups focus on building better cars. For instance, purchasing spends more time in parts supplier selection and relationship-building efforts. Materials handling personnel concurrently spend greater time planning outbound movements of cars. GM has seen the amount of paperwork decline as payments are consolidated. The bottom line has been lower costs and higher-quality cars.[45]

Contributing to New Offering Realization

Operations experts claim that about 80% of a product's or service's total costs are "locked in" prior to commercial production.[46] Once production begins, the costs associated with changing product or service specifications become extremely high. Firms intent on reducing their total costs carefully scrutinize the product design process. To make it more efficient, these firms partner with vendors through early supplier involvement (ESI) programs and include purchasing personnel in the design process via early purchasing involvement programs. Often, ESI programs entail joint value engineering projects to codevelop and codesign

BOX 3.4

Early Supplier Involvement in New Offering Realization by Mahindra & Mahindra Ltd.

Founded in 1945, Mahindra & Mahindra (M&M) is one of India's leading auto manufacturers. In 1991, the Vice Chairman of the group, Anand Mahindra, set about the task of transforming the image of the company to ensure that it remained competitive in the domestic auto industry. Launching the Scorpio was a key initiative in its move to become a world-class company.

The Scorpio project was initiated in 1997. Huge financial investments and infrastructure (a new plant) were required to support the manufacturing of the Scorpio. Further, the idea of designing a vehicle from scratch with the Indian customer in mind was new to the company. A significant part of the design was outsourced to suppliers to keep costs low and because M&M lacked the required expertise. Suppliers undertook the designing and engineering of all crucial systems, along with the testing, validation, and materials selection. M&M took to laying down performance targets and costs and integrated the components required to make the final product.

Unlike the conventional approach adopted by most global automakers, which carry out all design in-house giving suppliers a negligible role in design engineering, M&M took the unconventional route of early supplier involvement. For instance, in designing the air conditioning system for the Scorpio, the supplier was specified the temperature drop required over time, as against stating the number of air vents required. In this way, the supplier was allowed to apply past experience in deciding and creating the most cost-effective system as opposed to delivering a system devised by the automaker.

Working closely with the suppliers all through the design process helped M&M to build a bond of trust. This made economic sense. If a supplier was unable to deliver on a contract, M&M was willing to renegotiate. If the supplier was not very successful in producing cost savings, M&M assisted it in working out a solution that fell within the budget. The cooperation extended by M&M encouraged suppliers to look at all possible avenues of cost saving, which they reported to the company.

supplier components and materials. Box 3.4 relates Mahindra & Mahindra's noteworthy use of an ESI program.[47]

Increasingly, firms are involving purchasing personnel in the new offering realization process as active members of cross-functional development teams. Pundits commonly refer to such initiatives as early purchasing involvement (EPI) programs. Researchers in Europe identified potential purchasing contributions to the process. Among the most important of these contributions are helping senior management craft corporate strategy by identifying the firm's core competencies, funneling new technologies from suppliers to appropriate managers within the firm, selecting leading-edge suppliers for partnerships and alliances, and recommending sourcing options.[48]

During the crafting of corporate strategy and design of supply networks, purchasing managers serve as technology "matchmakers" between the firm and its suppliers. Because such matchmaking requires technical discussions, firms are increasingly hiring engineers to work within the purchasing department. For instance, IBM assigns procurement development engineers to design teams and R&D labs. These engineers scour the market for sources of new technology and help IBM form alliances with competent new vendors.

When relationships with individual suppliers are to be forged, purchasing managers provide a "reality check" concerning part costs and the capabilities of potential vendors. For example, at AT&T, purchasing managers reside in R&D laboratories and participate on cross-functional design teams in the Cost-Effective Product Introduction (CEPI) program. For major parts and components, purchasing managers scrutinize the process, alert engineers when they are about to specify high-cost, long lead-time, and overly customized parts, and recommend standard parts as alternatives. They identify and advocate suppliers with proven records for reliable delivery, quality, and capacity utilization. AT&T says that CEPI has reduced development costs, cycle time, and time to volume.

During single projects, purchasing managers keep designers "grounded" in the nature of operating costs. At Cisco Systems, a leading supplier of switches and routers on the Internet, purchasing managers serve as watchdogs for expensive and overengineered parts, and provide detailed cost estimates that help designers better forecast the total costs and profitability of new products. Finally, in the area of nontechnical service projects, purchasing managers serve as "catalysts." They take the lead in the service design process. Purchasing managers may even provide creative ideas behind the new service and help to map out procedures for its provision.

Understanding the Purchase Decision Process

In the final section of this chapter, we examine how firms secure products and services, technology, and knowledge from other organizations. With knowledge of the customer firm's purchasing process, business market managers are in a far better position to develop marketing strategies, sales presentations, and promotional efforts that can successfully inform and influence purchasing decisions. We start by discussing how supplier firms identify customer requirements as well as map activity and value cycles. Next, we use the BuyGrid Framework to describe the typical purchasing processes customers use. Finally, we investigate the procedures firms commonly use when evaluating supplier performance.

Understanding Customer Requirements and Preferences

Customer requirements and preferences serve as an essential guidepost for all business market management efforts. Over the years, scholars and consultants proposed a variety of frameworks and methods for surveying these guideposts. For example, Michael Porter outlined an approach that business market managers can use to first determine a customer's use criteria or specifications and then to rank them based upon their worth to that customer. He proposed that supplier managers organize use criteria into a 2 × 2 matrix. One dimension of the matrix is whether worth of the use criteria can be readily measured or is difficult to measure. The other dimension is whether the use criteria produce increased customer benefits or reduce the customer's total costs.[49]

Porter takes pains to point out that although a supplier can readily measure the worth of some use criteria, it may be difficult, if not impossible, to accurately measure the worth of others. When the worths of use criteria are difficult to measure, he recommends that firms investigate signaling criteria or those activities, attributes, promotions, and reputation of a supplier firm that indicate to a customer that the supplier's offering, in fact, delivers value.

As with Porter, Håkansson, Johanson, and Wootz suggest three sources of uncertainty that make it difficult for a customer firm to understand its own requirements and preferences. Need uncertainty refers to difficulties customers have in interpreting the exact nature and importance of goods and services that their firms require. For example, managers may have a tough time predicting how often a piece of machinery will break down and the severity of consequences. Market uncertainty reflects the buyer's inability to predict how many alternate suppliers will be available and what quality of goods and services will be forthcoming when a need arises. The fewer the suppliers offering high-quality solutions, the more the buyer will be willing to pay. Transaction uncertainty is inversely related to the customer's confidence that suppliers have easy-to-use procedures for doing business, processing orders accurately, and providing reliable and timely deliveries. Rather than ignore these uncertainties, Håkansson, Johanson, and Wootz encourage managers to evaluate them thoroughly when investigating customer requirements and preferences.[50]

Converge on Customer Requirements

In some instances, customer personnel have a better understanding of their own requirements, whereas in others the supplier has superior knowledge. Customers use the product or service and are often in a better position to define their requirements in terms of functionality and performance in specific applications. They have a better grasp of their firm's capabilities. At the same time, suppliers often know more about the offering's technology and can better match solutions to problems customers don't anticipate.

To converge on customer requirements, business market managers think in terms of a 2 × 2 **requirements matrix** where the rows and columns capture the extent of knowledge that the supplier firm and customer firm possess, respectively.[51] Then they conceive and initiate various research projects designed to yield insights from the perspective of each cell. When they complete the projects, business market managers aggregate findings into one comprehensive profile of customer requirements. In Figure 3.6 and Box 3.5, we present an illustration and explanation of the requirements matrix the customer support service group of Microsoft Corporation has designed and uses to converge on customer service requirements.

Figure 3.6 Microsoft Customer Support Requirements Matrix

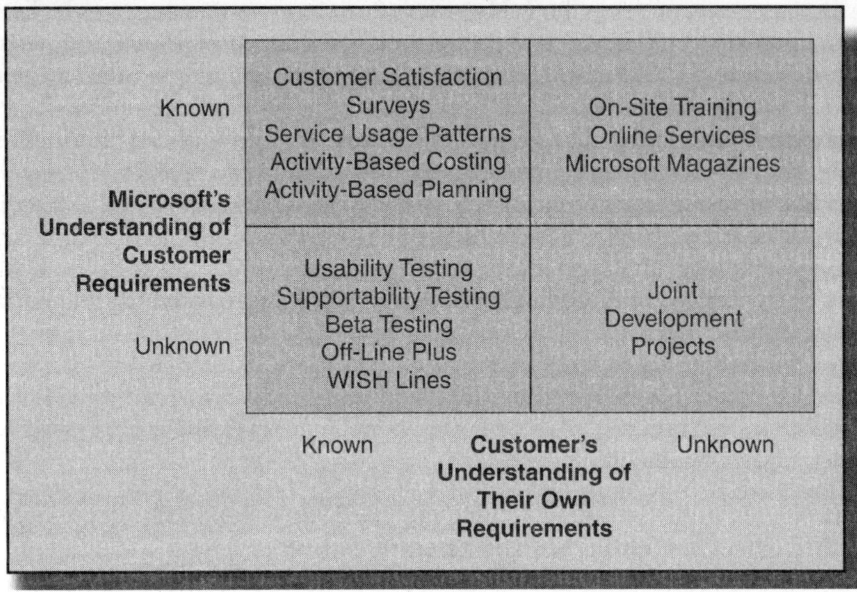

BOX 3.5
Microsoft Converges on Customer Support Services Requirements

Long ago, managers of the support services group of the Microsoft Corporation realized the complexity of their customer firms' information systems and the diversity of their technical support service requirements. Rather than using one method for probing customer needs, Microsoft managers devised the requirements matrix in Figure 3.6 and implemented a variety of ongoing research activities. The columns in the matrix capture requirements that the customer firm either knows or doesn't know. The rows, on the other hand, represent customer needs that Microsoft either knows or doesn't know.

To better understand requirements that are known to both firms, Microsoft managers periodically conduct customer satisfaction surveys and monitor service usage patterns, among other things. To learn about requirements customers are aware of but Microsoft isn't, managers test new software at customer locations through usability and beta testing. They use the Internet and special telephone numbers, Off-Line Plus and WISH Lines respectively, to gather suggestions on service improvements.

Microsoft educates customers to make them aware of the benefits of using Microsoft products and services. They use on-site training, online services, and several Microsoft magazines. In the final cell of the matrix, neither the customer nor Microsoft has a clear understanding of certain customer requirements. To come to grips with such needs, Microsoft initiates joint development projects with select customers. The partners then draw upon the customer's understanding of applications and Microsoft's knowledge of technology. Microsoft managers find that even though none of the techniques in the matrix provide full information, taken together they furnish a sharper image of the complete array of customer requirements.

Map Customer Activity and Value Cycles

Some managers assume that the value of an offering remains stable over its lifetime. For some products and services, particularly those that are time-sensitive, reusable, or acutely sensitive to the market forces of supply and demand, worth may actually ebb and flow. This fluctuation is due in part to the fact that benefits and costs accrue in different amounts and at distinct points in time in concert with the offering's activity cycle. The **activity cycle** refers to the steps required to produce, productively use, recycle, and dispose an offering, whereas the **value cycle** captures the changes in worth across these steps.[52]

Business market managers can map both cycles with the tools of business process engineering and value assessment. It is critical that they understand the activity and value cycles for their offerings in that these cycles may reveal sources for new and profitable, augmenting products and services. Figure 3.7 contains an illustration of the activity cycle for industrial containers. In Box 3.6, we discuss how Tetra Pak used an understanding of value cycles to create a new variety of packing for its customer, Health Foods Ltd.

Learning the Customer's Purchase Process

Many companies follow a structured and orderly process for acquiring goods. Scholars summarized this process in the **BuyGrid Framework**. The purchase

Figure 3.7 Activity Cycle for Industrial Containers

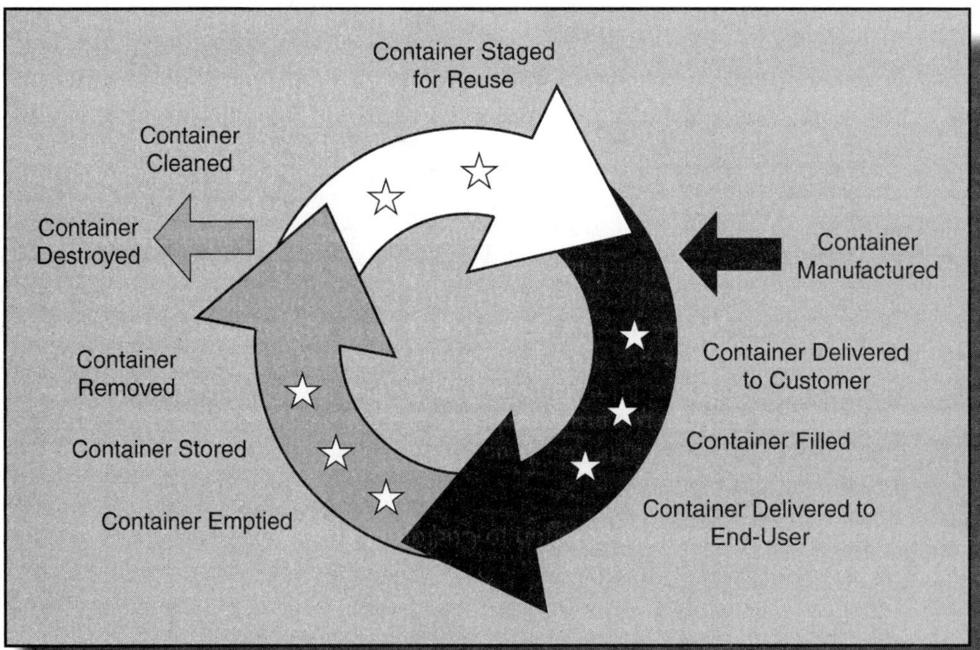

Source: Adapted from Gregory F. Wall, "Creating Customer Value: Greif Brothers Packaging Services," Presentation at Institute for Study of Business Markets Conference (January 2000).

BOX 3.6
Tetra Pak Introduces Innovative Solution to Customer Problem

Health Foods Ltd. (HFL, name has been changed for confidentiality) is a major packager and retailer of milk and juices in India. The packages for retailing are done using Tetra Pak technology, provided by the eponymous Switzerland-based company. Tetra Pak was HFL's sole (and monopolistic) supplier of packing material, given HFL's dependence on Tetra Pak-specific equipment.

Tetra Pak did not take the relationship for granted, nor did it abuse the oft-repeated *razor-blade* strategy: selling "razors" cheaply, building dependency, and then cashing in on the dependence by selling the "blades" at exorbitant prices for huge profits. Instead, Tetra Pak representatives maintained a continuous relationship with HFL managers and proactively assessed HFL's needs. Tetra Pak mapped the activity cycle for packaging milk and juices. They realized that since HFL was rapidly growing, it was inappropriate to have the same packing line to pack milk and juices, as this entailed considerable changeover time. Accordingly, Tetra Pak convinced HFL that its market had grown to a size where it should no longer be using the same technology for packing both milk and juices. Reviewing the activity and value cycles resulted in a clear insight: HFL's managers did not really want to buy Tetra Pak cartons. They were interested in transporting their products (milk and juices) securely from their plant to the markets to end customers. At the same time, they were interested in minimizing the time when the plant had to be stopped to change between packaging milk and juices.

After considerable interaction with HFL's managers, Tetra Pak managers developed a comprehensive value model to take into account each step of the activity cycle. There was a huge opportunity to add value to the customer firm and do so profitably for Tetra Pak, through looking at the situation from a holistic perspective, beyond just selling cartons to HFL. Tetra Pak, at its own initiative, brought to HFL a value proposition to upgrade its equipment at a reasonable price. Tetra Pak provided all the necessary services to HFL to make a smooth and orderly transition to the new way of doing things. HFL was given the ability to pack milk and juices without undergoing painful changeover procedures and has resulted in lost production time and constrained ability to shift production from one product line to the other at short notice.

Tetra Pak provided considerable value to the customer firm in this situation by identifying a need, designing the solution, and presenting the solution with quantifiable and non-quantifiable projected benefits to the customer. Having won the contract with ease due to its superior understanding of customer needs, Tetra Pak went on to supply the equipment, upgrade the existing line, and provide other services at its own cost, such as training the HFL staff and offering an extended warranty. Tetra Pak provided a total solution through maintenance services, spare parts supply, service level agreements that guaranteed minimal disruption to HFL's ongoing production schedules.

The solution transformed HFL's production planning outlook from that of a bulk manufacturer with heavy resistance to change its product mix, to a nimble, agile, and responsive manufacturer who could change its product mix at will. In this manner, HFL could better respond to its customers. This resulted in increased sales volume and improved operating margins through production efficiency. Tetra Pak benefited through increased demand for its products and, more importantly, a delighted customer!

Contributed by Bhaskar Kakuturu, Harish Chasmawalla, Kamesh Akundi, Prateek Gupta, Rachna Raniwala, and Senthil Govindam, Participants, PGPX Program, Indian Institute of Management Ahmedabad.

decision process begins with problem recognition, when someone within the firm identifies an opportunity or threat to address. For example, a production worker notices that stocks of a repair part are running low and need to be reordered. At this point, the employee provides a written general need description. This statement clearly identifies the problem or opportunity at hand and suggests a general solution. A purchasing manager then translates this need into product specifications. For instance, the purchasing manager takes the production worker's description of the repair part needed and describes it in terms of functional and technical specifications.[53]

Once specifications are known, purchasing managers conduct a supplier search to identify potential sources of the repair part. They begin with the firm's certified vendor list, then seek other vendors if necessary. The next stage is proposal solicitation. Purchasing managers send out written RFQs to certified vendors. With returned RFQs in hand, purchasing managers go through the supplier selection process. Depending on the purchasing orientation of the firm, purchasing managers select the supplier or suppliers that best meet company requirements. In the order-routine specification phase, the purchasing manager and vendor set up procedures for processing invoices and paperwork and receiving deliveries. Finally, the purchasing manager conducts a formal performance review of the supplier.

The BuyGrid Framework implies that the purchase process will vary across purchase situations. In a straight rebuy, a customer that has a track record of purchasing a given product from a given vendor can avoid many steps. In the new task situation, on the other hand, the customer has no experience purchasing the good or service. As a result, the customer must go through the entire process. We argue that a third dimension should be added to the BuyGrid Framework—ongoing versus new working relationships. In an ongoing relationship as with a straight rebuy situation, the customer may be able to eliminate some of the steps from the process. In a new relationship, the customer may have to go through a lengthier process.

One question frequently arises: "Is the purchasing process for services the same as that for physical products?" According to a market research study the Institute for Supply Management (formerly the National Association of Purchasing Managers) conducted in the United States among its members, the processes of purchasing a product and service are fairly similar. Only three significant differences stood out in the ISM study. First, managers have a more difficult time writing specifications for services because of their ambiguous nature. As a result, purchasing managers report encountering problems when it comes to acquiring services and evaluating vendor performance. Second, firms often have a tough time forecasting when they will need services. For example, a firm may not be able to predict precisely when it will need legal services and the nature of those legal services. Third, companies do not have sophisticated planning systems for services, such as ERP, MRP I, and MRP II. Scholars and practitioners have yet to develop them.[54]

Evaluating Supplier Performance

To make more productive use of external resources, firms are spending more time and effort evaluating supplier performance. Best practice companies are employing balanced scorecards, which assess performance using a set of pertinent measures.

Furthermore, they are turning to quantifiable performance measures whenever possible. However although supplier evaluations may be quantitative, the numbers may come from subjective judgments that can be influenced by social or personal considerations. Supplier performance evaluation systems tend to vary by purchasing orientation.[55]

Reviewing Price, Quality, and Availability

Companies that subscribe to the buying orientation evaluate suppliers largely in terms of realized price, quality, and availability. They draw on four types of analyses. In a subjective categorical summary, purchasing managers examine suppliers on several dimensions such as price, quality, and availability. To do so, they construct a survey instrument that features several questions for each performance category. The questionnaire is subjective in that respondents are asked to rate a given supplier on a scale ranging from poor to excellent. Managers from relevant functional areas within the firm complete the questionnaire. Buyers report results for each supplier in the form of averages for each question, then compare category performance across suppliers and across time periods.

Other firms summarize category results in the form of a single subjective index. For example, if managers believe that all the questions are of equal value, they might simply report the grand mean as an overall index of supplier performance. On the other hand, if managers believe that certain categories are more important than others, they might report a weighted grand mean. Thus, if they felt price represents 50% of performance, quality 30%, and availability 20%, they would multiply a supplier's price, quality, and availability ratings by 0.5, 0.3, and 0.2, respectively.

To be less judgmental, some firms replace the subjective questions with operational measures. However, managers still exercise considerable discretion in selecting categories. These are reported as objective categorical summaries. As an illustration, purchasing managers might subtract actual purchase price paid for a supplier's product this period from the purchase price paid last period and report it as an indicator of a supplier's performance on price. Concurrently, the firm might track the number of defective products delivered or the percentage rejection rate on products delivered as a measure of a supplier's quality. Managers might record reliability as percent of orders delivered on time or delivery accuracy in terms of the percent of items ordered that were delivered.

To convert these items into a single objective index of performance, managers would allocate a certain number of points for meeting acceptable performance standards for each price, quality, and availability measure; calculate; and then report the grand mean as the supplier's performance index. Alternatively, if managers believe that certain criteria are worth more than others, they can assign weights to each category and report the weighted grand mean. Even in more objective performance evaluations, managers exercise some judgment by choosing categories and weights.

Scrutinizing Total Costs

As firms migrate to a procurement orientation, they create performance measures that focus on TCO. Two cost-based supplier evaluation approaches have emerged. In the first approach, companies review the costs associated with supplier nonperformance.

For example, Monczka and Trecha created a supplier performance index (SPI) that recognizes cost attributed to supplier nonperformance on delivery, materials quality, and prices.[56] The SPI formula is

$$SPI_{(item)} = \frac{\text{extended purchase price} + \text{nonperformance costs}}{\text{extended purchase price}}$$

Extended purchase price represents the net price the customer firm pays after deducting discounts and allowances. Nonperformance costs are additional costs the customer firm incurs to correct mistakes the supplier made during a relevant time period, such as a year. Such costs might cover additional quality inspections, shipping defective parts back to the vendor, production downtime attributed to stockouts, and emergency shipments, among others.

Monczka and Trecha recommend that firms create and monitor SPI indices for each category of item purchased from each competing supplier. Procurement managers then use the resulting indices as indicators of the quality of alternate vendors. Customer firms can also multiply the resulting indices by the respective unit prices paid to each supplier to determine the costs per unit. They argue that using costs per unit rather than unit price is a superior means of comparing vendors.

In the second approach, customers audit and then calculate the TCO for a product or service during a prespecified time period. Procurement managers use results to determine how much each supplier has reduced the firm's total costs.

Tracking Supplier Value

Contrary to what many believe, supply managers conduct the most thorough and demanding evaluations of suppliers. Why? Because they expect more from suppliers. They also have fewer suppliers to review. These managers gather performance data from the techniques described previously. However, they take their analyses further. Utilizing the tools of value assessment and our fundamental value equation, supply managers evaluate vendors in terms of the value each contributes to their firm's market offering. Specifically, they estimate the benefits, total costs, and prices paid to each vendor. Some estimates will be qualitative in nature, such as the extent to which suppliers contributed to innovations achieved by the customer firm.

Consistent with the supply management orientation, these firms supplement direct vendor evaluations with studies of their own customers' satisfaction. Supply managers draw upon methods of gaining customer feedback we described in Chapter 2. The goal is to assess the impact of supplier contributions on end-user satisfaction. In this way, supply managers can better focus or redirect the efforts of the entire supply network toward the delivery of superior value to end-users.

SUMMARY

In this chapter, we examined how firms secure resources from the external environment and integrate them with their internal operations. Understanding firms as customers is the process of learning how companies rely on a network of suppliers to add value to their offerings, integrate purchasing activities with those of other functional areas and outside firms, and make purchase decisions. Business market managers must be familiar with the ways that both customer firms and their own firms handle this process. By understanding firms as customers, the business market manager is better able to craft responsive market strategies. By better comprehending one's own firm, the business market manager is in a better position to coordinate cross-functional efforts designed to deliver greater value to customers.

We began the chapter by exploring three purchasing orientations firms use in business markets. With a buying orientation, firms strive to obtain the best deal in terms of price, quality, and availability; maximize power over suppliers; and avoid risks wherever possible. As firms become more strategic, they tend to adopt a procurement orientation. Procurement managers work to improve quality of goods and services acquired, reduce TCO, and coordinate and integrate the activities of diverse functions not only within the firm but also with suppliers. Best practice organizations adhere to a value-based supply management orientation. Supply managers are actively involved with the integration and coordination of the value-adding activities not only among the diverse functions of their own firms but also with their customers, customers' customers, suppliers, and suppliers' suppliers.

We also looked at the ways progressive firms are working to integrate purchasing activities with those of other functions. Value management is an overarching framework for doing so. Firms that adopt a value management philosophy often turn to cross-functional groups such as buying teams to acquire goods and services, certify vendors, and conduct value analyses.

We concluded this chapter by reviewing the purchase decision process. First, we examined how managers gain a better understanding of the requirements and preferences of customer firms. Next, we described the purchase decision process using the BuyGrid Framework. The eight steps in the process range from problem identification to performance evaluation. Firms vary the extent of these activities as a function of the buying situation. Finally, we discussed alternate methods of supplier performance evaluation. We illustrated how firms rely upon a balanced scorecard of measures to more accurately assess supplier performance.

Endnotes

1. We chose buying, procurement, and supply management in order to be consistent with the work of Donald W. Dobler and David N. Burt, *Purchasing and Supply Management*, 6th ed. (New York: McGraw-Hill, 1996), xix.
2. We use the phrase *value network* instead of *value chain* to capture the diversity of relationships in business markets. For example, suppliers may buy from customers, firms may cooperate with direct competitors, and resellers may perform manufacturing operations.
3. Elliott R. Ross, "Making Money with Proactive Pricing," *Harvard Business Review* (November–December 1984): 148.
4. Ross, "Making Money," 305.
5. Dobler and Burt, *Purchasing and Supply Management*, 315; and Richard G. Newman and John M. McKeller, "Target Pricing—A Challenge for Purchasing," *International Journal of Purchasing and Materials Management* (Summer 1995): 16.
6. Anne T. Coughlin, Erin Anderson, Louis W. Stern, and Adel I. El-Ansary, *Marketing Channels*, 6th ed. (Upper Saddle River, NJ: Prentice Hall, 2001).
7. Niren Vyas and Arch G. Woodside, "An Inductive Model of Industrial Supplier Choice Processes," *Journal of Marketing Research* (Winter 1984): 30–45.
8. Newman and McKeller, "Target Pricing," 14.
9. David Hannon, "Technology Firm Minimizes Supplier Risk in Global Sourcing," *Purchasing* (February 15, 2007): 55–56.

10. David Ford et al., *The Business Marketing Course* (Chichester, UK: John Wiley & Sons, Ltd., 2002); Rob Rosenthal and Richard Villars, "The Online Sourcing Advantage," *IDC White Paper* (Framingham, MA: IDC, 2002).
11. Pierre Mitchell, "E-Sourcing Tools Can Improve Strategic Sourcing Processes, but Proceed with Caution," *Inside Supply Management* (March 2002): 46–52; Sari Kalin, "Reversal of Fortune," *Darwin* (February 2002): 12; Robert E. Hall, *Digital Dealing* (New York: W. W. Norton & Company, 2001); "GE GSN, The World's Largest Private Supplier Marketplace," GE Global eXchange Services (Gaithersburg, MD: GXS, cited August 2002), available at *http://www.gxs.com;* Sandy D. Jap, "The Impact of Online Reverse Auction Design on Buyer Seller Relationships, *Journal of Marketing* (January 2007): 146–159.
12. Hall, *Digital Dealing*, 71.
13. Arjan J. van Weele, *Purchasing and Supply Chain Management* (London: Thompson Learning, 2002).
14. Dobler and Burt, *Purchasing and Supply Management*, 24–30.
15. J.Y.F. Wynstra, "Purchasing's Development Role, The Internal and External Integration of Purchasing in Technological Development Processes," *Intermediate Report I, EUT/Bdk/73* (Eindhoven, The Netherlands: Eindhoven University of Technology Faculty of Technology Management & Uppsala University Department of Business Studies, 1995), 5.
16. Dobler and Burt, *Purchasing and Supply Management*, 182.
17. Dobler and Burt, *Purchasing and Supply Management*, 452.
18. *Total cost* is an alternate term for the life cycle cost of a product or service.
19. Carolyn Pye Sostrom, "Strategic Cost Management Programs: What's the Plan to Follow?" *Purchasing Today* (September 2000): 42; and Marc Wouters, James C. Anderson, and Finn Wynstra, "The Adoption of Total Cost of Ownership for Sourcing Decisions—A Structural Equations Analysis," *Accounting, Organizations, and Society* (February 2005): 167–191.
20. Susan Kuchinskas, "One-to-(N)one?" *Business 2.0* (September 12, 2000): 141–148.
21. Richard J. Palmer, "Survey Shows How Purchase Cards Save Time, Money," *Journal of Accountancy* (May 2000): 18–19.
22. Hall, *Digital Dealing*, 103; and Eric Young, "Web Marketplaces That Really Work," *Fortune* (Winter 2002): 78–84.
23. Philip B. Schary and Tage Skjøtt-Larsen, *Managing the Global Supply Chain* (Copenhagen: Copenhagen Business School Press, 2001).
24. James A. Narus and James C. Anderson, "Using Teams to Manage Collaborative Relationships in Business Markets," *Journal of Business-to-Business Marketing*, 3 (1995): 26.
25. Dobler and Burt, *Purchasing and Supply Management*, 179; and van Weele, *Purchasing and Supply Chain Management*, 192.
26. Virginia T. Freeman and Joseph L. Cavinato, "Fitting Purchasing to the Strategic Firm: Frameworks, Processes, and Values," *Journal of Purchasing and Materials Management* (Winter 1990): 9; and Peter Hines, "Purchasing for Lean Production: The New Strategic Agenda," *International Journal of Purchasing and Materials Management* (January 1996): 6–7.
27. Wynstra, "Purchasing's Development Role," II–XI; and James Brian Quinn and Frederick G. Hilmer, "Strategic Outsourcing," *Sloan Management Review* (Summer 1994): 43.
28. Carlos Niezen, Wulf Weller, and Heidi Deringer, "Strategic Supply Management," *MIT Sloan Management Review* (Winter 2007): 7–8.
29. Ravi Venkatesan, "Strategic Outsourcing: To Make or Not to Make," *Harvard Business Review* (November–December 1992): 98; and Quinn and Hilmer, "Strategic Outsourcing," *Sloan Management Review*, 45–47.
30. James P. Womack and Daniel T. Jones, "From Lean Production to the Lean Enterprise," *Harvard Business Review* (March–April 1994): 94.

31. Michael Hammer and James Champy, *Reengineering the Corporation* (New York: HarperBusiness, 1993); Louis P. Bucklin, "Postponement, Speculation, and the Structure of Distribution Channels," *Journal of Marketing Research* (February 1965): 26–31; and Schary and Skjøtt-Larsen, *Managing the Global Supply Chain*, 69.
32. Supply network models are also referred to as supply chain models.
33. Candace Arai Yano, "IIE Transactions Special Issue on Planning and Coordination of Supply Chains with Outsourcing," *IIE Transactions* (August 2002): IV–VIII.
34. Other popular supply network models include order-to-delivery, locate-to-order, and build-only-against-customer-order.
35. Adam Smith, *An Inquiry into the Nature and Causes of the Wealth of Nations* (1776) appearing in *Masterworks of Economics*, Volume 1 (New York: McGraw-Hill Book Company, 1946): 74.
36. Philip Kotler, *Marketing Management*, 11th ed. (Upper Saddle River, NJ: Prentice Hall, 2003): 482.
37. Peter Kraljic, "Purchasing Must Become Supply Management," *Harvard Business Review* (September–October 1983): 109–117; Schary and Skjøtt-Larsen, *Managing the Global Supply Chain*, 193–199; M. Bensaou, "Portfolios of Buyer-Supplier Relationships," *Sloan Management Review* (Summer 1999): 35–44; and Jan B. Heide, "Interorganizational Governance in Marketing Channels," *Journal of Marketing* (January 1994): 71–85.
38. van Weele, *Purchasing and Supply Chain Management*, 145–149; and Cees J. Gelderman and Arjan J. van Weele, "Strategic Direction Through Purchasing Portfolio Management: A Case Study," *Journal of Supply Chain Management* (Spring 2002): 30–37.
39. Much of this discussion is based on Commission of the European Communities Directorate General XIII Telecommunications, Information Market and Exploitation of Research, *Value Management Handbook* (Luxembourg: Office for Official Publications of the European Communities, 1995).
40. Lawrence D. Miles, *Techniques of Value Analysis and Engineering*, 3rd ed. (Washington, DC: Lawrence D. Miles Value Foundation, 1989).
41. Wesley J. Johnston and Thomas V. Bonoma, "The Buying Center: Structure and Interaction Patterns," *Journal of Marketing* (Summer 1981): 143–156. Although the term *buying center* has been widely used in academic literature, we prefer to use the word *team*, which has wider acceptance among practitioners. Furthermore, we believe that *team* is more appropriate because it conveys the key characteristics of a common orientation, mutual goals, and coordinated efforts. Finally, we use the word *buying* because of its widespread usage in this context, rather than to refer to any particular purchasing orientation.
42. Das Naryandas, *Note on Customer Management* (Boston, MA: Harvard Business School Publishing, 2002).
43. Patrick J. Robinson and Charles W. Faris with Yoram Wind, *Industrial Buying and Creative Marketing* (Boston, MA: Allyn and Bacon, 1967).
44. Mary Brandel, "Offshoring Grows Up," *Computerworld* (March 12, 2007): 25–27.
45. Tim Minahan, "GM Looks Outside to Fuel Internal JIT Initiatives," *Purchasing*, 5 September 1996, 40–41.
46. van Weele, *Purchasing and Supply Chain Management*, 186.
47. Tarun Khanna, Rajiv Lal, Merlina Manocaran, "Mahindra & Mahindra: *Creating Scorpio*," 22 February 2005, Harvard Business School Case 705-478.
48. Company examples in this section come from James Carbone, "A Buyer's Place Is in the Design Lab," *Purchasing*, 7 March 1996, 59–63; and Wynstra, "Purchasing's Development Role," 46–62.
49. Michael E. Porter, *Competitive Advantage* (New York: The Free Press, 1985), 146–150.
50. Håkan Håkansson, Jan Johanson, and Bart Wootz, "Influence Tactics in Buyer-Seller Processes," *Industrial Marketing Management*, 4 (1976): 319–332.

51. We attribute the design of this 2 × 2 matrix to Ron Kegarise, formerly of the ALCOA Corporation.
52. Mohanbir Sawhney, "Services-Led Growth Strategies for Difficult Economic Times," presented at Institute for the Study of Business Markets Conference (August 2002); and Robert G. Cross, *Revenue Management* (New York: Broadway Books, 1997).
53. Robinson and Faris, *Industrial Buying*, 14.
54. Carolyn Pye, "An Open Mike for Service-Industry Purchasers," *Purchasing Today* (December 1996): 24–26.
55. Robert S. Kaplan and David P. Norton, "The Balanced Scorecard—Measures That Drive Performance," *Harvard Business Review* (January–February 1992): 71–79.
56. Robert M. Monczka, Robert B. Handfield, and Robert J. Trent, *Purchasing and Supply Chain Management* (Cincinnati, OH: South-Western College Publishing, 2001); and Robert M. Monczka and Steven J. Trecha, "Cost-Based Supplier Performance Evaluation," *Journal of Purchasing and Materials Management* (Spring 1988): 2–7.

Chapter 4

Crafting Market Strategy

OVERVIEW

The business market processes of market sensing and understanding firms as customers provide supplier managers with an understanding of what particular market segments and customer firms value. These managers understand that the variation in requirements and preferences across market segments and customer firms means their business will not be able to serve all segments and customers equally well. In the last business market process for understanding value—crafting market strategy—supplier managers integrate their market and customer firm knowledge with an understanding of their business's resources to make decisions about where and how to create and deliver value.

Crafting market strategy is the process of studying how to exploit a business's resources to achieve short-term and long-term marketplace success, deciding on a course of action to pursue, and flexibly updating it as learning occurs during implementation. Studying how to exploit a business's resources draws on market sensing and understanding customer firms, yet involves more than just analysis. Studying also means contemplating the information and knowledge the business generates through market sensing and understanding firms as customers, and creatively thinking through its implications. Crafting market strategy is also more than simply making a plan and following it. It recognizes real-world complexity and the interplay between **deliberate strategy**, where the business decides on a course of action to pursue, and **emergent strategy**, where marketplace activities have a pattern to them that the business recognizes and acts upon in a coordinated way.[1]

Crafting market strategy requires significant participation from many functional areas besides marketing to decide what market segments and customer firms to pursue and how to deliver superior value to them. In an article titled, "What the Hell Is 'Market Oriented'?" Shapiro stresses that a firm's most important strategic decision is to choose its relatively important customers. He also stresses that collaboration among the firm's various functions is essential when pinpointing the market segments and customers that the firm will target.[2]

Because business market management regards value as its cornerstone, crafting market strategy is about understanding how the firm can be meaningfully different in ways that targeted market segments and customer firms value. This task requires understanding what the firm does, or is capable of doing, that would fulfill the requirements and preferences of targeted market segments and customer firms in a superior way—that is, better than the customer firms themselves or the supplier's competitors could do. At the same time, the firm must understand what it needs to do now to put itself in position to have market success in the foreseeable future. What resources will the firm have to invest in within and across its constituent functional areas to be able to deliver superior value over the long term?

We portray the process of crafting market strategy in Figure 4.1. This chapter parallels the flow of Figure 4.1.[3] We begin by considering business strategy as the context for market strategy. The firm first understands what resources it has and how it can best exploit them in one or more fundamental value-based business strategies. As we will see, the delineation between business strategy and market strategy has

Figure 4.1 Crafting Market Strategy

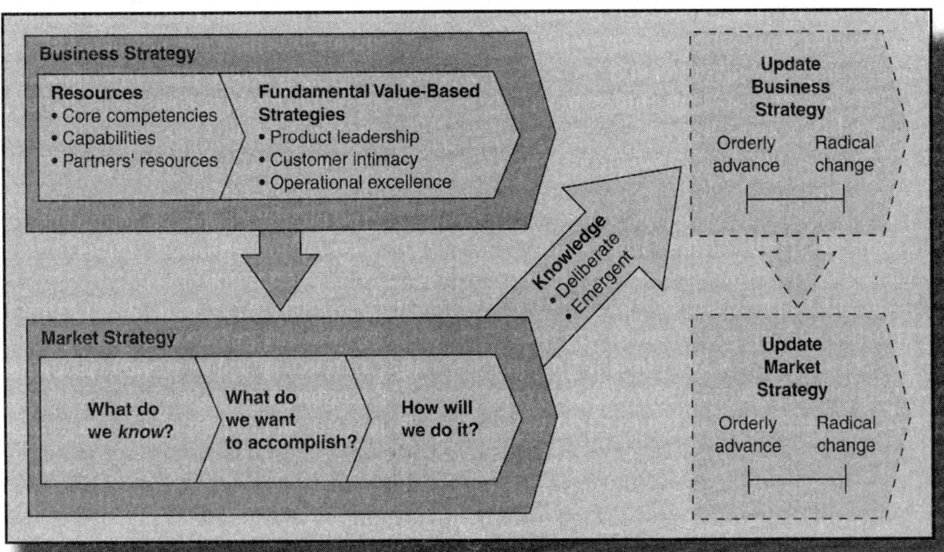

blurred somewhat. We next consider how the firm plans its market strategy. We organize our discussion of market strategy around three fundamental questions that firms must meaningfully answer. Planning the market strategy and implementing it provide the firm with gains in deliberate as well as emergent knowledge. The firm uses this knowledge to update its business and market strategies. Although business strategy often is seen as setting the constraints for market strategy, so too should market strategy inform and significantly influence business strategy. The nature of the changes in the updated strategies can range from orderly advances to radical change.

Business Strategy as the Context for Market Strategy

Strategy is written about more than any other topic in management practice. Advocates tout various prescriptive approaches for senior management to embrace. These approaches range from strategy as something that management designs and deliberately pursues to strategy as rapid learning and adapting from mistakes, experiments, and chance happenings in the marketplace.[4] Some strategy thinkers contend that senior management needs to move beyond strategy to defining an engaging purpose for the firm that workers will find fulfillment in accomplishing. One strategy expert even concludes that "strategic thinking is a necessary but overrated element of business success."[5]

In an article titled "What Is Strategy?" Porter contends that many firms fail to distinguish between operational effectiveness and strategy. **Operational effectiveness** "means performing similar activities *better* than rivals perform them." Firms that unwittingly pursue operational effectiveness as strategy find themselves in a continual race against competitors to extend the productivity frontier, with the differences among firms narrowing rapidly. Benchmarking each other's activities and the same set of best practice firms outside the industry, these firms become undifferentiated in the marketplace. In contrast, Porter says **strategy** "is the creation of a unique and valuable position, involving a different set of activities." **Strategic positioning** "means performing *different* activities from rivals' or performing similar activities in *different ways*." Significantly, strategy is about pursuing a course of action different from competitors and providing superior value to particular market segments. It is about making choices of what to do, and perhaps more important, what the firm will *not* do. Strategy is about putting together activities that generate superior value in complementary or synergistic ways. Because a strategic position is a fundamental course of action that a firm commits itself to pursuing, Porter contends that it should provide a competitive advantage for at least 10 years.[6]

We can think of business strategy as the overarching strategy that brings together sourcing strategy, technology strategy, and market strategy in ways that reinforce one another. **Sourcing strategy**, which we discussed in Chapter 3, specifies what the business should acquire from others and what it will produce itself. **Technology strategy**, which we discuss further in Chapter 6, concerns the design knowledge and process know-how that transforms inputs to outputs of greater value. Business strategy provides the context for a dialogue among these constituent strategies, with the intent of harmonizing them. Business strategy influences each of them and is itself influenced by each of them. Further, the distinction between business strategy, or simply strategy, and market strategy has blurred somewhat. As an example, consider this statement by Porter: "Deciding which target group of customers, varieties, and needs the company should serve is fundamental to developing a strategy."[7]

We focus our discussion on business strategy as it relates to business market management, which views the firm as a value-generating enterprise. Resources provide the capacity to produce offerings that fulfill particular market requirements and preferences in a superior way, thereby creating value. Consequently, we take a resource-based view of the firm, and then discuss some fundamental value-based strategies. We conclude by examining some alternative perspectives on strategy making.

A Resource-Based View of the Firm

The resource-based view of the firm "sees companies as very different collections of physical and intangible assets and capabilities. No two companies are alike because no two companies have had the same set of experiences, acquired the same assets and skills, or built the same organizational cultures."[8] As discussed in Chapter 1, **resources** are anything that firms (as collective actors) explicitly value, such as technical know-how, equipment, personnel, or capital, that can generate greater value for themselves and others. The resource-based view combines and builds upon the internal perspective of the firm, associated with concepts such as core competencies and capabilities, and the external perspective of the firm, associated with Porter's five-forces framework of industry analysis and more recent work on market-based assets.[9]

Resources are the building blocks for strategy. To be a source of competitive advantage, a resource must pass five external market tests of its value. The first test is *inimitability*, which is how difficult the resource is to copy or the length of time it will take for a competitor to replicate the resource. The second test is *durability*, which is how long a resource will last in providing value before it is overtaken by innovation either within the industry or outside of it. The third test is *appropriability*, which is the extent to which other firms or individuals can capture the value that the resource creates. The fourth test is *substitutability*, which is the ability of a different resource to provide similar functionality or performance at the same or lower cost. The fifth test is *competitive superiority*, which refers to a market assessment of how a resource compares to those of the firm's competitors. Management applies these tests to resources using empirical assessments in the marketplace, such as customer value assessment.[10]

Core competencies and capabilities are resources that are complementary building blocks of a value-generating strategy that provides competitive advantage. Brands represent a special resource through which suppliers can gain competitive advantage. Finally, the firm need not own all of the resources it requires to actualize its strategy. It may decide instead to engage those resources through alliances with partner firms.

Core Competencies

A **core competence** is "a complex harmonization of individual technologies and production skills."[11] As an example, 3M Company has core competencies in substrates, coatings, and adhesives that it has brought together in distinct ways to create a number of successful businesses. How can a firm sort out what are its core competencies?

> At least three tests can be applied to identify core competencies in a company. First, a core competence provides a potential access to a wide variety of markets. . . . Second, a core competence should make a significant contribution to the perceived customer benefits of the end-product. . . . Finally, a core competence should be difficult for competitors to imitate.[12]

Notice that these tests partly overlap those for resources. Reflecting the differences, though, some strategy thinkers draw a distinction between a core competence as something that the firm does particularly well and a **distinctive competence**, which is something that the firm does better than its competitors.[13]

The late strategy thinker Peter Drucker recommended that to measure and manage core competencies, a firm should carefully track its own and competitors' performances, looking particularly for unexpected successes and unexpected poor performances. He believed that these are revealing of what the market regards as core competencies in the firms, and changing market perceptions of them. Finally, he contended that innovation is one core competence that every organization must have, and that to appraise this, a business should study the record of innovation in its entire field during a given period.[14]

Capabilities

A **capability** is "a set of business processes strategically understood."[15] Product replenishment at Wal-Mart is an example of a capability, which closely coordinates business processes of Wal-Mart and its strategic suppliers to provide superior inventory turns. Although some strategy thinkers use the terms *core competencies* and *capabilities* interchangeably, others regard them as useful complements:

> Both concepts emphasize "behavioral" aspects of strategy in contrast to the traditional structural model. But whereas core competence emphasizes technological and production expertise at specific points along the value chain, capabilities are more broadly based, encompassing the entire value chain. In this respect, capabilities are visible to the customer in a way that core competencies rarely are.[16]

Day regards capabilities as "complex bundles of skills and collective learning, exercised through organizational processes, that ensure superior coordination of functional activities."[17] He recognizes that firms have numerous capabilities, not all of which they perform well, and uses **distinctive capabilities** to mean those the firm surpasses its competitors in performing. "The most defensible test of the distinctiveness of a capability is whether it makes a disproportionate contribution to the provision of superior customer value—as defined from the customer's perspective—or permits the business to deliver value to customers in an appreciably more cost-effective way."[18] He contends that market-driven organizations characteristically excel at *market sensing, customer linking*, and *channel bonding* capabilities. We considered market sensing as a business market process in Chapter 2. Customer linking refers to building and sustaining collaborative relations with customers, which we consider in detail in Chapter 10. *Channel bonding* refers to building and sustaining partnerships with resellers, which we consider in detail in Chapter 9.

Brands as Resources

Brands and brand building are concepts that are of growing interest and significance in business markets. A **brand** is a means of identifying a particular supplier and its market offerings as well as differentiating them from other suppliers and their offerings. To accomplish this, a brand draws on visual and verbal elements such as a name, logo, symbol, design, packaging, slogan, or some combination of these. A brand serves as a shorthand descriptor of the technical, economic, service, and social benefits that a particular supplier's market offering delivers to targeted market segments and customer firms.[19]

In business markets, brand elements may have no inherent meaning. Instead, they become endowed with meaning through the performance of the supplier and its market offering over time. For example, at DuPont Company, brand names most often are generated as two-syllable, nonsense words, which are pronounceable. Well-known examples are Teflon®, Kevlar®, and Tyvek®. Through their association with offerings that consistently deliver superior functionality and performance, brand elements such as brand names become a valuable resource themselves for suppliers.

Brand equity is a concept that is meant to capture the value of a brand and refers to how customers regard a brand relative to offerings of other competing suppliers (or an offering of an unnamed supplier), based on those customers' knowledge from experience with and learning about the brand. Brand equity is reflected in the following kinds of preferential actions or responses of present or prospective customers:

- Greater willingness to sample or trial the offering
- Reduction in time to close the sale of the offering
- Greater likelihood of purchasing the offering
- Willingness to award a larger share of purchase requirement
- Willingness to pay a higher price
- Greater unwillingness to switch to competitor offerings after price increases
- Less willingness to sample or trial competitor offerings

Suppliers build brand equity for their market offerings through the superior functionality and performance of those offerings, but also through the branding strategy that they pursue.

"A *branding strategy* for a firm identifies which brand elements a firm chooses to apply across the various products it sells." In business markets, the most significant aspect of branding strategy is deciding on the brand hierarchy to pursue.

"A *brand hierarchy* is a means of summarizing the branding strategy by displaying the number and nature of common and distinctive brand elements across the firm's products, revealing the explicit ordering of brand elements. . . . Because certain brand elements are used to make more than one brand, a hierarchy can be constructed to represent how (if at all) products are nested with other products because of their common brand elements." The potential levels of a brand hierarchy, from highest to lowest, would be corporate brand, family brand, individual brand, and modifier. An example of this brand hierarchy would be *IBM ThinkPad X30*. *IBM* is the corporate brand, *ThinkPad* is the family brand for all notebook computers (as contrasted with desktop computers), *X* Series is the individual brand that refers to extra-light, extra-small, and ultra-portable notebooks, and *30* is the modifier that refers to the Ethernet connection models (as contrasted with wireless network connection models, *31*).[20]

Properly understood and implemented, the brand hierarchy positions brands as resources enabling a supplier to leverage previous investments in brand building. The investment required to successfully gain awareness and purchase of the *IBM ThinkPad G* Series is much less because of the previous brand-building for the *IBM* corporate brand and *ThinkPad* family brand. Brand equity that has been built in one offering category can be leveraged to launch a brand extension in another offering category. The brand equity 3M Company has established for its Post-it® Notes was a resource to enable 3M to enter the market for flip-chart pads with its Post-it Self-Stick Easel Pads.

That a supplier's brands are valuable resources also is reflected in the acquisition prices paid by firms in business markets. Citigroup acquired Grupo Financiero Banamex-Accival in 2001 for $12.5 billion, the largest ever U.S.–Mexican corporate merger. Less than six months later, an integrated Citibank Mexico and Banamex began operating under the *Banamex* brand name. The acquiring firm must adroitly manage the newly acquired brands, deciding how best to fit them within the existing brands, brand hierarchy, and brand architecture of the firm. Oracle, which has extensive experience in this brand management, provides a noteworthy case, which we relate in Box 4.1.[21]

Reliance on Outside Partners for Resources

Firms use collaborative relationships with other firms to gain access to resources and to leverage their own resources. In rapidly changing, technology-driven markets, no one firm will possess all of the resources needed to create innovative products. Business relationships and business networks form to focus on specific market opportunities. The Light Conbat Aircraft business network that we discussed in Chapter 1 is an instance of this focus. Chapter 6 discusses the roles that outside development relationships and networks can play in a new offering realization strategy.[22]

Firms increasingly rely on the resources of outside logistics and transportation providers, such as United Parcel Service (UPS) or FedEx, to realize their business strategies. For example, Dell Computer restructured its order fulfillment process to leverage outside partnerships. In the past, the suppliers would ship the monitors first to Dell, which would in turn ship them on to the customer. Now, when Dell is ready to ship a computer, it sends an electronic mail (e-mail) message to its shipping

BOX 4.1

How Oracle Manages Large Number of Acquired Brands: Acquisition of i-flex

A significant reason for the rapid growth of Oracle Corporation over the years, the world's largest enterprise software company, has been its distinctive competence in identifying good acquisition targets and smoothly integrating these acquired companies into the Oracle brand. Many of these acquired companies have been successful in global markets and have powerful brands themselves. Oracle was able to manage these acquired brands in a superior manner, creating synergy in the marketplace. One such acquisition was i-flex, a hugely successful India-headquartered IT product company in the banking domain.

i-flex (earlier known as Citibank Information Technology Industries Limited), India's best-known product company, started as a spin-off from Citibank Overseas Software Limited. The name of the financial services product i-flex inherited from its parent, the Citi group, was Microbanker. Most of the customers who used Microbanker were banks, operating largely in Africa. This was an advantage as well as a disadvantage. Having all of its customers in one region helped i-flex as this was cost-effective for a small company with limited resources. On the other hand, i-flex was based out of India, a continent away. Initially, these customers were served by flying out teams from India. However, as the service requirements grew, this became no longer feasible. So, i-flex came up with a tiered model of service. It partnered with IT companies in the clients' local geographies to set up small offices in the same city, sometimes on the same premises as the client, which provided the first level of support to customers. For the next level of support, it set up state-of-the-art offices in India (Mumbai and Bengaluru) from where problems that could not be solved by the local partner were resolved. i-flex's superior way of servicing clients as well as continual product innovation resulted in its emergence as the market leader in Africa. The same strategy was subsequently applied to other geographies as well.

i-flex had over 550 customers spanning over 100 countries at the time it was acquired by Oracle in 2005. The acquisition was very successful from the perspective of both Oracle and i-flex. It gave i-flex the much-needed marketing power to more aggressively take its world-leading product to the developed markets. Meanwhile, the acquisition gave Oracle significant strength in the banking vertical. In 2008, Oracle, which owns 81% of i-flex, changed the name of i-flex to Oracle Financial Services Ltd. (OFSL). From the perspective of i-flex, the new identity was expected to help it better leverage the global reach, infrastructure and brand visibility of Oracle to accelerate its growth. It was also expected to bring synergies of scale, resources, expertise and efficiency across the two organizations. From Oracle's perspective, the new branding underscored the strategic importance it attached to the financial services sector. Oracle expected that OFSL would be the focal point of its investment in innovation and leadership in financial services. It would give Oracle the opportunity to put the credibility of the Oracle brand behind this strategic initiative of making strong inroads into the financial services sector. Oracle has proved, through the i-flex acquisition and dozens of others, its ability to protect the equity of the parent Oracle brand and leverage the equity of the acquired

BOX 4.1
Continued

brand where appropriate. It has repeatedly demonstrated its ability to manage multiple brands and effectively fold them into the mother Oracle brand.

Contributed by Rajiv Motwani, Participant, PGSEM Program, Indian Institute of Management Bangalore.
Sources: J. Ramachandran, Pravin Garg, "i-flex Solutions Limited: Winning Unconventionally," case developed for IIM Bangalore in 2006; "i-flex History And Times," *http://www.oppapers.com/*; "i-flex Solutions Ltd. to change its Name to Oracle Financial Services Ltd.," *http://in.sys-con.com/node/535152*, 4 April 2008.

partner, which coordinates the arrival of Dell's computer with the arrival of the ordered monitor from its supplier, and then delivers the complete order at the same time to the customer.[23]

A firm with an underutilized resource, such as an exceptionally proficient sales force or field service engineers, may seek out other firms that would value this resource *in exchange* for another. Two firms with complementary product lines may agree to comarket each other's product line. This approach can leverage the resources of each firm, particularly when the firms primarily operate in different country markets. In this way, each firm can offer and service a broader product line and achieve geographical diversity in its sales. For example, Delta Air lines offers service between Atlanta and Zürich, with a stop in Paris. The Atlanta–Paris leg is operated by Delta, whereas the Paris–Zürich leg is operated by code-sharing partner Air France. However, when business travelers purchase a ticket from Atlanta to Zürich from Delta, their tickets list only Delta as the operating carrier, with two Delta flight numbers for the entire route. In the same way, a business traveler purchasing a ticket from Air France for the Zürich to Atlanta route via Paris would find two Air France flight numbers listed.

A firm may look to *pool* its resources with those of one or more other firms so they all can pursue a strategy that none could do alone. The chemical distribution industry, for example, is consolidating to a few large players that offer worldwide distribution to chemical producers and customers. One medium-sized, privately held chemical distributor in the United States is talking with similar firms in Germany and Japan about a strategic alliance. Working together, the three firms would offer producers and customers worldwide distribution coverage and the superior flexibility and responsiveness of dealing with smaller, family-run businesses.

Relying upon outside partners for resources is a strategic decision, where senior management must consider the long-term as well as short-term benefits and consequences. What knowledge will be transferred between partners and what learning will take place? What resources will be expended, which will be replenished, and what new resources will result from working with the partner firm? Research indicates that alliances are most successful when firms carefully decide which resources will come from outside partners, select partners with which they are compatible, and engage in alliances where each firm contributes significant resources and treats the other as an equal.[24]

Fundamental Value-Based Strategies

At the core of every successful strategy is understanding what targeted market segments and firms regard as superior value and how to provide it to them. Not all markets nor firms within them value the same things, though, which means that a firm may provide superior value in multiple ways. Although prescriptions for fundamental strategies based on value vary somewhat, we consolidate them into three for discussion: product leadership, customer intimacy, and operational excellence. These basic value strategies are not mutually exclusive, and a firm that surpasses its competitors on two of them will have an extraordinary advantage.[25]

Product Leadership

Product leadership "means offering customers leading-edge products and services that consistently enhance the customer's use or application of the product, thereby making rivals' goods obsolete."[26] A firm that builds its strategy around product leadership pursues innovation relentlessly. It broadly seeks out technologies from other industries that it might creatively adapt to solve problems or further enhance its offerings' performance. Not content to have market offerings that deliver the best performance in an industry, it seeks to obsolete its own products before its competitors can. The firm uses its experience and learning to both speed up the realization process and lower its costs. Hewlett-Packard relies heavily on innovation and product obsolescence in its business strategy. More than half of its annual sales come from products introduced within the last two years.[27]

Customer Intimacy

Customer intimacy "means segmenting and targeting markets precisely and then tailoring offerings to match exactly the demands of those niches."[28] A firm that builds its strategy around customer intimacy recognizes that when it retains customers over time, it tends to gain more profits from them. This greater profitability comes from a deep understanding of the customers' requirements and preferences, and how the firm can adapt its market offerings to fulfill them in ways that are worth more or that lower total cost. When a firm pursues close relationships with its customers, it can better anticipate changes in requirements and preferences, which enables it to sustain its superior value. The supplier firm and its customers might work together to discover how they can make advantageous changes in requirements as well as processes for doing business together. Grainger Consulting Services' use of process mapping, which we discussed in Chapter 2, is an example. A worthwhile complement to these market sensing activities is for senior management to spend a day in the life of selected customers, gaining a firsthand understanding of their experiences and problems.[29]

Supplier's share of the customer's business is a critical measure for gauging the success of a customer intimacy strategy. Gaining a deep understanding of customers' requirements and preferences takes greater time and other resources. This effort is worthwhile only when the supplier receives a large share of their business. A supplier pursuing a customer intimacy strategy should also measure additional business in complementary areas that it gains from fulfilling its customers' purchase requirements in other related areas. After all, a deep understanding of targeted customers' needs should suggest some possibilities for the firm to broaden its business with those customers.

Operational Excellence

Operational excellence means "providing customers with reliable products or services at competitive prices and delivered with minimal difficulty or inconvenience."[30] A firm that builds its strategy around operational excellence organizes itself to provide market offerings that fulfill a defined set of customer requirements and preferences at the lowest cost. Such firms are creative in the design and implementation of their business processes, and continually search for ways to eliminate redundant activities that do not contribute to customer value. Dell Computer is an example of a firm that has pursued operational excellence. "By selling to customers directly, building to order rather than to inventory, and creating a disciplined, extremely low-cost culture, Dell has been able to undercut Compaq and other PC makers in price yet provide high-quality products and service."[31]

How does operational excellence differ from operational effectiveness, which we discussed earlier? Operational effectiveness means performing *similar* activities better than the firm's competitors. In contrast, operational excellence stems from performing *different* activities from competitors that enable the firm to provide comparable offerings at a lower total cost.

Strategy Making

How firms should develop a strategy is a topic of keen interest to senior management, business market managers, and strategy thinkers. The conventional view of strategy making is that senior management charts a course of action where the fit between the firm's resources and the requirements of markets it elects to serve is best. Some strategy thinkers challenge this view, and instead advocate a view of strategy making as radical change. However, although a radical view of strategy making has some merit, it neglects the fact that firms do pursue strategies over time and often achieve success with methodical progress. We attempt a balance in discussing who makes strategy, defining purpose, and strategy as orderly advances punctuated by radical change.

Who Makes Strategy?

The conventional view is that top management makes strategy. This view is reinforced by the business press, which regularly writes about senior executives who pioneered "Killer Strategies That Make Shareholders Rich."[32] Other firms claim to use a top-down, bottom-up process for strategy making where the more financially driven view of senior management informs and is informed by the view of lower management, which is closer to and more knowledgeable about the marketplace. Middle management traditionally transmits the views and mediates the disparities that occur between the financial results that senior management wants and the marketplace results that lower management believes it can produce. This critical intermediary role has become impoverished in many firms with the reduction of middle management.[33]

Recent management practice research has found that middle managers play critical, yet undervalued roles in strategy making and its successful implementation. The four primary findings of this research were:

> First, middle managers often have value-adding entrepreneurial ideas that they are able and willing to realize—if only they can get a hearing. Second, they're far better than most senior executives are at leveraging the informal networks at a company that make substantive, lasting change possible. Third, they stay attuned to employees' moods and emotional needs, thereby ensuring that the change initiative's momentum is maintained. And finally, they manage the tension between continuity and change—they keep the organization from falling into extreme inertia, on the one hand, or extreme chaos, on the other.[34]

An iconoclastic view is that in order to create innovative strategies, firms need to rely less on senior management, and instead, promote broader involvement of managers throughout the firm. This emergent view of strategy contends that imaginative thinking exists in many places within a firm as a result of experiments, mistakes, and learning. The challenge for the firm is to pull together and capitalize on this strategy-making resource. It requires a more democratic process for strategy making, where senior management encourages and actively seeks out revolutionary thinkers—wherever they are—in the firm. Three constituencies that are typically underrepresented in strategy making can have a disproportionate influence: employees who have youthful perspectives (not necessarily the same as young employees); employees at the geographic periphery of the firm (e.g., those in local country markets far removed from the corporate headquarters); and newcomers to the industry, who tend to a have a fresh perspective. Each of these constituencies can contribute thinking that challenges industry and firm beliefs, and produces strategy-making insight.[35]

Defining Purpose

The cornerstone of strategy making is defining the purpose of the firm. A firm may express its purpose in a **mission statement** or **vision statement**, which sets out a broad strategic charter for the course of action that the firm will pursue. As an example, consider the mission statement for R. R. Donnelley & Sons Company, whose traditional business has been printing: "It is the mission of R. R. Donnelley & Sons Company to be a preeminent worldwide provider of printing and related information and value-added services and products for owners, publishers, and users of information." This mission statement appears on a plaque near the elevators on the ground floor of corporate headquarters (and at other places throughout the building) to continually reinforce the firm's purpose. Notice that the statement suggests a strategic direction that broadens the business beyond printing. Reflecting this intention, R.R. Donnelley is pursuing business in related areas, such as database management, direct marketing, and mapping services.[36]

Hamel and Prahalad advocated that a firm define its purpose in a statement of **strategic intent**, which expresses "a desired leadership position and establishes the criterion the organization will use to chart its progress."[37] Komatsu, a Japanese manufacturer of bulldozers and construction equipment, expressed its strategic intent as "Encircle Caterpillar," the industry leader. Strategic intent also provides a bridge to strategy making by having the firm broadly specify the path to achieving its strategic intent, including establishing intermediate milestones and review mechanisms to track progress.

Other strategy thinkers contend that strategic intent can produce an obsessive focus on a competitor that makes the firm myopic to other strategic options for profitable growth. Komatsu's senior management was concerned that its strategic intent of "Surround Caterpillar" was causing its managers to become fixated on trying to surpass what Caterpillar was doing and overlook emerging growth markets, such as hydraulic excavators. In place of strategic intent, senior management defines the **purpose of the firm** as an ambition that engages its employees to develop, refine, and renew that ambition. So, Komatsu defined its purpose as "Growth, Global, Groupwide" to spur its managers' thinking on ways to grow through expanding geographically and leveraging the group's resources.[38]

The challenge for the firm is to define its purpose in a way that broadly guides strategy making, yet is still meaningful and motivating to employees. Most firms find this dual task difficult to do well. Thus, mission statements tend to have a dulling, generic sameness about them, which employees justifiably regard cynically. The firm improves its chances of having a meaningful and motivating definition of purpose by having a broad cross-section of employees participate in its creation, and then having senior management discuss the meaning of the purpose in dialogues with groups of employees throughout the firm. As part of these dialogues, senior management should sincerely solicit employees' thoughts on how the firm can realize its purpose.[39]

IBM has recently gone through a process to update its corporate values, which define its purpose or mission. Input from its top 300 executives and focus groups with more than a thousand employees yielded three proposed value statements. These candidate statements then were shared with IBM employees, who all were invited to participate in a live, company-wide conversation about them over 72 hours on the company intranet, called *ValuesJam*. An estimated 50,000 IBM employees checked out the discussion and about 10,000 comments were posted about the statements, some of them from Sam Palmisano, CEO of IBM. IBM relied upon a tailored-version of its e-classifier software to analyze the posted comments to extract significant themes, which the team responsible for the process factored into the final statements of corporate values. These corporate values or defining purpose for IBM are:

- Dedication to every client's success;
- Innovation that matters—for our company and for the world; and
- Trust and personal responsibility in all relationships.

To bring these to life and to show IBM employees that he was serious about using them to transform the company, Palmisano announced some initiatives to begin closing the gaps between the way IBM worked and the statements. For example, Palmisano allocated $5,000 annually to each of IBM's 22,000 first-line managers, which they could spend, no questions asked, to respond to extraordinary situations that would help win business or affect client success, or to respond to an emergency need of an IBM employee.[40]

Strategy as Orderly Advances Punctuated by Radical Change

Reacting to firms that pursue operational effectiveness as strategy, Hamel proposed the metaphor of "strategy as revolution." In this notion of strategy, firms pursue strategies that represent radical change in their industries. These revolutionary strategies break the established rules of competition within an industry. In implementing its strategy, the firm enacts new ones that give it unique advantages.[41]

This concept of strategy as revolution builds upon Hamel and Prahalad's earlier concept of "strategy as stretch and leverage." Firms that embrace this concept establish a strategic intent that is extraordinarily ambitious and that the firm cannot accomplish with conventional thinking. This situation spurs managers to creatively pursue ways to leverage their limited resources to attain the firm's strategic intent. Hamel and Prahalad outline five basic ways in which a firm can leverage its resources. First, it can *concentrate* its resources through astutely pursuing its strategic intent over time and focusing at any given time to accomplish more with limited resources. For example, Intel Corporation made a strategic decision in the early 1980s to concentrate its resources on developing its emerging microprocessor business, moving away from its past core business of dynamic random access memory (DRAM) chips. Second, it can *accumulate* resources through superior extracting of learning from its experiences and "borrowing" the resources of alliance partners. Third, a firm can *complement* resources, blending its resources in a superior way or balancing them to get the best return from the set of resources. Fourth, it can *conserve* resources in ways such as recycling them, coopting other firms to pursue a common objective, and shielding them from direct confrontations with entrenched competitors. Finally, the firm can *recover* resources by quickly generating revenue from them or otherwise making them available for redeployment.[42]

Although strategy making as the pursuit of radical change appears compelling in some respects, it does leave some unanswered questions. How frequently should a firm "revolutionize" its strategy? For what duration are individuals in a firm capable of pursuing (and going through themselves) dramatic changes before those changes become dysfunctional to the firm's performance? Is strategy making as revolution really just a search for dramatically different ways to enact the fundamental value-based strategies we discussed earlier? When multiple firms within an industry pursue strategy making as revolution, does this produce greater differentiation and industry profitability, or hypercompetition that is potentially damaging to the industry and its customers?

Progressive firms recognize the strengths and weaknesses of each kind of strategy making and alternate using them when each best suits their needs. The result is longer periods of strategy making as orderly advances punctuated by shorter periods of strategy making as radical change.[43] Mintzberg has found from his research on organizations over time that "clear periods of stability and change can usually be distinguished in any organization: while it is true that particular strategies may always be changing marginally, it seems equally true that major shifts in strategic orientation occur only rarely."[44] Further, he finds that more creative organizations, such as Canada's National Film Board, experience a more balanced pattern of stability and change, perhaps due to their willingness to experiment and their sensitivity and openness to external events that precipitate change.

The impetus for radical change may come from within the firm, such as bringing innovations to the market. It may come from the market, such as competitors or major customers enacting strategy as revolution. It may come from interaction between internal and external events, such as when a firm preoccupied with internal affairs becomes increasingly disconnected with changing market requirements and preferences. In any event, to prosper, the firm must pursue dramatically different ways to enact a fundamental value-based strategy. After the firm has settled on a strategy to pursue, a period of orderly advances ensues as the firm works to improve the fit among its activities to more fully realize its strategic positioning.

PLANNING MARKET STRATEGY IN BUSINESS MARKETS

"Chance favors the prepared mind."

The preceding quote by Louis Pasteur captures the essence of what the business attempts to accomplish with planning market strategy. Planning is a mechanism for learning. It should afford managers the time to validate their **market views**—the mental models that are simplified representations of the market and how it works. Planning also provides a way for the business to build its **institutional learning**, "which is the process whereby management teams change their shared mental models of their company, their markets, and their competitors."[45] Through planning, members of the management team compare, revise, and update their individual market views, with the intent of having them converge on a shared market view, which serves as the basis for discussing alternative courses of action for the business to pursue.

In many firms, though, planning as practiced has little to do with learning. Pressed for time and with little or no market research results to draw on, managers produce plans that are uninspired, straight-line extensions of the previous year's plan. In many cases, the plans are little more than the financial performance targets for the upcoming year. Devoid of market insights, such plans contribute little to running the business or reacting to changes that inevitably occur. Fortunately, recognition of the need for meaningful planning of strategy is growing.[46]

Firms employ many different planning processes and plan formats in their strategic planning efforts. The particular planning process and plan format are not what is important, though; it is the thinking that goes into the plan and the learning that results. We organize our presentation of planning market strategy in business markets around three fundamental questions:

- What do we know?
- What do we want to accomplish?
- How will we do it?

Regardless of planning process and plan format, businesses that can *meaningfully* answer these three questions will have constructed a market strategy that is worth pursuing.

What Do We *Know*?

We want to emphasize the word *know* in this question. To construct a market strategy, managers must distinguish among what they know, what they believe, and what they want to believe. Moreover, they must be willing to challenge what they think they know and ask themselves how they know it. Is this knowledge accurate and supported by data from internal assessments and market sensing? As Benjamin Disraeli perceptively observed, "To be conscious that you are ignorant is a great step to knowledge."

To answer what do we know, the management team should review recent performance, gather essential market information, and, when there is considerable uncertainty, construct scenarios.

Review Recent Performance

As a start, managers should review recent performance to see how it compares with prior plan objectives. Share of customer's business and sales of new products by market segments are examples of informative measures of market performance, and segment contribution (segment total sales minus total variable costs and assignable fixed costs) and customer contribution to profitability are examples of informative measures of financial performance. Divergence between planned and achieved results signals faulty assumptions, such as how well a market offering fulfills particular customer requirements and preferences.

Accurate explanation of past performance requires that managers have skill in **thinking backward.**[47] That is, to construct valid explanations for past performance, they must find relevant variables, put them in a causal sequence, and assess the plausibility of the causal sequence occurring. To improve their backward thinking, managers should take several steps:

- They should experiment with several metaphors as explanations, each of which might add to their understanding.
- They should recognize that an event or outcome may have more than one cause.
- Because a defining characteristic of insights is that they take us by surprise, the manager should go against what appear to be more probable causes to consider their opposites.

- Managers should assess candidate causal chains by the number and strength of their links; longer chains generally are less probable.
- Finally, managers should generate and test alternative explanations rather than simply settling on the first or seemingly most likely one.

Each of these steps can strengthen causal reasoning, enabling managers to learn more from past performance.

Reviewing past performance also connects planning market strategy with performance review. It establishes accountability for accomplishing the course of action in the prior market plan. Managers should provide explanations, supported by data, for significant variances between planned and achieved results. Reviewing past performance can also pinpoint problematic goal or objective setting and resource allocation. Overly ambitious goals or objectives that managers continually miss can cause dispirited performance and a growing disregard for taking goals or objectives seriously. Rather than working together to devise an ambitious yet achievable course of action, successive layers of management instead engage in game playing that wastes a valuable but often unaccounted-for resource: management time.[48]

Gather Essential Market Information

To build knowledge and reduce uncertainty, supplier firms must gather market information. Because managers' market views significantly affect the kinds of information they seek and use, they must challenge their market views using a variety of market information to forestall becoming market myopic.[49] We outline what we regard as essential market information for planning market strategy in business markets in Box 4.2. This market information would seem vital for meaningful discussions of alternative courses of actions to pursue, yet most businesses lack some of this information. Certainly additional kinds of market information would be useful to know, such as the identification of **lead-users** and **leap-froggers**—progressive firms whose present strong needs will become widespread in a market months or years in the future.[50]

BOX 4.2

Market Information Essentials for Strategic Market Planning in Business Markets

1. Alternative ways of segmenting the market that give the firm some leverage
2. Estimates of the size and growth of each market segment presently and potentially served
3. The distribution of estimates of the firm's share of customer's business for each market segment
4. Estimates of the value of the product offering and the value of the augmenting services for each market segment
5. Two or three strengths and two or three weaknesses where actionable improvements would significantly affect customer's perceptions of the firm's performance
6. Knowledge of the firm's most- and least-profitable products, and most- and least-profitable customer groups

We discussed gathering the kinds of market information in Box 4.2 in Chapter 2 as part of market sensing. We build on this earlier discussion here with a few comments related to crafting market strategy. Gaining estimates of the supplier's share of customer's business may not be easy, yet with some persistence and imagination it can be done. Box 4.3 recounts the experience of Dell India and how share of customer's business can produce insights for market strategy.

BOX 4.3
Dell India Researches Its Share of Customer's Business

Dell India Pvt. Ltd. is the Indian subsidiary of Dell Inc. that is headquartered in Austin, Texas. Dell India Pvt. Ltd. was incorporated in the year 1996 and began operations in 2000 from Bengaluru. With the growth of the IT and ITES segments in India as well as the overall growth in the GDP of the country, Dell India Pvt. Ltd. became an aggressive player in the Indian markets. The company has a manufacturing plant in Sri Perumbudur, near Chennai in Tamil Nadu, and sources some products from Penang in Malaysia. The annual revenues of the Dell India Pvt. Ltd. are currently about INR 4,600 crores.

At a broad level, Dell India Pvt. Ltd. segments its customers on the basis of size of the customer. A proxy for size of customer is number of employees. Accordingly, there are four segments of customers: large enterprises; public enterprises and the education segment, comprising mostly public sector enterprises; small and medium enterprises, typically having less than 400 employees; and, finally, the consumer segment having individual consumers. The large enterprises are further subdivided into large commercial accounts (LCA) with employee headcount of over 1,500; preferred accounts division (PAD) with an employee base of 400–1,500; and global customers, which are global companies with whom Dell has a global contract.

Another basis on which Dell India segments its customers is using share of wallet (SOW), that is, percentage of customer's purchases of relevant products and services that are awarded to Dell India. Dell classifies those accounts where it enjoys less than 10% SOW as acquisition accounts. Accounts where the SOW is between 10 and 50% are called development accounts, while those where Dell India enjoys a SOW of more than 50% are called retention accounts.

The above customer segmentation has been done on the basis of customer size as well as share of wallet (SOW). Therefore, it would be appropriate to analyze relationship-specific offerings based on both these classifications. There are about 4,500 customers in the B2B space in India. A comprehensive database is constructed classifying these customers based on SOW. The different segments enjoy different relationships with Dell India and are therefore addressed accordingly.

Acquisition customers, where Dell India enjoys a SOW of 10% or less, include non-customers of Dell, that is, where Dell has no presence. There are several challenges for Dell India with these accounts. The incumbent vendor is typically a competitor like HP India, Lenovo, Acer or HCL. These vendors have well-established relationships with the customer, making it difficult for new entry by another vendor. Therefore, unless the new vendor comes up with a "shattering value proposition" or competes on price, entry is very difficult. Another challenge is customer inertia. These customers are often happy with the incumbent vendor and therefore see little or no reason to shift. Salespersons of the new

BOX 4.3
Continued

vendor most often have to attempt a foot-in-the-door (FITD) approach to gain entry.

In order to address the challenges from its acquisition customers, Dell India runs several marketing promotions, seminars and targeted direct mailers to build awareness of Dell's product line. Customers who see value in Dell's offerings initiate talks with it by responding to the company's marketing efforts. Dell India attempts to show customers the value that they would get by dealing with it. Acquisition customers are generally hard to please. However, with the right kind of customer, Dell India has indeed built strong collaborative relationships. A significant proportion of these customers manifest a "buying orientation," at least initially.

The second category is development customers, with whom Dell India enjoys SOW between 10 and 50%. In order to maintain/improve the SOW, Dell India seeks to improve its penetration into these accounts. There is also an attempt to build long-term relationships with these customers. The nature of relationships and challenges in this segment are many and varied. For instance, Dell may or may not be the major supplier to these accounts. If Dell India only has 15% SOW, the challenges will be similar to those faced by acquisition customers. Several of these relationships may still be transactional in nature, where price becomes the only point of discussion. Development of these accounts requires significant upfront allocation of resources by Dell, with no guarantee of success in terms of increased SOW. A significant attempt is made by Dell India to offer relationship-based offerings to these customers. Although transactional relationships exist even in this segment, every attempt is made to move the customer into a more collaborative relationship.

The final category of customers is termed retention customers. Dell India enjoys more than 50% SOW of these customers. From the perspective of Dell India, these accounts have their own unique challenges. There is a threat of other vendors like HP, Lenovo, etc., pricing their products very aggressively to these accounts to take business away from Dell India. Additionally, these customers expect very high levels of service in return for the high SOW that Dell India gets from them. Since Dell enjoys preferred-vendor status with retention customers, it becomes imperative to sustain collaborative relationships by constantly ensuring "customer delight." A large part of the relationship involves creating superior value and sharing it mutually, which requires Dell to continually come up with innovative solutions.

Contributed by R. Kiran, Participant, PGSEM Program, Indian Institute of Management Bangalore.

Understanding strengths as well as weaknesses is critical for making changes consistent with different market strategies. Business marketing sage Irwin Gross contended, "Firms buy from you for what you are good at, and despite what you are bad at; for firms that do not buy from you, it is exactly the reverse." So, suppliers that pursue a **defensive market strategy**—one aimed at retaining present customers—may choose to strengthen what are already strengths. In contrast, suppliers that pursue an **offensive market strategy**—one aimed at gaining new customers—must remedy weaknesses that have kept firms from doing business with them. Of course, the firm also may craft a market strategy that represents a composite of both.

Profitability of market offerings and customer groups is something that most firms find difficult to know. It requires accurate tracking of the actual price the firm realizes from each market offering and customer transaction. It also requires an activity-based costing system that accurately conveys the costs of producing and providing the products and augmenting services, programs, and systems to particular customers.[51] Yet, even when the firm has this market information, it will need further research to understand the market strategy implications. It needs to understand what firms are purchasing the least-profitable and most-profitable market offerings, and for what applications they are using them. Isolating applications of most-profitable customers can suggest targeting of other firms with that application and comparable customer characteristics. Least-profitable products may be providing completeness of product line, which resellers and customers value overall, and that prevent potential competitor inroads.

Supplier firms that are in dynamic markets may argue that they do not have the time to gather much market information because it will slow their decision making. It is natural for these firms to be concerned about "paralysis by analysis," yet they must balance it against "extinction by instinct"![52] Interestingly, management practice research on firms in dynamic markets has found that fast-decision-making firms use as much or more information compared to their slow-decision-making counterparts.[53] The crucial difference is in the kind of information:

> Slow decision makers rely on planning and futuristic information. They spend time tracking the likely path of technologies, markets, or competitor actions, and then develop plans. In contrast, the fast decision makers look to real time information—that is, information about current operations and current environment which is reported with little or no time lag. . . . They prefer indicators such as bookings, backlog, margins, engineering milestones, cash, scrap, and work-in-progress to more refined, accounting-based measures such as profitability. . . . Fast decision makers also relay to each other external real time information such as new product introductions by competitors, competition at key accounts, and technical developments within the industry.[54]

So, it appears that fast decision makers use internal and market information to construct more elaborate market views, which they update frequently. This practice enables them to react quickly to changing events in the market.

Many firms use a **situation assessment** as a mechanism for pulling together market information and internal knowledge. Situation assessments typically consider the marketplace (customers and environment), competitors, and internal resources and capabilities. A critical aspect is for a firm to recognize the assumptions it implicitly makes about each of these areas. Comparisons of internal resources and capabilities with those of competitors define strengths and weaknesses, and comparisons of competitors with the marketplace define opportunities and threats. Situation assessments must be based upon market data and information, not simply managers' beliefs and opinions, to be worthwhile.

Construct Scenarios

When firms have considerable uncertainty about their markets, they find scenario analysis more useful than traditional forecasting.[55] A **scenario** is a plausible representation of a firm's possible future, where the pertinent factors basic to the representation relate to one another in a consistent way. A scenario analysis consists of multiple scenarios that portray provocatively different futures that, taken together, compel managers to contemplate the main forces driving the market, their interrelationships, and the crucial uncertainties. To keep from overwhelming managers, the number of scenarios should be limited to four or fewer.

Scenario analysis should cause managers to challenge their market views. In thinking through the set of scenarios, they should attempt to specify critical **milestones** or **signposts**, that signal whether a given scenario likely will, or will not, occur. The Royal Dutch/Shell Group has used scenario analysis to spur institutional learning. It provides scenarios as written cases in management games, where it challenges groups of managers to explore the question: "What will we do if this happens?" Shell has found that such games significantly accelerate institutional learning.

What Do We Want to *Accomplish*?

We want to emphasize the word *accomplish* in this question. We mean this not only in the sense of what the business wants to attain, but that if it does, it will provide a sense of accomplishment or fulfillment for the individuals responsible for achieving it. And, when the business prospers, the individuals who have collectively worked to produce it feel that they, not just senior management, will share in it.[56]

The length of time that firms consider in answering, "What do we want to accomplish?" will vary. A three- or five-year planning horizon for a market strategy is the most common. Often, the firm updates the plan yearly, with the first year of the plan serving as the firm's operating plan. In rapidly changing markets, such a long planning horizon may make little sense. The chief executive of a software firm once remarked that the market window—from idea to commercialization—for a new software program in his segment was six months. In such situations, answering the question "What do we want to accomplish?" might have a one-year horizon, with the firm revisiting the question each quarter.

The firm has more than one course of action that it might pursue. Business market managers should act as catalysts in structuring the market strategy alternatives and engaging the management team and their respective functional areas in a dialogue about them. Figure 4.2 shows how a management team can argue the alternatives, yet still get along. Rather than considering alternatives sequentially, the firm should work through multiple alternatives simultaneously. This approach promotes faster decision making, as comparative analysis sharpens preferences, builds confidence that a superior alternative has not been overlooked, and provides a better fallback position when the first alternative does not work out. By basing their arguments on market knowledge rather than opinion, the management team minimizes interpersonal conflict, which motivates team members to contribute ideas more freely. In reaching a decision on the market strategy alternative to pursue, the firm should use **consensus with qualification**, which means the management team attempts to reach a shared agreement. When agreement is not possible, the general manager and the senior marketing manager make the choice.[57]

The market strategy that the firm wants to accomplish begins with targeting. After selecting target market segments and customer firms to focus on, the firms

Figure 4.2 How Teams Argue but Still Get Along

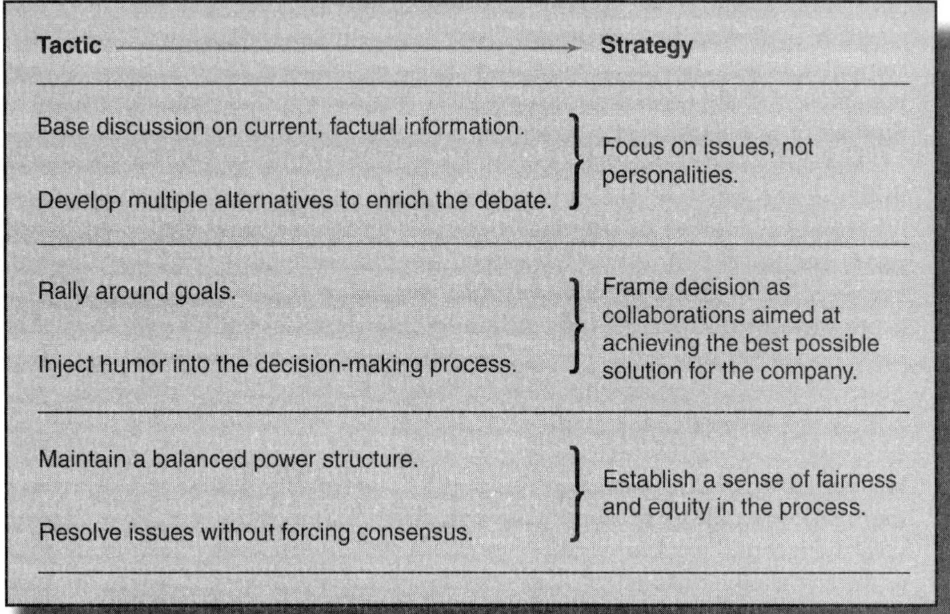

Tactic →	Strategy
Base discussion on current, factual information. Develop multiple alternatives to enrich the debate.	Focus on issues, not personalities.
Rally around goals. Inject humor into the decision-making process.	Frame decision as collaborations aimed at achieving the best possible solution for the company.
Maintain a balanced power structure. Resolve issues without forcing consensus.	Establish a sense of fairness and equity in the process.

Source: Kathleen M. Eisenhardt, Jean L. Kahwajy, and L. H. Bourgeois III, "How Management Teams Can Have a Good Fight," *Harvard Business Review* (July–August 1997): 82.

establish goals and objectives. Management also thinks through positioning and customer value propositions and, increasingly, brand building to decide what the firm wants to accomplish.

Targeting

Targeting refers to selecting particular market segments and customer firms that the supplier firm will focus its resources on serving. That is not to say that the firm will not sell to other market segments or customer firms, but instead, targeting specifies which segments and customer firms are of particular interest. As we mentioned in the chapter overview, collaboration among the various functions is essential when pinpointing the market segments and customers that the firm will target. As part of this targeting activity, each functional area should decide what constitutes its ordinary performance, and what it is prepared to do as extraordinary performance. Then, with the business market manager acting as a catalyst, the functional areas should collectively decide under what circumstances and for what customer firms they will provide each, and what they expect in return. For example, extraordinary performance may be extended to relatively important customers as standard in return for a larger share of the customer's business. For other customers, the firm may offer this extraordinary performance as an option and charge for it.

A firm may target particular market segments or customer firms for different reasons. Firms with a business-market management perspective will focus on segments and customers where value assessments demonstrate that their offerings provide superior value. They also target promising country markets for market development efforts. Expanding abroad allows a firm to leverage and deepen its strategic position.[58] As we discussed in Chapter 1, Indian SME automobile component manufacturers target narrow product markets, while achieving economies of scale, serving global markets. Firms also prefer to target growing segments and customer firms, because "a high tide raises all ships."

Finally, firms might target segments and customers for purposes of learning. That is, serving these markets or customers will build the firms' knowledge and capabilities in ways that are valuable elsewhere. As an example, Boeing Company's participation in the military aircraft segment enables it to develop cutting-edge design and production knowledge and know-how, which it then can use to sustain its market leadership in the commercial aircraft segment.

Setting Goals and Objectives

We use **goals** to refer to the longer-term, strategic directions that the firm pursues, which often are imprecisely stated or qualitative. Jeff Immelt, CEO of General Electric, has set the goal that GE will have organic revenue growth that is two to three times world GDP.[59] In contrast, we use **objectives** to refer to the near-term, more measurable standards that a firm uses to judge whether it achieved what it wanted to accomplish during a specific time period. In this way, objectives serve as milestones that enable the firm to chart its progress in attaining its goals. A firm pursues its strategic intent in this way, by broadly specifying the path to achieving it, and then establishing intermediate milestones and review mechanisms to track progress.

The business must specify measures that correspond to its objectives (and goals) or that signal the extent to which the firm has accomplished the market and financial performance it envisioned. Examples of informative measures of market performance include increased share of customer's total requirements by market segment (supplier share of customer's business), number of new customers by market segment, and sales of new products by market segment. Examples of informative measures of financial performance include segment contribution, customer contribution to profitability, and incremental revenues from optional, value-adding services.

Progressive firms should look at cash flow as a measure that bridges market performance and financial performance. Marketplace initiatives can accelerate and enhance cash flows, reduce their volatility and vulnerability, and enhance their long-term residual value. Cash flow is a critical measure of financial performance for a firm, as financial markets often use the net present value of cash flows as an indicator of shareholder value. Related to this, senior management at Siemens, for example, is compensated largely on the basis of accomplishing Economic Value Added (EVA®) objectives, which reflect the extent to which net operating profits after tax exceed the cost of capital employed.[60]

Successive layers of management translate the business's market goals and objectives into group and individual goals and objectives. Some firms use the **balanced scorecard**, which assesses customer, financial, internal business process, and learning and growth performance, as a mechanism to accomplish this.[61] Research has found that one of the best ways to gain superior cross-functional cooperation is to have some objectives, and rewards for accomplishing them, at the broader level of the cross-functional unit.[62] Even within the marketing and sales functional area, shared objectives and rewards significantly improve coordination. Also, senior management must prioritize and consider linkage implications among the objectives that the firm sets. For example, gaining new customers and lowering the cost of sales as a percentage of total sales most often have a negative linkage because getting new customers typically requires a number of sales calls before the first sale.

Often, significant slippage or disconnects occur between stated objectives and the measures that the firm uses for performance review and reward. Predictably, individuals in the workforce seek to excel on these measures, with business performance on the objectives falling short. This situation was captured in the title of a classic management article, "On the Folly of Rewarding A, While Hoping for B."[63] An often-occurring example in business markets is the folly of rewarding salespeople on revenue or volume, while hoping for profitability. Even in instances where some measure of offering or customer profitability is a part of the salesperson review and reward system, its weighting relative to revenue or volume measures often is insufficient to focus salesperson actions on profitability over volume or revenue. To remedy this problem, tighter linkages are needed between what senior management wants to happen and the measures that they put in place to evaluate the performance of the individuals who are responsible for accomplishing those objectives.[64]

Finally, the firm should set goals and objectives for learning about the marketplace. For example, a goal the firm might want to accomplish is to become and remain the industry leader in knowledge about customer requirements and preferences, and how they are changing. Setting learning goals and objectives should trigger the commitment of resources and specification of mechanisms for learning. The firm might increase the number of customer value assessments and market experiments that it conducts. Having goals and objectives for market learning also causes the firm to rethink the meaning of, and how it regards, failure. Even though initiatives fall short of their financial or market objectives, they might be strong contributors to the firm's learning and subsequent market success.[65] Each time the firm engages in planning, it wants to be better equipped to answer the question, "What do we know?" than it was previously.

Positioning in Business Markets

Positioning in business markets is absolutely critical for success, because it provides the conceptual cornerstone for constructing and managing marketing offerings (the topic of Chapter 5). By involving managers from all the relevant functional areas in the positioning process, at least to some extent, the creation and assessment of positioning statements provide a means of forging shared understanding of what the supplier is seeking to accomplish in the market. It puts into sharper focus which firms the supplier regards as the relatively important customers, what the supplier wants to emphasize about the market offering, and what promise the supplier is making to customers about the value they will receive. Everyone in the supplier's workforce ought to have a good grasp on these issues.

However, positioning is often either neglected or poorly understood by suppliers. Many managers think of positioning statements as just something that the marketing folks do to create business marketing communications, missing their potential contribution to superior business performance. The practice of positioning also is hindered, perhaps, by the lack of any generally accepted definition of positioning. For our purposes, **positioning** is the process of establishing (and sustaining) an intended meaning for a market offering in the minds of targeted customers.

Writing a positioning statement is the central element of the positioning process. Although guidance varies on writing positioning statements, the critical components are target, offering concept, and value proposition. The **target** component succinctly characterizes the specific type of customers for the market offering that are of most interest to the supplier. For example, "itinerant, Generation-X professionals" might be specified as the target for some advanced, intelligent network telephone services, such as single-number reach. The **offering concept** component specifies the essential attributes of the market offering for the selected target, out of the potentially larger set of attributes that an offering might possess. Because of its growing significance in business markets, we next discuss value proposition in greater detail.

Customer Value Propositions

Customer value proposition has become one of the most widely used terms in business markets in recent years. Yet, management practice research reveals that despite its growing use, there is little specificity or agreement as to what constitutes a customer value proposition or what makes one persuasive. From this management practice research, we can classify the substantially different ways managers use the term *customer value proposition* into three, basic alternatives. We provide these alternatives in Figure 4.3 and organize our exposition of them to address four fundamental questions that distinguish the alternatives from one another:[66]

- What does the value proposition consist of?
- What customer question is the supplier attempting to answer with the value proposition?
- What is required for a supplier to construct the value proposition and have the sales force deliver it?
- What is a potential pitfall of the value proposition?

We first consider the **All Benefits** customer value proposition, where supplier managers simply list all the potential benefits they believe that their offering might deliver to targeted customers. The more they can think of, the better. Management practice research has found that this is the meaning that supplier managers most frequently attach to the term. The explanation for its relatively frequent use is that it requires the least knowledge about customers and competitors and, thus, is the least demanding to construct.

Yet, this ease of listing all benefits has the potential pitfall of *benefit assertion:* claiming benefits for the offering that it does not actually deliver to target customers. Another pitfall of the All Benefits proposition is that many, if not most, of the benefits may be points of parity with the next-best alternative, diluting the effect of the few remaining points of difference. Recall from Chapter 2 our discussion of points of parity, points of difference, and points of contention.

Figure 4.3 Value Propositions in Business Markets: Which Alternative Conveys Value to Customers?

Value Proposition:	All Benefits	Favorable Points-of-Difference	Resonating Focus
Consists of:	All benefits customers receive from a market offering	All favorable points-of-difference a market offering has relative to the next-best alternative	The one or two points-of-difference (and, perhaps, a point-of-parity) whose improvement will deliver the greatest value to the customer for the foreseeable future
Answers the customer question:	"Why should our firm purchase your offering?"	"Why should our firm purchase your offering instead of your competitor's?"	"What is *most* worthwhile for our firm to keep in mind about your offering?"
Requires:	Knowledge of own market offering	Knowledge of own market offering and next best alternative offering	Knowledge of how own market offering delivers superior value to customers, compared to next-best-alternative offering
Has the potential pitfall:	Benefit assertion	Value presumption	Requires customer value research

Source: James C. Anderson, James A. Narus, and Wouter van Rossum, "Customer Value Propositions in Business Markets," *Harvard Business Review* (March 2006): 93.

The second customer value proposition, **Favorable Points of Difference**, explicitly recognizes that the customer has an alternative. The recent experience of a leading industrial gas supplier underscores this distinction. It received a request for proposal (RFP) from a customer for a major piece of business stating that the two or three suppliers that could demonstrate the most persuasive value propositions in their proposals would be invited in one month to visit the supplier and discuss and refine their proposals. After this meeting, the customer would select a supplier for this business. As this disguised example illustrates, "Why should our firm purchase your offering instead of your competitor's?" is a more pertinent question than "Why should our firm purchase your offering?" This question focuses supplier managers on differentiating their offering from the next-best alternative, which requires more detailed knowledge of it. A characteristic that the Favorable Points of Difference proposition shares with the All Benefits proposition, though, is that more is regarded as better. So, supplier managers strive to list as many favorable points of difference as they can.

Knowing that an offering element is a point of difference relative to the next-best alternative does not, however, convey what the *value* of this difference is to target customers. Further, a supplier's market offering may have several points of difference relative to the next-best alternative, complicating understanding of which of them delivers the greatest value to target customers. Without a detailed understanding of the customer's requirements and preferences, and what it is worth to fulfill them, suppliers may stress points of difference that deliver relatively little value to the target customer. Each of these can lead to the potential pitfall of *value presumption:* assuming that favorable points of difference must be valuable for the customer.

Although a Favorable Points of Difference proposition is preferable to an All Benefits proposition, we recommend that business market managers adopt the third customer value proposition alternative, **Resonating Focus**. Our rationale is that in a business world where customer managers are taking on greater responsibility and are increasingly pressed for time, to be successful, suppliers must deliver customer value propositions that are simple, yet powerfully captivating. They do this by making their offerings superior on the few elements whose functionality or performance matter most to target customers, demonstrate and document the value of this superior performance, and communicate it to target customer managers in a way that conveys to them that the supplier understands their business concerns and priorities. The Resonating Focus customer value proposition consists of the one or two points of difference, and perhaps a point of parity, whose improvement will deliver the greatest value to target customers for the foreseeable future.

The Resonating Focus proposition differs from the All Favorable Points of Difference proposition in two significant respects. First, more is not better. Although a supplier's offering may possess other favorable points of difference relative to the next-best alternative, the Resonating Focus proposition steadfastly concentrates on the one or two points of difference that deliver, and whose improvement will continue to deliver, the greatest value to target customers. To better leverage limited resources, a supplier might even cede to the next-best alternative previous favorable points of difference that customers value the least, so that the supplier can concentrate its resources on improving the one or two points of difference customers value most. Second, the Resonating Focus proposition may contain a point of parity. This occurs either when the point of parity is required for target customers even to consider the supplier's offering or when a point of contention, where the next-best alternative was thought to be superior but customer value research reveals it is not, is resolved in the supplier's favor.

To give practical meaning to the Resonating Focus value proposition, let's consider an example. Sonoco Products Company, a global packaging supplier headquartered in Hartsville, South Carolina, approached a large European customer, a maker of consumer packaged goods, about redesigning the packaging for one of its product lines. In this case, the next-best alternative was the present packaging that Sonoco was supplying. Although the redesigned packaging provided six favorable points of difference relative to the next-best alternative, Sonoco choose to emphasize one point of parity and two points of difference in its Resonating Focus value proposition, which it terms a *Differentiated Value Proposition* (DVP). Its value proposition to the customer was that the redesigned packaging would: have the same price as the present packaging, but deliver significantly greater manufacturing efficiency in the customer's fill-lines through higher-speed closing, and provide a distinctive look that consumers would find more appealing than the present packaging.

Sonoco chose to include a point of parity in its value proposition because, in this case, the customer would not even consider a packaging redesign if the price went up. The first point of difference in the value proposition delivered cost savings to the customer, allowing it to move from a seven-day, three-shift production schedule during peak times to a two-shift, five-day operation. The second point of difference in the value proposition delivered an advantage at the consumer level, helping the customer to incrementally grow its revenues and profits. In persuading the customer to change to the redesigned packaging, Sonoco did not neglect to mention the other favorable points of difference. Rather, it chose to place much greater emphasis on the one point of parity and the two points of difference that mattered most to the customer, thereby delivering a value proposition with resonating focus.

Resonating focus value propositions have the potential pitfall of *requiring customer value research*, which is necessary to provide the insights to construct them. Despite all of the talk about customer value, few suppliers have actually done customer value research. Customer value research is not easy, though, requiring time, effort, persistence, and some creativity. Yet, as the experience of a leading supplier of distributor and logistics services amply illustrates in the accompanying Box 4.4, doing customer value research may actually transform a commoditized offering into resonating focus.

Management practice research suggests that resonating focus customer value propositions can make a significant contribution to superior business performance.

BOX 4.4
Customer Value Research by Gati Transforms a Commoditized Offering into Resonating Focus

The distribution and logistics services catering to business markets in India are typically viewed by customers as being commoditized, with price as the primary determinant for choosing a logistics provider. However, as this example illustrates, there are exceptions. Gati, a leader in express cargo delivery and a pioneer in distribution and supply chain management solutions in India since 1989, has always been focused on providing value-added services. One of the primary sectors Gati operates is in the industrial/wholesale industry. It is fast changing and driven by consumer demand. Increased speed, reduced costs, more accurate fulfillment and value-added services are requirements that customers increasingly demand of their logistics service providers. Gati has focused on shortened lead time of its deliveries and provides real-time control and visibility of tracking each delivery.

The solution Gati provided to one of its customers, IFTEX Oil & Chemicals Ltd. (IFTEX), effectively illustrates how the company created a resonating focus in a commoditized industry. IFTEX is a market leader in manufacturing a wide range of petroleum additives for lubricating oils and fuels, high-performance lubricating oils for industrial/automobile/marine use, and coolants.

IFTEX wanted to have an end-to-end solution from its logistics provider, which could meet multiple requirements: pan-India presence, handling all sales tax-related matters in multiple states, delivery of its products to various petrol stations in the country, handling payment collection from customers and ensuring rapid realization of the money through local banks, online inventory visibility, single-window end-to-end solution, cost-effectiveness, and rapid customer order fulfillment through a very effective warehousing and distribution system.

Gati approached the problem by first identifying the key areas where it could provide value. It started the diagnostic process by using direct survey questions and field value-in-use assessment. The process included site visits, conducting interviews

BOX 4.4
Continued

and administering questionnaires. Along with assessing value directly, Gati carried out Strengths, Weaknesses, Opportunities, and Threats (SWOT) analysis of the entire IFTEX supply chain. These two research approaches helped Gati to identify areas which would provide customers with maximum value.

After conducting its initial diagnosis, Gati explored various supply chain options. They proposed a Supply Chain Model by first conducting a detailed audit and process mapping of the existing system. This led Gati to identify the process changes required, which resulted in a new model and strategies. Finally, new logistics options were explored, with a complete cost-benefit analysis done for each.

After conducting the initial analysis based on value assessment methods and exploring various options, Gati focused on translating the business issue into a project. It conducted a meeting with the customer to share the findings of customer value research and discuss points of parity and points of difference. This was followed by several steps such as mapping of critical processes, root cause analysis of existing problem areas, etc., which were undertaken to design a new re-engineered system. A comprehensive implementation plan covering people issues, investments to be made, and the benefits that would be derived from the new system was then presented to the customer. In this manner, Gati provided the customer a strong value proposition including several elements that were very important to the customer: an effective and responsive distribution network, more storage locations, more shelf space, minimum investment by the customer, standardized execution at all customer locations, and more proximate availability of inventory to the locations where the products are required.

Based on the above comprehensive approach and a deep understanding of customer needs, Gati provided IFTEX with a comprehensive end-to-end solution by supplying 100 square feet of warehousing space in each of 21 different cities. It assigned dedicated manpower to IFTEX and provided the customer with a shared information system and communication support. In addition, Gati implemented a Web-based software system, which helped implement superior order processing and capability to manage product returns better. It assigned an all-India co-coordinator at Mumbai and implemented centralized billing facilities. The daily MIS reporting helped in effective tracking of all consignments.

Gati's focus on customer value assessment enabled it to demonstrate the superior value it provided to IFTEX. Based on this, it implemented value-based pricing to derive equitable return for the superior value it delivers to the customer. Gati's solution resulted not only in reduced cost to the customer but also improved the performance of the supply chain and better profitability to Gati. The keys to their continued success include the ongoing practice of anticipating customer needs and competitor moves, examining the performance of the supply chain with a view to find drastic improvements, and eliminating processes that do not add customer value.

Contributed by Abhishek Khandelwal, Ananth Chandramouli, Prasanna Venkatesh Srinivasan, Puneet Arora, and Radha Rani Kizhanattam, Participants, EPGP Program, Indian Institute of Management Bangalore. *Sources:* Subrata Misra, "A Survey of the Third-Party Logistics (3PL) Service Providers in India," case study developed for IIM Calcutta in 2005; Report on Indian Logistics Sector by Goldman Sachs, May 2008.

We contend that properly constructed value propositions should serve as a "guiding beacon" (or touchstone) to direct all that a business does in its provision of a market offering to a targeted market segment. Thus, for example, the general manager of a business unit should be able to rely on a value proposition to guide decisions among conflicting tugs and pulls within the organization on how to further develop a market offering. In doing so, the general manager focuses scarce resources on making the offering outstanding on the few elements that targeted customers value most and would be willing to reward the supplier for providing.

Building Brands in Business Markets

Establishing and building their brands is something that managers in business markets increasingly seek to accomplish. They believe that by adapting the concepts and practices of their counterparts in consumer markets to the business-to-business setting, they can build brand equity and benefit from it. To guide their thinking about brand building, managers in business markets have been advised to ask, answer, and act on the following questions:[67]

- How does the brand strategy support our business strategy?
- What is our aspirational brand identity, and what do we need to do to get there?
- What value proposition is most valuable to our customers?
- How do I align my organization to make the brand and value proposition a reality?

Managers in business markets should meaningfully answer each of these questions and put responsive action plans into place prior to pursuing a brand-building initiative.

Some special considerations apply in building brands in business markets, as contrasted with consumer markets. Kevin Lane Keller, an expert in strategic brand management, offers the following additional guidelines for business markets:[68]

1. Adopt a corporate or family branding strategy and create a well-defined brand hierarchy.
2. Link non-product-related imagery associations.
3. Employ a full range of marketing communication options.
4. Leverage equity of other companies that are customers.
5. Segment markets carefully and develop tailored branding and marketing programs.

The non-product-related imagery associations refer to social benefits, such as "peace of mind" and "ease of doing business," which tend to be difficult to estimate in monetary terms. Nonetheless, they can affect customer managers' purchase decisions, especially when taken together with demonstration in monetary terms of the technical, economic, and service benefits a brand delivers. The brand also conveys other value placeholders, which contribute value but whose worth in monetary terms is not estimated in a customer value model.

Building a strong brand in business markets is critical whenever and wherever customer managers believe that formal assessments of value delivered are not worthwhile. In these instances, brand may serve as the sole basis for purchase. As an example, customer managers may feel that it is not worthwhile to conduct a formal value assessment for repositionable sticky notes and instead simply purchase 3M Post-it Notes, even if the price for them is slightly higher than lesser-known or generic brands.

The value proposition for a market offering serves as the cornerstone for brand building in business markets. What is the relationship of the value proposition to the customer value models we advocate in Chapter 2? The customer value model has the intent of estimating the worth in monetary terms of the points of difference and points of contention between the supplier's brand and the next-best-alternative offering in the minds of targeted customers. As noted in the previous discussion of value propositions, although a number of points of difference and points of contention may have positive estimates, we advise managers in business markets to focus on the one or two that have the most value to the target customer firms. And, at times when it is critical to establish comparable performance on some value element, a point of parity is added to complete the value proposition. Brand building for a market offering then would encompass devoting resources to significantly improve functionality or performance on those elements, demonstrating and documenting success in this with customer value management, and persuasively communicating this progress to target customers.

Building the corporate brand is of paramount importance in business markets in that it positions the firm or business unit in the minds of present and prospective customer firms. As we noted previously in our discussion of brands as resources, investments in building the corporate brand can provide dividends in brand building for specific market offerings. Building the corporate brand also can guide and energize the actions of the supplier's workforce in attaining the desired corporate brand identity.[69] The experience of Infosys in building its corporate brand, which we relate in Box 4.5, provides an outstanding case study.

BOX 4.5
Building the Infosys Brand

Infosys has never brought out a single major advertising campaign in India and yet receives frequent attention from various TV channels. It is the first brand that comes to mind when the Indian IT industry is mentioned. Infosys's brand value is about INR 310 billion. Clearly, Infosys seems to have done something right.

Infosys has always tried to stand out from the crowd, and this is probably the reason why the brand is highly remembered. One of its earliest initiatives in brand building was through employee recruitment. In advertisements placed in various newspapers, Infosys focused on ethics, integrity, and intellect, rather than on technical skills or certifications.

Other innovative ideas like giving away one-third of the company's equity as employee stock options (ESOPS); the large sprawling campus in Bengaluru and subsequently its learning center at Mysore, which is the world's largest learning facility for any corporation; the listing of Infosys on the NASDAQ as a sign of global arrival of the Indian IT Industry are some of the ways in which Infosys has succeeded in effective yet non-traditional brand building.

The CEOs of the company over the years have been no less instrumental in enhancing Infosys' brand. Chairman Narayan Murthy's life story, starting the company with his modest savings and taking the company through thick and thin, is no less than a modern-day fairy tale. It is the famous rags-to-riches story, which has ignited the imagination of India's youth. Co-founder Nandan Nilekani has

(continued)

contributed in his own way by increasing Infosys's visibility around the globe. Another method of brand building is through charity work carried out by Mrs. Sudha Murthy, the Chairman's wife, and other employees of Infosys through the Infosys Foundation. Infosys has also initiated partnerships with various universities around the world and even instituted awards like the Wharton Infosys Business Transformation Award which have only helped strengthen the brand.

Infosys won the Sharpening Brand and Competitive Differentiation Marketing Excellence Award from the Information Technology Services Marketing Association (ITSMA), USA, for its "Flat World" branding exercise. This was an initiative wherein Infosys wanted to communicate to its clients that it was not just another IT services and solutions provider, but rather its customers' business partner.

According to Mr. V. Balakrishna, Infosys' CFO, "Today, Infosys is known as one of the top notch global service providers in the world, and I think we've built a solid brand because of that. Our brand counsel meets regularly to take stock of what else we can do to enhance brand value. We don't feel we need to spend a large amount of money to build our brand. Rather, we do things like leverage our association with the Flat World Theme, engage deeply at the World Economic Forum, and work with universities around the world to improve their facilities and curricula." Infosys focuses on earning the respect of all its stakeholders. According to Mr. Aditya Nath Jha, Associate VP & Head (Branding), Infosys Technologies, "It is about doing the unusual thing, about staking a position in the market place, or in the minds of the employee, and then reinforcing that image. The branding exercise has been and will continue to be a priority for Infosys."

The "Win in the Flat World" initiative came from in-depth research of the changing business landscape. These changes resulted from opening of emerging economies, structural shifts in demographics, and ubiquity of technology and regulation. The companies listed in Global 2000 were looking for partners who could help them deal with the new business landscape. Infosys became just that—a partner offering a unique solutions portfolio. Infosys spent an estimated INR 460 million on this exercise worldwide, especially in those countries where it had a huge customer base. However, hardly anything was spent on brand building in India. As expected, its revenues and brand value increased dramatically as a result of this initiative. In fact, it can be stated that Infosys owes a large part of its success to its brand.

Contributed by Rajiv Motwani, Participant, PGSEM Program, Indian Institute of Management Bangalore. *Sources:* "Infosys Wins Marketing Award," *Dance with Shadows*, 21 November 2007, *http://www.dancewithshadows.com/tech/infosys-award.asp*; Shailesh Dobhal and Bhanu Pande, "Infosys Plans Brand Makeover, 18 July 2006, *The Economic Times*, *http://economictimes.indiatimes.com/articleshow/1767929.cms*; "Using Thought Leadership In Brand Building," *http://www.prayagextranet.com/document/confluence_final/confluence/vol2/pra_best_practices2.htm*; "Capitalizing on Globalization: CFO Strategies For Winning in a Flat World," *http://www.infosys.com/flat-world/usiness/documents/leveraging-local-talent.pdf*; Shivani Shinde, "TCS, Wipro, Infosys Increase Investments For Branding," 28 August 2007, *http://www.rediff.com/money/2007/aug/28brand.htm*; "Infosys Technologies wins ITSMA Marketing Excellence Diamond Award," 15 November 2007, Prdomain Business Register, *http://www.prdomain.com/companies/I/Infosys/newsreleases/2007111649054.htm*.

How Will We Do It?

This question is about thinking through implementation of the market strategy. Businesses can propose the most wonderful-sounding market strategies, but if they lack the requisite knowledge, skills, and abilities to put them into play, little will be accomplished.[70] Just as market strategy informs and guides implementation, implementation considerations should inform and guide the generation of market strategy. It is in answering the question, "How will we do it?" that the business develops action plans, designs sales and marketing programs, takes stock of its implementation skills, and prepares for learning and adapting.

Develop an Action Plan

An **action plan** translates the market strategy into the coordinated activities and specific resources the firm will use to attain what it wants to accomplish. It spells out the set of programs the firm will implement and mechanisms for coordinating them so that the firm best leverages its resources. Central to this task is gaining input from each functional area in the construction of the programs that affect them and their collective commitment to work together to produce seamless marketplace performance. The action plan associates each objective, or set of related objectives, in the market strategy with the program (or programs) the firm will carry out to achieve it.

Coordination of the various market initiatives is a must, but in firms organized around products rather than markets, it can be haphazard. We have heard resellers exclaim that such suppliers need a "traffic cop" to keep the various product managers from launching sales and marketing programs that "collide," competing with one another for the reseller's attention and effort. Coordinating the timing and complementarity of the programs the firm enacts in the market leverages rather than dilutes the firm's efforts.

Before putting an action plan "to bed," the management team should ask a retrospective question in advance: "Six months down the road, when this strategy has failed, what will have been the cause of it?"[71] Early in the process of developing the action plan, creativity and imagination need to be encouraged, and so negativity must be suspended. After the action plan has been tentatively set, though, it benefits from intense scrutiny and questioning. By institutionalizing this question as part of the market planning process, it becomes clear to managers that it is not meant to undercut their efforts, but to help them strengthen the plan prior to its implementation. When the question is phrased in this manner, managers do a surprisingly good job of isolating the plan's shortfalls. The management team then makes changes to buttress these shortfalls, which might mean allocating additional resources or shifting resources. To accomplish this, they may combine some programs or defer others to the next year.

Marketing and Sales Programs

A **sales and marketing program** is a set of connected activities that consumes resources to produce results in pursuit of some objective. The actors performing these activities may come from one functional area, such as sales, but more often the activities cut across functional areas, relying on actors from them. Examples of sales and marketing programs are a new offering introduction, participation in an industry trade show, or increasing the supplier's share of customer's business in a targeted segment. Box 4.6 provides a detailed example of how Philips India developed a market strategy for lighting up cricket stadiums in India.

Sales and marketing programs consist of two external elements "wrapped around" four internal elements. The external elements are an objective (or related objectives), which flows from the market strategy, and measures of feedback. A common problem with objectives is that they are missing or not sufficiently defined. For example, some firms do not set specific

BOX 4.6
Philips India Develops a Market Strategy for Lighting Up Cricket Stadiums in India

In 1993, the Sales & Marketing (S&M) team of the Lighting Division in Philips India comprised over 100 people. This division contributed over 50% of the top as well as over 60% of the bottom line of Philips India, the Indian subsidiary of Philips, Netherlands.

In 1993, the mother of all cricketing events, the "Reliance Cup," was scheduled to be played over several months in Kolkata, during a period when no rains were expected. This was to be a series of games that all the contesting nations had to play on a league basis. It was expected to involve teams from several cricket-playing countries. As the matches were to be played back-to-back, in order to minimize travel delays, reduce logistics-related problems, and in deference to the spirit of sportsmanship of the West Bengal cricket fans, it was decided that Kolkata would host several of the matches.

The Cricket Association of Bengal (CAB) invited bids from short-listed vendors for flood lighting the Eden Gardens Cricket Ground (an open-air stadium). Along with Philips India, local and international players such as Bajaj, Crompton Greaves, Siemens, and GE Lighting were invited to submit closed bids, comprising both technical and commercial parts, for the prestigious job. The customer (CAB) was keen to have high-quality lighting but was reputed to be price sensitive. The final decision was to be taken based not only on the bids submitted by the vendors, but also on discussions that CAB planned to have with each vendor to assess each vendor's solution in detail.

As per the tender specification released by CAB, there were four "lighting towers" to be constructed at four locations of the cricket ground. This was a fairly standard approach used in lighting up such stadiums. The games were to be played both day and night. From the organizer's perspective, the financial stakes in each of the matches were several millions of rupees, taking into account ticket sales, advertisement revenues, etc.

Word from the grapevine suggested that the other vendors of the stadium's lighting were bogged down with the normal placement of the towers and luminaires, complying with the specifications of CAB in its tender document. Their strategy was seemingly to get the order on the basis of L1 (lowest price), as CAB reportedly manifested "buying orientation." In the process, each vendor second guessed the price being quoted by the other vendors. They were all expected to quote as low a price as possible—in the range of INR 15 million for executing the entire contract. The explicit objective of each vendor was to bag the prestigious and very visible contract at any cost. This was expected to open the floodgates for lighting contracts for cricket stadiums in the Indian sub-continent and neighboring countries. Hence, it was not surprising that they reckoned that the key to success in the CAB tender was to quote the lowest price.

BOX 4.6
Continued

Philips Lighting is generally considered to be the product leader for lighting applications of various types, including stadium lighting. Consequently, it wanted to take an unconventional approach to the request for quotation (RFQ) from CAB. Philips was keen to find a way out of the inevitable price war, which CAB would leverage to get the best deal. Ideally, it would have liked to quote a price of about INR 50 million, based on its estimation of the financial health of CAB and the stakes involved in such a high-profile international event, as well as the value it felt it could provide to the customer. It wanted to fully leverage all of its capabilities. Philips India saw this as a "make or break" contract. Philips came up with an innovative idea to exit from the possible commoditization of the contract.

Only Philips thought the biggest challenge was that the winter sun on Kolkata would cast shadows from the towers onto the pitch during falling daylight. How was this to be avoided? Philips approached the Positional Astronomy Center in Kolkata and, using elaborate computer programs, charted out the exact minute-wise "sun path" throughout the day for every day of the year. On the basis of these path coordinates, the illumination engineers of Philips Lighting Design and Application Centre designed the placement of the towers so that there would be no shadow on the playing pitch, no matter where the sun was at any time of the day or year. None of the competitors had considered this, and their submissions were simply rejected on these grounds. So, while not being L1, Philips won the bid as the clear Number One.

Once the complex calculations relating to the optimal placement of the lighting towers were accomplished, the engineers at Philips designed the luminaires on each tower to provide steady high-intensity illumination, sufficient for the color TV cameras to telecast the game. The luminaires also promised to lower "glare" and reduce visual fatigue for the players. Philips got an expert flown in from its international team in Netherlands to endorse the work of the Indian team.

This was the first cricket stadium in the Indian sub-continent to have a sophisticated lighting system. The order was estimated at about INR 4 crores in 1993. It was designed and executed entirely by the team from Philips India. The success of Eden Gardens actually opened the floodgates for lighting other cricket stadiums in India and in the sub-continental region.

The Philips India market strategy leveraged the superior capabilities of Philips through an approach of high specifications and unique value addition to create a customized and creative solution to a complex lighting issue. The Philips example shows how the company made competition irrelevant by coming up with a superior marketing strategy which clearly placed it ahead of the competition.

Apu Bose, D. V. R. Seshadri, Shobitha Hegde, "Philips India: Bidding for Floodlighting Eden Gardens," case study developed for Indian Institute of Management Bangalore in 2009.

objectives for participating in a trade show, such as generating 100% awareness for a new equipment leasing program, gaining commitments to conduct field demos at 40 qualified prospect firms in a target segment, or learning the positioning of a competitor's new offering and specific details about the advanced technology it uses. Thus, after the show, the only things the firm's participants are in a position to evaluate are whether the bottles of Heineken® in the hospitality suite were cold or whether the jumbo shrimp were a bit mealy this year!

Simply put, measures of feedback are indispensable. They enable the firm to assess the extent to which the program accomplished its objectives. They signal needed modifications in programs to be responsive to changing marketplace conditions. They establish benchmarks, so that the firm can gauge the cost and returns on programs that are repeated over time and can have a baseline for evaluating refinements. Finally, they provide accountability for individuals who have ownership of the program or its constituent activities and serve as a basis for performance review.

The four internal elements of a sales and marketing program are the actions to be taken, the responsibilities defined, the timing, and the budget. The individual who has ownership of the program should detail each of its major actions and indicate who has taken responsibility for each action. The initials of the individual having primary responsibility for each major action (or group of activities) should appear in parentheses following it. The timing element lays out the program's sequential timeline; it specifies the date for completing each action. Finally, budgets refer to the resources, such as money or individuals' time, that the program requires and from whose budget(s) these resources will come.

Take Stock of Implementation Skills

Four behavioral skills of managers are fundamental in implementation: interacting, allocating, monitoring, and organizing.[72] **Interaction skills** are a manager's behavioral style of relating to others within the firm and outside the firm, such as resellers and customers. Interaction skills capture how a manager works together with others, uses influence strategies, and negotiates. **Allocation skills** refer to a manager's expertise in budgeting time, people, and money. **Monitoring skills** are a manager's ability to stay informed on what matters and to recognize when to intervene in ongoing activities. **Organizing skills** capture a manager's proficiency at drawing upon or, when necessary, circumventing the formal organizational structure to bring together the resources to accomplish a market task. Organizing skills reflect how adroit a manager is in connecting relationships and managing group dynamics, whereas interacting skills refer to one-on-one interaction adeptness.

Although each of these implementation skills is challenging to master, firms struggle most to strengthen the interaction skills of their managers. The increasing emphasis on working together more collaboratively, such as in closer cross-functional cooperation and partnering with customers, requires interaction skills. Significantly, when the senior management team has problems interacting with one another, cross-functional cooperation likely won't happen below them in the organization either. To align their interests and promote improved interaction, several years ago the 60 top executives of Baxter, Inc., a major health care company based in the United States took out personal notes to purchase, in total, INR 552 crores of Baxter stock. The deal was structured so that the dividends on the stock would pay the interest payments for five years. At that time, a balloon payment was due. If Baxter stock had risen a certain number of points, the executives would be at break-even; if the stock price was below that level, they were personally liable for the difference; if the stock price was above that level, they would gain. A senior executive commented that cooperation among the senior management team dramatically improved. Reflecting this cooperative attitude in part, the share price of Baxter stock rose significantly above the break-even share price.

Firms generally have difficulty making a knowledgeable and unbiased appraisal of their own skills and capabilities, no doubt because they are more familiar with their own capabilities and skills than they are with competitors'. In addition, firms tend to know what they do well; they tend not to know what they do not do well. That is, they tend to overestimate the number of capabilities and skills on which they are superior. To gain a more unbiased appraisal, firms often rely on outsiders, such as management consultants. Outsiders can assist them in producing a more objective appraisal, by performing comparative analyses using internal data as well as external customer and competitor data.

Learning and Adapting

"It is a bad plan that admits of no modification." Publilius Syrus made this statement in the first century B.C. So, although some may regard the emergent view of strategy as a recent phenomenon, the recognition that plans need to be adapted as learning occurs has existed for quite some time! At several points in this chapter, we have emphasized the criticality of learning and putting mechanisms in place to facilitate it. Here, we consider some ways to learn quickly to be able to make responsive adaptations or modifications in market strategy.

One way for businesses to excel at learning and adapting is to gain early feedback, either before or just after implementing parts of the market strategy. A **customer advisory board**, where the business brings together a group of its leading-edge and key customers to provide reactions, advice, and counsel, provides a valuable mechanism for learning and adaptation. Critical to the success of customer advisory boards are establishing a clear mission; recruiting qualified members; taking action so that board members can see that spending their time makes a difference (that matters to them); and communicating before and after meetings with board members.[73] Supplier management should make a 100% feedback commitment to board members: that the supplier will communicate back to the board members in a mutually agreed time interval what it will do as a result of board dialogue and counsel on each issue, even when that means explaining *why* the supplier will *not* pursue what the board may have counseled. Box 4.7 recounts how Wipro Technologies learns and adapts. Reseller councils, which we discuss in greater detail in Chapter 9, are also a potentially valuable mechanism for learning about changes in the market as well as gauging reactions to proposed market initiatives. Finally, business market managers must remember that in constructing sales and marketing programs, they need to devise feedback measures that provide some early indication of how a program is doing—postprogram evaluations are not enough.

Pilot programs are a valuable way of learning by doing. The firm should design them so that, to the extent possible, they are limited in scale and scope. The firm also should think through the conditions that will promote success, so that it can pick the best chances for a pilot program becoming a "success story." To maximize learning and guard against idiosyncrasies, whenever possible, the firm should implement at least two pilot programs of the same kind. This provides some estimate of the variance in outcomes the firm can expect and provides insights on the conditions for more consistent results.

BOX 4.7
Wipro Technologies Learns and Adapts

Being in the IT services sector, the employees of Wipro Technologies work closely with customers on a day-to-day basis. To build long-lasting relationships with existing customers as well as acquire new customers, it is essential for Wipro to make sure that all are happy with the value that they bring in. To track this on an ongoing basis, Wipro has taken some initiatives to ensure customer satisfaction.

Customer satisfaction is the no. 1 objective of every employee at Wipro and is tracked very closely in terms of customer feedback during and at the end of every assignment for each employee. Compensation is linked to this metric.

All customer satisfaction initiatives at Wipro are led by senior management. This sends a strong signal to the entire organization that Wipro is serious about its customers and values their feedback. It has various initiatives that indirectly affect customer satisfaction. For instance, its mission statement emphasizes quality and innovation, key drivers of customer satisfaction.

Wipro has a Web-based grievance-tracking system that can be used by customers to track their queries, and this ensures that customers' problems are resolved in a timely manner. They also have a robust C-SAT measurement system wherein transactional as well as relationship metrics are tracked on a per-customer basis. Last, Wipro organizes a customer forum called Mandala where key stakeholders such as customers, senior management and industry thought leaders meet and discuss issues, exchange ideas and discuss the future prospects openly.

Through these and other measures to continually learn and adapt, Wipro has been able to successfully manage its customer relationships and has grown to become a world leader with a market cap of over INR 28,800 crores.

Contributed by Rajiv Motwani, Participant, PGSEM Program, Indian Institute of Management Bangalore.

In the process of learning, business market managers must also consider the best method of disseminating what they have learned throughout the organization. At times, the medium of transmitting information can significantly influence the success and application of the learning within the firm. PIPSA-Mex, a Mexican paper company, uses a *grupo musical* (musical group) to communicate its market strategy, supplier relationships, and other critical information to its employees. The eight PIPSA musicians sing and play an assortment of folk instruments, ranging from guitars to the teeth of a donkey skull, in order to transmit information to the organization. Rather than rely upon more conventional written and spoken media, PIPSA management recognized and leveraged its employees' responsiveness to a more culturally familiar mode of learning.[74]

When firms do have success with an innovative market activity, program, or system, they often have difficulty reliably reproducing this best practice elsewhere in the firm. From their management practice research, Szulanski and Winter find:[75]

> People approach best-practice replication with the optimism and overconfidence of a neophyte stock trader out to beat the market. They try, for example,

> to go one better than an operation that's up and running nearly flawlessly. Or they try to piece together the best parts of a number of different practices, in hopes of creating the perfect hybrid. They assume, usually incorrectly, that the people running best-practice operations fully understand what makes them successful. As a result of this general overoptimism, people attempting to replicate a best practice are nowhere near as disciplined as they need to be.

What can business market managers do to improve their chances of successfully replicating best practices?

Although managers should consult the experts and the documentation on the best practice to be copied, these sources are not substitutes for carefully observing the best practice firsthand, to learn as much of the tacit detail as possible. They then should attempt to copy the working example in detail, as closely as they can, using it as a template to replicate. Intel developed its "Copy Exactly!" method to ensure the precise transfer of manufacturing know-how from the initial facility making a particular device to subsequent ones. Managers also should demonstrate decent results with the replicated best practice before beginning adaptations intended to improve performance. Rank Xerox requires managers first to demonstrate a comparable level of performance to that of the benchmark unit before they can initiate adaptations in the reproduced practice. Business market managers adhering to these guidelines then can use a search for discrepancies from the best practice example as a diagnostic device when implementation problems inevitably arise.

Finally, senior management must actively support a culture that values systematic market experiments. Progressive firms have at least several different market experiments underway at any time in pursuit of superior learning. For this culture to flourish, though, senior management must practice forgiveness and understanding for inevitable mistakes and failed experiments, provided that there is learning. Jeff Immelt, CEO of General Electric, expresses this reasoned support for failure nicely: "If you try something and it fails but you went about it the right way and you learned from it, that's not a bad thing."[76]

SUMMARY

Crafting market strategy is the process of studying how to exploit a business's resources to achieve short-term and long-term marketplace success, deciding on a course of action to pursue, and flexibly updating it as learning occurs during implementation. It requires significant participation from many functional areas, not just marketing, to make decisions about what market segments and customer firms to pursue, and what needs to be done to deliver superior value to them. Crafting market strategy recognizes real-world complexity and the interplay between deliberate strategy, where the business decides on a course of action to pursue, and emergent strategy, where marketplace activities converge into a pattern that the business recognizes and acts upon in a coordinated way.

Business strategy provides the context for market strategy. Although business strategy is often seen as setting the constraints for market strategy, so too should market strategy inform and significantly influence business strategy. We took a resource-based view of the firm, where core competencies and capabilities are complementary building blocks of strategy that generate value and provide competitive advantage. Product leadership, customer intimacy, and operational excellence represent fundamental value-based strategies. Disparate views are held on a number of issues in making strategy, such as who makes strategy and defining the purpose of the firm. Although the view of strategy as radical change appears compelling in some respects, progressive firms recognize the strengths and weaknesses of each kind of strategy making and alternate using them when each best suits their needs. The result is longer periods of strategy making as orderly advances punctuated by shorter periods of strategy making as radical change.

Through planning market strategy, members of the management team compare, revise, and update their individual market views, with the intent of having them converge on a shared market view, which serves as the basis for discussing alternative courses of action for the firm to pursue. We organized our presentation of planning market strategy in business markets around three fundamental questions: What do we know? What do we want to accomplish? and, How will we do it? Regardless of planning process and plan format, we contend that firms that can meaningfully answer these three questions will have constructed a market plan that is worth pursuing.

To construct a market plan, managers must distinguish between what they know, what they believe, and what they want to believe. Through reviewing recent performance, gathering essential market information, and, in situations of considerable uncertainty, constructing scenarios, the management team answers, "What do we know?" After considering multiple alternatives, the management team selects a market strategy it wants to accomplish. It targets market segments and customer firms to focus on, sets goals and objectives, and engages in positioning and constructing resonating focus value propositions to work out the implications of what the firm wants to accomplish. Brands and brand building are of growing interest and significance in business markets. In answering the question, "How will we do it?" the firm develops action plans and sales and marketing programs, takes stock of its implementation skills, and prepares for learning and adapting.

ENDNOTES

1. Henry Mintzberg, "Crafting Strategy," *Harvard Business Review* (July–August 1987): 66–75.
2. Benson P. Shapiro, "What the Hell Is 'Market Oriented'?" *Harvard Business Review* (November–December 1988): 119–125.
3. Although we use the term *firm* most often, our treatment of crafting market strategy is for a single business. Alternatively, we can view it as crafting market strategy for the smaller firm or for a business unit in a larger corporation. For focus, we do not discuss corporate strategy or strategy at the group or sector level for multiple business unit corporations. For discussion of these strategies, see Michael Porter, *Competitive Advantage* (New York: The Free Press, 1985).
4. For an interesting set of exchanges on the "design" versus "emergent" schools of strategy, see Henry Mintzberg, "The 'Honda Effect' Revisited: Introduction," *California Management Review* (Summer 1996): 78–79; Richard T. Pascale, "The Honda Effect," *California Management Review* (Summer 1996): 80–91; Henry Mintzberg, "Learning 1, Planning 0," *California Management Review* (Summer 1996): 92–93; Michael Goold, "Design, Learning and Planning: A Further Observation on the Design School Debate," *California Management Review* (Summer 1996): 94–95; Henry Mintzberg, "Reply to Michael Goold," *California Management Review* (Summer 1996): 96–99; Michael Goold, "Learning, Planning, and Strategy: Extra Time," *California Management Review* (Summer 1996): 100–102; Richard P. Rumelt, "The Many Faces of Honda," *California Management Review* (Summer 1996): 103–111; and Richard T. Pascale, "Reflections on Honda," *California Management Review* (Summer 1996): 112–117.

5. Christopher A. Bartlett and Sumantra Ghoshal, "Changing the Role of Top Management: Beyond Strategy to Purpose," *Harvard Business Review* (November–December 1994): 79–88. The quote is from Rumelt, "The Many Faces of Honda," 110.
6. Michael E. Porter, "What Is Strategy?" *Harvard Business Review* (November–December 1996): 61–78. The three quotes in the paragraph are from pp. 62, 68, and 62, respectively, with the emphases in the original. See also Keith H. Hammonds, "Michael Porter's Big Ideas," *Fast Company* (March 2001): 150–156.
7. Porter, "What Is Strategy?" 77. To some extent, this statement even blurs the distinction between strategy and marketing strategy.
8. David J. Collis and Cynthia A. Montgomery, "Competing on Resources: Strategy in the 1990s," *Harvard Business Review* (July–August 1995): 119.
9. Michael E. Porter, *Competitive Advantage: Creating and Sustaining Superior Performance* (New York: Free Press, 1985); and Rajendra K. Srivastava, Liam Fahey, and H. Kurt Christensen, "The Resource-Based View and Marketing: The Role of Market-Based Assets in Gaining Competitive Advantage," *Journal of Management*, 27, no. 6 (2001): 777–802.
10. Collis and Montgomery, "Competing on Resources."
11. C. K. Prahalad and Gary Hamel, "The Core Competence of the Corporation," *Harvard Business Review* (May–June 1990): 84.
12. Prahalad and Hamel, "Core Competence," 83–84.
13. Collis and Montgomery, "Competing on Resources."
14. Peter F. Drucker, "The Information Executives Truly Need," *Harvard Business Review* (January–February 1995): 54–62.
15. George Stalk, Philip Evans, and Lawrence E. Shulman, "Competing on Capabilities: The New Rules of Corporate Strategy," *Harvard Business Review* (March–April 1992): 62.
16. Stalk, Evans, and Shulman, "Competing on Capabilities," 66; see Pascale, "Reflections on Honda," for an example of the use of *core competence* and *capability* interchangeably.
17. George S. Day, "The Capabilities of Market-Driven Organizations," *Journal of Marketing* (October 1994): 38.
18. Day, "The Capabilities of Market-Driven Organizations," 39.
19. Most research and writing on brands and branding has been based on, and focuses on, consumer markets. Drawing on this work and our experience, we adapt it for application in business markets. For a comprehensive source on brands and brand building, which we draw on in this chapter, see Kevin Lane Keller, *Strategic Brand Management: Building, Measuring, and Managing Brand Equity*, 2nd ed. (Upper Saddle River, NJ: Prentice Hall, 2003).
20. Keller, *Strategic Brand Management*, p. 563 and p. 535 for the first and second quotes, respectively. IBM and Lenovo Group Ltd. signed a definitive agreement on December 7, 2004, under which Lenovo has acquired IBM's Personal Computer business for $1.75 billion, including $500 million as debt. IBM will receive $650 million in cash and $600 million in Lenovo stock. As part of the agreement, Lenovo will be the preferred supplier of PCs to IBM and will be allowed to use the IBM and Think brands for five years. See: Steve Lohr, "Sale of IBM PC Unit Is a Bridge between Companies and Cultures," *New York Times*, December 8, 2004, A1.
21. For a recent exposition on the brand value chain, which begins with marketing program investment and concludes with shareholder value, see Kevin Lane Keller and Donald R. Lehman, "How Brands Create Value," *Marketing Management* (May–June 2003): 26–31.
22. Kenichi Ohmae, "The Global Logic of Strategic Alliances," *Harvard Business Review* (March–April 1989): 143–154; Gary S. Ruderman, "Collaboration Adding Strength," *Chicago Tribune*, 8 July 2000, sec. 4, 1, 4.
23. Gary McWilliams, "Whirlwind on the Web," *Business Week*, 7 April 1997, 132.
24. David Lei and John W. Slocum, Jr., "Global Strategy, Competence Building and

Strategic Alliances," *California Management Review* (Fall 1992): 81–97; Louis P. Bucklin and Sanjit Sengupta, "Organizing Successful Co-Marketing Alliances," *Journal of Marketing* (April 1993): 32–46.
25. Michael Treacy and Fred Wiersema, "Customer Intimacy and Other Value Disciplines," *Harvard Business Review* (January–February 1993): 84–93; and Porter, "What Is Strategy?" We draw on both articles in this section.
26. Treacy and Wiersema, "Customer Intimacy," 85.
27. Edward Barnholt, "Fostering Business Growth with Breakthrough Innovation," *Research-Technology Management* (March–April 1997): 12–16.
28. Treacy and Wiersema, "Customer Intimacy," 84.
29. Francis J. Gouillart and Frederick D. Sturdivant, "Spend a Day in the Life of Your Customers," *Harvard Business Review* (January–February 1994): 116–125. We discuss sustaining customer relationships in greater detail in Chapter 10.
30. Treacy and Wiersema, "Customer Intimacy," 84.
31. Treacy and Wiersema, "Customer Intimacy," 86.
32. Gary Hamel, "Killer Strategies That Make Shareholders Rich," *Fortune*, 23 June 1997, 70–88; and "The Uncertain Return of the Hero Boss," *The Economist* (July 17, 2006): 63–64.
33. Henry Mintzberg, "Musings on Management," *Harvard Business Review* (July–August 1996): 61–67.
34. Quy Nguyen Huy, "In Praise of Middle Managers," *Harvard Business Review* (September 2001): 73.
35. Barlett and Ghoshal, "Changing the Role of Top Management"; Gary Hamel, "Strategy as Revolution," *Harvard Business Review* (July–August 1996): 69–82; Henry Mintzberg, "The Fall and Rise of Strategic Planning," *Harvard Business Review* (January–February 1994): 107–114.
36. James C. Anderson and James A. Narus, "Capturing the Value of Supplementary Services," *Harvard Business Review* (January–February 1995): 75–83.
37. Gary Hamel and C. K. Prahalad, "Strategic Intent," *Harvard Business Review* (May–June 1989): 64.
38. Barlett and Ghoshal, "Changing the Role of Top Management." For research on how a competitor-focused market strategy can produce lower profits for the firm, see J. Scott Armstrong and Fred Collopy, "Competitor Orientation: Effects of Objectives and Information on Managerial Decisions and Profitability," *Journal of Marketing Research* (May 1996): 188–199.
39. Jack Welch and Suzy Welch, "State Your Business," *Business Week* (January 14, 2008): 80. The Dilbert Web site makes fun of the generic, mindless nature of mission statements with its "Mission Statement Generator." See: *http://www.dilbert.com/comics/dilbert/games/career/bin/ms.cgi.* For more on how to have an honest conversation about defining purpose or strategy, see: Michael Beer and Russell A. Eisenstaat, "How to Have an Honest Conversation About Your Business Strategy," *Harvard Business Review* (February 2004): 82–89.
40. Samuel J. Palmisano, "The HBR Interview: Leading Change When Business Is Good," *Harvard Business Review* (December 2004): 60–70.
41. Hamel, "Strategy as Revolution"; and Gary Hamel, "Waking Up IBM," *Harvard Business Review* (July–August 2000): 137–146.
42. Gary Hamel and C. K. Prahalad, "Strategy as Stretch and Leverage," *Harvard Business Review* (March–April 1993): 75–84; and Robert A. Burgelman and Andrew S. Grove, "Strategic Dissonance," *California Management Review* (Winter 1996): 8–28.
43. Mintzberg, "Crafting Strategy"; Suzy Wetlaufer, "The Business Case Against Revolution: An Interview with Nestlé's Peter Brabeck," *Harvard Business Review* (February 2001): 112–119; and Gary Hamel, "Revolution vs. Evolution: You Need Both," *Harvard Business Review* (May 2001): 150–154.
44. Mintzberg, "Crafting Strategy," 71.
45. Arie P. de Geus, "Planning as Learning," *Harvard Business Review* (March–April 1988): 70.

46. John Bryne, "Strategic Planning," *Business Week*, 26 August 1997, 48–52; Mintzberg, "The Fall and Rise of Strategic Planning."
47. Hillel J. Einhorn and Robin M. Hogarth, "Decision Making: Going Forward in Reverse," *Harvard Business Review* (January–February 1987): 66–70.
48. Jack Welch and Suzy Welch, "Stop the B.S. Budgets," *Business Week* (June 26, 2006): 114.
49. George S. Day and Prakesh Nedungadi, "Managerial Representations of Competitive Advantage," *Journal of Marketing* (April 1994): 31–44.
50. Eric von Hippel, *The Sources of Innovation* (New York: Oxford University Press, 1988); James C. Anderson and James A. Narus, "Partnering as a Focused Market Strategy," *California Management Review* (Spring 1991): 95–113. We discuss lead-users and leap-froggers as sources of innovation that are of particular interest for a supplier firm to research in Chapter 6.
51. Michael V. Marn and Robert L. Rosiello, "Managing Price, Gaining Profit," *Harvard Business Review* (September–October 1992): 84–94; and Drucker, "The Information Executives Truly Need." We discuss monitoring transaction prices and activity-based costing in greater detail in Chapter 10.
52. Ann Langley, "Between 'Paralysis by Analysis' and 'Extinction by Instinct,'" *Sloan Management Review* (Spring 1995): 63–76.
53. Kathleen M. Eisenhardt, "Speed and Strategic Choice: How Managers Accelerate Decision Making," *California Management Review* (Spring 1990): 1–16.
54. Eisenhardt, "Speed and Strategic Choice," 3–4.
55. This section is based on de Geus, "Planning as Learning"; Paul J. H. Shoemaker, "Scenario Planning: A Tool for Strategic Thinking," *Sloan Management Review* (Winter 1995): 25–40; Pierre Wack, "Scenarios: Shooting the Rapids," *Harvard Business Review* (November–December 1985): 139–150; and Pierre Wack, "Scenarios: Uncharted Waters Ahead," *Harvard Business Review* (September–October 1985): 73–89. See also Ian Wylie, "There Is No Alternative to . . . ," *Fast Company* (July 2002): 106–110.
56. Aaron Bernstein, "Sharing Prosperity," *Business Week*, 1 September 1997, 64–69; and Robert D. Hof, "Stock Options Aren't the Only Option," *Business Week*, 14 April 2003, 60.
57. Eisenhardt, "Speed and Strategic Choice"; and Kathleen M. Eisenhardt, Jean L. Kahwajy, and L. H. Bourgeois III, "How Management Teams Can Have a Good Fight," *Harvard Business Review* (July–August 1997): 77–85.
58. Porter, "What Is Strategy?"
59. Jeffrey R. Immelt, "The HBR Interview: Growth as a Process," *Harvard Business Review* (June 2006): 60–70.
60. Rajendra K. Srivastava, Tassadduq A. Shervani, and Liam Fahey, "Market-Based Assets and Shareholder Value: A Framework for Analysis," *Journal of Marketing* (January 1998): 2–18; Peter Doyle, *Value-Based Marketing* (Chichester, England: John Wiley & Sons, 2000); and Phillippe Haspeslagh, Tomo Noda, and Fares Boulos, "Managing for Value: It's Not Just About the Numbers," *Harvard Business Review* (July–August 2001): 64–73.
61. Robert S. Kaplan and David P. Norton, "Using the Balanced Scorecard as a Strategic Management System," *Harvard Business Review* (January–February 1996): 75–85.
62. Ann Majchrzak and Qianwei Wang, "Breaking the Functional Mind-Set in Process Organizations," *Harvard Business Review* (September–October 1996): 92–99.
63. Steven Kerr, "On the Folly of Rewarding A, While Hoping for B," *Academy of Management Executive* (February 1995): 7–16.
64. The linkages between nonfinancial measures, such as employee satisfaction and customer loyalty, and business performance also need to be specified explicitly and tested. See: Christopher D. Ittner and David F. Larcker, "Coming Up Short on Nonfinancial Performance Measurement," *Harvard Business Review* (November 2003): 88–95.

65. Gary Hamel and C. K. Prahalad, "Corporate Imagination and Expeditionary Marketing," *Harvard Business Review* (July–August 1991).
66. This section is based on: James C. Anderson, James A. Narus, and Wouter van Rossum, "Customer Value Propositions in Business Markets," *Harvard Business Review* (March 2006): 90–99.
67. Daniel P. Morrison, "B2B Branding: Avoiding the Pitfalls," *Marketing Management* (September–October 2001): 30–34.
68. Keller, *Strategic Brand Management*, 737.
69. Colin Mitchell, "Selling the Brand Inside," *Harvard Business Review* (January 2002): 99–105.
70. Jeffrey Pfeffer and Robert I. Sutton, "The Smart-Talk Trap," *Harvard Business Review* (May–June 1999): 135–142.
71. We gratefully acknowledge Joseph Durette of Kraft General Foods for suggesting this question.
72. Thomas V. Bonoma and Victoria Crittenden, "Managing Marketing Implementation," *Sloan Management Review* (Winter 1988): 7–14.
73. Sean Geehan and Stacy Sheldon, "Connecting to Customers," *Marketing Management* (November-December 2005): 36–42.
74. Eric Matson, "You Can Teach This Old Company New Tricks," *Fast Company* (October–November 1997): 44–46. Pipsa-Mex, now owned by Grupo Industrial Durango (GIDUSA), was formerly Producer and Importer of Paper S.A. (PIPSA).
75. Gabriel Szulanski and Sidney Winter, "Getting It Right the Second Time," *Harvard Business Review* (January 2002): 62–69. The quote is from p. 64.
76. This quote is drawn from: Jena McGregor, "How Failure Breeds Success," *Business Week* (10 July 2006): 47.

Section III

Creating Value

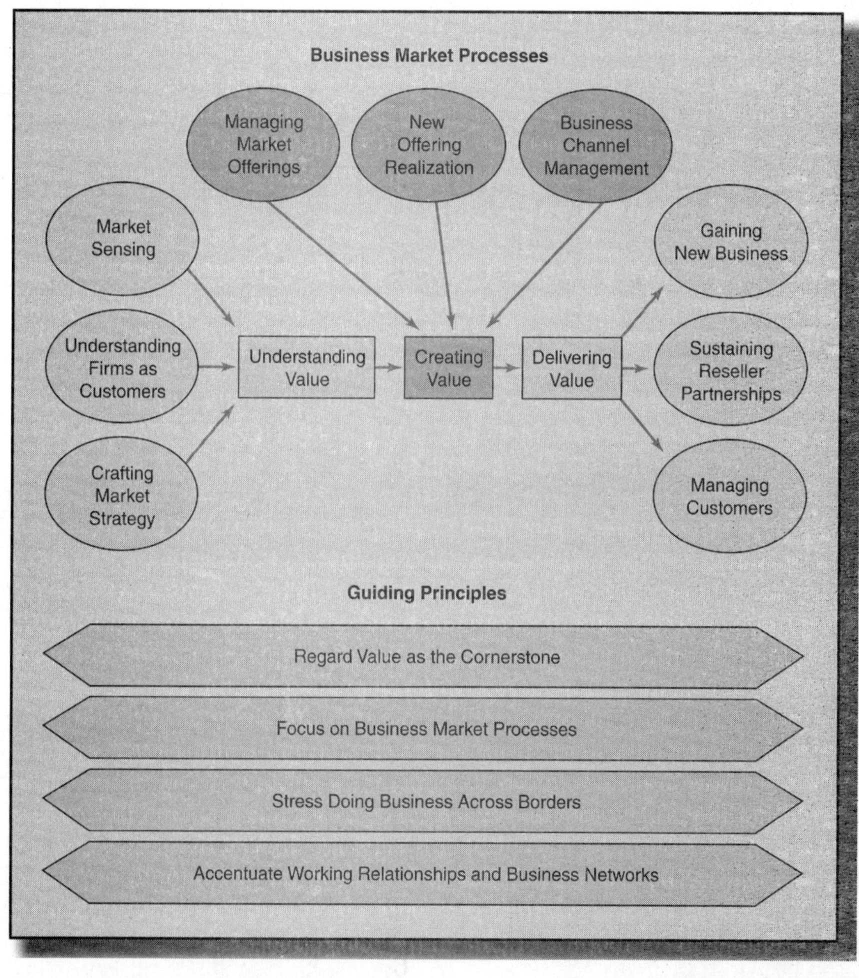

Chapter 5

Managing Market Offerings

Overview

The business market processes of market sensing, understanding firms as customers, and crafting market strategy provide supplier firms with an understanding of value. As Figure 1.1 portrays, the firm puts this understanding of value to use in creating value for the market segments and customer firms that it has decided are of greater interest. Creating value is composed of the business market processes of managing market offerings, new offering realization, and business channel management.

Managing market offerings is the process of putting products, services, programs, and systems together in ways that create the greatest value for targeted market segments and customer firms. The challenge for business market managers is to construct offerings that uniquely leverage a business's resources to provide this value. The process involves both responsively meeting targeted segment and customer requirements and managing their supplier expectations.

What exactly do we mean by *market offering*? To better understand this, we will unravel what in the past has been called a *product offering* and view it in several layers.[1] The **core product** is simply the fundamental, functional performance a generic product provides that solves a customer's basic problem. For example, the core product for an agricultural herbicide would be a specific chemical compound that has the ability to control particular broadleaf and grassy weeds. The **minimally augmented product** adds to this core product the least amount or number of services, programs, or systems that customers consider absolutely essential for doing business with *any* supplier. Examples of these essentials might include payment terms, delivery, and customer service for problems with the core product.

The **augmented product** adds to the core product those services, programs, and systems a supplier offers to meet a broader set of customer requirements and preferences, or to exceed the customer's expectations in ways that add value or reduce cost for the customer. Examples of augmenting services, programs, and systems offered in business markets appear in Figure 5.1. Finally, a **potential product** goes beyond the augmented product to encompass any imaginable product change or service, program, or system a supplier might create to add value or reduce cost in ways that set itself apart from others. As these potential additions are realized, they become a part of the augmented product. For example, an agrichemical supplier and dealer might consider jointly offering a "rain guarantee," whereby if the dealer applies the supplier's herbicide to the grower's fields and unexpected rain washes it away, the dealer will reapply the herbicide at no charge.

We prefer *market offering* to the more-often-used *product offering* as a way to capture these layers of meaning for three reasons. First, the core product may not be a concrete, palpable "thing" but instead may

Figure 5.1 Examples of Augmenting Services, Programs, and Systems

Services	
Fulfillment:	availability assurance, emergency delivery, installation, training, maintenance, disposal/recycling
Technical:	specification, testing & analysis, troubleshooting, problem-solving, calibration, customer productivity improvement
Programs	
Economic:	terms & conditions; deals, discounts, allowances & rebates/bonuses; warranty; guaranteed cost savings
Relationship:	advice and consulting, design, process engineering, product & process redesign, analysis of cost and performance, joint marketing research, co-marketing & co-promotion
Systems	
Linking:	order management intranet, automated replenishment & vendor-managed inventory, Enterprise Resource Planning (ERP), Computerized Maintenance Management (CMM)
Efficacy:	information & design assistance intranet, expert systems, integrated logistics management, asset management, responsiveness systems

Source: James C. Anderson, Nirmalya Kumar, and James A. Narus, *Value Merchants: Demonstrating and Documenting Superior Value in Business Markets.* Boston: Harvard Business School Press, 2007: 83.

be a service, such as management consulting or building maintenance. *Market* accommodates either equally well. Second, even when the core product is a concrete and tangible "thing," use of *market offering* emphasizes that what a supplier brings to the market is a package composed of a core product or service *and* a set of augmenting services, programs, and systems. The package as a whole, not simply the core product, must create value for the customer. In a number of instances, the augmenting services, programs, and systems provide the predominant part of the superior value over competitors' offerings. Finally, *market* reinforces an outward-focused perspective of what the supplier is trying to accomplish in the marketplace, as contrasted with *product*, which can promote an inward-looking or technology-driven perspective.

In this chapter, we discuss constructing and managing market offerings. After briefly considering some conventional thinking about market offerings, we present our approach, which we call **flexible market offerings**. We then discuss value-based pricing as a means for sharing created value with customers. We conclude by considering the potential complexities of managing market offerings across international borders. We depict the process of managing marketing offerings in Figure 5.2.

Figure 5.2 Managing Market Offerings

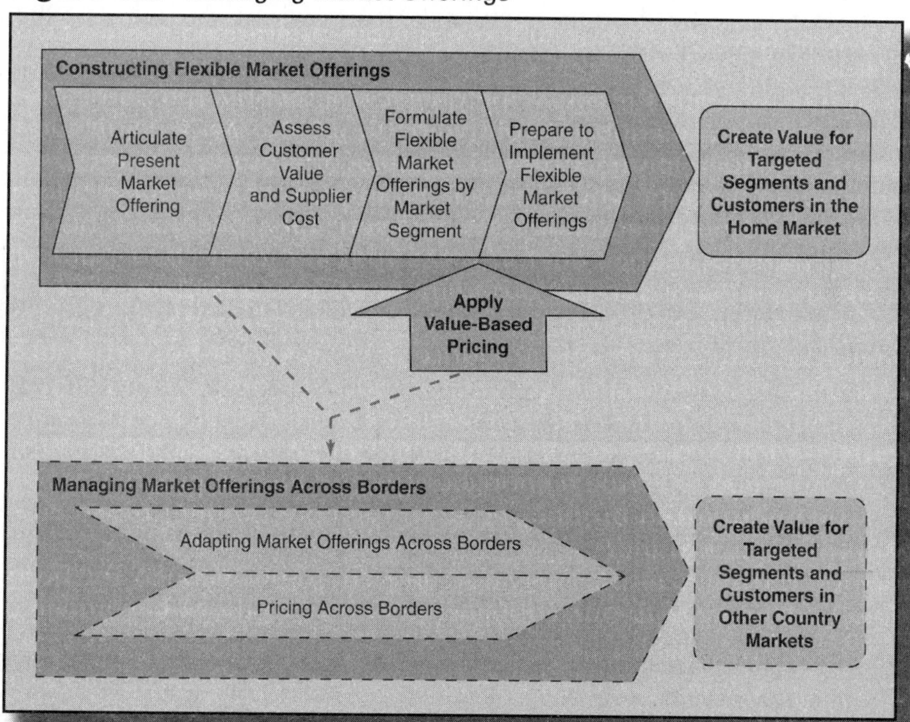

SOME CONVENTIONAL THINKING ABOUT MARKET OFFERINGS

Because business markets change and thinking about business marketing advances, even experienced business market managers need to periodically revisit their market views. It can thus be worthwhile to reexamine conventional thinking about what suppliers should and can do in the marketplace. Here, we reevaluate two often-encountered, conventional thoughts about market offerings to separate truth from apparent fiction.

The Tunnel Vision of Commodity Markets

If you think you are in a commodity market, you're thinking too narrowly about the market you're in.

Over the years, when discussing business marketing approaches for businesses to differentiate themselves from competitors, we have had a number of supplier managers respond with something to the effect of: "That is all well and good, but I'm in a commodity market!" Our response, most often, has been the preceding quote. As we saw in Chapter 3, the buying orientation tactic of **commoditization** is to convince suppliers that no differences exist among offerings. In turn, it is the responsibility of business market managers to persuasively demonstrate to customers that their offering is different in valuable ways.

Indeed, as products mature and customers gain extensive experience with them, there appears to be a routine narrowing of perceived differences among offerings in customers' minds and a corresponding unwillingness to pay anything different for them. In other words, the offerings over time tend to become undifferentiated in the minds of customers, with price becoming the sole basis for deciding among them. This is the definition of a **commodity**. The seemingly inexorable pull on a market toward commoditization has been referred to as the "commodity magnet."[2] To beat the commodity magnet, or at least to slow its pull over time, supplier managers must continually search for ways to differentiate their market offerings in ways that customers value.

In his classic article titled "Marketing Success Through Differentiation—of Anything," Levitt begins by stating:

> There is no such thing as a commodity. All goods and services are differentiable. Though the usual presumption is that this is more true of consumer goods than of industrial goods and services, the opposite is the actual case.[3]

As support, Levitt provides a number of examples of differentiation, two of which we would like to recount. Durum is a particular variety of wheat principally used in making pasta. Many readers would regard it as a commodity, and, in fact, grain elevator operators and food processors quote standard prices for durum wheat. Yet, closer scrutiny reveals that the prices growers actually receive vary, depending on the results of tests of the wheat's more elemental properties, such as its protein, moisture, farina, and gluten content. As Levitt notes, "Premiums and discounts for quality differences in a particular year have been known to vary from the futures prices on commodity exchanges by amounts greater than the futures price fluctuations themselves during that year."[4] By carefully studying how subtle variations in the core product's characteristics provide incremental value for certain sets of customers, such as pasta manufacturers in the example, suppliers may find meaningful ways to differentiate.

In some cases, though, the core products of alternative suppliers are essentially interchangeable. Still, augmenting services, programs, and systems present various ways for suppliers to set themselves apart from one another. As Levitt relates, although commodities dealers trade in totally undifferentiated core products, such as metals, grains, and pork bellies, they differentiate their offerings on their professed distinction in their execution of the trades and supporting activities for their clients. A supplier can discover potentially valuable ways to do business differently by more broadly considering all of the activities a customer undertakes and the resources it employs in using a supplier's offering.[5]

What can suppliers do to forestall or reverse this trend toward commoditization? The initial step for suppliers to take is to understand the true extent of commoditization for their offerings, which also uncovers some possibilities for differentiation. Armed with this knowledge, suppliers can pursue several strategies to rebuild their market offerings into differentiated offerings that customers value more than those of competitors.[6]

Understanding the True Extent of Commoditization

Oftentimes, suppliers simply conclude, "We're in a commodity business," because they are thinking narrowly about the core product or service. That is, the personal computer, hospital supplies, or letter-of-credit that the customer purchases may be very nearly or exactly the same across suppliers. But the market offerings that customers purchase typically are more than simply the core product or service. These market offerings contain supplementary services, programs, and systems that enhance the value of the core product (or service) and provide additional value to customers. Thus, before concluding they are in a commodity business, suppliers need to more carefully examine exactly what differences exist between their offerings and those of competitors, drawing on market and internal data. Specifically, they should gain estimates of the value that customers receive, validate their market pricing, and gain estimates of their share of customer's business.

Although much attention in recent years has been given to value and its provision to customers, remarkably few firms have the knowledge and capability to assess value in practice. We discussed customer value management in Chapter 2, which has as a central undertaking building customer value models. A supplier needs a fine-grained understanding of the value that a customer receives from its market offering relative to the next-best alternative. At the same time, suppliers should investigate what potential changes in their market offerings *would* be worth to customers. Although suppliers are more conversant with the technical and economic benefits of their offerings, they should not neglect service and social benefits, which can be significant sources of value.

Consider, for example, safety glasses (protective eyewear). Safety glasses provide the technical benefit of protecting workers' eyes from infrared and ultraviolet light and from foreign substances such as chemical stray. They provide the economic benefit of fewer lost days due to on-the-job injuries and lower insurance premiums.

To obtain these technical and economic benefits, however, the worker must wear the safety glasses, looking like a "dork." As a result, younger workers more concerned about how they look than about safety often do not wear them when they should. Taking a more comprehensive view of value, Dalloz Safety Products designed a line of protective eyewear that look like designer sunglasses. The glasses have contoured wrap-around frames that come in a variety of colors, with lenses in a selection of tints and colors. Now, workers actually like wearing their stylish Dalloz protective eyewear, making workplace compliance no longer a problem.

Gaining an accurate understanding of competitors' prices often is difficult in business markets. A supplier must *systematically* gather data from the field on the range of prices that customers are paying for competitor market offerings. A supplier also should investigate what supplementary services are and are not included in a competitor's quoted price for a market offering, to better understand offering comparability. Gathering these data will give the supplier a finer-grained understanding of variations in competitor pricing in the marketplace.

A supplier must also gather data about its own prices. Use of off-invoice rebates or allowances, whose percentages may depend on the amount of business that the customer has done with the supplier during the quarter or year, makes it difficult for a supplier to know at the time exactly what price it is realizing from a given transaction. Monitoring transaction prices enables a supplier to learn the extent to which exceptions are being made from set pricing strategy and tactics. One supplier discovered that 67% of its business was done on the basis of out-of-policy requests—transaction pricing that deviated from established pricing policy.

Finally, a supplier must gain an estimate of the percentage of each customer's total purchase requirements it obtains for each market offering it provides. Although most firms in business markets have some estimate of their market share, far fewer have estimates of their shares of each customer's business in the markets they serve. Yet, **share of customer's business** is much more diagnostic in that it pinpoints customer accounts that perceive the supplier's offering as superior to those of competitors and suggests sources of differentiation.

Suppose that a supplier has a 20% market share. It is unlikely that each customer in the market is purchasing 20% of its requirement from the supplier. Rather, some customers purchase nothing from the supplier and others are purchasing more than 20% of their requirements from the supplier. What differentiates large-share customers from minor-share customers, and what sources of differentiation are possible if the customer were to give the supplier a greater share of its business, or even a 100% share?

Rebuilding Differentiation

In business markets where the core product or service is seen as a commodity, it may be extremely costly or difficult to achieve a difference in the core product or service that customers would perceive as significant. By considering more broadly how they might deliver value to customers, suppliers can identify significant sources of differentiation. Supplementary services, programs, and systems most often are more profitable sources of differentiation that can significantly change the way customers value market offerings.

Suppliers can search for knowledge that would be valuable for customers to have, yet difficult for them to gain by themselves. We refer to this as *creating knowledge banks*.

One sort of knowledge is how the customer operations and ways of doing things compare with those of its competitors. Allegiance Healthcare, a leading distributor of hospital supplies, built a best practice database from the experiences of 100 leading hospitals for the 30 surgical procedures that drive 80% of a hospital's volume. This database details the activities performed and resources consumed for each of these surgical procedures. Armed with the knowledge this database provides, Allegiance clinical consultants work with hospital customers to identify where the hospitals deviate from best practice and assist in efforts to reduce costs and improve productivity.

Suppliers can search for problems or nuisances that a number of customers each experience, where the supplier could invest in expertise that could be shared across customers to solve or alleviate the problems. In doing so, the suppliers are able to provide superior solutions to customer problems, often at lower costs, and differentiate themselves from competitors. We refer to this as *building leveraging expertise.*

GLS Inc., a leading distributor of elastomers and specialty chemicals, recognized that it could leverage its superior expertise in environmental, health, and safety regulatory compliance as a value-adding service for its customers, which mostly are medium and small firms. GLS monitors the *Federal Register* and writes bulletins alerting customers on regulatory changes, as well as reminding them of existing standards. It provides customers with a regulatory compliance manual, performs audits of Environmental Protection Agency (EPA) and Occupational Safety and Health Administration (OSHA) regulatory compliance at customer locations, and assists smaller customers in preparing their annual toxic chemical release inventories and air emissions statements. Without GLS's assistance, these customers would find it difficult and costly to keep informed of regulatory changes and what they need to do to comply. Senior management at these customers greatly appreciates GLS's support, because failure to comply now can lead to criminal prosecution.

When corporate customers purchase personal computers (PCs), they often want to install software specific to their firms in addition to software licensed from firms such as Microsoft. To do this customization, though, typically takes an hour or two, costs between $200 and $300, and is a bother to both the user and the firm's PC support staff. Dell Computer recognized that it could build some leveraging expertise that would enable it to solve this costly nuisance for its major customers. It created a high-speed, 100-megabit Ethernet at its factory that can instantly download a tailored mix of software onto its major customers' PCs.[7]

Customers that focus on the core product or service tend to see only lowering price, not total cost, as a way of suppliers setting themselves apart from one another. Yet, suppliers that change the customer's frame of reference to total cost have much greater opportunities to add value, reduce costs, and differentiate themselves from competitors. We refer to this process as *changing the customer's frame of reference.* As an example, Boeing has 100,000 Dell PCs. Dell Computer has 30 employees on-site at Boeing, who work closely with Boeing managers in planning their requirements and configuring their network. Because of this arrangement, the Dell personnel are regarded more like Boeing's PC department than a PC vendor.

In exchange for 100% share of a customer's business, suppliers sometimes are able to change how they do business with the customer. As an example, a coatings supplier was willing to put a technician on-site to oversee the painting process and to quote a price per coated object rather than the customary price per liter of coating. And, after all, isn't price per coated object what the customer should really care about?

Finally, no matter how precisely a supplier segments a market, some residual variation in the product and service requirements of segment members will remain. That is, even though customers within a segment may be essentially the same in many of their requirements, they remain different in others. Rather than ignore residual variation, perceptive suppliers take advantage of it by *building flexibility into their market offerings*. Later in this chapter, we discuss at length constructing and managing flexible market offerings. Here, we simply mention that flexible market offerings do set a supplier apart from its competitors, which continue to offer a "standard" offering constructed for the "average" customer that "defines" each segment.

Services as Core Products in Market Offerings

Many of us are used to thinking of the core product as some tangible item. However, when the core product is a service, how does it affect our thinking about managing the market offering? Two views can be taken on this point. One is that services are fundamentally different.[8] In support of this viewpoint, four characteristics are thought to be unique to services[9]:

1. ***Intangibility.*** Services can't be touched but rather are experienced.
2. ***Inseparability of production and consumption.*** Services are consumed as they are produced.
3. ***Perishability.*** Following from this inseparability, services cannot be saved or stored for later use.
4. ***Heterogeneity.*** Because of their greater dependence on the provider, services have the potential for high variance in their performance.

The opposing view is that the differences between products and services are a matter of degree and that all market offerings can be thought of as falling along a continuum of tangibility. Further, few, if any, products or services are completely tangible or completely intangible. As Levitt notes, "Even the most tangible of products can't be *reliably* tested or experienced in advance." Based on this view, suppliers provide promises of performance satisfaction to prospective customers, which they attempt to tangibilize in their presentation.[10]

We concur with this latter view for two reasons. First, with some thought, we can identify services and products that are not consistent with the uniqueness characteristics listed previously. Cleaning services performed at night and market research studies are each produced separately and prior to their consumption or usage by customers. On the other hand, tangible products such as specialty organic chemicals are relatively perishable. Services themselves differ significantly in the tangibility of the outputs that they produce. Consider, for example, the range of tangibility for the following business services: architectural drawings, commercial banking, investment banking, tax attorney consultation, and commercial insurance. Second, in our experience, market offerings in the business marketplace are changing in ways that are moving them toward the center of the tangibility continuum. Services marketers appear to be increasingly seeking to "tangibilize" their market offerings, whereas product marketers appear to be increasingly wrapping their products with augmenting services.[11]

Constructing Flexible Market Offerings

Firms in business markets are learning that success depends upon adroitly balancing three pervasive, but often conflicting, marketplace requirements.[12] First, markets are becoming highly fragmented and customers are requesting, and getting, more customized offerings. Second, customers are uncompromising in their demands that market offerings be sold for either the lowest price or the lowest total cost. Third, because of the success of the Total Quality Management movement, many purchasers now take quality as a given and believe that few meaningful differences separate competing products. Customer firms increasingly expect suppliers to deliver added value and differentiation in the form of an augmenting bundle of **services, programs**, and **systems** such as those listed earlier in Figure 5.1. Hereafter, for simplicity, we most often refer to these value-adding elements inclusively as "services."[13]

However, few firms have discovered all the implications of these requirements. Instead, most choose to add layer upon layer of services to their market offerings at prices that reflect neither customer value nor their own costs, in the hope of keeping customers satisfied and gaining some competitive advantage. Box 5.1 illustrates how the market-offering practice of a telecom network equipment manufacturer ran amok owing to inadequate strategic thought to its market offering.

How can business market managers avoid such nightmares and confront seemingly paradoxical pressures to differentiate themselves from competitors, yet keep their own costs and prices to customers down? On the product side of the market offering, flexible manufacturing, modularization, and product platform design have each been part of the solution. This paradigm shift has challenged conventional thinking that it is impossible to provide product variety and low cost.[14] On the services side of the market offering, a counterpart paradigm shift is occurring. The businesses leading the way have begun to provide flexible market offerings, consisting of **naked solutions, with options**.

The Concept of Flexible Market Offerings

Business market managers start with the realization that no matter how precisely a firm segments a market, some residual variation in the product and service requirements of segment members will remain. That is, even though customers within a segment may be essentially the same in some of their requirements, they remain different in others. In the past, suppliers either ignored or were unable to deal with this variation, choosing instead to provide market offerings composed of "standard" bundles or packages of products and services designed to meet the needs of the "average" customer within each segment. Even worse, in many instances, suppliers have provided essentially the same "vanilla" offering across all segments. As a result, some customers felt that they were forced to pay for services they did not need, whereas others did not get the depth of service they required, even if they were willing to pay extra.

Rather than ignore residual variation, perceptive business market managers take advantage of it by building flexibility into their market offerings. They do so by first constructing **naked solutions** for each market segment—the bare minimum of

BOX 5.1
Market Offering Practice of GlobeFon Runs Amok

In 2004, PSTM (name disguised) invited tenders for expanding its GSM networks all over India. GlobeFon (name disguised), a global leader in telecommunication network equipment, was one of the lowest bidders as the company was desperate to enter the Indian market. PSTM was then one of the biggest telecom operators in the world. For GlobeFon, it was a strategically important customer. There were big celebrations in GlobeFon when it won the contract. However, from day one, it was clear that GlobeFon would not make money because of their low quote. The idea in quoting a low price was to get a foothold in India and ensure expansion projects from PSTM in the future, which would make up for the lost profits on the deal in hand.

PSTM, being a government undertaking, manifested buying orientation. It aggressively sought lowest price from its telecom network vendors. GlobeFon knew that the full service offering that it offered routinely for the developed country markets was not price competitive in India, especially with the aggressive buying behavior of PSTM. This forced GlobeFon to cut down on the associated services and programs that it usually provided to its customers to ensure that its systems perform flawlessly. The company was able to quote a lower price because of a modification of its market offering, deleting several product features and service offerings. After it had won the contract, its priority was to reduce the overall cost of deployment to reduce potential losses from the customer account.

PSTM designed the network and decided on the network node locations, while GlobeFon was to only supply the equipment, install it at the pre-decided sites, and test it. Such an arrangement would have worked well with a knowledgeable customer, but PSTM lacked the expertise to do a neat job in this regard. GlobeFon overestimated the customer's capabilities while designing its market offering, and this proved fatal for the performance of its equipment as well as the relationship between the two firms.

Within the first few months of the service roll out, PSTM's call drop rate increased, congestion on the network was bad, and the firm started losing revenue. PSTM blamed it on GlobeFon's equipments. GlobeFon responded by stating that similar equipment deployed in the United States and Europe by large telecom operators worked perfectly well. However, the actual problem lay in the way PSTM had designed its network. The network design was not properly configured for optimal capacity usage of the vendor's equipment. Later, GlobeFon had to spend extra effort, time, and money to correct some of the more important problems.

GlobeFon thought it had understood PSTM's requirements completely, which was not the case. It failed to package the offering with the right services and programs to maximize value for the customer. GlobeFon made huge losses in the deal (in excess of INR 2,250 crores) and PSTM lost revenue and customers because of poor service to its customers. PSTM blamed GlobeFon for the disaster. Both were at loggerheads, including litigation, for some time, and GlobeFon's chance of obtaining repeat business with this customer, as well as with other customers in the country, was adversely impacted.

In its anxiety to configure a low priced system, GlobeFon had ignored the fact that capabilities of customers differ across countries. A service that may be "optional" for a customer in the United States might be

BOX 5.1
(Continued)

"mandatory" for an Indian customer. The design of GlobeFon's market offering should have been done based on an accurate assessment of realistic needs of the customer, as well as understanding the customer firm's capabilities.

Contributed by Nikhil Popli, Niloy Das, Unus Ebrahim, Vishal Sharma, Vivek Gupta, Participants, EPGP Program, Indian Institute of Management Bangalore.

products and services that all segment members uniformly value. Importantly, naked solutions are sold at the lowest profitable price. In turn, naked solutions are wrapped with **options** that some, but not all, segment members value and are offered separately for those segment members that do value them.

Although flexible market offerings enable customers to tailor the offering to their own requirements and preferences to a greater degree, this concept is not the same as mass customization. **Mass customization** is the capability to offer individually specified products or services on a large scale. As Zipkin details:

> Mass-customization systems have three key capabilities: *elicitation* (a mechanism for interacting with the customer and obtaining specific information); *process flexibility* (production technology that fabricates the product according to the information); and *logistics* (subsequent processing stages and distribution that are able to maintain the identity of each item and to deliver the right one to the right customer). Those elements are connected by powerful communications and thereby integrated into a seamless whole.[15]

In contrast, flexible market offerings are composed of a few well-chosen naked solutions, each of which is wrapped with well-chosen options, where the supplier makes these choices prior to offering them to customers. Thus, flexible market offerings are more akin to the concepts of modularity and commonality in product design, which we discuss in Chapter 6. Our experience concurs with the views of pundits that most firms in business markets are not able to profitably offer mass customization. Moreover, we contend that these firms can gain most, if not all, of the benefits of mass customization at a much lower cost through flexible market offerings.[16]

Although flexible market offerings comprise both product components and services components, hereafter in this chapter we focus primarily on the services part of the market offerings. In many industries, business market managers find that services are the predominant means of creating value to differentiate their offerings from those of competitors. We discuss gaining flexibility on the product part of the market offering at lower cost in Chapter 6 as part of new offering realization.

How can suppliers move to flexible market offerings? In the following sections, we discuss how this approach is put into practice. In the process, we consider the difficulties business market managers can expect to encounter, and we suggest solutions.

Articulate the Present Market Offering for Each Market Segment

To start, business market managers need to take stock of how their firm is doing business by detailing their current market offerings for each segment. As an illustration, consider the service portion of Baxter Healthcare Corporation's market offering to two segments of interest: transactional hospital customers, which do business with Baxter on an order-by-order basis, and strategic customers, which are hospitals that have made a commitment to a closer relationship with Baxter (see Figure 5.3).[17] Baxter constructed these offerings to provide ordinary and extraordinary levels of services, programs, and systems that reinforce its commitment to fulfilling strategic customers' requirements and enhancing their medical services and financial performance. Even programs that are optional and charged for separately, such as Baxter Corporate Consulting, reflect this commitment because they provide value or savings that far exceed their cost to the strategic customer.

Figure 5.3 Baxter Healthcare's Market Offerings to Two Segments: Transactional and Strategic Hospital Customers

	Segment	
Market Offering Element	Transactional Customer	Strategic Customer
Services		
Product returns	standard	standard
Technical assistance	standard	standard
Single point-of-contact	not offered	standard
Future disease incidence forecast	not offered	option
⋮		
Programs		
Price deals	standard	standard
Corporate customer bonus (financial incentive)	not offered	standard
Executive perspectives	not offered	standard
Consolidated purchasing report summary	not offered	standard
ACCESS Program	not offered	option
Baxter Corporate Consulting	not offered	option
⋮		
Systems		
ASAP order entry system	standard	standard
COMDISCO technology assessment	not offered	standard
ValueLink stockless inventory program	option	option
COMDISCO asset management system	option	option
⋮		

Businesses that have market offerings as well-articulated and well-managed as Baxter's are rare. More often, managers' understanding of the services, programs, and systems their business offers within and across market segments is piecemeal, uneven, and inaccurate. For this reason, managers from all functional areas that "touch" the customers in some way should take part in a structured process to elicit the present market offerings for each segment. Meeting as a group, a facilitator systematically takes these managers through the various kinds of services, programs, and systems a business might offer. For each one, the managers are asked, "Are you doing something like this?" As a follow-up question, the managers are asked, "Are you doing this sometimes, for some customers?"

Supplier managers can gain at least three different kinds of insights from this process: the true breadth of the market offering, the arbitrary nature of charges, and lack of variation across segments.

The True Breadth of the Market Offering

Managers invariably spend more time, and have less difficulty, thinking about the product portions of their market offerings. On the other hand, most have trouble identifying the services their firms provide. Inevitably, the services portions of market offerings are found to be more extensive than managers realize.

The Arbitrary Nature of Charges

Another revelation is the lack of discipline in what is offered as "standard" at the package price, and what is marketed as an "option" for which customers pay separately. All too often, suppliers find that their sales forces are guilty of "fourth-quarter habits": that is, the practice of giving away service options "for free" at the end of the year in order to meet their sales quotas. In doing so, they cloud customer expectations of what services are standard and what are optional. Suppliers sometimes discover that certain customers are adept in circumventing charges, perhaps through knowing whom to call for a favor or special treatment.[18]

Lack of Variation Across Segments

A final insight that many suppliers gain from the examination of market offerings is the "vanilla" nature of their offerings across segments. In business markets, a number of firms still segment the market and then proceed to provide much the same, if not exactly the same, offering to each segment. As the marketing manager for a large chemical company related, "For 90% of our customers, we offer the identical mix of support services."

Assess Customer Value and Supplier Cost

Before supplier managers can formulate flexible market offerings for each segment, they need to gain an estimate of the value of each service and the cost to provide it. Having this knowledge would seem to be fundamental in managing market offerings. However, few businesses have undertaken any formal value or cost assessments.

Measuring Customer Value

How do leading-edge businesses measure the value of their augmenting services? Greif Inc., which manufactures fiber and plastic drums, routinely conducts what it calls *cost-in-use* studies to document the incremental cost savings, and thus the superior value, that a customer gains by using Greif products and services rather than a competitor's. To add credibility to the results, one of Greif's technical service managers works with customer managers to complete the research. In addition to examining manufacturing, the team undertakes a series of process flow analyses in which it diagrams the customer's business operations and estimates their current costs.

From these estimates, Greif managers brainstorm system solutions for the customer. For example, they might envision a complete materials handling system, including just-in-time deliveries, utilized delivery systems (e.g., placing rollers on trucks to facilitate unloading), and drum recycling. Importantly, Greif gives the customer a variety of service alternatives along with estimates of cost savings. In this way, customers can make informed purchase decisions based upon the worth of proposed system solutions to them.[19]

Coming to Grips with Service Costs

As for costs, activity-based costing (ABC) techniques would seem to enable the assessment of costs on a customer-by-customer basis. However, few companies appear to be using ABC in the management of their market offerings. Why? We find that three specific factors inhibit the application of ABC techniques in managing the services portion of the market offering: services definitions are often "fuzzy"; service costs are often buried in the fixed costs of staff departments; and many companies remain organized around the products they sell rather than around market segments or customers.[20]

Overcoming inertia and systems impediments is essential, because more fully and accurately allocated costs can provide quite a different picture of how costly some services actually are. In an activity-based costing study, drug wholesalers found that the returned goods service they provided to customers cost approximately 3.7% of the average wholesaler's gross sales, not 1% or 2% as was commonly thought. This substantial disparity was due to reliance on credited dollars as a percentage of sales as a measure of service cost, which did not recognize a number of "hidden" transaction costs for wholesalers.[21]

How do progressive companies understand the services costs associated with their market offerings? To eliminate the problems associated with fuzzy services and the tendency of sales reps to bury service costs, a manufacturer of food additives and seasonings revamped its service delivery and planning systems. For starters, the company more precisely defined its services and the levels of each it offered. Its sales force, which was composed of highly trained technical representatives, was required to handle all minor services, such as basic problem solving. Charges for such services account for a portion of the total yearly budget allotted to each sales representative.

All major services, such as detailed technical problem solving, were offered on a project basis and delivered by technical experts from departments such as customer service. Either the customer directly paid for the project, which was preferred, or a charge was placed against the allotted, discretionary budget of its sales representative. At the beginning of each year, managers at the manufacturer constructed a plan for each major customer account that defined financial and volume targets and specified the levels of services the manufacturer would provide. At the end of the year, the managers reviewed these plans, examined service costs and account profitability, and recommended changes in level of account services for the next year.

Significant progress is being made in activity-based costing for services, programs, and systems. Kaplan and Anderson have recently introduced the tool of **time equations**, which enable activity-based costing models to reflect how order and activity characteristics cause variation in processing times. A time equation expresses in simple words and mathematical operators the minutes to perform an activity and how those minutes are affected by variations in the activity, such as providing differing levels of service. Consider an example of a time equation that Kaplan and Anderson provide to capture the variation in minutes required to package a chemical for shipment to a customer, depending upon the requirement for special packaging or mode of transportation:

Packaging Time = 0.5 + 6.5 [if special packaging required] + 2.0 [if shipping by air]

This time estimate in minutes then would be multiplied by the cost per minute of supplying that capacity to provide a cost estimate for order packaging. We find that this time equation tool for simplifying activity-based costing is strikingly compatible with the value word equation tool that we present in Chapter 2. Together, they provide suppliers with methodical, yet practical means of precisely expressing and estimating the value and the cost of providing supplementary services.[22]

The Payoff from Value and Cost Assessments

What results can supplier managers expect when they perform customer value assessments in conjunction with cost assessments, as we advocate? Certainly, they can expect to make better decisions about the services, programs, and systems they provide in their market offerings and to manage them more profitably. Significantly, as part of this, it enables them to identify and eliminate **value drains**, which are services, programs, and systems that cost the supplier more to provide than they are worth to customers receiving them and have no strategic significance.

Tata Steel is a leading supplier in India. Through its *Customer Value Management (CVM)* process, it strives to find and eliminate value drains in doing business with its strategic customers. Since the launch of CVM, there has been a significant drop in costs across the value chain between Tata Steel and these customers, and a significant increase in business for Tata Steel from these customers. A value drain example comes from its tubes business, where Tata Steel supplies steel tubes to a boiler manufacturer located 1,000 miles away. The tubes, after manufacturing, are specially oiled to avoid rusting in route to the customer's plant. Bizarre as it may seem, the customer first cleaned the oiled surface and then treated the surface of the tubes to allow them to pick up rust in its plant! As the CVM assessment revealed, a little bit of rust on the tubes was desirable to create enough friction between the tube and the bobbin drum while making coil-type boilers. Eliminating the oiling process at Tata Steel and the subsequent cleaning process at the customers' end was a win-win solution for both firms. This has resulted in a savings for the customer of 30–40 USD per metric ton while lowering Tata's costs by eliminating the oiling step in its process.[23]

Gaining an estimate of the value of market offering elements is not always easy; having one, though, is essential. With an understanding of value, discussions with customers can focus on performance and meeting customer requirements. Without this knowledge, discussions center on price. At a minimum, managers are seeking to make a basic, categorical judgment about the value of each element. That is, what supplier managers are trying to do is to isolate elements within a segment that are uniformly highly valued from those that are highly valued by some but not others, and those that are not highly valued by any customers.

Much the same can be said about trade-offs between precision and cost in activity-based costing analyses. Suppliers should make an effort to improve their understanding of the cost of providing each service and how this cost varies. To start, if supplier managers have not already done so, they should establish baselines of services usage across customers within segments.

Formulate Flexible Market Offerings by Market Segment

When formulating flexible market offerings for each market segment, business market managers can choose from three strategic alternatives for each service element: Do not market the service; market it as standard for which there is no charge; or market it as an option for which there is a charge. Each service itself has one of three statuses: The service is a new one (meaning that it has not been previously marketed by the supplier although it may have been offered by some competitor); it is an existing standard service; or it is an existing optional service. We cross service status with service strategic alternative to provide nine unique combinations. A useful way to organize these nine resulting strategies is a **flexible market offering strategy matrix**, which we show in Figure 5.4. By arranging the services in their appropriate cells, this matrix can provide a systematic picture of the nature and balance of a supplier's market offering. It also can promote further inquiry and offering strategy development, as when, for example, managers find one or more cells empty of elements. We consider, in turn, the rows of this matrix. We then discuss the pricing implications of flexible market offerings.

Reevaluating Existing Standard Services

Because the overriding philosophy is to keep the standard offering as "naked" as possible, only those service, program, and system elements that all firms within a segment highly value should be standard. The first place to start putting this philosophy into practice is by reevaluating the existing standard services. By discontinuing, or "pruning," some of these services and recasting others as options, business

Figure 5.4 Flexible Market Offering Strategy Matrix for Services, Programs, and Systems

	Service Element Deployment		
Service Element Status	Do Not Market	Market as "Standard"	Market as "Option"
Existing "standard" service	Prune from standard offering	Retain in standard offering	Recast as surcharge option
Existing "optional" service	Discontinue option	Enhance standard offering	Retain as value-added option
New service	Keep on shelf	Augment standard offering	Introduce as value-added option

market managers retain just the subset of standard services that will serve as the base of an updated standard offering.

Suppliers are often far more reluctant to discontinue existing services than they are to add services. Nonetheless, managers need to scrutinize existing elements for pruning candidates. One source is those services that most segment members rarely use. The customers that still value the service are so few that it is not worthwhile for the supplier to continue to offer it. In the interest of these customers, though, the supplier can sometimes outsource the service, or suggest another firm that provides it.

Certain services are readily pruned. For example, value drains that provide low customer value yet incur high costs for the supplier are ideal candidates. Following detailed investigations, a chemical manufacturer learned to its chagrin that although each of its 186 services continued to incur annual fixed costs, many had not been used in the past year. Its managers responded by pruning a large number of these services. Many customers didn't even realize the services were discontinued.

Beyond the services that all customers within a segment value highly, in some circumstances a supplier retains additional services in the standard offering. The success of certain services, in terms of their value or cost, depends upon their widespread usage by customers. Web-based order placement and tracking systems and logistics management systems are examples.

Service elements that a supplier cannot readily differentiate from those of competitors are candidates for matching and, most likely, for inclusion in the standard offering. Such elements are often regarded as standard in industry market offerings and often make up a substantial part of the naked offering. The challenge in offering these parity services is to have customers perceive their value as not significantly less than competitors' comparable services, but at the same time manage their costs below those of the competitors. The rationale is that because customers typically do not place much value on these services, they do not factor into customers' decisions about changing suppliers as long as they are minimally acceptable.

Supplier managers report that recasting a standard service as a surcharge option is the most difficult of the nine strategies to implement. Customers may react angrily when told they must now pay for something they had expected to get for free. It is even more difficult when competitors continue to market the service for free as part of a standard offering. Nowhere is this issue more of a problem than in industries characterized by high levels of fixed costs, such as "commodity" industrial chemicals and fully integrated steel mills. In such industries, managers are hesitant to implement any scheme that may result in reduced sales volume because it may jeopardize their ability to reach profitable capacity utilization levels. As a result, they routinely add services to retain volume and rarely drop any.

Infrequently performed services that deliver value at specific points in time, such as training, installation, and retrofitting, are perhaps the best candidates for redeployment as surcharge options. By marketing these services as value-added options, suppliers retain the business of customers that still derive value from them and are willing to pay for them. Often, this approach provides a "litmus test" for services that customers claim have no value for them (or are said to be the same as those obtainable for free from other suppliers), but that suppliers believe are worth something to customers. Depending on the market response, in the next period suppliers can either continue them as value-added options or discontinue them.

Leading supplier firms use a variety of approaches to recast services as value-added options. To make the overhaul of its standard service package more palatable to its customers, one specialty chemical company implemented a variation of this strategy. Along with specialty organic chemicals, the company offers a variety of services including laboratory support, field consulting, on-site testing, and educational seminars, all of which are costly. Realizing that its customers value and use these services differently, the company offers customers a variety of levels for each service. If a customer purchases a minimum amount of products each year, it receives "basic" levels of services along with the standard offering. If that same customer wants to receive a higher level of service, it can either increase its annual purchases to a prespecified amount or pay extra. Thus, some level of each service that customers expect is available with each standard offering. Customers that place greater value on the service have the option to obtain more.

As a prelude to making some previously standard services value-added options, a large computer company began listing a charge for the provided services, which was then subtracted with the notation "Do not pay this." An accompanying letter explained that the company was pleased to have been able to provide the field service and stated what it estimated this service was worth to the customer, using market-based rates for independent industry consultants. In doing so, the company established a reference point for the value of its services in the minds of its customers and positioned the services as not necessarily being performed at no charge in the future. Thus, a sharp distinction can be drawn between offering an element separately, even as an invoice reduction "no charge," and simply "burying" it within the standard package.

Another alternative is to have the customer pay, in full or in part, for whatever options they value with "bonus dollars," earned from doing business with the supplier. Strategic customers accrued "Baxter dollars" based on the amount of and growth in their purchases from Baxter Healthcare, which they then applied to any of a number of optional services, programs, and systems. In this way, strategic hospital customers used a common "Baxter dollars" resource to tailor Baxter's market offering to their own individual requirements.

Reexamining Optional Services

Next, supplier managers should reexamine existing optional services to determine whether they should be discontinued, used to enhance the standard offering, or continued as options.

As is the case with the standard package, evaluation and construction of options menus should begin with a deliberate attempt to prune existing optional services. Optional services that were once good sources of revenue for the supplier but are no longer used enough to justify their fully allocated costs are pruning candidates. Similarly, services whose cost has outstripped customers' willingness to pay for them (because of changes in technology, necessary expertise, or insurance risk) are also candidates. For example, because of insurance risk, most manufacturers are unwilling to provide transportation for drums of solvents, even for an additional delivery fee. As with pruning standard services, suppliers sometimes can help customers that still need these services to outsource them from other firms.

At times, suppliers may fold into standard offerings services that they have marketed as options. Where the core product of the market offering is regarded as a "commodity," suppliers look to enhance the standard offering as a means of differentiating themselves in the market. Their underlying belief is that customers do business on the basis of which supplier has the best or most extensive set of services. Because customers within segments will vary in how they value these services, however, the supplier is often driven to offer more elements in the standard offering.

Instead, suppliers should consider trimming the standard offering to the naked solution, offering a set of options, and letting customers pay, in full or in part, for whatever options they value with "bonus dollars." The more customers concentrate their purchases with the supplier, the more bonus dollars they earn, and the more services they can purchase. Not only does this alternative allow customers to tailor the supplier's market offering to their own particular requirements, it reinforces to them that they do not have to pay for services they do not want, as is the case with the totally bundled offering. To underscore the value of the services it offers, a supplier can promise to give customers cash for any unused bonus dollars at the end of the agreement, as did Baxter Healthcare.

Building Flexibility with New Services

What are the sources of new services? Some suppliers rely on their own strengths and capabilities to identify new services to offer. Another source of ideas is to focus on the cost structures and strategic priorities of targeted key customers. What new services can the supplier innovate that will assist these customers in their own initiatives to lower costs or improve performance?

Because they have not been offered in the past, new services do not carry the "baggage" of customer expectations about how a supplier should provide them ("Now you want us to pay extra for something we used to get for free?"). Thus, new services provide the best means to build flexibility into market offerings. Even though they should try to preserve new services as stand-alone options, at times suppliers may elect not to offer them or use them to enhance the standard offering.

Suppliers may decide to not offer a new element because of a variety of market timing issues. It may be that customers have not yet recognized an element's value, the cost of providing it is still too high, or the present element it would replace is still deemed adequate. Akzo Nobel Industrial Coatings (ANIC) provides an example. They anticipated greater environmental concerns about current painting technologies and invested substantial time and resources in the technological development of a process for "water-borne" paint application. As a service to its customers, ANIC would consult with them on changing to this more environmentally benign technology. Unfortunately, although many customers were interested to learn that ANIC possessed this capability, no one was willing to pay extra for it. ANIC managers believed that customers would not value the process until environmental protection laws required a significant reduction in solvent emissions. As a result, they decided to keep the technology on the shelf until customer value increased.

Suppliers sometimes enhance the standard offerings with new services. Where suppliers segment the market by relationships, managers look for new elements that will sustain and invigorate the collaborative relationships. One way is to add new services that anticipate and are responsive to customers' changing requirements. Okuma, a Japanese builder of computer numerical control (CNC) machine tools, provides an example. In one year, it introduced a *24-Hour Parts Shipment Guarantee*, and in the next, it began to sell a *Guaranteed Trade-In Program*. Okuma management believed that in addition to being responsive to a changing marketplace, the practice forced its distributors and employees to be more efficient—they must learn how to ship parts anywhere in the United States in 24 hours. It also gave the sales force something new and interesting to discuss during sales presentations.

Shrewd suppliers also add new services to standard offerings to thwart or stymie competitors. Baxter Scientific Products' Industrial Division, for example, deliberately seeks out new services that customers value and that Baxter can perform better than the competition or at lower costs. By bundling them in with the standard offering, Baxter forces competitors to choose from a pair of unpleasant alternatives. If competitors decline to offer the service altogether, Baxter can tout its unique service to customers as an extra benefit of doing business with Baxter. If competitors attempt to match Baxter and offer the service, they must incur both added costs and time delays associated with learning how to deliver the new service. New elements that also are likely candidates for inclusion in the standard offering are those for which (1) most of the costs are incurred in their initial development or deployment; (2) continuing costs are relatively invariant over the number of customers actually using the element; or (3) usage of the element in some way reduces the supplier's own costs.[24]

Offering new elements separately provides value-added options for customers that seek them and allows suppliers to readily gauge interest in new services, programs, and systems. For example, although R.R. Donnelley Company's traditional business has focused around printing, binding, film preparation, and prepress work, its management believes that future growth and profits will come from innovative services, such as database management, consulting and training, dimensional and talking ads, direct marketing, layout systems, and mapping services. To test their viability in the marketplace, Donnelley has offered these services as value-added options.

"New" elements that a supplier can offer separately as value-added options can emerge from reconsidering services in the standard offering. For each service that is offered at a constant level, supplier managers should ask whether they can define alternate levels that would have different value for different customers. In one electrical wholesaler, an overworked inside sales force used overnight airfreight to cover mistakes in orders or delivery dates. It regarded this practice as "standard" (i.e., the sole service recovery element) when, in many instances, second-day UPS and third-day common carrier would have been viable options.

Pricing Implications

It is crucial to recognize that constructing flexible market offerings says little, if anything, about their pricing. Pricing is based on the supplier's strategy for each market segment. For example, suppliers that pursue enhancing the standard offering with additional services may alternately decide to raise the price, keep it the same, or even lower it. The market offering's price might be raised commensurate with the greater value provided, or raised less than the added value to "soften" the effects of a needed price increase due to rising costs. A supplier might keep the price the same in a stable marketplace to gain new or incremental business through superior value, or in a price-declining marketplace simply to hold price. The price might even be lowered in support of an aggressive market development or share of customer's business growth strategy.

Further, customers may value certain services offered as standard, but the only way they are affordable to a supplier is if it has all the customer's business. With single-sourcing, a supplier can take responsibility for the customer process in which its products play a principal role, such as a coatings supplier's taking responsibility for the whole painting process in a customer's paint shop. These single-source service arrangements can lead to innovative pricing, such as the customer's paying for the number of coated objects, rather than liters of paint. The supplier may even be paid more for lower rejects and rework on the coated objects.

Similarly, pruning elements has no inherent pricing implication, but again the effect depends on the segment market strategy. A supplier might lower its price equal to the cost of the discontinued services, thereby maintaining the competitive status quo. Alternatively, to improve contribution margins, a supplier might not lower the price at all, or lower the price but less than the cost of providing the service. This latter tactic has the dual advantage of improving the value of the offering to customers that did not value the pruned service, while providing an incentive for competitors that are similarly looking to improve their profitability to match the supplier's action. Suppliers might even raise prices in situations where they are pursuing a harvest strategy, taking as much profit out of the business as possible while letting it decline.[25]

Offering services separately provides flexibility not only to the customers within a segment, but to the supplier, too, in terms of pricing. Putting a price on a service (or a higher level of a service whose base level is standard) preserves the supplier's option of charging separately for it. The supplier then is able to either charge a customer for its provision or trade its provision for a larger share or more profitable mix of the customer's purchase requirement. One alternative is to show the service charge on an invoice and then "net out" the charge for a specific reason (e.g., initial use discount). This approach has at least three advantages. It provides a readily captured way of tracking service "giveaways." Suppliers employ it in a selective, transitory way, such as to close a deal, to blunt a competitive inroad, or to attract business in targeted new segments. For example, Mitsubishi Electric Industrial Controls offers as an option a proprietary software development tool, but to win targeted new accounts, it may provide the tool at no charge. Consulting on usage of this software tool, which it also offers separately, may initially be provided at no charge, but subsequent consulting is not. Finally, showing a charge establishes and reinforces the value of services to customers and the supplier's salespeople.[26]

Prepare to Implement Flexible Market Offerings

After constructing flexible market offerings, a supplier has several tasks to accomplish prior to implementing those offerings. The supplier needs to decide how it will present the flexible market offerings to the market. Presenting a flexible market offering as an option menu or as a tailored-value package are two basic alternatives. Branding each market offering is a means of differentiating it from other market offerings, particularly with respect to the value it delivers. A supplier must anticipate implementation problems with customers and how it will handle them. Finally, the supplier works through the issues involved in breaking away from the pack of competitors' market offerings.

Option Menu Versus Tailored-Value Package

What will the customer see in making its decision: an option menu or a tailored-value package? The option menu approach makes the flexible market offering transparent to the customer by listing all optional elements. Although the salesperson may provide consultation, the customer has the primary responsibility for tailoring the market offering to its perceived requirements. Apple Computer and Microsoft each provide detailed, multiple-page menus of technical support services with pricing options, and let customers decide.

Rather than treating all elements as options, suppliers often provide a standard package with a menu of options and let the customer craft its own market offering. Certainly, in negotiated bid situations, a preferred strategy is to start with a naked offering at the lowest possible bid price, to be selected for further negotiations. The supplier then uses consultative selling efforts to "trade up" the customer to select options that will provide value. Astute suppliers realize that if they do not have a competitively low bid price, they have no opportunity to do business, so they develop a two-part negotiations strategy.

In contrast, the **tailored-value package** approach keeps the flexible market offerings opaque to customers. Working with the customer, the salesperson develops a list of specifications and then crafts an offering based on a menu of options that only she sees. This method places greater responsibility on the salesperson to accurately comprehend and respond to stated customer requirements. In practice, salespeople would most often respond with several packages and let the customer choose among them. Purchasing managers may request several packages in an attempt to gain an understanding of the trade-offs the supplier is implicitly offering.

Sonoco Product Company's Industrial Products Division uses both approaches. The division manufactures fiber cores around which products such as newsprint, commercial printing paper, textiles, yarns, plastic films, and aluminum foil are wrapped. Its customers select from several market offerings. For customers that want the lowest possible price, it markets a naked solution comprised of parent cores (uncut cores in standard lengths ranging from 8 to 30 feet) plus a minimum of support services. Sonoco will also sell these customers trimming equipment to cut the parent cores into usable sizes. For customers that don't want to be bothered with the tasks and investments associated with cutting cores, Sonoco markets fiber cores that match customer specifications. Along with fiber cores, Sonoco offers a variety of optional services such as process redesign of customer packaging systems. Finally, for customers located great distances from Sonoco plants and concerned that deliveries won't arrive on time, Sonoco will even set up a satellite plant near the customer's location (often in space leased in industrial parks). There, Sonoco employees will cut the cores to customer specifications. Sonoco also offers these customers the optional services.

As mentioned, Sonoco sales representatives sell these market offerings in two ways. If the customer desires, reps will provide customers with a detailed menu of all Sonoco products and services along with their respective prices. The customer can pick and choose the products and services it desires. Alternatively, Sonoco sales reps can use their expertise to assemble several tailored packages of products and services. Along with the price of each proposed package, Sonoco sales reps provide a summary of the cost savings the customer can expect to gain if it buys the package. In this way, the customer can choose an appropriate package based not only on its price, but also on its value. Sonoco managers report that since they began offering customers such extensive choices, both division sales volume and market share have increased.

Branding Market Offerings

A **brand** is a shorthand descriptor of the promised value that a market offering delivers to targeted customers and a means of differentiating this value from that of other market offerings. These other market offerings may come from the same supplier, or they may come from its competitors. Branding market offerings allows suppliers to make intangible benefits tangible to targeted customers, build differentiation in near-commodity markets, achieve identity and preference with customers' customers, and differentiate market offerings that have the same or very similar core product but are augmented with different services, programs, and systems. We briefly consider each of these purposes of branding market offerings.

A market offering may provide a social benefit to customers. Because social benefits are intangible, branding can serve to make the intangible tangible. Exelon chose to brand its environmentally preferable power as Eco-Preferred® Power to make tangible its ISO 14042 certification that this energy has a reduced impact on human health and the environment when compared with competing sources of energy that serve the same purpose. Exelon is thus able to better convey this social benefit to its commercial, government, and industrial customers that have environmental stewardship as part of their strategies.[27]

In many business markets, customers regard the offerings of competing suppliers as basically the same. Yet, through gaining a more fine-grained understanding of how subtle changes in the product can affect its performance in target customer applications, progressive suppliers can differentiate their offerings from less astute competitors. They then persuasively communicate the significance of these subtle differences to target customers in branding initiatives to build **brand equity** for their market offerings. The experience of Tata Steel in building and sustaining brand equity provides an illustrative case, which we relate in Box 5.2.

When a supplier's market offering creates significant value for its customers' customers, pursuing a branding initiative enables the supplier to build identity and preference for its offering over those of competitors with the customers' customers. This is particularly the case when the presence of the supplier's product in its customer's product is not easily detectable by the customer's customers. The Intel Inside® branding initiative for its processors in personal computers is a well-known example. Pursuing an **ingredient branding strategy**, as this is sometimes called, is especially applicable when the customers' customers receiving the significant value are consumers. DuPont has pursued this strategy successfully with its STAINMASTER® brand of carpet protector, which it sells along with its fibers to carpet mills so that they can produce STAINMASTER carpet. In

BOX 5.2

Tata Steel: Branding Initiatives in a Near-Commodity Market

Tata Steel is the world's sixth largest steel company and has an annual crude steel production capacity of 30 million tonnes per annum. It was selling steel as a commodity. However, in the year 2000, the company decided to brand its steel. For this, Tata Steel improved its product mix, increased the differentiation in its products through branding, and constantly improved its processes to maintain cost competitiveness.

The company started its branding journey by making the organization customer-centric. A branding task force was set up, reporting to the managing director's office. In April 2000, Tata Steel launched its first brand, Tata Shaktee, for galvanized corrugated sheets. Subsequently, Tata Steel launched its second brand, Tata Tiscon, for rods used in the construction industry. Tata Steelium was launched three years later, in 2003. Tata Steelium was the world's first branded cold rolled steel. Tata Steel thus developed a portfolio of brands that also contained three generic brands: Tata Pipes, Tata Bearings, and Tata Agrico.

To connect with its consumers and create positive brand equity with its business customers, Tata Steel ran many successful ad campaigns. One such advertisement showed Tata Steel employees succeed in sports at a national level. The advertisement ended with the quote, "We make champions. We also make steel." Other advertisements showed Tata Steel contribute in societal development, environmental protection, human progress, poverty relief and concluded with the tag line, "We also make steel." These advertisements built on the emotional appeal of the brand and communicated that Tata Steel contributed to making life better in more ways than one, while also making steel. There were also campaigns to communicate the new customer orientation of the company.

Tata Steel then moved into the space of value-added products by focusing on brands such as Tata Agrico, a brand encompassing agricultural products such as hoes, sickles, pickaxes, crowbars, shovels and hammers. Branding efforts in this space was very important because brand value played an important role in the customers' decision-making process.

Tata Steel aggressively took to branding cold rolled steel as Steelium, since branding added value to the product and helped focus attention on the product in the otherwise fragmented market for cold rolled steel. Steelium was another product that Tata Steel took to branding in order to transform its image from manufacturer to marketer. When Steelium was launched, it was sold in the market at a high premium over the prices of competing unbranded cold rolled steel. The company was able to charge a premium because branding of the product had created a distinct identification that enabled customers recognize that it was a genuine product from Tata Steel and not a counterfeit product by a manufacturer of spurious CR steel. The company went on to brand many of its other products such as Tata Shaktee for its galvanized corrugated steel used for rural housing, Tata Wiron for its wires, and Tata Tiscon for its reinforced bars used for concrete-based construction. Each of these products today is a powerful brand individually, yet leverages the strength of the Tata brand. Creating the brand is an important component; yet, the bigger challenge is to ensure that the promise of the brand is fulfilled for which Tata Steel had to launch several initiatives in the marketplace. These included working closely with distribution channels, ensuring clear product identification, educating the

BOX 5.2
Continued

customer, price harmonization across the country to eliminate the possibility of opportunistic middlemen making money through unethical means, ensuring accurate weighing of the product at each point of sale, etc.

Contributed by Shreshth Sharma, Participant, PGP Program, Indian Institute of Management Bangalore.
Sources: Ishita Ayan Dutt, "We Also Brand Steel," 3 May 2003, *http://www.rediff.com/money/2003/may/03spec1.htm;* "Branding A Commodity – Tata Steel," *http://www.oppapers.com/essays/ Branding-A-Commodity-Tata-Steel/192066.*

either case, brand-building efforts are focused primarily on the customers' customers.[28]

Finally, branding market offerings enables a supplier to differentiate offerings where the core offering is essentially the same, but it has augmented the core offering with different services, programs, and systems to deliver superior value to target market segments having different requirements and preferences. The supplier then uses brand-building initiatives to reinforce the distinctive character of each brand and the value it delivers to its target customers. The experience of Taiwan-based Acer, Inc. in sustaining multiple brands that differentiate essentially the same product provides a noteworthy case, which we relate in Box 5.3.

Anticipating Implementation Problems with Customers

Suppliers can minimize implementation problems by understanding customer requirements and shaping customer expectations, through education and persuasion, about the superior value of the flexible market offerings. Suppliers need to manage service and pricing expectations. By developing collateral materials and case histories, they convey that less is more and can more easily combat the "We used to get it for free" gripes. These messages portray flexible market offerings from the perspective, "You don't have to pay for what you don't want."

Suppliers need to be relentless in communicating the value story to customers. As mentioned earlier, new services provide perhaps the best opportunity to implement flexibility in market offerings. As a rollout or phase-in, suppliers also might consider implementing flexible market offerings at the same time they make product changes or introductions.

Ross Controls, a maker of pneumatic valves, had to educate its customers about the value its new customized service offering provided. Ross's customers were used to making purchasing decisions based on price and did not see the benefit of spending a long time working with Ross to design custom valves for their specific applications. Because of its investment in computer-aided design tools and equipment automation, however, Ross could design and produce in several days what had taken up to 16 weeks in the past. To demonstrate this new service capability to design and produce custom valves quickly, Ross asked its customers to

BOX 5.3

Acer Sustains Multiple Brands That Differentiate Essentially the Same Product in Global Markets

In 2007, the Taiwan-based Personal Computer (PC) giant Acer, Inc. acquired California-based Gateway, a computer manufacturer in the United States. The Gateway purchase came along the budget PC line, eMachines. The deal was further complicated by Gateway's announcement that it would exercise its option to acquire European PC manufacturer Packard Bell. Acer was not strong in the United States, and it sought to increase its retail presence in this market by acquiring Gateway.

One of the key concerns of the acquisition was how the merged company would handle four brands—Acer, Gateway, eMachines, and Packard Bell, of which the first two were major world brands. This was the first time that Acer had had to deal with the challenge of carrying multiple brands.

Acer felt that Gateway and eMachines, the relatively low-end machines competing primarily on price, needed to be spruced up by adding faster processors and better designs. The newly combined Acer was keen on keeping the Gateway brand alive. Promoting a particular brand varied by market, depending on how successful the brand already was in that market. In Europe and Asia, Acer was a strong brand, while it was less true in the United States. In the United States, the company was therefore being forced to keep both Acer and Gateway. eMachines was positioned as a seller of budget-priced PCs.

There were many challenges in managing two distinct brands in the computer industry. Each of the computer makers had at least two major lines of products: computers (including desktops and servers) and laptops. There was a large product variety proliferation within each of these categories, compounded further by fast product obsolescence. Managing the service and support operations for the merged company was another challenge, given the differing precedents for service for the two companies. For example, in the United States, Acer performed its own repairs at a facility in Temple, Texas, while Gateway outsourced service to a third party. The existence of multiple languages in Europe led to support integration-related challenges.

Pre-acquisition, Gateway went to market directly, using the Internet. Acer by contrast extensively deployed channel partners. Consequently, evolving a coherent go-to-market strategy for the merged entity was a big issue. Acer needed to create adequate differential among the brands to make them appealing to retailers. Positioning and pricing the two brands was a huge challenge. There was a need to constantly explain to customers what the multiple brands stood for and why it was necessary to keep them. The Acer brand was perceived as highly innovative and attracted technologically savvy customers, while Gateway and Packard Bell attracted customers who were technologically less sophisticated. eMachines targeted users who were looking for efficiency and convenience in their personal computers.

In India, the company has been in operation as Acer India Pvt. Ltd. Its mission is to make computer technology easier and more affordable. In India, the company leveraged the more well-known Acer brand name. Keeping in mind the needs of the Indian market, the positioning of Acer includes providing highest levels of uptime of the computers through extensive service network, user-friendly products that can be used "straight

(*continued*)

BOX 5.3
(Continued)

out of the box," high reliability, and cost-effective ownership considering value-conscious Indian buyers.

In summary, the post-acquisition objectives were to avoid brand overlapping, communicate coherently to both internal and external stakeholders, maintain the identities of the companies, leverage their respective strengths, and finally to result in increased market share.

Sources: Melissa J. Perenson, *PC World*, 27 August 2007, "The Impact of the Acer-Gateway Merger," *http://www.pcworld.com/article/137462/acer_ceo_talks_gateway_acquisition_vista_rollout.html;* Harry McCracken, "Acer CEO Talks Gateway Acquisition, Vista Rollout," 21 September 2007, *PC World, http://www.pcworld.com/article/137462/acer_ceo_talks_gateway_acquisition_vista_rollout.html;* Timothy Prickett Morgan, "Acer Buys Gateway and Maybe Packard Bell Too," 27 August 2007, *http://www.itjungle.com/bns/bns082707-story02.html;* B2B Product Trade Portal, Bombay Harbour, *http://www.bombayharbor.com/Company/28836/Acer_India_Pvt_Ltd.html.*

provide prototype specifications. Within a few days, Ross provided them for free an actual prototype valve, which could cost as much as $20,000. Customers were delighted with Ross's responsiveness to their prototype specifications and were even willing to pay a premium for it. As a result, Ross has experienced growth in an otherwise stagnant-to-declining industry.[29]

Breaking Away from the Pack

In our field research, a number of managers wistfully expressed a desire for change, but were concerned about what competitors would do. These managers believed their competitors were similarly looking to improve profitability, but that they wouldn't match a move to flexible market offerings. In addition, there are timing and discipline concerns. Before discussing these issues, we first consider breaking away as a means of countering competitors' dubious parity claims.

One way to break away (which also works for services included in the standard offering) is to guarantee outcomes based on the service. The larger and more complicated the list of services a business markets, the more likely it is that competitors will promise, "We can do that." When this occurs, savvy marketers respond by transforming service claims into guarantees. For instance, when Okuma's competitors began to promise rapid delivery, Okuma announced its *24-Hour Shipment Guarantee.* If a customer orders a part and it is not shipped in 24 hours, the customer gets the part for free. Greif Inc. takes the guarantee one step further with its *Guaranteed Cost Savings Program.* If a customer requests that they be given a 5% price cut, the division guarantees to find at least a 5% cost savings. This arrangement is formalized into a written contract. If the customer doesn't realize the 5% savings, Greif agrees to pay the difference. If more than 5% of savings are found, the customer gets to keep it all. Greif has had no problem delivering as guaranteed. Furthermore, managers find that it is a great way to turn discussions away from price.

Knowing when to break away and unbundle is difficult. Is there an advantage to being the first, or is it better to be a rapid follower? To be an industry paradigm breaker, the first supplier must have tough resolve and be willing to "take the heat." An intermediate strategy is to pilot-test flexible market offerings in one of two ways: (1) either add two new services but offer them as options, or (2) pick two services from the present industry "standard" package and unbundle them, making them surcharge options. Going against industry standards can be the first step toward an industry paradigm shift and a market offering rule change.

Many companies refrain from implementing flexible market offerings because they fear they will lose certain customers by requiring them to pay extra for optional services. Instead, managers might adopt the philosophy of firms that have implemented flexible market offerings and found that while losing some accounts, they also gain new business because their market offerings now more closely meet customer requirements at reasonable prices. Other suppliers that have implemented flexible market offerings have found they now get a better return on their resources by focusing them on the segments and customers that value them.

Timing is always a concern. Akzo Nobel Industrial Coatings (ANIC) initiated its customer contribution to profitability approach in Europe about 10 years ago. Because revamping service offerings and pricing them to get an equitable return on the value provided was not only new to the industry, but internally controversial, ANIC decided to implement it first in the Netherlands and Germany, "home" markets where ANIC was strongest. It then rolled out the approach to Northern Europe. Southern Europe, the last to be converted, proved to be the most difficult markets to bring around because of sales force resistance (due to anticipated decreases in their commission incomes). Although ANIC lost some customers because they no longer got a variety of services for free, overall, its perseverance resulted in stable sales volume at significantly better profitability.

A final, paramount way to lead the pack is to be disciplined, operating within the imposed structures of the flexible market offerings. To maintain this discipline requires development of a most difficult-to-acquire customer skill: adroitly saying "no" to some customers. Flexible market offerings provide customers with choices from which they choose, but suppliers must be willing to say "no" to customers that want full-service packages at no-frills prices. Without this skill, flexible market offerings devolve to business as usual, "giving it away." Practiced deftly, it builds a reputation for the supplier within the industry as firm, consistent, and fair.

VALUE-BASED PRICING

How do business market managers decide upon a specific price for the market offering? "In most firms prices are determined by intuition, opinions, rules of thumb, outright dogma, top management's higher wisdom, or internal power fights."[30] This quote by Hermann Simon, an expert on pricing, accurately captures our experience in business markets. Even though superior pricing capability can have a significant impact on profitability, strangely enough, few firms in business markets attempt to systematically build and leverage their pricing capability.[31]

Pricing consideration ought to take place at the strategy level, at the tactics level, and at the level of the individual transaction.[32] In any market, we find a range of prices. **Pricing strategy** focuses on where within this range to position the market offering, and how to shift the range itself and the supplier's relative position within it. In contrast, **pricing tactics** focus on shifting the supplier's position within the existing price range and are often transitory in nature. Finally, **transaction pricing** focuses on realizing the greatest net price for each individual order. Our primary focus in this section is at the strategy level. In later chapters we take up pricing at the tactic and transaction levels.

The intent of pricing strategy is to establish the basic pricing for the market offering. Some approaches or methods can be used to inform this process, yet they can only provide guidance on the range of feasible prices with respect to the existing market price range. In our experience, although elaborate rationales are sometimes constructed to explain the prices selected for market offerings, supplier managers rely on what we call (somewhat in jest) **management numerology**—the belief that certain numbers are imbued with greater meaning and significance than others and thus make for more desirable prices. So, although a rationale is put forth that may appear internally quite consistent, when scrutinized, it has one or more implicit assumptions. Even though customer value assessment provides research-based guidance, ultimately some managerial judgment is required to select the specific price.

Traditional Pricing Approaches

Although we advocate a value-based approach to pricing, we have found that most firms rely on the traditional methods of cost-plus pricing or competition-based pricing. Each of these approaches may appear to give the business market manager some comfort as a basis for setting prices, but each has some problematic aspects.[33]

Cost-Plus Pricing

In **cost-plus pricing**, based upon knowledge of their own costs, supplier managers add some percentage onto those costs to arrive at the market offering price. First, let's consider the "cost" component that serves as the base. Often, cost is narrowly defined by what the supplier can readily measure: cost of goods sold, variable costs, or full costs. This approach assumes that the supplier has an accurate understanding of these costs, something many businesses lack. Even businesses that have instituted activity-based costing for their production, and thus have a relatively accurate understanding of cost of goods sold, may be neglecting the costs of the supplementary services, programs, or systems. Often, these latter costs are lumped into an overhead allocation component, "sales and general administration," which is subtracted out to provide the net profit margin.

The "plus" component represents the supplier's target profit. It may be a standard percentage that senior management sets for all businesses, or it may be specific to the business unit, perhaps representing historical margins on past market offerings. Target gross margin or net profit margin percentage commonly serve as the plus component.

Cost-plus pricing assumes that the customer cares about the supplier's costs, that they are somehow relevant to what the customer should pay for the market offering. Interestingly, some business market managers have related to us that their own sales forces have this belief, too. Consequently, they do not feel comfortable selling virtually the same market offerings (in cost) to different market segments at different prices. The value that the market offering provides to the customer is not considered, so the supplier risks either being uncompetitively high-priced or giving away value that it does not know it provides to the customer.

Although some may argue that knowledge of cost is relevant because it serves as the base for prices the supplier can charge and still make an operating profit, without knowledge of the value provided, this claim might not be true. Often, the cost numbers are based on assumptions of certain volumes being produced. If the market offering is uncompetitively high-priced, the number of units actually sold may fall below these forecasted volumes, making the acquisition prices of component materials and conversion costs higher than anticipated in the original costing calculations.

Competition-Based Pricing

With **competition-based pricing**, supplier managers simply set their price in relation to what the competitors' prices are. The price may be set exactly the same as the predominant competitors, signaling commodity, or it may be slightly higher or lower because of perceived minor reputation, quality, or service differences. Price changes by competitors tend to be imitated reflexively, with perhaps slight deviations as managers attempt to capture greater volume or margins. Supplier managers who use competition-based pricing are essentially giving control of a critical aspect of their marketing strategy to their competitors.

The supplier with the largest market share (and likely, industry capacity share) may provide price leadership.[34] As an example, Arcelor was created by a merger of Aceralia, Arbed, and Usinor in early 2002, making this Luxembourg-based steel producer the world's largest in flat carbon steel and long carbon steel products. In the third quarter of 2002, Arcelor announced that it would raise its prices €20 per ton for deliveries in the fourth quarter. In doing so, Arcelor not only gave its customers time to plan their purchases using this new pricing, it also exerted price leadership encouraging other steel producers to raise their prices as well, which they did.[35]

Competition-based pricing assumes that the supplier managers have an accurate understanding of competitors' prices, which may not be the case. Competitors may actively disguise their true prices through such tactics as off-invoice discounts, surcharges for services, and year-end bonuses or rebates, making exact comparisons difficult. Supplier managers may also receive misinformation about competitors' prices from customers or their own resellers. After all, each has self-interest that is better served with lower prices. For example, an already overworked field sales force may not have the time to validate all reseller requests for pricing relief to meet competitive pricing in their local markets. Unscrupulous resellers, seeking some extra margin, may invent "street prices" knowing that they will likely evade detection.

Even with an accurate understanding of competitors' prices, how many suppliers in a market can have the lowest price? One! But many suppliers are not content to accept this fact, and they willingly cut price to meet a competitor's lower price. Shrewd customers can orchestrate a downward-spiraling exchange among suppliers. Just as troubling is the message it sends to the market about the supplier: "Me, too!" That is, the supplier is essentially signaling that it regards its offering as no different from the competitor's. No wonder, then, that the sales force claims it can only sell on price! What's left?

Finally, just as with cost-plus pricing, without knowledge of their market offering's value, supplier managers may be giving value away. It seems less likely that their offering will be uncompetitive, because suppliers that embrace competition-based pricing may implicitly gain some coarse understanding of their offering's value by observing how pricing changes affect the volume sold. Seldom, though, is this knowledge the result of carefully planned market experiments. Rather, it is gathered piecemeal and anecdotally. Moreover, it presumes that the customer has an accurate understanding of the value of each competitor's market offering, which often may not be the case.

An Approach to Value-Based Pricing

Our philosophy is that price should be set in relation to a market offering's value, which is called **value-based pricing**. However, deciding upon a specific price is not simple, because there are other considerations. To help us understand these considerations, we next develop a framework for value-based pricing. Underpinning this framework is the **fundamental value equation** that we presented in Chapter 1:

$$(\text{Value}_f - \text{Price}_f) > (\text{Value}_a - \text{Price}_a) \quad \textbf{(5.1)}$$

where Value_f and Price_f are the value and price of the firm's market offering (Offering_f), and Value_a and Price_a are the value and price of the next-best-alternative market offering (Offering_a). In practice, a rearrangement of this equation better captures how customer firm managers decide between offerings:

$$(\text{Value}_f - \text{Value}_a) > (\text{Price}_f - \text{Price}_a) \quad \textbf{(5.2)}$$

$$\Delta\text{Value}_{f,a} > (\text{Price}_f - \text{Price}_a) \quad \textbf{(5.3)}$$

Often, value analyses or customer value assessments are performed on a comparative basis, where the differences in performance and total cost are ascertained for two market offerings of interest. Then these differences are expressed in monetary terms and summed to obtain $\Delta\text{Value}_{f,a}$. Equation 5.3 also represents a natural way that customer managers decide between two offerings: "What is the difference in the worth of the two offerings to my firm, and how does it compare to the difference in their prices?"

However, understanding Value_f, Value_a, and Price_a says nothing about a specific price that the firm should choose for Offering_f. We rearrange equation 5.3 to isolate Price_f on the left side of the equation:

$$\text{Price}_f < \text{Price}_a + \Delta\text{Value}_{f,a} \quad \textbf{(5.4)}$$

Figure 5.5 A Value-Based Pricing Framework

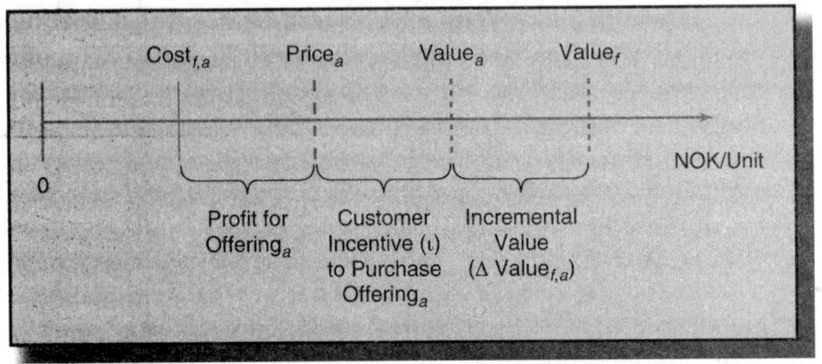

Given that Price$_a$ is known, which after some investigation is usually the case, equation 5.4 then defines the feasible range of prices the firm could charge and still maintain the inequality. Equation 5.4 also reveals an insight: competition-based pricing is a special case of value-based pricing, when $\Delta\text{Value}_{f,a}$ is either zero, the definition of a commodity, or unknown and regarded as though it were zero.

Selecting Price$_f$ depends upon some additional considerations. To begin, let's consider Figure 5.5. Because value is expressed as the worth in monetary terms, we provide a value continuum expressed in Norwegian kroner per unit (NOK/unit). For simplicity (and without loss of generality), we assume the cost of Offering$_f$ and Offering$_a$ are the same. The difference between Price$_a$ and Cost$_a$ defines the **profit** for Offering$_a$. The difference between Value$_a$ and Price$_a$ represents the **customer incentive to purchase** Offering$_a$ (labeled as ι). Note that in business markets, the value provided will likely exceed the price or else the customer will be indifferent. And, with the make-versus-buy consideration inherent in business markets, if the price equals the value received, the customer may be tempted to make rather than buy.[36]

Now, the difference between Value$_f$ and Value$_a$ represents the **incremental value** Offering$_f$ provides over Offering$_a$. What part of this incremental value to retain as profit and what part to share with the customer as an incentive to purchase is a strategic decision. Significantly, by sharing part of this incremental value with the customer, in essence, a supplier *creates* value for the customer.

Suppose we set Price$_f$ at Value$_a$. In this case, we would be giving all the incremental value to the customer as incentive to purchase Offering$_f$, with the relatively small remainder being the profit for the firm. Contrast this option with the alternative where we set Price$_f$ relatively close to Value$_f$, so that we are giving only enough of the incremental value as customer incentive to purchase to maintain the inequality of equation 5.3. The first alternative is sometimes called a **penetration pricing strategy**, because the firm intends to make its overall profit through selling a larger number of units at a lower profit per unit. The second alternative is sometimes called a **skimming pricing strategy**, because the firm intends to make its overall profits through selling fewer units at a higher profit per unit. A number of factors can support pursuing one or the other strategy, such as the market size and forecasted growth, the significance of any learning effects (e.g., experience curve or market knowledge), anticipated reactions by present or potential competitors, and how persuasively demonstrable the value proposition is.[37] The fundamental consideration that we want to emphasize, though, is that *pricing strategy can only be understood within the context of the business unit's market strategy for each segment.*

Furthermore, underlying the choice of a pricing strategy is the recognition that prospective customers vary in the value they place on a supplier's market offering and that this value may change over time. So, although we conceptually represent $Value_f$ and $Value_a$ as point estimates in equation 5.1 and Figure 5.5, when we broaden our consideration from a single, prospective customer firm to a market segment, these points become mean estimates of value distributions for the prospective customers in that segment. As we move $Price_f$ closer to $Value_a$, customer incentive to purchase $Offering_f$ over $Offering_a$ passes the threshold for a larger proportion of the distribution of prospective customers. That is, a greater number of those customers whose value for $Offering_f$ is less than the mean $Value_f$ will still have the inequality of equation 5.1 satisfied (using the individual $Value_f$ for their own firms).

Finally, consider the alternative where $Price_f$ is set so that the customer incentive to purchase $Offering_f$ is exactly equal to that of $Offering_a$, depicted as ι. Which offering will the customer choose? From equation 5.1, we might predict indifference. Yet in practice, we find that if one is the incumbent offering, say $Offering_a$, customers will continue to purchase it. Why? Generalized risk, or what might simply be called **inertia**. Even after all specific cost and value differences are accounted for in the respective value assessments, including any specific, identifiable risks in changing to $Offering_f$, a reluctance to change remains. Thus, to displace the incumbent offering, some additional portion of the incremental value must be given, a pricing tactic that we call **incentive to change**. Although the size of this incentive will vary by situation, based on some qualitative research with purchasing managers, we offer 5% to 7% as a rough heuristic. So, if the reduction in price (or gain in value) is less than this, purchasing managers are apparently unwilling to even investigate changing from the incumbent to another offering.

Because it is based upon what the customer is willing to pay for a market offering, value-based pricing is preferred over other approaches to pricing, and it is an essential component of a business market management philosophy. Yet, for firms to successfully implement it, some critical assumptions need to be met: (1) The supplier has an accurate understanding of either $Value_f$ and $Value_a$, or $\Delta Value_{f,a}$; and (2) the supplier has an accurate understanding of $Price_a$. To satisfy these assumptions, most often a supplier will need market sensing using the customer value assessment methods that we discussed in Chapter 2.

How do firms in business markets put value-based pricing into practice? Box 5.4 shows how Trilogy, an innovative software solutions company, uses value-based pricing. Box 5.5 describes how Manthan; the leader in business intelligence solutions for retail chains, has innovated its pricing model. Doing so enables Manthan to better demonstrate and document the value its offerings and thereby get better profitability.

BOX 5.4
Trilogy's Value-Based Pricing

Trilogy Software, Inc. was founded in 1989 by Joe Liemandt. The firm is a leading provider of enterprise software in a spectrum of industries including communications, insurance, and the automotive industry.

Though Trilogy had the best product, it was finding it difficult to sell new software. Existing customers were telling Trilogy that its "one size fits all" strategy was not good enough for them.

Liemandt decided to reinvent his company. Instead of trying to build the best products in the market, Trilogy would focus on only one thing: 100% customer success. Trilogy would tie all of its earnings to the success of its customers. How? By getting paid only after their customers achieved the business objectives that they themselves spelled out before adopting Trilogy's products. Trilogy simply moved its pricing from product based to success based. In this new mechanism, payments were made to Trilogy periodically by the client, based on the business value derived out of its software. Trilogy and the customer would agree on defined metrics, and these metrics were correlated to the price received by it.

To make gain-sharing work, Trilogy also made employee incentives dependent on customer success. It became the first company in the industry to implement customer-based compensation incentives. By 2003, Trilogy increased the success rate of its customers to three times the industry average, apart from increasing the customer's profitability.

Under a gain-sharing approach, the first step is to create a probability distribution of the value that can be delivered. This is based on consultations with experts and clients. The next step is to determine the percentage of maximum value attainable each year. This is based on the prediction of the time needed for ramp-up of the usage of Trilogy's software by the client. This can be determined based on past experience with clients of similar size in similar industries and other such factors. The expected life of Trilogy's software product is also considered. These steps when combined provide a sense of the value to be delivered to the customer over the life of Trilogy's product. Once the customer value is arrived at, an approximate percentage of this value can be charged to the customer as the price Trilogy gets for its product.

Customers benefited from such a gain-sharing scheme through improved value creation, risk mitigation, and lower up-front investment, as discussed in more detail in the following example. Typically, the functional specifications of enterprise software products are not fully and accurately known upfront. Instead, these tend to evolve as the product gets progressively developed. During the software product development, changes are made to the specifications on a continuous basis. In such a scenario, success is heavily dependent on a continuous collaboration between the client and the vendor. A gain-sharing pricing strategy in this situation will automatically result in better alignment of interests between the client and the software provider and thus result in superior value creation.

Furthermore, traditional pricing strategies focus on project delivery and do not encourage employees to develop software to deliver value. But under gain-sharing, effective pre-implementation and post-implementation tracking is done by a group comprising employees from both the client and the vendor to ensure that the promised value is delivered.

Because payments are made based on delivered value, the financial risk is transferred from the client to the vendor.

BOX 5.4
Continued

Considering the high failure rates of enterprise solution implementations, this transfer of risk encourages customers to try new solutions. This strategy also allows Trilogy to bring risk-averse customers into its fold.

Typical enterprise solutions require high capital investment from the client and hence only large companies may afford them. With gain sharing, even smaller clients are willing and able to invest in new products, since lesser up-front capital is required.

Trilogy's success rates improved with its transformation from a traditional strategy, because managers became concerned with the success of their customer firms, rather than merely focusing on product (or project) delivery. This helped Trilogy get more Fortune 500 clients. The strategy also provided a basis for it to differentiate itself from its competitors. Trilogy's profits improved since its pricing was directly linked to the extent of customer value delivered, which varied with each client's specific situation. The more the value created by Trilogy's software, the greater became the profits it earned.

Chinni Krishna Kommi, Sandeep Ray, D. V. R. Seshadri, "Creating a Crucible of Innovation at Trilogy India," case study developed for IIM Bangalore in 2005.

BOX 5.5
Manthan Systems' Innovative Pricing Model for Retail Chains

Founded in 2003, Manthan Systems, based in Bengaluru has emerged as the leader in providing specialized business intelligence (BI) software solutions for the retail and consumer-packaged goods industries. Its flagship product is ARC, a data warehouse and business intelligence suite, tailored for the retail industry. Possible clients include global retail chains such as Wal-Mart, Carrefour, and Spar, as well as Indian retail chains such as Reliance Retail, More, Shoppers Stop, Lifestyle, and Big Bazaar.

The ARC BI software solution enables better business decision-making by the retail chain by providing current and predictive views of retail business operations using data continually collected from the retail chain's information systems. ARC allows unique analysis of features such as stores, merchandise, inventory, and assortment. Although Manthan is relatively small as a company vis-à-vis large IT service providers such as Infosys, TCS, etc., it has leveraged its superior domain knowledge, deep knowledge of IT, and mastery of BI to emerge as the leader in this domain.

Manthan segments the market based on geography, kind of retail format, and size of retailer. Manthan categorizes retailers into four tiers. The retailers are further classified based on their retail segments such as lifestyle products, food and grocery, specialty retail, and general merchandise. The positioning of Manthan for each segment varies considerably. ARC is a versatile product, whose features are selectively configured for each segment of the market, based on Manthan's understanding of their unique needs. For

(*continued*)

instance, Manthan's positioning of ARC to Tier-1 retailers, which have annual sales of INR 80 crores or more, is that it will help them take certain key business decisions such as store productivity and benchmarking and store portfolio management.

The fashion lifestyle industry is very seasonal in nature. Styles change every season in the developed countries. It gets complicated due to the large scale of operations and merchandise categories. Comprehensive analysis covering size, color, season, consumer demography, etc., is facilitated by ARC's architecture for such chains. Fashion lifestyle retailers operate on high margins with low volumes, whereas, food and grocery retailing is relatively low margin but fast moving and high volume business. Food and grocery retailers thus thrive on operational efficiencies. For a retailer of same turnover, a food and grocery retailer's BI analytic application needs are very different from that of a fashion lifestyle retailer's. These subtle variations in the requirement of the BI system are facilitated by Manthan's ARC. For the Tier-4 retailers' customers, Manthan has reconfigured the product so that it is essentially a "plug and play" product, needing minimal interaction with Manthan. Rather than using direct selling channels, Manthan uses a distribution-based channel to take the product to these markets.

Manthan has an effective sales intelligence group that facilitates precise fit of customer need with Manthan's market offering. Segmentation of the market is based on size of retailer (turnover), retail format, geographic location, and stage of BI analytic evolution, that is, where the customer is on the BI lifecycle. Such information about the customer is gathered through the sales intelligence.

Manthan follows the license and deployment pricing model. This comprises two elements—a license fee for the product and implementation charges. Manthan has developed an internal pricing calculator. Pricing is a function of the retailer turnover, the segment in which the retailer operates, the retailer's profit margins, geography, number of stores, complexity for Manthan to implement the product at the client's site, and format (hypermarket, supermarket, etc.) of the retailer.

Manthan does not charge the customer on a "per user" basis. Most companies in this line of business charge on a "per user" basis so that if they provide a new module, then they can charge the customer based on the number of users who would use that module. However, Manthan charges its customers a "per store" price, which is independent of the number of users. This gives a lot of comfort to the client. The implementation charges are variable depending on the nature of services provided. Services provided include training and providing customized analytics, reports and presentations for senior management meetings, etc. These are charged additionally as specific services that are wrapped around ARC. These services provide a regular annuity stream of revenues to Manthan. In summary, however, Manthan's pricing is strongly correlated to the value that the customer derives from its offerings.

D. V. R. Seshadri, James A. Narus, Shobitha Hegde, "Opportunities and Challenges Galore," case study developed for IIM Bangalore in 2006.

Managing Market Offerings Across Borders

Because business markets are predominately about functionality and performance, they are inherently more global in nature than consumer markets, which are predominately about aesthetics and taste. Quite often, then, business market managers will have the responsibility of managing market offerings across borders. Although regions or countries might be regarded as simply another basis of market segmentation, some considerations beyond what we've already discussed occur in managing market offerings across borders. In this section, we consider how the market offering may vary across borders and how to manage pricing strategy across borders.

Adapting Market Offerings Across Borders

The extent to which business market managers adapt their market offerings when doing business across borders typically depends on their firm's stage of international market development. When coordinating market offerings across borders is a concern, managers should consider flexible market offerings and global branding.

International Market Development

Douglas and Craig provide a framework for international market development that is useful for thinking about how managing market offerings across borders evolves as firms gain experience in international markets. Firms progress through three phases. After a preliminary phase of pre-internationalization, where the firm focuses on serving its home market, subsequent phases are: (1) initial foreign market entry, (2) local or national market expansion, and (3) global rationalization.[38]

Firms in the initial foreign market entry phase typically vary their market offering little from that of the home market. As Douglas and Craig observe, "Attention is centered on pinpointing the closest match between the firm's current offerings and market conditions overseas so that minimal adaptation of products or market strategies is required."[39] So initially, other than required changes in distribution, the market offering remains virtually the same as in the home market. In fact, firms appear to decide which national markets to enter first based on their perceived similarity to the home market. Supporting this, 60% of U.S. companies that do business in only one foreign country do business in Canada.[40] As a result, managing market offerings across borders is not a significant issue.

Firms in the local market expansion phase attempt to broaden their base of business in each country market by gaining greater market penetration of presently served segments and constructing market offerings that better meet the requirements and preferences of new segments. The focus is on tailoring the market offerings to the unique, local requirements of each country market. "The emphasis shifts from 'export' of strategy and its direction from the domestic market base, to development of strategy on a country-by-country basis."[41] Because of this shift, although firms may have multiple market offerings corresponding to the country markets in which they participate, little attention is given to managing the market offerings across borders. Instead, the supplier often manages the market offerings for each country locally, with perhaps the home office providing or supporting some common core of services, programs, and systems.

It is only when firms progress to the third phase, global rationalization, that managing market offerings across borders becomes a paramount concern for firms. The growing openness of borders for international trade, overlaid with continuing developments in integrated logistics systems, challenges the business market manager to truly grasp what it means to "think global, act local."[42] To provide superior value and lower costs in local markets, firms should develop **transnational capabilities**: "The ability to manage across national boundaries, retaining local flexibility while achieving global integration."[43] Ericsson, the Swedish telecommunications firm, uses its national company boards as one mechanism to foster this process. "At least one, and often several senior corporate managers are members of each board, and subsidiary board meetings become an important means for coordinating activities and channeling local ideas and innovations across national lines."[44]

Providing Transnational Market Offerings

A framework for thinking through the provision of transnational market offerings is the *AAA Triangle*, where the A's stand for the three distinct types of global strategy[45]:

- ***Adaptation*** seeks to boost revenues and market share by maximizing a firm's local relevance.
- ***Aggregation*** attempts to deliver economies of scale by creating regional or sometimes global operations; it involves standardizing the product or service offering and grouping together the development and production processes.
- ***Arbitrage*** is the exploitation of differences between national or regional markets, often by locating separate parts of the supply chain in different places—for instance, call centers in India, factories in China, and retail shops in Western Europe.

Because of the tensions that are inherent among these A's, businesses are advised to excel at the one or two of them that best meet their businesses' requirements and priorities. As examples, businesses that do a lot of advertising would strive to excel at Adaptation, whereas businesses that have a high percentage of R&D spending to sales would strive to excel at Aggregation. "Success in 'AA strategies' takes two forms. In some cases, a company wins because it actually beats competitors along both dimensions at once. More commonly, however, a company wins because it manages the tensions between two A's better than its competitors do."[46]

The underlying logic and philosophy of flexible market offerings—naked solutions with options—readily generalizes to transnational market offerings and adroitly managing the tension between adaptation and aggregation. A supplier would design its product offering and service offering platforms around regional or global requirements to offer them at lower cost. At the same time, it would tailor augmenting features and supporting services, programs, and systems to local market requirements to provide superior value. These product offering and service offering platforms would be (much) fewer in number than the country markets served. How, though, does the firm go about deciding what will constitute its product offering and service offering platforms?

Managers first must step back and decide which country markets are most significant and interesting to their business. Making decisions about which subset of all the countries the business serves are the *relatively* important markets is essential. Rather than designing a product to meet the average requirements of a regional (or global) market, business market managers would instead pursue what Nissan terms a *lead country* model: "A product carefully tailored to the dominant and distinct needs of individual national markets."[47] Within each region, the firm designates as the lead country that country market it deems most important. It designs product offering platforms that will provide the greatest value in each lead country. Then, managers in other country markets are asked whether small changes can make one of these platforms acceptable to their local markets.

So, too, are business market managers advised to construct lead country service offerings and marketing programs, which local managers in the other country markets can modify to better meet their requirements. Again, flexibility is critical for accomplishing the difficult balance between global (or regional) and local. Often, "backroom operations" that are characteristic of most systems and many programs can be advantageously integrated across borders, providing arbitrage. The "face" to the customer, though, must remain local. However, this does not necessarily mean that the supplier is located locally. For example, a supplier may provide customer service in Belgium, the Netherlands, and Germany from one customer service center, staffed by nationals from each country market. Customers, dialing a local telephone number, may be completely unaware that the call is being routed to a service center in another country. Moreover, they may not even care as long as the voice on the other end is a native-speaking one. However it is accomplished in practice, the goal of the firm is to be regarded as a local company in every country market in which it participates.[48]

Global Branding

As we discussed in Chapter 1, because business markets are predominantly concerned about functionality and performance, business market management stresses doing business across international borders. Most often, customers in country markets in the Americas, Asia, and Europe are seeking essentially the same functionality and performance from market offerings. In our discussion of brands as resources and brand building in business markets in Chapter 4, we emphasized the paramount importance of corporate brands in business markets, such as 3M and IBM. Taken together, the implication is that firms in business markets should pursue global branding of their market offerings. Yet, a number of circumstances can make this sort of branding difficult to accomplish in practice, with the result being that the firm may have global brands, regional brands, or local country brands for their market offerings.[49]

When customer requirements and preferences vary across regional or country markets, suppliers may pursue regional or local country branding to reflect these variations. The overarching goal, though, should be to strive for as much consistency and standardization in the brand strategy and brand building as possible. Country managers often have a tendency to believe that their market situation is unique, and consequently global (or regional) brand-building initiatives will not work in their markets. To counter this notion, the firm must assign global responsibility for the brand strategy of a market offering to one individual, who may accomplish managing the market offering globally through leading a team composed of regional or country brand (or marketing) managers. Senior management should require country managers to adopt global or regional brand-building efforts, unless they can persuasively document their claims of uniqueness with data from the local market.

Having different brands for the same market offering in different parts of the world also occurs through acquisition of firms that have strong corporate or family brands in particular regional or local country markets. The acquiring firm may be reluctant to change brands in this situation and may instead opt to manage the greater complexity of multiple brands for essentially the same market offering. Citigroup, opting to operate under the Banamex brand name in Mexico after it acquired Grupo Financiero Banamex-Accival (discussed in Chapter 4), is an instance of this. Finally, a firm may find that it must alter the positioning of its market offering in particular country or regional markets because of the presence of an entrenched formidable competitor. In this circumstance, the firm may choose to use an alternate brand for its market offering to avoid confusion with its positioning of the market offering in other regional or country markets, where it may be the market leader.

Launching a new brand in business markets appears to be an outstanding opportunity to use a global brand. This appears especially so for technology-driven firms and market offerings, where it is more likely that customer firms in developed markets around the world are seeking essentially the same functionality and performance. The experience of Wipro Technologies® in launching its global brand provides an instructive case, which we recount in Box 5.6.

Pricing Across Borders

Pricing market offerings within the home market is a vexing enough task for most business market managers. Pricing across borders often is even more daunting. Firms in the initial foreign market entry and local or national market expansion phases of international market development have the primary concern of pricing relative to local competitors. When firms reach the global rationalization phase, they face the added concern of harmonizing pricing across borders.

Pricing in Local Markets

An implication of equations 5.1 and 5.2 for foreign markets is that what is regarded as the next-best-alternative offering may change, depending on the local market competition. In some country markets, local competitors may provide offerings that are state-of-the-art, while in others, the local competitors are not

BOX 5.6
Wipro Technologies Decides upon Global Branding

Up until the mid-1980s, Wipro operated in the fast moving consumer goods (FMCG) industry before diversifying into personal computers and subsequently software services. Prior to the 1990s, Wipro's branding reflected its role as a producer of FMCG products. The company forayed in the mid-1980s into software business as a low-cost software services provider. Over time, the company started to aspire to move up the value chain by offering higher-order services. The company had a unique challenge in that its brand identity had to be in tune with the major business of the company, namely, software services, and at the same time incorporate elements of its FMCG business, which was a well-established business.

The company did a survey among its stakeholders as to what the Wipro brand meant for them and how the customers would want to see the brand in future. The answers from stakeholders, both internal and external, included descriptors such as *solid, caring, high on values, innovation, technology, versatility, diverse, etc.* The company decided on a multicolor sunflower logo, representing diversity and innovation, which represented a majority of these values.

In early 2000, Wipro had started to move up the software services value chain from a low-cost provider of software services to a one-stop shop for end-to-end business solutions. At the time, however, the company lacked a strong, coherent, and appropriate brand identity to signal the strategic shift of moving up the value chain. Wipro's offerings did not differentiate it from other suppliers of software services such as TCS and Infosys. In response to this need, the company came up with the "Applying Thought" branding strategy. "Applying Thought" as the branding for the company was easily understood internally by the employees as well as externally by the company's customers and clarified the company's unique competence. Through this branding effort, it also sought to create a unique identity for itself, differentiating itself in the international markets from other large Indian IT service providers such as TCS and Infosys.

Wipro's focus on out-of-the-box solutions was symbolized by its "Applying Thought" advertising campaign. The company wanted the brand to communicate superior quality standards, better understanding of the customer's needs, and technical excellence. Another element of its brand identity, which the company hoped to change, was its perception as an India-centric company. The new Wipro brand was expected to represent a company with a global outlook.

The company's next step was to devise an action plan for executing its branding strategy. The company marketed itself externally among its customer base as well as internally within its own workforce. As part of its effort towards building a brand that stood for out-of-the-box thinking and innovation, councils and centers of excellence were set up. Customer Forum and Relations was an initiative towards market sensing, so as to better understand the customer issues and build thought leadership as a means of differentiation. Likewise, in the social domain, "Applying Thought" in schools was an initiative towards improving the quality of education by training the teachers as well as involving parents in the education process.

Wipro has successfully transformed its brand identity in its journey from a

(*continued*)

BOX 5.6
Continued

manufacturer of FMCG products to a knowledge and IT industry major. The company correctly identified the two inflection points where the brand identity and value proposition required a transformation and also effectively executed its branding strategy. All these have had a significant positive impact on the company's business performance.

Contributed by Tarundeep Singh, Participant, PGSEM Program, Indian Institute of Management Bangalore. *Sources:* B. Rao and B. Mulloth, "Building a Global Brand: The Case of Wipro," *http://ieeexplore.ieee.org/Xplore/login.jsp?url=http%3A%2F%2Fieeexplore.ieee.org%2Fiel5%2F4349300%2F4349301%2F04349459.pdf%3Farnumber%3D4349459&authDecision=-203;* "What Does Wipro Identity Stand For?," *http://www.wiprocorporate.com/Brand/What_Wipro_Identity_Stand_For.asp; Wipro, http://www. spiritus-temporis.com/wipro/history.html.*

nearly as strong as those the firm confronts in its home market.[50] The competitors in the local market may be national companies or foreign subsidiaries of firms from other countries in the region or the world at large. So, the incremental value that a firm's market offering provides likely varies across its country markets. In some, the value even may be at parity, but the prices of the local market offerings are much higher, perhaps reflecting a higher cost structure of local firms.[51] Finally, foreign suppliers may encounter difficulty, at least initially, demonstrating to potential customers in the local markets the superior value of their offerings (that is, $\Delta\text{Value}_{f,a} > 0$), and Price_a for the best local competitor may be lower than in the supplier's home market.

Perceived superior value relative to local market offerings would seem to be a critical factor in initial foreign entry decisions, yet we have not seen this issue discussed much. Moreover, firms typically have not conducted formal customer value assessments to support these decisions. Instead, firms tend to focus on price, with a subjective, and often sketchy, understanding of the relative value of the locally available competitive market offerings ($\Delta\text{Value}_{f,a}$). Apart from this, firms that employ a cost-plus approach to pricing may view foreign markets simply as a place to gain additional business, thereby improving capacity utilization. Therefore, they are willing to accept even a lower price than in the home market—a practice known as **dumping**. Finally, the incentive to change that a firm needs to offer prospective customers in the local country markets will likely be greater than in its home market. How much greater this incentive needs to be depends on the strength of the firm's reputation or corporate brand equity in that local market.[52]

Harmonizing Pricing Across Borders

Firms in business markets face increasing pressure to harmonize pricing across borders. More and more firms are now in the global rationalization phase. Customers that operate across borders increasingly expect unified pricing from their suppliers. For example, companies that do business in each country within the European Union may demand pricing rationalization from their suppliers. One consequence of a single European currency is to put pressure on suppliers to move to a single European price, expressed in euros.[53]

The growing openness of borders for international trade coupled with advances in integrated logistics systems has led to a disconcerting number of instances of cross-border arbitrage. Customers purchase a product in a country where it has a lower price, transport the product themselves to another country for use, and still incur a lower total cost than if they had purchased the product at the higher price in that country. This cross-border arbitrage forces suppliers to confront their widely varying prices across countries.

Yet, harmonizing pricing is a thorny undertaking. Local country managers with lower relative pricing often claim that they cannot raise prices to meet regional or global pricing targets without a significant loss of sales. This claim may have some substance in that these managers may face national competitors that sell only in their home market. Conversely, senior management is loath to lower pricing in the country markets with relatively higher pricing and thus forgo incremental profit.

One approach is to move to **pricing bandwidths**, where pricing within each country market is within an agreed-upon range around the target pricing. For example, a coatings supplier set a target price ±10% to create an acceptable pricing bandwidth. Subsidiary business unit managers whose local markets are outliers are asked how they plan to move within the bandwidth, and their progress is closely monitored. New products are introduced within an even smaller bandwidth. As Box 5.7 recounts how Cheslind harmonizes its offering and pricing across borders, thereby creating superior customer value.

BOX 5.7
Cheslind Harmonizes Its Offering and Pricing Across Borders

Cheslind Textiles Ltd., headquartered in Bengaluru, is a textile yarn manufacturing company with 65,000 spindles. It exports its products to about 15 countries around the globe. Its major markets are Korea, Hong Kong, Indonesia, Taiwan, Italy, Spain, Turkey, Bangladesh, and Mauritius.

Cheslind's core product is cotton yarn in various counts, but the company tailors its market offerings for each country's market to match their different requirements for quality, services, programs, packaging, and price terms. It is instructive to study how Cheslind manages its market offerings across different countries and how the problem of pricing across borders is handled. The company offers tailored, flexible market offerings: naked solutions with various value-added services, programs, and systems for different markets.

For instance, Cheslind offers different packing for the products in different markets. This may even vary within a particular market as different customers may have different packing requirements. For example, European customers want pallet packing; that is, they prefer that the yarn cones are packed in wooden pallets. In countries such as Bangladesh, packing is usually done in export-worthy paper cartons. Cheslind offers these

(*continued*)

BOX 5.7
Continued

flexible packing options to different customers in different markets so that it can satisfy all their packing requirements. The company offers these flexible offerings and charges different prices for different kinds of packing.

In another example, Cheslind got an order for 100% cotton weaving twist yarn NE-60/2 from its customer, Youngdo Velvet Co. Ltd., South Korea. This customer required yarn for producing velvet fabric, which it was exporting to its end customer in the United States. Cheslind's manager knew that for velvet, knitting twist yarn is considered better. Moreover, knitting twist yarn is cheaper to produce. Cheslind sent some samples of knitting twist yarn to Youngdo Velvet's factory in Gumi, South Korea. Youngdo was happy after testing and, in fact, ready to pay a higher price for this new yarn than for the normal weaving twist yarn. From the perspective of the customer, Cheslind delivered superior customer value. At the same time, this resulted in better profitability for it. This was made possible by better understanding the requirements of a cross-border customer and by offering a tailor-made product instead of a standard offering.

In yet another example of better understanding of the local context of the customer firm, different countries have different payment terms. Cheslind offers its products at different terms to different customers around the world, based on local practice. For example, the normal payment terms in South Korea are a letter of credit (L/C) on an at-sight basis, which means the supplier can get the credit for the material supplied when the material is loaded on international carriers such as ship or aircraft. In Hong Kong, Indonesia, and Mauritius, the normal payment terms are L/C on a 90-day basis (i.e., there is a credit period of 90 days). Cheslind adapts its payment terms to suit such local variations.

As can be seen from the Cheslind example, the supplier firm should tailor product offering and service offering platforms as well as augmenting features and supporting services, programs, and systems to suit customer requirements. In doing so, it is necessary to factor in variation in common business practices across countries. The big challenge, however, while designing tailored market offerings, is to also find a way to harmonize offerings and prices across borders, lest customers arbitrage variations in prices and product features to their advantage. The fact that Cheslind is a high growth export-oriented company suggests that it has found a way to delicately balance the seemingly opposing requirements of tailored market offerings and harmonization across international borders.

Contributed by Nikhil Popli, Niloy Das, Unus Ebrahim, Vishal Sharma, Vivek Gupta, Participants, EPGP Program, Indian Institute of Management Bangalore.

Finally, fluctuating currency exchange rates also add to the complexity of harmonizing pricing across borders. Movements between currencies that are relatively predictable can be built into the pricing bandwidths, whereas structural changes (currency devaluations, loss of confidence in a local market currency by the international banking community) require case-by-case market strategy adjustments.

SUMMARY

Managing the market offering is the process of putting products, services, programs, and systems together in ways that create the greatest value for targeted segments and customers. We began by considering some conventional thinking about market offerings. Business market managers can overcome the tunnel vision of commodity markets by first understanding the true extent of commoditization and then rebuilding differentiation through strategies that focus more broadly on how to deliver value, such as creating knowledge banks and building leveraging expertise. Regarding the distinction between products and services, we prefer the view that differences between products and services are a matter of degree, and that all market offerings can be more usefully thought of as falling along a continuum of tangibility. Further, market offerings in the business marketplace are changing in ways that are moving them toward the center of the tangibility continuum.

Recognizing the variation in customer requirements that remains no matter how finely a market is segmented, flexible market offerings provide naked solutions consisting of offering elements that all segment members highly value, augmented with optional offering elements that some, but not all, segment members value. We advocate flexible market offerings as an approach for managing market offerings. Business market managers begin by articulating the present market offering for each market segment, which most often turns out to be far greater than any manager realizes. Business market managers next assess customer value and supplier cost for each service. Armed with this knowledge, they construct flexible market offerings for each market segment, specifying which service elements will be standard, which will be options, and which services they will not offer (but which perhaps a third party will provide). We considered some implementation issues, such as whether a supplier should provide flexible market offerings as naked solutions with option menus or as tailored-value packages; how branding a market offering provides a means of differentiating it from other market offerings, particularly with respect to the value it delivers; and how to break away from the pack to move to flexible market offerings.

Although supplier firms have traditionally relied upon cost-plus or competition-based approaches to pricing, each of these has its problems in practice. Instead, we advocate that business market managers pursue value-based pricing, where they select a price from the feasible range defined by what the customer is willing to pay for the market offering. We developed a framework for understanding how to accomplish value-based pricing, and discussed penetration pricing and skimming pricing as alternative pricing strategies.

Finally, the extent to which business market managers adapt their market offerings when doing business across borders typically depends on their firm's stage of international market development. When coordinating market offerings across borders is a concern, our approach of flexible market offerings proves useful in constructing transnational offerings. Firms in business markets should pursue global branding of their market offerings, yet a number of circumstances can make this sort of branding difficult to accomplish in practice, with the result being that the firm may have global brands, regional brands, or local country brands for their market offerings. Pricing market offerings within the home market is a vexing enough task for most business market managers, yet pricing across borders often is even more daunting. Firms in the early phases of international market development have the primary concern of pricing relative to local competitors. When firms reach the global rationalization phase, they face the added concern of harmonizing pricing across borders.

ENDNOTES

1. Theodore Levitt, "Marketing Success Through Differentiation—of Anything," *Harvard Business Review* (January–February 1980): 83–91.

2. V. Kasturi Rangan and George Brown, "Beating the Commodity Magnet," *Industrial Marketing Management*, 21 August 1992, 215–224.
3. Levitt, "Marketing Success," 83.
4. Levitt, "Marketing Success," 89.
5. Ian C. MacMillan and Rita Gunther McGrath, "Discovering New Points of Differentiation," *Harvard Business Review* (July–August 1997): 133–138, 143–145.
6. The following two subsections draw heavily on James C. Anderson and Gregory S. Carpenter, "Escaping the Commodity Trap in Business Markets," in Tim Dickson and Neville Hawcock, eds., *Mastering Marketing* (London: Pearson Education, 1999), pp. 241–246.
7. Joan Magretta, "The Power of Virtual Integration: An Interview with Dell Computer's Michael Dell," *Harvard Business Review* (March–April 1998): 72–84.
8. See, for example, A. J. Magrath, "When Marketing Services, 4Ps Are Not Enough," *Business Horizons* (May–June 1986): 44–50; or Ralph W. Jackson and Philip D. Cooper, "Unique Aspects of Marketing Industrial Services," *Industrial Marketing Management*, 17 May 1998, 111–118.
9. Valarie A. Zeithamel, A. Parasuraman, and Leonard L. Berry, "Problems and Strategies in Services Marketing," *Journal of Marketing* (Spring 1985): 33–46.
10. Theodore Levitt, "Marketing Intangible Products and Product Intangibles," *Harvard Business Review* (May–June 1981): 94–102. The quote is drawn from p. 95, with emphasis in original.
11. For some examples of the "servicization of products and the productization of services," see Regis McKenna, "Marketing Is Everything," *Harvard Business Review* (January–February 1991): 65–79.
12. This sections draws heavily from the same research project as the previously published article: James C. Anderson and James A. Narus, "Capturing the Value of Supplementary Services," *Harvard Business Review* (January–February 1995): 75–83.
13. "The Secrets of the Production Line," *The Economist*, 17 October 1992, 5–6; Fay Rice, "The New Rules of Superlative Service," *Fortune* (Autumn–Winter 1993): 50–53; and Rahul Jacob, "Beyond Quality & Value," *Fortune* (Autumn–Winter 1993): 8–11.
14. Steven C. Wheelwright and Kim C. Clark, *Revolutionizing Product Development* (New York: The Free Press, 1992); B. Joseph Pine II, Bart Victor, and Andrew Boynton, "Making Mass Customization Work," *Harvard Business Review* (September–October 1993): 108–119.
15. Paul Zipkin, "The Limits of Mass Customization," *MIT Sloan Management Review* (Spring 2001): 82.
16. Zipkin, "The Limits of Mass Customization"; and "A Long March," *The Economist*, 14 July 2001, 63–65.
17. Baxter International Inc., based in the United States, split into two separate entities. Baxter Healthcare in this example and the following ones became Allegiance Corporation in 1996. Allegiance Corporation merged with Cardinal Health, Inc., in February 1999 and is now known as Allegiance Corporation, a Cardinal Health company.
18. Michael V. Marn and Robert L. Rosiello, "Managing Price, Gaining Profit," *Harvard Business Review* (September–October 1992): 84–94.
19. We provide other company examples and discuss assessing customer value in detail in Chapter 2.
20. Robin Cooper and Robert S. Kaplan, "Profit Priorities from Activity-Based Costing," *Harvard Business Review* (May–June 1991): 130–137; and William Rotch, "Activity-Based Costing in Service Industries," *Cost Management* (Summer 1990): 4–14. For some work in this area, see Barry J. Brinker, ed., *Emerging Practices in Cost Management* (Boston: Warren, Gorham & Lamont, 1992).
21. William R. Benfield and Dale B. Christensen, *Keeping the Wholesaler's House in Order: How Attention to Returned Goods Processing Can Improve the Bottom Line* (Reston VA: National Wholesale Druggists' Association, 1993).
22. Robert S. Kaplan and Steven R. Anderson, "Time-Driven Activity-Based Costing," *Harvard Business Review* (November 2004):

131–138. The time equation example comes from p. 135.
23. James C. Anderson, Nirmalya Kumar, and James A. Narus, *Value Merchants: Demonstrating and Documenting Superior Value in Business Markets*. Boston: Harvard Business School Press, 2007.
24. The Scientific Products' Industrial Division of Baxter was acquired by VWR in September 1995.
25. Philip Kotler, *Marketing Management,* 11th ed. (Upper Saddle River, NJ: Prentice Hall, 2003).
26. "The Price Is Wrong," *The Economist*, 25 May 2002, 59–60.
27. James C. Anderson and Florent G. Carbonneau, "Exelon: Eco-Preferred® Power," Kellogg School of Management, Northwestern University, January 2003.
28. DuPont sold its Textiles & Interiors Division, along with the STAINMASTER® and LYCRA® brands, to Koch Subsidiaries in April 2004. This business is now called Invista and operates as a separate company.
29. Mark Ingebretsen, "Mass Appeal: Ross Controls Builds Customers for Life with Mass Customization," *Business Marketing* (March 1997): 1, 14, 52; and Carol L. Karnes and Larry P. Karnes, "Ross Controls: A Case Study in Mass Customization," *Production & Inventory Management Journal* (Third Quarter 2000): 1–4.
30. Hermann Simon, "Pricing Opportunities—And How to Exploit Them," *Sloan Management Review* (Winter 1992): 55–65.
31. Shantanu Dutta, Mark Bergen, Daniel Levy, Mark Ritson, and Mark Zbaracki, "Pricing as a Strategic Capability," *MIT Sloan Management Review* (Spring 2002): 61–66.
32. Elliot B. Ross, "Making Money with Proactive Pricing," *Harvard Business Review* (November–December 1984): 145–155; and Michael V. Marn and Robert L. Rosiello, "Managing Price, Gaining Profit," *Harvard Business Review* (September–October 1992): 84–94.
33. G. Dean Kortge and Patrick A. Okonkwo, "Perceived Value Approach to Pricing," *Industrial Marketing Management* (May 1993): 133–140.
34. Stuart U. Rich, "Price Leadership in the Paper Industry," *Industrial Marketing Management* (April 1983): 101–104.
35. Arcelor merged with Mittal Steel in June 2006 to form ArcelorMittal.
36. Thus, although the adage by Publilius Syrus (first century B.C.) that "Everything is worth what its purchaser will pay for it" is true in that an offering is worth *at least* that much, it is likely an underestimate of the actual value of the offering. Note also that when building customer value models as we advocate in Chapter 2, to make the task manageable, suppliers estimate $\Delta\text{Value}_{f,a}$ and so do not know the customer incentive to purchase Offering_a. This assessment does not matter in practice, though, since Supplier_a is giving this value away, so too must Supplier_f. Thus, it is an unknown constant that does not affect purchase decisions between the two offerings.
37. For further discussion on these factors, see Simon, "Pricing Opportunities"; and Hermann Simon, *Price Management* (Amsterdam: Elsevier-North Holland, 1989), Chapter 6.
38. Susan P. Douglas and C. Samuel Craig, "Evolution of Global Marketing Strategy: Scale, Scope and Synergy," *Columbia Journal of World Business* (Fall 1989): 47–59.
39. Douglas and Craig, "Evolution of Global Marketing," 51.
40. Pankaj Ghemawat, "Regional Strategies for Global Leadership," *Harvard Business Review* (December 2005): 98–108.
41. Douglas and Craig, "Evolution of Global Marketing," 54.
42. William Taylor, "The Logic of Global Business: An Interview with ABB's Percy Barnevik," *Harvard Business Review* (March–April 1991): 91–105.
43. Christopher A. Bartlett and Sumantra Ghoshal, "Organizing for Worldwide Effectiveness: The Transnational Solution," *California Management Review* (Fall 1988): 54–74.
44. Bartlett and Ghoshal, "Organizing for Worldwide Effectiveness," 71.
45. Pankaj Ghemawat, "Managing Differences: The Central Challenge of Global Strategy," *Harvard Business Review*

(March 2007): 58–68. The quote is drawn from page 60, with emphasis in the original.

46. Ghemawat, "Managing Differences," p. 63.
47. Ohmae, "Management in a Borderless World," 155.
48. John A. Quelch and Edward J. Hoff, "Customizing Global Marketing," *Harvard Business Review* (May–June 1986): 59–68; "Outsourcing to India: Back Office to the World," *The Economist*, 5 May 2001, 59–62; Taylor, "The Logic of Global Business"; and Ohmae, "Managing in a Borderless World." ABB Asea Brown Boveri Ltd. refers to this process as creating a "multidomestic enterprise," whereas Ohmae refers to this process as "insiderization."
49. As we noted in Chapter 4, most research and writing on brands and branding has been based on, and focuses on, consumer markets. This bias is perhaps even more the case for global branding. So, again, drawing on this work and our experience, we adapt it for application in business markets. In this section, we draw on David A. Aaker and Erich Joachimsthaler, "The Lure of Global Branding," *Harvard Business Review* (November–December 1999): 137–144; and Kevin Lane Keller, *Strategic Brand Management: Building, Measuring, and Managing Brand Equity*, 2nd ed. (Upper Saddle River, NJ: Prentice Hall, 2003), Chapter 14.
50. Niraj Dawar and Tony Frost, "Competing with GIANTS: Survival Strategies for Local Companies in Emerging Markets," *Harvard Business Review* (March–April 1999): 119–129.
51. In some instances, the value of the firm's market offering may be lower than that of local alternatives. The firm still may enter the foreign market, offering a relatively lower price to maintain the inequality of equation 5.2, with the intent of competing in the "low end" of the market.
52. Because business ethics and legal systems vary across countries, in some country markets, managers in customer firms may expect bribes or other similar payments as additional incentive to change when they award their business to foreign suppliers. See: "Business in China: Dirty Dealing," *The Economist*, 4 August 2007, 55; Tina Rosenberg, "The Taint of the Greased Palm," *The New York Times Magazine*, 10 August 2003, 28–33; and Jean-Claude Usunier, *Marketing Across Cultures*, 2nd ed. (London: Prentice Hall Europe, 1996), Chapter 14.
53. "When the Walls Come Down," *The Economist*, 5 July 1997, 61–63.

Chapter 6

New Offering Realization

OVERVIEW

The intent of a new market offering is to fulfill the requirements and preferences of target market segments and customers better than previous offerings of the supplier. Businesses *create value* with new offerings by increasing the difference between what these offerings are worth to target customers and the total costs of providing them. A new offering can create value in a number of ways: (1) it lowers the customer's total costs; (2) it provides superior performance in the customer's application; (3) it meets the customer's changing requirements and needs; or (4) it lowers the supplier's own costs, a savings that it wholly or partly passes on to customers in the form of lower prices. It is critical to marketplace success that a supplier's new offering also be superior to the offerings of its competitors in one or more ways that target segments and customers value.[1]

New offering realization is the process of developing new core products or services, augmenting them to construct market offerings, and bringing them to market. Realization encompasses all the actions a supplier takes to transform an idea into a market offering that it commercializes. New offering realization comprises understanding and implementing the means of consistently producing the core product or service, and the design and delivery of augmenting services, programs, and systems that enhance the value of the core product or service.[2] Firms strive to commercialize new market offerings with greater speed, lower total cost, and greater marketplace success than they have previously achieved or than their competitors can achieve.

To accomplish these goals, a firm needs a realization strategy that coordinates, prioritizes, and guides its various realization

Figure 6.1 New Offering Realization

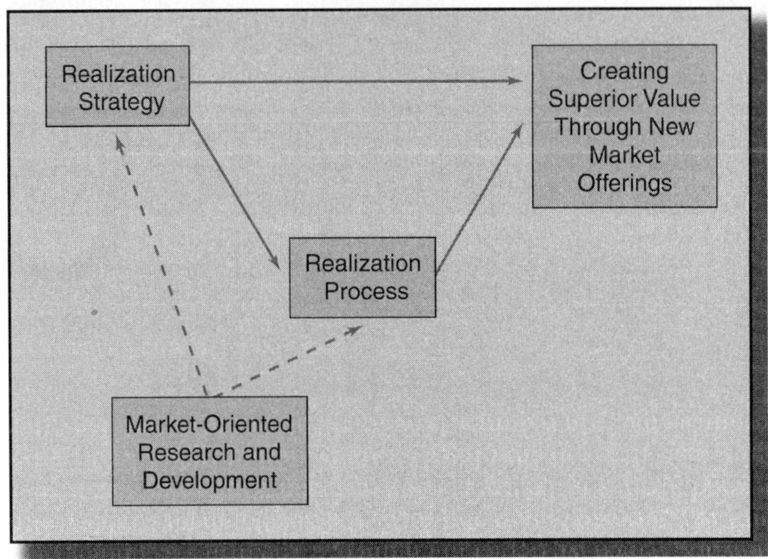

efforts. This chapter begins with an approach to realization strategy that suppliers can use to strengthen their realization performance. We next survey a number of realization process models that firms in different industries use to direct and manage individual realization projects. We then present a general realization process model and relate the firm models we survey to it. The last section of the chapter focuses on how firms can make new offering realization more market oriented. We depict new offering realization in Figure 6.1.

REALIZATION STRATEGY

New offering realization has the potential to provide significant outcomes in three areas: It can strengthen the firm's market position; it can improve the firm's resource utilization—enabling the firm to reuse product and process know-how—and it can be a vehicle for organizational enhancement and renewal.[3] Most firms, though, find that new offering realization all too seldom delivers these rewards. In fact, it is commonly estimated that 35% to 80% of all new offerings efforts are failures.[4] As examples, NeXT, Inc., spent $200 million of investment funds developing and marketing its sleek black NeXT desktop computer before discontinuing it in 1993.[5] The telecom downturn in 2001 is littered with write-downs of goodwill and business losses from new product development activities of various suppliers in this industry. For example, JDS Uniphase announced in late July 2001 a write-down of goodwill and then the largest loss in business history: $45 billion. Especially hard-hit were the ambitious R&D programs related to producing new, cutting-edge 40 Gbit/sec and 10 Gbit/sec products that were terminated as the customer requirements and preferences quickly shifted back to marginal improvements in existing legacy 2.5 Gbit/sec data rate products.

Wheelwright and Clark, experts in product development, suggest the following causes for why new offering realization often falls short in practice: unanticipated shifts in technology or market requirements, mistaken expectations of other functional areas' performance, unexpected technical problems, problem-solving delays, and unresolved policy issues. In a 2007 study focused on critical success factors that underlie excellent new product performance, Cooper and Kleinschmidt found that the strongest driver of profitability was the existence of a high-quality, rigorous new product process—one that emphasized up-front homework, tough Go/Kill decision points, sharp early product definitions, and flexibility. By contrast, they found that merely having a formal new product process has no impact at all on performance.[6] Along similar lines, in a study of more than 700 new product development projects, Lynn and Reilly found several significant processes that differentiated the blockbuster teams from the rest:

- Senior management commitment,
- A clear vision of immutable goals for the product that the team had to deliver,
- Rather than a structured, linear development process to bring the idea from concept to market, an improvisation process in which the teams were flexible and quickly tried many ideas and iterations in the marketplace until they developed a prototype that clicked with their customers,
- A diversified communication portfolio that went beyond formal reports and memos and included a variety of informal media ranging from coffee klatches to video conferencing, and
- Teams that focused on achieving goals and objectives without being fixated on bonding with each other or even on insisting that everyone like each other.

Lynn and Reilly assert that if teams ignore these five practices or perform them poorly, their chances of launching a blockbuster are only 1%. If, however, teams do all five and excel at them, chances of overall product success increase to 98%, and chances of launching a blockbuster product increase to 72%.[7]

To overcome or minimize realization shortcomings, Wheelwright and Clark advocate that firms generate a **development** or **realization strategy** that encompasses the following[8]:

- Creating, defining, and selecting a set of development projects that will provide superior products and processes
- Integrating and coordinating functional tasks, technical tasks, and organizational units involved in development activities over time
- Managing development efforts so they converge to achieve business purposes as effectively as possible
- Creating and improving the capabilities needed to make development a competitive advantage over the long term

Wheelwright and Clark visually capture these activities in a development strategy framework, which we depict in Figure 6.2. The firm's technology strategy and market strategy serve to bound and focus the development strategy, although as the two-headed arrows in Figure 6.2 suggest, some interplay occurs between these strategies. The firm's **technology strategy** defines what knowledge and know-how resources the firm requires, how it will attain them, and how they will

Figure 6.2 Development Strategy Framework

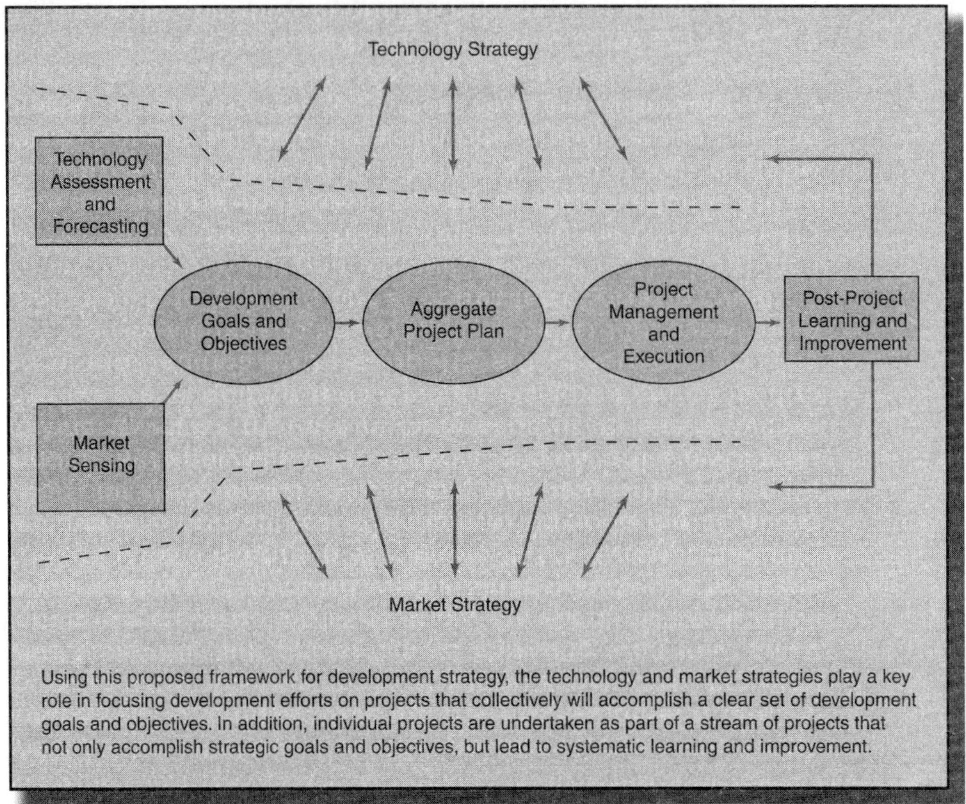

Using this proposed framework for development strategy, the technology and market strategies play a key role in focusing development efforts on projects that collectively will accomplish a clear set of development goals and objectives. In addition, individual projects are undertaken as part of a stream of projects that not only accomplish strategic goals and objectives, but lead to systematic learning and improvement.

Source: Adapted from Steven C. Wheelwright and Kim B. Clark, *Revolutionizing Product Development: Quantum Leaps in Speed, Efficiency, and Quality* (New York: The Free Press, 1992): 35.

translate into market advantages for the firm. Market strategy, as we discussed in Chapter 4, defines the target market segments and customers and a course of action that the firm will pursue to deliver superior value to them. Note also at the end of the development "funnel" the presence of a Post-Project Learning and Improvement step, which then feeds back to both technology strategy and market strategy. Wheelwright, Clark, and others have stressed the need for firms to make learning a formal part of new development projects.[9] To accomplish this, firms should specify learning objectives in their new development project planning, have project leaders conduct a "learning audit" at the end of each project, and adopt a performance review system that monitors and rewards these activities.

Wheelwright and Clark added Development Goals and Objectives and the Aggregate Project Plan as crucial preproject mechanisms for generating and implementing realization strategy. They argue these mechanisms allow managers to resolve policy issues and concerns that run across multiple projects, and better coordinate and integrate the firm's development efforts. We next examine development goals and objectives, and the aggregate project plan in greater detail. We then discuss the contributions that concurrent engineering can make to realization performance.

Finally, we consider the role of outside development relationships and networks in realization strategy.

Development Goals and Objectives

In defining its development goals and objectives, a business specifies what it is seeking to achieve in new offering realization. Obviously, it wants greater success, but defining what exactly "greater success" means is crucial. In doing so, management confronts conflicts that exist among the goals and objectives, and through debate and discussion, makes the required trade-offs. Further, management needs to distinguish between goals for new offering realization as a whole and objectives for individual development projects.

Overall Development Goals

Because of different business strategies that they are pursuing, firms may vary in the overall goals they set for new offering realization. The overall goals of learning, efficiency, and speed-to-market should be of interest to management regardless of the business strategy the firm is pursuing, although the relative emphasis placed on each may vary depending on the business strategy.[10] **Learning** refers to gains in design and process knowledge and know-how and is paramount for organizational enhancement and renewal to occur. To gain the most, a firm needs to manage learning across all realization efforts. Chaparral Steel, a steel minimill located in Texas, does three things that maximize its overall learning from its development efforts:

> First, it requires every development project to advance the company's capabilities. Second, it carefully plans which series of projects to undertake and how to carry them out so that altogether they will strengthen the company's overall set of capabilities. And third, after each project has been completed, Chaparral analyzes it to find out what it achieved or failed to achieve so the organizational lessons—not flow charts and organization structures but the way people actually worked best together—can be passed on to subsequent projects.[11]

Although learning is considered to be an important outcome, there is evidence that not many firms conduct formal reviews that capture the lessons learned in development projects.[12] To ensure learning from each project and create knowledge, firms need to institute formal processes that capture the most important experiences directly after each project milestone, using external neutral moderators, that are then evaluated collectively and interactively.[13] The Siemens example in Box 6.1 offers an example of how firms can leverage learning by converting information into knowledge using collaborative networks.

Efficiency concerns getting the most out of available resources. As with learning, to gain the most, a firm needs to manage efficiency across all realization efforts. For example, one measure that Hewlett-Packard uses to monitor its overall realization efficiency is "'project team change-over waste': the cost of time and resources spent between the end of the previous effort and the point at which all team members are again fully engaged in value-adding activity."[14] In the pharmaceutical industry, which is characterized by complex product systems that are continually evolving, firms such as GlaxoSmithKline (GSK) and AstraZeneca have enhanced the efficiency

BOX 6.1

Siemens: Leveraging Learning by Converting Information into Knowledge in Collaborative Networks

The primary reason for Siemens AG, Germany, to establish a corporate technology (CT) division in India was the realization that India is a significant emerging market with distinct needs as well as product and price challenges. India has huge infrastructural needs in the areas of energy production and distribution, transportation, health care, information technology, and communication. Technology deployed to address these needs must be appropriate to Indian conditions and must be affordable. To develop such technologies is the primary mandate of the Indian CT division of Siemens Ltd. For instance, there is a huge potential demand for low-cost, high-performance ECG equipment that can work under adverse conditions of power supply, dust, etc., common to semi-urban and rural hospitals and clinics. To meet this demand, the engineers of the CT division worked closely with various stakeholders, both internal as well as external (such as the Government of India and top-notch hospitals and doctors), to understand their specific needs.

Siemens's Corporate Technology (CT) focuses solely on research in collaboration with the various strategic business units (SBUs). When an SBU faces difficult systems-related product issues or has a particular innovative product feature in mind to gain a competitive market advantage, it engages with the CT division.

The ideas on which CT spends time and resources come from four sources:

From the product evolution itself. Every company that manufactures a product knows the future logical road map of that product. In the case of the ECG, once a cost-effective model that works in Indian conditions has been created, the next logical step is to miniaturize it so that it is easy to carry around.

From specific SBU requirements. The SBU's competence is the engineering of the product whereas CT's competence is the design. When there are system issues, SBU approaches CT to come up with a solution. There are also times when the issue is not a routine issue but a specific challenge from the SBU on a feature that it was working on and could not implement.

From Siemens customers. When a customer using a Siemens product has a systems or process problem—for example, a manufacturing unit reports to Siemens that it wants to save on total energy costs—then Siemens CT engineers visit the customer and study the system. Out of this study emerges a specific solution for the customer. Often, out of the solution also come ideas for future development.

From the market analysis team. The market analysis team continuously scans the environment to understand various competing products in the marketplace, the features built into them, what customers are looking for, etc. Based on these findings, the market analysis team comes up with recommendations on the features missing in Siemens products. CT takes the feedback from the marketing analysis team but independently verifies it with industry contacts to understand the relevance of each of these features. If the feature is relevant and has the potential to strengthen the market offering of Siemens, then CT initiates development effort of the feature.

The CT division gets the inputs from an extensive network of partner groups both

BOX 6.1
Continued

within the company and outside, which are then converted into databases. Based on these inputs, CT sets out a roadmap for the things that the teams should be working on for the next one, five, and ten years. An idea is moved forward in stages of invention disclosure to patent, patent to prototype, and finally prototype to product.

Contributed by Wilson Thankachan, Participant, PGSEM Program, Indian Institute of Management Bangalore; Discussions with Dr. Antony Louis Priyakumar, Siemens Corporate Technology, India.

of their development processes by conducting internal projects to develop complex genetic databases and networks that are exploited by scientists to improve the discovery of high-quality drugs and lower the risk of failure in development. GSK does this by implementing projects as part of an integral top-down strategic move—based on a vision of how genetics would transform drug discovery. AstraZeneca follows a different path to the same goal. It uses small projects to conduct proof-of-concept studies. The results are then used to bid for internal funds for larger studies that eventually lead to the creation of major new research projects to develop and exploit genetic technologies.[15]

Speed-to-market refers to the time it takes to complete a development cycle. Improving speed-to-market has become almost a mantra for new offering realization in business markets. Yet, the firm must understand what advantage speed-to-market provides and how it gauges performance for this goal. As an example, the semiconductor company Analog Devices uses the concept of half-life to gauge its performance on speed-to-market: The time to complete a realization project should decrease by half for each constant period of time, such as every two years.[16] So, the time-to-market should decrease from 36 months to 18 months to 9 months over successive two-year periods. The move toward speed-to-market and reduced cycle time is being adopted by an increasing number of firms, as shown in a 2005 survey conducted by *IndustryWeek*, which found that manufacturers across a variety of industries are succeeding in shortening their product development cycle times.[17]

The returns for cycle time reduction can sometimes be limited and can even potentially backfire on firms. For example, Analog Devices might need to revise how they gauge performance on this goal at a point when becoming faster no longer will provide an advantage, suggesting that other goals will become predominant. Von Braun has cautioned firms about the harmful consequences of an acceleration trap, where technology-driven firms introduce and discontinue products faster and faster.[18]

Managing speed-to-market at the overall level can dramatically affect the speed-to-market of individual projects. Demands for the same resource from multiple projects, such as support technicians who perform testing of prototypes, can create bottlenecks that cause lengthy project delays. Adler, Mandelbaum, Nguyen, and Schwerer found that if firms lowered their planned usage of development resources from 90% to 80% of overall capacity, they could decrease development cycle times by 30% or more.[19] So, building in slack can reduce overall development times.

Defining the overall goals of new offering realization (and the measures that will assess their achievement) brings the conflicts that exist among these goals into sharper focus for management. The previous example illustrates a trade-off between efficiency and speed-to-market as overall new offering realization objectives. Similarly, learning as a goal will adversely affect speed-to-market and efficiency in that establishing learning goals and conducting learning audits takes time and other resources. The trade-off in favor of having learning as an overall goal is based upon the belief that it will eventually pay significant dividends in increasing the speed-to-market and efficiency of realization efforts as a whole. Management needs to validate such beliefs over time with internally generated data, just as it needs to validate market views with market data.

Finally, as an overall assessment of new offering realization performance, some firms use the sales or profits that new offerings generate. Medtronic, a leading medical device company, has as its stated policy that 70% of revenue should come from products launched within the past two years. In 2007, new products (launched within the past five years) were expected to account for over 35% of DuPont's revenues—a substantial improvement from 22% in 2001.[20]

Project Objectives

Individual development projects play different roles in a firm's realization efforts, as we discuss in the next section on aggregate project plans. Thus, the relative emphasis management places on specific objectives will vary across projects. Smith and Reinertsen, product development consultants, contend that firms must balance four key objectives in managing individual development projects[21]:

- *Development speed or time-to-market,* which is "the time between the first instant someone could have started working on a development program and the instant the final product was available to the customer"[22]
- *Product cost,* which is the total cost of the product to the supplier, including all costs it incurs in marketing, sales, and support services (which are part of the purchase price customers pay)
- *Product performance,* which is how well the product meets the requirements and preferences that target customers have specified
- *Development program expense,* which consists of all the one-time development costs a specific project incurs

Smith and Reinertsen observe that every development project will have to confront trade-offs among these four objectives, and making them correctly is paramount for project success. For example, outsourcing some part of a project adds to the development program expense, but it lowers the time-to-market. To guide managers in making these trade-off decisions, Smith and Reinertsen recommend comparing different cases using cumulative profits over the life of the product as the criterion measure. They advise managers to construct an economic model using spreadsheet software to explore the effects of trade-offs on cumulative profits. This kind of analysis can produce insights, but managers must be cautious about relying too much on the apparent certainty of quantification. The accuracy of the data used and the assumptions made in constructing the relationships among the variables are crucial in determining a model's practical worth. For example, although cumulative profits may be a worthwhile indicator of financial success, as we have seen, managers may want to consider other realization goals, such as learning, as well. Taking them into account will lead managers to make more complicated, qualitative judgments on trade-off decisions.

To understand the varying roles or contexts of individual projects, Dolan advocates that the firm use a **newness map** that has two dimensions: the newness of the developed product or service to the firm (low to high), and the newness to the market (low to high).[23] A firm can portray its portfolio of projects on this map to recognize what the paramount marketing issues will be for each project. As an example, when the anticipated outcome of a project is an offering that will be low to moderate in newness to the firm and newness to the market, cannibalization versus incremental sales is a paramount marketing issue. **Cannibalization** is when a new offering takes a portion of its sales from an existing offering of the firm. The firm may be willing to endure some cannibalization when its objective for the new offering is to blunt inroads made by a recently introduced competitor's offering. Alternatively, its objective may be to maximize cannibalization, as, for example, when the new offering has greater profitability than the existing offering. Thus, management sets the objectives for projects based on its understanding of their context.

What measures do firms use to assess the achievement of project objectives? To capture variation in project roles, Griffin and Page constructed six development scenarios that systematically vary along the two dimensions of the newness map.[24] Experienced practitioners judged which measures were most useful for evaluating the success of individual projects for each of these six scenarios. The set of measures that the practitioners evaluated comprised customer-based, financial, and technical performance measures of success. With *new-to-the-world projects* (high newness to the firm and to the market), practitioners regard marketplace reaction measures such as customer acceptance and customer satisfaction as most useful. For *line extensions* (moderate newness to the firm and to the market), meeting profit goals, competitive advantage, and market share are the most useful measures.

Best-practice firms do not simply rely on postproject measures to evaluate project performance. They also devise measures that can be used *during* a project to provide early warning signals and suggest corrective actions. Recognizing and responding to development problems as they occur increases the rate of project success. "Therefore, smart innovators add leading in-process indicators that measure, for example, anticipated break-even time, quality of planning, conformance to best-practice, time spent with customers, timeliness of deliverables, thoroughness of early engineering analysis, and quality of resources."[25]

The Aggregate Project Plan

An **aggregate project plan** is a mechanism "to ensure that the collective set of projects will accomplish the development goals and objectives and build the organizational capabilities needed for ongoing development success." It allows management to think through in a systematic way how the firm can achieve realization performance that is greater than simply the sum of the projects done. Management should select, sequence, and manage individual development projects to create and leverage interdependence, synergy, and learning across the set of development projects. Three basic steps in constructing an aggregate project plan are: (1) mapping the varying kinds of development projects, (2) making capacity decisions, and (3) making provisions for gaining critical skills and capabilities.[26]

Mapping the Kinds of Development Projects

The first step in generating an aggregate project plan is to understand how the firm is allocating resources across varying kinds of development projects and look at the mix of projects that the firm is doing. Wheelwright and Clark advise creating a map having two dimensions: the extent of product change and the extent of process change. They find these two dimensions most useful for organizing projects because each determines the amount of realization resources a project requires. We reproduce the resulting development project map in Figure 6.3. Product change ranges from "derivatives and enhancements" to "new core products," whereas process change ranges

Figure 6.3 Mapping the Five Types of Development Projects

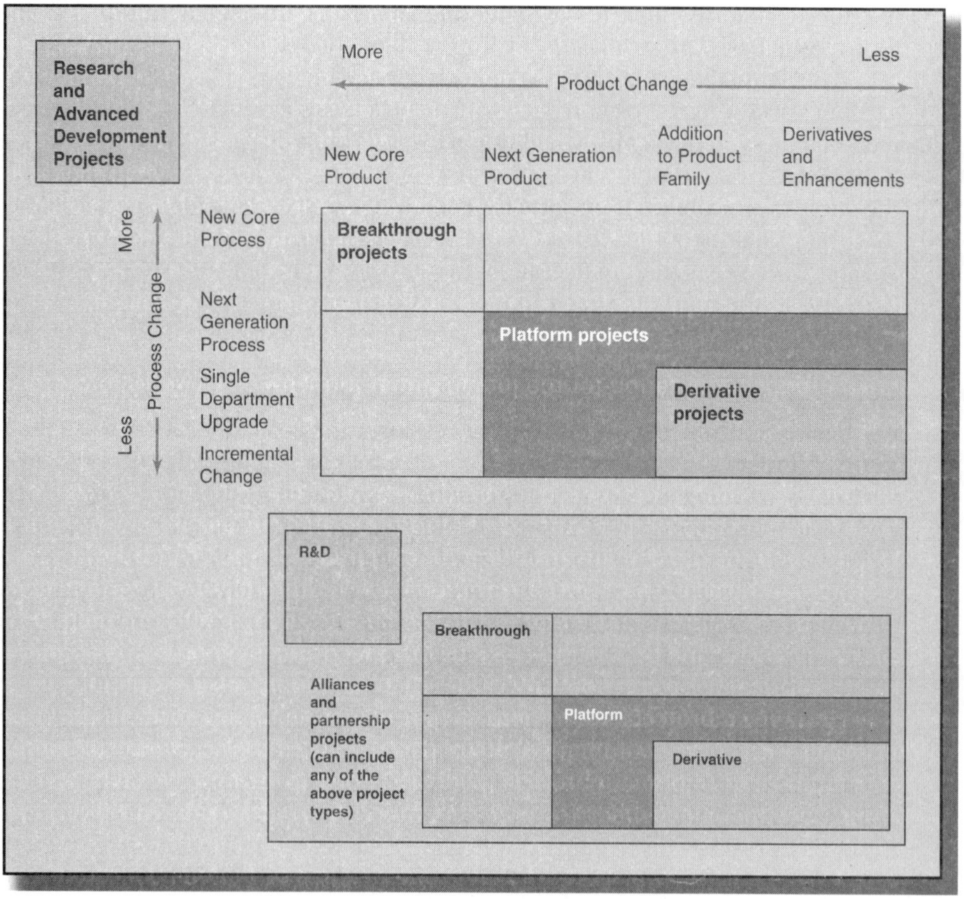

Source: Steven C. Wheelwright and Kim B. Clark, "Creating Project Plans to Focus Product Development," *Harvard Business Review* (March–April 1992): 74.

from "incremental change" to "new core process." Wheelwright and Clark delineate five kinds of development projects that correspond to areas of the map. Management arranges the projects within these areas, based on each project's expected outputs.

Derivative projects are initiatives that realize small advances in the firm's current offerings or production processes, such as making cost reductions in existing products, providing product line extensions by adding or subtracting secondary features, and devising incremental improvements for an existing production process. Derivative projects have shorter durations and require relatively little management involvement or other realization resources. However, they can produce profitable products and enhance the firm's capabilities. As an example, we consider in Box 6.2 how EWAC Alloys Ltd. created a continuous wired electrode as a derivative product

BOX 6.2
Derivative Product Realization for the Indian Sugar Industry by EWAC Alloys Ltd.

Sugarcane crushing mills are used all over India and internationally in the sugar industry. A crushing mill is very much like the sugarcane juicers we see in sugarcane juice centers all over India, only much larger. The typical rolls used to crush sugarcane in the modern sugar industry have a diameter of over one meter and a length of two to three meters. These rolls have projections similar to gear teeth running all around the circumference. Two rolls are mounted, one over the other, so that their teeth mesh and produce an effective crushing action.

EWAC Alloys Ltd. (EWAC) makes various types of welding rods, wires, and electrodes as well as diamond plates for protection against abrasion and erosion. Its welding rods are extensively used in most industries, including the sugar industry. With growing competition, EWAC was experiencing pricing pressures and its products were perceived as commodities. EWAC realized a need to consolidate its market position in the sugar crushing mills business.

Sugarcane and other materials fed into the crushing mill form a highly abrasive mixture. It causes continuous wear on the teeth, making their surfaces very smooth. Smooth surfaces are unable to grip the sugarcane and result in a loss of crushing efficiency. To avoid this, the teeth flights are periodically roughened by welding. Small weld metal beads are deposited all along the flight of the teeth to provide a better gripping action. The deposited weld alloy is wear-resistant and designed to be durable to avoid frequent repairs.

Until a few years ago, to provide such a rough surface on the face of the teeth of the geared wheels, the sugar industry in India deployed a process that used stick electrodes to deposit the weld material on the face of the teeth. Stick electrodes are 350 to 450 mm in length and weigh approximately 70 to 100 grams each. Naturally, there is a limit to how much weld material can be deposited using one electrode. After the electrode is consumed, the welder has to stop the welding process to remove the left-over stub and replace it with a new electrode. This creates a discontinuity in the operation, which is typically carried out *in situ* while the rolls are in motion. The welding process is physically very exhausting to the person doing the job. During one of its brainstorming sessions to find a solution to this problem, there was a suggestion to convert the stick electrode welding technique into a flux-cored continuous welding process, so that there are no interruptions to the process.

(*continued*)

BOX 6.2
Continued

The idea was taken forward for investigation and possible implementation. After a series of studies, EWAC developed a satisfactory flux-cored continuous welding technique that used a wire as weld material that would be deposited on the face of the teeth. The wire was made available in the form of a spool weighing 12.5 kg and could weld continuously for extended periods. EWAC identified this as the perfect product to differentiate itself and further consolidate its hold in the sugar crushing mills business.

The product was named continuous wire electrode (CWE) and was classified as a derivative product, since it used one of the previously available alloys. The five distinct steps of the new product development process were idea generation, internal design, verification, validation, and launch. At each of these stages, there were several challenges to overcome. For instance, during the verification stage, when this product was tested at selected sugar mills, some safety issues arose. Typically, the welder would lie down on a makeshift platform that was constructed over the operating mill. The welder would then weld on the teeth of the crushing rolls. There was always a danger of the operator slipping, resulting in serious accidents. To overcome this, EWAC also redesigned the welding torch. The length of the welding torch was increased from 150–200 mm to more than one meter. This made it possible for the welder to stand at a safe distance from the operating mill and carry out welding. It was even possible to introduce semi-automatic welding by mounting the torch rigidly on a stand.

Once the product was completely approved in a series of trials with several customers, it was launched. The combination of a continuous welding wire with a modified torch has been a big success in the sugar industry and has helped L&T break into a virtual monopoly.

Contributed by Hrishikesh Tinaikar, Ravishankar Savita, Sandeep Desale, and Yogesh Soman, Participants, PGPX Program, Indian Institute of Management Ahmedabad.

that provided a profitable product and significantly expanded its capacity to service its customer firms in the sugar industry.[27] Building upon the letters of credit (LC) platform product, the LCS project required incremental process changes and realization resources to provide a worthwhile addition to the LC product family.

At the opposite end of the development gamut, **breakthrough projects** generate new core products and processes that are fundamentally different from previous generations. Breakthrough products create new markets or are in response to nascent markets with unique requirements. As an example, we consider in Box 6.3 how Tata Motors created Tata Ace as a breakthrough product in response to changing market needs.

Platform projects "are in the middle of the development spectrum and are thus harder to define. They entail more product and/or process changes than derivatives do, but they don't introduce the untried new technologies or materials that breakthrough products do."[28] Platform products represent the natural starting point for the core product part of **flexible market offerings**.[29] Initially, the platform product is the "naked solution" for the product component for the target market segments and customers. The initial platform product provides little flexibility, offering few or no options that some, but not all, segment members value. Over time, derivative

BOX 6.3
Breakthrough Project: Tata Motors' Launch of the Tata Ace

Tata Motors was established in 1945 and is now India's largest automobile company. It was focused solely on the manufacturing of commercial vehicles until 1991, when it entered additionally into the passenger vehicle segment. It has many firsts to its credit, including Tata Ace, India's first indigenous light commercial vehicle; Tata Safari, India's first sports utility vehicle; Tata Indica, India's first indigenously manufactured passenger car; and most recently, Tata Nano, the world's cheapest car.

Tata Ace was launched in 2005, as the country's first versatile and indigenously developed mini-truck. The Ace, which was suitable for both rural and urban use, was a diesel-powered, low-maintenance, safe and reliable vehicle. It had sporty car-like features that provided comfort in ride and handling and was priced at about INR 230,000. Through this product, Tata Motors introduced a new category in the commercial vehicle industry into the Indian market, the small commercial vehicle segment (SCV), which has since attracted the attention of several other Indian auto majors.

The idea of creating this vehicle came through a deep understanding of the market and customer needs. Worldwide, auto manufacturers segment the automobile market into commercial vehicles and passenger cars. The market for commercial vehicles is segmented further into goods vehicles (such as trucks) and passenger vehicles (buses). Goods vehicles are classified based on gross vehicle weight (GVW, which includes vehicle weight and maximum weight that can be loaded into the vehicle): into light goods vehicles (GVW up to 7.5 tons), intermediate goods vehicles (GVW between 7.5 and 12 tons), medium goods vehicles (GVW between 12 and 16.2 tons), and heavy goods vehicles (GVW in excess of 16.2 tons). Each of these classes of vehicles is characterized by different engine capacity, payload capacity, wheel base, loading platform size, and turning circle diameter.

The model for goods transport in the country was changing from point-to-point to a hub-and-spoke model, where the spokes were increasingly being serviced by light GVW carriers. The Indian roads program to connect remote villages, the huge investments in highway infrastructure, and a host of other initiatives launched by the central and state governments also pointed to a huge market opportunity for Tata Motors.

Interested to get into a high growth segment, Tata Motors studied the light goods vehicle segment closely. It already had two products in this segment: a pick-up for GVW of less than 3.5 tons and, another, a higher-end vehicle for GVW between 3.5 and 7.5 tons. Light goods vehicles owners represented the bottom of the pyramid of commercial goods vehicle operators. They were owner-drivers, operating three-wheelers (rickshaws) as goods carriers, as well as small fleet operators (SFOs), who owned less than five vehicles, mostly rickshaws and a few trucks, to provide last mile connectivity for the transported goods. The fastest growth was taking place for the three-wheeler goods carriers.

A detailed study was done to understand the needs of customers in this bottom of the pyramid segment of goods carriers. Topmost of their needs included: safety (which the three-wheelers did not have), fuel efficiency, and low-maintenance cost. Two other very interesting conclusions emerged from this study. The owner-drivers and SFOs used the three-wheelers for transporting goods up to 1 ton for short distances of 50–100 km (intra-city), while

(*continued*)

BOX 6.3
Continued

the lowest end of Tata Motors' commercial vehicle, for GVW of 3.5 tons, was used to carry three tons of weight for inter-city transport (200–250 km). Owners of three-wheelers (rickshaw-wallahs, as they were derogatorily referred to), who provided the last mile connect for goods transport, felt that the Tata 3.5 GVW vehicle was an overkill. Owning a three-wheeler did not give them much stature and prestige in the society.

From this deep market and customer understanding was born the idea of Tata Ace, a four-wheeled vehicle that could carry loads up to one ton for intra-city hauling of loads, to provide the last mile connectivity in the emerging hub-and-spoke model. At the time it was conceived, it was a new core product for the Indian market, as no such vehicle existed. It also required major changes in the way commercial vehicles were designed and manufactured, requiring radical change in processes. For one, this vehicle had to compete with three-wheelers that were available at a price of INR 60,000. The vehicle had excellent fuel efficiency, sporty car-like interiors, low noise and vibration levels, safety features, low turning radius, low-maintenance cost, etc. Accessories included vehicle protection systems, music systems, and even Lord Ganesha idols. The launch of Tata Ace was a great success and adversely impacted the sales of three-wheelers as goods carriers. It also enhanced the prestige of the owners and made them more eligible in the marriage market!

Contributed by G. S. Sundar Rajan, Participant, PGP Program, Indian Institute of Management Bangalore. *Sources:* "Commercial Vehicle Review," July 2007, Report published by Crisil Research; Soorya Tejomoortula, Rajiv Fernando, "Tata Motors: Serving an 'Ace' of Success," ICMR Centre for Management Research, *http://www.icmrindia.org/casestudies/catalogue/Marketing/MKTG139.htm;* "Launching an Ace on the Roads," *The Financial Express, http://www.financialexpress.com/old/print.php?content_id=141984;* "Tata Targets A New Truck Segment," 9 May 2005, Media Reports, Tata Group, *http://www.tata.com/company/Media/inside.aspx?artid=ZRgoeNDhk88=.*

projects provide product options that some, but not all, members of initially targeted segments value. The value proposition could also be extended to other segments that the firm decides to target. We consider positioning for offerings from platform and derivative projects in Box 6.4.

As an example of a platform product, consider how Asea Brown Boveri (ABB) standardized its offering of power plants. Because the price of a power plant is several hundred million dollars, ABB had to provide some flexibility in the product part of the market offering. Yet, this requirement does not necessarily mean that each power plant must be a one-off, custom-designed and -built product. Rather, ABB's insight was to recognize where flexibility created significantly greater value for the customer than the incremental cost of ABB providing it. Figure 6.4 depicts which power plant subsystems to standardize, which to customize, and the "boundary" subsystems that needed to be negotiated, depending upon the customer's requirements. Having a reference power plant of modular construction and repetition in building that power plant product were critical for gaining advantage for ABB. In return, ABB could provide these *reference power plants* at a significantly lower price to customers and, importantly, deliver the plant in a significantly shorter period of time, allowing the customer to begin earning revenue from the generated electricity.[30]

BOX 6.4
Generic-Naked Offering – Value-Based Pricing

Conceptualizing development projects as breakthrough, platform, or derivative can also provide a meaningful way of *positioning* the resulting products to prospective customers. The platform product should emphasize the essential attributes to the target customers and provide the overarching value proposition. The firm subsequently positions derivative products relative to the platform product position. These derivative products might strengthen the value proposition for subsegments within the originally targeted market segments that come to have special requirements. Alternatively, derivative products might add attributes that are essential to other market segments, or might delete attributes from the platform product that other market segments regard as superfluous. In each case, the derivative product strengthens the value proposition for the targeted segment.

The derivative product positioning to the prospective customers would communicate differences from the established meaning of the platform product, making it easier for them to understand. Moreover, whether attributes are added or deleted, the firm would frame the differences as gains in value for the target customers. As an example, Mahindra & Mahindra, an Indian automobile major, launched the Bolero by adding features and positioned it as a more expensive and feature-rich Pik-up vehicle (the name Mahindra used for its vehicles that are used for pick-up services) than Mahindra Maxx Pik Up. Bolero Camper is targeted at small-to-medium businesses that would prefer to use these vehicles for weekend rentals for catering to tourist traffic. The attributes that have been added in Bolero vis-à-vis Maxx are essential to this market segment. The Bolero Pik-up line is targeted at another market segment as well: frequent out-of-town travelers in consumer markets, who also value the additional features of the Bolero. The Mahindra Bolero was so successful that it achieved the no. 1 SUV/MUV (sports utility vehicle/multi-utility vehicle) status in India for three years in a row.

Two kinds of development projects management needs to include in the aggregate project plan appear outside the boundaries of the development map in Figure 6.3. **Research and advanced development projects** "aim at inventing new science or capturing new know-how so that required knowledge will be available for application in specific development projects."[31] Wheelwright and Clark draw a sharp distinction between this kind of development project and commercial development projects, which consist of breakthrough, platform, and derivative projects. They stress separating invention from application, and that whenever possible, an invention's applied workability should be demonstrated prior to its use in a commercial development project. Yet, research and advanced development (RAD) projects and commercial projects must be part of the same plan because they compete for development resources, and management must provide mechanisms to ensure smooth exchange of knowledge back and forth between RAD and commercial projects.

Alliances and partnership projects are those done in conjunction with one or more outside firms. The projects may be RAD or commercial in nature, and the extent of involvement of the firm in the project can range from minimal oversight to

Figure 6.4 Standardization of Combined Cycle Power Plants at ABB

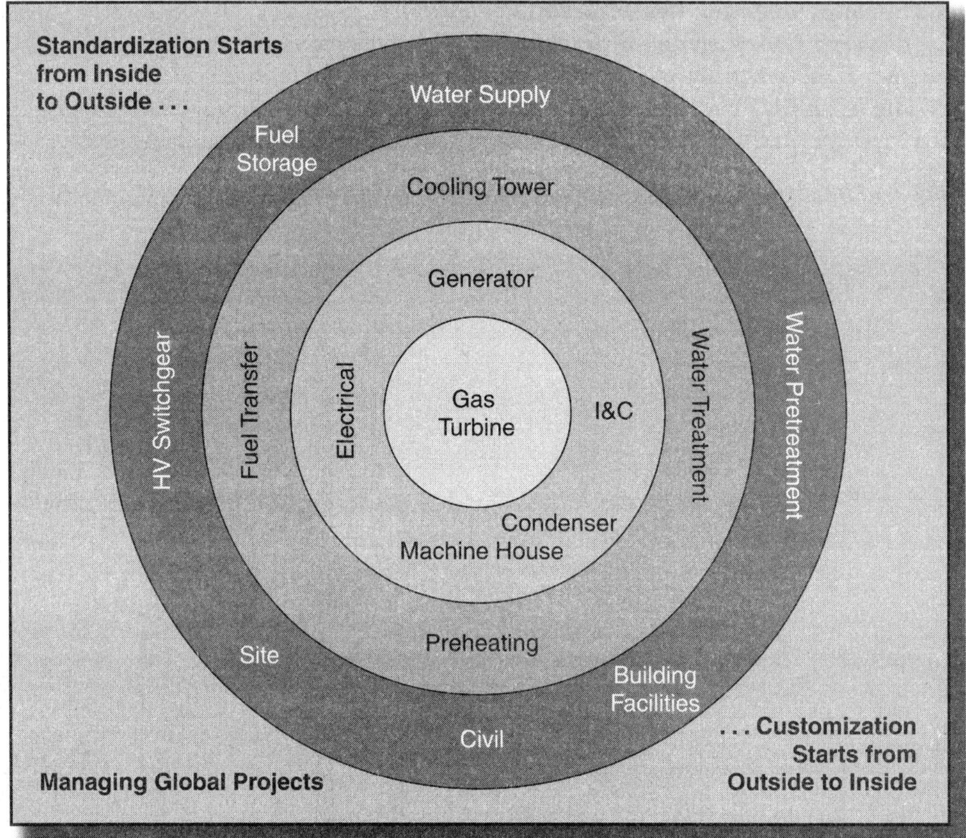

extensive interaction and involvement. "Even when the partner company takes full responsibility for a project, the acquiring company must devote in-house resources to monitor the project, capture the new knowledge being created, and prepare for the manufacturing and sales of the new product."[32] We discuss the role of supplier relationships and networks in innovation in the next section.

Making Capacity Decisions

After understanding the number of proposed and current projects, and the mix of these projects, management must make some hard decisions about the number and mix of projects to start or complete with the resources they have. "When organizations overextend their resources, productivity declines, the number of projects 'in process' increases, projects take longer to complete, and the rate of project completions declines."[33] Wheelwright and Clark observe that it is not unusual for firms to find that their project commitments greatly exceed available development resources, sometimes by more than twice their capacity!

Management has several related capacity decisions to make. First, it likely needs to reduce the number of projects being done at any one time. Management must postpone some projects, and it needs to adroitly refuse or cancel others that do not appear promising. Second, it likely needs to resequence some projects to provide a better mix or flow of projects. For example, a particular sequence of projects may enable the firm to build upon its learning and knowledge in a way that reduces the overall time required to complete the sequenced set of projects. Taking projects out of the order of when individuals requested them may go against an implicit policy of "first-in, first-out" project scheduling and execution and may anger those whose projects are "bumped." Finally, management must decide upon a preferred level of development capacity utilization. This decision will depend, in part, on the mix of projects being done and the resource bottlenecks that are likely to occur. As we discussed earlier, building in slack can reduce overall development times.

Gaining Critical Skills and Capabilities

As a final step in constructing an aggregate project plan, management needs to consider how the set of candidate development projects will enable the firm to build or acquire the critical skills and capabilities it will need for future development and marketplace success. As Wheelwright and Clark contend, "Possibly the greatest value of an aggregate project plan over the long-term is its ability to shape and build development capabilities, both individual and organizational. It provides a vehicle for training development engineers, marketers, and manufacturing people in the different skill sets needed by the company."[34]

Three aspects to consider are building technical knowledge, cross-functional cooperation, and project leadership capability. Assignments to project teams should be made to build technical knowledge for the organization and in the individuals themselves. For example, a firm can use job rotation between the research and advanced development group and the commercial development group to alternately deepen and broaden individuals' technical knowledge and capability. Building and reinforcing cross-functional cooperation is paramount to technical and marketplace success. A study of commercialization by McKinsey & Company found that:

> High-performing companies emphasize a set of skills notably different from their less successful counterparts. They value cross-functional skills, while other companies pride themselves on their functional strengths. High performers boast, "We've got the best project managers in the world." Low performers say, "We've got the best circuit designers."[35]

Participating in cross-functional work teams for projects, training, and job rotation across functional areas builds cross-functional skills and appreciation for how each area contributes to marketplace success. Finally, the preceding quote also points to the critical importance of project leadership. To build this capability, individuals need to receive training on how to work in teams and have a series of project assignments with increasing responsibility. Project leadership would progress from derivative projects to platform projects to breakthrough projects.

Concurrent Engineering in Realization Strategy

To significantly improve speed-to-market and realization efficiency, a number of best-practice firms make concurrent engineering a part of their realization strategies. **Concurrent engineering** is where firms work on the process for making a product while they are still in the process of designing it.[36] Firms that practice concurrent engineering purposely overlap stages of their development processes that have traditionally been strictly sequential. They form cross-functional teams composed of members from design, engineering, manufacturing, procurement, and marketing who are responsible for a realization project from its inception through its market launch. To facilitate communication and social interaction among team members, management often **collocates** the team; that is, it has them work together in a single place throughout the project.[37] Primary suppliers play a more active role in concurrent engineering and may even provide **resident engineers**—engineers a supplier temporarily assigns to the customer's location to work closely with the cross-functional project team.[38] We first look at point-based versus set-based approaches to concurrent engineering, then show a relationship between set-based concurrent engineering and flexible market offerings.

Point-Based Versus Set-Based Approaches to Concurrent Engineering

In a point-based approach to concurrent engineering (CE), individuals responsible for the design of a product generate a number of alternatives and select what appears to be the most promising design solution. Then, they and their counterparts responsible for the process of making the product go back and forth with the design, making successive improvements until both groups arrive at a mutually satisfactory solution.[39] The CE practice of collocated, cross-functional teams accelerates this process. Yet, the process still has a sequential, though iterative, character. Individuals responsible for making the product encounter obstacles that require backtracking for reevaluations and modifications by the design team. This backtracking slows down the realization process, and those responsible for the process of making the product may wait until most or all of the design parameters are settled before proceeding with their work on the manufacturing process.

A set-based approach to CE offers a way around the shortcomings of point-based CE. **Set-based concurrent engineering** "refers to a deliberate effort to define, communicate about, and explore sets of possible solutions, rather than modifying a point solution—and in some cases, these sets may be deliberately more constrained than common industry practice."[40] A firm uses its accumulated knowledge about its design and manufacturing capabilities to specify what the feasible ranges are for design parameters (as well as noting problems that have occurred outside these ranges). Critically, research suggests that downstream engineering should pursue set-based concurrent engineering for those areas where upstream engineering understands the structure of the problem and the set of relevant variables but is uncertain what the specific values of those variables will be. When there is ambiguity about the structure of the problem and what the relevant variables might be, iterative coordination and problem-solving are preferred.[41] Ward, Liker, Cristiano, and Sobek find that Toyota uses audit sheets to track deviations from designated constraints, organize communication between affected groups, and provide a mechanism for resolving problems:

> These sheets give the nature of the problem, a countermeasure suggested to alleviate the problem, the suggesting department, and a sign-off for the affected functional areas. Often the suggestions resolve the problem to all parties' satisfaction. However, if they are unable to find a common

ground, a functional group (say, die design) may develop a new technology or process advance to make the design feasible, and then revise the lessons-learned book.[42]

Box 6.5 considers how set-based CE might have altered a point-based CE project failure at PWR Company.

BOX 6.5

New Product Development Programs: The Need for Set-Based Concurrent Engineering

PWR Company (a disguised name) is a manufacturer of uninterruptible power supplies (UPS), products that protect computers and other hardware from fluctuations in electric power quality. Recently, PWR initiated a new product development program, named 510, to significantly increase its sales to performance-oriented customers. The 510 program had a clear business objective: leverage existing technology to quickly deliver a reliable, modular product to the mid-range UPS market.

To help ensure the success of the 510 program, PWR embraced four key elements of concurrent engineering (CE): (1) establish a cross-functional team to achieve early simultaneous influence; (2) collocate team members; (3) use computer and information technology; and (4) implement in-process design controls. In spite of seemingly successful use of these elements, after six months, only the electrical engineering (EE) design group was working. Other engineering groups, as well as purchasing and product management, indicated that any further progress on their part was now dependent on EE decisions. Concurrent engineering had become sequential engineering with downstream resources waiting for upstream decisions. As a result, the 510 program made slow progress, and senior management canceled it in its eighth month. CE had failed.

Subsequent to the failure, one team member conducted an analysis to determine why success was not achieved. Although CE provided noticeable benefits early in the program, the point-based approach to CE that PWR was practicing had devolved into an "over the wall," sequential design paradigm. If management had recognized the need to change this design paradigm to a set-based approach, the 510 program might have been saved.

For example, the EEs at PWR hesitated to communicate the circuit design options they were in the process of evaluating. Had they communicated the options, the team would have observed that each option required surface-mount technology to meet dimensional constraints. With this information, manufacturing engineering could have started evaluating equipment capable of handling surface-mount technology, which was currently beyond PWR's capability. With set-based CE, designers communicate to other team members those aspects of the design alternatives that they are considering that are constant across the set. Parallel development proceeds on the basis of what is known.

The PWR manufacturing engineers would not have known the exact surface-mount equipment specifications, but they could have anticipated the future demand for surface-mount capability and begun to research machine options. They could have learned enough even to make an equipment purchase decision without incurring prohibitive risk. With the information a set-based approach to CE provides, downstream team members can anticipate, act upon, and, with surprising consistency, meet program challenges before they adversely affect the development timeline.

Contributed by Samuel Bachman, Kellogg Graduate School of Management, Northwestern University.

Set-Based Concurrent Engineering and Flexible Market Offerings

We use Nippondenso, a world leader in radiators and alternators based in Japan, to show a relationship between set-based concurrent engineering and flexible market offerings. Through its participation in an early supplier involvement program with Toyota, Nippondenso learns about Toyota's upcoming requirements for all of its prospective models. Armed with this knowledge and knowledge gained from its other customers, Nippondenso uses set-based CE to converge upon a single design concept that it uses to define a product family that collectively will satisfy the requirements for an entire set of automobiles. Significantly, it produces all the variants of the product family on the same line. Nippondenso refers to this approach of providing extensive product variety (e.g., more than 700 different alternators) while standardizing the production process as *standardized variety.* "For example, the development group will develop a modularized plan to standardize the various components of the alternator to meet all requirements. It might develop three different body types, nine different wire specifications, four different regulators, etc., all mutually compatible."[43]

Standardized variety is a means of providing flexibility at lower cost in the product component of the market offering. Notice that modularity (with compatibility) is a design constraint in set-based CE. It is a design imperative. In much the same way, senior management can make commonality of parts a design imperative, imposing it as a design constraint in set-based CE. This reduces the number of like parts across a product family that are uniquely different in ways that do not contribute value. Ford Motor Company's Expedition sport utility vehicle and F-150 truck share about half of their parts. This is a result of the company's Ford 2000 initiative, which had as one of its goals greater commonality of parts.[44] Modularity and commonality provide greater flexibility while lowering acquisition, manufacturing, and after-sales service costs.

Outside Development Relationships and Networks in Realization Strategy

In business markets, a crucial part of a firm's realization strategy is understanding what role outside development relationships will play. Firms may require resources that are technical, economic, social, or even political in nature for successful new offering realization. The latitude senior management has in deciding whether to develop the resource in-house or to seek it from outside sources will vary considerably, depending on the kind of project and the resource required. We discuss alternative development structures the firm might pursue, the various aims firms have for outside relationships, and factors that senior management should consider in making their decisions about outside development relationships and networks.

Alternative Development Structures

A firm can pursue a number of development structures to gain needed resources. The firm might outsource a technical resource—simply acquire it from an outside supplier that develops it for sale to the firm. The firm might license the technology, which involves gaining the intellectual property rights. In rapidly developing fields, such as semiconductors and electronics, firms often exchange intellectual property rights through cross-licensing arrangements, where any discrepancies in the value between the firms' respective patent portfolios are compensated for with royalty payments. Not only does this provide firms with greater intellectual property resources, it also provides them with freedom to design and operate without fear of patent infringement litigation.[45]

The firm might collaborate with an outside firm to co-develop a technical resource it needs. This outside relationship can be with another firm, such as a supplier or customer. The "outside" relationship even may be with a development group from another business unit, subsidiary, or division of the same firm. When Lockheed Martin, the large defense and aerospace firm, bids for a new contract, it creates a "'virtual company,' a new unit that draws on several parts of the vast firm."[46]

The collaboration may be with two or more outside development partners: that is, a business network focused on research and advanced development, or commercial development. As an example, consider the development of a comprehensive market offering by Huawei to one of India's leading telecom service providers, which is presented in Box 6.6. In this example, Huawei had deep understanding of the customer firm's needs and used this information to develop a winning market offering.

BOX 6.6

Realization of Strategy by Working Closely with Outside Partners: Reliance Communication and Huawei

As the growth rates in the developed markets become stagnant, emerging markets become the scene of action for the telecom majors. Consequently, these markets are witnessing an all-out war among the telecom service providers (telecom companies or telcos). In India, the story is no different. The price wars put enormous downward pressure on bottom lines of all the major players in the domestic market. This pressure gets transmitted to the upstream of the telecom industry value chain, mainly to the direct suppliers of hardware for the telcos.

Despite this intensely competitive business environment in the Indian telecom industry and its modest brand equity, China-based Huawei was able to create a sizeable and successful footprint in this market, by working closely with customers, understanding customer needs, and coming up with new products that meet these needs in a superior manner, resulting in its becoming the preferred supplier for most telcos within a short time span. Huawei's first major breakthrough came working closely with Reliance Communications, one of India's largest telecom service providers.

Being a late entrant into the telecom services field, Reliance Communications was saddled with a host of challenges while it tried to gain market share. Improving service level reliability turned out to be one of the defining factors in the competition. This had become more important as mobile companies shifted their focus from densely populated urban areas to the sparsely populated tough terrain of rural India in order to be able to provide comprehensive coverage to mobile users. Maintaining service quality in this challenging environment was a tough proposition for Reliance. Another challenge was to install a system that would support future expansion. Any network design which did not consider compatibility with future devices would be a

(*continued*)

BOX 6.6
Continued

huge investment disaster. Before the expansion drive, Reliance had already made some investments in network systems and was providing telecom services, and all future expansion had to be compatible with these existing equipments.

The mobile usage growth rate in India clocked in over 150% per year. Competitive pressure required the players to install and implement network systems in the shortest possible time to capture the rapidly expanding market, which was another important criterion that any telecom equipment supplier had to fulfill.

While Reliance was grappling with these issues, Huawei was trying to get a foot in the door in the Indian market. All the leading network vendors were in the fray to get the Reliance order. On the competitive front, Huawei India was at a disadvantage since it neither had a valued brand name nor did it have any prior execution experience in the Indian market.

At the outset, the marketing and business development team from Huawei India had concluded that in this deal, price was not going to be the only important criterion from the customer's perspective. The company realized that coming up with a market offering that was based on comprehensive understanding of the operational challenges of Reliance, while keeping costs down, would maximize its chance of winning the order. Huawei was in an unenviable position of facing a new customer with new needs in a new business environment.

For instance, the average temperature is 45°C in northern India in the summer, and power supply is unreliable. Most network equipments fail in this environment. In addition to temperature and power challenges, the physical terrain is complex. Despite these constraints, the customer requires easy installation and maintenance of the equipment. To address Reliance's expanding footprint into remote areas, Huawei India proposed its innovative BTS3606C. Huawei's BTS3603C is a high-tech, leading outdoor macro-base station (which is one of the many building blocks in a telecom network.) Huawei's BTS has many exclusive features such as large capacity, high reliability, low power consumption, and easy maintenance, which enable BTS3606AC to be the ultimate time- and money-saving solution for building telecom networks. This solution was designed to function in hostile ambient conditions.

Operations at these sites have been trouble-free since installation. Huawei BTS3606AC not only performs well in complex terrains, it also has high reliability even in the absence of good infrastructure. Huawei's market offering to Reliance included effective end-to-end planning, implementation, commissioning, and operationalizing and maintenance processes. Huawei India offered a time-compressed, rapid deployment commitment. This customized and innovative "Total Solution" offer from Huawei enabled it to get the Reliance order. The offering protected Reliance's existing investment and at the same time enhanced its capabilities for future-oriented service expansions and service quality.

True to its commitment for faster deployment, Huawei was able to achieve its first connection within 10 days of the order and had installed base stations at the rate of 50 per day. This resulted in Huawei India becoming the preferred vendor for Reliance, handling about 65% of its network-related supply and service requirements. The success of Huawei with Reliance opened the doors for the company working with other telecom operators.

BOX 6.6
Continued

Huawei's success is attributable to the fact that it was able to leverage its product leadership to offer innovative end-to-end solutions that met the customer firm's exacting requirements and packaging a host of services with the product to create a winning market offering. This enabled Huawei to move out of the low-cost/low-price paradigm. It crafted a winning market strategy by positioning itself as a partner to telcos. In this manner, it was successful in aligning its strategy with the business strategy of its customer firms.

Contributed by Amit Tambi, Chandrasekar Lakshmanarao, Debojyoti Dey, Prasad Nair, Rajesh Khanna, Participants, EPGP Program, Indian Institute of Management Bangalore.

The actors that make up the network can be suppliers, competitors, or customers to one another. As we saw in Chapter 1, the firms may have **multiplex relations**, taking on more than one role with respect to other actors. The actors in the network can all be outside firms or a mix of inside-the-firm and outside partners. For example, the Mercedes unit of Daimler-Benz is collaborating with Daimler's Dornier and MBB aerospace units, as well as an outside firm, Canada's Ballard Power Systems, to develop a vehicle powered by a fuel cell.[47] To develop next-generation fuel cell powered vehicles such as the NEBUS (New Electric Bus), DaimlerChrysler, Ballard, Johnson Matthey, Mobil, and Shell established a collaborative network alliance covering all major components of a fuel cell system. Automaker DaimlerChrysler in partnership with competitor Ford saw its role in the alliance as being centered around the integration of fuel cell technology into vehicles it manufactured. Ballard was responsible for developing the fuel cell stack. Johnson Matthey, a leading company in materials technology and precious metal–based fuel cell catalysts, helped develop the fuel cell electrodes. Finally, Mobil and Shell, the oil companies in the alliance, focused on fuel reformer technology using their vast resources and experience in hydrocarbon processing and catalytic technologies. Within DaimlerChrysler, the management unit *Projekthaus* was responsible for supervision of all fuel cell–related activities. DaimlerChrysler's R&D division was responsible for continued research on proprietary fuel cells and fuel reformers, as well as vehicle-related issues. Temic, the automotive electronics and semiconductor subsidiary of DaimlerChrysler, developed electronic controls for the fuel cell vehicle prototypes, and dbb Fuel Cell Engines, a majority owned joint venture of DaimlerChrysler with Ballard, was responsible for control systems and the fuel processing unit.[48]

Aims of Development Relationships and Networks

What purposes do outside development relationships and networks serve that firms are not able—or choose not—to fulfill in-house? We can broadly group the aims as technical, economic, social, or political (a notable kind of social aim), and each can be present to varying extents in seeking outside relationships. Outside suppliers might have technical resources that the firm does not have, such as design expertise, process engineering know-how, or technological artifacts. The firm may view these resources as peripheral to its realization strategy or may recognize that developing them internally would significantly slow its speed-to-market.

Using the resources of an outside supplier can significantly lower development costs, because the outside supplier may have an advantage in a resource that would be prohibitively expensive to duplicate. Another economic aim is that by pooling resources, two or more firms leverage their respective technical capabilities while lowering the development costs to each.

Another kind of economic aim is for two or more firms to collaborate on common design and technical specifications for products that do not provide any of them with an advantage. In this way, participating firms lower the costs of products that each purchases and also improve their efficiency. For example, General Motors, Ford Motor, and Chrysler are collaborating to reduce "more than 100 different wiring connectors to fewer than 10, which would be standard throughout the industry, lowering parts costs, reducing the difficulty of building cars, and making them easier to repair."[49]

A social aim of outside relationships and networks might be to have a number of firms commit to developing and using a particular technology. Adobe Systems has furnished programming tools such as software development kits and application programming interfaces to outside developers for free. In doing so, Adobe gains the support of these developers in upholding its Portable Document Format (PDF) as the dominant format, enhancing the value of its full-version Acrobat product.[50] Apart from these consensus-building effects on reducing risk, by pooling resources, outside relationships and networks also allow firms to reduce their risks through sharing the financial burden of development. Finally, firms may use outside relationships and networks for political aims to persuade industry associations, regulatory agencies, or governments to adopt standards that favor their developed technology over rival technologies.

Decision Considerations

Our discussion of the aims of outside relationships and networks has touched on some considerations for senior management to use in making decisions. Senior management will find that it must consider social as well as strategic factors. It also must understand the technology cycle and the resource demands of different kinds of development projects.

Eisenhardt and Schoonhoven studied product development alliances in the semiconductor industry over an eight-year period.[51] Their research sought to determine what strategic and social factors predict the formation of development relationships or alliances between firms. Firms with innovative technologies, that were competing in emergent markets, or that had larger numbers of competitors were significantly more likely to form alliances. Although these strategic factors are not so surprising, Eisenhardt and Schoonhoven also found that social factors related to top management characteristics were significant. "Firms with top management teams that were large, experienced, and well-connected through former employers and high-level previous jobs formed product development alliances at higher rates."[52]

Hamel, Doz, and Prahalad stress that firms considering outside relationships (with current or potential competitors) must delimit cooperation carefully and guard against competitive encroachment:

> A strategic alliance is a constantly evolving bargain whose real terms go beyond the legal agreement or the aims of top management. What information

gets traded is determined day to day, often by engineers and operating managers. Successful companies inform employees at all levels about what skills and technologies are off-limits to the partner and monitor what the partner requests and receives.[53]

They also observe that firms that benefit most from outside relationships put in place practices and mechanisms to learn as much as possible from the partner, even in areas outside the formal agreement.

Drawing on a number of examples of technological evolution, Tushman and Rosenkopf propose a **technology cycle** consisting of four sequential stages: technological discontinuity, an era of ferment, the emergence of a dominant design, and an era of incremental change. Tushman and Rosenkopf stress that a firm must forge outside relationships and networks that serve social and political purposes for it to prevail in the latter three stages. For example, a firm must recognize that technical prowess or economic strength may be insufficient for it to bring about a **dominant design**, which is a single architecture that becomes the acknowledged standard in a product class. "Where technological discontinuities may be driven by random events or strokes of genius . . . dominant designs are driven by the visible hand of organizations interacting with other organizations and practitioner communities to shape dimensions of merit and industry standards to maximize local needs."

In fact, superior interorganizational network skills can prevail over superior technology, as was the case for Matsushita's VHS format versus Sony's Betamax format for videocassette recorders.[54] A similar story played out in February 2008, when Toshiba announced it was pulling out of the high-definition DVD market even though its HD-DVD technology compared very favorably to its only competitor, Sony's Blu-ray technology. In the weeks leading up to Toshiba's decision, Warner Bros., a longtime Toshiba partner, had made a pivotal decision to side exclusively with Blu-ray. This was followed by announcements from retailing giants from Best Buy Co. to Wal-Mart Stores Inc. that they would stop stocking HD-DVD discs and only sell Blu-ray products in their stores. Compounding the impact of these alliance partners' decisions was the increase in sales of Sony's PlayStation 3 home videogame console, which also worked as an inexpensive Blu-ray player.[55] At the end of the day, in addition to the broad Hollywood support and the channel partners' decisions, Sony's own content businesses, non-video content partners such as games developers and music labels, and subsidized hardware were just too much for the HD-DVD camp to compete with.

REALIZATION PROCESS MODELS

One of the captivating aspects of business markets is their marvelous diversity. Examining a number of realization process models from different business markets provides some appreciation for this diversity. We also will see that some common characteristics emerge. We then present a general realization process model that has these characteristics, is market oriented, and emphasizes cross-functional coordination. We conclude by considering some next-generation changes in realization process models.

A Variety of Realization Process Models

We briefly examine the realization process models for Smallfry Industrial Design, Akzo Nobel Coatings, Kleinwort Benson Investment Management, ABB Asea Brown Boveri Ltd. large system projects, and ABN-AMRO Bank Global Transaction Services. These models run the gamut from investment products to power plants. Each provides us with further understanding of the new offering realization process in practice.

Smallfry Industrial Design

Smallfry Industrial Design is a specialist industrial design consultancy based in England. Its success lies in closely supporting its clients' business objectives by applying a strategic approach to design projects. Smallfry's stated aims are to increase added value, improve product quality, and reduce manufacturing costs for its clients by carefully interpreting marketing, customer, and technical requirements into effective manufacturing solutions. Its capabilities cover all aspects of design realization, from seeking out new product opportunities and concept generation through to compiling full manufacturing specifications for a new product offering.

Smallfry acts as an external design resource for client companies with a wide range of design experience and product types. Consequently, its realization process needs to work alongside a variety of internal process models that client firms use. Smallfry has carefully developed its Product Development Flow Diagram, which we reproduce in Figure 6.5, to give a clear overview of the key design stages and highlight the critical activities under each stage. This overview ensures that Smallfry's work ties in with the client's own process and activities and helps to prevent vital steps from being overlooked in the realization process. The flow diagram breaks down the process into 12 stages from project setup to final manufacture and marketplace sales. It is intended as a prompt for activities that need to be addressed throughout the realization process, clarifying the contribution that an external design resource can make and the major points of interaction with the client firm.

To accommodate the majority of scenarios, Smallfry's flow diagram assumes that the client has a clear understanding of the nature of the product it wishes to develop and has assembled information on the core factors governing the product's realization. As an aid to assembling this information, Smallfry offers a Product Design Specification Checklist, which we reproduce in Figure 6.6. This checklist highlights the critical aspects of marketing, technical performance, manufacturing, usage, maintenance, and contractual considerations that will directly affect the scope of the subsequent realization work.

By necessity, Smallfry's all-encompassing realization model is a simplified, linear version of a range of complex activities that often run concurrently. Still, it has proved of great benefit in describing the general process to client firms that are not experienced in running design realization projects or do not have a formalized process for these activities themselves. It also helps provide personnel from the cross-functional teams within an organization who only participate in certain stages of the process with a better understanding of where their contribution fits into the overall picture.

Akzo Nobel Coatings

At Akzo Nobel (AN) Coatings, Innovative Research, which is the research and advanced development unit, feeds into Product Development, which is the commercial

Figure 6.5 Smallfry's Product Development Flow Diagram

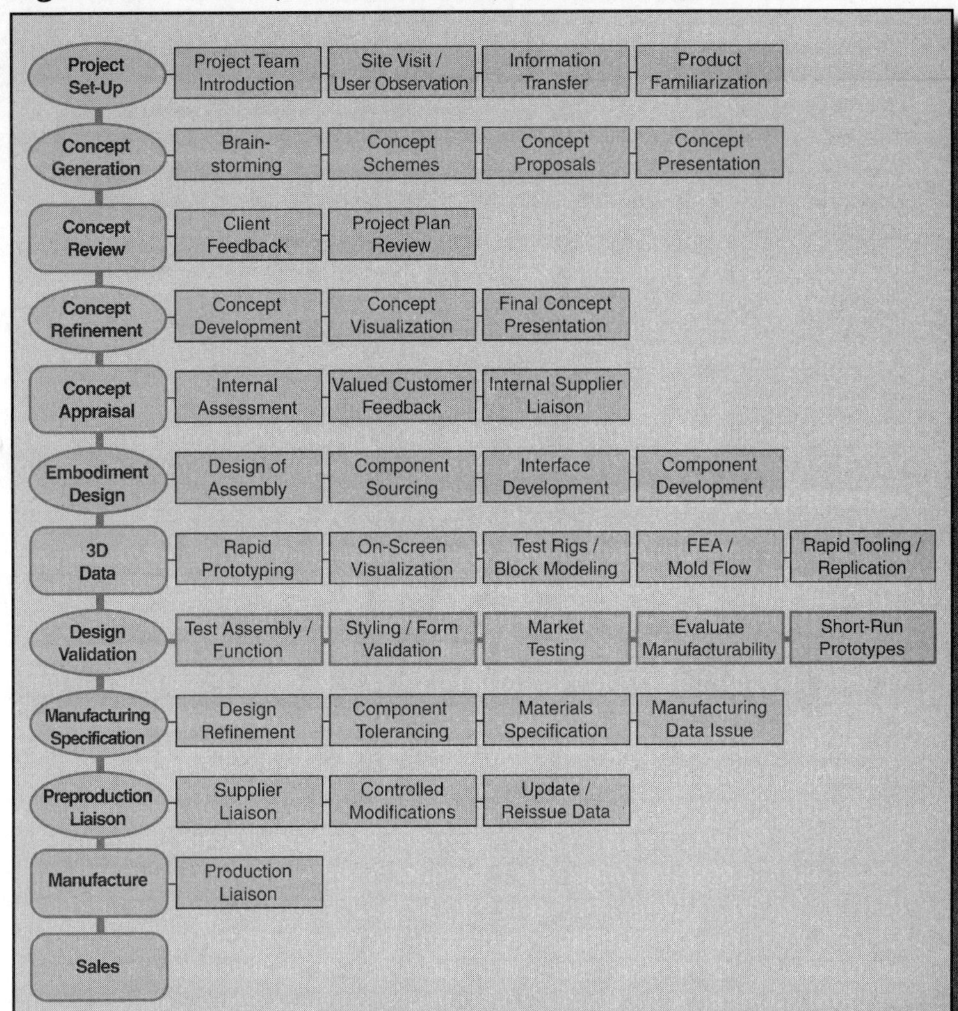

development unit. Product Development has international and local country market product development responsibility, and it also has technical support responsibility for the local country markets. On the international side, new offering realization can be a joint Business Unit Coatings North and South (Europe) effort; an international brand initiative, such as for the Sikkens[56] professional line of coatings; or a multibrand initiative, in which the same technology underlies a product that has a different brand name in each country market. A local initiative is a product that is of interest to one country market.

We reproduce the AN Coatings realization process model in Figure 6.7. The process begins with an *idea phase*, in which anyone in the business unit can contribute a short idea paper. The business unit management team meets every three months to consider idea papers and project proposals, and to give approvals. Following idea approval, AN Coatings names a project manager and forms a project

Figure 6.6 Smallfry's Product Design Specification Checklist

1 Marketing
1.1 Product justification
1.2 Primary use
1.3 Secondary uses
1.4 Product features
1.5 Associated client products
1.6 Target market
1.7 Competitive situation
1.8 Projected introduction
1.9 Product life
1.10 Future developments
1.11 Pricing strategy
1.12 Visual precedents
1.13 Graphic identification
1.14 Corporate identity
1.15 Sales outlets
1.16 Sales distribution
1.17 Packaging

2 Technical Performance
2.1 How does the product work?
2.2 What elements does it consist of?
2.3 How are the elements related?
2.4 Performance requirements
2.5 Power supply—variations
2.6 Dimensional constraints
2.7 Ambient operating conditions
2.8 Applicable standards
2.9 Applicable regulations

3 Manufacturing
3.1 Available facilities
3.2 Preferred materials
3.3 Target production rate
3.4 Total production quantities
3.5 Proposed batch size
3.6 Packaging methods
3.7 Distribution method
3.8 Size/Weight restrictions
3.9 Tooling amortization policy

4 Usage
4.1 Storage means
4.2 Installation or preparation method
4.3 Environmental requirements
4.4 Product operation sequence
4.5 Operation duration and frequency
4.6 Where used?
4.7 Type of operator
4.8 Effects on other people

5 Maintenance
5.1 What maintenance required?
5.2 Frequency of maintenance
5.3 By whom?

6 Contractual
6.1 What is the patent situation?
6.2 Copyright
6.3 Confidentiality

Figure 6.7 The Realization Process Model at Akzo Nobel Coatings

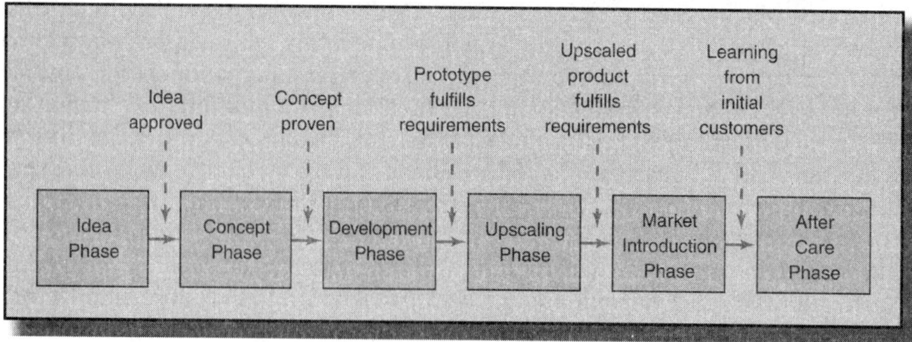

team, which has primary responsibility for the remaining phases of the realization process.

A noteworthy aspect of the AN Coatings process is that it does not end at the completion of the *market introduction phase*; there is a subsequent *aftercare phase.* This phase takes place about 12 months after AN Coatings introduces the offering to the market, when AN coatings makes small improvements, if needed, based on customer remarks and feedback. AN Coatings has found that small technical adaptations can make a significant difference in the market acceptance of a new product.

Kleinwort Benson Investment Management

Kleinwort Benson Investment Management (KBIM) is a unit of London-based Dresdner Kleinwort Benson, an investment bank. Several years ago, KBIM had a sales orientation that led to a proliferation of mutual funds and other products for company pension funds and other institutions. The result was a large portfolio of marginally profitable products. These events led KBIM to create a Marketing Committee, which recognized the need for a more structured new-product development process.

Drawing on its own experience as well as those of some other banks, KBIM constructed the product development process that we reproduce in Figure 6.8. The purpose of the process was to ensure that individuals sponsoring a new product idea would consider the necessary elements of a new product's development in time scales appropriate to allow others to carry out other necessary work, while controlling the overall cost and risk to KBIM.

Four committees provide oversight and guidance in the new offering realization process:

1. *Marketing Committee* (MC), comprising 12 members selected from KBIM division heads, designed to be more imaginative, yet objective.
2. *Risk Management Committee,* comprising 6 to 8 members, focuses on credit limit approval and exposure to Kleinwort Benson. The head of the private bank serves on this committee, and the others are knowledgeable and experienced in finance and treasury.
3. *Investment Committee,* comprising 6 to 8 members, with the Chief Investment Officer as chair.
4. *Investment Management Executive Committee* (IMEC), which is an interlinking committee in that each member is on at least one of the other committees.

The sponsor of the initial idea forms a project group that goes through the process, beginning with initial product development and continuing through launch plan management. Notice that the project would go to either the Risk or Investment Committees (rarely would both need to sign off), depending upon whether it was a debt, equity, or bond product.

KBIM has worked hard to move project groups from viewing the MC as a hurdle to viewing it instead as a resource that adds value by offering "builds" on initial product ideas. For example, recently the MC suggested to a project group that rather than going to the market directly with a new investment product, they consider using Building Societies as strategic distribution partners that would take the marketing risk. Further, the MC gave a qualified, initial approval to the project subject to further research (which subsequently supported the reorientation to indirect participation).

Figure 6.8 Kleinwort Benson Investment Management's Product Development Process

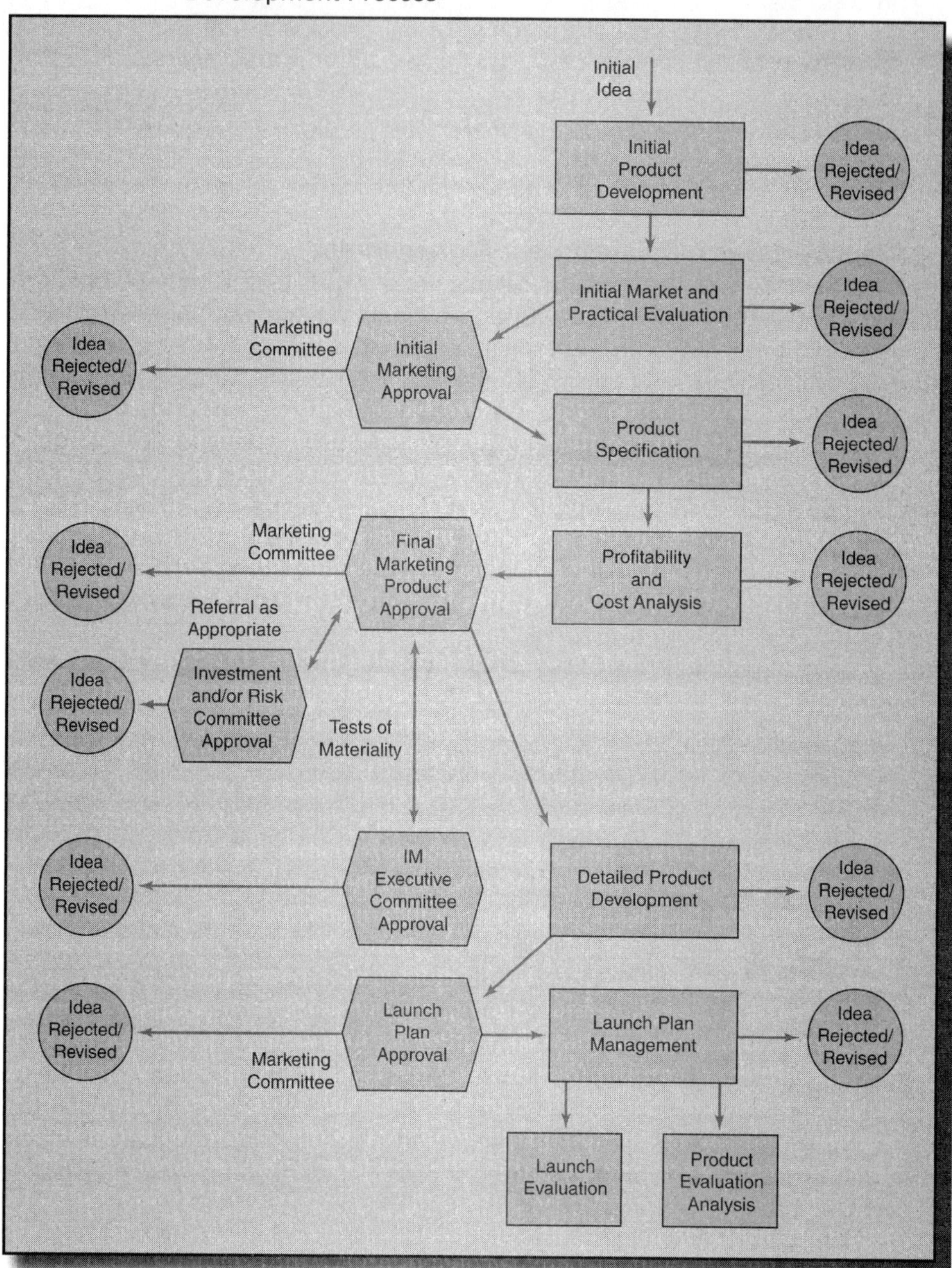

KBIM recognizes the intent of its new offering realization process is not to enforce a rigid, bureaucratic process that stifles product development. Some flexibility is needed. One way the KBIM MC provides this flexibility is through *qualified project approvals,* subject to further research that will supply critical information needed for a decision. This allows other development activities to proceed while the specified research is done. Another way it provides flexibility is through a *fast-track option,* where an idea sponsor requiring rapid approval is permitted to call a meeting with at least two members of the MC who can approve the initiative if they both believe it to be in KBIM's overall interest. The idea sponsor can then present the project with supporting documentation at a later meeting of the full MC. This flexibility has proved to be important where a prospective client has initiated a request for KBIM to design a specific solution that is typically a deviation of an existing product.

ABB Asea Brown Boveri Large-System Projects

ABB Asea Brown Boveri (ABB) defines **large-system projects** as those priced at greater than $15 million. Power plants and paper and pulp mills are examples. Large systems projects are becoming an increasingly significant way of doing business for ABB in that they now account for about one-third of ABB's annual turnover. ABB has constructed a realization process model for large-system projects, which we reproduce in Figure 6.9. This model outlines a systematic process for ABB to understand which projects to pursue, to capture the projects it wants, to manage risk, and to lower the costs of executing the projects for customers.

We can use gas-fueled power station projects to illustrate several aspects of the realization process. Fifty percent of the cost per kilowatt produced is the fuel. ABB uses its design expertise and technical knowledge to increase the efficiency of the plant to lower this cost. Fifteen percent of the cost is financing. ABB uses predesign to accelerate completion of the project, thereby reducing finance cost and generating earlier revenues. Thirty percent of the cost is equipment. ABB has established linkages among participating ABB units to lower total costs through superior fit and process. An internal ABB consortium or network can supply all of the equipment for a power station. Finally, 5% of the cost is power plant operations and maintenance.

Figure 6.9 ABB—How to Pursue the Business Opportunity

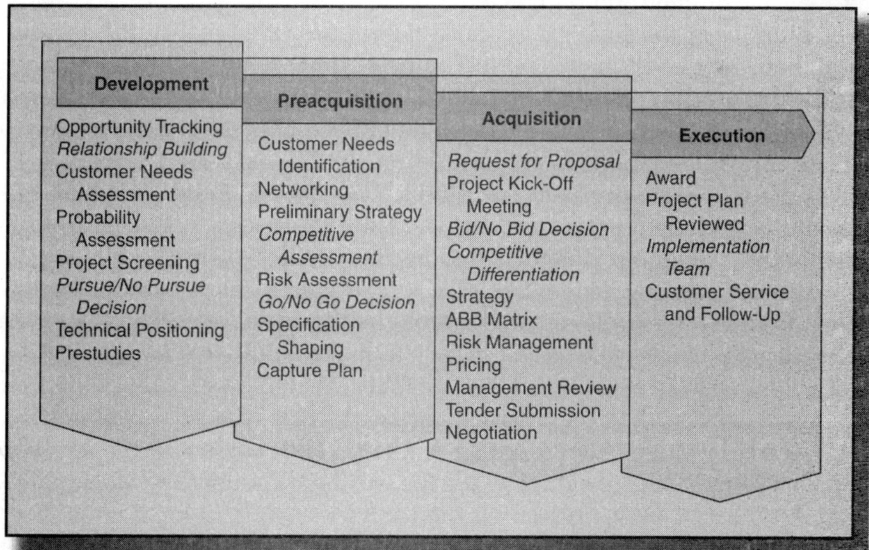

ABB uses its knowledge and experience to do this at a lower cost, offering service contracts to customers.

ABN-AMRO Bank Global Transaction Services

The Global Transaction Services (GTS) Unit of ABN-AMRO Bank (AA) has embedded its new offering realization process within its overall process for product management. The new offering realization process has four phases: idea filtering, product development, performance management, and close down.

A spark of inspiration from a member of the GTS organization often sets off the process. The *idea filtering* stage is an investigation into the consequences of pursuing an idea. It begins with secondary research, but proceeds to primary market research and initial logic designs. The business decides whether to pursue the idea based on the fit with other activity that is going on, current (or expected) capabilities, and how persuasive the evidence is that a sufficient return on investment is available. In the proposal subphase, the product manager must delineate the opportunity and convince the business that it is worth performing a fuller investigation of the feasibility and viability of the idea. In the justification subphase, the product manager must convince the business that the idea is worth committing the major resources necessary to develop the product. A significant part of this is that the initiative must have the commitment of all functional areas that would be involved in its development and support.

The purpose of the *product development* phase is to turn the idea into reality and develop the product up to its market launch. This phase has a strong project-management orientation. In fact, a professional project manager is appointed to work with the product manager, and formal project control is implemented. Multiple subprojects are likely, with at least one per functional area typical. It is also typical that each functional area appoints a subproject manager for the duration of development. However, the product manager does not take a "back seat." It remains the product manager's primary responsibility to see that resources are used efficiently; risks, assumptions, and dependencies are controlled; and a market-ready product is made available on time and budget.

The purpose of the *performance management* phase is to realize the return on the initial and ongoing investment, and it encompasses the launch, growth, maturity, and decline of the product. As such, it calls on a wide range of skills from the product manager, who effectively acts as the managing director of the product, responsible for its profitability and continued competitiveness. In the market launch subphase, customers begin to use the product. The product manager courts early adopters whose usage will drive opinion in the marketplace. The market launch subphase is an intensive period of ironing out unanticipated bumps in the service that inevitably occur despite the best planning and testing. Once the product is in the market, it needs to be modified recurrently to fulfill (changing) requirements and preferences of customers.

The purpose of the *close-down* phase is to make an orderly withdrawal from an unsustainable market position. The close-down stage is a delicate operation. Customers will be used to the product, and there is likely to be resistance to change to a newer, replacement GTS product. Alternatively, customers may be switching rapidly to a competitor's product, while the existing product is being clung to internally at AA. Judged by its impact on the Bank, AA GTS considers withdrawal of a product from the market just as important as the launch of a new product. In fact, it believes that products should be designed with withdrawal in mind. Finally, the postmortem enables AA GTS to capture and integrate its learnings from its entire experience with a product.

A General Realization Process Model

Given the diversity in the realization process models we have reviewed, is there a general realization process model that pulls together their common characteristics? A general realization process model that we prefer is one that Wheelwright and Clark provide, which we reproduce in Figure 6.10.[57]

This model emphasizes cross-functional integration and provides the primary activities of engineering, marketing, and manufacturing for each development phase. Wheelwright and Clark broadly define these functional areas, intending marketing to include market research and sales, and manufacturing to include process development, manufacturing engineering, and plant operations. This model also specifies the key milestones and key decisions for each phase. Because approval acts as a "gate" through which a project must pass to progress to the next development phase or "stage," this kind of model of the realization process is called a **stage-gate model**.

Wheelwright and Clark maintain that new offering realization requires more than cross-functional coordination; it requires **cross-functional integration**, which means that management or the project team add specific activities that support cross-functional work. "For example, engineering builds very early system prototypes in order to support marketing's desire to develop richer customer insight early in the process."[58] To reinforce this integration, Wheelwright and Clark express the milestones in Figure 6.10 to focus attention on how the different functional activities in each phase fit together. They recognize that cross-functional integration truly occurs when individuals from different functional areas work together to accomplish interdependent tasks. In so doing, those individuals gain appreciation and respect for what each functional area contributes to new offering realization. Not every development project requires cross-functional integration, though. When the project involves substantial continuity and experience from past realization efforts and marketplace change is methodical, cross-function coordination is sufficient.

Another aspect of the model that we find desirable is the inclusion of a market introduction phase. This phase encompasses all activities that are part of the market launch for the new offering and concludes with its demonstrated commercial viability. Often, firms mistakenly believe that their new product development process is finished at the end of the detailed design and development or commercial preparation phase. A market launch that is inadequate or poorly done is one of the leading causes of new product failure.[59]

We relate the various realization process models that we have examined to this general realization process model in Figure 6.11.

Each of them is consistent with the general realization process model, with the variations reflecting each firm's unique strategy, circumstances, and marketplace. For example, Smallfry Industrial Design's model is more elaborate earlier in the realization process than later, in keeping with its focus as an industrial design consultant. Some of the process models appear simpler, but recall that each phase has a number of subphases that we did not detail. The ABB Asea Brown Boveri Ltd. is

Figure 6.10 A General Realization Process Model

Functional Activities Under Cross-Functional Integration

Functional Activities	Phases of Development					
	Concept Development	Product Planning	Detailed Design and Development: Phase I	Detailed Design and Development: Phase II	Commercial Preparation	Market Introduction
Engineering	Propose new technologies; develop product ideas; build models; conduct simulations	Choose components and interact with suppliers; build early system prototypes; define product architecture	Do detailed design of product and interact with process; build full-scale prototypes; conduct prototype testing	Refine details of product design; participate in building second-phase prototypes	Evaluate and test pilot units; solve problems	Evaluate field experience with product
Marketing	Provide market-based input; propose and investigate product concepts	Define target customer's parameters; develop estimates of sales and margins; conduct early interact with customers	Conduct customer tests of prototypes; participate in prototyping evaluation	Conduct second-phase customer tests; evaluate prototypes; plan marketing rollout; establish distribution plan	Prepare for market rollout; train sales force and field service personnel; prepare order entry/process system	Fill distribution channels; sell and promote; interaction with key customers
Manufacturing	Propose and investigate process concepts	Develop cost estimates; define process architecture; conduct process simulation; validate suppliers	Do detailed design of process; design and develop tooling and equipment; participate in building full-scale prototypes	Test and try out tooling and equipment; build second-phase prototypes; install equipment and bring up new procedures	Build pilot units in commercial process; refine process based on pilot experience; train personnel and verify supply channel	Ramp up plant to volume targets; meet targets for quality, yield, and cost
Key Milestones	• Concept for product and process defined	• Establish product and process architecture • Define program parameters	• Build and test complete prototypes • Verify product design	• Build and refine 2nd phase prototype • Verify process tools and design	• Produce pilot units • Operate and test complete commercial system	• Ramp up to volume production • Meet initial commercial objectives
Key Decisions	CONCEPT APPROVAL	PROGRAM APPROVAL	DETAILED DESIGN APPROVAL	JOINT PRODUCT AND PROCESS APPROVAL	APPROVAL FOR FIRST COMMERCIAL SALES	FULL COMMERCIAL APPROVAL

Source: Steven C. Wheelwright and Kim B. Clark, *Revolutionizing Product Development: Quantum Leaps in Speed, Efficiency, and Quality* (New York: The Free Press, 1992), p. 173.

Figure 6.11 Relating the Various Realization Process Models to the General Realization Process Model

General Realization Process Model:	**Concept Development**	**Product Planning**	**Detailed Design and Development**	**Commercial Preparation**	**Market Introduction**	**[Post Project Learning and Improvement]**
Smallfry Industrial Design Model:	Project Set Up Concept Appraisal	Embodiment Design	3D Data Manufacturing Specification	Preproduction Liaison; Manufacture	Sales	
Akzo Nobel Coatings Model:	Idea Concept		Development	Upscaling	Market Introduction	After Care
Kleinwort Benson Investment Management Model:	Initial Product Development; Initial Market and Practical Evaluation	Product Specification; Profitability and Cost Analysis	Detailed Product Development	Launch Plan Management		Launch Evaluation; Product Evaluation/ Analysis
ABB Asea Brown Boveri Ltd. Large System Projects Model:	Development	Preacquisition	Acquisition	Execution		
ABN-AMRO Bank Global Transaction Services Model:	Idea Filtering	Product Development			Performance Management	Close Down

an example. Finally, the formal inclusion of a phase following market introduction in the Kleinwort Benson Investment Management, Akzo Nobel Coatings, and ABN-AMRO Bank Global Transaction Services models is in keeping with the Post-Project Learning and Improvement phase depicted at the end of the development process "funnel" in Figure 6.2.

Augmenting Services in Realization Process Models

We elaborate on this model by considering the planning, design, development, and delivery of the augmenting services, programs, and systems that enhance the new core product's or service's value. Planning for the augmenting services for the core product or service should begin in the *product planning* phase. Devising, designing, and prototyping these augmenting services should occur in the second phase of *detailed design and development*. The firm also should estimate the resource requirements and costs of providing the augmenting services. The firm should run pilot programs for the augmenting services during the *commercial preparation* phase with customers that are testing the new product, and make final refinements in the services, estimates of resource requirements and costs, and customer feedback mechanisms. At the *market introduction* phase, the firm is able to deliver the augmenting services at the requisite levels to support the market launch of the new offering.

"Next-Generation" Realization Process Models

New product development is an area of active inquiry, where academic researchers, consultants, and pundits continually suggest new developments and refinements in the new product development process. Cooper has proposed a next-generation product development process that he contends is fundamentally different from stage-gate models of the realization process in four ways[60]:

1. ***Fluidity:*** It is fluid and adaptable, with overlapping and fluid stages for greater speed.
2. ***Fuzzy gates:*** It features conditional Go decisions (rather than absolute ones), which are dependent on the situation.
3. ***Focused:*** It builds in prioritization methods that look at the entire portfolio of projects (rather than one project at a time) and focuses resources on the "best bets."
4. ***Flexible:*** It is not a rigid stage-and-gate system; each project is unique and has its own routing through the process.

Cooper recognizes that these characteristics also have the potential to produce more mistakes because the process becomes more unstructured, and it shifts some decision responsibility from senior management to project managers and teams. Adler, Mandelbaum, Nguyen, and Schwerer also advocate more fluidity and flexibility and propose that firms construct *processing network models* that capture the overlap and simultaneous nature of development across functional areas.[61]

Supplier firms that compete in dynamic marketplaces, such as high-technology markets, take advantage of the greater agility that "next-generation" realization processes provide. By overlapping concept development and implementation phases, a firm can incorporate late-breaking changes into its product design without sacrificing overall speed-to-market, as measured from project start until market

BOX 6.7

Leveraging Uncertainties in a Firm's Realization Process to Create Value

Any new product development that seeks to harness market opportunity must be innovative. Innovation is inextricably linked with uncertainty, and even risks. Firms therefore have to find ways of managing these risks. While firms need to ensure that their realization processes are efficient in terms of resource utilization, they also need to be agile in terms of converting evolving opportunities into innovative products and services. This can be achieved through rapid experimentation and testing in the marketplace. When testing reveals that the product creates little value for customers, firms need to quickly change track and in extreme cases even abandon projects, to ensure that resources are not wasted on ideas that have little potential. Resources are instead directed to those ideas that show promise and potential, through a process of constant iteration, till a winning product is developed. Often, to mitigate the risks, companies attempt to simultaneously develop several new products. The essence of such an approach is rapid prototyping followed by quick marketplace testing.

Manthan, a Bangalore-based software development company that offers products and services in the domain of business intelligence (BI) for the retail industry, illustrates this. At the time of its inception in Decenber 2003, Manthan began to work simultaneously on three different products that leverage BI analytics: Astra, Promax, and ARC. These products span three different application areas within the retail industry.

Astra was a tool to measure the effectiveness of strategy execution. Despite its seemingly considerable potential, the product was discontinued quickly, as there was not much traction for it in the marketplace. Manthan, however, captured and used the learning that had evolved from developing this product.

Promax provided a powerful BI layer to Enterprise Resource Planning (ERP) product companies who sold their products to the retail industry. Manthan's offering was expected to be an add-on product to ERP software vendors, who sell their ERP products to retail chains. Manthan did not have an effective manner in which to take this product to markets. This, and the fact that the value creation was not apparent during market testing, resulted in Manthan discontinuing further development of Promax. But learnings from this development experience were also captured as part of the organization's collective knowledge.

The third product that Manthan developed was ARC—its flagship in the retail BI suite of products—that went through rapid prototyping, market testing, and evolution, and ultimately proved to be an outstanding success.

Manthan developed and launched three products simultaneously because they saw much opportunity in the fast-growing retail industry. Three different groups of thirty each developed and test-marketed the three products parallelly. This helped Manthan save time and avoid costly mistakes, while ensuring that it did not miss out on any significant opportunities in its chosen domain.

D. V. R. Seshadri, James A. Narus and Shobitha Hegde, "Manthan Systems: Opportunities and Challenges Galore," case study developed for IIM Bangalore in 2008.

introduction. These changes may be in response to evolving customer requirements, technological advances, or new knowledge of competitors' products.[62]

Another "next-generation" variation in realization processes is to take a short hiatus in the middle of the development phase for a new platform product. Firms use this hiatus to define and initiate the realization processes for derivative products that will fill openings in the market that the new platform product will create. By purposively overlapping its realization processes in this way, the firm improves the speed-to-market of its derivative products and thwarts rapid-response competitors from beating them to market niches.[63]

We can see these next-generation characteristics reflected in the various realization process models that we considered. ABB's use of established linkages among participating ABB units in large-system projects provides fluidity. Indeed, the cross-functional integration of the Wheelwright and Clark realization process model strives to provide fluidity. KBIM's use of qualified project approvals is an instance of fuzzy gates, and its fast-track option provides flexibility in its realization process. Finally, the aggregate project plan of Wheelwright and Clark is a focus mechanism for prioritizing projects and allocating resources across a set of projects. In Box 6.7 we present thinking on how firms can leverage uncertainties in their realization process to create value.

MARKET-ORIENTED REALIZATION

Firms in business markets should have the intent of being market oriented and customer focused in their realization efforts. Learning about the requirements and preferences of target market segments and customers early in the realization process, and collaborating with selected customers should increase speed-to-market, reduce realization cost, and improve marketplace success. Yet, many firms have difficulty understanding what this means for them and how to accomplish it in practice. Moreover, it is comfortable for research and development groups (as well as other functional areas) that view themselves as largely removed from the marketplace to remain, or revert to being, inward looking.

We have discussed a realization strategy and a realization process that are market oriented. Here, we consider further how to make new offering realization market oriented and customer focused. We first suggest ways in which a firm's research and advanced development group can be market oriented. We then offer ways in which a firm's development process can be market oriented.

Market-Oriented Research

Research and advanced development (hereafter, simply Research) has a pioneering or scouting mission in most firms; it is responsible for generating new scientific and technical knowledge. It seeks to push back the knowledge frontiers in science and technology in ways that create value over the long term. The intent is that Research's work will translate into technology that firms can commercialize in new offerings. In contrast, Commercial Development (hereafter, simply Development) has a more practical and short-term mission: It uses, adapts, or further develops known technologies to produce new core products or services for the firm to offer to the market. Research and Development (R&D) have a critical linkage; each is dependent upon the other, at least partly, for its own success within the firm. So, R&D must work together to translate generated knowledge resources into products for commercialization, and marketplace understanding into direction for future Research efforts.

Businesses are placing greater demands on Research to be market oriented.[64] R&D budgets are either stagnant or growing slowly at most firms. Firms appear to be placing more emphasis and spending more on research than in recent years, restoring the balance compared with the proportion spent on development, but in return they are insisting that Research interact regularly with marketing and other executives from the business units. Each of these reflect senior management discontent with the marketplace results that Research has produced with their resources. Senior management increasingly wants Research to demonstrate how it is contributing to an advantage in the market.

To excel with limited resources, Research needs to focus its efforts and leverage its resources with outside relationships. Furthermore, Research needs to connect itself with the market. We briefly examine each of these in turn.

Creating Focused Research Centers

Research management in consultation with senior management needs to make choices about which basic areas of science and technology research the firm will pursue actively. As an example, General Electric has reduced the number of areas for long-term research from 20 to just five.[65] An organizational mechanism that a firm can use to focus its scientists and other resources on particular areas is the *research center*. Akzo Nobel Coatings' Innovative Research unit focuses on six research areas: high solids, water-borne, color, powder, pigment dispersants, and new coating chemistry. It has created a research center for each of these areas. Innovative Research has also established a number of mechanisms to facilitate sharing information across research centers, such as having common raw material codes so each center knows what the others are using.

Scientists in focused research centers need to make decisions about how they can best leverage their allocated resources. What knowledge should they generate internally, what knowledge should they cogenerate through collaborative relationships and research networks, and what knowledge should they acquire from outside research sources? One concept that should influence these decisions is **sticky information**: that is, the extent to which it is costly to transfer knowledge or information from the place where it resides to another location and have it in a form the information seeker can use.[66] Information might be sticky because of its nature, such as being tacit rather than explicit. Alternatively, information might be sticky because of the amount a provider needs to send the seeker, because the seeker cannot specify in advance what parts will be germane.

A focused research center can pursue collaborative relationships with universities, government-funded laboratories, research institutes, or other firms' research units. Intel is supporting a number of small labs, staffed by 20 to 30 researchers, that it terms *lablets* and which are located adjacent to leading universities. Each lablet is focusing on a nascent technology and is directed by a faculty member who has taken a temporary leave of absence. A focused research center also can participate in research networks that comprise a mix of outside partners. For instance, the pharmaceutical firm Pfizer has teamed up with academic researchers and small biotech firms at its Discovery Technology Center to develop computerized methods for screening thousands of potential drug molecules per day. This Center is located in Cambridge, Massachusetts, apart from its main R&D facility in Connecticut.[67]

As part of its activities, a research center should actively monitor science and technology developments both within and outside its industry. Kodama maintains that firms should engage in collaborative research with a variety of firms across many different industries. In doing so, the firms can gather intelligence on how existing technologies might be combined to create hybrid technologies, which he calls *technology fusion*.[68]

Finally, a research center should not overlook the potential benefits of having its scientists participate in social networks with academic scientists. Rather than having the commercial intent of a business network, a **social network** is "a collectivity of individuals among whom exchanges take place that are supported only by shared norms of trustworthy behavior." A study of two new biotechnology firms' use of social networks found that scientists at one firm collaborated with academic researchers at 144 different external institutions over a 10-year period, whereas scientists at the other firm collaborated with academic researchers at 147 different external institutions over a comparable 9-year period. Interestingly, although both firms were located in the United States, 29% of the collaborations for the first firm and 43% of the collaborations for the second firm were with researchers at institutions outside the United States. Commenting on their results, the researchers stated, "This evidence suggests that Firms X and Y continued to gain benefits from research collaborations during the period studied in terms of prospecting for innovations, reducing their direct R&D costs, accessing the knowledge of immobile external scientists, and attracting and retaining scientist-employees."[69]

Connecting Research with the Market

"Selling only on price. Where is the fun in it?" A director of a basic research unit made this to-the-point observation. He understands that the role of Research is to add value in the marketplace. He recognizes that his business unit needs innovation so that when there is market pressure on price, the business has something different it can offer, something that provides greater value to its customers than the products of its competitors. How can other firms get their researchers as connected with the market as this director is?

Regular, scheduled interactions with the design engineering, manufacturing engineering, field engineering, and advanced marketing groups appear to be the best answer. These interactions should include a mix of one-on-one information exchanges and more structured group-to-group exchanges. We recommend an alternating "home and away" schedule for these interactions, where participants take turns visiting and spending time at each other's location. General Electric built meeting and conference facilities at its Nishkayuna, New York, central research lab. Its head of global research and development has found that some of the best ideas come during off-hours, when employees from across the company are having a meal together or relaxing in the lounge.[70]

In one-on-one meetings, field engineers and marketers can relate to research scientists changes in customers' requirements and advances in competitors' offerings. It is especially important to communicate to Research (and to Development) as early as possible new or anticipated entrants whose offerings use different technology. In meetings with design engineers and manufacturing engineers, researchers can communicate their progress on research projects as well as learn of difficulties that the developers are having in working with, adapting, and further developing new and existing technologies. Research should periodically put on research symposia or innovation fairs, where it presents recent research advances to design engineering, manufacturing engineering, field engineering, and advanced marketing groups. At these more structured meetings, Research also can apprise symposium participants of technological advances that it sees occurring in other areas; speculate on their relevance, with further innovation, in the firm's markets; and gain valuable feedback for future research initiatives from the symposium participants. Finally, Research can participate in "home and away" research overviews with research units of strategic customers, where supplier development groups facilitate and also attend these meetings.

Eaton Corporation's aerospace operations, which developed the hydraulic and wing fluid distribution systems operating on Airbus's latest A380 aircraft, uses "innovation summits" and "design bursts" to propel its product development process. Innovation summits are two- or three-day events that involve representatives from multiple levels and functions across the corporation including program management, engineering, sales and marketing, customers, competitors (seen as potential alliance partners), and external experts with the objective of generating new ideas. Design bursts are "deeper dives" into the three to five ideas generated in the innovation summits. They also last two to three days. The outcomes of these events are concrete ideas about appearance and the associated investments, as well as the potential payback. Such a process allows Eaton to look for new product realization opportunities across the division and the corporation.[71]

Market-Oriented Development

Predicting the applications of an innovation other than its initial one has proven extraordinarily difficult for companies. For example, Motorola initially saw cellular phones as replacement technology for its two-way radios in vehicles; at the time, it never envisioned that customers would use them outside of a vehicle! Tellis and Golder found that enduring market leadership is due not to being first to market, but instead to envisioning a larger potential market, managerial persistence, financial commitment, and relentless innovation (improvement of the invention). Robinson and Min found that first entrants in a new industrial market face the greatest market and technological uncertainties, but compensating for this, they benefit from first-mover advantages that might include introducing follow-on offerings that better meet the requirements and preferences of developing market segments. This research suggests how critical market-oriented development is to enduring market leadership.[72]

We consider four ways for the firm to be market oriented in its development of new offerings: (1) use positioning statements as a market-focusing mechanism; (2) research customer requirements and preferences and translate them into design specifications; (3) guide realization efforts with customer value assessment; and (4) tailor market introductions of new offerings.

Positioning Statements as a Market-Focusing Mechanism

Positioning statements can assist in focusing a project team on the market throughout the realization process. At each phase, senior management should require the project team to provide a positioning statement as part of its review materials. Each positioning statement would contain the three critical components we discussed in Chapter 4: target, offering concept, and value proposition. Although the team might state elements of the positioning statement in broad or coarse terms in the initial phases, senior management would expect to see refinement and greater specificity as the project moves through the realization process. This expectation pushes the team to think about the characteristics of target customers, the essential attributes of the offering for customers, and the worth of the new offering to the customer. To reach this specificity, the team would have to translate customer requirements and preferences into design specifications and conduct value assessments with target customers.

Researching Market Requirements and Translating Them into Design Specifications

Simply put, there is no substitute for market research on the requirements and preferences of target customers to inform and guide realization efforts. Such research can take a number of forms, such as field qualitative research by a firm's development engineers or an outside engineering consulting firm, focus groups, and quantitative field survey research by an outside market research firm. Astute firms employ more than one method, seeking convergence in the results they obtain. Market research complements reports from the sales force and field engineering, which are also valuable sources of information about customer requirements and preferences, and how they are changing.

What customers are of particular interest for the firm to research? Customers that have knowledge or experience that can significantly contribute to a firm's realization efforts are of interest. These customers may be current users, prospective customers, or even customers that have recently switched to competitors' offerings. When Boeing Company began to design the 787 passenger jet in October 2002, executives of the aircraft manufacturer met with a group of global airline representatives at a conference center on the Seattle waterfront. The executives desperately were trying to figure out what to build next to hold off a soaring Airbus. One Boeing executive drew a graph on a whiteboard, the axes being cruising range and passenger numbers. Then he asked the airline representatives to locate their ideal position on the graph. The distribution of the data points showed the company that airlines favored efficiency over speed—the exact opposite of what Boeing was thinking. Two months later, Boeing ditched plans for a high-speed high-cost jetliner to embark on a new program, the 7E7—E for efficiency—that has changed global aviation and airframe manufacturing.[73]

Indeed, evidence shows that lead-user customers are often sources of innovation to supplier firms.[74] **Lead-users** are current or prospective customers who are experiencing problems or needs that will become widespread in the market in the foreseeable future. They would derive significant value immediately from an innovative solution. Such customers may have begun problem-solving activities themselves. Studies have shown how lead users also are often connected with other innovative users in user networks that can exert enormous influence in the design, development, and diffusion of an innovation, as in the case of open-source software (OSS).[75] Finally, firms can also use lead-users to help relaunch failed products by using the lead users to teach the firm about possible user-defined and new-to-the-firm uses or applications of the product.[76]

Another kind of customer that is of interest to research is the **leap-frog customer**, which is a small aggressive firm, possibly a newer entrant, that is pursuing a riskier development strategy to gain market share.[77] Finally, the firm should seek to participate in early supplier involvement (ESI) programs of large strategic customers. We view these ESI collaborations as a kind of participant-observer research.

The kind of input about innovation that a supplier solicits from present or prospective customers can make a difference in how worthwhile that input turns out to be. Ulwick advises against asking customers what they want in an offering or suggesting solutions for problems they experience with current offerings; instead, solicit from them changes in the *outcomes* that they seek from an offering. "A well-formatted outcome contains both the type of improvement required (minimize, increase) and a unit of measure (time, number, frequency) so that the outcome statement can be used later in benchmarking, competitive analysis, and concept evaluation." Examples of outcome statements from a study of improvements for angioplasty balloons used to clear blocked arteries of cardiac patients are "Minimize restenosis (or the recurrence of a blockage)" and "Minimize the amount of force required to cross the lesion with the balloon." Ulwick recommends soliciting these outcomes from a diverse set of customers and not just lead-users, whose recommendations may have limited appeal to the broader market.[78]

Translating target customer requirements and preferences into design specifications is a crucial step in connecting the marketplace with realization efforts. Often, gaps occur between the way a customer expresses the performance it is seeking and the way a supplier specifies how it makes products. As an example, an appliance customer might want *formability* in a steel coil that allows it to perform a deep, reverse-draw operation to create the inner tub for a washing machine. The problem is that a steelmaker characterizes the products it produces in terms of *chemistry* and *metallurgy*. What specific chemistry and metallurgy will provide the desired formability? A firm can pursue several translation approaches: quality function deployment, prototyping, beta testing, and realizing flexible product components.

Quality function deployment (QFD) is a set of methods and tools for translating target customer requirements and preferences into internally understood engineering and manufacturing parameters. The *house of quality* is a prominent QFD methodology that brings together in a "house" configuration a list of customer attributes (CA) the firm generates from market research; a list of engineering characteristics (EC) that will likely affect the CA; the relationships between CA and EC; the relationships within EC; objectives measures of EC; and judgments of the technical difficulty, imputed importance, and costs of achieving target levels of EC. QFD can be a valuable methodology in the concept development and product planning phases of the realization process, and its use can extend to manufacturing process design. Further, Hauser and Griffin found that use of QFD led to greater communication among cross-functional team members and communication patterns that were more horizontal, rather than "up-over-down" through management. The downside was less communication with others in the firm outside the team.[79]

The project team should attempt to gain feedback on its translation as early as possible in the realization process. **Prototypes** are a research tool that allows selected customers to experience in a rough form the functionality or performance of a new offering and give feedback to the project team. Firms are looking for ways to lower the cost of prototypes, and some have turned to computer simulations rather than constructing physical prototypes. Boeing Company estimated that it saved $21 million during the engineering and manufacturing development phase of its realization process for the Osprey V-22 helicopter by eliminating physical mock-ups and instead relying on computer-simulated prototypes to verify clearances and accessibility.[80] Not only do computer-simulated prototypes reduce realization costs, they also speed up the realization process. "Millennium Pharmaceuticals in Cambridge, Massachusetts, for instance, incorporates new technologies such as genomics, bioinformatics, and combinatorial chemistry in its technology platform for conducting experiments. The platform enables factory-like automation that can generate and test drug candidates in minutes or seconds compared with the days or more that traditional methods require."[81]

Later in the realization process, a firm can use **alpha testing**, where individuals within the firm simulate the target customer's use of a nearly realized product. After making any necessary adjustments or refinements, the firm proceeds with **beta testing**, where the firm provides select customers with the new offering and gains feedback on it from the customers' experiences. The firm uses this feedback to make any final adjustments or refinements in the new offering before its market introduction. Dolan and Matthews conclude from their research on beta testing that beta-testing is most valuable when

1. users are heterogeneous;
2. potential applications of the product are not fully understood;
3. alpha testing is unable to guarantee a "bug-free" product;
4. product complexity limits the potential sample size in product-use tests;
5. the decision-making unit for a purchase is complex, so the opinions of a variety of people within an organization must be understood; and
6. opinion leadership phenomenon is operative.[82]

Finally, in certain cases, it is extraordinarily difficult to know the customer's application of a new offering; that is, the customer's application information is "sticky."[83] In such a case, a firm can respond with a product that provides flexibility through two components: one component that is standard across all applications, and a user-friendly component that enables customers to tailor the standard component to their own requirements. An example would be an integrated circuit supplier providing standard silicone wafers along with a CAD software package to its custom circuit users so that they can produce application-specific integrated circuits (APSIC). Another example is a software company providing a standard software package along with a user "tool kit" that enables customers to customize the program to their diverse applications.[84]

Guiding Realization Efforts with Customer Value Assessment

Although customer value assessment is a kind of market research, we discuss it separately because most market research that firms use to understand the requirements and preferences of target customers does not address the question, "If we accomplish this, what is it worth to the customer in its application?" Knowing that an improvement in some functionality is important does not tell a firm whether the customer is willing to pay what it will cost to provide that improved functionality. Value assessment provides this essential information to guide realization efforts.

In realization projects that are **technology push**, where the firm's new offering will introduce new technology into the market, it can use value assessment to persuasively demonstrate to prospective customers how the new technology provides greater value or lower cost to them. This demonstration is especially critical when the new technology gives the market offering a higher price than competitors' offerings using more established and familiar technologies. At the same time, the firm can learn how the value of its new technology varies across applications, customer capabilities, and usage situations. Box 6.8 provides an example of how FlowServe has a unique program called Life Cycle Advantage[85] to demonstrate the value of its offering.

In realization projects that are **market pull**, where the firm is developing its new offering in response to customer requests or demands, it can use value assessment to provide guidance on what improvements are worthwhile for it to pursue, and the priority it should give to potential advances. The value assessment can examine the incremental value target customers would place on changes in the market offering from its present levels of functionality or performance to levels that represent short-term achievable development objectives. The firm can have managers in different functional areas of the customer firm respond to offering attributes for which they are primarily responsible. For example, a chemical pigment producer had customer firm managers in production and R&D perform a conjoint task for short-term achievable changes in technical attributes, such as gloss and dispersability. It also had general management and purchasing managers perform a conjoint task for short-term achievable changes in commercial attributes, such as delivery service and payment terms.

Tailoring Market Introductions of New Offerings

A firm should tailor its market introductions of new offerings, striving for commonality and consistency where it can, yet recognizing where it needs to remain flexible. This is particularly true where the firm is introducing the new offering into a number of country markets. Aurolab's market launch of intraocular fens, which we recount in Box 6.9 provides a noteworthy case study of market introduction.

AN Coatings management focuses on three critical activities in the market introduction phase of new offering realization:

1. ***Know the local market.*** For example, how important is drying time? Further, environmental concern is lower in some countries.
2. ***Internal selling.*** It is essential to gain the commitment of local country managers. Approach them in their local languages.
3. ***Motivate channel partners.*** Motivate the paint dealers to stock and market the product. Clearly communicate the economic advantages of the product to them in their local languages.

Notice that having downstream actors involved earlier (than the market introduction phase) in the realization process contributes to success in the preceding activities, as when AN Coatings had all the European country market managers participate in the decision to use Austria as the test market.

BOX 6.8
Flowserve's Value Assessment Tool

Flowserve is one of the world's leading manufacturers and after-market service providers for valves, pumps, and sealing solutions. Its core competency is in flow control systems, which require high reliability and are often delivered to critical service applications. It also provides after-market equipment services, such as diagnostics, detailed analysis of the existing systems, consulting, as well as repair and service of flow control systems.

Flowserve initially started its Indian operation as a 100% export-oriented unit. With the growth of the Indian economy in recent years, Flowserve has started focusing on the domestic market. The market has largely been commoditized, with the lowest bidder in terms of price getting the order. To come out of this commodity trap, Flowserve provides its customers the choice of a host of augmented services to its basic offering. This approach has resulted in the customer perceiving greater value from its offering despite its higher price. These efforts have yielded results. For instance, Flowserve obtained an order from Indian Oil Corporation's Gujarat Refinery for supplying a special coke-cutting pumping system that will be used for the heavy oil upgradation project. The value of the contract is estimated to be about INR 78.2 crores.

Flowserve has a unique program called LifeCycle Advantage, specifically designed to deliver more value and to help customer firms achieve greater cost savings. The company offers services such as analyzing equipment performance, streamlining inventory management, standardizing equipment for procurement, efficiency enhancement, training, and problem solving. Flowserve approaches its customers not as vendors but as partners in business. Flowserve promises documented cost savings through its LifeCycle Advantage program. It analyzes customer's needs and implements some of the industry's best practices, which ultimately save money through better equipment management and improved efficiency. The process is customized for each customer's individual needs. Through this program, Flowserve has been able to quantifiably minimize customers' equipment downtime, streamline inventory, reduce costs on part replacements, and extend the lifetime of the equipment. For example, one oil-refining company reported approximately INR 216.2 crores savings over a seven-year period by using Flowserve's solutions.

Once the customer has signed up for the documented cost saving program, a team of engineers from Flowserve form a taskforce along with the customer firm's engineers. The team first does a complete audit of the existing system and documents its maintenance history in order to identify critical and underperforming equipment. Then, a root-cause analysis is performed, and corrective actions are identified for immediate improvement in equipment downtime. Key performance indicators are established, and solutions are recommended to significantly increase efficiency and decrease equipment downtime. From time to time, meetings are held between Flowserve managers and the customer firm's managers to assess the program's performance.

Contributed by Kiran Prabhakara, Participant, PGSEM Program, Indian Institute of Management Bangalore.

BOX 6.9

Aurolab's Tailored Market Introduction of Intraocular Lenses

Aurolab was set up by Aravind Eye Care System (AECS), Madurai in 1992. Aurolab was to complement Aravind Eye Hospitals' vision of providing affordable eye care through the production of high-quality intraocular lenses (IOLs) at low cost to reduce the overall cost of eye surgery, making it accessible to all. IOL is an artificial lens that is implanted into the patient's eye to replace the cataract-affected natural lens. Aurolab's creation stemmed from its socially responsible business model of having two free patients for every paying patient, which necessitated it to have total control of all aspects of the eye care value chain. Initially set up as an in-house captive manufacturing division, through innovation, Aurolab reduced the production cost of IOLs, resulting in a unit price of less than INR 100, vis-à-vis the then prevailing imported price of over INR 4,600, while maintaining international quality standards.

Due to growing number of cataract surgeries in the country and consequent increased demand for quality IOLs at affordable prices, Aurolab started supplying its products to other hospitals and non-profit non-government organizations (NGOs) in India and in over 120 countries from the developing world. Gradually, the product portfolio was broadened to include sutures, surgical blades, and pharmaceutical products.

As a result of these sustained efforts, Aurolab was successful in setting up a competitive ecosystem for ophthalmic products by forcing competitors to drastically lower the prices of their ophthalmic products. Today, Aurolab's product portfolio comprises hundreds of stock keeping units (SKUs) of IOLs and other ophthalmic products. The industry is characterized by frequent introduction of new products.

For export of IOLs, given its relatively small sales and marketing team, Aurolab concentrated on selling to international NGOs (INGOs) and large hospitals. It enjoys a global market share of 7%. Pricing to programs by INGOs are typically much lower, due to large volumes that they source from Aurolab. Under these programs, INGOs donate IOLs to hospitals in developing countries free of cost, as part of their social charity work. When the beneficiary hospitals need additional supplies, they approach Aurolab directly for their needs. Through word of mouth, other hospitals in the country also source IOLs from Aurolab, which results in dealers in these countries approaching Aurolab and wanting to distribute its products in that country. From this perspective, dealers are not chosen deliberately, but emerge.

Medical supplies in each country are governed by different laws, which are local to each country. There are different standards to be complied with in terms of packing, labeling in the local language, providing the product brochures (referred to as IFU or information for use) in the local language, etc. For surgical products such as those manufactured by Aurolab, international protocol requires standardized markings on the packaging. This enables doctors to recognize the product easily. Aurolab has to comply with such stipulations as well. For instance, a notation, "2X" on the packing might represent that there is no need to re-sterilize the product before use.

It is mandatory for Aurolab to get registration in these countries to sell its ophthalmic pharmaceutical products. However,

(*continued*)

BOX 6.9
Continued

in some of the developing countries, such registration is not needed for IOLs due to newness of the products in these markets and hence the lack of knowledge by the registration authority on how to treat them. In many of the developing countries, the process of registration is not transparent, and Aurolab may often not know the undercurrents that prevail for obtaining the registration. Aurolab has to rely on the dealer to get local registration for its products. Often the dealers may not be knowledgeable about the procedures involved in getting the registration. Market potential in some of the smaller countries may be so low that it may not be worth Aurolab's time, effort, and money to get these registrations. Many of these countries end up sourcing much costlier ophthalmic pharmaceutical products from the developed world at much higher prices than what Aurolab can supply, due to the difficulties Aurolab has in getting registration for them. One of the significant challenges for Aurolab in exporting to these countries is to make the right SKU physically available at the right place, at the right time. Besides, in these markets, Aurolab has to compete with well-established and large international competitors who have access to huge financial and other resources.

D. V. R. Seshadri, A. Gautam , R. Karthik, V. Badrinarayanan, "Aurolab: Excellence in Sight and Beyond," case study developed for IIM Bangalore in 2010.

One other aspect of market introduction that we want to address is pricing new offerings. As we discussed in Chapter 5, we strongly recommend value-based pricing. Pricing new offerings requires some elaboration on our earlier framework. Because a new offering ranges from low to high in "newness to the market," firms typically need to provide prospective customers with a larger **incentive to change**: that is, initially give an additional part of the offering's incremental value as monetary motivation to try something different. It is critical for the firm to think about this pricing tactic and manage it separately from the pricing strategy for the new offering.

Some firms mistakenly blur the two, introducing a new offering at a "low introductory price," with the intent of raising the price as the offering becomes established in the market. Customers view the fairness of prices relative to a reference point rather than in absolute terms.[86] By introducing at a low price, the firm establishes an expectation, or reference point, with the customer of what the price should be for the offering. When it attempts to raise price, customers react angrily because the firm is asking the customer to pay more than it expects for the offering, with no noticeable change in its value. Instead, the firm should introduce the new offering at the higher price that represents its pricing strategy, and then discount off this price with initial use discounts. An **initial use discount** is a pricing tactic that is an invoice reduction used to encourage prospective customers to try an offering that is new to them. The offering's actual price is listed on the invoice, then reduced by the incentive to change, with the notation "initial use discount." In this way, the firm establishes the reference point that represents the pricing strategy of the offering while it signals the incentive to change. Note that this initial use discount may be large, as much as 100% of the reference price in the case of trial samples, such as AN Coatings' paint kit.

Finally, marketing communication tools can influence the size of the incentive to change a firm needs to provide. When a firm can give prospective customers a low-cost, low-risk "experience" with the new offering, it may not need to offer as large an incentive to change. As an example, AN Coatings provides *Color Advice* as a value-added service, where it takes a photograph of a building, digitally scans it into a computer, and then uses proprietary software to show the building owner what the building would look like painted in various ways.

SUMMARY

New offering realization is the process of developing new core products or services, augmenting them to construct market offerings, and bringing them to market. Realization encompasses all the activities a firm does to transform an idea into a market offering that the firm commercializes. New offering realization has the potential to create value for the firm and its customers. It can strengthen a firm's market position, improve its resource utilization, and contribute to organizational enhancement and renewal. A firm generates a realization strategy as a means of accomplishing its realization objectives. As part of its realization strategy, a firm defines its goals and objectives for overall development efforts and for individual projects, and resolves conflicts that occur in pursuing them. It constructs an aggregate project plan that maps the mix of derivative, breakthrough, and platform projects it is doing; enables it to make resource capacity decisions; and outlines how it will gain critical skills and abilities. As a final part of realization strategy, we considered what roles and purposes outside development relationships and networks can serve in the firm's realization efforts.

Realization process models delineate the phases and decision points through which development projects progress. The realization process models of Smallfry, Akzo Nobel Coatings, Kleinwort Benson Investment Management, ABB Asea Brown Boveri Large-System Projects, and ABN-AMRO Bank Global Transacion Services convey the wonderful diversity of business markets, yet some common characteristics emerge. We presented a cross-functional, general realization process model that has five phases—concept development, product planning, detailed design and development, commercial preparation, and market introduction—and provides the key milestones and decisions for each.

Firms in business markets should have the intent of being market oriented and customer focused, yet many firms encounter difficulty understanding what this means for them and how to accomplish it in practice. Some ways for Research to be market-oriented are to create focused research centers that support the firm's long-term business strategy, and to connect itself with the market through regular, scheduled interactions with design engineering, manufacturing engineering, field engineering, advanced marketing groups, and research units of strategic customers. A firm can be market oriented in its development of new offerings by using positioning statements as a market-focusing mechanism; researching customer requirements and preferences, and translating them into design specifications; guiding realization efforts with customer value assessment; and tailoring market introductions of new offerings.

ENDNOTES

1. Robert G. Cooper, *Winning at New Products: Accelerating the Process from Idea to Launch*, 2nd ed. (Reading MA: Addison-Wesley Publishing Company, 1993).
2. George Stalk, Philip Evans, and Lawrence E. Schulman, "Competing on Capabilities: The New Rules of Corporate Strategy," *Harvard Business Review*

(March–April 1992): 57–68. Because of the growing significance of augmenting services, programs, and systems to marketplace success, we prefer the term *new offering realization* to the traditional term *new product development*, where often augmentation of new products has been treated almost as an afterthought and considered just prior to their market introduction. In addition, some managers still narrowly view new product development as the activity of the research and development (R&D) department. New offering realization, in contrast, both emphasizes the critical nature of the design and delivery of the augmenting elements, the cross-functional nature of transforming ideas to new market offerings, and forces the manager to move beyond the conventional process view of considering the development of new offerings as a linear process involving stages from idea generation to market launch (Cooper, *Winning at New Products*) to adopting a view that products must be continuously developed so they continue to evolve and stay relevant to the marketplace (Becky Philipps and Larry Stauffer, "Managing Product Development Projects When Manufacturing is Overseas," *Engineering Management Journal* (December 2006): 23–27). When we do use the term *development* in this chapter, it carries this broader meaning.

3. Steven C. Wheelwright and Kim B. Clark, *Revolutionizing Product Development: Quantum Leaps in Speed, Efficiency, and Quality* (New York: The Free Press, 1992).
4. Joe Tidd, John Bessant, and Keith Pavitt, *Managing Innovation: Integrating Technological, Market and Organizational Change* (John Wiley and Sons, 2005).
5. Christopher Power et al., "Flops," *Business Week*, 16 August 1993, 76–82; Herb Brody, "It Seemed Like a Good Idea at the Time," *High Technology Business* (October 1988): 38–41.
6. Robert G. Cooper and Elko J. Kleinschmidt, "Winning Business in Product Development: The Critical Success Factors," *Research Technology Management*, 50 (May–June 2007): 52–67.
7. Wheelwright and Clark, *Revolutionizing Product Development*, 29–31; Gary S. Lynn and Richard R. Reilly, *Blockbusters: The Five Keys to Developing Great New Products* (New York: HarperCollins Publishers, Inc., 2002). In contrast, a recent meta-analysis of 24 predictors of new product performance found that product advantage, market potential, meeting customer needs, predevelopment task proficiencies, and dedicated resources have the strongest effects on new product success. See David H. Henard and David M. Szymanski, "Why Some New Products Are More Successful Than Others," *Journal of Marketing Research* (August 2001): 362–275.
8. Wheelwright and Clark, *Revolutionizing Product Development*, 34.
9. H. Kent Bowen, Kim B. Clark, Charles A. Holloway, and Steven C. Wheelwright, "Development Projects: The Engine of Renewal," *Harvard Business Review* (September–October 1994): 100–120.
10. Abbie Griffin and Albert L. Page, "The PDMA Success Measurement Project: Recommended Measures for Product Development Success and Failure," *Journal of Product Innovation Management* (November 1996): 482.
11. Bowen et al., "Development Projects," 119.
12. K. Saban, J. Lamosa, C. Lackman, and G. Peace, "Organizational Learning: A Critical Component to New Product Development," *Journal of Product and Brand Management* (2000), 9(2), 99–119.
13. M. Schindler and M. J. Eppler, "Harvesting Project Knowledge: A Review of Project Learning Methods and Success Factors, *International Journal of Project Management*, 21 (2003): 219–228; Ursula Koners and Keith Goffin, "Learning from New Product Development Projects: An Exploratory Study," *Creativity and Innovation Management*, 14 (2005): 334–344.
14. Herman J. Vantrappen and Philip D. Metz, "Measuring the Performance of the Innovation Process," *Prism* (Fourth Quarter 1994): 25–26.
15. Andrew Davies and Michael Hobday, *The Business of Projects: Managing Innovation in*

Complex Products and Systems (Cambridge, UK: Cambridge University Press, 2005).

16. Vantrappen and Metz, "Measuring the Performance."
17. Bruce Vernyi, "2005 IndustryWeek Value-Chain Survey," *IndustryWeek*, 1 September 2005.
18. Christoph-Friedrich von Braun, "The Acceleration Trap in the Real World," *Sloan Management Review* (Summer 1991): 43–52. See also George Stalk, Jr., and Alan M. Webber, "Japan's Dark Side of Time," *Harvard Business Review* (July–August 1993): 93–102.
19. Paul S. Adler, Avi Mandelbaum, Viên Nguyen, and Elizabeth Schwerer, "Getting the Most out of Your Product Development Process," *Harvard Business Review* (March–April 1996): 134–152.
20. "Devices and Desires," *The Economist*, 2 September 2002, 66; and Crit Thomas, "New Products Bring Energy to DuPont Sales," *Dayton Business Journal*, 26 January 2007.
21. Preston G. Smith and Donald G. Reinertsen, *Developing Products in Half the Time* (New York: Van Nostrand Reinhold, 1995).
22. Smith and Reinertsen, *Developing Products,* 18.
23. Robert J. Dolan, *Managing the New Product Development Process* (Reading, MA: Addison-Wesley Publishing, 1993).
24. Griffin and Page, "The PDMA Success," Figure 2, 489.
25. Vantrappen and Metz, "Measuring the Performance," 26.
26. Wheelwright and Clark, *Revolutionizing Product Development*. The quote is drawn from p. 48.
27. EWAC Alloys Ltd. (EWAC) is an associate company of South and South East Asia's largest engineering and construction company, Larsen and Toubro Ltd., based in Mumbai.
28. Steven C. Wheelwright and Kim B. Clark, "Creating Project Plans to Focus Product Development," *Harvard Business Review* (March–April 1992): 73.
29. We focused primarily on the augmenting services, programs, and systems part of flexible market offerings in Chapter 5.
30. The power generation business of ABB was merged with the power generation business of ALSTOM in June 1999 to create a new Netherlands-based joint venture, ABB Alstom Power, owned 50:50 by ABB and ALSTOM.
31. Wheelwright and Clark, *Revolutionizing Product Development*, 49.
32. Wheelwright and Clark, "Creating Project Plans," 75.
33. Wheelwright and Clark, *Revolutionizing Product Development*, 50.
34. Wheelwright and Clark, "Creating Project Plans," 81.
35. T. Michael Nevens, Gregory L. Summe, and Bro Uttal, "Commercializing Technology: What the Best Companies Do," *Harvard Business Review* (May–June 1990): 162.
36. Jeffrey K. Liker et al., "Involving Suppliers in Product Development in the United States and Japan: Evidence for Set-Based Concurrent Engineering," *IEEE Transactions on Engineering Management* (May 1996): 165–178.
37. Allen Ward et al., "The Second Toyota Paradox: How Delaying Decisions Can Make Better Cars Faster," *Sloan Management Review* (Spring 1995): 43–61.
38. Jeffrey H. Dyer, "How Chrysler Created an American Keiretsu," *Harvard Business Review* (July–August 1996): 42–56.
39. Liker et al., "Involving Suppliers."
40. Ward et al., "The Second Toyota Paradox," 44.
41. Christian Terwiesch, Christoph H. Loch, and Arnoud De Meyer, "Exchanging Preliminary Information in Concurrent Engineering: Alternative Coordination Strategies," *Organization Science* (July–August 2002): 402–419.
42. Ward et al., "The Second Toyota Paradox," 52.
43. Ward et al., "The Second Toyota Paradox." The quote is taken from p. 55.
44. Marjorie Sorge, "Expedition Takes a Walk on the Wild Side: Ford Cuts Development Costs, Tries New Manufacturing Ideas with Its New SUV," *Automotive Industries* (August 1996): 49.

45. Peter C. Grindley and David J. Teece, "Managing Intellectual Capital: Licensing and Cross-Licensing in Semiconductors and Electronics," *California Management Review* (Winter 1997): 8–41.
46. "Missile to Queen's Rook Four," *The Economist*, 17 May 1997, 74.
47. "Electrifying," *The Economist*, 20 December 1997, 98–99; "New Power," *The Economist*, 30 August 1997, 17; and Peter Coy, with Neil Gross, Silvia Sansoni, and Kevin Kelly, "What's the Word in the Lab? Collaborate," *Business Week*, 27 June 1994, 78–80. For an interesting perspective on gaining new ideas for innovation from outsiders, see Darrell Rigby and Chris Zook, "Open-Market Innovation," *Harvard Business Review* (October 2002): 80–89.
48. Steinemann, Patrick (1999), "R&D Strategies for New Automotive Technologies: Insights from Fuel Cells," International Motor Vehicle Program (IMVP), Massachusetts Institute of Technology.
49. Port, "Talk About Your Dream Team," 79.
50. "Trapeze Artists," *The Economist*, 14 December 2002, 22–23.
51. Kathleen M. Eisenhardt and Claudia Bird Schoonhoven, "Resource-Based View of Strategic Alliance Formation: Strategic and Social Effects in Entrepreneurial Firms," *Organization Science* (March–April 1996): 136–150.
52. Eisenhardt and Schoonhoven, "Resource-Based View," 146.
53. Gary Hamel, Yves L. Doz, and C.K. Prahalad, "Collaborate with Your Competitors—and Win," *Harvard Business Review* (January–February 1989): 134.
54. Michael L. Tushman and Lori Rosenkopf, "Organizational Determinants of Technological Change: Toward a Sociology of Technological Evolution," in *Research in Organizational Behavior*, vol. 14, B. Staw and L. Cummings, eds. (Greenwich, CT: JAI Press, 1992), 311–347. The quote is taken from p. 322.
55. Yukari Iwatani Kane, "Toshiba Exits HD DVD Business, Ceding Market to Sony's Blu-ray," *Wall Street Journal Online*, 19 February 2008, http://online.wsj.com/article/SB120342115442976687.html; "Toshiba quits HD DVD business," *CNNMoney.com*, 19 February 2008, http://money.cnn.com/2008/02/19/technology/toshiba.ap/
56. Dresdner Bank, the corporate parent of Dresdner Kleinwort Benson, was acquired by Allianz AG in July 2001.
57. Wheelwright and Clark, *Revolutionizing Product Development*.
58. Wheelwright and Clark, *Revolutionizing Product Development*, 174.
59. Cooper, *Winning at New Products*.
60. Robert G. Cooper, "Third Generation New Product Processes," *Journal of Product Innovation Management* (January 1994): 9.
61. Adler et al., "Getting the Most."
62. Marco Iansiti and Alan MacCormack, "Developing Products on Internet Time," *Harvard Business Review* (September–October 1997): 108–117.
63. Behnam Tabrizi and Rick Walleigh, "Defining Next-Generation Products: An Inside Look," *Harvard Business Review* (November–December 1997): 116–124.
64. Peter Coy, "Research Labs Get Real. It's About Time," *Business Week*, 6 November 2000, 51; Barrett, "DuPont Tries to Unclog a Pipeline;" Michael Arndt, "3M: A Lab for Growth," *Business Week*, 21 January 2002, 50–51; Erika Jonietz, "Economic Bust, Patent Boom," *Technology Review* (May 2002): 71–72; and Rachel Emma Silverman, "GE Goes Back to the Future," *The Wall Street Journal*, 7 May 2002, B1, B4.
65. Silverman, "GE Goes Back to the Future."
66. Eric von Hippel, "'Sticky Information' and the Locus of Problem Solving: Implications for Innovation," *Management Science* (April 1994): 429–439.
67. Wade Roush, "Lean Mean R&D Machines," *Technology Review* (December 2001): 71–73.
68. Fumio Kodama, "Technology Fusion and the New R&D," *Harvard Business Review* (July–August 1992): 70–78.
69. Julia Porter Liebeskind et al., "Social Networks, Learning, and Flexibility: Sourcing Scientific Knowledge in New Biotechnology Firms," *Organization Science* (July–August 1996): 428–443. The first

quote is taken from p. 430 and the second from p. 437.
70. Silverman, "GE Goes Back to the Future."
71. Jill Jusko, "Out to Launch," *Industry Week* (February 2008): 47–49.
72. "The Shock of the Not Quite New," *The Economist,* 18 June 1994, 81; Gerard Tellis and Peter N. Golder, "First to Market, First to Fail? Real Causes of Enduring Market Leadership," *Sloan Management Review* (Winter 1996): 65–75 (additionally, Tellis and Golder found that a fifth factor, asset leverage, enables late entrants to gain market leadership through exploiting advantages that they possess, such as related technologies or established distribution channels); and William T. Robinson and Sungwook Min, "Is the First to Market the First to Fail? Empirical Evidence for Industrial Goods Businesses," *Journal of Marketing Research* (February 2002): 120–128.
73. Coco Masters/Everett, "How Boeing Got Going," *Time,* 17 September 2007, 49–52.
74. Eric von Hippel, *The Sources of Innovation* (New York: Oxford University Press, 1988).
75. Nikolaus Franke and Sonali Shah, "How Communities Support Innovative Activities: An Exploration of Assistance and Sharing among End-Users," *Research Policy,* 32 (2003): 157–178; Eric von Hippel, "Horizontal Innovation Networks—By and For Users," *Industrial and Corporate Change,* 16 (2007): 293–315.
76. Debbie Harrison and Alexandra Waluszewski, "The Development of a User Network as a Way to Re-launch an Unwanted Product," *Research Policy,* 37 (2008): 115–130.
77. James C. Anderson and James A. Narus, "Partnering as a Focused Market Strategy," *California Management Review* (Spring 1991): 95–113.
78. Anthony W. Ulwick, "Turn Customer Input into Innovation," *Harvard Business Review* (January 2002): 91–97. The first quote is taken from p. 95 and the second from p. 97.
79. John R. Hauser and Don Clausing, "The House of Quality," *Harvard Business Review* (May–June 1988): 63–73; and Abbie Griffin and John R. Hauser, "Patterns of Communication Among Marketing, Engineering and Manufacturing—A Comparison Between Two New Product Teams," *Management Science* (March 1992): 360–373.
80. Stanley W. Kandebo, "V-22 Modifications Focus on Cost, Producibility," *Aviation Week and Space Technology,* 22 May 1995, 35.
81. Stefan Thomke, "Enlightened Experimentation: The New Imperative for Innovation," *Harvard Business Review* (February 2001): 68.
82. Robert J. Dolan and John M. Matthews, "Maximizing the Utility of Customer Product Testing: Beta Test Design and Management," *Journal of Product Innovation Management* (September 1993): 318–330.
83. von Hippel, "Sticky Information."
84. von Hippel, "Sticky Information"; and Stefan Thomke and Eric von Hippel, "Customers as Innovators," *Harvard Business Review* (April 2002): 5–11.
85. Gerald E. Smith and Thomas T. Nagle, "Frames of Reference and Buyers' Perception of Price and Value," *California Management Review* (Fall 1995): 98–116.
86. Smith and Nagle, "Frames of Reference."

Chapter 7

Business Channel Management

Overview

As core products and services become more commodity-like, business market managers often turn to their marketing channels as a source of competitive differentiation. They realize that channels can augment their market offerings through the creation of a highly valued *total customer experience*. To deliver an intended total customer experience to targeted segments, business marketers draw upon emerging information, logistics, and supply management technologies and increasingly configure novel value-adding networks—multiple channels, modular channels, hybrid channels, and integrated multi-channels. These channel networks combine elements of the supplier firm's direct sales forces, traditional reseller firms, pioneering online formats, and third-party service providers. Such thinking has enabled firms to meet customer requirements and preferences in superior ways, but it has also created challenges, prompting managers to reformulate the process of business channel management.[1]

Coughlin, Anderson, Stern, and El-Ansary formally define **marketing channel** as "a set of interdependent organizations involved in the process of making a product or service available for use or consumption."[2] Building upon this definition and incorporating recent trends, we describe **business channel management** as the process of designing a set of marketing and distribution arrangements that create superior customer value for targeted market segments and customers, and executing those arrangements directly through supplier firm sales forces and logistics systems or indirectly through resellers and third-party service providers. We diagram this process in Figure 7.1 and examine each step in detail in this chapter.[3]

Figure 7.1 Business Channel Management

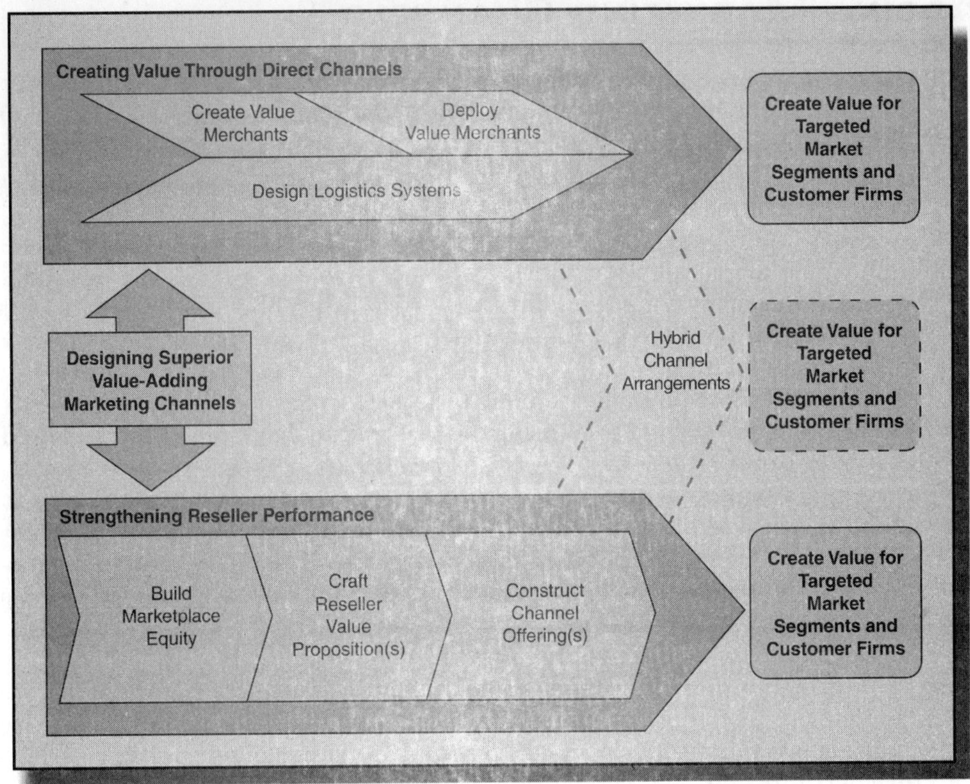

To begin, we present a framework for designing superior value-adding marketing channels. Pivoting on a thorough customer value assessment and the creation of tailored total customer experiences, the framework guides business market managers through the tasks of assembling a channel network and forging capabilities-sharing arrangements that enable the supplier firm to consistently and profitably meet customer requirements and preferences. In contrast to organizations that serve the consumer marketplace, firms in business markets are much more likely to do business directly with customers in some or all targeted market segments. Thus, in the second section, we discuss how firms add value through direct channels focusing on sales force and logistics systems issues.

In the final section, we turn our attention to situations where suppliers rely on a network of resellers and third-party service providers to add complementary value to their market offerings. When suppliers do so, they must devise programs and systems that encourage partners to contribute their capabilities, to aggressively market resulting offerings, and to deliver intended total customer experiences to customers. We contend that suppliers can and do elicit outstanding performance through a technique called channel positioning.

DESIGNING SUPERIOR VALUE-ADDING MARKETING CHANNELS

Marketing channels add value to a market offering through the creation of what consultants call the total customer experience. The **total customer experience (TCE)** entails all aspects of a customer firm's encounter with a supplier firm. Ideally, the TCE should be a positive, seamless, and memorable interaction that matches the customer firm's purchasing requirements and preferences.[4]

Based upon extensive research, consultant Brent Grover has identified two requirement categories—*immediacy of fulfillment* and *extent of augmenting value-added services*. While many supplier and reseller firms rush to offer a wide variety of value-added services with the intent of achieving competitive advantage, Grover urges them to focus on fulfillment, because his research indicates that firms that do so also tend to be the more profitable. Among the five essential customer requirements that encompass immediacy of fulfillment are the breadth and depth of products and services in a supplier's market offering, the availability of those products and services at supplier warehouses and/or showrooms, timing and reliability of delivery, installation, and payment terms and conditions. So-called value-added services cover a wide range of pre-sale, point-of-sale, and post-sale services that are commonly offered as "for-fee options." As these customer requirements tend to be more tangible than preferences, managers assess their worth using the tools of customer value management that we discuss in Chapter 2.[5]

Although supplier managers would prefer to differentiate their firms by meeting specific customer requirements, reseller managers often have no choice but to look to customer preferences for sources of competitive advantage because other resellers in their territories may be selling nearly identical products and services at similar prices. Consultants Friedman and Furey describe customer purchasing preferences in terms of how customer managers like to *learn*, *shop*, *buy*, and *get help*. As these preferences tend to be more difficult to quantify in monetary terms than requirements, managers assess their worth using a variety of perceptual research techniques such as conjoint analysis and focus groups which we describe in Chapter 2 as well as order cycle management techniques which we describe in Chapter 3.[6]

Importantly, it is possible for supplier or reseller firms to use elements of their intended TCE as part of their overall competitive positioning. Consultants have identified four TCE-based positions. **The efficient, low-cost transactional experience** provides inexpensive, convenient, self-service exchange relationships with minimal value-added service, often through Internet Web sites or other direct marketing media. For example, Grainger.com offers an electronic catalog of more than 890,000 items from which industrial customers can order online conveniently from their own offices. **The high-touch, consultative experience** furnishes extensive consultation and advice, customization of offerings, frequent face-to-face encounters with supplier personnel, and a complete range of value-added services. Composites One, a leading distributor of fiberglass and plastics materials, relies on teams of highly trained sales persons, engineers, and technical support persons, to design, implement, and service complex fiberglass solutions for its strategic accounts.

The flexible, multi-access-point experience allows the customer the ability to choose to purchase a supplier's offering intact or piecemeal from several integrated or stand-alone channels on a transaction-by-transaction basis. For example, in some of its markets, Oracle relies upon the Internet, direct mail, and telemarketing to identify sales leads. These leads are transferred to business partners who are responsible for order generation, fulfillment, and new customer relationship development. Oracle and its business partners share responsibilities for long-term customer care and support. **The one-stop shopping experience** enables customers to purchase a wide-variety of complementary products and services from a single source. In Chapter 9, we will discuss Yahoo! India, which positions its operations exclusively around this TCE. Basically, Yahoo! India sets up consortia of complementary specialty distributors that provide integrated supply management for large customer firms.[7]

The first challenge of marketing channel design is strategic in nature. Business market managers must conceptualize a superior and distinctive TCE that targeted segments require and prefer. Naturally, the foundation for such a conceptualization will be a thorough customer value assessment. The second and equally important challenge is operational in nature and demands that business market managers decide whether to insource the provision to customers of some or all TCE elements or to outsource them to resellers or third-party service providers. As with other sourcing decisions, managers must seek to generate the greatest customer value profitably by drawing upon the firm's core capabilities and competencies while leveraging the complementary resources of channel partner firms. A key difference between traditional sourcing and channel sourcing is that a contracted channel partner is likely to maintain the "face" before the customer. As such, issues concerning "ownership" of customers arise that are not of concern in more familiar outsourcing situations.

We now examine the six steps of designing superior value-adding marketing channels.

1. Specify marketing channels goals and objectives.
2. Assess the customer value of potential TCE elements.
3. Envision a value proposition for each targeted market segment.
4. Reformulate the intended TCE for each targeted market segment.
5. Configure the channel network.
6. Finalize marketing and distribution arrangements.

Specify Marketing Channels Goals and Objectives

As part of a broader strategic planning process, business market managers must identify the goals they hope to achieve through their marketing channels. Although these goals will vary from company to company, three predominate—maximize market access, optimize value-added, and minimize cost-to-serve. In turn, these goals provide managers with platforms for specifying short-term objectives and performance metrics.[8]

Market access refers to the extent to which business channels enable a supplier firm to reach, develop, and serve targeted segments and customer firms. Ideally, supplier firms seek channels that provide coverage and exposure to as many profitable customers as possible. To set short-term and tactical market access objectives as well as assess performance to date, business market managers draw upon four primary metrics—trade area served or the geographic area the channel services, market penetration or the percent of all potential segments and customers purchasing the supplier's offering, market share or the percent of current industry sales for which the supplier's offering accounts, and share of customer business or the percent of a specific customer's "total spend" that the supplier's offering has gained.[9]

Value-added in the context of business channels entails the augmenting products and services channel partners contribute to the supplier firm's market offering. Naturally, a supplier firm wants to provide a total customer experience to each market segment that creates the greatest possible value. As mentioned previously, channel value-added comes from meeting customer requirements in terms of immediacy of fulfillment and pre-sale, point-of-sale, and post-sale services as well as from satisfying customer preferences regarding learning, shopping, buying, and getting help. Business market managers specify short-term channel value-added objectives and assess performance based upon service output levels. For example, reliable and accurate delivery might be defined in terms of the percent of on-time deliveries and the percent of delivered items versus items ordered. Alternatively, preventative maintenance performance might be measured in terms of percent of machine up-time versus total available operating hours.

Cost-to-serve captures the total expenditures required to deliver the intended total customer experience to targeted segments and customers. Perhaps the principal reason that supplier firms turn to indirect channels is the desire to dramatically reduce distribution costs. Business market managers typically state cost-to-serve objectives and performance metrics in terms of percent of sales; however, activity-based costing systems allow progressive suppliers to state them in monetary amounts. Among the most common are fulfillment costs as a percent of sales, marketing communications costs as a percent of sales, and technical service costs as a percent of sales.

Although business market managers may seek the best possible outcome for the three goals, they should exercise caution, because trade-offs and adjustments may be required. These channel goals often work at odds with one another, and each may be more important during different product life cycle phases. For example, focusing on maximizing market access may lead a supplier firm to franchise far too many resellers in hopes of reaching every possible customer. As a result, the firm may select some resellers that are incapable of delivering the desired value-added services. Alternatively, partnering exclusively with specialty, high-value-added resellers may result in excessive costs-to-serve and uncompetitive prices. As for the impact of the product life cycle, during introduction and growth phases, a supplier firm may need to place primary emphasis on achieving market access. Early in the maturity phase, the supplier firm may have to shift emphasis to optimizing value-added in order to differentiate its offering from the competition. Later on in the maturity phase, minimizing cost-to-serve may become critical as competition focuses primarily around low price. As we will discuss in Chapter 9, conflicting goals and objectives are often the principal challenge to successful business channel management.

Assess the Customer Value of Potential TCE Elements

Consistent with our overall approach to business market management, managers should begin the channel design process with a thorough customer value assessment.

Assuming that the supplier firm has already assessed the value of its core market offering, business market managers should turn their attention to those value elements that may contribute to the total customer experience. They use two central questions to guide their inquiries. (1) What purchasing requirements and preferences do targeted segments have in regard to the TCE? (2) How much is the delivery of a TCE that meets those requirements and preferences worth to customers? In Chapter 2, we explain a variety of value assessment techniques that managers can use to answer these two questions.

When conducting the customer value assessment of TCE requirements, business market managers should focus on service outputs and their monetary worth.[10] Examples of fulfillment service output levels are 95% on-time delivery, 24-hour availability of 50,000 stock-keeping units (SKUs), and $250 minimum order size. As to value-added services, managers should pay particular attention to five—integrated supply, local customization, emergency delivery, technical support, and product standardization—and their related service output levels. These services will strongly indicate the type of channel network the supplier firm should adopt. For example, if integrated supply is an essential value driver, the supplier firm may require the assistance of a reseller to bundle the supplier's offering along with complementary products and services possibly from other vendors into a total solution. On the other hand, if local customization is the key, the supplier firm may have to hire third-party service providers such as assemblers or value-added resellers to make final modifications in the product.

Using perceptual techniques, managers then turn their attention to assessing customer preferences. The evaluation of customer preferences for learning, shopping, buying, and getting help are critical as they shape the "soft" side of the total customer experience. They indicate to the business market manager such things as whether the customer wants to deal face-to-face with a sales representative or interface with an impersonal Web site, whether the customer prefers to buy directly from the supplier firm all of the time or is willing to purchase from different channels as a function of the situation, whether the customer would like a "hands-on" demonstration of a new product or will settle for looking at detailed photographs, and whether the customer would like premium "high-touch" or cheap "no-frills" technical service.

The key findings of these customer value assessments will be a prioritized list of TCE elements and an indication of the prices that segments and customers are willing to pay to receive them. By matching the customer value of TCE elements to estimates of the supplier costs that will be incurred to provide them, business market managers will be able to gauge the profit potential of serving those segments and customers.

Envision a Value Proposition for Each Targeted Market Segment

Business market managers adopt the customer firm's perspective asking, "What is most worthwhile for our firm to keep in mind about your offering?" Using inputs from the customer value assessment, managers answer this question by envisioning a distinct value proposition for each targeted market segment. To do so, they meld essential value drivers from the supplier's core market offering with newly uncovered and critical TCE elements. In Chapter 4, we addressed the task of writing value propositions in business markets. Importantly, the customer value proposition serves as a beacon for all the supplier firm's channel network design efforts.

Reformulate the Intended TCE for Each Targeted Market Segment

For each targeted market segment, business market managers now ask, "How can the TCE be reformulated to better support the intended value proposition?" In Chapter 5, we discuss an approach for building flexible market offerings, which provides the guidance and tools for answering this question. Simply stated, managers add, delete, or modify products and value-added services as well as fulfillment and communications processes to more closely meet the critical TCE requirements and preferences of the targeted segment.

If the supplier firm has been marketing an offering for some time, business market managers should compare the current TCE to the reformulated version. Minor differences may indicate that only incremental channel improvements are necessary. Such improvements might entail bolstering technical service capabilities through reseller training programs, adding third-party service providers to enhance emergency delivery capabilities, or partnering with another supplier to secure complementary product lines for a total solution. On the other hand, major differences may point to the need for radical channel redesign. In this case, business market managers may have to develop an entirely new channel network to deliver the intended TCE. Whether the reformulation is incremental or radical, the output of this step will be a description of the intended TCE including specification of fulfillment and value-added service output levels as well as an indication of how customers will learn, shop, buy, and get help.

Configure the Channel Network

Managers next pose the question, "What type of channel network will enable the supplier firm to achieve its market access, value-added, and cost-to-serve goals while delivering the intended TCE to targeted segments?" To answer this question, managers simultaneously consult and consider the classic channel strategies related to exposure and coverage, postponement and speculation, and functional acquisition and functional spin-off. Then, they meld their strategic preferences into a channel network design that can profitably deliver the intended TCE to targeted segments.

Maximize Market Access by Balancing Exposure and Coverage

Business market managers realize that to gain desired market access, channels must provide sufficient exposure and coverage. **Exposure** is the degree to which targeted customer firms are actually reached and served by the appropriate kind and number of channels. It further demands that managers match customer TCE requirements and preferences with the capabilities of alternate channels. For example, if the supplier firm seeks rapid market penetration for a new-to-the-world product and targeted customers desire a high-touch consultative experience, then the supplier firm may choose to market through a network of manufacturer's representatives. Alternatively, if the supplier firm wants to sustain its market share for a commodity offering and targeted customers prefer an efficient, low-cost transactional experience, then the supplier firm may service demand through its own Internet Web site.

A firm's approach to segmentation also indicates the appropriate exposure strategy. If a supplier firm is pursuing undifferentiated marketing, then managers are likely to rely on a **single-channel strategy** whereby all products are marketed either directly or through one type of reseller. Alternatively, if the supplier firm has adopted target marketing, business market managers may turn to a **multiple-channel strategy** and use a separate channel to reach each targeted segment. For example, an electrical product supplier may have to use two different channels to reach the large-scale electrical contractor and "gypsy" electrical contractor segments. Large-scale contractors buy large quantities and assortments of electrical products and services and typically receive greater value from electrical distributors such as Graybar. In contrast, gypsy contractors work on small repair projects, often out of the back of a pickup truck. For this reason, they purchase small quantities and limited assortments of products, and they commonly get better service when they shop at a building supplies store, such as Home Depot.[11]

Coverage refers to the number of resellers authorized or direct sales persons assigned per geographic trade area. By adjusting the level of coverage, the supplier makes it more convenient for the customer to purchase an offering. In the case of indirect channels, coverage entails a choice of a **distribution intensity strategy**: **exclusive**, where a supplier authorizes one reseller per trade area; **selective**, where it authorizes a limited number of resellers per trade area; or **intensive**, where it essentially authorizes all resellers that want to carry its line. The three distribution intensity strategies can be further differentiated in terms of the supplier's share of the reseller's business: (1) the reseller sells only the supplier's offerings, as with Swagelok distributors; (2) the reseller sells one of the supplier's lines along with the lines of other firms, as with GE® Lamps at W.W. Grainger; or (3) the reseller sells only one of the supplier's products plus an assortment of other firms' products, such as a Hytrol conveyor belt at a full-service materials handling equipment distributor. As we will discuss in Chapter 9, the more exclusive the relationship and the greater the supplier's share of the reseller's business, the more control over the reseller's efforts the supplier will have.[12]

Business market managers should ground their exposure and coverage strategy decisions in reliable, accurate, and timely estimates of demand for each trade area. They must seek to gain a deep understanding of customer requirements, the target-market penetration capabilities of alternate channels, and the segments on which resellers are focusing. As part of this learning process, they conduct market research to estimate the market potential of their firm's offering in each segment and to determine with which resellers customers prefer to do business.

Armed with an appraisal of demand and segment preferences, managers then determine the maximum number of customers to which a reseller or alternate channel can provide the desired levels of service outputs. Then, they estimate the number of resellers to authorize by dividing projected demand by reseller service capacity for each targeted trade area. In practice, the decision turns out to be more of an art than a science because of limited supplier knowledge and wide variation in number of customers that each available reseller or alternate channel can adequately service. Thus, firms often start with a minimum per trade area and add new resellers or alternate channels as they learn about unfulfilled demand.

One firm that has mastered exposure and coverage is the Parker Hannifin Corporation (PHC). Realizing that customers in the lumber, fishing, and aircraft industries in the Pacific Northwest purchase its line of pneumatics, PHC has designed a unique channel network. Rather than authorizing one or two industrial distributors, as it does in most of the United States and Canada, Parker Hannifin utilizes three separate channels there—forestry equipment distributors, marine distributors, and industrial distributors. PHC directs each channel at a separate target segment. In the Seattle area, two of these three types of distributors are located across the street from one another. Little conflict arises among the three distributors because they don't serve the same segments. As a result, PHC maximizes penetration in each of the three market segments.

Consultants Freidman and Furey recommend that business market managers summarize their exposure and coverage strategy in chart form. Figure 7.2 contains a channel exposure and coverage model for an electronic controls supplier firm. The rows list the firm's three target market segments—electronic components manufacturers, scientific testing equipment manufacturers, and process control manufacturers. The columns categorize the firm's offerings—standard items, specialty items, and customized solutions. The shaded areas contain the exposure and coverage strategies: (1) no coverage for electronic components manufacturers for standard items, (2) direct marketing through a Web site and inside sales reps of standard items to process control manufacturers, (3) indirect sales of specialty items to electronic component manufacturers through electronic distributors, to scientific equipment

Figure 7.2 Channel Exposure and Coverage Model for an Electronic Controls Supplier Firm

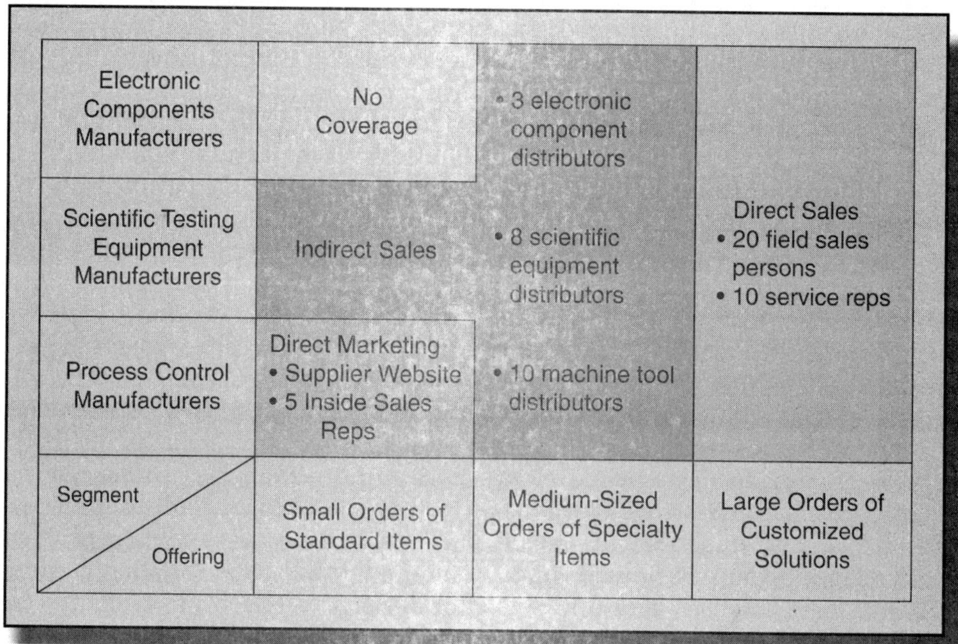

Source: Adapted from Friedman and Furey 1999.

manufacturers through scientific equipment distributors, and to process control manufacturers through machine tool distributors, and (4) direct sales of customized solutions to all three target segments through a field sales force and service reps.[13]

Optimize Value-Added Through Postponement or Speculation

Bucklin's classic postponement and speculation strategies furnish a sound foundation for designing direct and indirect channels that optimize the value-added delivered to customer firms. The strategies pivot on the predictability of demand, quantity of production, and the amount of inventories held in reserve as well as the required proximity of customization activities and inventory to customer locations.

Through a **postponement strategy** a supplier firm undertakes product design, customization, and value-added service augmentation as geographically close to the customer firm as is possible. Typically, this entails *direct sales* of highly tailored, design-to-order offerings via a technically competent and consultative sales team, just-in-time inventory deliveries, and a high level of end-to-end customer service provided in person at the customer firm's location. At the other extreme is a **speculation strategy** where the supplier firm manufactures standard products in large quantities well in advance of demand at a plant site that is often distant from customers' locations. Speculation strategies often entail *indirect sales* and intensive distribution. Reseller firms stock inventories, take orders, make deliveries, and provide minimal value-added service.[14]

When customers gain significant value from last-minute and minor physical adjustments to offerings yet demand low price, managers draw upon manufacturing postponement and speculation. The traditional remedy, **manufacturing postponement**, relies upon *indirect sales* through local assembly, fabrication, compounding, or extrusion firms that customize the supplier's products to the unique requirements of regional customer firms. More recently, the Internet and logistics firm have spawned a popular alternative, **manufacturing speculation**, which features *direct marketing*. Here, the supplier uses a build-to-order model, taking orders from customers directly over the telephone or Internet, mass customizing products from platforms and modules, and shipping final products directly to customers via third-party logistics firms.[15]

For situations where emergency resupply of parts and/or services for mission-critical applications is critical to customers, supplier firms turn to logistics postponement and speculation. As local inventory storage and 24-hour delivery have long been seen as a raison d'être of distribution, **logistics postponement** via *indirect sales* has long been the preferred solution. In this case, a reseller would either reserve stocks of an item in its local warehouse for a customer firm and provide immediate delivery in an emergency or leave the items on consignment within the customer's plant site. More recently, suppliers have turned to **logistics speculation** for their largest and most profitable customers. This approach involves *direct sales* and vendor-managed inventory programs whereby the supplier firm takes responsibility for managing all customer inventories and ensuring emergency delivery of bottleneck items.[16]

Minimize Cost-to-Serve via Functional Acquisition and Functional Spin-Off

When operations management experts seek to reduce the cost-to-serve customers, they often turn to the tools of business process engineering and attempt to create a lean enterprise. A **lean enterprise** is a group of individuals, functions, and legally separate but operationally synchronized companies. In building a lean enterprise, managers focus on improving business processes by allocating functions to the most capable partner firms, bolstering their partners' ability to perform those tasks, coordinating and integrating the efforts of all firms in the lean enterprise, and eliminating unnecessary redundancies in efforts.[17]

Progressive business market managers apply the Womack and Jones lean enterprise approach to the design of their channel networks. To do so, they conceptualize channel networks both horizontally within each channel level and vertically across all channel levels. When they view channels horizontally, business market managers see **functions**, or the tasks that a specific channel partner firm performs. These functions include buying, selling, breaking bulk, assembling the offering, providing credit, transportation, warehousing, and post-sale servicing. When they consider a channel vertically, they see a set of **business processes**, such as facilitating exchange, providing market access, and augmenting the marketing offering. Significantly, channel members must coordinate functions across firms to complete a business process.[18]

Experts urge firms to focus on functions whenever incremental channel improvements are needed. When they do, business market managers often turn to Mallen's classic marketing channels strategies of **functional acquisition** and **functional spin-off** to lower system costs. Through a process referred to as "shifting and sharing," the supplier firm either acquires functions from or spins off functions to various resellers within the channel network. For example, many chemical companies have spun off the drumming function to chemical distributors who perform the task more efficiently. Chemical distributors not only incur lower costs and investments associated with drumming but also they reap greater profits from the value-added service.[19]

Figure 7.3 demonstrates functional acquisition and functional spin-off through a pair of functional allocation charts where key functions are listed as rows and channel members as columns. The upper chart shows the original channel design where a supplier produces the product, advertises it, and conducts field sales calls. Electrical wholesalers generate leads, furnish fulfillment services, provide customer credit, and undertake repair work. To reduce costs and make the channel more effective, the supplier adds manufacturer representatives and reallocates functions as illustrated in the lower chart. Although the supplier continues to produce and advertise the product, it has spun off field sales calls to manufacturer representatives and acquired customer credit from electrical wholesalers. At the same time, manufacturer's representatives have acquired the lead generation function from electrical wholesalers. Electrical wholesalers retain the fulfillment and repair work functions.

As management consultants point out, the vertical or business process perspective is most appropriate when radical channel redesign is necessary. Through business process reengineering, the supplier firm is often able to eliminate resource and effort redundancies within the entire channel network, thus lowering total system costs, while strategically deploying channel members' capabilities to maximize the total value delivered. Such reengineering typically brings new types of channel partners and distribution arrangements.

In years past, managers viewed competition in channels as horizontal in nature with suppliers competing against suppliers, resellers against resellers, and customers against customers. The Japanese revolutionized our view of competition within marketing channels with their strategic alliances known as *keiretsus.*

Figure 7.3 Functional Allocation Charts for Electrical Products Supplier

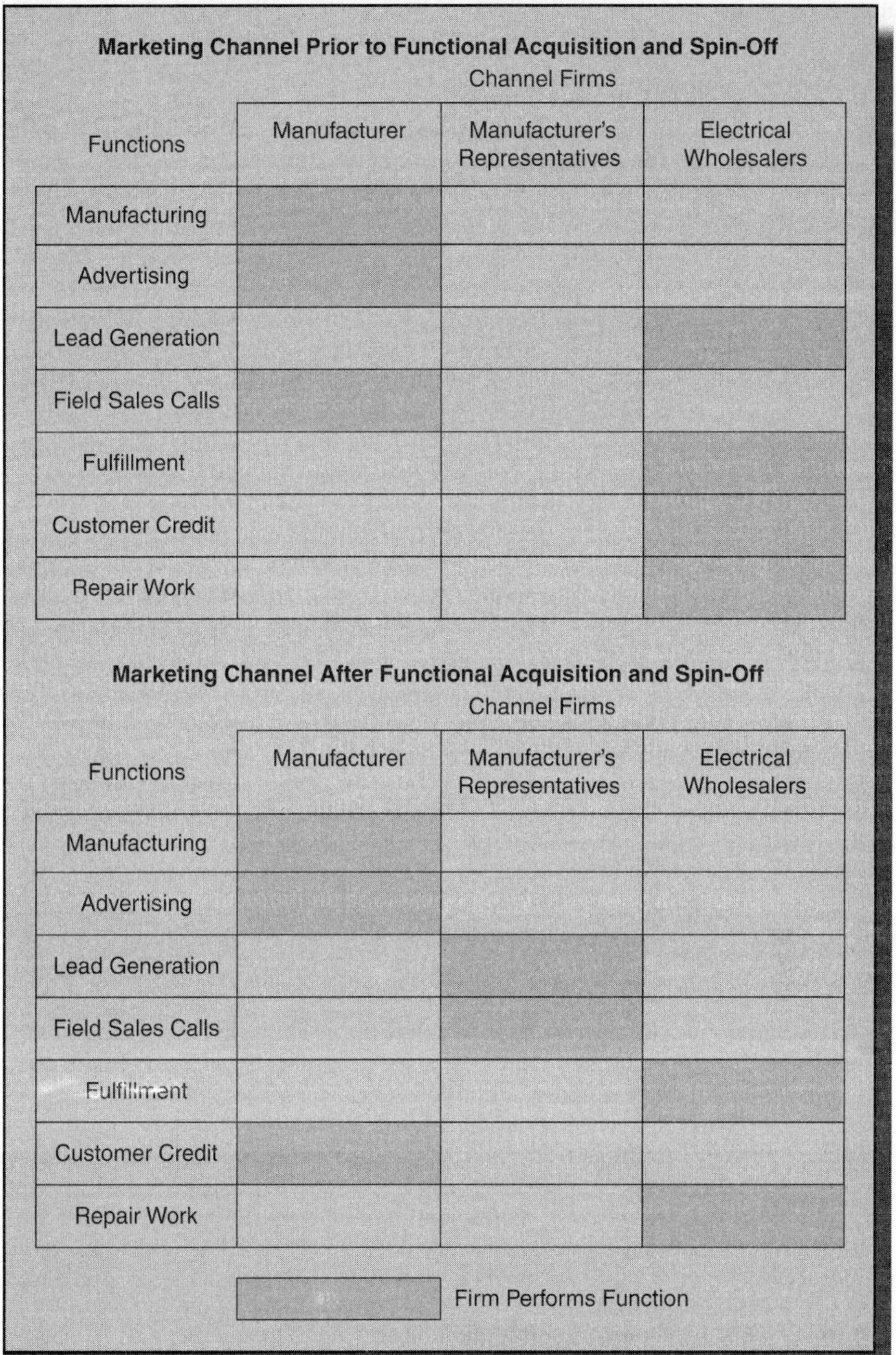

Marketing Channel Prior to Functional Acquisition and Spin-Off

Channel Firms

Functions	Manufacturer	Manufacturer's Representatives	Electrical Wholesalers
Manufacturing			
Advertising			
Lead Generation			
Field Sales Calls			
Fulfillment			
Customer Credit			
Repair Work			

Marketing Channel After Functional Acquisition and Spin-Off

Channel Firms

Functions	Manufacturer	Manufacturer's Representatives	Electrical Wholesalers
Manufacturing			
Advertising			
Lead Generation			
Field Sales Calls			
Fulfillment			
Customer Credit			
Repair Work			

Firm Performs Function

BOX 7.1
Japanese Keiretsus

Three basic types of keiretsu are relevant to marketing channels. The first is referred to as a **horizontal keiretsu**. It is composed of a group or "wheel" of companies from a variety of industries. Typically, a major bank is at the center of the wheel to provide financing for members. A major trading company that handles domestic and international distribution of products provides the "glue" that binds participants. Member companies are linked by cross shareholding, interlocking directorates, and a president's club composed of chief executives who meet periodically. The largest keiretsu is the Mitsubishi Group, which has more than 190 member companies, over 300 billion yen in sales, and more than 360,000 employees. Others include the Mitsui, Sumitomo, Fuji, DKB, and Sanwa Groups.

A **vertical keiretsu** represents a union among highly specialized manufacturers and service providers within a particular industry that spans significant portions of a value-added chain. They can include raw materials processors, primary materials manufacturers, resellers of various types, and original equipment manufacturers. Typically, a core manufacturer provides leadership and control over the affairs of other members. Often, this manufacturer assembles the components smaller members produce into finished products. The 12 big vertical keiretsus have combined annual sales of 10 trillion yen and employ more than 200,000 employees. The largest include Nippon Steel, Hitachi, Nissan, Toyota, Matsushita, Toshiba, Tokyu, and Seibu.

The third type of alliance is called a **distribution keiretsu**. It is composed of a manufacturer and the various types of wholesalers, distributors, and retailers in its marketing channels. The purposes of distribution keiretsus are to achieve market access and coverage, build a uniform brand image, secure customer feedback, and enforce reseller price maintenance. Matsushita, Toshiba, and Toyota lead the largest distribution keiretsus. Given that these distribution keiretsus are dominated by a manufacturer, it is difficult for outside producers (especially from abroad) to obtain their services.

Nakato Hirakubo, *An Analysis of the Japanese Market: Consumer, Distribution System, and Market Structure* (New York: Center for Applied Research, Pace University, 1992).

As described in Box 7.1, keiretsus are networks of specialized organizations linked together with the purpose of serving a specific market or markets. Of particular interest are vertical keiretsus, which are organized around value-added chains. Competition here is vertical in nature. A keiretsu competes against another keiretsu at the customer level. Their rivalry is focused on delivering high-quality products and relevant augmenting services at the lowest total cost. At the same time, within a given keiretsu, firms work together closely and perform whatever tasks are necessary, even noncustomary ones, to meet customer requirements. We refer to this form of business market contention as **streams of competition**.[20]

Build a Channel Network Model

A **channel network model** maps out the business processes and functions required to provide the reformulated TCE to targeted customer firms. The model also specifies whether the supplier firm, resellers, third-party service providers, or customer firms will complete these required processes and functions. There are four general network models—conventional channels, modular channels, hybrid channels, and integrated multi-channels. When selecting a model, managers must weigh each alternative in terms of its abilities to achieve the supplier firm's market access, value-added, and cost-to-serve goals, to deliver the intended TCE, and to garner reasonable profits given the resource limitations of the firm.

Conventional channels resemble linear pipelines when diagrammed. Various channel member firms appear as nodes in the pipelines. Products and services flow from a supplier firm either directly or indirectly through resellers to a market segment or customer firm. Along the way, each firm completes clusters of business functions. The unique group of functions performed distinguishes one type of channel member from another. For example, a manufacturer's agent primarily makes technical sales calls and takes orders for a supplier. On the other hand, a distributor purchases and takes title to the supplier's products in bulk, breaks bulk, stores local inventory, assembles assortments or total solutions for customer firms, makes promotional sales calls, takes orders, and provides financing, as well as furnishing a host of other services. Typically, one dominant firm serves as **channel captain**, managing and coordinating all distribution efforts and investing in and cultivating brand or reseller equity.[21]

In direct conventional channels, the supplier firm performs all the required business functions, maintains the "face" or contact with the customer firm, "owns" the customer relationship, and captures all resulting profits. In indirect conventional channels, business functions are allocated among the supplier firm and reseller firms. Both sets of firms work as partners, sharing profits through various discounts, commissions, and allowances. The reseller firm often manages the face before the customer and may even claim ownership of the customer relationship. In some indirect conventional channels the supplier firm may not know who the ultimate customers are or in which applications they use the supplier's product. In Figure 7.4, we illustrate a conventional channel for an electrical product marketed to original equipment manufacturers (OEMs) and maintenance, repair, and operating supplies (MRO) customers. The sequence of boxes and arrows captures the way that the product "flows" to market.

Emerging information and logistics technologies have given rise to **modular channels**, which appear on paper as complex networks of relationships among firms.[22] They too can be either direct or indirect channels. Managers from one firm serve as **system integrator**. They envision the channel network, select participating firms, and manage ongoing relationships.[23]

The system integrator begins by **deconstructing** all the business processes required to provide the reformulated market offering down to individual functions or tasks.[24] Then, the managers determine which type of firm is best suited to perform each function. The system integrators hire the selected firms as subcontractors and compensate them on a fee-for-service or retainer basis. Importantly, the system integrators maintain the "face" before the customer, retain sole ownership of the customer relationship, manage the network, and promote its own brand equity. Often, coordination and integration of all modular channel activities is done electronically via partner relationship management (PRM) systems, which we discuss in Chapter 9. In Box 7.2, we describe a modular channel from Mahindra Shubhlabh Services Ltd.[25]

Figure 7.4 Conventional Channel for an Electrical Product

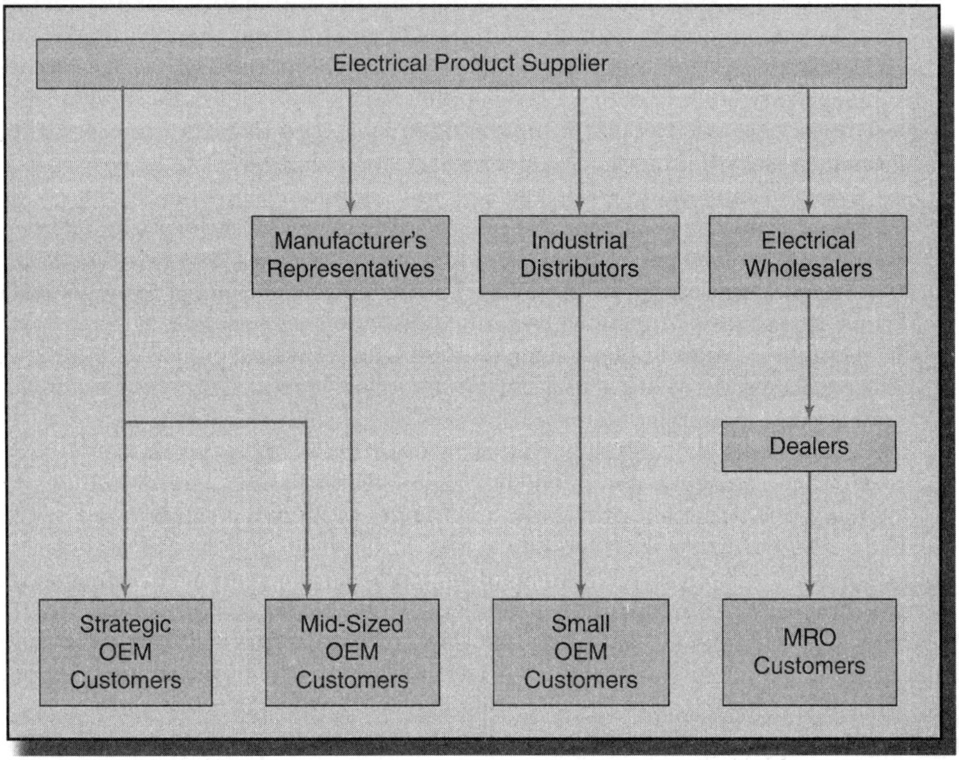

BOX 7.2
Mahindra Shubhlabh Services Ltd. (MSSL) Develops an Innovative Channel

Agricultural production in India is generally low owing to a failure to integrate quality inputs, scientific farming techniques, and finance. The industry is heavily dependent on the monsoon. Any fluctuation in the monsoon has a great impact on production. The industry is mainly credit driven. Vertically coordinated supply chains help to eliminate inefficiencies in agricultural marketing arising from intermediaries sucking away a major chunk of the margins. Agriculture marketing lacks proper infrastructure and technology, which further aggravates disparities.

Mahindra Shubhlabh Services Ltd. (MSSL), headquartered in Mumbai, was set up in April 2000 to integrate the farm supply chain and maximize profitability for farmers. It provides a one-stop channel for both the pre- and post-harvest management of farm produce and helps farmers achieve the required output quality. Its two major goals are commodity trading and providing a one-stop solution for all the needs of farmers. To better reach remote villages, MSSL adopted a hub-and-spoke model through franchises. In the process of setting up the system, the company also generated a number of jobs in rural

BOX 7.2
Continued

areas through agricultural extension, retailing, logistics, and farm equipment operations.

Each agricultural service center (known as Mahindra Krishi Vihar) is either a subsidiary or franchisee, delivering basic services to farmers. Each hub provides farmers with various services. The first is an agricultural input retail (selling seeds, fertilizers, chemicals) with guidance provided on their application. Equipments may be rented, especially for those machines that farmers use sparingly, making it unviable for them to be individually owned. MSSL hubs provide agronomics support, market information, farm input and advisory services, and financial support through crop loans with commercial banks. Lastly, they assist in selling the produce through tie-ups with other retailers and exporters. These services bring down cultivation costs and increase yields by 15–50% for each farmer.

To further penetrate the local market, 10 local Internet-based kiosks (spokes) are placed around each hub ASC. Farmers get their inputs and services through these spokes. The spokes are manned by trained supervisors who visit the fields and supervise critical farm operations. Where franchises are deployed for providing the hub-and-spoke services, they are expected to invest a non-refundable sign-up fee and provide access to the villages. The franchises gain significantly through improved margins from sales to registered farmers, consultancy fees for services provided, margins through distribution/sale of farm produce, and rental income through renting equipment to farmers.

MSSL provides a wide range of fertilizers from manufacturers such as Madras Fertilizers Limited and FACT; pesticides from major players such as Bayer, Syngenta, Aventis, Rallis, and Lupin; and market-leading brands of seeds. Farmers availing themselves of MSSL services have access to products at reasonable prices. Over a period of time, the company has expanded its product range to cover various crops including paddy, soya, potato, banana, cotton, fresh fruits, etc. Following the model's proven success, the company has progressively expanded its geographical footprint to cover newer locations throughout India.

Contributed by V. Vinupriya, Participant, PGSEM Program, Indian Institute of Management Bangalore.
Sources: Mahindra Newsletter, April–June 2006, *http://216.198.202.132/Newsletters/M&M%20Newsletter%20Issue%202%202006/M%20and%20M%20April-June%202006/html/GroupCompany.htm*; Rakesh Singh, "New Farm Supply Chain Initiatives In Indian Market," *www.greatlakes.edu.in/pdf/farmsupplychain.pdf*; V. Rasheed Sulaiman, Andy Hall, and N. Suresh, "Effectiveness Of Private Sector Extension in India And Lessons For The New Extension Policy Agenda," Network Paper No. 141, January 2005, AGREN, *http://www.odi.org.uk/networks/agren/papers/agrenpaper_141.pdf*.

In a **hybrid channel**, business market managers combine features of both conventional and modular channels. For example, a supplier firm might choose to complement a conventional channel network with backup support from a modular channel. As in Figure 7.5, let's say that a computer software producer distributes its programs through computer dealers and retailers. Because many of these resellers might not have technical capabilities, the software producer may choose to create a network of design consultants and authorized technical support providers to work jointly with the resellers. In this way, the producer enhances the ability of resellers to furnish a total solution of software and value-adding services without unnecessarily forcing them to expand the

Figure 7.5 Hybrid Channel for Computer Software

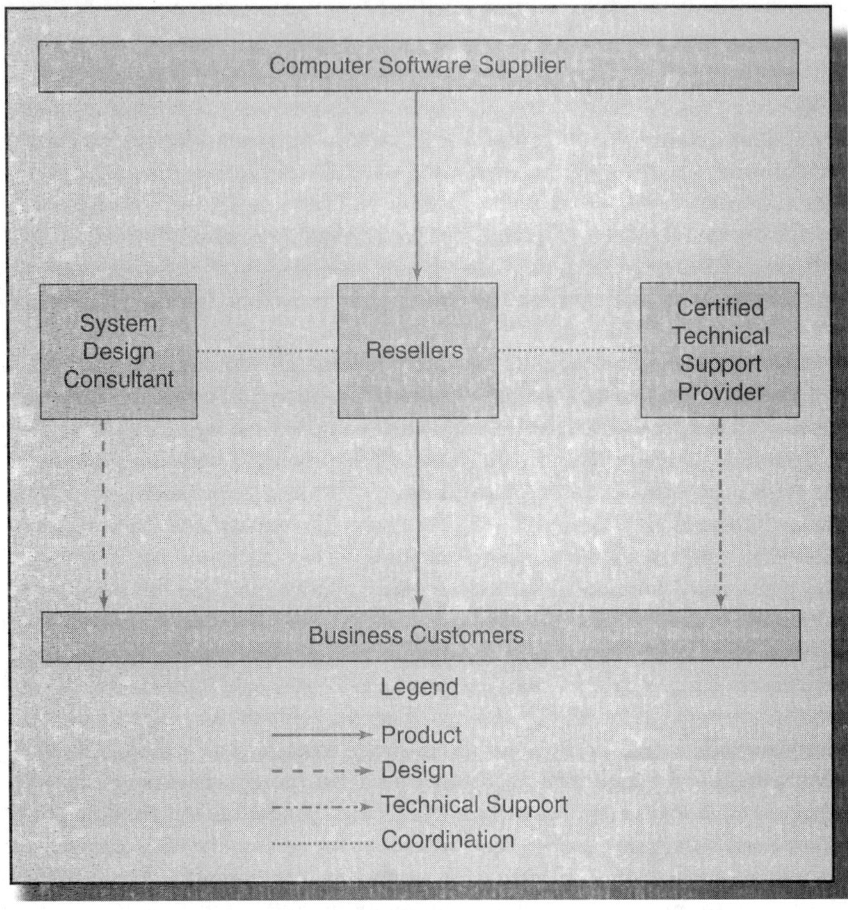

scope of operations outside their core capabilities. **Adaptive channels** are a special hybrid in which suppliers, resellers, third-party service providers, and customer firms agree to share complementary capabilities for prespecified compensation to fulfill critical yet infrequent customer requirements. Because adaptive channels improve the effectiveness of channel partnerships, we discuss them in Chapter 9.[26]

In recent years, the Internet has diluted the traditional strategic intent of channels. Rather than purchasing products from the same channel every transaction, customer managers routinely search the Internet for the best deal across all channels. The practice has given rise to more frequent channel conflicts and gray markets. To accommodate, if not capitalize on this trend, many supplier firms have adopted more flexible networks called **integrated multi-channels** that empower customers to select from different resellers or channel formats as their requirements change from transaction to transaction. Instead of competing with one another for the loyalty of a given customer, the supplier and resellers work together to serve their mutual customer.[27]

Figure 7.6 provides a process map for an integrated multi-channel. In the example, the supplier's inside sales force, direct marketing group, and Internet Web site

Figure 7.6 Integrated Multi-Channel Process Model

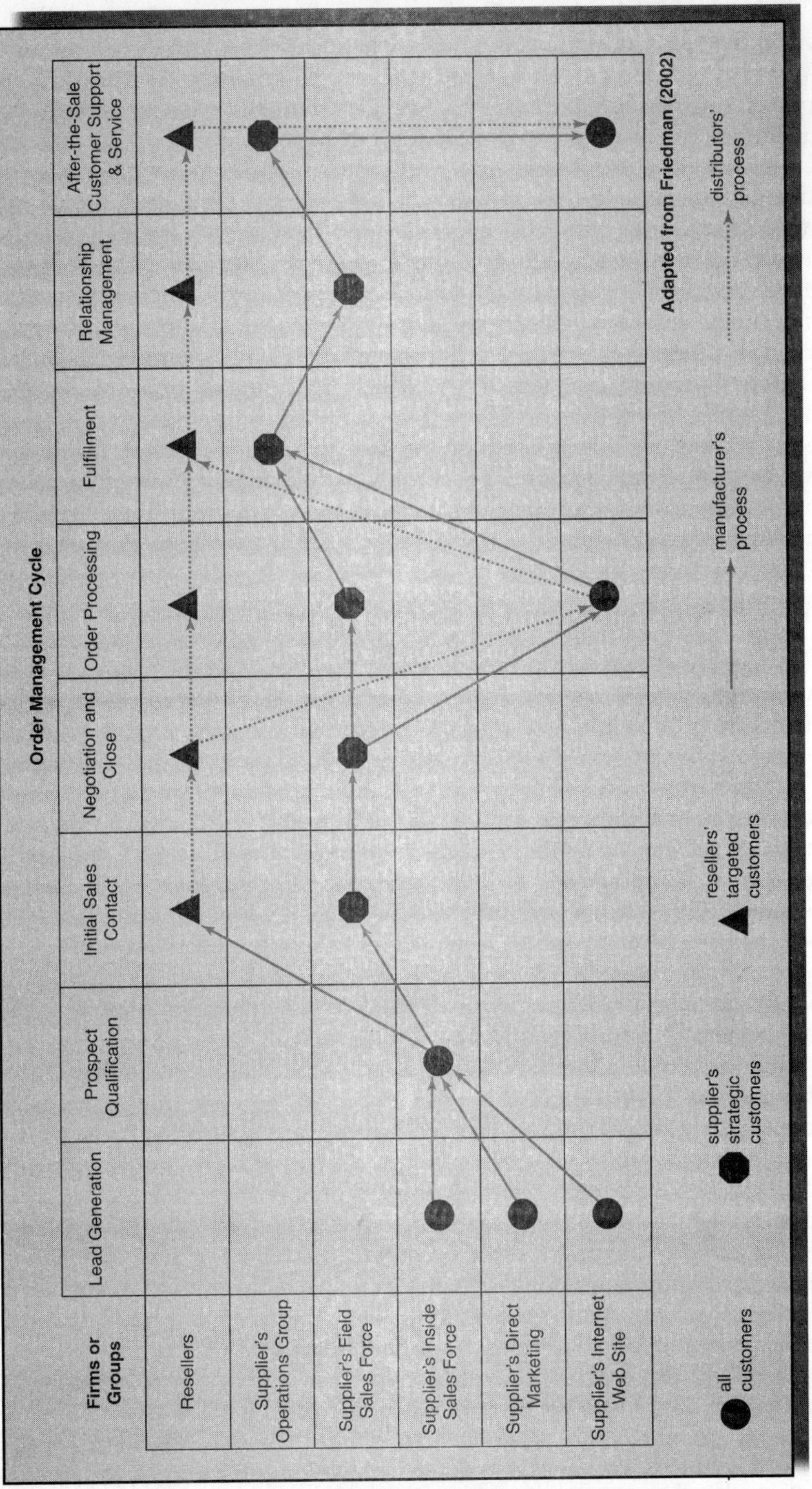

gather leads for all channel members. The inside sales force qualifies all prospects. They turn prospects that meet preestablished criteria to reseller firms for initial sales contact, negotiations, and closing. Resellers' targeted customers might be small to medium-sized firms, companies that order in small quantities, or firms that value services resellers provide. Concurrently, the inside sales force turns over designated strategic prospects to the supplier's field sales force for cultivation. On subsequent transactions, newly won customers can elect to be served through traditional channel arrangements—strategic accounts through the supplier's operations group and resellers' targeted customers through reseller operations. Alternatively, the customer may choose to order through the supplier's Web site and designate how the order will be fulfilled. For example, a reseller customer may require a huge quantity of the supplier's product and elect to have it delivered directly from the supplier firm. In this instance, the reseller would automatically be compensated via a drop-shipping fee or prespecified commission on the sale. In another example, a strategic account may desperately need an emergency delivery of a small volume of the product. Here, the Web site would direct the order to the reseller firm the customer selects for fulfillment. Finally, all customers can use the supplier's Web site for customer support.

Finalize Marketing and Distribution Arrangements

With a channel network design in hand, business market managers ask the final questions: "Which firms will we ask to participate in the network, and what will their roles be?" Mindful that channel partnerships require "gives & gets," business market managers devise a feasible profit model for all proposed participants before selecting partners and assigning responsibilities. Next, they carefully choose channel partners, deliberately seeking out top-performing and forward-thinking resellers that have proven capabilities and apparent motivation to achieve the supplier's market access, value-added services, and cost-to-serve goals while delivering the intended TCE. Whenever appropriate, managers adopt supporting electronic business (e-business) and wireless technologies to bolster partner productivity and adapt international channels to local customs and established distribution practices. Finally, the supplier firm and all selected channel partners come to agreement on contract terms, conditions, and time frames.

Devise Profit Models

Before asking firms to join a channel network, business market managers must think through viable profit models not only for their own firm but also for prospective partners. As supplier expectations and requirements for channel network partners have changed, so too have compensation methods. Traditionally, supplier managers set suggested resale prices and then provided resellers with a combination of trade discounts, volume discounts, rebates, and special incentives to entice full-service resellers to market their product lines. They intended that trade discounts would cover reseller costs and afford a reasonable profit. With rudimentary accounting tools at their disposal, supplier managers often used industry averages for reseller costs and profits when setting trade discounts. Noting that suppliers often kept trade discount amounts unchanged for years rather than adjusting them in parallel with rises in service costs, reseller managers have long disparaged the practice. As for resellers engaged primarily in selling tasks—manufacturer's representatives, agents, and brokers—supplier firms commonly offered commissions and bonuses based on realized sales.

These long-standing models have begun to break down. Among full-service resellers, cutthroat competition has compelled many firms to price well below suggested resale prices. This practice trivializes trade discounts and has forced many reseller firms to earn a living off meager volume discounts, rebates, and incentives. Given the volatility of sales in some markets, manufacturer's representatives, agents, and brokers are increasingly requesting that a greater percentage of their compensation come in the form of guaranteed salaries or fees.

In response, business market managers have begun to experiment with alternative compensation schemes. For example, McKinsey & Company, Inc., developed a cost-to-serve (CTS) model, which it advocates that supplier firms use in place of traditional trade discount schemes. Under the McKinsey CTS model, participating wholesalers are compensated for each service they perform for a supplier. Payments cover the actual costs a specific wholesaler incurs plus a prespecified profit. Critics argue that the CTS model is more difficult and costly to implement. To participate, wholesalers have to create activity-based costing systems that monitor the ongoing costs of providing each service. They also have to enter into complex negotiations with suppliers over compensation for each service. However, McKinsey consultants counter that the CTS model not only serves as a strong incentive for superior wholesaler performance but also enhances supply chain efficiency.[28] In modular channels, where firms serve as subcontractors and perform prespecified tasks, CTS models or a "retainer contract" variant have become commonplace.

Realizing that resellers stand to gain far greater profits from providing services to customers than from merely selling products, supplier managers have also begun to create forward-thinking certification programs and franchising and licensing agreements through which resellers can charge service fees for such things as applications design, installation, maintenance, and consulting. Finally, as more and more resellers turn to e-business, supplier firms have shown them how to gain incremental profits from their Web sites through commissions on referrals, advertising charges, and syndication fees.

Carefully Select Channel Partners

Business market managers identify and then select existing or potential channel-partner firms that can best perform the channel functions required to meet market access, value-added service, and cost-to-serve goals and to provide the intended TCE. Of course, managers realize that their choice of channel partners is often constrained. To begin, they specify those channel capabilities the supplier firm seeks in terms of such things as technical competence, sales force deployment, warehouse and delivery capabilities, financial stability, and leadership. Next, business market managers internally generate a comprehensive list of candidates for each reseller type targeted or acquire them from governments, database marketing firms, or trade associations. For example, the U.S. Department of Commerce keeps track of resellers through its North American Industry Classification System, while the National Association of Wholesaler-Distributors monitors reseller firms in more than 105 industries. Suppliers also can gather general and financial information about these firms from public and commercial sources such as Dun & Bradstreet. Managers eliminate those resellers that do not meet screening requirements.[29]

Managers then conduct a market research survey to assess customer preferences for, and satisfaction with, specific reseller firms. As part of the survey, respondents evaluate reseller firms in terms of their abilities to deliver necessary service outputs to create a list of prospective reseller partners. Then, they reconcile this list with the one we described in the previous paragraph to create a list of prospective and preferred resellers. To validate the research, managers visit each reseller firm, particularly those located outside of the supplier firm's domestic market, to tour facilities, assess capabilities, and gauge management interest.

Consider E-business and Wireless Technologies

Considerable debate surrounds the issue of whether evolving e-business and wireless technologies constitute new marketing channels or are merely computer and telecommunications-based tools that enable existing channels to function more efficiently. Regardless of the eventual outcome of that debate, managers should use the technologies wherever they stand to increase the value of the offerings that the channel network provides. In particular, they need to determine whether new types of resellers might complement or replace existing channel members and whether new transaction formats might augment modular and hybrid channels.[30]

The Internet has given rise to two new types of resellers: infomediaries and metamediaries. An **infomediary** is a broker that finds, retrieves, sorts, processes, and analyzes information from the World Wide Web. Infomediaries typically receive subscription or other fees from firms for conducting information searches, seeking buyers or sellers, aggregating orders, making referrals, and consulting. Internet portals and browsers, such as Google, Yahoo!, and Microsoft Network (MSN), are among the most successful. Another form of infomediary is the *comparison agent*. It allows customers to search the Internet for sources of supply and to compare vendor prices. By paying infomediaries listing fees and charges for banner and pop-up advertisements, a supplier firm can further enhance market awareness of its offerings.[31]

Metamediaries are Web sites that furnish multivendor, multiproduct, and multiservice market space for customer firms. Suppliers commonly pay such firms in the form of commissions on sales. Grainger and Marshall Industries are two prominent metamediaries in business markets. Metamediaries are a particularly attractive option when a supplier firm needs to bundle its market offering with complementary products and services into a total solution.

Four electronic transaction formats facilitate delivery of added value: communities, catalogs, auctions, and exchanges. They are particularly useful in the case of modular and hybrid channels because managers can use these formats to improve the performance of specific channel functions. A **community** is a hosted, though unmoderated, cyber forum where users exchange information about a particular product or service, technology, or industry. For example, in the software industry a common practice for suppliers is to set up and operate a Web site where users can come to find answers to pressing program problems. Volunteer programmers may even staff "for free" and solve user problems for the personal satisfaction it brings.[32]

With a **catalog** format, a firm posts detailed information about the company and its market offerings. In more advanced systems, customer firms have access to pricing information, use an "electronic shopping cart" to select items for purchase, configure more complex offerings, and are able to order products or services 24 hours a day, 7 days a week (24 × 7). Catalog sites are perhaps the most common because they are relatively easy to set up and operate, and customers are familiar with the practice from personal experiences.

In an **electronic auction**, one firm posts an offering and other parties submit bids. In a forward auction, a supplier firm lists products or services and potential customers bid for them, with the highest bidder winning. In Chapter 3, we addressed reverse auctions where a customer firm manages the process. Supplier firms tend to use forward auctions opportunistically and tactically to sell items of unknown value, perishable goods, surplus or discontinued items, and used equipment.

A business-to-business (B2B) **exchange** is an electronic forum where multiple buyers and sellers can make bids or accept offers for a variety of products and services. Buyers and sellers can accept any price offered at any time and either party can withdraw or revise a bid. In some exchanges, electronic bidding is followed up with face-to-face negotiations. Vertical exchanges are industry specific, such as for auto parts, chemicals, or steel; horizontal exchanges are service specific, such as for advertisements, accounting services, or consulting. Suppliers, customers, or industry associations can sponsor exchanges. Much ballyhooed during the latter 1990s, exchanges have had limited success. Covisint, ChemConnect, Elemica, and Exostar are among the surviving B2B exchanges.[33]

The convergence of wireless communications, mobile computing, and the Internet may have major implications for channel network design in the near future. These **wireless technologies** range in complexity from beepers to personal digital assistants to mobile telephones. Widely popular in the consumer arena, particularly in Europe and Japan, this evolving technology has already yielded two proven applications in business markets. The first is remote, 24×7 tracking of order, payment, and delivery status. Perhaps more promising, the second is contact management. This application is particularly useful in modular channels where personnel from several companies interact with customer firms. Functioning as a communications medium for PRM systems, text and instant messaging features of mobile phones or other wireless devices enable all contact personnel to have immediate access to sales leads, service requests, summaries of previous sales and service calls, and sensor readings, as well as to process invoices.[34]

Build International Marketing Channels

Those firms that currently operate or are expanding internationally should anticipate longer business processes and additional functions in their marketing channels. They must cover additional geography and adhere to export and import regulations of each country market as well as its local culture and TCE expectations. In addition, international business market managers should expect the division of functions among channel members to vary from region to region and from country to country.[35] We provide a brief description of the various types of international resellers in Box 7.3. In general, managers have four basic choices concerning international channels and resellers.[36]

A firm can rely upon domestic reseller-exporters to handle international marketing functions. Domestic reseller-exporters operate within the supplier's home country and provide services from offices within that home country. Although specific responsibilities vary across nations, two general categories exist: agents and merchants.

BOX 7.3
Examples of International Marketing Channels and Resellers

I. Resellers Involved in International Marketing

A. Domestic Reseller-Exporters

- **Export management company (EMC):** An international sales organization that functions as the exclusive export department for a group of noncompeting manufacturers. An EMC handles the entire exporting operation for a client, functioning as the manufacturer in the eyes of international customers. They work under contract and are paid by salary, commission, or retainer plus commission.
- **Manufacturer's export agent (MEA):** Operating within limited markets and under a short-term contract, an MEA acts as a firm's sales representative in an international marketplace. This type of firm offers far more limited services than an EMC and is paid on a commission basis.
- **Commission agent (CA):** A CA represents international customers interested in buying domestic products. They are paid a commission by the international buying organization.
- **Domestic trading company (DTC):** A domestic trading company provides a full range of exporting services for clients within its home country. These services can include international warehousing and physical distribution, financing, insurance, marketing research, market development, and selling. A DTC handles goods from numerous manufacturers.
- **Export broker (EB):** Working on a commission basis, export brokers bring domestic manufacturers together with prospective international buyers. They do not take title or physical possession of goods.
- **Cooperative exporter (CE):** A CE is another manufacturer that has an international marketing channel already established. Serving as either EMCs or CAs for manufacturers that lack international distribution, they market others' goods along with their own.

B. International Reseller-Importers

- **Import broker (IB):** Located abroad, this type of broker establishes contacts for a supplier with potential customers within the broker's home country.
- **Managing agent (MA):** An MA serves as a manufacturer's agent in another country. It performs related selling activities.
- **International trading company (ITC):** Headquartered in another country, an ITC performs similar functions to a DTC.
- **Import jobber (IJ):** An IJ is a jobber located in another country that specializes in importing goods. It performs the typical array of wholesaling functions.

II. Countertrade Arrangements

- **Barter:** In its simplest form, barter entails the exchange of products without the use of money.
- **Clearing arrangement:** This is a type of barter in which a number of transactions are consolidated into a single contract to purchase a specified amount of goods and services. Credit is often involved in such agreements.

BOX 7.3
Continued

- **Switch trading:** Switch trading is a triangular, barter arrangement in which a third-party is brought into the deal to dispose of merchandise.
- **Buy-back:** Under this form of barter, an exporter agrees to set up and operate a plant in another country and contracts to buy a percentage of that plant's output for a set period of time.
- **Offset:** An agreement in which an exporter sells goods at a set price and is paid in currency. A reciprocal arrangement is made for that exporter to in turn buy a certain amount of goods from the client.

Subhash C. Jain, *International Marketing,* 6th ed. (Cincinnati, OH: South-Western College Publishing, 2000); and Anne T. Coughlin, Erin Anderson, Louis W. Stern, and Adel I. El-Ansari, *Marketing Channels,* 6th ed. (Upper Saddle River, NJ: Prentice Hall, 2001).

Agents, such as export management companies, a manufacturer's export agents, and domestic trading companies, largely perform selling activities without taking title to goods and are paid either a commission or a fee for service. Merchants such as export merchants, cooperative exporters, and export vendors, on the other hand, take title and physical possession of goods and perform other marketing functions. They make their profit from the resale of products in other countries.

A firm can choose to deal with international reseller-importers. These resellers are based in the country that managers target and specialize in importing goods from abroad. Among these agents are brokers, managing agents, international trading companies, import jobbers, and national distributors and dealers. Like their domestic counterparts, international reseller-importers vary in terms of the marketing functions they perform, whether they take title to goods, and the manner in which they are compensated.

A supplier can decide to market directly in the targeted nation. It might establish an in-country sales and service office. Or the supplier might acquire or set up its own production facilities and develop a direct sales force for the nation or region. Some resource-rich suppliers may even choose to acquire a local distributor or dealer firm to handle channel functions. Although marketing directly may at first seem to be a high-risk and resource-intense strategy, international business market managers may find that they have no choice when penetrating certain markets. For example, in Japan where working relationships in vertical keiretsus are long-running and close, access to the best channels and resellers may be blocked. Furthermore, where access is possible, resellers may give low priority to imported lines out of loyalty to traditional suppliers.[37]

Finally, a firm might engage in countertrade. Broadly defined, countertrade is the exchange of goods or services for the promise to reciprocate through the purchase of the other party's goods or services. The most common types of countertrade include barter, clearing arrangements, and switch trading. Countertrade partners often include governments and businesses, as well as individuals.

Business market managers often find international channels, especially those in emerging markets, to be particularly challenging. Not only must managers be imaginative and design new channels that meet unique local requirements, they must also be prepared to quickly alter their channel strategies whenever market conditions shift dramatically.

Formalize Partnership Agreements

With all channel network design investigations completed, business market managers now enter into partnership negotiations with prospective and preferred resellers. Following productive negotiations, the supplier and its resellers summarize the terms, conditions, and time frame of their partnership in a sales agreement. The agreement will identify the responsibilities of all parties for completing channel functions and the rewards that each will receive. There are four principal types of sales agreements in business channels—handshake agreements, written contracts, licensing agreements, and franchise agreements.

Handshake agreements are arguably the oldest form of channels contracts. Once managers of the two firms come to agreement on the terms and conditions of their partnership, they give their word to follow through on their promises and meet their responsibilities. Such agreements remain common in some industries such as produce and air conditioning equipment as well as in many international channels. In cultures where a person's word and honor are paramount, handshake agreements are the norm for doing business. In more litigious cultures such as in the United States and Western Europe, where firms don't want to rely on memories of past oral promises as the basis of dispute resolution, business market managers turn to written contracts. A **written contract** is a legal document grounded in the country's commercial codes that specifies in detail the responsibilities and rewards of both supplier and reseller firms. A time frame for the contract is specified as well as renewal or termination conditions and procedures.

As outsourcing has become a more prevalent business strategy, supplier firms have increasingly turned to licensing and franchise agreements to structure their channel partnerships. Through a **licensing agreement**, a supplier firm grants legal permission to a channel partner to use a manufacturing or service process, trademark, patent, or trade secret for a fee or royalty. Such an agreement enables the supplier firm to gain access to a new market with limited investment and risk. The channel partner gains a well-known brand name or manufacturing process. A **franchise agreement** is a more comprehensive and all-encompassing form of licensing. Franchising entails the sale for fees or royalties of the rights to market a brand using the methods, trademarks, names, products, know-how, production techniques, accounting methods, and marketing processes of a supplier firm. Franchisees are typically required to follow specified procedures for the production and marketing of the supplier's brands. And, the partnership is most often exclusive. In Chapter 9, we will discuss the example of Yahoo! India.[38]

Creating Value Through Direct Channels

Firms in business markets are more likely to market their offerings directly to customer firms than their consumer market counterparts. Customer firms are far fewer in number. Furthermore, customers tend to purchase products in large quantities, require extensive technical support, and prefer a TCE featuring close supplier relationships. Taken together, these factors provide a powerful economic incentive for supplier firms to serve customers directly. In addition, popular direct marketing tools such as catalogs, e-mail ordering systems, and e-business make direct channels both practical and cost effective.

When a supplier firm chooses to "go it alone," it faces unique implementation challenges. Among the most important issues include building and maintaining a sales force and a logistics system. In this section, we explore issues related to executing a direct channel network. Given that we advocate a value-based market management approach, we begin by discussing the training programs, sales tools, and compensation systems that suppliers use to develop a sales force of value merchants. Then we describe how suppliers deploy these value merchants among potential customers to maximize profits. To physically deliver products or services to customers as well as the intended TCE, supplier firms must create appropriate infrastructure, which often includes order entry and processing systems, inventory management systems, warehouses, and delivery vehicles. Thus, we explore logistics systems and describe how supplier firms can draw upon emerging technologies to do so.

Creating a Sales Force of Value Merchants

In today's demanding business environment, a supplier's sales force must be comprised of highly skilled professionals. Each salesperson must be able to investigate customer requirements and preferences, demonstrate value, negotiate terms and conditions, and take the order. As if these tasks are not enough, the salesperson is increasingly responsible for the profitability of each customer account to the supplier firm. We contend that a supplier firm must create a sales force of value merchants to ensure that each of these demanding tasks is performed competently.

A **value merchant** recognizes the supplier's own costs and the value to the customer for each market offering and works to obtain a fair return for both the supplier firm and customer firm. The value merchant stands in stark contrast to the all-too-common **value spendthrift**, who either cuts price needlessly or gives away extra services "for free" to gain the next sale. To create value merchants, the supplier firm must instill a value philosophy and culture, train the salesperson on value-selling techniques, and compensate the sales force as a function of value delivered.[39]

Internally Promote a Value-Based Marketing Philosophy and Culture

To inspire value merchants, senior management needs to put a philosophy in place that the firm generates value with both its core offering and its augmenting services, and that the firm expects to receive an equitable return for this value. For instance, the Sonoco Products Company's corporate culture reinforces to each salesperson the preeminence of value in the firm's overall market strategy. From the day they are hired, sales representatives learn that Sonoco products are typically higher priced than those of competitors. They also quickly discover that Sonoco prospers because it provides value to its customers in the form of technologically superior products and outstanding services. From these lessons, salespersons readily conclude that if they are to succeed at Sonoco, they must sell value and not price. Moreover, the Sonoco "value story" is repeatedly reinforced through such things as annual reports, brochures, company newsletters, case histories presented at sales meetings, and sales tools. A firm can further invigorate a value merchant culture through salesperson titles and designations, marketing communications, and celebrations of successful value-based selling.

Train Value Merchants

Giving value away is easy. Obtaining an equitable return on the value provided to customers is quite the opposite. A first step in countering the tendency to cut price is for senior management to provide salespersons with an adequate understanding not only of the value services provide, but also of their cost and profitability. Management must also inform their salespersons about the relationship between sales volume and account profitability. Based on this information, the sales force focuses its efforts and those of service providers toward those accounts that have the greatest profit potential.

Next, business market managers must develop and instill a value-selling process among their value merchants. A more insightful salesperson intuitively follows a methodological process to investigate customer requirements, puts together and proposes responsive market offerings, demonstrates that they are superior to those of competition, negotiates a fair price, and then makes sure that the business delivers on what the salesperson has promised. The purpose of putting a formal value-selling process in place is to make this practice explicit and complete, so that even less skillful salespeople can follow it consistently to produce superior results. As an example, Kennametal is a leading global supplier of tooling, engineered components, and advanced materials that are consumed in its customers' production processes. Kennametal finds that having a global value-selling process in place provides a consistent, reliable, and repeatable process for continuously improving the way they do business with their customers. Its process consists of six steps: (1) target customers, (2) discover needs, (3) develop customer-specific value proposition, (4) build detailed sales plan, (5) execute relentlessly, and (6) listen and modify. Sales training focuses on honing the salesperson's skills in each of these areas.

To ensure that the value-selling process is executed effectively, management equips its salespeople with tools that enable them to persuasively demonstrate and document the superior value of their market offerings to targeted customers and to obtain a fair price. In Chapter 2, we discussed value calculators and value-based case histories as prime examples. In addition to these "snapshot" value-based selling tools, progressive suppliers employ a complementary value-accumulation tool that documents the value provided to a customer over time. Such a tool arms salespeople with a proactive response to customer questions of "What have you done lately?" Astute suppliers create this tool, train salespersons in its use, and compensate them for taking the time to keep score on the value created in the relationship.

Salespeople typically gain their initial experience with value-based selling tools through role-playing exercises during the training. Even though considerable effort may be put into making the role-playing exercise realistic, it is not the same as using the value-based sales tools with customers in the field. Because of this difference, suppliers that are serious about transforming their salesforces into value merchants make certain that they follow up the sales training with in-the-field practice, with the salesperson receiving "hands-on" coaching and support. SKF has its *area value champions* work one-on-one with its salespeople, spending a week driving around with them, conducting joint sales calls. Over the course of the week, the two use SKF's Documented Solutions Program (DSP) value-based selling tool in customer visits, with the salesperson increasingly taking the lead during the calls. In doing so, the salesperson gains confidence and comfort in his or her ability to use the DSP tool through firsthand field experience.

Compensate Value Merchants Based on Profitability of Accounts

Value merchant compensation is based on short-term and long-term profitability. SKF Corporation provides a noteworthy example. SKF salespeople have 50% of their incentive compensation based on individual targets, such as DSP activities completed, sales growth in their territories, and introduction of specific products. The remaining 50% is based on *total value added*, which is defined as net profitability after subtracting the cost of capital and is calculated based on the geographic area, business unit, and division performance. SKF, interestingly, uses the *number* of activities a salesperson quantifies in monetary terms using the DSP tool as its measure for the sales force compensation plan. It believes that the number is more important than the actual monetary amounts because it wants its salespeople to make use of the DSP tool a part of their daily activity.

More fine-grained criteria for value merchant compensation emerge when the supplier gains the capability of monitoring which products and services each customer uses. Senior management must guard against compensation schemes that reward salespeople for selling separately as many products and services as they can to the customer. Although this practice will most likely provide a short-term spike in customer contribution to profitability, long term it will undermine credibility with the customer and sacrifice future business. The challenge is for sales management to integrate short-term performance with long-term results. This goal suggests the need for an inclusive set of measures that captures how well the firm is meeting customers' present and envisioned requirements. In Box 7.4, we discuss how Hitech Servers revamped its sales incentive program to create a sales force of value merchants. [40]

Deploying Value Merchants

When staffed with a limited number of value merchants, supplier firms deploy them selectively among prospective customers to yield the greatest possible sales and profits. First, if necessary, suppliers create separate sales forces to serve distinct market segments. Second, they determine the number of value merchants needed to provide appropriate market coverage. Third, supplier firms designate individual areas of responsibility. Finally, they assign value merchants to specific areas of responsibility.[41]

Establish Necessary Sales Units

Recognizing differential sales and profit potential among targeted segments, suppliers increasingly divide the sales force into several units. Managers make this decision based on the knowledge required to adequately market the offering and on the types of working relationships required in each targeted market segment. In Chapter 10, we explore relationship-building efforts in detail.

Shapiro identified four types of field sales forces. Each type has different responsibilities and organization. In a **transactional field sales force**, each salesperson is

BOX 7.4
Hitech Servers Revamps its Sales Incentive Program

Hitech Servers (name disguised) is the leader in providing high-performance computer servers. To protect its market leadership, Hitech Servers revamped its marketing strategy and changed its incentive plans for its sales and services teams. This initiative was meant to encourage the sales team to sell not just a product but a complete solution, including the software stack, applications, etc.

Before the revamp of the incentive system, the sales force was quota driven. Each salesperson was given a target in terms of revenue to achieve for the year for each product under his/her responsibility. The incentive was linked directly to performance towards the assigned quota.

The new criteria measuring the performance of a salesperson consisted of a primary element such as revenue, secondary elements such as profit, as well as specific individual challenges. This was a significant departure from the earlier incentive program, which focused purely on meeting or exceeding specified revenue targets. The behavior of salespersons changed considerably to push high-margin products rather than merely pushing products to complete quota obligations.

To emphasize a sales process based on solutions, not products, requires collaborative work across different product lines. The modified incentive structure facilitates such collaboration. Sales teams are aligned to specific industries. In such a team-based working, different product experts work together within one team. Based on field engagement report, each team is assigned a team quota. This is in addition to individual quotas that are applicable to each salesperson. Finally, salespersons can choose the incentive plan from a few available options that they would like to be part of. These changes have translated into significantly enhanced sales success. Hitech Servers re-established itself as the market leader by 2008.

Contributed by Sharyathi Nagesh, Participant, PGSEM Program, Indian Institute of Management Bangalore.

responsible for calling on customers in a defined territory. They perform traditional selling activities—making presentations, asking for orders, and making after-sale calls. Their efforts revolve around discrete exchanges or series of exchanges.[42]

In a **systems sales force**, salespersons from several product groups or divisions within a company work together. They temporarily band together in a team, to sell a solution comprising products or services from their respective groups. A team sales effort is appropriate in these situations because no one salesperson has the technical knowledge of all components of the system. Customers benefit from systems selling in that they don't have to listen to separate presentations from sales representatives from each group.

As the sales and profit potential of accounts grows, firms turn to dedicated sales teams. A **major account sales force** takes one of two forms. When important customers have multiple divisions located across the nation or world, suppliers often rely on contracts. A **major account contract** creates uniform pricing and coordinated servicing for all customer divisions. A major account manager is responsible for the account and spends much time calling on the national headquarters of the customer firm, because the customer firm's senior managers who sign the major account contract and then coordinate its implementation across divisions are typically located there. The major account manager also supervises those field sales representatives who call on customer plants within their territories. The selling team is composed of all individuals who call on that customer. For larger and more collaborative relationships, firms turn to **major account programs**. Teams are made up of cross-functional personnel charged with developing all aspects of the relationship. Cross-functional personnel serve several accounts at once.

For accounts with the greatest potential, suppliers use **strategic account management**. A strategic account team comprises cross-functional personnel who are permanently assigned to one customer. They may even maintain offices at the customer's facility. Their task is to manage the entire customer relationship. Strategic account management teams spend less time on sales and marketing, and more time on such tasks as joint research and development than their transactional field sales force counterparts.

In addition to these four types of field sales forces, supplier firms commonly have an inside sales force. Inside salespeople maintain relationships via telephone, fax, or other electronic media with customer firms that are too small or strategically insignificant to justify frequent field sales calls. Suppliers sometimes organize inside sales into three groups. A **telemarketing group** is responsible for making proactive and outgoing calls on customers to solicit orders. An **order center** takes incoming calls from customers and processes transactions. A **customer service group** provides technical problem-solving assistance over the telephone, by fax, or via the Internet.

Determine the Number of Value Merchants Needed

Managers routinely use one of two methods for estimating necessary sales force size. In the **breakdown method**, they begin by forecasting total annual sales in monetary units in the market. Then managers assess how much sales a single salesperson can generate annually acting alone or as part of a team. To determine how many representatives are needed, managers simply divide the annual sales forecast by the sales a single representative can generate.

Realizing that accounts frequently require different levels of service, that all geographic areas do not contain an equal number of prospects, and that salespersons have unique capabilities, progressive companies turn to the workload approach. With the **workload approach**, business market managers estimate the total efforts that sales personnel must undertake to serve the entire marketplace. They measure total efforts as a function of such things as number of accounts, calls needed per account in a given time period, the amount of time spent per call with each account, and the geographic distance to be covered. Managers then divide this estimate by the total amount of work a single salesperson can handle.

Designate Areas of Responsibility

Next, business market managers develop areas of responsibility or portfolios of accounts for sales representatives to manage. Their goal is to allocate accounts equitably in terms of sales potential and amount of work. By doing so, managers boost sales force morale, minimize disputes over fairness, and simplify the performance evaluation process. The nature of these portfolios or areas of responsibility varies by type of sales force. For example, in a strategic account program, the business market manager identifies all key accounts. Then, the manager assigns each key account to a separate strategic account team.

With a transactional sales force, managers design geographic territories. To do so, they first select the most appropriate geographic control unit. Among the units widely used are states or provinces, counties, trading areas, cities or metropolitan areas, and postal code zones. Then they estimate potential sales, number of accounts, and dispersion of accounts within potential territories. At this stage, managers perform a workload analysis and delineate tentative territories. More sophisticated firms utilize one of many sales force planning models that are currently available on interactive computer software. Two of the most popular of these models are CALLPLAN and MAPS. After reviewing the tentative territories and making modifications, managers formally map sales territories.[43]

Assign Value Merchants to Areas of Responsibility

Finally, the business market manager determines which value merchant or sales team should be assigned to each designated area of responsibility. Managers use their familiarity with each value merchant's capabilities, personality, and preferences to match each salesperson to an area of responsibility that is most likely to be productive. Customer feedback and preferences should also play a significant part in these assignment decisions.

Designing a Logistics System That Creates Value

According to Fuller, O'Connor, and Rawlinson, logistics systems represent a vast untapped arena for creating customer value. Although 10% of the typical manufacturing firm's operating costs are related to logistics, few firms have applied the rigorous tools of Total Quality Management and business process engineering to them. As customer firms increasingly consider acceptable quality and competitive price as "table stakes" in doing business, suppliers must create a highly valued TCE in the form of logistics-related services that provide customers with convenience, reliability, and support.[44]

In response, companies are implementing integrated logistics systems. **Integrated logistics systems** (ILSs) entail the interfirm and cross-functional planning, implementation, and control of the flow and storage of raw materials, in-process inventories, finished goods, and related information from supplier firms to customer firms. They encompass three management activities: materials management, material flow systems, and physical distribution. ILS systems are closely linked to the firm's information technology (IT) systems. Often, third-party suppliers design and manage these ILS systems. Notable among these suppliers are FedEx Logistics Services, Roadway Express, CSL Logistics, USCO Logistics, GATX, and Caterpillar Logistics Services.[45]

When designing an ILS system, business market managers conduct the following tasks:

- Segment the market into logistically distinct businesses.
- Establish differential service standards for each market segment.

- Tailor unique logistics systems to deliver differential services.
- Exploit economies of scale among the different logistics systems.

Segment the Market into Logistically Distinct Businesses

As with other business market management tasks, senior managers charter a cross-functional team to design the ILS system. The team's first task is to group customers into segments that operations experts call logistically distinct businesses. A **logistically distinct business** (LDB) is a set of customers that have unique physical distribution service requirements. A supplier firm must build a separate logistics system and strategic business unit to serve each. In business markets, common LDBs include systems contracts; maintenance, repair, and operating supplies (MRO) replenishment; emergency orders; special orders for customized offerings; bulk shipments to stock; and items that have special handling requirements. These aspects correspond to the supply management models that we discussed in Chapter 3.[46]

Establish Differential Service Standards for Each Market Segment

For each LDB, the team specifies the firm's service standards. For example, in the case of systems orders, the team determines which product bundles to provide to each customer, which suppliers will provide complementary items or services, when and where to deliver products, and how to enter products into the customer's inventory system. When planning for emergency orders, the team identifies which items are highly critical to customers, how much inventory of each critical item to hold in reserve for crises, and how to provide immediate delivery. For special-handling situations, the team evaluates such things as packaging alternatives, transportation mode options, environmental control systems, and delivery procedures.

Tailor Unique Logistics Systems to Deliver Differential Services

The cross-functional team designs a logistics system for each LDB that creates superior value by meeting or exceeding service standards. Each system entails order receipt and processing, warehousing, materials handling, transportation, and control and tracking. When deciding on each component of a logistics system, the team considers the value each element creates for customers and its cost. They may decide to outsource some or all of the system elements.

Exploit Economies of Scale Among the Different Logistics Systems

Before implementing a separate logistics system for each LDB, team members determine whether they can achieve any cost economies by consolidating two or more of the proposed systems. For example, it may be possible for the firm to combine systems that deliver emergency orders, special orders for customized products, and items that have special handling requirements. Alternatively, the supplier may employ a single logistics system to handle systems contracts and MRO replenishment. When making the decision to consolidate LDBs, the team must trade off reductions in costs with lower service levels. Here, knowledge of the value that customers place on each service is essential.

STRENGTHENING RESELLER PERFORMANCE

An essential ingredient for executing an indirect channel network is a comprehensive program of reseller support. We contend that such an approach should be based on a simple concept—that the best way to ensure resellers deliver superior value to customers is for the supplier to create superior value for resellers. Channel positioning is a way to do so.[47]

Drawing on the bedrock marketing principles of segmentation, targeting, and positioning, we define **channel positioning** as the process of establishing and sustaining the supplier's reputation among targeted resellers for providing superior value. Several prerequisites and building blocks of channel positioning need to be addressed. Suppliers need to consider the reseller as a partner and to develop a working relationship that builds mutual self-interest. With significant mutual self-interest, both the supplier and the reseller recognize the importance of each other's contribution and coordinate efforts to better satisfy the requirements of customers.[48]

The supplier must conceive a potent **reseller value proposition** and provide it through a distinctive bundle of core products, capability-building programs, and incentives that we refer to as the **channel offering**. The channel offering not only compensates resellers in part for their efforts, but also encourages them to contribute augmenting services to the TCE that they provide to customers. Then the supplier must gain a reputation or **channel position** among resellers for delivering superior value.

Channel positioning involves four steps:

1. Determine reseller performance expectations.
2. Assess the reseller value of channel offering elements.
3. Craft a reseller value proposition and channel offering.
4. Communicate the reseller value proposition.

We begin our discussion of channel positioning by introducing the concept of marketplace equity, which prompts managers to think strategically about the contributions that they and their resellers are making to provide value to targeted market segments.

Build Marketplace Equity

Equity is a concept that captures the past, present, and future value a market offering provides to a customer. When a supplier reaches customers through resellers, business market managers need to further elaborate the equity concept, decomposing marketplace equity into its constituent components: brand, reseller, and channel equities. Cultivating and sustaining each of these equities are central tasks of channel management.[49]

Decompose Marketplace Equity

Marketplace equity represents the value that a customer firm receives from acquiring a particular supplier's product or service through a particular reseller in its local trade area. Marketplace equity is a joint result of reseller equity and brand equity. **Reseller equity** is the value of acquiring a supplier's offering from a particular reseller versus other authorized resellers in the local trade area, whereas **brand equity** is the value of acquiring a particular supplier's offering versus other competing suppliers' offerings. **Channel equity** captures the value a reseller receives from the channel offering a supplier provides. Significantly, channel equity may consequently contribute to reseller equity. We conceptually depict this decomposition in Figure 7.7.

The relative contributions of brand equity and reseller equity to marketplace equity determine not only the nature of the partnership between a supplier firm and its reseller but also respective profit margins. Economist Robert Steiner explains the linkage in terms of a hypothetical, purchasing "moment of truth." At some point in time, a customer manager contacts a reseller firm with the intention of buying a branded product. When the manager asks the reseller salesperson for the item, the salesperson responds that the product is out of stock. The customer manager has two choices, and Steiner represents each as a cross-elasticity of demand. In scenario 1, the customer manager remains steadfast in his or her desire to purchase the branded product and contacts other reseller firms until he or she can secure it. In scenario 2, the salesperson convinces the customer manager to purchase a competitor's comparable product that is in stock.[50]

Brand equity is clearly superior to reseller equity in scenario 1. The supplier firm has a power advantage over resellers, directs overall marketing efforts, and takes the

Figure 7.7
Decomposing Marketplace Equity

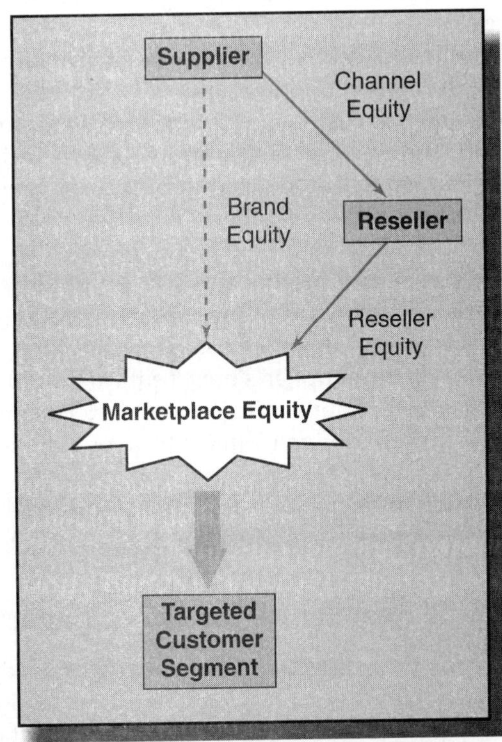

lion's share of profits the product generates. This scenario develops whenever the customer firm believes that the supplier provides the essential value through such things as innovation, product quality, and technical service. Conversely, reseller equity dominates brand equity in scenario 2 and the reseller has the advantage. This case arises when the customer firm believes that resellers furnish key value elements via such things as product availability, 24 × 7 delivery, and liberal credit policies. Of course, in a third scenario the customer managers believe that brand equity and reseller equity are essentially equivalent. This is perhaps the more common and preferred instance in that both firms recognize that they each significantly contribute to marketplace equity and must work together for mutual gain.

Cultivate Brand and Reseller Equity

Profound implications for both supplier and reseller managers arise in the management of marketplace equity. For supplier firms, we underscore the importance of developing and sustaining strong brand equity among targeted customers. Yet, too often supplier firms treat resellers as the "final customer," lose track of actual customers and their applications, and neglect to cultivate brand equity. For example, a supplier of recessed lighting that sells its products through mass merchants, such as Home Depot or Lowe's, should not focus its equity building efforts solely on the mass merchant. Instead, it should continue to reinforce brand equity with small electrical contractor customers through marketing communications and support services, such as a toll-free, installer assistance line that is staffed 18 hours a day, 7 days a week. Building equity with the customer is essential to create the "pull" necessary to avoid having mass merchants regard the supplier's products as "commodities."

Simultaneously, reseller firms must strive to keep their equity strong by customizing the market offerings and TCE that they offer to customer firms, by improving the quality of customer services such as on-time delivery, routine maintenance, and credit, and by aggressively promoting their firms to customers. For the reseller, building equity with the customers ensures long-term loyalty, yields continuous opportunities to cross-sell other products and services, and enables the firm to avoid intense price competition.

As supplier and reseller firms face significant "streams of competition," they must work together to build superior marketplace equity. Two channel-management tasks ensure a high level of coordination. First, firms must select their partners wisely. Ideally, the supplier's brand equity should complement the partner's reseller equity. Second, the supplier firm must develop significant channel equity by providing resellers with superior value in the form of a channel offering. Such an offering must not only bolster any weaknesses in the reseller's customer-serving capabilities, thus strengthening reseller equity, but must also encourage the reseller to enthusiastically promote the supplier's product lines.

Determine Reseller Performance Expectations

Channel positioning begins as supplier managers determine their expectations of reseller performance. Following candid discussions with resellers, supplier managers should summarize the supplier's expectations, taking into account both marketplace realities and the supplier's channel goals. Suppliers that intend to target several market segments and to reach them through separate channels should develop expectations for each type of reseller they authorize. Managers formalize these expectations in oral or written sales agreements, policy statements, and annual objectives or quotas. They should communicate these expectations and explain specific points to all authorized resellers through personal contacts and correspondence.

It is essential that supplier managers explicitly state expectations in terms of market access, value-added services, and cost-to-serve goals, the intended TCE, and management professionalism so they can design appropriate support programs. Earlier on in this chapter, we outlined specific channels objectives and performance metrics. At the same time, to ensure that market-offering augmentation is done properly, suppliers may require resellers to provide such things as facilities and personnel, technical and marketing expertise, and repair and service work. Finally, managers define reseller professionalism in terms of such things as the extent of strategic planning, financial management, operations management, and succession planning.

Assess the Reseller Value of Channel Offering Elements

As Figure 7.8 shows, channel offerings have three major components: channel core elements, capability-building programs, and incentive programs. **Channel core elements** are those basics that resellers must have from all their suppliers, such as adequate financial returns and strong brand equity for the supplier's line within the reseller's home country. **Capability-building programs** enable resellers to strengthen their own performance and to enhance the value they provide to customers. Examples are training programs, information-sharing systems, and collaborative policies. Given that competing suppliers often offer similar core elements, we find that capabilities programs represent the most potent, strategic means of differentiating a supplier's offerings. **Incentive programs** motivate short-term improvements in reseller and salesperson performance. These programs commonly entail bonuses for the supplier's salespeople, growth rebates for the reseller firm, and contests for reseller sales forces.

To gather input for the channel positioning process, supplier managers assess the reseller value of channel offering elements and construct a channel positioning matrix. We urge managers to use a variety of qualitative and quantitative techniques to first gain a general understanding of reseller requirements and then to identify those handful of channel offering elements that create the greatest value. During the process, business market managers must be mindful of what elements competitors are providing resellers.

The value of channel offering elements to a reseller firm will likely depend upon the nature of the supplier's product or service and how it fits into the bundles or solutions that the reseller in turn markets. We differentiate between a **bundle**—a collection of loosely connected products and services that a supplier firm consolidates in a transaction typically for a discounted price—and a **solution**—a deliberately engineered and integrated group of products and services that the supplier firm markets for a premium price.[51] A supplier's product or service can play one of

Figure 7.8 The Channel Offering

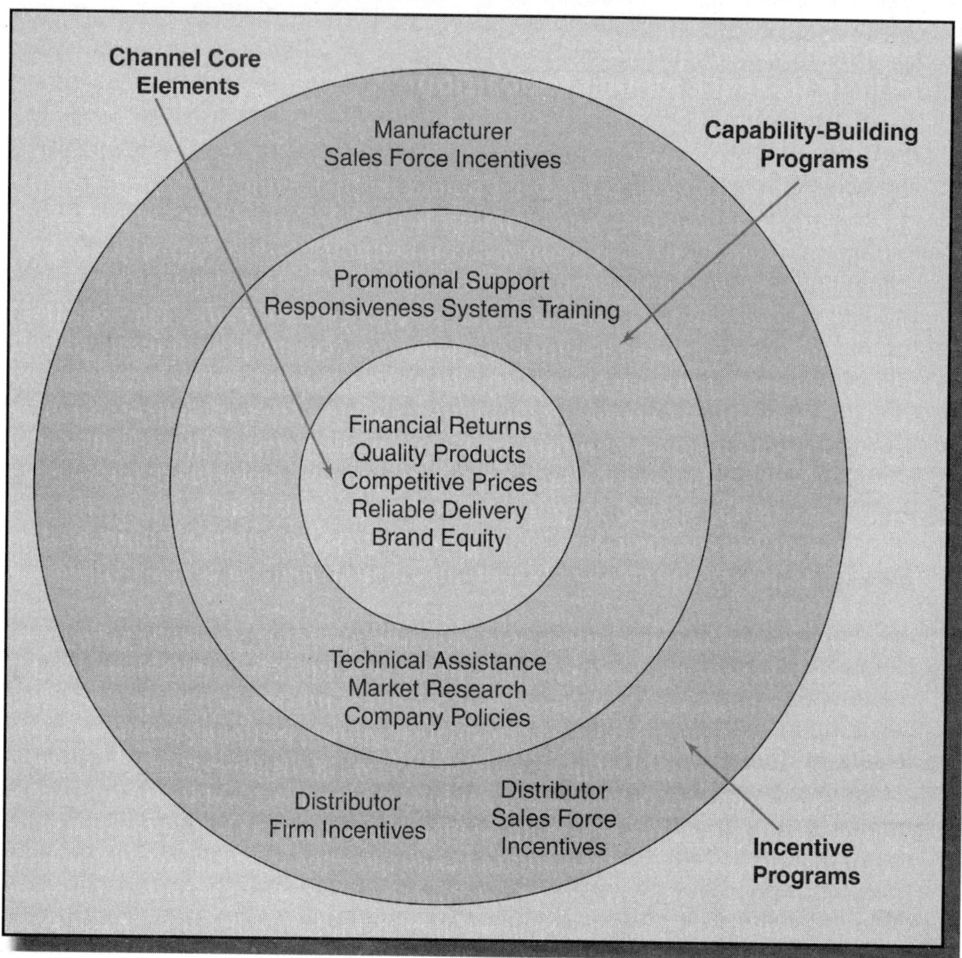

Source: James A. Narus and James C. Anderson, "Strengthen Distributor Performance Through Channel Positioning," *Sloan Management Review* (Winter 1988): 33.

three general roles in a reseller's offering. A **reseller-offering platform** is a product or service upon which the bundle or solution is assembled. It tends to be a high-turnover and lower margin item that a customer firm deliberately seeks out and scrutinizes intensely. It drives the transaction with the customer firm. A **reseller-offering peripheral** or add-on item is a component, subassembly, or complementary item that functions in conjunction with the platform. Its turnover and margins typically fall in the moderate range. A **reseller-offering accessory** is an extra, noncritical item that is often added onto a transaction without forethought. It may or may not be complementary to the platform and peripherals. Such items tend to have slower turnover but high margins. Before designing support programs, supplier managers clearly understand how their offering contributes to the reseller firm's bundles and solutions.[52]

Construct a Channel Positioning Matrix

A **channel positioning matrix** refers to a detailed comparative analysis of what a supplier provides to its resellers, what its competitors provide, and what its resellers' requirements are. Business market managers should construct a separate channel positioning matrix for each type of authorized reseller. We present a channel positioning matrix in Figure 7.9. As we see in the figure, managers begin by listing in the left-hand column the key elements of channel offerings common to the industry. In a second column, managers summarize the elements of the channel offering that resellers require. Next, they describe the supplier's current channel position and offering in the third column. Last, managers state the positions and offerings of relevant competitors in additional columns.

Some suppliers find it useful to add a column in which they construct a **best practice composite**. For each element, they list the supplier firm that provides the best program or system. It may be the supplier firm, one of its direct competitors, or a firm that markets a complementary line to the same resellers. Because it is unlikely that one firm will be the best at all elements, what results is a composite of the best practices of a number of competing suppliers. The logic for constructing a best practice composite is that resellers' experiences with all their suppliers shape their expectations of each supplier's performance. Simply being the best within the set of direct competitors may not be enough. Business market managers can benchmark the best practices of noncompeting firms that market complementary lines. In exchange, managers allow these noncompeting firms to benchmark their own firm's best practices.

The results of the channel positioning matrix analysis suggest changes for the supplier to pursue that will contribute most to a reseller value proposition. Managers might decide to bolster competitive strengths, where the supplier already does a superior job in furnishing the offering elements that resellers value. They most often pursue unfulfilled requirements—where the reseller values an offering element, yet no one in the industry comes close to delivery of an acceptable version—as the source of a distinctive, reseller value proposition. The supplier might close other gaps as a matter of "defensive" channel positioning. Importantly, they also prune support programs that resellers do not value. The supplier might pass on cost savings from such program terminations to resellers in the form of discounts or rebates. Given the intense competition in most industries today, managers are likely to find only a handful of gaps. However, managers should remember that they can establish a potent reseller value proposition with only a few points of difference.

Craft a Reseller Value Proposition and Channel Offering

Based on the value assessment and channel positioning matrix, business market managers devise a reseller value proposition using the process that we described in Chapter 4. Ideally, the reseller value proposition should reinforce the envisioned customer value proposition and intended TCE. Suppliers that serve several market segments through different types of resellers may at this point choose to develop a distinct value proposition for each type of reseller. The most potent reseller value

Figure 7.9 The Channel Positioning Matrix

	Distributors' Requirements	MicroChem Offering	CLT Equipment Offering
Channel Position	**Not Applicable**	**Low Price Leader**	**Computer Networking Leader**
Core Elements			
Functional Discount	32% off suggested resale price	32%	32%
Payment Discount	2/10/net 30	2/15/net 60	None/net 45
Quality Discount	3% on orders of 50–100 units 5% on orders of 100+ units	4% on orders of 50–100 units 7% on orders of 100+ units	3% on orders of 50–100 units 5% on orders of 100+ units
Quality Measured in Life Cycle Costs*	$225	$250	$225
Suggested Resale Price Per Unit	$35	$25	$35
Completeness of Product Line (# of complementary products)	7 out of 12 items	6 out of 12 items	7 out of 12 items
Reliability of Delivery	90% of orders filled in one week	85% of orders filled in one week	95% of orders filled in one week
National Reputation Development	$1 million in annual national televising	$750,000 in annual national televising	$1.25 million in annual national televising
Capability-Building Programs			
Promotional Support	Product literature and catalogues	Product literature and catalogues	Product literature and catalogues
Responsiveness Systems	None	None	Computerized order entry expert systems
Training	One-week sales course	One-day sales course	One-week sales course plus videotapes Three-day course on computer systems
Technical Assistance	5–10 tech reps	2 tech reps	10 tech reps Portable problem-solving computers
Company Policies Distribution Selectivity	120 distributors for United States; few per trade area	250 distributors for United States; many per trade area	131 distributors for United States; few per trade area
Return Policies	10% of annual purchases	5% of purchases	10% of purchases
Incentive Programs			
Manufacturer's Sales Force Programs	Commission on sales to distributors	Commission on sales to distributors	Bonus on sales over quota to distributors
Distributor-Firms Programs	Rebates on purchases made prior to peak sales periods	Rebates	Rebates Price reductions in orders placed by computer
Distributor's Sales Force Programs	Spiffs Annual sales contests	Spiffs	Spiffs Monthly contest based on sales and computer utilization Blazers awarded to best salesperson of the year

*Life cycle cost refers to the total costs of using a product or service over its productive lifetime.

Source: Adapted from "Strengthening Distributor Performance Through Channel Positioning," James A. Narus and James C. Anderson, *Sloan Management Review* (Winter 1988): 38, by permission of publisher.

propositions tend to be closely related to the role the supplier's offering plays in reseller bundles or solutions. For example, a supplier firm is most likely to tout the high turnover rate or increased reseller traffic when its product is a reseller-offering platform. On the other hand, if the product is a reseller-offering peripheral, the supplier firm is likely to stress the ability of the partner to cross-sell the item along with the reseller-offering platform, thus contributing to the reseller's lines per order and enhancing its transaction profitability. When the supplier firm's item is a reseller-offering accessory, managers are likely to promote its ability to unexpectedly sweeten transaction profitability. Taking these issues into consideration, managers must now reformulate their channel offering to bolster the reseller value proposition.

Devise and Pretest the Channel Offering

To reformulate a channel offering, business market managers identify key elements and determine the level that the firm is prepared to offer. Obviously, a reseller is likely to put in extra effort toward the promotion of a line that brings it outstanding profits. When an industry is highly competitive in terms of core elements offered to resellers, capability-building programs are likely to be the most useful. As an example, companies such as DuPont and Parker-Hannifin have long relied on technical training programs and market research to provide their resellers with the specialized skills and sales leads necessary to take advantage of emerging market segments.[53]

Incentive programs are least likely to result in a long-term value proposition because competitors can readily copy them. Managers should only consider them after they have completed the other two sections of the offering, and they should use incentives sparingly to reinforce the more long-lasting changes they seek in the capability-building programs. Research suggests that of the three types of incentives, those directed toward the reseller firm are preferable to those targeted at reseller employees, mostly because reseller managers want to direct the activities and efforts of their own employees.

The role the supplier's product plays in the reseller's bundle or solution provides clues as to the nature of the ideal channel offering. For example, when the supplier's product is a reseller-offering platform, perhaps the best support the supplier can offer to resellers is to aggressively use "pull" promotions to build brand preference among customer firms and steer them to reseller firms for servicing. In the case of reseller-offering peripherals, potent channel offering elements would include training on how to cross-sell the supplier's item along with the reseller-offering platform as well as incentives which reward such cross-selling efforts. Last, in the case of reseller-offering accessories, suppliers should provide merchandizing assistance as well as special deals to promote impulse buying.

Having assembled a tentative channel offering, supplier managers should pretest it to be certain that it will be effective. One way to accomplish these tasks is to formally present the offering at the firm's reseller council meeting and solicit evaluations and suggested improvements. We discuss reseller advisory councils fully in Chapter 9.

Improve Reseller Target-Marketing Efforts via Tailored Channel Offerings

By carefully crafting channel offerings, supplier managers can significantly improve resellers' target marketing efforts, while reducing the likelihood of interchannel conflict. Consider the example of a manufacturer of three lines of power saws. The first is a basic line of saws that a supplier targets at small and gypsy contractors for use in home repairs and remodeling. The supplier markets the line through home improvement centers such as Home Depot, Lowe's, and Builders' Square largely on the basis of competitive price. To ensure the performance of the home improvement centers, the supplier developed a channel offering featuring generous functional discounts that enable resellers to keep prices competitive, minimal stock-keeping units (SKUs) to reduce the resellers' inventory commitments, and instructive and eye-catching packaging that allows the product to sell itself.

The supplier sells a second line of professional saws that they target at larger contractors that specialize in building housing developments. They market the line through contractor supplies distributors. In this market segment, contractor customers require a broad line of professional saws and supplies for highly specialized applications. To support distributors, the firm created a wide range of SKUs, substantial quantity discounts that can be passed along to contractors that purchase a large number of saws annually, and cooperative advertising funds that can be used only in trade journals targeted at home builders.

For large-scale contractors that build offices and commercial buildings, the supplier markets a line of top-end saws that cut concrete and steel girders. They sell these saws exclusively through specialty cutting-tool distributors. Compared to the first two categories of resellers that make their profits primarily from the sale of products, these specialty distributors emphasize value-added services. Such services include construction-site layout design, materials processing systems planning, and recommendations on proper tool usage. For this reason, the supplier's channel offering among specialty cutting-tool distributors revolves around its distributor capability-building services. Thus, it provides a range of highly technical training programs for resellers' service engineers, joint sales calls and design assistance for key contractor customers, and a technical center staffed with engineers who can promptly answer a reseller's most difficult applications questions.

Communicate the Reseller Value Proposition

To secure the desired channel position, the supplier firm actively communicates the value proposition to resellers relying upon the full range of promotional tools available and appropriate to the industry. To sustain each value proposition, the supplier must deliver what it has promised. In addition, business market managers should reinforce the value proposition at every opportunity. Given that many of the most distinctive aspects of a channel offering are eventually duplicated by competitors, managers must constantly monitor the marketplace. They should record any competitive moves as adjustments to the channel positioning matrix. To track channel perceptions, managers should conduct reseller satisfaction studies at least annually. In Box 7.5, we present an example of the process.

BOX 7.5
An Example of Channel Positioning

Incorporated in 1997, Canon India Pvt. Ltd. is a 100% subsidiary of Canon Singapore Pte. Ltd., the world leader in imaging technologies.

In 2001, Canon India made a conscious decision to promote a pro-active channel management strategy. First, a direct Canon salesperson was installed in each state. This strategy was given a regional thrust with four regional distributors—Compuage in the west, Wellwin in the south, Supertron in the east, and Tech Pacific in the north. The regional distributor model allowed distributors to build up Canon's brand image while providing a strong regional presence.

Canon identified service as one of the key elements of the market offering that customers rated highly, along with the core product offering. However, at that time, service was extended through the Tier-1 partners who were also involved in the sales of high-end imaging devices to corporate clients. The Tier-2 partners were mainly involved in the sales of lower-end products. As part of its revamped channel management strategy, Canon graduated its Tier-2 partners to selling additional high-end enterprise solutions. The Tier-1 partners were handed the exclusive responsibility of services. They were happy with the focus on the high-margin service provided by this channel reconfiguration. Tier-2 partners also benefited from their new ability to climb up the value chain by selling high-end enterprise solutions. The empowered Tier-2 partners were instrumental in increased market penetration, while Tier-1 partners benefited from the resulting higher installed base and thus higher service revenues. As a consequence, customers received better overall support both before and after the sale.

Canon launched three incentive programs for its partner firms and partner firms' employees, under the Canon Empowered Partners (CEP) program. High-performing partners were offered free trips to overseas locations, star performers from the sales force of channel partners were rewarded, and various other partner-level incentives were provided. Canon also launched a unique channel education program, Gurukul, to enhance the skill sets of its authorized partners' salespersons. In addition, it had an agreement with an MNC bank to extend credit to the CEP, resulting in the partners' credit limits more than doubling. Canon enhanced channel equity through initiatives such as margin assurance and price fluctuation protection. This served to increase monetary returns to the resellers. Likewise, Canon followed a policy of using a single mandated reseller price for each item, thereby avoiding price wars between resellers.

These initiatives resulted in a very motivated set of channel partners. They contributed over 90% of Canon India's revenues in the year 2008. The remaining 10% was contributed by the specialized internal sales force.

There are several lessons that business marketers can learn from Canon's effective channel management strategy. Canon India has emerged as a leader in the industry by empowering its channel partners to provide value to end customers. It has sought ways to sustain and enhance channel profitability. It incentivizes star performers, including those in the channel partner ecosystem. It invests significantly in enhancing the skills of its channel partners. All this translates to better channel positioning by it. While working on enhancing its brand equity, it

(*continued*)

BOX 7.5
Continued

also takes concrete steps to enhance its channel equity, thus creating significant enhancement of reseller equity and marketplace equity.

Contributed by Amardeep Varma, U. Krishnakumar, Niloy Das, Unus Ebrahim, Vishal Sharma, and Vivek Gupta, Participants, EPGP Program, Indian Institute of Management Bangalore. *Sources:* N. Geetha, "Canon Plans Channel Expansion For Enterprise Imaging Solutions," *Channel Business, http://www.channelbusiness.in/index.php?option=com_content&task=view&id=368&Itemid=97*; "Canon Offers Singapore Trip on Laser Printer Sales," *http://www.channeltimes.com/India/News/Canon_Offers_Singapore_Trip_on_Laser_Printer_Sales/551-87955-766.html*; "Canon Successfully Executes 7th Season Of 'Wings Of Glory'," 14 March 2010, *http://www.financialexpress.com/news/canon-successfully-executes-7th-season-of-wings-of-glory/461955/*.

SUMMARY

Business marketing channels augment the customer value of a supplier's offering and create competitive advantage through the delivery of total customer experience. A TCE entails all aspects of a customer firm's encounter with a supplier. It should be a positive, seamless, and memorable interaction that matches the customer firm's purchasing requirements and preferences. Channel-related purchasing requirements pivot on immediacy of fulfillment and augmenting value-added services, whereas purchasing preferences encompasses the manner in which customers want to learn, shop, buy, and get help. Working together to implement an intended TCE, the supplier firm, resellers, and third-party service providers leverage each others' capabilities to create and share value far in excess of what they could be acting alone.

Business channel management is the process of designing a set of marketing and distribution arrangements that create superior customer value via tailored total customer experiences for targeted segments and customers, and executing those arrangements either directly through supplier firm sales forces and logistics systems or indirectly through resellers and third-party service providers or through an integrated combination of direct and indirect methods. To design superior value-adding channels, business market managers conduct a thorough customer value assessment and envision a superior value proposition. Using sourcing procedures, they reformulate their current TCE drawing upon supplier firm capabilities while leveraging the strengths of potential channel partners. Rather than just selecting from conventional direct and reseller channels, managers combine elements of the supplier firm's direct sales force, traditional resellers, innovative online formats, and third-party service providers, into more dynamic and flexible networks.

When a supplier firm chooses to serve the marketplace directly, it must furnish many of the capabilities, resources, and functions that reseller firms normally provide. To ensure that the direct channel creates the intended TCE, the supplier must build a sales force of value merchants. A value merchant recognizes the supplier's own costs and the value to the customer for each market offering and works to obtain a fair return for both the supplier firm and customer firm. To cultivate value merchants, suppliers must offer training programs, provide value-based sales tools, and construct compensation systems that reward personnel for providing value to customers. Once value merchants have been trained, suppliers deploy them to maximize profits. To physically deliver products or services to customers, supplier firms must construct an appropriate integrated logistics system with order entry and processing procedures, inventory management programs, warehouses, and delivery vehicles.

Suppliers turn to channel positioning to ensure that resellers will enthusiastically market their products and services as well as deliver the intended TCE. The approach calls for managers to identify a distinctive reseller value proposition and to devise a channel offering composed of core elements, capability-building programs, and incentive programs. That offering provides resellers with the tools and incentives necessary to create the intended TCE. Suppliers promote the reseller value proposition via advertising, sales presentations, and communications to the trade. When managers' efforts are successful, the supplier's brand equity combines with reseller equity to create competitive advantage in the form of marketplace equity. Marketplace equity represents the value that a customer firm receives from acquiring a particular supplier's offering through a particular reseller in its local trade area.

ENDNOTES

1. For the sake of simplicity and consistency, we define key marketing channel members as follows. A *supplier firm* produces the core product or service of a marketplace offering. A *reseller firm* takes the core product or service, adds value to it with augmenting products and services, and then markets the enhanced offering. We see *reseller* as less confusing than terms such as *intermediary, middleman, distributor, wholesaler,* and *dealer,* which often have industry-specific meanings and usage. A *third-party service provider,* such as a trucking firm, public warehouse, or information system vendor, furnishes additional augmenting services on a fee basis to suppliers and resellers. Finally, a *customer firm* acquires a market offering from a supplier or reseller for the customer's own use, or for inclusion into the products or services it produces.
2. Anne T. Coughlin, Erin Anderson, Louis W. Stern, and Adel I. El-Ansary, *Marketing Channels*, 7th ed. (Upper Saddle River, NJ: Prentice Hall, 2006), 2.
3. In an *indirect channel,* the supplier firm employs reseller firms to market its products and services to customer firms. In a *direct channel,* the supplier firm markets those products and services to customer firms.
4. Lawrence G. Friedman, *Go To Market Strategy* (Oxford, UK: Butterworth Heinemann, 2002).
5. Brent R. Grover, *More to the Bottom Line* (Washington, DC: Distribution Research and Education Foundation, 2004).
6. Lawrence G. Friedman and Timothy R. Furey, *The Channel Advantage* (Amsterdam: Butterworth Heinemann, 1999).
7. Friedman, 128–129.
8. Roger J. Best, *Market-Based Management*, 4th ed. (Upper Saddle River, NJ: Pearson Education, Inc., 2005): 274–277; Friedman, Chapter 7.
9. A *trade area* is the geographic area within which firms operate. Firms commonly specify their trade area as a function of the size of potential business and logistics or other resource constraints.
10. Louis W. Stern and Frederick D. Sturdivant, "Customer-Driven Distribution Systems," *Harvard Business Review* (July–August 1987): 34–41; and Louis W. Stern, Frederick D. Sturdivant, and Gary A. Getz, "Accomplishing Marketing Channel Change: Paths and Pitfalls," *European Management Journal* (March 1993): 1–8.
11. Philip Kotler, *Kotler on Marketing* (New York: The Free Press, 1999).
12. Coughlin, Anderson, Stern, and El-Ansary, *Marketing Channels*; and Gary L. Frazier and Walfried M. Lassar, "Determinants of Distribution Intensity," *Journal of Marketing* (October 1996): 39–51.
13. Friedman and Furey, Chapter 6.
14. Louis P. Bucklin, "Postponement, Speculation, and the Structure of Distribution Channels," *Journal of Marketing Research* (February 1965): 26–31.
15. Philip B. Schary and Tage Skjøtt-Larsen, *Managing the Global Supply Chain* (Copenhagen: Copenhagen Business School, 2001): 69.

16. Schary and Skjøtt-Larsen, 69.
17. James P. Womack and Daniel T. Jones, "From Lean Production to the Lean Enterprise," *Harvard Business Review* (March–April 1994): 93–105.
18. Michael Hammer and James Champy, *Reengineering the Corporation* (New York: HarperBusiness, 1993); and Bert Rosenbloom, *Marketing Functions* (Washington, DC: The Distribution Research & Education Foundation, 1987).
19. Bruce Mallen, *Principles of Marketing Channel Management* (Lexington, MA: Lexington Books, 1977).
20. Nakato Hirakubo, *An Analysis of the Japanese Market: Consumer, Distribution System, and Market Structure* (New York: Center for Applied Research, Pace University, 1992).
21. Coughlin, Anderson, Stern, and El-Ansari, *Marketing Channels*, 16.
22. Modular channels are also referred to as *deconstructed channels, virtual channels, demand networks, value-engineered channels,* and *networked channels.*
23. Charles C. Snow, Raymond E. Miles, and Henry J. Coleman, Jr., "Managing 21st Century Network Organizations," *Organizational Dynamics* (Winter 1992): 5–19.
24. Lawrence G. Friedman and Timothy R. Furey, *The Channel Advantage* (Oxford, UK: Butterworth-Heinemann, 1999).
25. *http://www.mahindra.com/Farm_Equ_sec/agribusiness.html*
26. Frank V. Cespedes and E. Raymond Corey, "Managing Multiple Channels," *Business Horizons* (July–August 1990): 67–77; and R. T. Moriarty and Ursula Moran, "Managing Hybrid Marketing Systems," *Harvard Business Review* (November–December 1990): 146–157.
27. Friedman, Chapter 7. Academics alternatively refer to these as "concurrent channels." Alberto Sa Vinhas and Erin Anderson, "How Potential Conflict Drives Channel Structure: Concurrent (Direct and Indirect) Channels, *Journal of Marketing Research* (November 2005): 507–515.
28. "McKinsey Study Backs Cost-to-Serve Wholesale Model," *CM/Circulation Management* [Internet] (Overland Park, KS: PRIMEDIA Business Magazines Media Inc., cited January 2002); Karlene Lukovitz, "McKinsey Study Backs Cost-to-Serve Wholesale Model," *Circulation Management* (January 2002): 20–26.
29. Arthur Andersen & Co., *Facing the Forces of Change 2000* (Washington, DC: Distribution Research & Education Foundation, 1992).
30. Kevin L. Webb, "Managing Channels of Distribution in the Age of Electronic Commerce," *Industrial Marketing Management* (April 2002): 95–102.
31. E-business definitions in this section are adopted from Steven Kaplan and Mohanbir Sawhney, "B2B Marketplaces," *Harvard Business Review* (May–June 2000): 97–103; Mohanbir Sawhney and Steven Kaplan, "Let's Get Vertical," *Business 2.0* (September 1999): 1–7; and Mohanbir Sawhney, "Making New Markets," *Business 2.0* (May 1999): 1–5.
32. Friedman and Furey, *The Channel Advantage*.
33. Eric Young, "Web Marketplaces that Really Work," *Fortune* (Winter 2002): 78–84.
34. Ravi Kalakota and Marcia Robinson, *M-Business: The Race to Mobility* (New York: McGraw-Hill, 2002).
35. David Arnold, "Seven Rules of International Distribution," *Harvard Business Review* (November–December 2000): 131–138.
36. International channel definitions adapted from Subhash C. Jain, *International Marketing*, 6th ed. (Cincinnati, OH: South-Western College Publishing, 2000); and Coughlin, Anderson, Stern, and El-Ansari, *Marketing Channels*.
37. Jack G. Kaikati, "Don't Crack the Japanese Distribution System—Just Circumvent It," *Columbia Journal of World Business* (Summer 1993): 34–45.
38. Philip Kotler and Kevin Lane Keller, *Marketing Management*, 12th ed. (Upper Saddle River, NJ: Pearson Prentice Hall, 2006): 676; and Coughlin, Anderson, Stern, and El-Ansary, *Marketing Channels*, 518-520.
39. Examples in this section are drawn from: James C. Anderson, Nirmalya Kumar, and

James A. Narus, *Value Merchants: Demonstrating and Documenting Superior Value in Business Markets*, (Boston, MA: Harvard Business School Press, 2007).

40. Robert S. Kaplan and David P. Norton, "Putting the Balanced Scorecard to Work," *Harvard Business Review* (September–October 1993): 134–149.
41. This discussion is based on Gilbert A. Churchill, Jr., Neil M. Ford, Orville C. Walker, Jr., Mark Johnston, and Greg Marshall, *Sales Force Management with Excel Spreadsheets*, 7th ed. (New York: McGraw-Hill/Irwin, 2003); and Andris A. Zoltners, Prabhakant Sinha, and Greggor A. Zoltners, *The Complete Guide to Accelerating Sales Force Performance* (New York: AMA-COM, 2001).
42. Benson P. Shapiro, "Close Encounters of the Four Kinds: Managing Customers in a Rapidly Changing Environment," *HBS Note 9-589-015* (Boston, MA: Harvard Business School, 1988).
43. R. S. Howick and M. Pidd, "Sales Force Development Models," *European Journal of Operations Research* (October 1990): 295–310; Leonard M. Lodish, "CALLPLAN: An Interactive Salesman's Call Planning System," *Management Science* (December 1971): 25–40; and Zoltners, Sinha, and Zoltners, *The Complete Guide to Accelerating Sales Force Performance.*
44. This section draws on Joseph B. Fuller, James O'Connor, and Richard Rawlinson, "Tailored Logistics: The Next Advantage," *Harvard Business Review* (May–June 1993): 87–98; and Donald J. Bowersox, "The Strategic Benefits of Logistics Alliances," *Harvard Business Review* (July–August 1990): 36–45.
45. Bob Deirlein, "Fleet Speak," *Beverage World* (March 1997): 106–110; and "Integrated Logistics: Journey to the Ultimate Customer," *Materials Handling Engineering* (March 1996): 63–66.
46. Fuller, O'Connor, and Rawlinson, "Tailored Logistics."
47. This section draws heavily from James A. Narus and James C. Anderson, "Strengthen Distributor Performance Through Channel Positioning," *Sloan Management Review* (Winter 1988): 31–40.
48. James A. Narus and James C. Anderson, "Turn Your Industrial Distributors into Partners," *Harvard Business Review* (March–April 1986): 66–71.
49. Kevin Lane Keller, *Strategic Brand Management*, 2nd ed. (Upper Saddle River, NJ: Prentice Hall, 2002).
50. Robert L. Steiner, "The Inverse Association Between the Margins of Manufacturers and Retailers," *Review of Industrial Organizations*, 8 (1993): 717–740.
51. We attribute this distinction to our colleague Professor Nirmalya Kumar, of the London Business School.
52. Grover, *More to the Bottom Line.*
53. Rajagopalan Sethuraman, James C. Anderson, and James A. Narus, "Partnership Advantage and Its Determinants in Manufacturer and Distributor Working Relationships," *Journal of Business Research* (December 1988): 327–347.

Section IV

Delivering Value

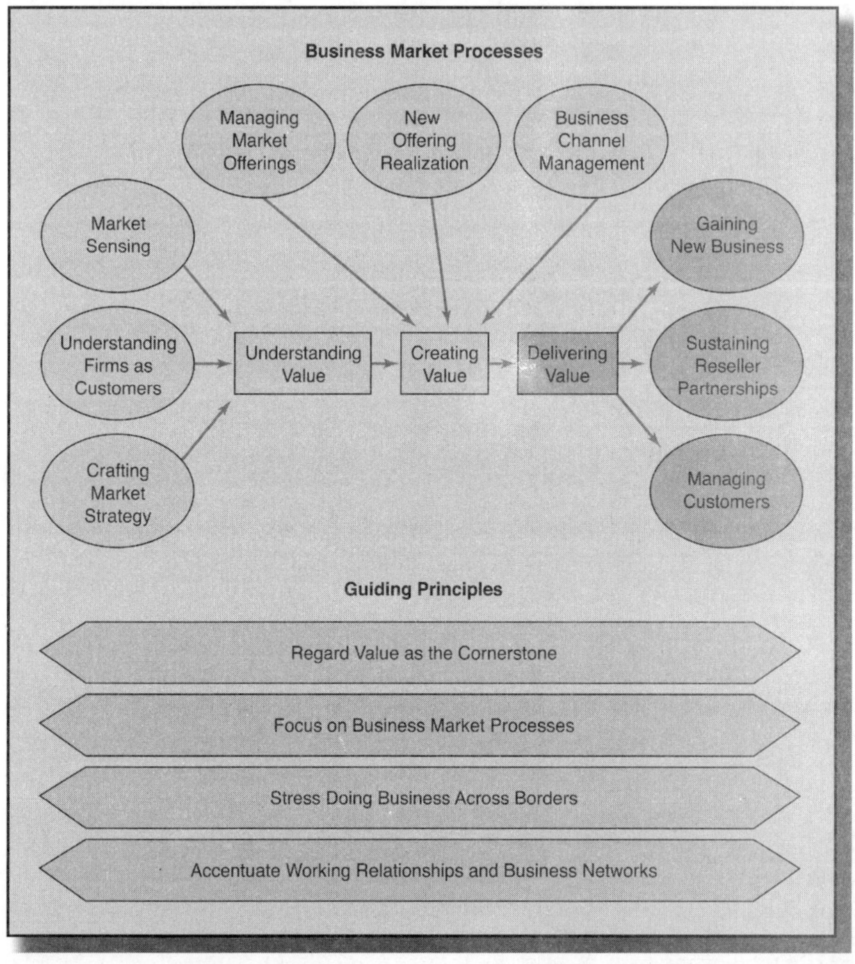

Chapter 8

Gaining New Business

OVERVIEW

According to Professor Philip Kotler, "Marketing is the science and art of finding, keeping, and growing profitable customers."[1] In the final chapters of this book, we address these tasks through three related business market processes. Gaining new business focuses on finding, qualifying, and delivering value initially to new demand opportunities, whereas sustaining customer relationships concentrates on keeping and growing profitable customers. Sustaining reseller partnerships examines all three activities when a firm chooses to deliver value indirectly to customers through a channel network of resellers and third party service providers.

Gaining new business is the process of differentiating business opportunities, prospecting for new business, assessing the fit with supplier offerings and priorities, gaining the initial order, and fulfilling it to the customer's complete satisfaction. We depict this business market process in Figure 8.1. Leading business market managers view gaining new business as a winnowing process in which a supplier firm begins with a large pool of potential customers, sequentially eliminates candidates where opportunities to deliver and share value are poor, and finishes with a significant number of profitable new business customers.

In the first section of this chapter we differentiate among the various types of potential new business that business market firms are typically faced with, that is, orders and customers, and the differential impact these opportunities could potentially have on the firms' capabilities. In the second section, we discuss the process of finding these new opportunities. We argue that business market managers must coordinate two distinct but related

Figure 8.1 Gaining New Business

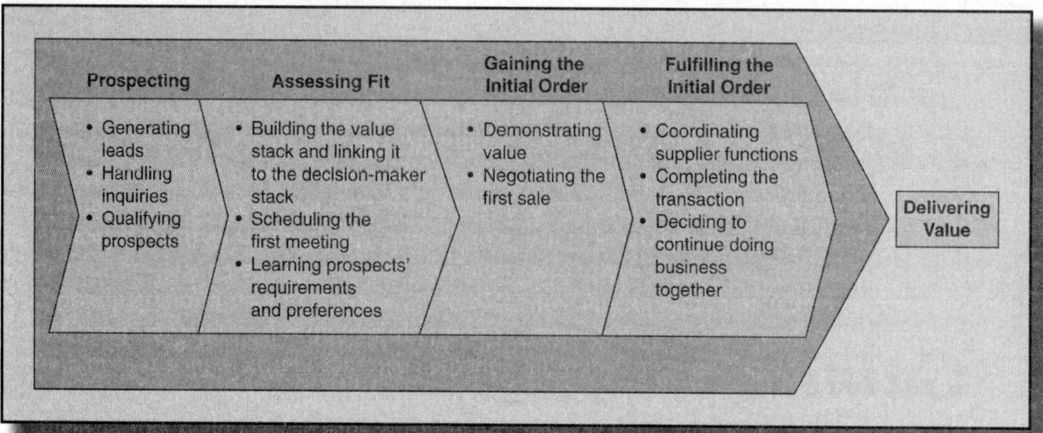

prospecting activities: generating leads via databases and prompting inquiries via integrated marketing communications. Further, we stress that suppliers must follow up and qualify leads and inquiries based on the business opportunity type. In the third section, we discuss how suppliers can learn about the customer's requirements and preferences, determine whether a match exists between customer requirements and supplier abilities, and develop a clear understanding on the value elements being offered in the initial transaction with linkages to the appropriate personnel in the buying unit. We urge business market managers to have the discipline not to dilute their limited resources pursuing potential business that does not accomplish the firm's strategic ends.

In the fourth section, we highlight different selling techniques that business market firms can use to prospect and gain the initial transaction across the different business opportunity types. Through these techniques, sales representatives can tailor the value proposition and presentation style to unique prospect requirements and preferences. Moreover, they can competently demonstrate the value of the offering and negotiate an equitable transaction with the customer firm. In the fifth section, we strongly assert that progressive supplier firms must be concerned with fulfilling the initial transaction and examine how suppliers can better coordinate functions to seamlessly fulfill initial customer requirements and provide complete customer satisfaction. Finally, in the last section, we consider follow-up actions that the supplier must take—to validate the initial designation of the opportunity type and then to realign their efforts in case of any mismatches. Consistent with guiding principles of business market management, firms should manage transactions and/or cultivate long-term relationships with customers depending on the situation so as to be able to deliver and equitably share the greatest value.

DIFFERENTIATING POTENTIAL BUSINESS[2]

Marketing strategy has always emphasized the importance of market selection. With a lot at stake, including enormous investments of resources, firms spend significant amounts of time in defining the markets and segments they should enter. We argue that firms need the same discipline when it comes to selecting individual opportunities to serve. Once a firm has carefully thought through the set of opportunity selection decisions, other questions arise. Should all opportunities be managed similarly? Or, should individual opportunities be managed to different objectives, capabilities, and resources?

Our argument is based on the fact that not all demand opportunities that business market firms are presented with are equally attractive. Further, it is important to note that every demand opportunity that a firm chooses to serve can potentially affect its overall business positively or negatively. As a result, it is sometimes better, as in all relationships in life, to say "no" at the outset. Firms need to be mindful that their choice of customers defines their skill set over time (*Whom we serve affects what we are*) and, in turn, their abilities affect their choice of customers (*What we are affects whom we can serve*).

To understand the impact of customer choice on a firm's skill set, consider Fabtek, a traditional custom fabricator of titanium structures. Through a series of opportunistic customer selection decisions, the firm had landed in an anomalous situation of operating unprofitably at full capacity with dissatisfied customers. Under these circumstances the firm was presented with four potential opportunities. The first, from Refco, Fabtek's largest customer, was an opportunity to produce in much larger volumes a product similar in design to past orders. This new order could potentially put Fabtek at risk of becoming too dependent on a single customer relationship. The second opportunity, an order from Pierce-Pike, which had done business primarily with Fabtek's competitors, represented the culmination of a four-year sales effort by Fabtek's head of sales. An order from Worldwide Paper for a standard product line presented an opportunity for Fabtek to shift from custom orders fabricated in a job-shop environment to large-volume standardized orders manufactured on a production line. The final opportunity, an order from Kathco for titanium electrodes, was a "one-shot" deal that would not tax Fabtek's specialist titanium welding capability, its current resource constraint. As one can see, each order had its own idiosyncratic issues that were likely to pull Fabtek in different directions.[3]

To understand how a firm's abilities affect the choice of customers it can serve, consider the case of Dell Computer Corporation, which eliminated channel intermediaries and sold customized PCs directly to corporate and individual customers. For this approach to work, customers had to be able to tailor systems to their requirements with minimal help from Dell. Moreover, because the products were delivered directly to them, customers had to be skilled enough to install and use their systems right the first time. As a result, Dell's direct model constrained the firm to serve only sophisticated customers, a point captured by Dell's Vice-Chairman Morton Topfer's remark, "We want to sell to only the educated customer who is buying their third or fourth PC." Dell's entire go-to-market strategy was explicitly designed to avoid the unsophisticated and focus only on the educated customers.[4]

Beyond recognizing the interplay between customer choice and skill set, business marketers need to understand that opportunities present themselves in two types: orders and customers.

Orders are predetermined, and little can be done to change them. An automotive component supplier that responds to an automobile manufacturer's request for quotation (RFQ) for the purchase of component parts is one such case. Not only the features and performance capabilities of the component part, but also the timing of delivery and quantities have been predetermined by the customer. In this situation, it might potentially be excessively expensive and very likely futile for the supplier to try to change the specifications or influence the nature, quantity, and timing of customer demand generated. When little or no effort is spent trying to create customer demand, the key to success in managing orders is discipline in effort expended in locating and sizing customer demand, then pricing appropriately to win the business and allocating resources to concurrently satisfy customer demand and maximize order profitability.

There are times when historical and future considerations prevent suppliers from taking the transactional view of orders discussed earlier. This is the case, for example, when an opportunity is part of a stream of orders. Although the nature and timing of customer demand remain beyond the supplier's control, the future implications of how a single order is bid and served need to be considered. Discipline in not trying to create customer demand is still needed, given the objective of satisfying preexisting customer demand in the best way possible, but the emphasis now is on maximizing not the profitability of the current order but that of the anticipated stream of orders. The decisions the supplier must make to ensure future revenues while enhancing the probability of securing all orders and maximizing order stream profitability include the pricing offered to the customer for each order; the level of service to be provided to and costs to serve the customer; and any concessions and ongoing efforts between orders.

For **customers**, as opposed to orders, suppliers do have to create demand. Customers might have some understanding of, but seldom know the solution to, their requirements or problems. A supplier creates customer demand by first educating the customer and then winning and satisfying the business that is generated. The resource allocation needed to win customers is typically much greater than that needed to win orders. How a customer opportunity is subsequently managed is determined by (a) the number of alternatives available to the customer, and (b) whether the opportunity constitutes a single transaction or is part of an ongoing relationship. As they do orders, suppliers serve customer opportunities that are limited to individual transactions differently than they do those that are part of ongoing streams of opportunities. Sourcing strategy affects how suppliers manage opportunities when alternatives are available to the customer. Switching costs or a supplier's excellent past performance, for example, can inhibit a customer from considering available alternative suppliers. Industrial customers that seek assured sources of supply and healthy price competition, on the other hand, routinely split their total purchases at any given time across a select set of suppliers.

Managing Single Transactions

Only when a customer is single sourcing by choice and the opportunity is restricted to a single transaction does it make sense for the supplier to directly maximize customer profitability. Firms that sell long-lived capital equipment with little or no after-sales service or spare parts requirements operate exclusively in this space.

In the presence of alternative suppliers, suppliers manage the quality of share of customer business, that is, cherry-pick the best parts of the customer's total purchase volume. This approach presumes that not all of a customer's business is equally attractive. A supplier fares better not only by picking off favorable portions of a customer's business, but also by saddling the competition with the most difficult, harder to satisfy, parts. Managed right, this can yield an additional benefit. That "they told us to give some of our business to their competition signals to us they are looking out for our interests, not just trying to make money," is how a customer is likely to interpret this approach.

Managing Long-Term Customer Relationships

When the horizon expands beyond a single transaction, a supplier's focus should become twofold: manage the current opportunity; and ensure favorable future customer behaviors. The nature of the actions taken and manner in which the current opportunity is managed are not uniform across customers, but depends on the role a customer plays in a supplier's portfolio.

Customers play different roles, for example, relative to purchase volumes, margins, and such other strategic considerations as supplier learning, showcase effects, preempting competition, and counter-cyclicality. We discuss several of these customer types in greater detail next.[5]

Volume customers purchase in large quantities and can be problematic as well as beneficial to suppliers. Because they keep production lines running, for example, large-volume customers are especially important to suppliers with high fixed costs. But their purchase volumes also make such customers powerful enough to extract price reductions and services that could potentially negate the volume benefits. Suppliers, with marginal control over price levels should focus on managing the costs to serve the current opportunity and improving the mix of customer business (if the customer uses multiple sources).[6]

Margin customers are willing to pay higher prices. Margins are the prices paid by customers less supplier costs. Among the reasons customers are willing to pay higher prices are greater perceived value, ignorance, and ineptitude. A supplier can reduce its costs to serve customers through scale economies and by minimizing customer demands and increasing its own effectiveness. Firms should manage prices paid in the current opportunity with the former type of customers and manage costs to serve the current opportunity with the latter.

Strategic consideration customers can affect suppliers' revenues and costs in a variety of ways. Supplier learning in a relationship, for example, can be a source of product feature improvements and new product innovations as well as enhance operations, logistic capabilities, and other functional areas such as marketing and sales. *Transferability* refers to a supplier's ability to leverage focal customer relationships to serve other customers more efficiently. Customers impressed with a supplier's performance, for example, are more likely to convince other customers to do business with that supplier. Similarly, suppliers develop relationships with high-profile customers that they use as showcase accounts to attract other business. Counter-cyclical customers balance dips during downturns in a supplier's business cycles. Finally, a supplier might choose to do business with a customer simply to preempt the entry of competitors. Managing strategic consideration customers is more complex than managing revenues received or costs to serve; suppliers need to monitor and manage revenues from other customers that are attributable to the focal relationship and associated changes in costs to serve other customers.

In Box 8.1, we discuss an example of how a firm decided to serve different customer types differently.

BOX 8.1
Different Customer Types Need to Be Managed Differently

Bosch Rexroth India Limited (BRIL), based in Ahmedabad, is a wholly owned subsidiary of Bosch Rexroth AG, Germany, and is part of Robert Bosch GmbH. Bosch Rexroth contributes about 12% of Bosch's approximately INR 2,32,000 crores overall turnover. Bosch Rexroth's primary products encompass hydraulics, pneumatics, AC servo drives, linear motion, and assembly technologies. The hydraulics division is further divided into industrial and mobile products. Industrial hydraulics comprises bulk products and projects. Bulk products are standardized while projects are customized systems or component products.

Hydraulic products are used in a wide variety of applications. BRIL's typical customers are corporations and government organizations that include steel plants, power plants, naval applications and offshore projects, manufacturers of injection molding machines and hydraulic presses, aviation systems and flight simulators, etc. Price is often an important criterion for awarding the contract.

Since BRIL manufactures modules used in building larger equipment and systems, its customers are often original equipment manufacturers (OEMs). It is these OEMs who in turn sell their equipment to end customers. For these end customers, price is an important decision criterion. This price pressure passes upstream to BRIL. To counter the price pressure, BRIL leverages its reputation for impeccable technical expertise to convince buyers, including governmental agencies, to raise their technical specifications to filter out low-cost/low-quality competitors. Government customers give high importance to references based on past performance, where BRIL scores highly over competitors. In order to achieve and maintain its reputation, it regularly conducts tradeshows and training programs for customer firms.

Despite its price being the highest and delivery times being the longest in the industry, BRIL is able to maintain market leadership because it quantifies and communicates value in monetary terms to the customer. It leads in energy efficiency, life expectancy (especially for critical components), operational cost, and maintenance cost. In addition to "quality," it also leads in application know-how and its after-sales support network. For many customers, the quality of after-sales support is the deciding factor in favor of BRIL. In convincing customers to look

BOX 8.1
Continued

beyond price, it argues that its products cost more despite the advantage of it being the global leader and having the highest economies of scale because BRIL truly offers superior customer value. Moreover, due to its technical pre-eminence, it is often the first company to enter new segments, such as wave research, and establish itself ahead of its competition. Until the competition catches up, Rexroth can thereby command premium pricing for such projects.

Customer relationships at BRIL depend on whether the product is bulk or project. For the former, the relations are with the dealer rather than the OEM. The company offers bulk discounts and volume incentive schemes to dealers to promote sales of commodity products. Where its systems are used by OEMs to design a product, it guarantees that the product will perform to expectation. It works jointly with the customers to obtain approvals from various governmental agencies. Since the end customer (the OEM's customer) trusts the Rexroth brand, the approvals are easier to obtain. Such service orientation is highly valued by OEMs.

Although BRIL's customer accounts in the hydraulics division were profitable when aggregated, its management had some concerns about the profitability of particular accounts. A study of the 500 customers of the hydraulics division based on a combination of the 80/20 principle (20% of customers contributing to 80% of business) and ABC analysis (A: most important customers, B: customers of medium importance, and C: least important customers) found that of all the loss-making accounts, five customers were responsible for 80% of the losses. Of these five, the division's top revenue generator also contributed to most of the losses. To redress the situation, the company investigated the cause of the losses. It found that the reason for the losses from this account was feature creep (later additions in scope) and the unwillingness of the salesperson to charge for the newly requested features. BRIL addressed the situation by working closely with the customer to standardize its configurations, slowly raising price over two years and instituting a new assembly concept to reduce time spent on welding and assembly of the product, thus reducing its cost of manufacture. Rexroth let go two of the "C" class loss-making customers who had unreasonably low-price expectations.

The outcome of the ABC analysis was customer segmentation into classes A, B, and C, based on contribution. Separate profit target guidelines were set for each class. However, the company found this gross classification by contribution margin was inadequate. It then did a second-level classification by industry, such as steel plant, power plant, machine tools, etc. Consequently, it developed a customer matrix, which revealed an important insight: sales in the machine tool segment were determined primarily by price and this segment also had a well-established competitor. The company reduced its contribution target for this segment while continuing to compete on value in other application segments. The allocation of overhead to various business lines was also rationalized. BRIL understood the strategic imperative of handling the needs of different types of customers differently, which resulted in the company's superior financial performance.

Contributed by Bhargavi Ramachandran, Debananda Pati, Rahul Shah, and Vinod Kuberkar, Participants, PGPX Program, Indian Institute of Management Ahmedabad.

Figure 8.2 The Divergent Effects of Orders and Customers

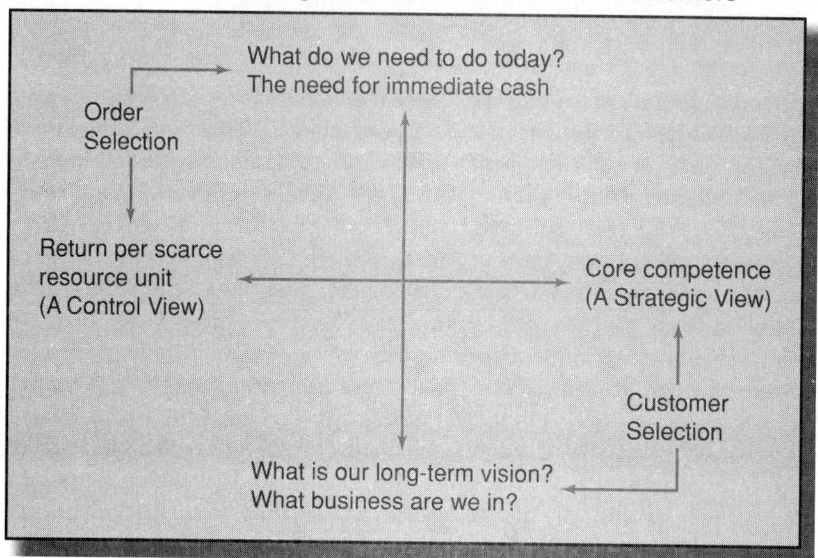

Impact of Selection Decisions on Suppliers

The divergent effects of orders and customers can wreak havoc with a supplier's organization, resources, and skills. In an ideal situation customer choice and order selection would be aligned, but in most business markets there is disconnect between the two (see Figure 8.2). Given preset demand, a supplier's decision to serve an order is typically based on availability of resources, that is, it is primarily a capacity decision. The need to create customer demand and the resources required to customize solutions for individual customers, on the other hand, tend to affect (and be affected by) the supplier's capabilities. Consequently, order selection tends to be affected by resource and capacity constraints (Where are the production bottlenecks? What are the shortfalls? What can we do in the short term?), and customer choice tends to be based on long-term strategic vision and to affect skill set and capabilities (What business are we in?).

If not managed appropriately, the disconnect between orders and customers can occasion interfunctional conflict between marketing and manufacturing, with marketing pursuing the right set of customers with no regard for the impact of its decisions on the plant and production capacities and manufacturing trying to establish discipline at order level without considering the long-term implications of its decisions for customer choice. Box 8.2 elaborates on how Bharat Forge, the world leader in industrial forgings, benefits from diligent customer selection.

BOX 8.2

Bharat Forge Ltd. (BFL) Benefits from Diligent Customer Selection

Bharat Forge Ltd. (BFL), based in Pune, has had a successful track record in acquiring major customer accounts. BFL started off in 1961 much like any other forging company of its time, with a hammer shop. However, following a series of investments and upgrades,

BOX 8.2
Continued

by the 1980s, it boasted world-class plant infrastructure. Ever since, it has targeted developed market customers. BFL has a careful process for selecting potential customers to target. Once it determines to acquire a customer, it pursues the account aggressively through a superior market offering.

The first big break came from Rockwell International (currently ArvinMeritor), the United States, which offered a contract for supplying 30% of its requirements. BFL acquired this customer through an innovative approach. BFL kept tabs on all the joint venture partners of its parent, Kalyani Group, of which one was Rockwell. When BFL heard of Rockwell's plans to shut down its forging plant in Newcastle, Pennsylvania, it reasoned that Rockwell would need to source significant supplies from outside. BFL immediately expressed interest to be a vendor for Rockwell's forging requirements. BFL realized that Rockwell's order would open the gates to many more customer accounts in the developed world. At the same time, it acknowledged the stigma prevalent then with "Indian suppliers" in the developed markets. Based on thorough research of customer requirements, it found that Rockwell was trying to minimize its inventory holding costs. It was keen on tying up with a supplier who would work closely with it on all aspects of developing forged components. BFL came up with a proposal that documented these aspects in the form of a detailed proposal. Additionally, it offered a very price-competitive bid. Rockwell found its proposal compelling, resulting in BFL acquiring its important first major customer from the United States.

This opened the floodgates for many more orders from customers in the developed world. In another example, a new manager at Metroline, the United States, recommended BFL when Metroline's existing U.S. forging supplier compromised its quality standards. Metroline contacted BFL for a proposal. BFL's response, 16 pages in length, arrived within five days. It explained, with detailed diagrams and illustrations, the key issues on which the client wanted clarity. Impressed with the proposal and the two-hour teleconference call that followed, Metroline expressed its interest in visiting the BFL production facility before making the decision to award the contract. On arrival, the Metroline team was taken around BFL's production facility. When the team reached the press shop, it observed that the part being forged at the shop was indeed for Metroline. Surprised by what they saw, Metroline executives asked the reason why BFL was making Metroline parts when the order had not even been placed with BFL. BFL believed that Metroline would be interested in finding out whether BFL was capable of manufacturing the parts required by them and instead of leaving room for doubt, BFL thought it best to undertake sample manufacture of the parts that would prove BFL's capabilities. The Metroline team carried the sample parts to their laboratory in the United States for testing. After testing, they called back BFL and told them that the program was on! Such is the aggressiveness with which BFL demonstrates its capability and relationship commitment to acquire targeted customers.

At BFL, customer relationship management is a single-minded pursuit. Often, the chief guests for BFL new plants are the CEOs of its major customer firms. This sends out strong signals of continued interest to do business with one another.

Contributed by S. Jayachandra Sekhara Rao, Participant, PGSEM Program, Indian Institute of Management Bangalore. *Sources:* Case study of Bharat Forge, *http://www.ibscdcorg/Case%20Studies/Abstracts/Strategv/Growth%20Strategies/GRS0248K; http://www.bharatforge.com/index.asp;* J. Ramachandran, Sourav Mukherji, "Bharat Forge Limited – Forging Leadership," case study developed for IIM Bangalore; Bharat Forge Annual Report 2001–02, *http://www. bharatforge.com/investers/annualreport.pdf; http://www. bharatforge.com/company/history.asp; http://www.thehindubusinessline.com/businessline/2000/03/28/stories/022818kd.htm; http://www.bharatforg.e.com/companv/ philosophy.asp.*

Prospecting for New Business Relationships

Having established the importance of being selective in the choice of business to pursue, we now discuss the nuts and bolts approach that business market firms can use to locate new business opportunities. For discussion purposes, we distinguish among three types of sources that supplier firms can use to prospect for potential opportunities to serve. **Leads** are names of possible clients that business market managers generate from computer databases. **Inquiries**, on the other hand, are customer-initiated business contacts with the supplier firm. **Prospects** are leads and inquiries that the supplier firm has qualified as having significant sales and profit potential. Thus, **prospecting** entails the related activities of internally generating leads from databases, prompting and gathering inquiries externally from the marketplace, and qualifying leads and inquiries as significant prospects. As we illustrate via the dashed lines in the prospecting "funnel" in Figure 8.3, these related

Figure 8.3 The Prospecting Funnel

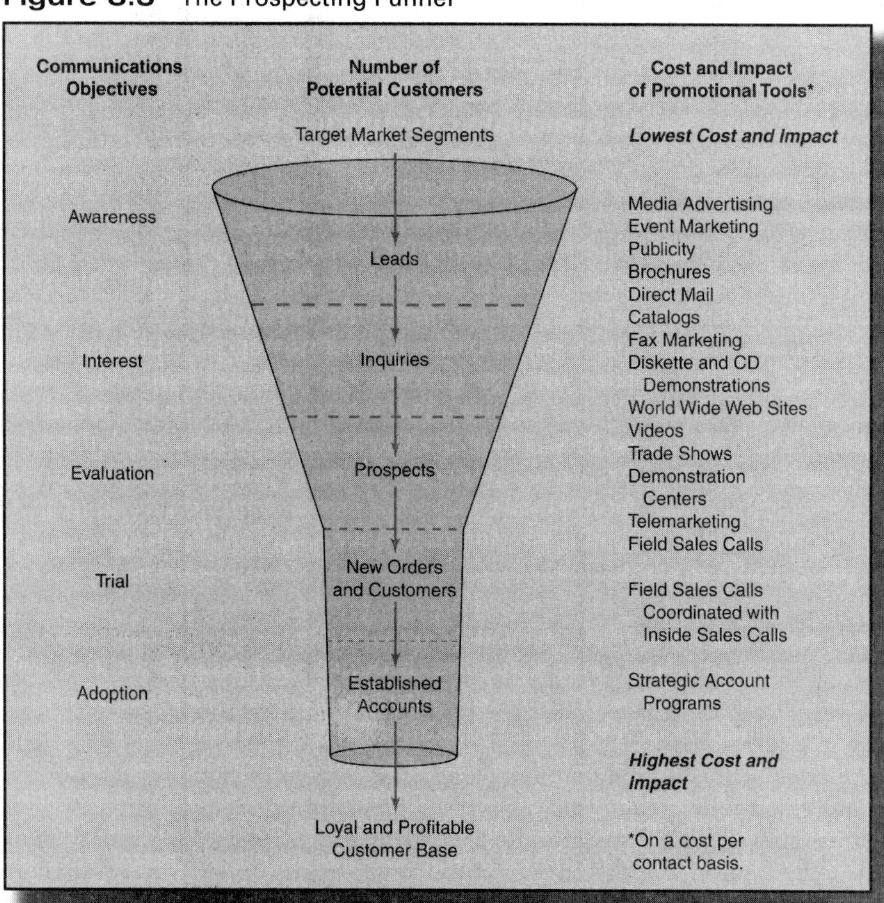

prospecting activities serve as ever finer "screens" through which only the highest potential customer firms pass.[7]

Although all prospecting efforts encompass these three activities, their nature varies as a function of the total number of potential customers, how readily the supplier firm can enumerate them, the type of market offering sold, and the firm's overall strategic intent in gaining customers. For example, an electronics company that seeks to market an innovative weather-tracking device for commercial airplanes will not have to use a computer database system to generate the names of major aircraft manufacturers. In other markets, readily identifiable potential customers may not exist. The supplier firm will have to "create" customer firms before it can market offerings to them.

Generating Leads from Business Market Databases

Conceptually, the task of generating leads from databases is deceptively simple. As we discussed in Chapter 2, the business market manager first develops a profile of the key descriptors of firms or managers in each targeted market segment. Then, using a variety of statistical programs, the manager scans readily available databases and isolates company or manager names that closely match the target segment profile. As an example, consider A/E/C Systems International.

A/E/C Systems is a small firm that runs computer trade shows for the design and construction industries. Over the years, the firm has developed a database of more than 50,000 names and addresses of construction engineers and architects worldwide. The firm obtained these names from the registration lists of previous conferences and from commercial list suppliers. Based on their experience and statistical analyses of descriptive data from past conference participants, A/E/C Systems managers have identified 39 key attributes of potential customers that are most likely to attend seminars. These encompass such things as job title, employer sales and industry, geographic location, project specialization, and primary interests. Information on each of these 39 attributes appears in the database, along with the 50,000 names and addresses. When planning an upcoming conference, A/E/C Systems managers develop a profile of desired attendees and exhibitors from a subset of the 39 attributes. Then they search the 50,000 entries for matches with the profile. The firm mails each of these leads a conference announcement, a package of personalized information, and a registration form.[8]

Unlike A/E/C Systems, most business market firms do not do a good job with lead generation. For starters, most firms have only a vague notion of their target market segments. As a result, they find it very hard to narrow their list of leads down to a manageable, high-potential group. In a 2007 survey of more than 700 professional service firms, of all the new leads these companies generated, only about 25% were found to be sales-ready, whereas 50% needed further nurturing, and the final 25% were quickly disqualified.[9] Perhaps more troubling is the fact that many suppliers' databases either are hopelessly out of date or contain irrelevant data. In the aforementioned study, only 77% of the firms could identify a general profile of the customer firms they wanted to target. Further, asked to be more specific with their target markets, only 58% could give the titles of the decision-makers they needed to reach, 55% knew the names of the specific organizations they wanted to target, and only 30% knew the names of specific decision-makers they would target in generating new leads.[10] In addition to all the complexity of the tasks involved in creating credible lists, business market firms typically also lack the statistical skills necessary to accurately probe the databases for leads. As a result, many business market firms tend to outsource the entire lead-generation process to database marketing consultants.[11]

Supplier firms that choose to do the work internally rely on a **customer relationship management (CRM) system**, which is defined as "the set of tools and processes a firm uses to identify, attract, and retain customers and to leverage its relationships with customers."[12] The heart of the CRM system is an updated, reliable customer database supplemented with market databases. A **customer database** is the supplier firm's repository for all relevant information about past and present customers. For each customer, it should contain transaction prices and profits from past orders, costs to serve, an estimate of the supplier's share of the customer's business, a forecast of potential sales, important customer firm characteristics, the names of buying team members and their roles in purchase decisions, previous account call reports, product or service applications, and relevant buying practices, policies, and patterns. Firms should further supplement their customer database with research findings from value assessments and estimates of the lifetime value of each customer.[13]

A **market database**, on the other hand, contains names of key contacts, their direct mail and e-mail addresses, corporate locations, and Web-site information, plus limited descriptive information on each competitor in the defined market. Most often, supplier firms rent or acquire such databases in the form of industry lists from commercial list suppliers. In the United States, Dun & Bradstreet, American Business Information, Database America, Trinet, R. L. Polk, and TRW are the leading list suppliers. Once managers obtain these industry lists, they commonly merge them or run them in parallel with their in-house customer database to create a comprehensive database that reflects market potential. In doing so, they eliminate duplicate entries.[14]

Prompting and Gathering Inquiries via Integrated Marketing Communications

Recent marketplace trends have altered the nature of prospecting, placing greater importance on prompting and gathering inquiries. The emergence of Internet-based search engines has made it increasingly feasible and cost effective for customers to actively search for suppliers on their own. As a result, virtually all business market firms are now using online search as a low-cost way to encourage prospects to visit their Web sites through a search engine, and leave their contact details. For example, Rackspace, a Web hosting business firm, uses online search marketing to generate more than half its new business leads. However, there is a growing consensus that online search is just another layer in a multi-channel world, and smart business marketers will have to use a combination of channels to reach prospects, establish communications, and generate inquiries.[15] One way to accomplish this task is to link prospecting activities with an integrated marketing communications plan.[16]

Use Integrated Marketing Communications to Reach the Target Market

Within the context of business market management, **integrated marketing communications (IMC)** can be defined as

> a concept of marketing communications planning that recognizes the added value of a comprehensive plan. Such a plan evaluates the strategic role of a variety of communications disciplines—for example, general advertising, direct response, sales promotion, and public relations—and combines these disciplines to provide clarity, consistency, and maximum communications impact through the seamless integration of discrete messages.[17]

IMC entails four closely coordinated activities. First, business market managers set sequential communications objectives, often relying on one of the many response hierarchy models to guide the process. **Response hierarchy models** describe the cognitive, affective, and behavioral stages that a customer goes through during the purchasing process. For example, Rogers' Diffusion-Adoption Model proposes five: awareness, interest, evaluation, trial, and adoption.[18]

Second, managers develop a complementary and cost-effective mix of promotional tools to achieve each communications objective. For example, targeted e-mails, online banner advertising and industry/trade magazine advertising are well suited for generating awareness; trade shows and exhibitions, online white papers, technical brochures and Webinars generate interest; product samples and special discounts prompt trial; and the sales force can persuade customer managers to adopt the product as part of their firm's specifications. The manager's choice of specific promotional tools is tempered by cost considerations. Typically, tools with the lowest cost per contact such as mass media advertising have the least impact, whereas high-impact tools such as a sales call have high costs per contact. As Figure 8.3 indicates, when seeking new business, managers are likely to begin with lower-cost and lower-impact promotions to generate inquiries and progress to higher-cost and -impact promotions targeted toward their best prospects.[19]

Third, as we discussed in Chapter 4, business market managers create a value proposition and communicate it through a variety of promotions vehicles. Consider the case of Greif Incorporated. Greif produces fiber drums, plastic drums, and intermediate bulk containers for food products and chemicals manufacturers. Rather than competing on a price-per-container basis, Greif markets complete packaging systems. Greif's value proposition, *total cost-based packaging* (TCBP), promises that its systems can significantly reduce a customer's total costs of packaging. Greif account managers communicate TCBP via promotional brochures that highlight potential cost savings, videotapes that demonstrate how Greif containers save money, and presentations in which they report cost-of-use analysis findings.

The final challenge of IMC is to synchronize the efforts and build consistency of messaging across all the online and offline communication channels used as business marketers shift more of their budgets to evolving online digital channels. In fact, firms such as Intel and Microsoft expect more than 50% of their marketing spending to be online by 2010.[20] With a myriad of online and offline communication options, business market firms are faced with the challenge of devising complex multi-channel

IMCs that can reach as many customers and prospects as possible without diluting the overall impact of the campaign and the brand equity over time.[21]

Encourage and Process Inquiries

To cost-effectively stimulate inquiries from specialized target markets, business market managers have typically used direct response advertisements (DRAs) placed in highly focused industry magazines or trade association (or special interest group) Web sites. DRAs are print or online promotions that feature a special offer and a request for the reader to contact the supplier for "further information." The supplier includes either a business reply card (BRC), a toll-free telephone number, or a Web site address to facilitate inquiries.[22]

To qualify internally generated leads, business market managers typically tend to use direct mail in the form of newsletters and information packets to communicate with internally generated leads. For example, Panasonic's Factory Automation (PFA) Division produces two newsletters. *Automation Line* is a four-page, two-color newsletter it mails quarterly to leads identified from Panasonic's *market* database. The newsletter contains general-interest stories and basic information on Panasonic products. Panasonic managers use the newsletter to prompt inquiries via BRCs or toll-free numbers during market development and diversification initiatives. The PFA Division mails *The Panasert Technical Bulletin* to Panasonic customers that have made major capital investments in Panasonic factory automation technology. Managers base these mailings on the firm's *customer* database. In contrast to the first newsletter, the *Bulletin* contains detailed, technical information on the productive use of Panasonic products, changes in automation technology and processes, product and engineering developments at PFA, and new PFA products. PFA managers use the *Bulletin* to encourage inquiries during market penetration and product development efforts.[23]

With the growth and maturity of online marketing, business marketers are experimenting with mixing online and traditional media channels and moving beyond just advertising, direct mail, and telesales to encourage and process inquiries. For example, Crossbeam Systems, a company that markets network security appliances, uses social networking coupled with a multi-touch e-mail strategy to spur interest from prospects. The company picks up leads at the local level through 150 to 200 Webinars and in-person events such as seminars, luncheons, and dinners. E-mail is the primary way Crossbeam invites prospects to these events, working with channel and application partners to assemble invitation lists. For Webinars the average list of invitees might number in the tens of thousands, whereas an in-person dinner at a nice restaurant, for example, might only draw a few hundred, depending on how targeted the topic is. E-mail invitations are sent twice. Once people register, they get another e-mail with details about the event location and time. A reminder goes out 48 hours before the function. Personal interviews during the events and Webinars help the further qualify the prospect quality.[24]

In another example, Internet security software provider Computer Associates (CA) launched an IMC in 2006 that involved a combination of online and offline channels. A direct mail pack was sent to prospects, inviting them to attend a seminar. Once they had signed up, prospects were then sent an e-mail with a link to an exclusive Web site where they could find further information on the seminar alongside an invitation to dinner with some of the speakers. Recipients could also tailor their particular interests via the Web site, after which there were e-mail updates alerting them to relevant product news.[25]

IMC plans also rely on trade shows and exhibitions to stimulate inquiries. These interactive media formats typically feature product demonstrations and educational sessions for prospects while providing suppliers with access to tens of thousands of active and informed businesspeople from all functions in one location and in a short period of time.[26] The Internet allows business market managers to take this format to the next level. For example, a content-rich Web site serves as an interactive "electronic trade show," where potential customers can enter at will, 24 hours a day, 7 days a week (24 × 7), from anywhere in the world, search and download company information and product specifications, read promotional materials and answers to frequently asked questions (FAQs), and perhaps even obtain price quotes. Often the site sponsor provides a toll-free telephone number for customers to call to speak with a salesperson or place orders.

Moving further down the purchasing process are online catalog sites that not only contain product information and price lists but also provide interactive service and order entry systems to customers. Catalog sites are effective in generating inquiries as well as orders for generic products. Forward auction sites that companies such as Grainger and GXS run, as well as B2B exchanges such as Covisint, ChemConnect, and Exostar, similarly furnish opportunities for prospective customers to find suppliers and to acquire products and services online. They are often useful in marketing leverage and bottleneck items.[27]

Foster Strong Brands

Even though generating inquiries is an important short-term objective of IMC, business market managers should never lose sight of a more important strategic goal—bolstering brand equity. As we discussed in Chapter 4, brands play two critical roles in business markets. In the case of generics and leverage items, purchasing managers may limit their "choice set" in buying situations to well-known brands in order to reduce risk and time-related costs. In the case of critical and bottleneck items, purchasing managers may use a brand name as a shorthand descriptor for previously demonstrated value. This practice saves them time and effort, in that they don't have to complete a value assessment each time they acquire an offering. Thus, a strong brand may be the most effective tool that the business market manager has to gain customers. As a result, supplier firms should use every IMC program to build awareness and to reinforce the value of their brands.[28]

Current Challenges in Designing Effective Integrated Marketing Communications Campaigns

There is considerable rethinking going on about the use of e-mails in business market firms' IMC. Issues of e-mail data decay, the reality that up-to-date e-mail lists are actually scarce, and stringent spam filters at customer sites that trap bulk e-mails have forced business marketers to be innovative in integrating e-mail campaigns with other traditional communication media. Research carried out by Experian, for example, shows that starting with direct mail, then following up with a call, a targeted and customized e-mail, and a subsequent call is one of the most effective ways of increasing response rates and improving the quality of leads generated.[29]

A dramatic shift is already in the works in the use of online search as part of business market firms' IMC. In the early years, leveraging search engines to uncover customer leads involved a combination of buying keywords from the search engine for sponsored links and optimizing the company's own Web assets to be ranked highly by the search engines. Major online search engines now offer so-called "blended search" interfaces that expand the content of a search results page beyond text links to many kinds of content, such as maps, video, images, audio, news, and blogs. For example, Google announced its Universal Search interface in May 2007 that offered such blended search capabilities. A month later, search engine Ask.com launched Ask3D that makes a variety of content available on a single page of search results. These next-generation search capabilities are forcing business market managers to begin to optimize much more than text elements on their Web sites and include other types of content such as videos and podcasts.[30]

Business market firms are also beginning to experiment with other Web 2.0 applications including blogs, podcasts, social networks, and virtual worlds. For example, Intel has a presence in virtual world Second Life, where it holds virtual events and press conferences. It also regularly uses blogs, podcasts, online video, and social networks to connect with its prospects.[31]

Qualifying Leads and Inquiries

Business market managers typically tend to immediately pass along internally generated leads and externally gathered inquiries to the field sales force. This rush to pass results in unqualified, lower quality leads. As a result, it is not surprising that as many as 70% of the leads generated by marketing tend to be ignored by the sales force.[32] With the average cost of a sales call ranging from $250 to $500, and the average "yield" from leads hovering between 1% and 2%, it is imperative that companies qualify leads and inquiries as prospects early in the process.

To qualify a lead or inquiry, the supplier (or contracted third parties) contacts the potential customer via direct mail, fax, e-mail, or telephone and asks a series of preliminary questions to confirm that the firm has significant sales and profit opportunity.[33] When Actuate Corporation, a software provider for enterprise reporting applications, introduced customer self-service software for financial firms in 2005, it discovered that key contact managers didn't carry the same job or function title across firms in its prospect list. To build a new list of qualified prospects, Actuate started with a purchased list of the top 450 financial-services companies and found the right prospects by using secondary resources or by calling the companies directly.[34]

At the center of qualifying efforts is a brief questionnaire. Experts urge suppliers to ask all prospective clients at least five questions: (1) Is the potential customer currently using a similar product or service? (2) Is the firm considering purchasing the offering? (3) When does the firm plan to execute the transaction? (4) Is the individual contacted the ultimate decision maker? and (5) Has funding been approved for the acquisition?[35]

A supplier has several options for distributing the qualifying questionnaire. Managers can embed it on direct-response advertisements or direct mail pieces within BRCs so that inquiries prequalify themselves when they request further information. To qualify prospects that use online channels, the supplier can require all visitors to complete the questionnaire during "registration" as a prelude to gaining access to Web site information. Another approach that is gaining popularity is fax or e-mail qualification. Here, the supplier faxes or e-mails the questionnaire to the lead or inquiry, often along with a specification worksheet. In turn, the potential customer faxes or e-mails the forms back to the supplier. Perhaps the most common method, and definitely the preferred one for high-potential accounts, is telephone qualification. Using an automated script, a telemarketing rep prompts a potential customer through the questions and probes for additional information.

Over a period of time, market researchers from the supplier firm should evaluate questionnaire responses and develop a scheme for prioritizing prospects. Often, researchers rely on statistical tools such as discriminant analysis to sort accounts based on sales and profit potential and the opportunity for the supplier to deliver value. For example, Belden Wire & Cable Company, a U.S.-based specialty steel supplier with annual sales of approximately $750 million, devised a ranking matrix that rates prospects as "hot," "warm," or "cold." Each category is based upon the prospect's responses to a qualification questionnaire, past sales history with Belden, expected product usage, and current wire and cable purchases. Now when Belden marketing personnel qualify leads or inquiries, they designate them as hot, warm, or cold prospects based on ranking matrix criteria. Then they turn hot prospects over to the field sales force and warm prospects over to the telemarketing unit for follow-up.[36]

We conclude this section with an observation. Progressive business market managers encode all pertinent information they gain during lead generation, inquiry gathering, and prospect qualification in the firm's CRM databases. In this way, they upgrade and refine the databases and ensure that the firm's future prospecting efforts will be more productive.

Getting the Sales Force to Follow Up with Prospects

As discussed earlier, the lack of follow-up by the sales force on leads generated by marketing is one of the key reasons for the failure of many firms' prospecting efforts.[37] Clearly, to improve the yield from prospecting, suppliers must gain the commitment and support of the sales force. To do so, business market managers must create programs and systems for the sales force that deliver four critical elements: knowledge, motivation, experience, and sales support.[38]

Provide Knowledge to Create an Informed Sales Force

It goes almost without saying that sales representatives must possess sufficient product and market knowledge to be successful. This knowledge is particularly important when product development, market development, and diversification strategies call for reps to sell new products or penetrate new markets. Furthermore, sales reps may require cutting-edge selling skills to gain new customers. Logically, business market managers gain sales force commitment first and foremost by providing training on product and market knowledge as well as selling skills.

Sales personnel often attribute their failure to follow up with prospects to a lack of understanding of the role that it plays in overall company strategy. All too often, reps are left "out of the loop" when prospecting programs are introduced and explained. To remedy this problem, business market managers if not senior management must keep the sales force informed about how following up with prospects fits into the firm's goals and strategies. Some companies create sales advisory councils to do so. A sales advisory council is a cross-functional group comprising respected salespeople, product managers, direct marketing personnel, advertising agency account representatives, and customer service personnel, as well as senior managers. The council meets periodically to discuss proposed company goals, strategies, and programs and to suggest ways to integrate interdepartmental efforts. By participating in council meetings, sales personnel gain an appreciation for their role, contribute to the design of corporate plans, and commit to following up on leads and inquiries.[39]

Motivate Sales Representatives to Follow Up

Sales representatives, as well as other professionals, tend to complete tasks they are paid to do. Therefore, one of the strongest ways to motivate them to follow up on prospects is to link their compensation packages to new account development. To do so, business market managers devise a series of activity quotas linked to prospecting. These quotas might include such things as the number of sales calls on prospects to be made per quarter, number of new accounts to be gained, and sales or turnover to new accounts. In turn, managers tie performance to base salary increases or to bonuses. In general, the larger the salary component or bonus linked to the quota, the more time reps will devote to follow-up.[40] Having instituted a comprehensive lead qualification process to generate high-quality leads, Gates Corporation, an industrial power transmission equipment manufacturer, then achieved considerable success by instituting an incentive program to get reps to follow up on 100% of their leads.[41]

To inspire sales force efforts, business market managers often involve salespeople in the planning and design processes for prospecting programs. For example, at Motorola, managers actively seek continuous two-way dialogue with all salespeople concerning lead generation and inquiry-gathering efforts. Before any new program is announced, managers contact all sales representatives by mail, by telephone, or in person. Sales reps learn the details of the program, its purpose, the target audience, timing, and how resulting prospects should be handled. More important, business market managers ask salespeople to share their thoughts on the proposal and to offer suggestions. Motorola managers make it a point to implement as many sales force recommendations as are feasible. Once programs have been introduced, Motorola managers maintain sales force enthusiasm by providing "extra" local support in the form of increased direct mail, advertising, and trade show coverage to sales reps who actively participate. Finally, Motorola gives the sales force "the credit" for prospecting program success, which serves as a potent social recognition or reward for outstanding efforts. To do so, managers publish case histories and success stories in company newsletters.[42]

Focus on Quality and Timeliness of Leads

Pundits claim that many salespeople fail to actively pursue prospects because they require "cold" calls. After all, few salespeople really like making cold calls. For business market managers, solving this problem demands that they remove the "cold" from the call. The obvious way is to qualify the prospect well in advance. Sales reps at Draeger Medical, a medical instruments manufacturer, were reluctant to follow up on trade show leads they were provided with—a result of the fact that, historically, over

80% of such leads were dead-ends. To solve this problem, the firm decided to use a telemarketer to follow up on the leads and inquiries generated at trade shows. The telemarketer's calls achieved two objectives, both qualifying the lead and also providing timely, consistent follow-up to contacts made at the trade show. In the end, the sales team received only 200 qualified prospects, down from the original list of more than 700 inquiries, which included full contact information, notes about the conversation, and a ranking that indicated how hot the lead was. The new qualified set of leads was very well received by Draeger's sales reps, who now were focused on making appointments only with high-quality prospects, going to the appointment and closing the business, rather than trying to find a couple of needles in a haystack.[43]

Give Sales Representatives Experience Dealing with Prospects

Suppliers should give their sales reps plenty of practice so that they feel at ease dealing with prospective new customers.[44] A number of innovative training programs are useful here. To begin with, sales managers can create role-playing situations by having sales reps make prospecting calls on the firm's own purchasing department or on managers from cooperative customers. Some firms videotape such calls, using them to work with trainers to build and refine selling skills. Then salespeople meet as a group to critique one another and vote for the one they felt did the best. The sales manager reinforces the process by providing some reward, either social recognition or a small remuneration, to the winner.

Another proven training approach is to use field joint sales calls as a transition to field sales competency. The supplier has each field salesperson make calls with a technical specialist or a sales manager, who takes a less active and more supportive role as the calls progress, letting the field person work with a "technical safety net." Of course in both of these approaches, sales managers must provide constructive feedback on progress and coaching. In Chapter 9, we further discuss the importance of coaching to sales force and marketing channel performance.

Furnish Abundant Sales Support

A final way to gain sales force commitment is to provide reps with sales support that makes following up with prospects an easier task. Traditionally, such support came in the form of market research, collateral materials, and technical information. Emerging information technologies and communications media enhance not only the quality but also the availability of sales support.

Baan, the ERP software and Internet-enabled business solutions group of London-based Invensys, PLC (annual sales of more than $11 billion) furnishes its sales personnel with an online system, *Publish on Demand*, which enables them to customize brochures for prospects. Following preliminary discussions with a prospective client, a Baan salesperson can go online to a company-restricted Web site. There, the salesperson finds templates for solution-specific brochures along with an inventory of photographs and standardized paragraphs. Using his or her knowledge of customer requirements and preferences, the salesperson can electronically tailor a brochure by inserting and editing desirable paragraphs and photos on a template. Because company policy requires that each brochure conclude with a value proposition, the salesperson can create a proposition specifically for a prospect. When the draft of the brochure is done, the salesperson electronically sends it to the director of marketing and communications for reviewing, editing, and printing. According to Baan managers, the final brochures are available in about two days. Now, when a Baan salesperson gives an important sales presentation to a prospect, he or she can distribute a customized brochure to listeners.

Progressive firms are now also using CRM systems to improve sales force productivity. The most popular and effective CRM modules address lead distribution, prospect sales cycle tracking, contact management, product configuration, pricing, call reporting, and territory management. When deployed effectively, these CRM modules allow all supplier employees who "touch" the prospective customer to know in real time what actions the firm has taken for each prospect, what further steps need to be taken, and what support and cooperation will be needed to land the account.[45]

After refining the list of qualified prospects to those that the supplier firm cannot serve exclusively via indirect means such as catalogs, direct mail, the Web, or resellers, the business market manager instructs either a field or inside salesperson to initiate direct contact, or "sales calls." Through these calls, the salesperson assesses the opportunity to deliver and equitably share value and, ideally, takes the first steps in building a long-term business relationship. In these initial contacts, the rep will likely find significant diversity in selling situations across the pool of prospects. These selling situations vary by industry and within an industry as a function of each prospect's philosophy of doing business, purchasing orientation, purchasing portfolio matrix category, technological sophistication, capabilities, and market offering usage and applications.[46]

Recognizing the variation in selling situations, sales professionals practice **adaptive selling**, or "the altering of sales behaviors during a customer interaction or across customer interactions based on perceived information about the nature of the selling situation."[47] Of these behavioral changes, modifying the sales approach is the most pertinent. Salespeople can also alter their communication style, for instance becoming more or less technical, to better match a purchasing manager's competence and personality. They can also modify message content, perhaps varying emphasis placed on certain offering benefits. Last, salespeople can change their call strategy by deviating from the call plan.[48]

Assessing Fit*

Having qualified the leads, irrespective of whether it is an order or a customer, to make a detailed assessment of the fit between the opportunity and the firms' skills, suppliers need to first understand the value they can potentially create in the given situation. The supplier's objective is to link the costs of creating value to the revenues generated, just as the customers are likely to trade off the value of the benefits being offered against the price being asked. In answering this question, the supplier might also be able to answer the subsequent question of which opportunities should be pursued further, and which abandoned?

*This section is adapted from Das Narayandas, "Building Loyalty in Business Markets," Harvard Business Review (September 2005): 131–139.

Understanding and Communicating Value

Digital lighting pioneer Color Kinetics Inc. (CKI) had a number of options for developing a value proposition to pitch its diode-based intelligent lighting systems as a replacement for incandescent and fluorescent-bulb designs used by commercial customers.[49] An example of the firm's product would be the multicolored "Loews" blade sign at New York's Times Square that is 60 feet tall by 8 feet wide and visible up to six blocks away. A purely economic case could be made using benefits such as bulb replacement (in excess of 100,000 hours of use versus a few thousand hours for incandescent bulbs), reduced power consumption (diodes consume a fraction of the power consumed by equivalent incandescent and fluorescent bulbs), and lower equipment costs (for diodes, standard power supplies were sufficient; incandescent bulbs needed high-voltage power systems). CKI could also focus on product attributes; the deep saturated light, color washes, cross-fades, and strobe lighting effects that were possible using the 16.7 million color shades generated by diode-based lighting systems permitted lighting designers to create signs that were more pleasing to the eye. CKI realized that these latter benefits were not as easily quantified and their value was more difficult to communicate to customers. Nor was it certain that customers, unless they experienced these benefits, would accept a suggested value.

As the CKI example illustrates, a supplier's understanding of and ability to deliver the benefits it offers, when in pursuit of a prospect, is but one part of the equation. It is also important that a supplier take into account the customers' (or *prospects'*) ability to comprehend and appreciate the value offered in terms of the various individual benefits. Benefits that customers or prospects fail to perceive or to believe in are unlikely to enter into their value equations and thereby generate a willingness to pay a price for them.[50] This dyadic perspective suggests four types of customer benefits as shown in Figure 8.4.

Marketing is often called the art of creating, extracting, and delivering customer value. It is important to add "communicating the value created in a timely manner" to this definition. When customer benefit types are prioritized across the various combinations of opportunities, the following general rules emerge.

- When pursuing orders, focus on economic, tangible benefits and leverage market reputation and brand equity (if available) to create differentiation.
- Acquire new business by first establishing competitive parity on economic, tangible benefits and use non-economic, tangible benefits to differentiate your offerings.
- Build strong customer relationships and ensure the continuity of order streams by migrating customer focus from economic and non-economic, tangible benefits and toward non-economic, intangible benefits.

Once they understand the customer benefit types, the process of quantifying the value, that is, the benefits, and the decisions of which set of customer benefits to communicate (and to whom) are complicated by a number of factors peculiar to business markets including:

- Complex value propositions
- Business purchases being made by complex purchasing units that employ multistage purchase processes

Figure 8.4 Typology of Customer Benefits

Typology of Buyer Benefits

Supplier's Ability to Communicate the Benefit to the Customer (Hi → Lo) / Benefit type (Hi → Lo)	Hi	Lo
Economic Benefits (Hi)	Economic, Tangible Benefits Focus on comparing with current alternatives available to customer – show superior price to performance.	Economic, Intangible Benefits Burden of proof is on the supplier. Typical approaches–benchmark studies, pilot tests, or guarantees to offset customer risk.
Non-economic Benefit (Lo)	Non-economic, Tangible Benefits Focus on building market reputation and brand image.	Non-economic, Intangible Benefits Not a viable option for acquiring customers, but the glue that holds buyer-seller relationships together over time.

- Individual members of the customer's purchasing unit typically being exposed only to pieces of suppliers' total value propositions

Business market firms will find the *Value Stack* a framework for systematically addressing these complexities and efficiently quantifying and communicating the value created.

Building the Value Stack

The *Value Stack* depicted in Figure 8.5 helps suppliers mobilize and communicate value by stacking the benefit elements one on top of the other. This both facilitates suppliers' understanding of the level and importance of benefits being offered and captures the essence of supplier efforts to communicate to customers the value of their offerings.

To successfully quantify and communicate value, suppliers must identify the motivations and power bases of all of the purchasing unit members as well as the specific concerns of these individuals and, consequently, the value elements on which each is focused.

To help companies manage that process, one can link the value stack to a purchase decision-maker stack (Figure 8.6). Every supplier must list all the benefits it offers, placing the more important at the base of a stack. This exercise, we find, facilitates marketers' understanding of the relative significance of benefits they offer. The supplier should then create a stack of purchase decision makers, listing the main concerns, motivations, and power bases of each member of the purchase committee, and place it beside the

Figure 8.5 The Value Stack

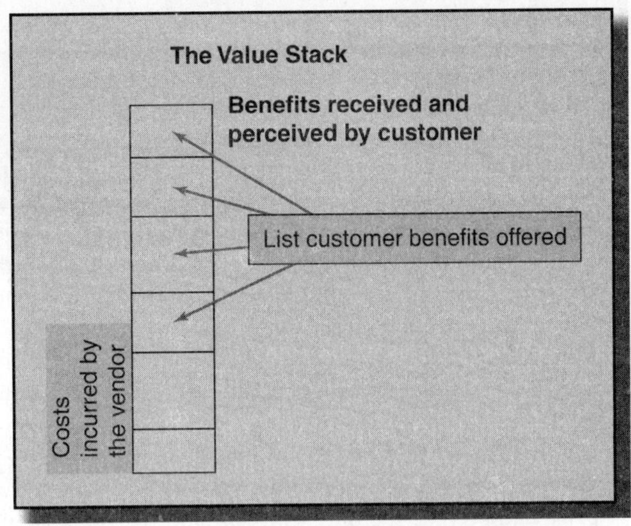

Figure 8.6 Linking the Value Stack to the Decision-Maker Stack

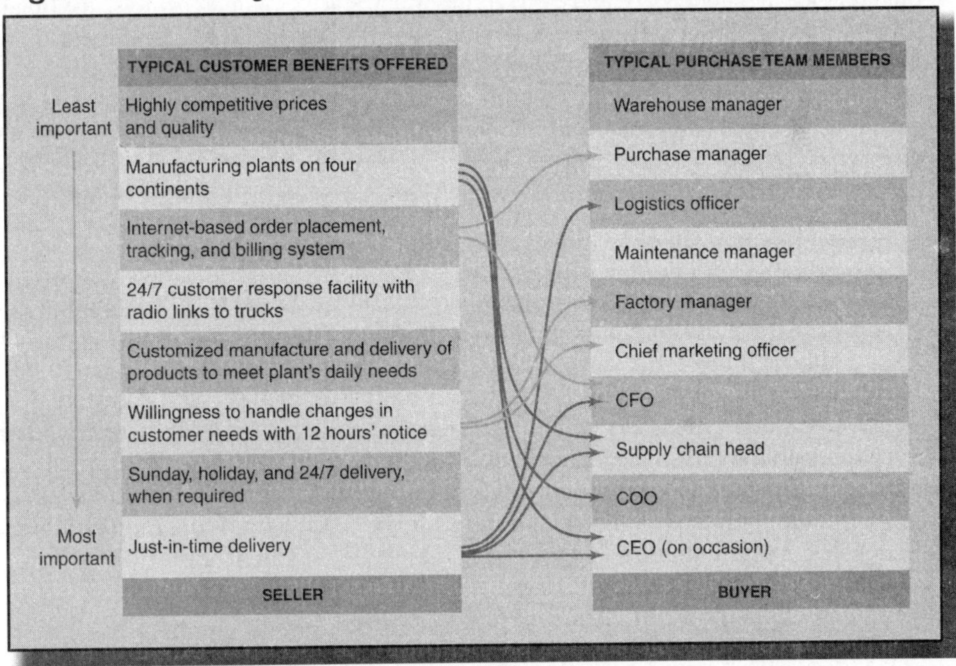

Source: Das Narayandas, "Building Loyalty in Business Markets," Harvard Business Review (September 2005): 131–139.

value stack. By linking the two stacks, the supplier can systematically tackle each decision maker's concerns and communicate how it will meet his or her specific requirements. Marketers must also brief each customer manager about the concerns of the other people in the stack, as well as the solutions the supplier proposes, so that the entire committee gets the full picture. Box 8.3 provides details on how Kone, an elevator manufacturer,

BOX 8.3
The Benefits of Linking the Value Stack to the Purchase Decision Maker Stack

In 1996, the $2.5 billion Kone introduced an elevator system in Germany that was superior to other products in three ways. The MonoSpace was more energy efficient, its motor didn't have to be housed in a rooftop structure, and its installation and maintenance costs were much lower. However, Kone had traditionally been a low-end player and had marketed its products only to contractors.

The performance of the top five elevator systems in the market being roughly the same, price had become the only differentiator. In this environment, Kone wanted to charge a premium for the MonoSpace and decided to study the market afresh to figure out a way of doing so. The company found that decisions about elevators were made jointly by owners, architects, structural engineers, and building contractors. Owners were interested in keeping project costs low and, to a lesser extent, in minimizing maintenance costs; architects were interested in the elevator's aesthetics and design; engineers worried about how elevators affected buildings' structural integrity; and contractors, the company knew, sought to reduce the costs of installing elevators. Kone began its marketing campaign by educating owners about the MonoSpace's lower operating and maintenance costs and by explaining its design benefits to architects. When Kone's executives met with purchase teams, they found that most engineers were neutral because the new product didn't affect buildings' structural integrity. Architects sold the MonoSpace's value to owners, and, together, they usually convinced contractors to install the new product. Kone found it tough to reinvent its selling process to communicate the MonoSpace's benefits. But when it succeeded in doing so, the company doubled its share of the German elevator market in three years.

was able to increase its marketing effectiveness and grow sales by linking the value stack to the purchase decision maker stack for its MonoSpace elevator products.

Although the value stack can help the suppliers monitoring changes in the different customer benefits, the level of each benefit as perceived by the customer, and the link to different members of the customer purchasing unit while accommodating for new benefits and purchasing unit members, it still does not help the supplier decide on how much effort to expend in maintaining or growing a relationship over time. To do so, the supplier needs to be able to calculate the returns on its ongoing efforts in a relationship. We will discuss this approach in greater detail in Chapter 10.[51]

ORGANIZING THE SELLING EFFORT

Having determined the nature of the opportunity, business market firms need to organize the selling effort. Consultants Rackham and DeVincentis distinguish between three sales approaches: transactional, consultative, and enterprise selling. **Transactional selling** focuses on gaining an order as quickly as possible. In fact, advocates urge salespeople to structure the entire sales call as a prelude to closing or "asking for the order." With **consultative selling**, the sales representative becomes a long-term, trusted, and value-adding resource for a customer firm by gaining an in-depth understanding of its operations and by contributing analytical expertise to resolve pressing problems. Acting as a consultant, the rep crafts and recommends a total solution or bundle of products and services designed to precisely meet customer firm requirements and preferences. Seeking a strategic alliance or even a joint venture with an important customer to exploit a market opportunity, a supplier's senior management uses **enterprise selling** to convincingly elaborate the benefits of combining and sharing complementary competences and capabilities across firms. In enterprise selling, the offering is a partnership and not just products and services.[52]

Because sales representatives routinely use both transactional and consultative selling while gaining new business, we will address them in detail in this chapter. Although experts have devised various consultative selling methods in recent years, we focus our attention on one, SPIN® selling.[53] We believe that SPIN selling is the most consistent with business market management's emphasis on value. In Figure 8.7, we contrast transactional selling with SPIN selling. Enterprise selling, on the other hand, is an approach for securing partnerships between firms. We will further examine it in Chapter 10.

As we outlined in Figure 8.1, the first part of assessing mutual fit is the salesperson scheduling the first meeting with a prospect. After discussing this, we examine how the salesperson and prospect manager learn each other's requirements and preferences. Through these interactions, managers determine whether it is in the supplier and customer firm's best interests to do business together. To account for the variation in selling situations, we contrast how assessing mutual fit differs in transactional and SPIN selling.

Scheduling the First Meeting

In today's hectic workplace, salespeople frequently find making an initial appointment with a prospect to be a major challenge. With most managers' agendas overfilled with pressing work, few have time for "get acquainted" sessions. Technology often poses a barrier, as witnessed by the difficulties one encounters trying to get through a company's automated voice-mail system. How the sales representative arranges for that first meeting is a function of the selling situation.

Getting Started for Orders

As discussed earlier, in the case of an order, the customer firm typically requires an offering of low importance and minimal risk such as a generic item. In general, these customer managers fully understand the basic attributes and applications of the offering they require and do not need a technical explanation. These relatively simple sales situations correspond to the **straight rebuy** or **modified rebuy** buying situations we discussed in Chapter 3 and typically apply to orders. A purchasing manager typically has sole authority and can make the purchase immediately, often based on lowest price. Examples of simple sales are the acquisition of corrugated packaging materials and printing.

When confronted with an order, sales representatives can use the techniques of transactional selling. Here, "timing is everything" for the salesperson. The prospective customer commonly makes such purchases either when a problem arises unexpectedly within the firm or when an existing supplier botches an order. Thus, the salesperson

Figure 8.7 Contrasting Transactional and SPIN® Approaches to Selling

Selling Stage	Traditional Selling	SPIN Selling
Planning the Call	Study call reports and files	Same
	Set call objectives	Same
	Prepare presentation	Same
	Review offering knowledge	Same
	Reflect on offering benefits	Review value elements
Opening the Call	Relate to buyer's personal interests	Get down to business quickly
	Complement, mystify, or intrigue buyer	Begin asking questions
	Make an opening benefit statement	Don't offer solutions too soon
Investigating Requirements	Ask general open-ended questions to uncover customer problems	Uncover implied requirements and develop them into explicit requirements via situation, problem, implication, and requirement-payoff questions
Proposing Solutions	Sell benefits	Demonstrate capabilities
	Personalize benefits to unique customer requirements	Show how offering meets explicit requirments and articulate value
	Handle objections	Prevent objections
Gaining the Order	Close early and often	Obtain the right commitment in the form of advances and orders
		Make additional calls on the customer as needed
Following Up After the Sale	Check to be sure the offering has been delivered	Same
	Correct installation and start up problems	Same
	Ensure customer satisfaction	Same
		Ascertain the value promised has been delivered
		Seek new ways to add value

makes periodic and routine "cold" calls on prospects. The rep gains access to the purchasing manager by promising special "deals" or by making an attention-getting new claim about her product. If the purchasing manager has spare time or faces a crisis situation revolving around the product, he meets with the salesperson.

Initiating Dialogue for New Customer Opportunities

In the case of customer opportunities, the prospect seeks an offering of greater significance and associated risk such as a bottleneck or critical item. More than likely, these customer managers are not fully aware of their firm's requirements or how those requirements might best be satisfied. Because of this lack of awareness, the **buying team** of customer managers will require detailed explanations about the performance of alternative market offerings. New customer opportunities correspond to the modified rebuy or **new task** buying situations we discussed in Chapter 3. Examples of a complex sale are a government's acquisition of a 300-megawatt power plant, or a firm's purchase of a pension plan for its employees.

In such a sale, the customer firm conducts analyses of alternate offerings and requires a longer period of time to decide what to purchase. The customer's buying team may demand multiple sales calls from cross-functional representatives of the supplier firm. Based on its analyses, the team recommends a purchase based on an offering's value or total cost to the customer firm. Importantly, the buying team will most likely make its decision when supplier representatives are not present. To handle the sale, representatives turn to a consultative selling approach, such as SPIN selling.

Given that a buying team makes the decision in these cases, a salesperson must skillfully identify the team's **gatekeeper** and schedule the initial meeting with that person. The gatekeeper is the person who has principal responsibility for regulating the flow of information to and from the buying team as well as providing the sales rep with access to specific team members.

Learning Prospect Requirements and Preferences and Communicating Value

In most cases, a salesperson will spend a portion of the initial encounter with the prospect getting acquainted and learning about their requirements and preferences. However, in the case of orders, the prospect and the salesperson often are able to articulate the potential customer's requirements after a short period of interaction. As a result, experts in transactional selling instruct the sales representative to quickly close the sale, then negotiate the terms and conditions of the order.

In the case of customer prospects, neither the prospect nor the sales representative may fully comprehend customer requirements. Since considerable risk is involved and both firms frequently seek a long-term relationship, neither supplier nor customer representatives are in a hurry to consummate the deal. Thus, in a consultative selling approach, such as SPIN selling, the salesperson devotes several sales calls to surface and specify prospect requirements and preferences. Typically, the rep will uncover these requirements by calling on purchasing and other customer managers during visits. We now compare how learning differs between transactional and SPIN selling. As in Figure 8.7, we contend that the salesperson learns in three selling stages: planning the call, opening the call, and investigating requirements.

Plan the Call

When using transactional selling, a salesperson selects a prospect for an upcoming call and develops a call plan. In a **call plan**, the representative briefly identifies key objectives to accomplish during the call, selects topics to discuss, formulates a presentation, and considers selling tactics. While preparing the call plan, the rep reviews call reports from previous encounters, if any, with the potential customer and examines customer files to glean information about possible customer requirements. A rep will also study pertinent market offering information and major benefits.

The sales representative follows similar procedures under SPIN selling with a few minor differences. To begin with, the salesperson uses the call-planning period to become reacquainted with the specific value elements of the firm's market offerings. Most important, the representative's objectives are likely to be more detailed. In the case of orders, the salesperson may be able to get the order during the first meeting. Therefore, call objectives will likely revolve around closing. Because customer opportunities often entail a long sales cycle, the rep may use the first call to learn about the prospect's business philosophy, mission and goals, and purchasing orientation. The salesperson's major objective during the first call on a prospect may be to get invited back.

Open the Call

The salesperson arrives at the prospect firm, greets the purchasing manager, exchanges business cards, and engages in small talk for about 5 to 10 minutes. This scenario comprises the **opening** of the presentation.[54] In both transactional and SPIN selling, an important objective during the opening and initial portion of a sales call is to establish trust. **Trust** is "the firm's belief that another company will perform actions that will result in positive outcomes for the firm, as well as not take unexpected actions that would result in negative outcomes for the firm."[55] Consultants have identified five trust-builders that sales personnel use to establish trust between organizations: candor, dependability, competence, customer orientation, and likeability. The rep demonstrates **candor** by speaking openly and honestly about the supplier's market offerings and their potential fit with customer requirements. The salesperson cultivates a reputation for **dependability** by fulfilling promises such as getting answers to a prospect's technical questions or delivering samples on time. He displays **competence** through a professional demeanor, command over relevant product and application knowledge, and problem-solving skills. A sales professional shows a **customer orientation** by learning more about customer requirements, empathizing with prospects' problems, and providing advice that helps customers resolve difficulties. Finally, the representative establishes **likeability** by being courteous and polite, making efficient use of the customer manager's time, and finding points of commonality as they relate to both business and personal affairs.[56]

When utilizing transactional selling, the salesperson strives to find common personal interests during the opening. For instance, a rep who spots a football pennant on the wall talks about the local football team's latest game. When the salesperson has established rapport with the purchasing manager, it's time to grab the manager's attention by making an intriguing claim about the product, perhaps making a riveting benefit statement.

Although the opening is similar in SPIN selling, the rep does not try to contrive or force points of common personal interest. Furthermore, the salesperson does not make a benefit statement immediately. After all, a rep does not really understand the customer's requirements and preferences. Instead, the rep gets down to business quickly and moves on to the next critical stage of SPIN selling—investigating requirements.

Investigate Prospect Requirements and Preferences

The salesperson devotes a significant part of the sales call to exploring the prospect firm's requirements and preferences. Gaining an understanding of a prospect firm's requirements may seem relatively straightforward, yet understanding individual managers' preferences often is not. For example, the salesperson must attempt to discern the extent to which internal political considerations at the customer firm will positively or negatively affect prospects of doing business. The company culture also will often exert a subtle, though significant, influence on individual managers' preferences. Connected relationships with other firms that either the salesperson's firm has or the prospect firm has also may influence the customer firm's willingness to do business with the salesperson's firm. So, although individual managers' preferences may not be apparent, at least initially, it is worth investigating them thoroughly. Accommodating them may be the deciding factor in purchase decisions.

In the case of orders, the prospect's requirements typically tend to be basic and straightforward, and the investigation phase tends to be brief. Here, advocates of transactional selling urge the salesperson to ask a series of general open-ended questions to encourage the purchasing manager to elaborate any current problems. When the purchasing manager describes a problem that the supplier's market offering can resolve, the representative launches into a formal sales presentation or "pitch."

As a consultant, the salesperson asks a series of focused SPIN questions during calls. Through these questions, the rep helps the customer manager uncover **implied requirements**, which are vaguely defined areas of discontent, dissatisfaction, and discomfort with current operations, and to develop them into **explicit requirements**, which are precise specifications of products and augmenting services that resolve the customer's problems. The sales representative uses **situation questions** to gather general background information about the customer firm. Experts suggest that salespeople use these sparingly because clever reps can and should obtain most background information from secondary sources during call planning. The rep should pose at least two situation questions: Who are the other members of the buying team? and, what roles do buying team members play in the purchasing process?

Moving on as quickly as possible, the salesperson asks a series of **problem questions**, which seek to pinpoint the customer firm's difficulties and dissatisfactions. Most likely, customer managers will answer in generalities or with imprecise statements. Some examples of problem questions are: Why are you dissatisfied with your current computer system? What happens to your production line during peak loads? How quickly does your current maintenance contractor respond to your equipment breakdowns, and how long does it typically take them to repair machines?

To this point, the questioning strategies of transactional and SPIN selling are similar. They begin to diverge when the salesperson as consultant poses **implication questions**, which require customer managers to fully articulate the consequences of not resolving the firm's difficulties. Importantly, the skilled sales rep prompts the prospect whenever possible to define both incurred costs and lost benefits in monetary terms. To structure implication questioning, sales representatives often turn to the total cost of ownership (TCO) analyses that we discussed in Chapter 3. For example, account representatives from major consulting and information technology firms routinely begin engagements with diagnostic TCO assessments. Through these TCO assessments, reps and purchasing managers jointly identify and quantify major "points of pain" or cost drivers for the prospect company that might not otherwise be apparent. Then they configure a total solution that dampens the impact of these cost drivers.

The following are sample implication questions:

- You've pointed to a bottleneck in your main production line. How many sales have you lost during the past month because you could not get product out the door on time?
- You state that 10% of your MRO purchases are unplanned. What are your firm's total costs associated with an unplanned purchase?

The final phase of questioning is the most important because it yields arguments that each customer manager can use to sell the supplier's market offering to other members of the buying team when the sales representative is not present. **Requirement-payoff questions** help the customer manager assess the worth of the solution that the supplier firm's market offering provides. Ideally, the skillful salesperson uses such questions to prompt the customer manager to specify the worth in monetary terms. Requirement-payoff questions take the following form:

- Suppose that you had a material that was 50% easier for your machine operators to use. How would that cut your current rejection rate? What would those cost savings be worth to your firm?
- How much would you be willing to pay per month if you could restrict long-distance calling privileges solely to authorized personnel?

To assist customer managers to quantify a solution's worth, sales representatives should use Internet-based or laptop computer-based value models or worksheets such as the BT Compass we discussed in Chapter 2.

GAINING THE INITIAL TRANSACTION

Transaction Versus Consultative Selling

At the close of the assessing mutual fit portion of the gaining new business process, the business market manager along with the salesperson determines whether it is in the best interests of the supplier firm to do business with the prospect. If the answer is an emphatic "yes," the sales representative takes deliberate steps to gain an initial transaction. If the answer is an unqualified "no," the salesperson directs her attention to another prospect firm.

In many instances, to proceed with gaining the initial transaction, the supplier must first gain approved-vendor status. By conveying **approved-vendor status**, purchasing managers indicate that they are confident the supplier firm will dependably deliver the value that its representatives promise, and formally recognize it as a potential supplier to their firm. To gain designation as an approved vendor, the salesperson, working together with other supplier personnel, provides product samples to the customer firm for testing, evidence of quality or conformance to ISO 9000 series standards, and proof of management capability and technical competence.

Often, a cross-functional team from the customer firm will visit the supplier firm and tour its facilities as part of the process.

In this section, we discuss how the salesperson demonstrates the value of the supplier firm's market offering and convinces the prospect to acquire it. We conclude by examining how the salesperson negotiates for the initial transaction. As in the previous section of this chapter, we continue to contrast the nature of these activities within the context of transactional and SPIN selling.

Demonstrating and Documenting Value

Armed with a clear understanding of prospect requirements, the salesperson practices adaptive selling, modifying the supplier's value proposition and market offering elements to better align them with customer requirements and preferences. In Box 8.4, we discuss how Zyme Solutions introduces high technology based market offering to help some customer firms' vexing problems with regard to getting accurate channel information. During its discussions with prospective customers, Zyme times to identify at least one "shattering value." A shattering value is an element in Zyme Solutions' offering which is clearly worthwhile. Using these insights, the Zyme salesperson customizes the firm's value proposition for the prospect.

BOX 8.4

Zyme Solutions Introduces High Technology into Markets which were Traditionally Managed with Low Technology

Zyme Solutions, Inc., based in Bengaluru, is a hosted data intelligence service provider specifically focused on helping high-tech product companies gain visibility into their sales in the indirect distribution channel. These high-tech companies typically have thousands of channel partners located around the globe, which individually report critical sales, inventory, and incentive claims information on a daily or weekly basis. Ironically, although these channel partners distribute products for the high-tech industry, hundreds of thousands of channel partners worldwide operate with low levels of IT sophistication. On a weekly or daily basis, they report to the product companies what stock information they hold for various models of products, sales, etc.

This self-reported information is subject to a wide variety of quality issues, including timeliness, completeness, and accuracy, all of which render the data suspect for use in executing channel processes, maintaining financial compliance, and making decisions. Zyme's flagship channel intelligence service solves this problem by collating millions of records of sales transactions from thousands of distributors and retailers in 140 countries each week and providing timely operational insights to its technology product clients.

When Zyme Solutions was founded in 2004, its principal motivation was to construct a practical and valuable solution to the problem of poor downstream data visibility in the high-tech industry. The reality about channel data is that they are intrinsically of low quality since they are cross-enterprise, non-standard data originating from multiple systems. Yet, companies rely on these data to transact billions of dollars each year in commercial incentive

BOX 8.4
Continued

programs and a number of other critical business decisions. Zyme recognized that to really solve this problem for its clients, it would need not only a deep software platform capable of accurately processing, cleansing, and analyzing high volumes of channel sales data but also a highly trained and knowledgeable team of analysts who could reach out to hundreds of global distribution partners around the world to negotiate and resolve disputes and discrepancies in the reported sales information. Zyme went about building software and related services to address this problem.

Zyme's assumption, which has since been validated, is that if it could solve this problem for one high-tech OEM, it could solve the same problem in a similar way for hundreds of other companies. This led to the idea that it could "productize" the service offering and build a far more scalable business: one that would increase its value to customers with growth, while increasing its own profits with each additional customer, thereby allowing further cycles of increasing R&D spending, new customer offerings, and customer value creation.

From the very beginning, Zyme focused on building a platform business. It realized that having multiple unconnected services offerings, all of which look different from one another, would make it impossible to build a services platform. It made a deliberate choice from its inception that the services offered to each subsequent customer would closely resemble the services provided to prior customers. This enabled Zyme to leverage organizational learning and economies of scale in a very real way.

Because its focus is on a single market and single-solution footprint, ultimately the asset built by Zyme embeds the deep accumulated domain knowledge coming from continuous immersion into the channel visibility problems facing its clients in a very real way.

As a result of its focused approach, Zyme has a ringside view of the channel data problem across an entire industry. This information is converted into insight and new services to add incremental value to its clients. The company has invested its time in building a client services management team with a dual focus on operational excellence and continuous innovation. It treats new client relationships as the beginning of a value journey, not the end—and it continually raises the bar on the value added to clients. The success of Zyme hinges on its understanding that success is rooted in delivering high-quality operational value, week after week, without slowing down.

D. V. R. Seshadri and Shobitha Hegde, "Bucking the Trend: A look at Zyme Solutions Non-linear Business Model for IT Services from India," case study developed for IIM Bangalore in 2008.

As another example, in Box 8.5, we describe how account managers for Ingersoll-Rand's Air Solutions Division work with potential customer managers to research their current air compressor costs, use a cost-of-use approach to design solutions that reduce those costs, and then incorporate the results of those analyses in sales presentations. Ingersoll-Rand gets a second use from its value assessment efforts by documenting them in case studies so that account managers can use them when marketing its solutions to other prospects.

After selecting a market offering that meets prospect requirements, the salesperson enters the presentation stage of the interaction with the prospect. As in Figure 8.7, the rep must persuasively propose solutions and gain the order.

BOX 8.5
The Air Solutions Division of Ingersoll-Rand (India) Deploys Cost-of-Use Approach to Marketing

Ingersoll-Rand, Inc., the United States, a global major in the manufacture of a wide range of equipment catering to diverse industries, established its Indian presence in 1921 by incorporating a private limited company under the name Ingersoll-Rand (India) Pvt. Ltd. in Kolkata, West Bengal. Known to be one of the first Indo-American ventures in India, Ingersoll Rand (India) (IRL) commenced business as a trading company. IRL subsequently established significant manufacturing bases in Bengaluru, primarily focusing on making heavy construction equipment, and at its Ahmedabad Air Solutions Division to make a wide variety of compressors, including reciprocating, screw, and heavy-duty centrifugal compressors.

During the early 2000s, IRL's Air Solutions Division experienced significant commoditization pressures for many of its complex engineered products such as centrifugal compressors. Going forward, the company was faced with two choices. The first was to continue doing business as before, winning some orders, and losing some. However, it was unlikely that this approach would result in dramatic growth of IRL's large compressor business unit. The second option was to change the way the company gained new customers, which required a radical departure from the past. It entailed seeing the entire process from the customer's perspective, delivering value and ceasing to fight over price, in order to make a sale.

The company adopted the latter approach, which was christened "SolutionizingTM." What this strategy entailed was to deliver superior customer value through holistic solutions that saved money for the customer. Such a solution would be initiated by performing an audit for the customer on its compressed air system. Based on a deep understanding of the customer domain, IRL would work closely with the customer firm and come up with stretch targets on parameters critical to the functioning of the compressed air system such as cost of operating the system, air quality, system reliability, etc. This entailed much more than just the compressor as a product and required IRL to take the responsibility of the entire system including piping, filters, point of use nozzles, and much more, many of which were supplied by vendors other than IRL. To achieve these stretch targets required joint working of IRL with the customer over several months, with detailed documentation of value delivered at every stage of the process. "SolutionizingTM" was successful in moving IRL from a transactional dealing with the customer to a loyal, continuous relationship with the customer, resulting in Ingersoll-Rand (India)'s dramatic growth in revenue, profitability, and, most importantly, credibility in the Indian marketplace.

D. V. R. Seshadri and Shobitha Hegde, "Ingersoll-Rand (India) Ltd.: The Air Compressors Business at the Crossroads (A)," case study developed for IIM Bangalore in 2005.

Propose Solutions

Again, how the salesperson approaches the presentation varies across transactional and SPIN selling. During transactional selling training programs, instructors counsel salespeople to build the value stack and personalize market offering benefits to customer requirements via the FAB approach. The FAB approach entails translating

Figure 8.8 Drilling Down to Worth with Value Mapping

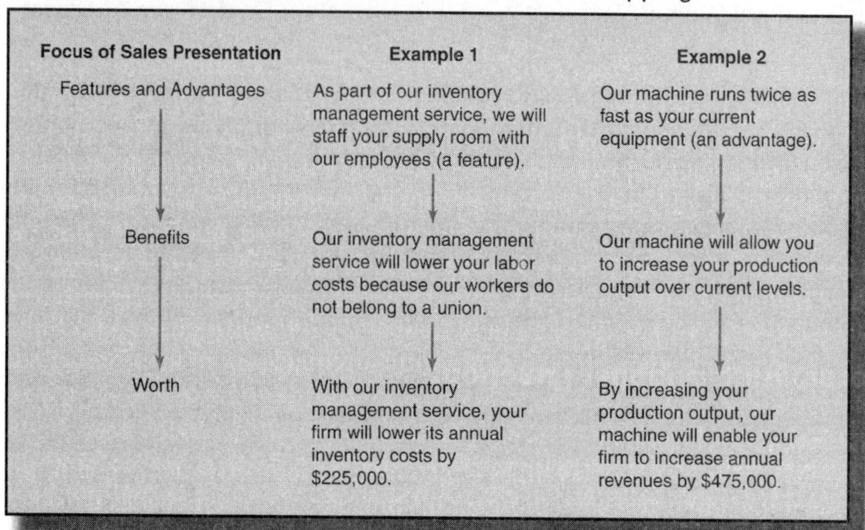

features, which are product characteristics or specifications, and **advantages**, which are functions that the supplier's product performs better than competitive models, into customer-specific **benefits**, which summarize how the product will help the prospect. In Figure 8.8, we provide two examples of how a salesperson converts a feature and an advantage into benefits.

In SPIN selling, the salesperson explains how the supplier firm's market offering meets the explicit requirements of the customer firm. As illustrated in Figure 8.8, this goes beyond stating benefits to explicating the worth of the supplier firm's market offerings. Business market managers refer to this practice—building the value stack by translating features and advantages to benefits and ultimately to worth—as **value mapping** or value stream mapping. Progressive suppliers often "explode" value maps backward to determine which internal business processes yield specific offering features and advantages. In this way, they can take deliberate steps to improve the value of their offerings by reengineering related business processes.[57] Box 8.6 recounts a noteworthy case on how VUTEk enables its salespeople, working along with customer managers, to measure the value of their offerings.

When proposing solutions, salespeople can expect to encounter objections from prospects. In transactional selling, experts view objections, or resistance to the sales message, as a sign of prospect interest. Salespeople handle objections by first listening carefully to objections and then answering each one thoroughly. Given that reps commonly hear the same objections across customers, managers advise them to prepare "canned responses" prior to the sales call.

Another key difference between transactional and SPIN selling is that advocates of SPIN selling urge sales reps to prevent objections rather than to just handle them. How does the salesperson prevent objections? First, the rep makes a greater effort at qualifying prospects and reduces the likelihood of calling on a firm that has no need

BOX 8.6
VUTEk Gains and Grows Customers via Its Documented Solutions™ Program

VUTEk, Inc., pioneered superwide format printers used for outdoor graphic arts advertising such as billboards and hoardings for corporate branding. These outdoor billboards and hoardings form the backbone of the booming signage industry in India and many other countries. In 2005, VUTEk was acquired by EFI, headquartered in California, the United States. The company has a significant software development center in Bengaluru.

Advertising companies hire a media planning agency to design the ad campaign, which in turn places orders to print shops located in various parts of the country. The print shops employ four key resources for delivering the order: printers (wide or superwide), printware (or media), ink, and labor. Of these, procuring the printers requires a major upfront investment for the print shops. For printing companies, even as the printers themselves represent a huge capital investment, it is the ink that accounts for a significant portion of the recurring costs. Often, printer-manufacturing companies price their printers aggressively because selling the printers enables them to achieve a loose kind of long-term lock-in for selling inks.

VUTEk's printers enjoy tremendous brand equity because of their top performance, durability, and stability. VUTEk printers are priced at least 40% higher than those of its nearest competitor. VUTEk's prohibitive prices made customers contemplate acquiring cheaper printers from competitors.

Two other factors influenced a typical customer's decision. First, print jobs were becoming highly commoditized. For print shops to run, they needed large corporate customers to place orders in bulk. Given their volume, these corporate customers tended to give a very low price for their orders, resulting in lower profits for the print shops. With corporate deals forming the bulk of their revenue, print shops owners were consequently reluctant to invest in the higher-priced VUTEk range of machines.

The second reason was that, by 2005, VUTEk's competitors started slashing their prices even further. EFI refused to be drawn into this price war. The company management reasoned that the high cost of VUTEk machines was not due to the high premium charged but due to the high-quality components used. As such, competing on price was not a tenable option for EFI. VUTEk printers accordingly began to lose market share.

In India, the outdoor ad market was changing with the explosion of multinational players. VUTEk decided to make a pitch to these corporate customers on the benefits of deploying VUTEk-printed ads. It realized that if corporations were willing to pay a premium for quality work, print shop owners would be able to invest in quality equipment and would turn to VUTEk printers. The company thus decided to focus on its customers' customers.

EFI decided to educate corporations about the benefits of using VUTEk-printed billboards. These companies had to be convinced to pay a premium on print orders and to specify to the print shops that their prints be done using VUTEk printers and inks while giving them orders to make the billboards. EFI decided to leverage its vast experience in color management software and hardware with its customers' customers. EFI offered this expertise to corporations. Armed with this knowledge, corporate customers (i.e., customers of print shops) in turn mandated that print shops should use VUTEk printers

(continued)

BOX 8.6
Continued

and inks, since it was the color management expert that was best suited for the job.

To address durability concerns, EFI offered corporations a warranty on the banners' life, ranging from 3 months to 2 years. That is, if a hoarding started deteriorating in quality during its agreed upon lifetime, the corporation would get a free replacement. This was a unique India-specific arrangement. It represented substantial value for EFI's customers' customers. By adding this major, tangible, and easy-to-understand value element to its market offering, EFI hoped that it could convince corporations to pay a premium for the high quality and service of VUTEk-generated prints. This in turn would help EFI's customers (print shops) to get better margins while pursuing large deals with corporate customers. With more margins, the print shops could now invest in quality equipment and this represented a great opportunity for EFI. Within a year of implementation of this approach, EFI sold a large number of high-end VUTEk printers to print shops at considerable price premium compared to competition.

Contributed by Utanka Sarma, Participant, PGSEM Program, Indian Institute of Management Bangalore.

for the supplier's offering. Second, the rep shrewdly uses implication and requirement-payoff questions to get purchasing managers to "sell it to themselves." Third, the salesperson who has a deeper understanding of the prospective customer's requirements and preferences can propose more tailored offering options that are worthy of serious consideration.

Gain the Initial Transaction

Because it is possible for a salesperson to take an order on the first sales call with a prospect, the most important part of transactional selling is closing. According to traditional thinking, the sales rep must "always ask for the order" when making a sales call. In fact, sales courses routinely instruct salespeople to close early and often and at least five times during the call. To help reps with their closing techniques, pundits have written many books that summarize snappy and clever, if not high-pressure, closing lines. Among the classic closes are:

- *Assumption Close*—Where do you want it delivered?
- *Alternative Close*—Do you want the three-year or four-year maintenance contract?
- *Standing-Room-Only Close*—If you don't order now, I'll have to sell it to another customer firm that has expressed an interest in it.
- *Last-Chance Close*—This special offer ends today. If you wait until tomorrow, you'll have to pay full price.
- *Order-Blank Close*—The salesperson begins to fill out the order form before the customer has agreed to the purchase.

Although closing is considered to be essential in SPIN selling, the ultimate goal is obtaining commitment from the customer. In Chapter 10, we discuss in detail the importance of commitment within customer and supplier working relationships.

Commitment "captures the perceived continuity or growth in a relationship between two firms."[58] According to research from the Dartnell Corporation, a leading sales management consulting firm, the typical sales professional makes an average of about four calls on a prospect to close a business sale.[59] For this reason, advocates of the SPIN selling approach urge salespeople to seek increasing customer commitment with each contact rather than to mindlessly try to close during every call. In fact, they argue that asking for the order too early and too often during the sales cycle may actually alienate and anger the prospect.

As per adaptive selling, the salesperson must assess the events during a given call and seek an appropriate level of commitment from the prospect. SPIN selling divides possible commitments into two broad categories. **Advances** represent progress in the purchasing process, whereas **orders** are actual sales. Examples of advances include such things as making appointments with other members of the buying team, getting approval from the customer to deliver a sample product, and making definite plans for a follow-up sales call. To be successful, the salesperson pursues an appropriate advance from a prospect at each stage of the sales cycle, working up to the initial order.

Negotiating the First Sale

In business markets, a prospect firm's tentative decision to buy prompts more detailed negotiations with the supplier firm. Three aspects that we single out for consideration are pricing the initial offering, negotiation approaches, and understanding the best alternative to a negotiated agreement (BATNA).

Pricing the Initial Offering

As a prelude to price discussions, the two firms must come to a preliminary agreement on the precise nature of the market offering the supplier will provide. Although supplier and prospect may concur on the makeup of the naked solution, they may have different views as to which optional services are to be included at what total price. As per our discussions of managing market offerings in Chapter 5, supplier and prospect firm representatives may be willing to trade product or service elements for price modifications. For example, in the case of defeaturing or cooperative pricing, the supplier firm may lower a product's price if the prospect firm relaxes specifications that in turn allow the supplier to produce the offering at a lower cost.

Of course, supplier and prospect must negotiate a final price. As part of this negotiation, the supplier might use the pricing tactic of an **initial use discount**, which appears as a price reduction on the invoice. The supplier may use this tactic as an additional inducement for change or as compensation for perceived or actual switching costs that the prospect will incur. The initial use discount has the advantage of establishing in the customer's mind what the supplier believes is the equitable price for the value the offering provides, and one that the prospect should expect to pay on subsequent purchase occasions. **Trade-in allowances**, another form of initial use discounts, are credits a prospect firm receives from a new supplier in exchange for that firm's used equipment or unused supplies.

Suppliers also commonly use a number of other pricing tactics. **Early payment discounts** allow prospective customers to deduct a percentage from the invoice for paying within a specified number of days. **Volume discounts** provide lower unit prices in return for larger-quantity orders. **Freight allowances** are invoice reductions that compensate prospects and customers for transportation and delivery charges. **Rebates** or **bonuses** cover a variety of schemes where suppliers provide money or additional products and services at no charge as a reward based on the amount of business a customer has done with the supplier during some time period.

Finally, once both sides have come to agreement on the final configuration of the market offering and its price, they must also finalize terms and conditions. These include such things as when and where deliveries are to be made, the nature of payment schedules, the particulars of return goods policies and warranties, and installation procedures. **Extended dating**, where the customer gets an unusually long period to pay for its purchase, serves as another pricing tactic.

Negotiation Approaches

As we mentioned in Chapter 3, the sales rep must be familiar with two approaches to bargaining. In **distributive negotiations**, the two sides assume that the value "pie" is fixed and haggle over one item, typically price. With this approach, each party views gains for one party as coming at the expense of the other, and acts accordingly. In **integrative negotiations**, the two sides first prioritize their own requirements and then trade off elements that are less important to their respective firms for those that are more important. With this approach, the two parties work together to find ways to expand the outcomes available, which they equitably share.

Naturally, as part of adaptive selling, the salesperson must select the bargaining approach that fits the situation. Typically, selling and bargaining approaches go hand in hand. For example, when discussing price in a simple sale with a purchasing manager whose firm has a buying orientation, the salesperson will most likely draw on the techniques of transactional selling and distributive negotiations. On the other hand, when working out the final details of a market offering in a complex sale with a major account that adheres to a supply management orientation, the representative will likely utilize consultative selling and integrative bargaining.

Of course, even when a prospect firm and supplier firm use integrative bargaining to expand the value pie, they ultimately must split the expanded value. So, a distributive bargaining phase follows integrative bargaining. Yet, firms typically find it easier to split an expanded pie, in part because they each recognize the greater present and future value that they can generate by preserving goodwill in their relationship.

Understanding BATNA

Regardless of the negotiation approach taken, the salesperson should develop what Fisher and Ury call a **best alternative to a negotiated agreement (BATNA)**. A BATNA is the most favorable option that the supplier can pursue if the supplier firm cannot reach an equitable agreement with a prospect. Thus, the BATNA is a standard for comparison during bargaining. If the terms of an agreement exceed the BATNA, the sales representative accepts the terms of the deal. On the other hand, if it falls below the BATNA, the rep declines and either makes a counteroffer or terminates the discussions.[60]

In business markets, a BATNA might entail seeking out another promising prospect or market segment if the prospect refuses to pay an equitable price for a highly augmented market offering. Alternatively, the supplier firm might choose to market new offerings if the firm couldn't make a profit from existing offerings. With a BATNA in mind, the salesperson is more objective in dealings with a prospect. Rather than caving in on price to gain the order, the salesperson knows the alternatives in advance. By understanding the BATNA, the rep has the confidence to say "no" to a bad deal. Lost orders are not necessarily failures. Sometimes it is better to let a competitor "win" a bad deal.

INITIAL ORDER FULFILLMENT

Contrary to what many sales and marketing experts apparently believe, the process of gaining new business does not end with the receipt of an initial order. Instead, we argue that business market managers must take deliberate steps to ensure that the offering is delivered as promised and meets prospect requirements to their complete satisfaction. We refer to these activities as **order fulfillment**. In all too many firms, though, order fulfillment falls short of being seamless and error free. Responsibilities for order fulfillment typically cut across many functional groups, and rarely does one person oversee and coordinate cross-functional activities. Furthermore, no one has a clear understanding of how order fulfillment works in its entirety. As a result, order fulfillment systems are often poorly coordinated and suffer from communications lapses, resulting in certain tasks going uncompleted and others suffering from duplication and redundancy in efforts across functional groups.

As outlined in Figure 8.1, we begin this final section of the chapter by recommending actions that supplier firms can take to coordinate cross-functional order fulfillment efforts. Next, we turn our attention to completing the initial transaction. Once the initial order has been fulfilled, the business market manager reflects on the process and makes another essential screening decision—whether to continue doing business with the customer.

Coordinating Supplier Functions

Managers and experts in the field of operations commonly embed order fulfillment within a larger order management cycle.[61] Depicted in the second column of Figure 8.9, the typical **order management cycle (OMC)** is a 10-step process from planning to post-sales service that defines a company's business system.[62] As Shapiro, Rangan, and Sviokla illustrate in the chart, most firms divide responsibilities for performing each of these steps among diverse functional groups and rarely, if ever, put a single senior manager or function in charge. With many handoffs between functions, the likelihood that customers will "fall through the cracks" and receive poor service increases dramatically. To fill in these cracks, Shapiro, Rangan, and Sviokla urge companies to coordinate the activities of diverse functions in several ways.

To begin with, they argue that senior management must promote internally a systems philosophy based on customer responsiveness. They do so by providing training to managers from all relevant functions about the importance of OMC and their group's role in it. To reinforce the systems philosophy, senior management simultaneously creates individual rewards based on cross-functional performance of OMC tasks. Obviously, when functional groups are compensated for working

Figure 8.9 The Order Management Cycle

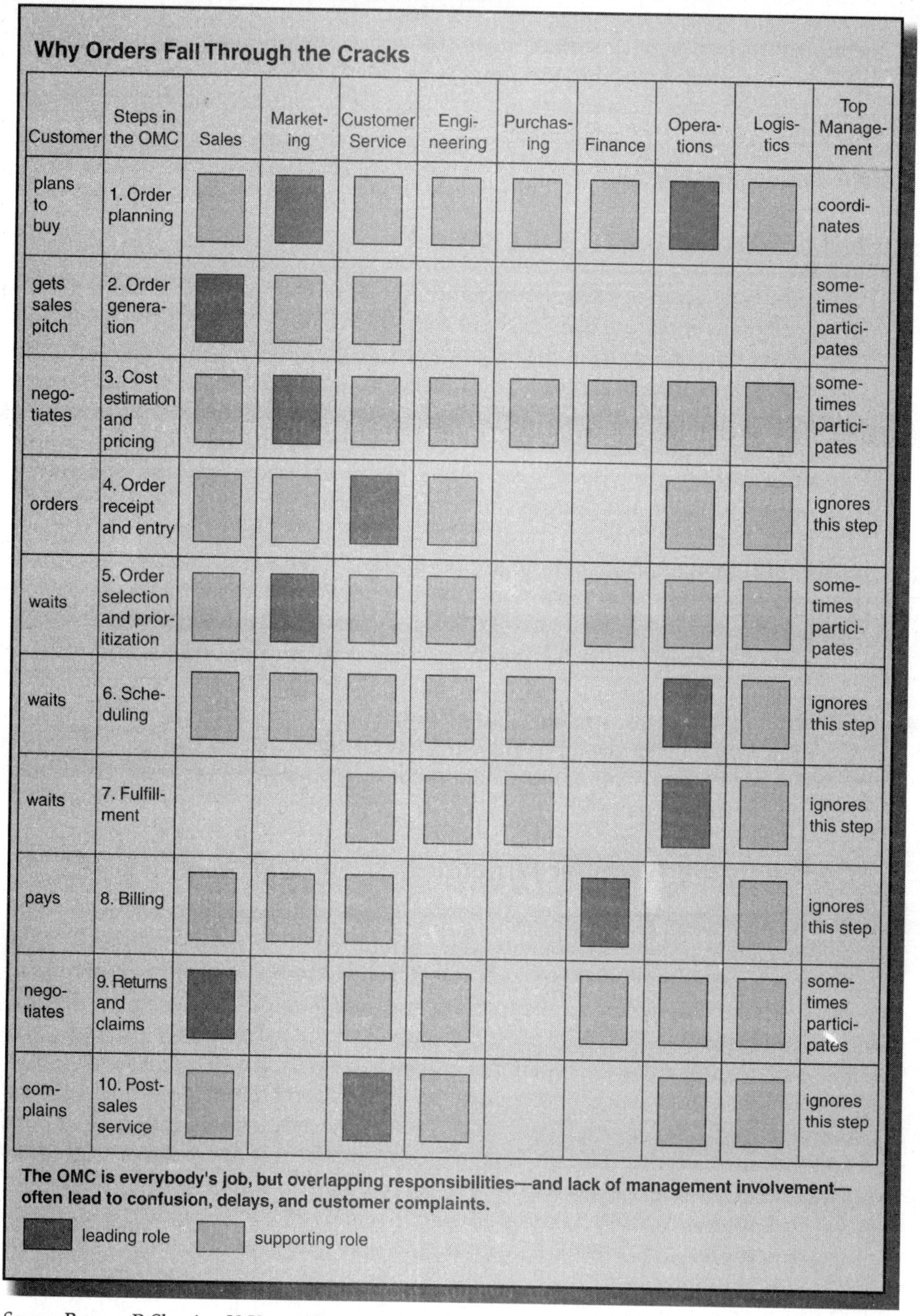

Why Orders Fall Through the Cracks

Customer	Steps in the OMC	Sales	Marketing	Customer Service	Engineering	Purchasing	Finance	Operations	Logistics	Top Management
plans to buy	1. Order planning	□	■	□	□	□	□	■	□	coordinates
gets sales pitch	2. Order generation	■	□	□						sometimes participates
negotiates	3. Cost estimation and pricing	□	■	□	□	□	□	□	□	sometimes participates
orders	4. Order receipt and entry	□	□	■	□			□	□	ignores this step
waits	5. Order selection and prioritization	□	■	□	□		□	□	□	sometimes participates
waits	6. Scheduling	□	□	□	□	□		■	□	ignores this step
waits	7. Fulfillment			□	□	□		■	□	ignores this step
pays	8. Billing	□	□	□			■		□	ignores this step
negotiates	9. Returns and claims	■		□	□		□	□	□	sometimes participates
complains	10. Postsales service	□		■	□			□	□	ignores this step

The OMC is everybody's job, but overlapping responsibilities—and lack of management involvement—often lead to confusion, delays, and customer complaints.

■ leading role □ supporting role

Source: Benson P. Shapiro, V. Kasturi Rangan, and John J. Sviokla, "Staple Yourself to an Order," *Harvard Business Review* (July–August 1992): 118.

together, they develop better ways to handle customer order "handoffs." Next, working as a team, key managers from relevant functional areas use business process mapping to chart the firm's OMC. Then, drawing upon business process reengineering, they redesign the OMC to make it more responsive to customer requirements. Reengineered OMC systems often use management information systems such as CRM and partner relationship management (PRM) to streamline order fulfillment and link functional groups.

To sustain the practice of interfunctional cooperation, Shapiro, Rangan, and Sviokla urge senior managers to periodically assign projects to these cross-functional teams associated with OMC issues. Finally, to ensure long-term cross-functional cooperation, progressive firms place a senior manager in charge of the overall OMC process. Armed with the appropriate authority, this manager resolves differences between groups and inspires the functions to work together.

Completing the Transaction

In addition to cross-functional integration, Shapiro, Rangan, and Sviokla argue that customer-responsive order fulfillment hinges on order selection, prioritization, and scheduling, as well as cost estimation and pricing. These are steps 3, 5, and 6 in the OMC in Figure 8.9. In this section, we present the technique of revenue or yield management as a means of addressing these related issues. Then we examine the salesperson's task of following up to make certain that the final four steps of the OMC are executed to the customer's complete satisfaction.

Manage Revenue[63]

"**Revenue management** is the application of disciplined tactics that predict consumer [customer] behavior at the micromarket level and that optimize product availability and price to maximize revenue growth."[64] Widely practiced in the airline and hospitality industries, revenue management is applicable to market offerings that share some or all of certain characteristics. They include perishable products and opportunities, markets featuring seasonal or periodic demand, differential offering value across market segments, competition for offerings between small-quantity and short-term users and large-scale and long-term users, and frequent discounting to meet competition. In business markets, revenue management is particularly useful in such industries as business travel and lodging, and consulting and research. Revenue management can also be used very effectively in business services contexts such as after-sales service of specialized, complex, and expensive capital equipment including semiconductor manufacturing machines, power generation systems, and robotic systems used in manufacturing.[65]

In Figure 8.10, we summarize the seven core concepts of revenue management. The central idea is that firms can optimize profits by balancing supply and demand at the microsegment level via price rather than at the mass-market level via capacity modifications. To do so, firms segment markets in terms of value and set prices as a function of those differential values rather than costs.

Often, time is a determinant of value, with time-sensitive customers willing to pay more for assurances that they will receive a service immediately when they require it. Critically, supplier firms reserve or restrict a certain portion of their products and

Figure 8.10 The Seven Core Concepts of Revenue Management

The Seven Core Concepts of Revenue Management

- Focus on price rather than costs when balancing supply and demand.
- Replace cost-based pricing with market-based pricing.
- Sell to segmented micromarkets, not mass markets.
- Reserve sufficient product for most valuable customers.
- Make decisions based on knowledge, not suppositions.
- Exploit each product's value cycle.
- Continually reevaluate revenue opportunities.

Source: Adapted from Robert G. Cross, "Launching the Revenue Rocket," *Cornell Hotel and Restaurant Administration Quarterly* (April 1997): 33.

services for these high-value and high-profit-potential customers. If the firm ever "stocks out," it is on low-value offerings targeted toward low profit-potential customers. Thus, rental car companies always reserve a certain number of premium-priced cars for price-insensitive business travelers, who will drive them for several days, rather than renting them at a discount to bargain-hunting vacationers, who will use them for just one day.

Another time-based concept that comes into play in revenue management is that of the value cycle, which we described in Chapter 3. The **value cycle** captures ebb and flow of benefits and costs that accrue to a customer firm over time across an offering's activity cycle. Of particular importance in revenue management is the urgency with which segments require an offering after its commercialization and the price premium that each segment is willing to pay to acquire it as soon as possible after introduction. Armed with knowledge of an offering's value cycle, the business market manager can tactically adjust its price as a function of time from introduction in order to maximize profits.

In gaining new customers, the business market manager can use revenue management concepts to guide order selection, prioritization, and scheduling, as well as for cost estimation and pricing decisions. The supplier should target market segments and prospective customers within those segments that receive the greatest value from a market offering. Furthermore, it should focus its market or product development initiatives on them. In situations in which capacity is overbooked, inventory should be held in reserve for these segments. Importantly, managers should price the offering as a function of the value it creates for the segment. As for the remaining segments, their place in the order fulfillment queue is a function of their location in the value cycle and their profit potential for the supplier firm.[66]

Follow Up with Prospects After the Sale

As order fulfillment activities on the initial sale wind down, the salesperson makes follow-up calls to the new customer. As Figure 8.7 summarizes, the purpose is to ensure that the correct offering has been delivered in the appropriate amounts and that it is performing correctly. If problems have arisen, the sales representative resolves them. Post-sales service may also be provided in the form of maintenance and repair work. In addition, the salesperson must be certain that the customer readily understands the invoice it received is accurate and pays promptly. In the rare cases when products are defective, the sales representative may be responsible for managing product returns and claims procedures.

Although these tasks are basically the same in transactional and SPIN selling, some important differences are noteworthy. When practicing SPIN selling, the salesperson must ascertain that the supplier has delivered on its value promise. For example, in high-tech markets salespeople commonly return to the customer firm after a reasonable period of time to perform a value audit. Using the value assessment techniques we described in Chapter 2, they assess the performance of the supplier's offering. Often, salespeople report these results in terms of **return on investment (ROI)**, comparing delivered benefits and cost savings to resources expended to acquire and operate the offering. The high-tech consulting firm The Gartner Group, among many others, has developed and markets ROI models, programs, and services that enable both supplier and customer firms to perform and interpret such analyses.

Last, the salesperson should confirm that the customer is completely satisfied with its initial experience in doing business with the supplier. A part of this is actively probing for any areas of discontent. In the process, the salesperson constantly searches for new opportunities to add value to customer-specific offerings.

Validating the Initial Designation of Order Versus Customer

At the conclusion of the first iteration of gaining new business, business market managers need to perform one final screening task. This is the ideal time for managers to make a determination of opportunity type because they have superior information for assessing fit at this point. It is important for firms to recognize that, even after careful initial screening, some "false positive" selections are inevitable and that the initial classification of an opportunity as an order or customer opportunity might not have been the right one. Were it the case that an opportunity was actually an order and was incorrectly classified as a customer, the supplier firm needs to take immediate action to pull back resources that it has deployed in pursuing and fulfilling the customer requirements. If it were the opposite, that is, the opportunity was a customer while the supplier firm had classified it initially as an order, then the supplier firm needs to quickly redirect efforts and pursue the opportunity beyond just fulfilling the initial transaction. Suppliers, in fact, may provide extraordinary responsiveness to such customers to signal their interest in further developing the relationship.

In addition, as we discussed in Chapter 2, the supplier should also tailor the customer feedback it seeks from new business customers. For example, how easy was it to do business with the supplier? Feedback is critical for making process improvements, because ease of doing business is critical for attracting additional new business in the future. Further, gaining immediate customer feedback enables the supplier to learn quickly of any problems or mistakes, giving the supplier an opportunity to remedy them and improve its chances of fulfilling the initial transaction and, in the case of customers, retaining them. Finally, gaining new feedback can suggest worthwhile market offering modifications.

SUMMARY

Gaining new business begins with a clear understanding of the opportunity type and selection criteria. At all times, new business opportunity selection decisions need to consider the short- and long-term impact on the supplier firm's resource (capacity) constraints and skills (capability) development goals. The next steps in the process of prospecting for new business entails the related activities of generating leads internally from databases, prompting and gathering inquiries externally from the marketplace, and qualifying leads and inquiries. Although all prospecting efforts encompass these three activities, their nature varies as a function of the total number of potential new business opportunities, how readily the firm can enumerate these prospects, and the supplier firm's overall strategic intent in gaining new business. To improve the yield from prospecting, a supplier must gain the commitment and support of its sales force, which requires the provision of knowledge, motivation, experience, and sales support.

Next comes the important step of assessing the fit between prospects' requirements and preferences and supplier offerings and priorities. We propose a detailed analysis of the customer benefits being offered and using the value stack to understand the total potential value that can be created in each opportunity. In assessing mutual fit, the salesperson schedules an initial meeting with a prospect, often followed by others, to learn the prospect firm's requirements and preferences. Through this interaction, managers determine the opportunity type and, therefore, the sales approach. For expositional clarity, we examine two fundamental approaches to selling: transactional selling and consultative selling, as embodied in the prominent SPIN selling process. Transactional selling focuses on gaining the immediate order as quickly as possible, whereas with consultative selling, the salesperson becomes a long-term, trusted, and value-adding resource for a customer by gaining a deep understanding of customer operations and offering problem-solving assistance.

To gain the initial business, the supplier firm demonstrates the value of its market offerings and convinces the prospect to acquire it. Following this step, the salesperson negotiates the initial sale. Settling on the market offering that the supplier will provide and its pricing is critical to this step. The supplier and prospect alternatively may use distributive or integrative bargaining in these negotiations. The supplier salespeople must recognize the best alternative to a negotiated agreement (BATNA) to avoid making deals that are not in the supplier's best interests.

After obtaining the initial order, the supplier firm strives to fulfill its promises. Yet, few firms have developed an integrated order management cycle (OMC) process to provide seamless, error-free order fulfillment. To coordinate participating OMC functions, progressive firms analyze their current system via business process mapping and seek a systems solution, cultivate a systems philosophy across the entire organization, reward all functions for working together, and place a senior manager in charge of the entire process. Rather than simply taking orders on a "first-come, first-served" basis, a supplier can use techniques of revenue management to focus efforts on high-value segments, price based on value, and give fulfillment preference to customers in high-value segments in overbooking situations. Once the initial transaction is completed, the salesperson follows up to ensure complete customer satisfaction. At the conclusion of the process, supplier managers decide whether their initial classification of the new business was indeed the correct one and, in case of false positives, take the appropriate remedial actions.

ENDNOTES

1. Philip Kotler, *Kotler on Marketing* (New York: The Free Press, 2001), 121.
2. This section is adapted from Das Narayandas, "Note on Customer Management," *HBS Note 9-502-073* (Boston, MA: Harvard Business School, 2002).
3. Benson P. Shapiro and Rowland T. Moriarty, "Fabtek (A)," *HBS Note 9-592-095* (Boston, MA: Harvard Business School, 1992).
4. Das Narayandas and V. Kasturi Rangan, "Dell Computer Corporation (A)," *HBS Note 9-596-058* (Boston, MA: Harvard Business School, 1995, revised 25 September 1996).
5. Manohar U. Kalwani and Narakesari Narayandas, "Long-Term Manufacturer-Supplier Relationships: Do They Pay Off for Supplier Firms," *Journal of Marketing* 59-1 (1995): 1–16.
6. Das Narayandas, John A. Quelch, and Gordon Swartz, "Global Pricing Contracts," *Sloan Management Review*, 42-1 (2000): 61–70.
7. Managers, pundits, and academics use the terms *leads*, *inquiries*, and *prospects* interchangeably. We use the following definitions to illustrate how suppliers screen firms during prospecting and to draw a managerially useful distinction between categories of potential customers.
8. Anne Field, "State of the Art Precision Marketing," *Inc. Technology*, 2 (1996): 54–58.
9. Karen E. Klein, "Is Cold-Calling Really Dead?," *BusinessWeek Online* (March 7,2007). Web address http://www.businessweek.com/print/smallbiz/content/mar2007/sb20070306_143154.htm
10. Klein, "Is Cold-Calling Really Dead?"
11. Randy Bean, "Business-to-Business Direct Marketing: The Most Commonly Asked Questions," *Direct Marketing* (June 1995): 27–29, 78; and Kenneth M. Culpepper, "Database Maintenance Planning: Scheduling, Updates & Results," *Direct Marketing* (December 1996): 16–20.
12. Andris A. Zoltners, Prabhakant Sinha, and Greggor A. Zoltners, *The Complete Guide to Accelerating Sales Force Performance* (New York: AMACOM, 2001): 389.
13. Robert C. Blattberg, Gary Getz, and Jacquelyn S. Thomas, *Customer Equity* (Boston: Harvard Business School Press, 2001): 53.
14. Arnold Fishman, "List Industry Overview," *Direct Marketing* (August 1991): 46–47.
15. Claire Foss, "The Search is Now On," *Marketing Direct*, (June 2007), 37–39.
16. Michiel R. Leenders and David L. Blenkhorn, *Reverse Marketing* (New York: The Free Press, 1988).
17. Philip Kotler, *Marketing Management*, 11th ed. (Upper Saddle River, NJ: Prentice Hall, 2003): 583. Summarized from American Association of Advertising Agencies statement.
18. Everett M. Rogers, *Diffusion of Innovation*, 4th ed. (New York: The Free Press, 1995).
19. This discussion and the third column of Figure 8.3 are adapted from Benson P. Shapiro and John Wyman, "New Ways to Reach Your Customers," *Harvard Business Review* (July–August 1981): 103–110.
20. Kate Maddox, "Marketers Face Challenges from Economy to Ecology," *B to B* 92 (2007): 1–4.
21. Kim Benjamin, "The Importance of Being Integrated," *Marketing Direct* (February 2007): S5–9.
22. Jakki Mohr, *Marketing of High-Technology Products and Innovations* (Upper Saddle River, NJ: Prentice Hall, 2001).
23. Kent Hanson, "Working Customer Databases," *Business Marketing* (May 1993): 71.
24. Beth Negus Viveiros, "Networking Opportunity," *DIRECT Newsline* (February 2008): 13.
25. Benjamin, "The Importance of Being Integrated."
26. S.H. Godar and P.J. O'Connor, "Same Time Next Year—Buyer Trade Show Motives," *Industrial Marketing Management* 30 (2001): 77–86; Ling-yee Li, "Relationship Learning at Trade Shows: Its Antecedents and Consequences," *Industrial Marketing Management* 35 (February 2006): 166–177.

27. Robert E. Hall, *Digital Dealing* (New York: W.W. Norton & Company, 2001).
28. David A. Aaker, *Building Strong Brands* (New York: The Free Press, 1996).
29. Benjamin, "The Importance of Being Integrated."
30. Carol Krol, "Marketers Prepare for Blended Search" *B to B* 92 (September 2007): 1–2.
31. Maddox, "Marketers Face Challenges from Economy to Ecology."
32. Harry Watkins, *Bridging the Great Divide: Process, Technology, and the Marketing/Sales Interface* (Aberdeen Group, Wellesley, MA, 2003).
33. Philip Kotler, *Marketing Management;* and Tom Eisenhart, "Going the Integrated Route," *Business Marketing* (December 1990): 24–28.
34. Julia Chang, "Hitting the Target," *Sales and Marketing Management* 158 (July 2006): 16.
35. Robyn Griggs, "Give Us Leads!" *Sales & Marketing Management* (July 1997): 66–72.
36. Griggs, "Give Us Leads!"
37. Timothy M. Smith, Srinath Gopalkrishna, and Rabikar Chatterjee, "A Three-Stage Model of Integrated Marketing Communications at the Marketing–Sales Interface," *Journal of Marketing Research* 43 (November 2006): 564–579.
38. Jeff Abugel, "Ad Bust: Slowpoke Marketers Lose Billions," *Business Marketing* (May 1997): 1, 33; and Joyce K. McArdle, "How to Create New Business Prospects: A Telemarketing Guide for Economic Developers," *Economic Development Review* (Winter 1996): 57–59.
39. Eisenhart, "Going the Integrated Route."
40. Gilbert A. Churchill, Jr., Niel M. Ford, and Orville C. Walker, Jr., *Sales Force Management,* 5th ed. (Burr Ridge, IL: Irwin, 1997).
41. Kate Maddox, "Integration Key to Lead Generation," *B to B* 91 (10 July 2006): 1–2.
42. Libbie Bramson, "Make Sales a Partner in Lead Generation Programs," *Sales & Marketing Management* (July 1990): 94–96.
43. Charlotte Woolard, "Separating Leads from Inquiries Central to Draeger's Success," *B to B* 92 (12 March 2007): 35–36.
44. Tom Przybylski, "BtoB Direct," *Marketing Tools* (January–February 1995): 54–62.
45. Bob Fernekees, "CRM Magazine Best Practices Series: Sales Force Automation," *Customer Relationships Management,* 11 (2007): 2; Zoltners, Sinha, and Zoltners, *The Complete Guide to Accelerating Sales Force Performance.*
46. Although we use the phrase *sales representative* throughout the rest of the chapter, a supplier actually may have a sales team making the call and continuing the process. We discuss sales teams further in Chapters 7 and 10.
47. Barton A. Weitz, Harish Sujan, and Mita Sujan, "Knowledge, Motivation, and Adaptive Behavior: A Framework for Improving Selling Effectiveness," *Journal of Marketing* (October 1986): 175.
48. John F. Tanner, Jr., "Adaptive Selling at Trade Shows," *Journal of Personal Selling & Sales Management* (Spring 1994): 15–23; David N. Stievater, Alexander Peterson, and Rahul Bhatia, "Sewing Up New Sales," *Pharmaceutical Executive* 26 (September 2006): 98–103.
49. Das Narayandas, "Color Kinetics Incorporated (A)," *Harvard Business School Case 9-501-077* (Boston, MA: Harvard Business School, 2001).
50. Douglas Bowman and Das Narayandas, "Linking Customer Management Effort to Customer Profitability in Industrial Markets." *Journal of Marketing Research* 41 (November 2004).
51. Das Narayandas, "Measuring and Managing the Benefits of Customer Retention: An Empirical Investigation," *Journal of Service Research* 1–2 (1998): 108–127.
52. Neil Rackham and John DeVincentis, *Rethinking the Sales Force* (New York: McGraw-Hill, Inc., 1999).
53. We base this discussion on Neil Rackham, *SPIN Selling* (New York: McGraw-Hill, 1988).
54. Pundits alternately refer to the opening as *the approach* or *the preliminaries* in the case of SPIN selling.
55. James C. Anderson and James A. Narus, "A Model of Distributor Firm and

Manufacturer Firm Working Partnerships," *Journal of Marketing* (January 1990): 45.

56. Stephen X. Doyle and George Thomas Roth, "Selling and Sales Management in Action: The Use of Insight Coaching to Improve Relationship Selling," *Journal of Personal Selling & Sales Management* (Winter 1992): 59–64.
57. R. Eric Reidenbach, Reginald W. Goeke, and Gordon McClung, *Dominating Markets with Value* (Morgantown, WV: Rhumb Line Publishing, 2002); Jonathan Gutman, "A Means-End Chain Model Based on Consumer Categorization Processes," *Journal of Marketing* (Spring 1982): 60–72; and Thomas J. Reynolds and Jonathan Gutman, "Laddering Theory, Method, Analysis, and Interpretation," *Journal of Advertising Research* (February–March 1988): 11–31.
58. James C. Anderson, Håkan Håkansson, and Jan Johanson, "Dyadic Business Relationships Within a Business Network Context," *Journal of Marketing* (October 1994): 10.
59. "It Takes 3.9 Calls to Close a Sale," *The American Salesman* (August 1995): 8–9.
60. Roger Fisher and William Ury, *Getting to Yes* (New York: Penguin Books, Ltd., 1981).
61. This discussion is based on Benson P. Shapiro, V. Kasturi Rangan, and John J. Sviokla, "Staple Yourself to an Order," *Harvard Business Review* (July–August 1992): 113–122.
62. Shapiro, Rangan, and Sviokla, "Staple Yourself to an Order."
63. This discussion is based on Robert G. Cross, *Revenue Management* (New York: Broadway Books, 1997); and Robert G. Cross, "Launching the Revenue Rocket," *Cornell Hotel and Restaurant Administration Quarterly* (April 1997): 32–43.
64. Cross, "Launching the Revenue Rocket," 33.
65. Robert Obrtter, "Revenue Managment for the Capital Equipment Service Industry," *Journal of Revenue and Pricing Managmnt* 1 (July 2002): 183–189.
66. For a detailed description of procedures and mathematical models of revenue management, see Fedeick H. Haris and Peter Peacock, "Hold My Place, Please," *Marketing Management* (Fall 1995): 34–46.

Chapter 9

Sustaining Reseller Partnerships

OVERVIEW

In an indirect marketing channel, a supplier and its resellers must leverage their complementary resources to find, keep, and grow jointly targeted customer firms. They must work together to deliver value in the form of an intended total customer experience (TCE) and achieve their mutual self-interests. Over time, the supplier and select reseller firms commit to reseller partnerships and actively work to sustain them.[1]

A **reseller partnership** refers to "the extent to which there is mutual recognition and understanding that the success of each firm depends on the other firm, with each firm consequently taking actions so as to provide a coordinated effort focused on jointly satisfying the requirements of the customer marketplace."[2] We further define **sustaining reseller partnerships** as the continuing process of aligning the mutual self interests and complementary resources of partner firms in stable marketplaces, responding adaptively to incremental marketplace changes, and transforming channels in the face of disruptive forces. Figure 9.1 depicts this process of sustaining reseller partnerships.[3]

In this chapter, we explore the process of sustaining reseller partnerships. To begin, we define and examine the challenging task of aligning the mutual self-interests and complementary resources of channel partner firms. Next, we discuss actions that supplier and reseller firms must take to strengthen their partnerships when marketplaces are relatively stable. Then, we discuss ways in which progressive firms can adapt their partnerships to incremental changes in marketplace conditions. Finally, we explore various ways to transform channels when highly disruptive forces threaten.

Figure 9.1 Sustaining Reseller Partnerships

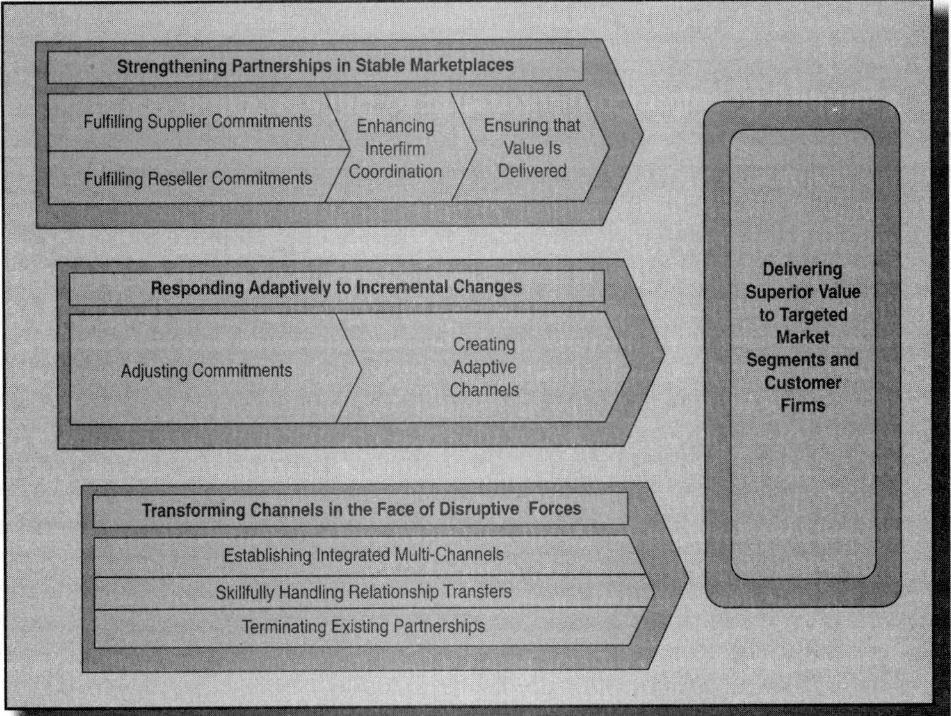

Aligning Mutual Self-Interests and Complementary Resources

Implicit in the definition of sustaining reseller partnerships just given is the realization that each firm in a business marketing channel is striving to accomplish not only shared goals but also distinct individual goals. A supplier firm and reseller firm partner because their respective managements understand that by sharing complementary resources and capabilities, they are more likely to achieve their respective self-interests than if they act alone. Importantly, if both firms meet their individual goals, then the partnership continues to thrive. If either firm or both fails to meet their individual goals, then the partnership becomes marked with intensifying conflicts and may eventually dissolve. Thus, scholars argue that for a partnership to succeed both firms must continuously align and strengthen their **mutual self-interests**.[4]

Alignment captures the extent to which goal congruence exists among partner firms' self-interests and the degree to which complementary resources and capabilities enable the partner firms to capitalize on marketplace opportunities. Pundits argue that a pivotal task of business market managers is sustaining the alignment of the mutual self-interests and complementary resources within their reseller partnerships. Although this task appears to be straightforward, it remains a challenge for supplier and reseller managers alike.[5]

Consultants Marks, Horan, and Emerson attribute alignment difficulties to two principles—the law of legitimate cross-purposes and the law of perpetual change. The *law of legitimate cross-purposes* refers to the fact that supplier firms and reseller firms rely upon different profit models that are sometimes at odds with one another. By producing and shipping large quantities of a limited number of products, supplier firms profit through economies of scale. Ideally, they would like reseller firms to direct their undivided attention to selling large quantities of the supplier's products to each prospective customer firm. Resellers, on the other hand, profit through economies of scope from selling unique bundles or solutions composed of small quantities of a wide variety of products and services to each of their customer firms. Ideally, they would like to distribute a portfolio of products from numerous supplier firms that can be readily assembled and consolidated into high-value, customized bundles or solutions. To bring a partnership into alignment, business market managers must seek ways to reconcile these conflicting cross-purposes.[6]

The *law of perpetual change* reflects the fact that evolving marketplaces may dramatically and unexpectedly alter the goals and resources of channel partners.[7] As mutual self-interests and complementary resources diverge more and more, they prompt counterproductive actions that threaten the continued prosperity of a partnership. For example, as the Internet becomes more cost effective and the preferred means of doing business, some supplier firms are tempted to terminate long-standing agreements with resellers and market directly to customer firms. On the other hand, as a current supplier's products become low-margin commodities, some reseller firms are prompted to sell private labels. To bring a partnership back into alignment in the face of marketplace change, business market managers must seek ways to adapt and/or transform the very nature of the business marketing channel.[8]

Scholars have long pointed to a third and more pernicious though less common threat to channel alignment—opportunism. In contrast with the legitimate pursuit of individual firm goals, **opportunism** refers to "self-interest seeking with guile."[9] In a destructive reseller partnership, a firm may resort to "lying, stealing, cheating, and calculated efforts to mislead, distort, disguise, obfuscate, or otherwise confuse" in order to claim a greater share of relational benefits than warranted under existing contracts.[10] Extensive research has identified four principal mechanisms through which managers can achieve channel alignment under the threat of opportunism: (1) careful selection of honest and trustworthy partner firms, (2) provision of incentives designed to thwart counterproductive behaviors, (3) diligent monitoring of partner firm activities, and (4) socialization of partner firm managers to the norms and values associated with the pursuit of shared goals.[11]

Insuring Alignment

Perhaps one of the biggest challenges to sustaining reseller partnerships occurs when business market managers are blindsided by unpredicted and significant changes in partner firm goals, resources and capabilities, and/or marketplace conditions. There are several actions that managers can take to avoid this trap. And, they should get in the habit of doing them beginning in the channel design phase, which we describe in Chapter 7.[12]

To begin with, it is essential that business market managers develop a deep understanding of their channel partners' business models and the legitimate though counterproductive tendencies they spawn. Supplier firms tend to be fixed-asset intensive. Their managers are consumed with the desire to achieve optimal capacity utilization of production facilities and fixed-asset turnover. They are inclined to be product-oriented and are driven to achieve growth in sales and market share for each of their offerings. As a result, supplier managers frequently try to "load" their reseller partner firms with excess inventory in order to increase return on investment by simultaneously increasing sales recorded on the supplier's income statement and reducing inventory assets on its balance sheet. Furthermore, supplier managers expect their resellers to focus almost exclusively on their lines and aggressively market them to all their customers. All too often, supplier managers interpret reseller efforts directed toward the products of any other suppliers that they carry to be a sign of disloyalty.[13]

Reseller firms, on the other hand, tend to be short-term asset intensive (i.e., inventory and accounts receivable). Their managers are primarily concerned with cash flow management. They are more likely to be customer-oriented and are driven to increase the share of customer business and profitability of each customer account they serve. According to research conducted by Brent Grover for the National Association of Wholesaler-Distributors, the most profitable resellers tend to sell a greater median number and dollar amount of items per transaction, take greater advantage of supplier's cash discounts, turn their inventories faster, and hold less short-term debt than less profitable resellers. As a result, shrewd resellers have a tendency to heavily discount products in order to add items to a given transaction, sell whatever products that their customers request, and drop supplier lines whenever demand plummets or the sales cycle lengthens. Reseller managers constantly fret that supplier firms will "do an end-run" and sell directly to the reseller's customers, thus cutting that reseller out of hard-earned business. For this reason, reseller managers are hesitant to provide suppliers with the names and sales data for any of the resellers' customer accounts.[14]

Through joint annual planning or periodic surveys of partner managers, business market managers should monitor changes in partner goals, resources, and capabilities and use them as diagnostics of misalignment. In Chapter 7, we identified key channel goals as maximizing market access, optimizing value added, and minimizing cost-to-serve. Naturally, firms may have other idiosyncratic marketing, operational, and financial goals that should be considered as well. Discrepancies among partner firms as to the importance and prioritization of these goals may indicate looming partnership problems and the need for corrective actions. For example, a common source of misalignment stems from market access priorities. Supplier firms typically give greater weight to expanding market penetration and growing market share for their offerings, whereas reseller firms are keen to increase the share of customer business. Significant differences among the market access goals of supplier and reseller firms may indicate misalignment—the supplier firm may have franchised general line distributors when in fact manufacturers' representatives or specialty distributors would have been more appropriate.

In another common case of misalignment, a supplier firm may expect resellers to deliver a total customer experience that focuses on intensive and time-consuming customer service. Locked in bitter price wars with local competitors, the supplier's resellers may forgo the provision of such value-added services in order to lower operating costs and hence prices. Such discrepancies in value-added service priorities may indicate the need for the supplier firm to devise new methods for delivering customer services such as through its Internet Web site. Last, some supplier firms aggressively seek out new ways to reduce costs-to-serve customer firms. This priority may conflict with the reseller's desire to provide a highly personal and responsive TCE. These differences may suggest the need for new distribution arrangements such as hybrid or integrated multi-channels.[15]

Another diagnostic of misalignment that business market managers should monitor on an ongoing basis is the amount of conflict within their marketing channels. By **conflict**, we mean "the overall level of disagreement in the working partnership. As such, conflict is determined by the frequency, intensity, and duration of disagreements."[16] Scholars have found that the three principal causes of channel conflict are differences in goals, understandings of the allocation of partnership responsibilities, and perceptions of the marketplace. In their research for the National Association of Wholesaler-Distributors, Marks, Horan, and Emerson found that conflict often masks misalignment and that the tendency of both suppliers and resellers to avoid or "gloss over" conflicts often has detrimental consequences for all parties. Instead, they argue that business market managers should address disputes early and decisively even if that means changing channels and terminating partnerships. In coming sections of this chapter, we will discuss various conflict resolution mechanisms.[17]

Business market managers must identify and pay particular attention to changes in the marketplace that stand to misalign the mutual self-interests of partner firms. Rangan states that the market forces that have the greatest impact on business marketing channels are customer demand requirements, channel member capabilities, costs-to-serve customers, the distribution of power among channel members, and competitive actions. Product and transaction technologies may also be added to his list. As changes in these forces may be subtle and come unexpectedly, managers must take the time to monitor them and to predict their consequences.[18]

When business market managers initially design and implement a new channel, it is highly likely that mutual self-interests are aligned. Rather than assuming that these conditions will remain the same indefinitely, managers should plan for three distinct scenarios of action: strengthening partnerships in a stable marketplace, responding adaptively to incremental marketplace changes, and transforming channels in the face of disruptive forces.

Strengthening Partnerships in a Stable Marketplace

When a marketplace is relatively stable and supplier and reseller firms' mutual self-interests and resources are reasonably well aligned, the principal channel management tasks are fulfilling commitments, enhancing interfirm coordination, and ensuring that value is delivered. **Commitment** "captures the perceived continuity or growth in the relationship between two firms."[19] It entails a "desire to develop a stable relationship, a willingness to make short-term sacrifices to maintain the relationship, and a confidence in the stability of the relationship."[20] In essence, each firm formally or informally promises to invest certain resources and capabilities in the partnership, perform certain channel tasks, and share profits. Once they make such commitments, supplier and reseller firms must strive to consistently fulfill them.

Fulfilling Supplier Commitments to Deliver Value

Clearly, the greatest component of customer value the supplier firm contributes is its products and services. However, as we pointed out in Chapter 7, progressive managers think more broadly in terms of the total customer experience and marketplace equity it creates. When they do, managers realize they can ensure that superior value is delivered to customer firms by assisting reseller firms on tasks the resellers cannot efficiently complete by themselves. Thus, supplier firms commonly make commitments to provide resellers with help in the form of training and coaching, responsive sales and marketing programs, pricing support in competitive situations, and operational and technical assistance.

Train and Coach Partner Firms

Perhaps the most direct way to strengthening a partner firm's resources and capabilities and helping them to reach their goals is through training and coaching. **Training** entails imparting knowledge and skills in a systematic manner through courses, seminars, and demonstrations. Increasingly, not only are supplier firms offering such programs for their resellers, but resellers also are providing them to supplier firms. Whereas supplier training programs focus on such things as product knowledge, selling skills, and technical competence, reseller courses concentrate on such things as customer applications, changing customer needs, and operational procedures.

Training efforts commonly take two forms: certification programs and skills training. Through a certification program, one firm requires that personnel from its partner take a series of technical courses and demonstrate competence, often through an examination, before the partner firm is officially allowed to perform certain tasks or offer particular services. For instance, the Microsoft Corporation requires third-party service engineers to become certified to deliver value-added business solutions or technical support using Microsoft products. To become certified, technicians complete a series of courses and demonstrate proficiency with Microsoft programs through certification exams. When they pass these exams, individuals are formally recognized as Microsoft Certified Professionals. They can include this designation on their resumes and promote it to prospective customers.

Skills training entails courses on focused topics. For example, a supplier might offer reseller sales reps a course in how to sell to major accounts. Alternatively, a reseller firm might provide supplier operations and information systems personnel with a course on reseller-industry bar-coding standards. Whereas in the past, firms provided skills training largely in a classroom setting, they are increasingly using emerging technologies to enable personnel to study at their own convenience in locations of their own choosing. For example, the Mita Corporation, a supplier of photocopying equipment, created a CD-ROM–based sales training program for its dealers. Using their own personal computers, the sales reps walk through all the steps associated with selling copier equipment. Moreover, because the CD-ROM program is interactive, the sales reps can participate in role-playing exercises. Via a keyboard, the sales rep "speaks" to a hypothetical customer, making a sales presentation, handling objections, and asking for the sale. At the end of the exercise, the program rates the rep and offers suggestions on how to improve.[21]

The Ford Motor Company created the satellite-based Fordstar Network to beam training programs and technical information directly to its dealers in the United States, Canada, and Mexico. The first Fordstar Network program furnished training on how to repair onboard electronics on Ford vehicles. Service engineers at more than 6,000 dealer sites and 300 Ford locations participated. At the dealerships, these service engineers sat around conference tables and viewed an instructor on a monitor. An audio interaction feature of the network enabled the instructor to question participants and listen to their responses. The instructor used computer programs, videotapes, and a laser disc player to perform mathematical calculations, demonstrate repair procedures, and convey technical information. Importantly, Ford reports that the network dramatically reduced training costs per students and cut by half the amount of time dealer personnel had to spend away from their dealerships for training.[22]

Research demonstrates that most participants forget more than 80% of what they learned within one month after attending a training program. Such findings indicate the importance of a second performance enhancement tool—coaching. **Coaching** entails the improvement and reinforcement of desired skills, behaviors, and performance through periodic assistance, counseling, and practice. Partner firms coach each other at both the strategic and skills levels.[23]

Senior or middle-level managers provide strategic coaching or conceptual guidance during the joint annual planning, implementation, and review processes. During those meetings, the coach shares the wisdom of experience with partner managers and helps them to craft a set of goals, strategies, and activities for the coming year. Skills coaching serves to strengthen the partner's behavior at the tactical level. For example, a supplier that conducts a technical selling training program for reseller salespersons might follow it up by having its field engineers make a series of joint sales calls with the salespersons. The field engineers provide advice and act as a technical "safety net," allowing the reseller salespersons to fearlessly practice their newly learned skills.

Provide Responsive Sales and Marketing Programs

Some reseller firms do not have sufficient resources or capabilities to conduct periodic market research studies. As a result, they may have difficulty identifying emerging customer prospects or adapting their TCE to better meet changing market preferences. Let's consider how the Parker Hannifin Corporation helps resource-constrained distributors overcome these deficiencies.

Parker Hannifin Corporation (PH) supports distributor sales and marketing efforts through its Industrial Distribution Marketing System (IDMS). By contract, PH requires its distributors to forward copies of all customer invoices involving PH products to the manufacturer's market research department. Analysts code these invoices by customer and industry numbers and enter the sales data into the IDMS database. This database contains extensive profiles on existing and potential PH customers worldwide. Rather than using the invoices opportunistically, PH creates a marketing tool, Product-Market Sales Analysis (PMSA) reports. Periodically, PH sends each distributor a customized PMSA report that analyzes the distributor's product line sales by geographic region, by market segment, and by customer firm, as well as a compact disc containing the research data and analytical software. The report identifies prospects and forecasts sales. To aid with the selling process, PH furnishes contact information on these prospects to distributors and proposes a strategy for cultivating new business from existing and potential accounts. This strategy includes recommendations on how to customize offerings for local customers and how to cross-sell the full line of PH products. Distributors, too, are given the option of analyzing the data and generating marketing development strategies as they see fit.[24]

Back Up Resellers with Pricing Support

When faced with cutthroat price competition, many reseller firms forgo well-conceived, value-based marketing strategies and slash prices indiscriminately. All too often, this response precipitates a downward price spiral within an industry and jeopardizes reseller profitability. To keep resellers focused on delivering value, leading supplier firms promise pricing support. For example, the Lincoln Electric Company, a manufacturer of welding equipment and supplies, devised what it calls the Guaranteed Cost Reduction Program to help its distributors cope with intense price competition from other welding product manufacturers. The program works as follows. Whenever a customer demands that a distributor lower prices on Lincoln supplies and equipment to meet those of competitors, Lincoln and that distributor guarantee in writing that they will find cost reductions in the customer's plant that meet or exceed the price difference. All the customer has to do is continue buying Lincoln Electric products from the distributor.[25]

If the customer agrees, a Lincoln sales rep and a distributor counterpart survey the customer's operations, identify possible cost reductions, and help to implement them. At the end of a prespecified time period, an agreed-upon third party independently audits performance. If the cost savings do not match promises, then Lincoln Electric and the distributor pay the difference to the customer. Lincoln contributes 70%. Since the program was initiated, Lincoln has failed to deliver promised cost savings in only two instances![26]

On occasion the supplier adjusts its pricing so resellers can obtain customer business, in part, through lower price. In exchange for a large order, the reseller may offer a customer a price discount, and the supplier sometimes supports this lower price by reducing its invoice price to the reseller. These large-order price discounts are a pricing tactic that suppliers and resellers should use selectively to win business in pursuit of their market strategy. The supplier sometimes also supports its resellers in their efforts to gain new customers by providing additional gross margin to partially compensate the resellers for the initial-use discounts they give. Finally, a supplier and its reseller sometimes pass on the lower costs of a transaction to a customer in the form of a lower price. This is an instance of defeaturing pricing, where the customer absorbs one or more functions that the supplier or its reseller normally would perform. An example would be a supplier drop shipping a large quantity to a single customer location. The customer either uses the large quantity at that location, or breaks bulk and further distributes it internally.

Furnish Operational and Technical Support

Increasingly, supplier firms can reduce the cost-to-serve customers for an entire marketing channel by maintaining and providing operational and technical support in the form of inventory control, logistics, and customer service systems for other channel partners. By eliminating redundancies, the supplier firm enables reseller partners to offer a broader array of services at far lower costs than they could acting alone. The following examples demonstrate how suppliers help their resellers deliver value in these ways.

The Panduit Company, a manufacturer of electrical components, established a Vendor Managed Inventory (VMI) system to reduce the inventory investments and related warehousing costs of its distributors. Through its VMI system, Panduit continuously receives withdrawal and inventory balance information from its distributors via electronic data interchange and automatically replenishes those inventories to a predetermined level. Panduit sets these levels to yield the lowest total operating costs at a given customer service level for each distributor. Panduit then arranges shipments, consolidates loads, and schedules deliveries. It also provides electronic order acknowledgments, shipping notices, and invoices. Whenever Panduit's VMI system shows that distributors are maintaining too much stock of slow-moving items, Panduit generates a return order with no restocking charges and takes the inventory back. Distributors claim that the system has reduced their operating costs, enabled them to provide better service to customers, and minimized out-of-stock occurrences.[27]

Okuma has instituted *Okuma Care* (Constantly Available Resource Experts), a 24-hour, seven-day-a-week, 52-weeks-a-year (24 × 7 × 52) customer-service support program for its North American Market, to improve its distributors' technical and service capabilities. Through Okuma Care, Okuma makes technical expertise and repair parts available to distributor service personnel. Whenever an Okuma distributor runs into a technical or service problem that its technicians cannot solve, the distributor can contact Okuma's Charlotte, North Carolina, headquarters for technical service counsel or parts, anytime of the day or week. Based upon the immediacy and severity of the problem, the distributor chooses from three levels of support. The distributor can use Okuma's online portal to download files on how to service machines. Alternatively, the distributor can telephone toll-free to an answer line and speak to a service engineer. Finally, if the problem is critical, Okuma will dispatch a technical rep or team to the customer's site.

Fulfilling Reseller Commitments to Deliver Value

Resellers, too, must meet commitments to deliver value in the form of the intended TCE. Perhaps the most important way in which resellers work to meet commitments is by consistently providing superior service to customer firms. However, reseller firms also promise to contribute in other ways. They do so by innovating in the local marketplace and by actively participating in the supplier firm's new offering realization and quality improvement programs. In these ways, reseller firms not only boost their own reseller equity but also enhance the supplier's brand equity.

Provide Consistently Superior Service to Customer Firms

To be sure that they are providing excellent service, resellers are turning to techniques popularized by the quality movement. For example, customers sent Central States Industrial Supply (CSIS), a distributor of pipes, valves, and fittings, a "wake-up call" via a market research survey. According to survey results, CSIS provided no exceptional services to customers. Managers quickly discovered that customers believed the quality of CSIS's services was highly inconsistent.[28]

To ensure that CSIS consistently delivered service superior to its competitors as well as to eliminate work process redundancies in the company, CSIS management decided to pursue ISO 9002 registration. Senior managers appointed an ISO coordinator. She attended ISO training schools and joined a local network group of firms undergoing the ISO process. With the help of cross-functional employee teams, the ISO coordinator devised standard procedures for performing the firm's services and a quality management system. After testing the procedures and verifying that they worked properly, the firm implemented the system. Then the ISO coordinator documented those procedures for ISO registration purposes. Following detailed audits by ISO representatives, CSIS received its ISO 9002 registration. Today, CSIS management is confident that the firm delivers consistently superior services to its customers.

Innovate in the Local Marketplace

Because they are "closer" to the market, resellers are often in a better position to detect changes in local requirements and exploit them. For instance, as a new market segment emerges, a progressive reseller might customize existing supplier offerings with appropriate augmenting services and begin to develop new accounts. Alternatively, as technology evolves, a reseller may be able to put those developments to use for customer firms in the form of new support services. By acting promptly in both cases, the reseller firm creates a high-value total customer experience that increases sales for its own firm and the supplier. Boxes 9.1 and 9.2 provide outstanding examples of two firms that have innovated in the marketplace by deploying an extensive network of resellers.[29]

Enhance the Supplier's Brand Equity

A reseller firm can help the supplier deliver superior value to customer firms by offering new product ideas and by participating in quality improvement efforts. For example, the Cameron & Barkley Company (Cambar) enthusiastically cooperates with suppliers in the new offering realization process. Cambar sales representatives routinely study customer applications for needs that current products do not meet. For example, Cambar reps learned that welders needed a welding shield that would fit on full-face respirators. They relayed this insight to a supplier that developed and then marketed the desired shield. Furthermore, the firm conducts an annual market research survey of customers to identify new product ideas and summarizes major findings for its suppliers. When select supplier partners introduce new products, Cambar frequently tests prototypes at customer locations or participates in test markets. Often, Cambar ideas lead to innovative products. Working closely with Dalloz Safety Products, Cambar managers convinced the supplier's R&D group to design safety goggles with frame colors and lens options that mirrored the styles of popular sunglasses young people wear. The result was a successful line of stylish safety goggles.[30]

BOX 9.1
Yahoo! India Pioneers an Important Offering for the Small and Medium Business Marketplace

Yahoo! India Small Business (YISB) is a Web-hosting package from Yahoo! India, providing business Web site building services to small businesses and entrepreneurs. The package includes domain registration, a Web site hosting package, business e-mail, and Web site development tools.

Yahoo! India soon realized the necessity of a strong channel partnership. Many small and medium businesses prefer third-party agents to develop and publish their sites. This segment was estimated to be larger than the self-service segment in India. YISB's strategy to target this segment effectively was to develop a strong sustaining reseller network which had the reach and competence to take its products and services to the Do-It-For-Me (DIFM) segment, which needed third-party agents. Yahoo! India began aligning with resellers to push up its sales and target new markets it had been previously unable to reach.

YISB had only online payment gateways set up to accept payments. It soon realized that a significant set of customers wanted to pay using only cash or cheque. A significant portion of the Indian customer base is still averse to doing business through online payment mechanisms. YISB could still serve its cash or cheque-paying customers by channeling them through resellers. In addition, Yahoo! India could take advantage of the deep reach of local players in the Indian market.

YISB realized that some of the resellers in the Indian market have far more local reach which Yahoo! India could take advantage of. With a total of 10 million small and medium businesses in India (online and brick-and-mortar), spread throughout metropolitans and remote semi-urban towns, Yahoo! India realized that the existing market was huge and could be effectively tapped by piggy-backing onto resellers. Yahoo! India could also direct the leads it generated through the Web to resellers, who would in turn track them to realize an actual sale. To this end, Yahoo! India provided resellers functionality which allowed them to capture, track, and manage leads to closure. This enabled both Yahoo! India and the resellers to penetrate the Indian small and medium business market more effectively.

Contributed by Abhishek Dan, Participant, PGSEM Program, Indian Institute of Management Bangalore.

Dealers are actively involved in Caterpillar's product quality, cost reduction, and manufacturing improvement efforts. The *Partners in Quality Program*, for example, links personnel responsible for building a particular machine with select dealers. These individuals meet quarterly as a team to discuss quality issues. Dealers also audit each Caterpillar machine they receive, and if anything is wrong, they feed that information back to the plant immediately so that corrections can be made. As an illustration, a dealer discovered that hoses in a new grader model had been installed incorrectly and immediately notified the factory. Caterpillar retrained the assembler, fixed the machines still in the factory, and notified other dealers to repair the machines in their inventories. In another instance, Caterpillar's dealer in Thailand concluded that a pump in a new line of hydraulic excavators was not durable enough to meet local working conditions. It persuaded Caterpillar to use a different pump on the machines until engineers could redesign the one in question.[31]

BOX 9.2
Tata Motors Creatively Supports Its Customers through an Extensive Dealer Network

Tata Motors has been in the automotive business since 1954. The company originated with manufacture of commercial vehicles (trucks and buses), which even now accounts for a significant portion of the company's revenues. It has the biggest dealer and service network in the commercial vehicle market. Its distribution channel consisting of 19 distributors and approximately 1,000 retail outlets has been designed with the goal of increasing customer satisfaction and loyalty. Tata Motors believes that its channel network is the company's unique selling proposition and is very effectively used to counter international competition.

Lately, Tata Motors has been trying to consolidate its distribution business into a new company called TML Distribution Company Limited (TDCL). It is a 100% subsidiary of Tata Motors Limited (TML) and engages in dealing and providing logistics support for distributing the company's products throughout the country. As a supplier, TML ensures that dealers are comfortably positioned to achieve the sales and services objectives of the company and builds a strong partnership with them. Tata dealers understand the importance of partnership and value their association with Tata. The dealers contribute to the partnership by committing to run their businesses upholding long-standing Tata group values, capturing customer feedback to provide key inputs for sales and operations planning, and providing valuable input for new product development initiatives. The supplier–dealer relationship at Tata Motors is continuously evolving with new initiatives and programs being developed to deliver superior value to both channel partners and customers.

In 2003, Tata Motors launched an initiative to integrate customer relationships and dealer management efforts on an IT system. The integrated system supports over 15,000 users within the company and across 1,000 dealer locations in India and abroad to conduct all customer-facing transactions. The real-time availability of customer and product information enables the company and its channel partners to improve response time and customer service. As an effort towards incentivizing dealers, Tata Motors has created structured and periodic training programs with a view to integrate dealers as important stakeholders in the company. Dealers have direct access to top management for addressing grievances.

A deeply penetrated, well-established dealer network coupled with a company committed to being customer-centric has ensured a highly agile channel network. There is a high degree of involvement of the dealer network in the development of new products and services. The company believes that the dealer network is its major strength. The dealer network is also a major source of feedback from the marketplace to the company in that the dealers deeply understand customers' needs and requirements. They play a significant role in channeling them to the company for appropriate response in terms of coming up with new products and services, etc.

Contributed by Mayank Jha, Participant, PGP Program, Indian Institute of Management Bangalore.
Sources: Tata Motors Annual Report 2008; Oracle Press Release, 30 August 2007, *http://www.oracle.com/global/in/pressroom/tataMotorsDealerOutlets.html*; "Tata Motors Rejigs Dealer Network," *Business Standard*, 29 September 2006, *http://www.business-standard.com/india/news/tata-motors-rejigs-dealer-network/260065/*; "Tata Motors May Outsource Distribution To A New Unit," *LiveMint.com*, July 19, 2008, *http://www.livemint.com/2008/07/18233746/tata-Motors-may-outsource-dist.html*.

Strengthening Interfirm Coordination

Through **coordination**, the customer firm and supplier firm synchronize their activities, resources, and capabilities to accomplish a collective set of tasks. Firms achieve better coordination by participating in joint annual planning, improving communications, clarifying roles and responsibilities through written agreements, and synchronizing efforts with a partner relationship management system.[32]

Participate in Periodic Joint Annual Planning

One way to ensure that partners' mutual self-interests are aligned and that appropriate resources and capabilities are being directed toward delivering the intended TCE is to engage in joint annual planning. Quite simply, when the supplier and resellers participate in the planning process, they are more likely to view the plan as theirs and work hard to implement it. To reinforce these commitments, a supplier and its resellers conduct both planning and review sessions at least once a year, preferably at each reseller's home office. During these meetings, managers discuss the three fundamental questions for planning market strategy that we discussed in Chapter 4: (1) What do we know? (2) What do we want to accomplish? and (3) How will we do it?

After these individual sessions, the business market manager summarizes perspectives in an annual **reseller marketing plan**, both for each reseller partnership and for the channel network as a whole. Such plans typically begin with a situation analysis, which assesses strengths, weaknesses, opportunities, and threats for the supplier and reseller. The next section lists mutual objectives that the supplier and reseller commit to accomplishing. The next two sections are a basic requirements section that spells out the kinds of support that resellers will need, and an action program section that delineates the actions the supplier and reseller will take separately and together in the marketplace. The last section is implementation and control, which charts a timetable for program implementation, assigns responsibilities for execution, and defines performance measures and expectations. Supplier managers should meet with each reseller quarterly to review each firm's performance versus the plan and to initiate corrective actions.

Clarify Roles and Responsibilities Through Written Agreements

Progressive companies improve channel coordination by writing more equitable sales agreements, policy manuals, and policy statements. Each of these documents has a special purpose. The sales agreement, in the form of a written contract, formally and legally specifies the rights and responsibilities of both parties within the partnership. By specifying such working conditions, the written sales agreement serves to sharpen expectations and direct the actions of both firms.

Although companies generally write sales agreements in broad, legal terms, they clarify those terms and conditions in policy manuals and policy statements. A policy manual contains far more detailed descriptions of tasks each member should perform, such as the layout of material data and safety sheets, handling procedures, and product labeling. It provides a summary of key supplier and resellers' policies. A policy statement is a detailed statement of changes and modifications in a specific policy. Key examples might include pricing sheets, payment terms, and product line specifications. The supplier issues these statements periodically to reflect changes in market conditions and company strategy.

Improve Communications Through Bridging

Communication is "the formal and informal sharing of meaningful and timely information between firms."[33] Supplier and reseller managers use bridging to improve interfirm communications. **Bridging** entails establishing and sustaining communications between partner firms across functions and management levels. Dayco Products Inc. has long required that its president, distributor marketing managers, and key operations personnel call on distributors each year to demonstrate the importance of their partnership. Bridging should also be practiced across careers and generations. Composites One has a policy of tracking the careers of all the supplier sales reps and marketing managers that they have dealt with over the years. Normally, this tracking entails occasional phone calls, letters, and holiday cards. By doing so, CompositesOne has managed to maintain contacts at various organizational levels within their supplier partners. In the case of a multibillion-dollar chemical supplier, this continuous contact includes the chairman of the board of directors.[34]

Synchronize Efforts with a Partner Relationship Management System

Partner relationship management (PRM) is a business regimen that enhances the ability of a supplier firm, resellers, and third-party service providers to seamlessly integrate and synchronize their operations, selling, marketing, and servicing efforts. PRM system functionality facilitates communication with partner firms, the provision of technical support, order processing and tracking, and the improvement of selling effectiveness. PRM systems often entail Internet or extranet-based software. Supplier firms create or acquire PRM software modules individually as applications arise. These modules are configured to draw upon accounting and operations data from the firm's enterprise resource planning (ERP) system and marketing data from its customer relationship management (CRM) system. In fact, firms can purchase PRM functionality as part of a new ERP or CRM system.

Perhaps the easiest and often the first modules to be added to a PRM system seek to sychnronize communications between the supplier, resellers, and customer firms. For example, publish-on-demand capabilities enable resellers to download and print up-to-date product information, promotional materials, brochures, and manuals 24 × 7. These capabilities frequently empower resellers to customize standard documents to better meet the requirements of local customers. More advanced communications applications include contact management. Contact management modules keep sales, service, and operations personnel aware of the nature and content of all calls that supplier, reseller, and third-party providers make on each customer firm. With these modules a supplier can forward such information immediately to all relevant personnel via personal computers or mobile telephones.

Through its Web site, a supplier can furnish resellers with repair manuals and technical problem-solving search engines. Some suppliers even provide technical training exercises and simulations for reseller personnel to use. And, PRM software can route technical service requests immediately to an appropriate authorized service provider for resolution. Another popular PRM application addresses order management concerns. For example, online order placement systems allow reseller managers to electronically scan available inventories, place orders, track deliveries, and review account billing records. Such modules not only reduce transaction costs but also improve the accuracy and timeliness of deliveries.

To improve the selling and marketing effectiveness of resellers, supplier firms increasingly distribute qualified sales leads through their PRM systems. Product configuration and proposal generation modules help resellers specify feasible offerings that better meet customer requirements and write more persuasive sales proposals. Pricing configurators that enable resellers to match proposed product and service specifications with their own firm's costs and profit rules can help ensure that resellers gain a reasonable return on their efforts. Finally, partner life cycle management modules empower suppliers to monitor ongoing reseller performance.

Okuma America Corporation provides an excellent example of a PRM System. Okuma managers have developed a suite of online applications to provide distributors vital information for sales, service, and support of their products. Distributors can access data through any Internet location or portable handheld device. Okuma provides three sources of support for through the system. One is CRM. It includes a history of sales calls and transactions made across the distribution network and a communications tool through which distributor personnel can contact the sales representatives who made those calls. Another is called *Diamond Lane*, a Web-based directory portal where a distributor representative can pull up information on anything from technical specifications to brochures to training presentations. Last, all parts, feature options, and machines, can be viewed and ordered in real time via Okuma's *BaaN System* from any of the 46 distributor locations in the western hemisphere.

In Box 9.3, we describe how Tata Steel synchronizes its reseller sales and service efforts.

Ensuring That Value Is Delivered

Periodically, supplier and reseller managers take stock of overall channel performance to determine whether they have fulfilled their commitments to deliver customer value. They conduct market research to learn whether the TCE promised to customer firms has in fact been provided. In addition, supplier and reseller firms conduct financial analyses to determine whether they have received an equitable return on the value they have delivered. Supplier and reseller managers use the insights they gain from these evaluations to improve their value-delivery efforts.

Conduct Market Research

Using procedures we discussed in Chapter 2, business market managers perform both customer satisfaction and customer value assessment studies. For instance, drawing on customer firm names from its IDMS system that we described earlier, Parker Hannifin managers conduct an annual customer satisfaction study. The study assesses how well PH and its distributors meet customer expectations and identifies ways PH and its distributors can improve their market offerings. Best practice examples of value assessment in marketing channels are the SKF Documented Solutions Program and the Applied Industrial Technologies Documented Value-Added Reports, which we describe in Chapter 2. In both cases, managers return to customer firms and conduct value-in-use studies to document benefits provided and costs saved.

Business market managers use the findings of these research projects in several ways. First, reseller and supplier managers reexamine what each contributes to the delivery of the intended TCE to determine whether a reformulation of channel tasks

BOX 9.3
Tata Steel Synchronizes its Reseller Sales and Service Efforts

Historically, Tata Steel had focused its sales on large business market customers. It had little knowledge of retail markets and did not deeply understand the retail steel customer. However, during the early 2000s, the company saw a huge growth opportunity in retail markets due to a dramatic growth in infrastructure caused by strong thrust from the government. Hitherto, this market had been the domain of small regional producers with local brands. Leveraging its strong corporate "Tata" brand, the company decided to redefine the rules of retailing steel in India through its innovative Retail Value Management (RVM) initiative.

RVM seeks to upgrade the retail network and to bring about transparency in retail operations. Its goal is to deliver the true value of the brand to the consumer. This not only entails offering a quality product but also differentiated services. Together, these constitute the "market offering" of the company to the targeted consumer market segments.

The RVM process addresses two basic levers for improving the performance of the company's retail channel. The first lever is efficiency, answering the question, *Which specific markets and retailers should the company focus on?* The second lever is effectiveness, addressing the question, *What strategies should the company adopt to realize the full potential of the channel and the brand?*

The RVM initiative was implemented for each state in the country by a specially formed team comprising the territory's designated customer account manager (CAM) from Tata Steel, a key manager from the distributor for the state, and a full-time facilitator (essentially an RVM process expert). Typically the CAM, who is a Tata Steel salesperson, is responsible for the state's retail sales and works closely with a designated distributor for the state. However, in the past, Tata Steel had no visibility into the market beyond the distributor. All this was set to change with the implementation of RVM.

The RVM team was mandated to revisit each operation and challenge every assumption of the retail channel. The objective was to ensure that brands offered by the company in the retail market were the products of choice for the end consumer. Simultaneously, the channel had to develop the capacity and motivation to sell higher volumes at better profitability as per the market share objectives of each respective brand. For this purpose, the RVM implementing team took on stretch targets that were closely monitored by top management through a very structured process.

The result of RVM's implementation was closer work between Tata Steel and its channel partners, both distributors and retailers. This reduced inefficiencies in the channel, thereby reducing costs. It also improved profits for the company as well as for the channel partners.

Anand Sen and Peeyush Gupta, "Redefining Retail of Steel in India," Internal Paper of Tata Steel, 2006; Arabinda Tripathy, Peeyush Gupta, D. V. R. Seshadri and Subodh Pandey, "Reinventing Marketing at Tata Steel," case study developed for IIM Bangalore in 2004; Arabinda Tripathy, Peeyush Gupta, Kulvin Suri and D. V. R. Seshadri, "Retail Value Management at Tata Steel," case study developed for IIM Bangalore in 2004.

and rewards is necessary. For example, they might eliminate products and services from their respective offerings that they find are value drains. Another result of the research might be that the supplier adapts its channel offering to better motivate and enable its resellers to serve customers. Finally, the research findings might also point to needed improvements in supplier and reseller firm coordination.

Getting an Equitable Return on Delivered Value

As a complement to customer satisfaction and value assessment studies, supplier and reseller managers routinely evaluate channel financial performance. They do so for two important reasons. First, they want to ascertain that the supplier and its reseller firms have realized the financial returns they expected. Obviously, partner firms are more motivated to continue delivering superior customer value if these expectations have been met or surpassed.[35] Second, managers hope to find new ways to achieve their cost-to-serve goals. For example, if they learn that the channel's delivery costs are out of line with industry standards, they would investigate how to strengthen their logistics system. Commonly, managers evaluate financial performance through diagnostic measures and profitability analyses.

A diagnostic measure signals that a problem may exist with a channel. Traditionally, managerial accountants have relied upon ratio analyses as diagnostics. The process runs as follows. First, managers calculate a given ratio for the firm's channels. A ratio contrasts two or more income statement or balance sheet items for a specific firm. Second, the manager compares it to industry averages. Trade associations and consulting firms commonly compile and publish these industry averages in **performance and activity reports (PARs)**. In theory, if a firm's ratio is close to the industry average, then it is doing acceptably well on that dimension. Third, managers use ratios to track performance over time, to compare relative performance of two firms, and to make cross-industry comparisons. Suppliers and resellers rely on different sets of performance ratios.

Suppliers frequently use distribution-related costs-to-serve customers as channel performance diagnostics. In companies that sell exclusively through resellers, distribution-related costs can exceed 40% of total revenues. The most readily available diagnostics are **expense-to-revenue (E/R) ratios**. Suppliers evaluate four categories—customer communications, paperwork flows, physical distribution, and financial risk assumptions. Suppliers use them to learn whether certain costs are under control and to contrast the efficiency of one channel versus another.[36]

Resellers that stock inventory, such as wholesalers, distributors, and dealers, regard three diagnostics as critical. **Turns × earns** is the product of annual inventory turnover times average gross margin. Resellers evaluate it for the firm as a whole and for major product lines. Turns × earns captures two critical performance dimensions for resellers: how quickly they are turning inventory and how much gross profit they make on these sales. **Gross margin return on inventory (GMROI)** is average gross margin divided by average inventory. Managers use GMROI as a surrogate for return on assets. **Gross margin return on receivables (GMROR)**, on the other hand, is average gross margin divided by average account receivables. Receivables are resellers' second largest investment category. Because GMROI and GMROR are readily calculated, they provide "quick and dirty" measures of asset turnover.[37]

For resellers that do not carry inventory, managers evaluate activity measures rather than asset turnover. Thus, they spend greater time examining such things as return on equity, gross margin, and E/R ratios. Furthermore, managers review personnel productivity measures in great detail. These items include such things as the number of billable hours charged, the ratio of potential to charged billable hours, and E/R ratios related to employee activities.

Although performance diagnostics serve to flag potential problem areas, they frequently do not provide sufficient insight into the nature and cause of these difficulties.

To gain such perspectives, managers turn to profitability analyses. Manning proposed an activity-based costing (ABC) approach for exploring distribution channel profitability from the supplier's perspective, called **strategic cost management (SCM)**. SCM recasts the direct costing income statement around distribution-related activities.[38]

The SCM approach has four steps. First, managers divide the organization's costs into activity costs, such as order processing and selling costs, and into nonactivity costs such as regional advertising or trade-show participation. At the same time, they estimate the amount of expenditures associated with activity and nonactivity costs. Second, managers subdivide and classify these costs as channel-related or specific reseller-related costs. Third, managers trace each cost back to individual channels or resellers. Tracing entails developing approximations of the cost required to perform a specific task. Fourth, either managers estimate revenues channels or resellers generate them, and then they construct direct costing income statements. With these analyses, managers can readily examine the profitability of channels or resellers.

As part of the widespread acceptance of ABC costing and SCM among accounting professionals, supplier and reseller managers have begun to redirect their profitability analyses away from those grounded in gross margin and toward contribution margin or net marketing contribution. **Contribution margin** is calculated as sales minus variable costs, whereas **net marketing contribution** is contribution margin minus controllable marketing fixed costs. Accountants see these numbers as better indicators of marketing performance because they more precisely reflect those revenues, costs, and portions of profit for which business market managers are responsible and can control. Greater use of these accounting techniques has also enabled both supplier and reseller managers to assess profitability at the transaction level. In the past, business market managers would assess and then develop support programs around the gross margin of a supplier's product. Today, they focus on the contribution margin and/or net marketing contribution that a reseller gains from the total solution or bundle of products and services that the customer buys in a given transaction. In this way, they better understand how the supplier's product contributes to a transaction's profitability (i.e., as a solution platform, peripheral, or accessory) and can develop more appropriate incentive and promotional support programs.[39]

Responding Adaptively to Incremental Marketplace Changes

To this point, we have examined the process of sustaining reseller partnerships within a relatively stable marketplace. What happens when conditions change incrementally? Given the dynamic nature of the marketplace, partner firms occasionally need to adjust their commitments. To do so, they need a mechanism to alert them of such changes and a process for adapting their partnerships.[40] Thus, we begin this section by examining one means of detecting and responding to marketplace changes, the reseller advisory council. Next, we examine how firms reformulate the gives & gets of the partnership to restore equity. In turn, these reformulations require the partner firms to modify joint annual plans, taking into account changing market conditions. And, business market managers may turn to influence strategies to ensure that the new plans are implemented. Because change often precipitates disagreements, we then turn our attention to the need to set up a conflict resolution process and procedures. Last, incremental marketplace changes may necessitate a more flexible set of channel arrangements. We conclude this section by exploring one such arrangement—adaptive channels—that enables partner firms to cope with altered conditions.

Adjusting Commitments

Establish a Reseller Advisory Council

In Chapter 2, we discuss a variety of research methods for monitoring marketplace change. One commonly used channels method for doing so is the reseller advisory council. A **reseller advisory council** is a consultative forum typically composed of key managers from a supplier firm and 10 to 15 of its reseller firms. The council typically meets once or twice a year for one to two days to discuss issues of common concern and to suggest improvements in product lines, supplier policies, marketing programs, market trends, and so on. The forum is not a legislative body, a bargaining unit, or a gripe session. Rather, it is an advisory group that offers counsel to the supplier.

Advisory councils function as a means of incremental channel improvement. They share characteristics with other commonly used problem-solving teams, such as quality circles, labor-management committees, task forces, and focus groups. Run properly, councils improve market response, new product and service marketing, and channel management both domestically and internationally. Here are a few examples of how firms have used them.[41]

Toro, a major manufacturer of lawn mowers, relies on its reseller advisory council for local market intelligence. The firm and its resellers, in turn, use such intelligence to respond to competitive threats before they become acute. At one of its council meetings, for instance, Toro managers learned from a North Carolina dealer that a new German company had introduced a greens-cutting machine into the golf course market in the United States. Another council member verified that the competitor had entered the Florida market as well. More important, the Florida dealer explained how the firm's sales force successfully sold against the new product by highlighting the superior value of Toro's equipment and the dealer's repair services. From these discussions, Toro and reseller managers quickly devised a value-based training program for dealer salespeople and a cooperative merchandising program. Working together, Toro and its resellers launched a successful counterstrike.

Business market managers frequently use reseller advisory council meetings to brainstorm product line extensions and new customer services. For example, several years ago, Fort Howard Paper Company's council identified growing plastic plate usage among institutional food users. Resellers pointed to major "gaps" in Fort Howard's plastic plate line that prohibited them from capitalizing on this surging demand. Following council suggestions, Fort Howard acquired a plastic plate manufacturer whose lines filled those gaps. With a full line, Fort Howard resellers successfully penetrated the emerging segment.

Loctite, a subsidiary of The Henkel Group, manufactures specialty adhesives. At a reseller advisory council meeting in Europe, Loctite managers verified the need for a new label adhesive in the French marketplace. Because of "green" environmental regulations, the French recycle bottles often. For this reason, processors prefer adhesives that permit them to remove labels easily. Based on these insights, Loctite developed a label adhesive exclusively for the French market.

Reformulate Channel Partners' Gives & Gets

To sustain or enhance high levels of channel performance, business market managers must periodically examine and adjust the balance in partner firms' gives & gets. **Gives** are the specific investments and resources a firm contributes, such as knowledge, personnel, fixed assets, and cash. **Gets**, on the other hand, are the specific gains a firm receives, such as greater expertise, enhanced capabilities, and additional profits. It is here that disconnects often occur; what one channel member thinks it is giving to a partner firm is significantly different from what that partner perceives it is getting.

Often, business market managers can trace inequities in gives & gets back to the vagaries of traditional channel compensation practices. In Box 9.4, we describe traditional discounts and allowances. Even though the traditional methods of reseller compensation are widely practiced, many managers question their practicality and equity. As we mention in Chapter 7, resellers complain that trade discounts, determined as a function of industry standards or average gross margins, underestimate the true costs they incur. And because of intense price competition, resellers rarely receive the suggested resale price on products and hence never gain the gross margins that trade

BOX 9.4
Traditional Reseller Discounts and Allowances

The **trade** or **functional discount**, stated as a percent reduction from the suggested resale price, ideally covers the reseller's costs of performing assigned tasks and provides the reseller with a reasonable profit. Suppliers derive trade discount amounts for specific products from one of three sources: historical industry discounts, industry gross margin averages, or turns × earns ratios.

Firms supplement the trade discount with a **quantity** or **volume discount**, designed to motivate resellers to buy in large quantities and store local inventory. Suppliers state quantity discounts as a percent reduction either from suggested resale price or from the reseller's net or invoice price. They commonly offer tiers of quantity discounts reflecting the supplier's economies of scale in production and logistics. For example, a supplier might offer a progressively higher discount to a reseller for buying a product in box loads, truckloads, and rail carloads.

Suppliers offer resellers a **payment discount** to encourage them to pay for goods immediately. The payment discount is stated as a percent reduction off the invoice price. Perhaps the most common payment discount, 2/10/net 30, is a 2% reduction off invoice price if the reseller pays within 10 days. The net amount is due in 30 days. Shrewd suppliers periodically change this discount to reflect their current cost of capital.

An **allowance** is an extra payment designed to gain reseller participation in special programs. Cooperative advertising, merchandising, and delivery allowances are perhaps most common. Suppliers exercise their own discretion in selecting allowance amounts; however, they must make them available to all their resellers. They pay allowances through a reduction in invoice prices.

discounts are supposed to provide. As a result, far too many resellers believe that they are not receiving adequate compensation for their efforts and investments.

How can progressive firms eliminate inequities? They begin by evaluating both their own gives & gets and those of their channel partner. At a joint management meeting, both reseller and supplier managers construct two sets of T-accounts, as in an accounting ledger, one for each firm. In one column, managers comprehensively list the gives, and in the other column, the gets. Supplier and reseller managers then use these T-accounts to surface and discuss discrepancies in perceived gives & gets and negotiate changes in the structure of gives & gets to attain equity. As we point out in Chapter 7, business market managers may need to rethink channel partners' profit models.

To better reflect channel partner gives & gets, some progressive suppliers have migrated toward a **functional allowance**. Here, the supplier pays a reseller a set percent off the reseller buy price for performing specific tasks. Several years ago, the CompositesOne Corporation, a major distributor of composite materials and thermoplastic elastomers, agreed to become the exclusive supplier of Shell Chemical's Kraton® thermoplastic-rubber compounds for plastic molded goods applications in the United States. Kraton rubber is a versatile material and, in addition to plastics molding, has many substantial applications, such as adhesives, lubricants, asphalt, and polymer modification.

The plastics molding opportunities are smaller and fragmented. Shell wanted to apply more of its resources to develop sales in larger applications, so it turned to CompositesOne for assistance. In response to this challenge, CompositesOne created its own applications support laboratory and staffed it with two chemists and a materials engineer. Additionally, the firm hired sales engineers and trained them to provide product specification and applications assistance as well as to give technical sales presentations. For its efforts, CompositesOne received a functional allowance for market development, which was paid as a percent reduction off the acquisition price of Kraton, plus sales growth bonuses.

Another innovative compensation approach that some suppliers use is paying resellers a **fee-for-service**. Under this arrangement, a supplier pays its reseller partners a prespecified amount for performing a particular function. Microsoft, for example, pays authorized support centers a fee for providing technical assistance to customers. The fee allows the support centers to cover the costs of personnel and equipment as well as to make a profit. LaBlond Makino, a Japanese-owned machine tool builder, has taken this approach one step further. It specifies the amount of technical service days or hours it expects its distributor partners to provide to customers. In essence, LaBlond Makino keeps distributors **on retainer** because they are paid whether or not they provide service.

Make Responsive Adjustments to the Joint Annual Plan

Although reseller marketing plans provide a coordinated course of action to pursue, business market managers recognize the necessity of responding to incremental market changes. Not only do market conditions change, but the supplier and its resellers also learn through implementing the plan, which may prompt them to make changes. Rather than waiting until the next formal planning session, progressive suppliers and resellers adjust the existing marketing plan when necessary. The following examples illustrate how two leading firms successfully adapt ongoing reseller marketing plans.

To further penetrate the mining and heavy construction industries, Caterpillar designed and introduced a revolutionary new tractor, the D9L. Caterpillar expressly created the D9L to deliver improved traction, reduced stress on the undercarriage and fast-wearing parts, easier and faster repairs, and improved productivity to mine operators and construction firms. Caterpillar priced the D9L significantly higher than traditional tractors and encouraged dealers to actively promote it in the United States and Middle East. Conditions changed soon after the marketing plan was implemented. Komatsu entered the marketplace with aggressively priced models. Perhaps more ominously, D9L models in the field began to fail after 2,500 hours of operation. It turned out that a variety of parts used in the new design were not durable enough to withstand severe operating environments. Clearly, Caterpillar and its dealers had to modify their marketing plans.[42]

Working as partners, Caterpillar and its dealers initiated both strategic and tactical remedial actions. To begin with, Caterpillar redesigned failing systems and rushed superior replacement parts to dealers. Dealers, in turn, implemented a comprehensive program for repairing equipment in the field, even replacing parts on machines that had not yet failed. Interfirm teams of mechanics flew to dealerships that were overwhelmed with repair calls and serviced crippled D9Ls. Looking to the future, Caterpillar repositioned the D9L to be more competitive with Komatsu models. As a result of these joint efforts, D9L downtime was minimized, customer dissatisfaction evaporated, and the D9L become a popular product in the mining and heavy construction industries.

When PSS World Medical Inc., the medical supplies distributor, began targeting physicians, the firm promised next-day delivery and charged premium prices for its services. By the mid-1990s, demands for heath-care reform in the United States and insurance company demands for lower costs prompted physicians to demand lower prices on supplies. In addition, a number of discounters entered the market, causing prices to deteriorate even further. Rather than clinging to the marketing plans PSS had forged with its suppliers, PSS management modified its strategies.

The firm began by dropping prices on 300 of its most popular items. PSS then initiated a buying club called *Network Plus* for physicians. PSS provided a lower price to participating physicians in exchange for contractual commitments for greater shares of customer business. Importantly, even though PSS shifted its strategy to be more price competitive, management did not abandon its profit-based incentive systems. This direction prompted employees to aggressively pursue cost reductions instead of just slashing prices. They also significantly lowered selling and administrative costs at PSS. As a result of the change in strategy and its profit-based incentives, PSS witnessed an increase in both market share and profit margin during a period in which most competitors suffered major losses in sales and profits.[43]

Seek Influence Among Channel Partner Firms

When mutual self-interests begin to diverge because of changing marketplace conditions, business market managers may have to increasingly rely on power and influence to keep the partnership functioning. By *power* we mean the ability of one firm to get its partner to undertake activities that the partner firm would not do on its own. Some managers believe that gaining and using power is the best way to achieve coordination. The use of power has serious drawbacks, though. Most firms dislike being "told what to do" and aggressively seek to "get even." Thus, managers should be prudent and sparing in their reliance on power. Scholars have identified six influence strategies for gaining and using power—information exchange, recommendations, promises, threats, legalistic pleas, and requests.[44]

A key question that often arises relative to power is: How can the weaker firm ensure that its more powerful partner will treat it fairly? The answer is through dependence-balancing operations, which are courses of action that the weaker firm pursues to equalize the importance of the partnership to both firms. For example, the weaker firm might make greater investments in the partnership until the resources both firms have committed are roughly the same. Alternatively, the weaker firm might seek out other partners. By doing so, the firm would reduce its dependence on the partnership. In a related move, the weaker firm might try to change nonredeployable assets into redeployable assets by finding new uses for them.[45]

Establish a Process and Procedures for Conflict Resolution

By anticipating channel conflict and putting conflict resolution mechanisms in place, progressive managers turn potentially destructive disputes into opportunities for improvement. Box 9.5 describes some practical means for reducing and resolving reseller and supplier conflict. When implemented properly, these conflict resolution mechanisms enable partners to vent frustrations and create mutually acceptable solutions to common problems.

Creating Adaptive Channels[46]

A handful of forward-looking companies have altered their channel networks to make them more flexible and responsive to changing marketplace requirements. A form of hybrid channels we discuss in Chapter 7, they are known as **adaptive channels**. The managers who deploy them progressively view their distribution channels as webs of capabilities embedded in an extended enterprise. They realize that by sharing their resources and capabilities in novel ways, they can take advantage of profit-making opportunities that they could not exploit alone.

To act on this realization, these managers first identify infrequent yet critical customer requirements that they cannot routinely fulfill on their own. Then they make progressive, cooperative arrangements with other channel members for assistance that will enable them to meet those requirements. The partner firms define in advance the nature of such assistance, the procedures for providing it, and the appropriate remuneration. Often, PRM software furnishes the interfirm interfaces necessary to activate these prearranged agreements when appropriate.

We divide adaptive channel initiatives into three broad categories. In the first, channel partners design arrangements that ensure they are routinely able to cope with unpredictable or unusual demands for products and services. In the second, adaptive channel arrangements focus on meeting customers' growing demands for broader market offerings—products and services that the channel member does not normally provide. In the third, the objective is to improve the quality of service throughout the distribution channel by substituting the superior capabilities of one member for the subpar capabilities of another.

BOX 9.5
Resolving Reseller-Supplier Conflict

A low-cost yet effective means to resolve reseller-supplier conflict is to train **boundary-spanning personnel**, or individuals who are in contact with the partner firm on a regular basis, to be sensitive to inherent trouble spots. For a supplier, boundary-spanning personnel are likely to be field sales reps and inside customer service reps, whereas for resellers, they are likely to be purchasing managers or general managers. These persons should learn to identify emerging problems and try to resolve them informally and immediately before they escalate into relationship-threatening crises.

An alternative is to establish a regular **employee exchange program**, in which firms assign personnel for periods of time to channel partner operations. In the first of two varieties of these programs, the employee spends several weeks at the partner firm, rotating through a variety of positions. In this way, the individual becomes familiar with the tasks and problems that the partner firm must address. Hopefully, this experience leads to empathy and better understanding of the partner's plight. In the second, the employee actually works on-site at the partner firm. For example, a staff member from the firm's order center might be assigned to the purchasing department of a particularly large reseller firm. At the reseller's establishment, the individual would take the reseller's orders, transmit them to the supplier, and oversee delivery.

Firms can better understand issues and concerns of channel partners through **trade association membership**. Many reseller associations, for example, offer associate memberships for suppliers. By attending conferences and receiving newsletters, both channel partners can learn how the other operates and what problems they must routinely address.

Finally, some suppliers have established the office of **ombudsman**. The ombudsman is typically a retired reseller manager or principal employed by the supplier, who has credibility with both parties. Serving as the "friend" of the reseller, the ombudsman listens to reseller concerns, draws on experience to assist the supplier in finding equitable solutions, and helps explain them to resellers.

For intractable disputes, business market managers turn to mediation or arbitration. **Mediation** is the process where a third party is brought in to help resolve a dispute by either refocusing discussion on key issues or suggesting viable solutions. In general, their role is to promote clear understanding of each firm's position and to encourage the open discussion of issues. Under **arbitration**, the firms legally agree to have a third party settle the disagreement. The decision of the third party, often a professional arbitrator, is final and legally binding. For these extreme conflict resolution mechanisms to function properly, firms need to agree ahead of time what types of concerns will trigger either mediation or arbitration and who can be brought in as an acceptable mediator or arbitrator.

Louis W. Stern, Brian Sternthal, and C. Samuel Craig, "Managing Conflict in Distribution Channels: A Laboratory Study," *Journal of Marketing Research* (May 1973): 169–179; Bruce A. Jacobs, "Tell It to Bob," *Industry Week* (September 1982): 62–63; and, Roy J. Lewicki and Joseph A Litterer, *Negotiation* (Burr Ridge, IL: Irwin, 1985).

Provide Support in Extraordinary Situations

Through **auxiliary support systems**, distribution channel members cope with unexpected or unusual demands for products and services by sharing inventories and support services in return for prespecified remuneration. What makes auxiliary support possible is information technology that monitors the availability of offerings and processes orders, as well integrated logistics systems that deliver those offerings rapidly from distant locations to customers' sites. In Box 9.6, we

BOX 9.6

Okuma and Its Distributors Share Inventory Across Three Continents

Okuma America Corporation, a subsidiary of Japanese machine tool builder Okuma Corporation, provides an outstanding example of how distributors can routinely satisfy unexpected demands by sharing the burden of maintaining safety stocks and making emergency deliveries. The expense of stocking a full line of machine tools, which often cost more than $160,000 apiece, along with a complete assortment of repair parts, which number in the thousands, is prohibitive. Historically, it has hampered the ability of distributors to provide responsive service. To overcome the problem, Okuma created its own auxiliary support system.

Okuma requires each of its 46 distributor locations in North and South America to carry a minimal number of machine tools and select repair parts in inventory. The company tries to ensure that nearly all Okuma machines and parts are in stock either in its warehouse in Charlotte, North Carolina, or somewhere in the distribution channel. Okuma's BaaN system keeps distributors informed about the location and availability of machine tools, spare parts, and used equipment in Okuma warehouses throughout North and South America, Europe, Asia, and Japan.

When a customer orders a machine tool or part that the distributor does not have, the distributor checks the BaaN system to determine whether the item is in stock at Okuma facilities. If it is available, the distributor can order it electronically. If it is not, the distributor can use the BaaN system to scan other Okuma distributors' inventories or e-mail them directly to find the closest location where items are available. Then, the manager phones or e-mails a counterpart at the stocking site and arranges for delivery of the item directly to the customer's plant site. Both distributors, in turn, share the commission on the sale of the machine tool or parts. Okuma further supports the availability of repair parts with a 24-Hour Shipment Guarantee—if parts are not shipped within 24 hours of order receipt, the customer receives them for free.

The benefits of Okuma's auxiliary support system are significant. Investments and costs associated with stocking and handling inventory were reduced for the total channel system. Simultaneously, Okuma has created numerous potential pathways—its 46 distributors plus global company warehouses—for their products and services to reach each customer. As a result, the likelihood that a distributor will lose a sale because the needed item is out of stock has been dramatically lowered. Furthermore, customer satisfaction has increased because the superior service promised by Okuma is being consistently delivered.

Adapted from "Rethinking Distribution: Adaptive Channels," James A. Narus and James C. Anderson, *Harvard Business Review* (July–August 1996): 112–130.

describe how Okuma America Corporation created a network that enables the firm and its distributors to exchange machine tools and repair parts when the need arises.

Responsively Broaden the Market Offering

Sophisticated companies sometimes choose to outsource their supply management function via integrated supply management (ISM) contracts to a single distributor to reduce their total transaction costs. Even though ISM contracts provide a tremendous opportunity for distributors to increase both sales and profits, fulfilling them requires a broader market offering as well. In addition, customers are likely to expect the reseller to handle their infrequent or emergency requests for unusual products and support services.

To capitalize on this opportunity, some distributors have turned to **reseller alliances**. In these alliances, members agree to pool their resources and capabilities and broaden one another's market offerings. By joining forces, they can exploit opportunities that they could not on their own, and they can meet demands that fall outside their traditional areas of specialization. In return for its contribution, each member shares the resulting sales and profits.

One such reseller alliance is a consortium. To form a consortium, resellers of complementary lines contribute equity and create a separate corporation. This new corporation markets the collective product lines and services of its members, primarily to ISM customers. Through the consortium, member firms can serve customers individually when they want only specialty products and technical service, or collectively when they want broader offerings. Consortium members can also draw on partner inventories when a traditional customer wants something out of the ordinary. Participating reseller firms share consortium profits in the form of dividends, capital gains, or both. In Box 9.7, we present Yahoo! India's innovative approach for building reseller consortia.

Share Capabilities with Other Channel Members

Ideally, every participant in the distribution channel should provide the same high-level service to every customer. In practice, of course, such consistency is virtually impossible because neither the supplier nor any of its resellers is likely to excel at everything. Instead, companies tend to do an outstanding job with some services and a mediocre job with others. To overcome these discrepancies, suppliers and resellers are adopting **capabilities-sharing agreements**. Through such agreements, the superior service of one channel member substitutes for the subpar service of another. In turn, channel members receive appropriate compensation for sharing their superior service capabilities.

In Box 9.8, we relate Su-Kam's experiences creating centers of excellence among its resellers to leverage their distinctive capabilities. Independently owned channel members can achieve similar gains through capabilities-sharing contracts with more resourceful partner firms. The technical problem-solving arrangement between Oracle and its partners, to leverage their capabilities through Oracle Communities, provides an outstanding illustration, which we recount in Box 9.9.

BOX 9.7
Yahoo! India's Approach to Reseller Consortia

Yahoo! India Small Business (YISB), as presented in Box 9.1 earlier in this chapter, is a Web-hosting package from Yahoo! India, targeted at small and medium businesses to help them develop effective Web presence. One of the primary issues YISB faced during the launch of its Web-hosting package was that its targeted customers, small businesses and entrepreneurs, did not perceive the product to be adding significant value to their businesses. One reason for this was that customers were ill-informed about the usage of online portals and did not know how to successfully use online presence to boost sales.

Resellers proved to be immensely helpful in this regard. Local Web designers with their own core competencies were able to not only sell the Web-hosting platform, but also provide a customized one-stop solution to customers. They provided assistance at different stages of the Web-hosting process from domain registration, Web design to putting the business Web site online. They also provided solutions for search optimization, which enabled the customers' sites to be highlighted by search engines. Detection of a company's Web site by search engines was a key prerequisite to drive more business to the company. Consequently, the resellers could actually convert a passive business Web site into an active one.

Moreover, resellers could more effectively follow up with potential customers to obtain sales for the Web-hosting package. With its lean sales force, Yahoo! India could not be as effective in generating sales from such a fragmented market base.

The consortia of resellers and Yahoo! India were effectively working as a single extended entity, providing superior value to their customers. Yahoo! India offered 24/7 technical and customer support to ensure that issues were resolved immediately and within defined service level agreements (SLAs), which are key metrics to measure performance between the supplier and channel partner, thus providing superior customer experience.

The direct online sales model, wherein customers procure the Web-hosting package directly from Yahoo! India, entails a flat price. However, if the customer elects to purchase through the reseller channel, pricing is variable. The resellers charge the base price with a premium for their services, with pricing for the add-on services being customer specific. However, for most small-business customers, going through a reseller is more convenient as a one-stop solution; they need not learn the details of Web design and integrate their Web site with search engines, since all these aspects are taken care of by the reseller. There is an equitable revenue-sharing arrangement between Yahoo! India and the resellers, wherein resellers are compensated for the services they render to each specific customer. The resellers also have targets. They are paid additional incentives on achieving those targets. There are several models of reseller compensation that are available to provide flexibility. This strategy of developing an effective reseller channel resulted in significant additional revenue and an expanded customer base for Yahoo! India.

Contributed by Abhishek Dan, Participant, PGSEM Program, Indian Institute of Management Bangalore.

BOX 9.8
Su-Kam Establishes Excellence in Serving its Customers through its Distribution Network

Su-Kam is the biggest supplier of home and industrial power backup solutions in India, manufacturing inverters specifically designed to handle extreme power fluctuations, sold through an elaborate network of distribution channels. It has over 6,000 channel partners and expects to grow this number steadily over the next several years. Its revenues exceed INR 6 billion and account for over 50% of India's inverter business market. Its success is attributable to its innovative response to a huge opportunity, creating a superior product and configuring and operating a superior distribution channel.

Before Su-Kam's entry, the industry was highly fragmented. There were a large number of small manufacturers in the country, catering to local markets. However, their products were not very reliable and did not perform well, given the extreme fluctuations in the electric power supply in most areas of the country. Consequently, inverters frequently failed on the field and needed service. Customers who purchased inverters often found they did not have the backup power they needed during a power outage.

After successful product testing using in-house knowledge and indigenous Indian technologies, Su-Kam licensed state-of-the-art technology from a foreign collaborator. The resulting product was of much higher quality and lower price than the inverters supplied by the other Indian inverter manufacturers. The company also developed and announced an ambitious product roadmap that promised year-on-year, continuous improvement on key performance parameters of its future-generation inverters.

Since Su-Kam had no established distribution channels to reach the customers across the country, both in business and consumer markets, it developed an innovative method to get channel partners onboard. First, small inverter manufacturers, concerned about their inability to compete with Su-Kam's inverters in both quality and price, became distributors of Su-Kam's products. Small, local dealers of batteries (one of the essential modules used to manufacture inverters) were enrolled as Su-Kam's dealers. Support to this two-tier channel structure was provided by a team of the company's sales and service executives, who worked closely with channel partners to motivate them to deliver high performance.

To rapidly create widespread visibility across the country in a cost-effective manner, the company approached small tea shops and eating places across the country with a proposal to display Su-Kam signage. On this signage, the name of the small tea shop or eating place was also conspicuously displayed. This was an attractive proposal for these shops, since, being quite small, they did not earlier have their own high-quality signage. This was the first time any business had thought about such an approach for creating massive awareness in the marketplace. This approach was replicated by many other companies subsequently. Su-Kam's innovative approach to create brand awareness resulted in instant, countrywide visibility for Su-Kam and its products. This, coupled with a well-prepared and motivated channel for delivery and service, helped Su-Kam achieve rapid success in the market place. All of its meteoric growth occurred in the last 10 years.

Porus Munshi, "Making Breakthrough Innovation Happen: How 11 Indians Pulled Off The Impossible," *Collins Business* (New Delhi: HarperCollins, 2009): 217–232.

BOX 9.9
Oracle and its Partners Leverage Their Capabilities through Oracle Communities

Oracle is the world's leading supplier of software for information management. Oracle prefers to call its resellers "partners" to emphasize the equal importance accorded to them. Oracle has more than 20,000 partners with whom it forms the formidable Oracle communities, providing industry leading solutions and services that address business needs of customers around the world.

The Oracle Partnership Network is a program created to help resellers succeed by offering value to customers. For an annual fee, it offers partners access to all tools, resources, and benefits needed to support the entire business cycle with Oracle.

Oracle has a very strong base of software products capable of generating business. Oracle believes that more value is delivered when it is able to assist resellers on issues that they may not be able to resolve on their own. Apart from creating brand equity among the channels, this also creates brand equity for Oracle products. Oracle offers different value elements to different partners depending on the type and nature of markets they operate in. Oracle clearly communicates the benefits it offers to the partner, as well as the tangible and intangible value elements that the partner will derive from the program.

Further, Oracle has come up with the Oracle Partner Network Innovation Award, which rewards initiatives that apply Oracle's products and technology innovatively to create value for the customer and generate new business. This program encourages partners to continually innovate on Oracle's products, thus enhancing customer value. Oracle constantly evaluates the performance of its channels through information received from the marketplace. Since Oracle has a large number of partners, the company promotes healthy competition among them, forcing each to create and deliver maximum possible value to customer firms.

Oracle has very innovatively created a partner structure wherein each of the partners is placed in a certain tier. Based on the amount of value each partner generates for Oracle, enhanced services and support are offered. Thus, its low-importance, simpler tasks may be done by partners at the entry level with little investment into the relationship by both Oracle and the partner. On the other hand, for critical tasks, it offers the partner firm more support and services on terms that are mutually agreed. Such relationships are typically exclusive. This is done so that together they generate the highest value for the customer firm.

Contributed by Rahul Bhalla, Participant, PGP Program, Indian Institute of Management Bangalore.

Transforming Channels in the Face of Disruptive Forces

Periodically, disruptive forces emerge that portend major structural changes within a marketplace. Among the forces that have had a profound impact upon business marketing channels during the past decade are the growth of the Internet and mobile telephones as a method of directly communicating with and fulfilling the requirements of customer firms, the shift in power from supplier firms to customer and reseller firms, global outsourcing and importing, the commoditization or technological obsolescence of many products, and the growing importance of service as the primary source of customer value. Importantly, when truly disruptive forces surface, business market managers must rethink and transform not only the way their firms do business but also their existing channel structure. The channel transformations that enable firms to handle disruptive marketplace changes include the creation of integrated multi-channels, relationship transfers, and—in the worst-case scenario—the termination of long-standing partnerships.[47]

Creating Integrated Multi-Channels

In Chapter 7, we introduced integrated multi-channels as an alternative channel design. The idea for this innovative channel format can be traced to integrated marketing communications. In the context of promotions, business market managers realized many years ago that customers received and responded to communications messages from a variety of sources and that all of those messages needed to be coordinated. More recently, pundits have argued that the same logic should be applied to marketing channels. Rather than restricting purchases of a given offering to one channel, customer firms routinely search and patronize multiple channels. Instead of bickering over "whose customer is it," pundits contend that both supplier and reseller managers should integrate and synchronize their efforts at serving their mutual customers. Doing so requires that one channel member—the supplier, the reseller, or a third-party service provider—serve as the **channel steward** and coordinate activities for mutual benefit.[48]

An integrated multi-channel can be constructed around either the sales or fulfillment cycle. Basically, the channel steward outlines the sales or fulfillment processes and functions that must be performed to deliver various high-value total customer experiences to targeted customer segments and firms. Those functions are assigned on a single-function basis among several channel firms (i.e., the supplier, resellers, and third-party service providers) simultaneously, thus creating several potential and parallel pathways to market. A shared information system (e.g., CRM, PRM, or ERP) is often used to take a customer's order, select the most appropriate channel configuration given the required TCE, and synchronize the efforts of participating channel partners. Customer firms are also given the option of using multiple access points to the channel on a transaction-by-transaction basis; that is, they can seek service, order, or communicate with the supplier, resellers, or third-party service providers or work through the shared information system as they see fit. The customer's primary supplier and hence the channel may vary from one order to the next as a function of the TCE that they require for that given transaction. Importantly, revenues are shared among partners as a function of their contributions to a given transaction.

Integrated multi-channels differ from adaptive channels, which we discussed previously, in that they are more routine arrangements that address all sales and fulfillment tasks rather than infrequent yet critical problems. Because integrated multi-channels provide business market managers with numerous alternative channel configurations, they can quickly respond to changing customer requirements regardless of the consequences of disruptive forces. Although the concept of integrated multi-channels is still in its infancy, a number of firms have reported success with them, including Charles Schwab, Dell Computers, Hewlett-Packard, Marriott Hotels, and Oracle.[49]

Skillfully Handling Relationship Transfers

When establishing an integrated multi-channel is not practical, business market managers may respond to disruptive marketplace forces by transferring customer relationships between a supplier and its resellers. For example, in the past, the principal working relationship was between a supplier and a customer firm. Now, as the customer's typical order size and annual purchases of an offering shrinks dramatically, the principal responsibility for the relationship needs to shift to one of the supplier's resellers. Successful relationship transfers require especially close coordination between the supplier firm and the reseller firm. For instance, they may make joint sales calls on the customer during a transition period. As time progresses, one of the partners (the reseller in our example) makes more and more of the contacts. The supplier should try to maintain some sort of relationship with the customer firm, although it is significantly diminished.

To sustain the strength of the working relationship and to keep the customer's loyalty, managers must take steps to adroitly manage the transfer. In advance, both reseller and supplier managers must agree on the conditions under which the principal responsibility for serving an account will shift from one firm to another. Then, they must spell out equitable compensation, if necessary, for transferring the relationships from one firm to the other.

Delineate Relationship Transfer Criteria

The breadth and depth of the market offering a customer account purchases and the account's TCE requirements are among the key indicators that a relationship transfer is needed. In general, the greater the volume and the more limited the assortments of products and services required, the more efficiently a supplier can serve the customer. This efficiency can be attributed to greater economies of scale in production and logistics, which translate into significant cost savings for the customer. In the reverse situation, the customer is often more efficiently served by a reseller because resellers are better able to exploit economies of scope by spreading out fixed transaction costs over a broader assortment.

The key for both channel partners is to identify the relevant sales breakpoint. For example, CompositesOne and one of its plastics suppliers have specified the breakpoint as one truckload, or 40,000 pounds of resin, per month for an extended period of time. If CompositesOne sales to a given account routinely exceed this amount, CompositesOne transfers the account to the supplier. On the other hand, if a customer's purchases from the plastics supplier routinely drop below the breakpoint, the supplier transfers the account to CompositesOne.

Changes in customer TCE requirements may also indicate the need to transfer relationships. For example, as customer requirements for technical assistance become more complex, direct sales by the supplier become more feasible because the supplier is often the best source of technical expertise for a particular product. Alternatively, as customers increasingly require integrated supply management contracts, the importance of the reseller increases because they offer one-stop shopping.

As an example, consider how Technische Unie, a Dutch electrical wholesaler owned by Sonepar, and Draka, the cable manufacturer, handled the relationship transfer of KPN, the Dutch telephone company. Technische Unie markets integrated supply contracts to large customers and has established procedures for transferring accounts from suppliers. Several years ago, senior management at KPN demanded that its operations group reduce costs by 25% while increasing the availability of electrical equipment and parts to the firm's installers. At the time, only 70% of required supplies were available when needed. To capitalize on this opportunity, Technische Unie's managers went to Draka, a major supplier of KPN, and asked to supply all Draka cable and supplies to KPN. By offering Draka products along with those of other suppliers, Technische Unie would be able to provide an integrated supply contract to KPN. Draka agreed, and Technische Unie became the single-source supplier of electrical equipment and supplies to KPN. Within a short period of time, KPN gained access to 96% of its requirements in 24 hours and a reduction in costs that exceeded senior management's 25% goal.

Establish Equitable Compensation for Relationship Transfers

One of the best ways to ensure that relational transfers are made smoothly is to compensate the partner for loss of the customer. For example, CompositesOne managers report that one supplier pays them a transfer fee and a 5% finder's fee for a transferred account for a period of six months to a year. Technische Unie demonstrates to suppliers how their infrastructure will be reduced through fewer warehouses, less inventory, and fewer employees following a relationship transfer. At the same time, Technische Unie furnishes suppliers with detailed market information on what the transferred customer is purchasing. Furthermore, Technische Unie encourages the supplier to continue sales and technical service calls on the customer.

Terminating Partnerships

As a result of certain disruptive marketplace changes, business market managers may have no choice but to terminate all existing partnerships and go-to-market via a completely different channel. Although many of the guidelines for termination mirror those of relationship transfers, there are several critical additions. To begin with, supplier, reseller, and third-party service provider managers should enter into partnerships with the sober realization that the arrangements are not likely to last forever. Instead, they should include a "contract renewal clause" into written agreements that specifies that they will be reviewed at periodic intervals and then either be continued or discontinued depending upon whether mutual self-interests are being met. Conditions under which partnership termination are likely (e.g., disruptive marketplace changes) should be addressed in the agreement. Procedures for termination should be delineated. These include such issues as advance notification of termination date, inventory buy-back, and equitable compensation for past efforts. Most importantly, terminations should be conducted in a civil and courteous fashion in order to prevent ill-will and conduct that may be detrimental to the firms' brand equity. Such behavior is also warranted because the business market manager may need the terminated partner's services in the future.

SUMMARY

In this chapter, we examined the process of sustaining working partnerships within distribution channels. To sustain reseller partnerships, supplier and reseller managers must continuously align their mutual self-interests and complementary resources by: (1) strengthening partnerships in stable marketplaces, (2) responding adaptively to incremental marketplace changes, and (3) transforming channels in the face of disruptive forces. These tasks constitute a never-ending challenge for business market managers. To rise to the challenge, managers must develop a deep understanding of their channel partners' business models and the counterproductive tendencies they spawn. Through joint annual planning or periodic research surveys, managers should monitor the extent of changes in both partner goals and marketplace conditions, and then undertake decisive actions to maintain alignment.

The nature and extent of realignment efforts varies as a function of marketplace conditions. When a given marketplace is relatively stable and mutual self-interests are reasonably well aligned, the principal managerial tasks are fulfilling commitments to one another, ensuring that customer value is delivered, and enhancing interfirm coordination. As conditions within a marketplace begin to change markedly, business market managers must respond adaptively. They do so by establishing a reseller advisory council and following its recommendations, modifying joint annual plans, and promptly and equitably resolving conflicts. Another way to cope with altered conditions is for channel partners to share their resources and capabilities in novel ways to create an adaptive channel.

When marketplace changes are disruptive, the channel steward must act to transform the channel network. One way to do so is through the establishment of a highly flexible integrated multi-channel. Through an integrated multi-channel, customers firms gain multiple access points to the supplier, resellers, and third-party service providers on a transaction-by-transaction basis. When establishing an integrated multi-channel is not feasible, managers may have to skillfully transfer customer relationships among channel partner firms. Last, when disruptive forces are acute, business market managers may have no choice but to terminate existing reseller partnerships and shift to a different channel network. Such terminations should be made in accordance with contract conditions and in a civil and courteous manner.

ENDNOTES

1. As in Chapter 7, we use the following terms. In an *indirect channel*, a supplier firm employs reseller firms to market its offerings to customer firms. A *supplier firm* produces the core product or service of a marketplace offering. A *reseller firm* takes the core product or service, adds value to it with augmenting products and services, and then markets the enhanced offering. A *third-party service provider*, such as a trucking firm, public warehouse, or information system vendor, furnishes additional augmenting services on a fee basis to suppliers and resellers. Finally, a *customer firm* acquires a market offering from a supplier or reseller for the customer's own use, or for inclusion into the products or services it produces.
2. James C. Anderson and James A. Narus, "A Model of Distributor Firm and Manufacturer Firm Working Partnerships," *Journal of Marketing* (January 1990): 42.
3. Academics often refer to this process as *interorganizational governance*. To read more about governance issues, read Jan B. Heide, "Interorganizational Governance in Marketing Channels," *Journal of Marketing* (January 1994): 72.
4. Rodolfo Vázquez, Víctor Iglesias, and Luis Ignacio Alvarez-González, "Distribution Channel Relationships: The Conditions and Strategic Outcomes of Cooperation between Manufacturer and Distributor," *International Review of Retail, Distribution*

and Consumer Research (April 2005): 125–150.

5. Sandy D. Jap, "Pie-Expansion Efforts: Collaboration Processes in Buyer-Seller Relationships," *Journal of Marketing Research* (November 1999): 461–475; Sandy D. Jap and Erin Anderson, "Safeguarding Interorganizational Performance and Continuity Under Ex Post Opportunism," *Management Science* (December 2003): 1684–1701; Kenneth H. Wathne and Jan B. Heide, "Relationship Governance in a Supply Chain Network," *Journal of Marketing* (January 2004): 73–89; and David Wallace, Jean Johnson, and U.N. Umesh, "The Role of Channel Alignment Capabilities in Effective Multiple-Channel Distribution Systems," *ISBM Report 6-2006* (June 2006).
6. Mike Marks, Tim Horan, and Mike Emerson, *Working at Cross-Purposes: How Distributors and Manufacturers Can Manage Conflict Successfully* (Washington, DC: Distribution Research and Education Foundation, 2006): 5.
7. Academics alternatively refer to this as *environmental dynamism*. Jap, "Pie-Expansion Efforts."
8. Marks, Horan, and Emerson, 6; Anne T. Coughlan, Erin Anderson, Louis W. Stern, and Adel I. El-Ansary, *Marketing Channels*, 7th ed. (Upper Saddle River, NJ: Pearson Prentice Hall, Inc., 2006): 134; V. Kasturi Rangan with Marie Bell, *Transforming Your Go-to-Market Strategy: The Three Disciplines of Channel Management* (Boston, MA: Harvard Business School Press, 2006).
9. Oliver E. Williamson, *Markets and Hierarchies: Analysis and Antitrust Implications* (New York: The Free Press, 1975): 6.
10. Oliver E. Williamson, *The Economic Institutions of Capitalism* (New York: The Free Press, 1985): 47.
11. Kenneth H. Wathne and Jan B. Heide, "Opportunism in Interfirm Relationships: Forms, Outcomes, and Solutions," *Journal of Marketing* (October 2000): 36–51; James R. Brown, Chekitan S. Dev, and Dong-Jin Lee, "Managing Marketing Channel Opportunism: The Efficacy of Alternative Governance Mechanisms," *Journal of Marketing* (April 2000): 51–65; Jan B. Heide, Kenneth H. Wathne, and Aksel I. Rokkan, "Interfirm Monitoring, Social Contracts, and Relationship Outcomes," *Journal of Marketing Research* (August 1007): 425–433.
12. Sertan Kabadayi, Nermin Eyubogulu, and Gloria P. Thomas, "The Performance Implications of Designing Multiple Channels to Fit with Strategy and Environment," *Journal of Marketing* (October 2007): 195–211.
13. Mike Marks, Tim Horan, and Mike Emerson, *Working at Cross-Purposes.*
14. Brent R. Grover, *More to the Bottom Line: Customer Profitability Tools for Wholesaler-Distributors* (Washington, DC: Distribution Research and Education Foundation, 2004).
15. Lawrence G. Friedman, *Go To Market Strategy* (Oxford, UK: Butterworth Heinemann, 2002).
16. This quote is drawn from Anderson and Narus, "A Model," 44.
17. Coughlin, Anderson, Stern, and El-Ansary, *Marketing Channels*, 24; and Marks, Horan, and Emerson, *Working at Cross-Purposes*, 6.
18. V. Kasturi Rangan with Marie Bell, *Transforming Your Go-To-Market Strategy: The Three Disciplines of Channel Management* (Boston, MA: Harvard Business School Press, 2006).
19. James C. Anderson, Håkan Håkansson, and Jan Johanson, "Dyadic Business Relationships Within a Business Network Context," *Journal of Marketing* (October 1994): 10.
20. Erin Anderson and Barton Weitz, "The Use of Pledges to Build and Sustain Commitment in Distribution Channels," *Journal of Marketing Research* (February 1992): 19.
21. Andy Cohen, "Dealer Training Goes Interactive," *Sales & Marketing Management* (December 1995): 31–32.
22. Larry Conley, "Head of the Class," *Satellite Communications* (October 1995): 26–34.
23. Neil Rackham and Richard Ruff, *Managing Major Sales* (New York: HarperBusiness, 1991).
24. N. Mohan Reddy and Michael P. Marvin, "Developing a Manufacturer-Distributor

Information Partnership," *Industrial Marketing Management* (1986): 157–163.
25. James A. Narus and James C. Anderson, "Turn Your Industrial Distributors into Partners," *Harvard Business Review* (March–April 1986): 66–71; and *Guaranteed Cost Reductions* (Cleveland, OH: Lincoln Electric Company, cited August 2003), available at *http://www.lincolnelectric.com.*
26. Anita Lienert, "A Dinosaur of a Different Color," *American Management Association Management Review* (February 1995): 29.
27. Arthur Hughes, "How Panduit Did It," *Marketing Tools* (March–April 1996): 4–7; and Tom Andel, "Manage Inventory, Own Information," *Transportation & Distribution* (May 1996): 55.
28. Victoria Fraza, "Documented Success," *Industrial Distribution* (January 1997): 54–56.
29. JuxtConsult India Online 07; *in.business.yahoo.com; www.tatamotors.com.*
30. "Relationships Develop Products," *Industrial Distribution* (October 1996): S6–S8.
31. Donald V. Fites, "Make Your Dealers Your Partners," *Harvard Business Review* (March–April 1996): 88–89.
32. Jakki Mohr and John R. Nevin, "Communication Strategies in Marketing Channels: A Theoretical Perspective," *Journal of Marketing* (October 1990): 36–51.
33. This quote is drawn from James C. Anderson and James A. Narus, "A Model of Distributor Firm and Manufacturer Firm Working Partnerships," *Journal of Marketing* (January 1990): 44.
34. Narus and Anderson, "Distributor Contributions."
35. Nirmalya Kumar, Lisa K. Scheer, and Jan-Benedict E. M. Steenkamp, "The Effects of Supplier Fairness on Vulnerable Resellers," *Journal of Marketing Research* (February 1995): 54–65.
36. E. Raymond Corey, Frank V. Cespedes, and V. Kasturi Rangan, *Going to Market* (Boston: Harvard Business School Press, 1989).
37. Peter L. Mullins, *Effective Financial Management for Wholesaler-Distributors* (Washington, DC: National Association of Wholesaler-Distributors, 1979); and Peter L. Mullins, *Measuring Customer and Product Line Profitability: Beyond "Turn & Earn"* (Washington, DC: Distribution Research & Education Foundation, 1984).
38. Kenneth H. Manning, "Distribution Channel Profitability," *Management Accounting* (January 1995): 44–49.
39. Roger J. Best, *Market-Based Management: Strategies for Growing Customer Value and Profitability*, 4th ed. (Upper Saddle River, NJ: Pearson Prentice Hall, 2005): 43–44; and Grover, *More to the Bottom Line.*
40. Sandy D. Jap and Erin Anderson, "Testing a Life-Cycle Theory of Cooperative Interorganizational Relationships: Movement Across Stages and Performance," *Management Science* (February 2007): 260–275.
41. For a discussion on how to run a reseller advisory council, see James D. Hlavacek and James A. Narus, "Early Warnings in the Channel," *Marketing Management* 1, no. 4 (1993): 50–59.
42. Fites, "Make Your Dealers . . ."
43. Thayer C. Taylor, "Sales Automation Cuts the Cord," *Sales & Marketing Management* (July 1995): 110–115.
44. Anne T. Coughlan, Erin Anderson, Louis W. Stern, and Adel I. El-Ansary, *Marketing Channels*, 6th ed. (Upper Saddle River, NJ: Prentice Hall, 2001); Gary L. Frazier, "Interorganizational Exchange Behavior in Marketing Channels: A Broadened Perspective," *Journal of Marketing* (Fall 1983): 68–78; Gary L. Frazier and John O. Summers, "Interfirm Influence Strategies and Their Application within Distribution Channels," *Journal of Marketing* (Summer 1984): 43–55; and Gary L. Frazier and Jagdish N. Sheth, "An Attitude-Behavior Framework for Distribution Channel Management," *Journal of Marketing* (Summer 1985): 38–48.
45. Jan B. Heide and George John, "The Role of Dependence Balancing in Safeguarding Transaction-Specific Assets in Conventional Channels," *Journal of Marketing* (May 1988): 20–35.

46. This discussion is drawn from the article, James A. Narus and James C. Anderson, "Rethinking Distribution: Adaptive Channels," *Harvard Business Review* (July–August 1996): 112–120.
47. Jonathan D. Hibbard, Nirmalya Kumar, and Louis W. Stern, "Examining the Impact of Destructive Acts in Marketing Channel Relationships," *Journal of Marketing Research* (February 2001): 45–61.
48. Lawrence G. Friedman, *Go To Market Strategy* (Oxford, UK: Butterworth-Heinemann, 2002); and Rangan, *Transforming Your Go-To-Market Strategy*.
49. Friedman, *Go To Market Strategy*, 229–268.

Chapter 10

Managing Customers

Overview

Increasingly, business market managers seek to maximize their firms' financial returns by balancing efforts to gain new business with activities designed to retain and expand profitable share of business among existing customers. To do so, they build and sustain a portfolio of customer relationships. Some of these relationships will be collaborative and last many years, others will be short-lived, transactional, and opportunistic. Some will be extensive in scope, others narrow. Some will be just beginning, others ending. Having discussed the process of gaining new business in Chapter 8, we turn our attention to those activities associated with managing customer relationships.[1]

Managing customers is the process of differentiating transactional and collaborative customers, delivering offerings that fulfill the respective requirements and preferences of a portfolio of customers in a superior way, and getting a fair return in exchange. This definition emphasizes that to deliver value, supplier managers must develop and continually update a detailed understanding of transactional and collaborative customers' requirements and preferences and actively communicate with customers about how these requirements and preferences are changing. The supplier must anticipate and capably respond to these changes. By marketing tailored yet flexible offerings, the supplier strives to make itself indispensable to the customer. In exchange, the supplier retains and expands a profitable share of the customer's business that meets the goals of its market strategy.

In this chapter, we address each aspect of managing customers. We begin by differentiating between transactional and collaborative customers. This differentiation rests on the concepts of a relationship continuum and industry bandwidths, the careful selection of different customer types, and a clear trajectory on how to cultivate and grow particular working relationships by changing the value to be delivered over time in the form of relationship-specific market offerings. In the second section, we discuss the foot-in-the-door and all-at-once approaches to growing a customer relationship profitably over time. We highlight how progressive suppliers can add value and reduce costs by using innovative business arrangements such as single-sourcing, facilities management, and outsourcing. We then provide guidance on how a supplier firm can get the customer comfortable with these innovative ideas while ensuring an equitable sharing of the value they create through risk-sharing and gain-sharing agreements.

In the third section, we discuss the need for suppliers to manage their portfolio of customer relationships, which is based on the dimensions of customer loyalty and the cost-to-serve customers. We detail how suppliers can develop appropriate metrics to measure customer loyalty and cost-to-serve customers, and then construct the customer portfolio matrix. We then provide guidance on how suppliers can use this matrix to profitably execute customer migration strategies to optimize customer value and enhance customer profitability. Finally, in the last section we discuss how suppliers need to look ahead and continually revisit their customer selection decisions because their skills and capabilities are affected by the customers they choose to serve, and that, in turn, affects their ability to serve other orders and customers in the future. Suppliers need to continually assess and improve their ability to deliver superior value and get a fair return in exchange. In a way, we come full circle on the process of customer value management in business markets.

Differentiating Transactional and Collaborative Customers

As we argued in Chapter 4, managers must be selective in choosing which customers to serve and which requirements to fulfill. To accomplish this goal, in Chapter 8 we highlighted how managers need to first think strategically about opportunities they select to serve, and then deliver superior value in the form of relationship-specific market offerings. We further expand on this issue in this section.

Thinking Strategically About Relationships[2]

When serving order streams or customers (as discussed in Chapter 8), all customer and supplier firms that do business together have some sort of working relationship that extends beyond the initial order or transaction. Jackson discussed a working relationship continuum along which industries fall.[3] We diagram this continuum in Figure 10.1. Purely **transactional relationships** (as defined in Chapter 8 as the

Figure 10.1 The Working Relationship Continuum and Industry Bandwidths

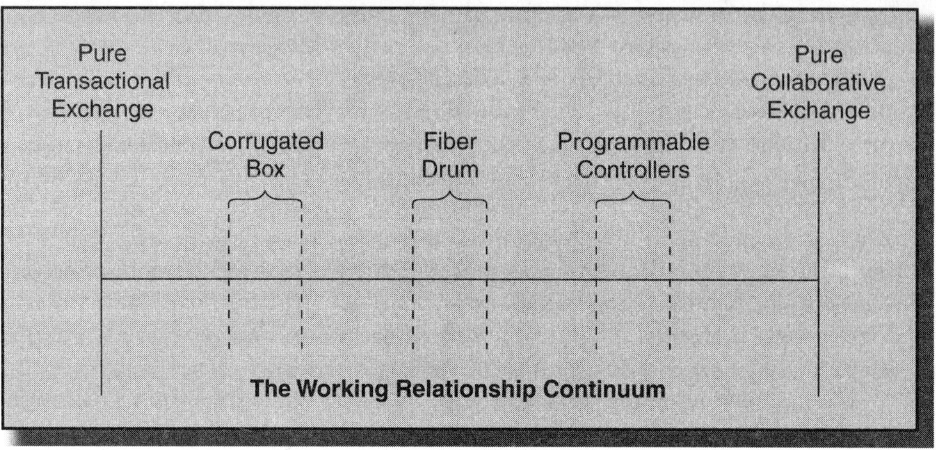

Source: Adapted from James C. Anderson and James A. Narus, "Partnering as a Focused Market Strategy," *California Management Review* (Spring 1991): 95–113

business of serving *order streams*) where the customer and the supplier focus on the repeated and timely exchange of basic products for highly competitive prices, anchor one end. Purely **collaborative relationships** anchor the other end. This latter kind of relationship comes about through **partnering**, which is a process where a customer firm and supplier firm form strong and extensive social, economic, service, and technical ties over time. The intent of partnering is to lower total costs or increase value, thereby achieving mutual benefit.[4]

Consider Industry Bandwidths

The nature of working relationships in business markets suggests that we need some further elaboration with respect to Jackson's rudimentary premise. Rather than occupying a single point on the continuum, each marketplace is better characterized as a range of customer relationships that are more collaborative or more transactional in nature relative to that marketplace's norm. We refer to this range as the **industry bandwidth of working relationships**. This bandwidth reflects the explicit or implicit customer relationship strategies that suppliers pursue in an industry. Firms either attempt to span the bandwidth with a portfolio of relationships or treat all customers more or less alike, thereby having a narrower range of relationships than the industry bandwidth.

Naturally, industry bandwidths for various markets fall along the entire continuum of working relationships. Even the most transactional relationship in one industry might be more collaborative in nature than the most collaborative relationship in another industry, and vice versa. For example, compare the corrugated box, fiber drum, and programmable controller industries that we depict in Figure 10.1. Because the underlying technology in the programmable controller industry is the most complicated and is still developing, collaborative relations in this industry can be all encompassing, ranging from codesign of manufacturing systems to installation, training, and maintenance. Collaborative relations in the fiber drum industry tend to be more circumscribed and focus on helping customers modify their systems and procedures in areas such as lifting and stacking fiber drums. Finally, because many customers consider corrugated boxes a commodity, long-term supply contracts and just-in-time inventory programs generally represent the extent of potential collaboration.

Partnering as a Focused Market Strategy

Business market managers recognize that not all customer firms want the same kind of relationship with a supplier, nor can the same kind of relationship deliver the same value to all customers. Instead, they draw on the bedrock marketing concepts of segmentation, targeting, and positioning (STP), which we discussed in Chapters 2 and 4, to formulate a relationship strategy. Business market managers first segment the marketplace, using progressive bases such as customer application, capabilities and business priorities, and usage situation. They then estimate the value of their offerings in these segments. Such information indicates how a supplier firm can enhance market offerings, if at all, through working relationships.

Next, managers target one or more segments for collaborative emphasis versus transaction emphasis. Specifically, they target segments where a firm's offering has superior value relative to the competition for collaborative emphasis and segments where its offering does not provide superior value for transaction emphasis. Segments where the firm has superior value represent natural places for the firm to allocate resources for relationship-building efforts. Customers in these segments are more likely to be receptive to such initiatives and may be proactive themselves in suggesting closer relations.

Having targeted specific segments, supplier managers then turn their attention to individual accounts. In Chapter 8, we discussed how managers must distinguish between customer selection and order selection. *Customer selection* is based on the supplier firm's mission and strategic intent and takes competencies and capabilities into consideration. *Order selection*, on the other hand, is tactical in nature and focuses on short-term resource utilization. Ideally, the supplier firm should deliberately seek out profitable orders from strategic customers. All too often, undisciplined firms take any order from any potential customer in order to make short-term sales quotas. Furthermore, managers frequently fail to discriminate between "bad orders from good customers" and "good orders from bad customers." Such short-sightedness reduces supplier profitability and diminishes its competitive advantage.

In partnering as a focused market strategy, managers diligently concentrate on customer selection, identifying likely prospects for partnerships versus transactional relationships. Later in this chapter, we will discuss a methodology that suppliers can use to assign the appropriate relationship form for each customer in their customer portfolio and manage each customer relationship optimally over time. Here, we illustrate the activities of partnering as a focused market strategy through an example from Titan Industries in Box 10.1.

Pursuing Growth and Continuity

Once the supplier firm has established a working relationship with a customer firm, business market managers pursue growth and continuity. By **growth**, we mean that the supplier firm works to increase its profitable share of the customer's business and

BOX 10.1
Titan Industries Sets Priorities for Serving Market Segments

The Indian eyewear market is worth around INR 1.6 billion and growing at a rate of 15–20% per year. Only about 10% of this market is organized. Watch and jewellery retail major Titan Industries forayed into this market in 2007 and within a span of two to three years grew to around 250 stores.

The consumer segmentation used by Titan is very progressive. Titan divides the market by "customer outlook towards eyewear" into four distinct segments. These are further divided based on income level to give at least eight sub-segments. The four main segments are as follows:

Eyewear as medication (segment A). The users in this segment consider eyewear a bane. They do not like the idea of being bespectacled. They are at best apathetic to eyewear and use glasses/contact lenses for purely medical reasons. They dislike interference caused by eyewear and would rather not make any choices regarding the same. This segment is 15% of the overall market.

Eyewear as a functional tool (segment B). This segment consists of consumers with no reservations against eyewear but who would still prefer to use eyewear sparingly. They are not conscious of any specific brand or look. They are content with what they wear and do not expect better. 27% of the market falls in this segment.

Eyewear as look enhancer (segment C). Consumers in this segment wear eyewear to enhance their looks. For them, eyewear may or may not be prescriptive. This segment is 43% of the market.

Eyewear as hi-fashion (segment D). Eyewear is more than an accessory for the consumers of this market. It is a statement in *haute couture* and part of standing out in the crowd. They account for 15% of the market.

With this unique segmentation and value recognition, Titan has formed its marketing strategy. It would not target Segment A, as eye power correction is not its strength. It can add immense value in Segments B and C, because it knows Indian consumers better than others. For example, it knows that for Indians, the distance between one eye and the other over the nose ridge is two mm lesser than for a European or American of similar body structure. Information like this can make a huge difference in manufacturing and developing superior products. Finally, Titan recognizes that it would not be able to add value to Segment D with its own products vis-à-vis already well-established, mostly international brands. However, Titan, with its excellent distribution channels, could add great value by providing a superior network to sell these brands.

Contributed by Shashank Gupta, Participant, PGP Program, Indian Institute of Management Bangalore.

to become an irreplaceable partner. As we discussed in Chapter 1, relationship development progresses through a series of exchange episodes and interwoven business strands. Thus, the supplier firm pursues growth through broadening the scale and the scope of its business with the customer firm over time. As for **continuity**, we mean that the supplier firm strives to retain the working relationship as long as it enables both supplier and customer to each achieve their respective strategic objectives.

We begin this section offer guidance on how firms can grow profitable working relationships by proposing and implementing an explicit growth strategy for each relationship over time. We also highlight innovative business arrangements such as single-sourcing, facilities management, outsourcing, and risk-sharing gain-sharing agreements. Then we examine how firms can manage the behavioral aspects of working together and foster relationship continuity. Finally, we explore CRM as a comprehensive system and set of procedures for finding, keeping, and growing profitable customers.

Pursuing Growth in a Customer Account

As business market managers search for profitable growth, a natural option for them is doing more business with current customers. After all, it appears to be conventional wisdom that it is easier and less costly to gain incremental sales from loyal customers than from new ones. Yet, many suppliers lack sufficient knowledge to devise anything but the most simplistic growth strategies, such as "use cross-selling and upselling to get customers to buy more." Without a more fine-grained and disciplined approach, chasing incremental customer business with steeply discounted prices or closing deals through the provision of supplementary services "for free" may grow customer share but often wrecks a supplier's profits.

Estimate Share of Customer's Business

To grow an account, it is important for a supplier to first understand the total volume of business attainable in a customer relationship and its current share of the customer business.[5] In Box 10.2, we discuss how Tata Steel measured its share of each customer's business and embarked on a process, which it named as Customer Value Management, to increase its share of customer's business.

BOX 10.2

Customer Value Management at Tata Steel Increases Share of Customer's Business

The opening up of the Indian economy in the early 1990s resulted in the Indian steel industry reckoning with the forces of liberalization. Inefficient operations, large-scale project delays, and a "big plant" mindset characterized the Indian steel industry during the preliberalization era. Post-liberalization, the old business paradigm suddenly appeared to have lost its relevance. In the past, the basis of obtaining an order was the lowest price. Steel was a commodity product, and supplier–customer relationships were largely transactional. The steel industry operated on a "one size fits all" approach.

Tata Steel had a large and fragmented customer base. It served more than 2,000 customers. Two hundred customers accounted for over 85% of its sales. Of these, the top 50 customers accounted for 60% of sales. Until 2000, the company considered itself a commodity supplier to both business and consumer markets. With a capacity of about four million tons per annum, translating to about 15% of India's steel manufacturing capacity, the company supplied steel to large users in business markets. Throughout the 1990s, the drive was to improve operational efficiency. By the turn of the century, Tata Steel became one of the lowest-cost steel producers in the world. However, in the changing scenario, cost competitiveness alone did not guarantee success.

(continued)

BOX 10.2
Continued

After commissioning its cold rolling mill in 2000, Tata Steel's challenge lay in its ability to serve a fragmented customer base in business markets, with stringent quality norms, large number of stock-keeping units, and different specifications to cater to varied applications. Most of the company's new customers had exacting requirements from steel suppliers. A large part of the value addition responsibility was now shifting to Tata Steel.

Based on detailed analysis of the customer base of Tata Steel, the company came up with three categories of original equipment manufacturer (OEM) customers: potentially large, long-term accounts called enterprise accounts (about 80 accounts); commercial accounts called key accounts (about 150 accounts), and distribution (customers accessed through over 50 distributors across the country). The most important basis for obtaining customer orders, however, continued to be price. The company tracked its share of business from each of its customers in these three categories.

In response to the challenge posed by the commodity trap in which the company found itself, Tata Steel launched the Customer Value Management (CVM) program. The primary objective of this program was to grow Tata Steel's share of business with select customers by developing a non-price agenda wherein Tata Steel could add value in ways other than just by dropping price. CVM envisaged the company working closely with the customer firm to eliminate value drains and implement new value-creating ideas.

Using well-defined criteria, about 30 customers were selected for the CVM program. Tata Steel put mechanisms in place to deliver extraordinary value to these customers through generating and implementing ingenious ideas, working across cross-functional teams, and working across customer–supplier boundaries. The CVM program resulted in contributing significantly to the top line and bottom line of the company. In many cases, it resulted in a steep increase in the customer firm's share of wallet for the company.

D. V. R. Seshadri, Arabinda Tripathy, Peeyush Gupta, and Subodh Pandey, "Reinventing Marketing at Tata Steel," case study developed for IIM Bangalore in 2004; D. V. R. Seshadri, Arabinda Tripathy, Peeyush Gupta, and Subodh Pandey, "Tata Steel: Drive on Institutional Sales," case study developed for IIM Bangalore in 2004; D. V. R. Seshadri, Arabinda Tripathy, Peeyush Gupta, and Subodh Pandey , "Customer Value Management at Tata Steel," case study developed for IIM Bangalore in 2004.

Having established the total volume of customer business and their current share, suppliers need to next answer two questions: Which customer share growth prospects are worth pursuing, and which are better left to competitors to fight over? How should we grow business with a customer over time? The answers to these questions together with knowledge of customer value for their offerings enable progressive suppliers to accurately target the most profitable growth prospects and devise new ways of doing business that add value or reduce costs. Next, we examine two generic approaches to growing share of a customer's business over time.

Two Generic Approaches to Building Share over Time

To understand the pattern of growth in a relationship, it is important to revisit the issue of how business market firms initiate a customer relationship. Given an understanding

Figure 10.2 Different Paths to Building Customer Share

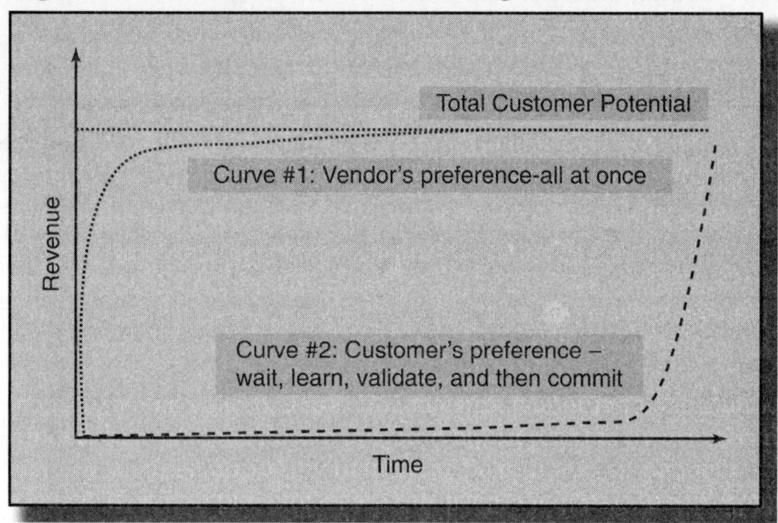

of customer business and the attractive opportunities to pursue profitably, one could argue that a supplier's objective would be to try to capture all the dollars a customer can potentially spend as early as possible (curve #1 in Figure 10.2). However, a customer with little or no experience with either supplier or product is unlikely to exhibit such behavior. The customer might prefer to evaluate products and supplier capabilities prior to committing to a purchase that yields a revenue trajectory that resembles curve #2 in Figure 10.2.

Curves #1 and #2, being incompatible, inevitably lead to adversarial relationships in which one party stands to gain only at the expense or forbearance of the other. For example, a supplier might be powerful enough to insist that customers purchase an entire bundle up front or a customer (a large-volume purchaser) capable of demanding extensive supplier compliance without reward.

Breaking down the total offering into multiple, independent components constitutes a "foot-in-the-door" (FITD) approach. The first component sold becomes the proverbial "foot in the door." A supplier's revenue trajectory from this approach would resemble that in Figure 10.3.

Although the size of the first sale is relatively small, time and effort required to close the sale are lower and the probability of closing the sale is higher, which together have the potential to translate into customer profitability at a much earlier stage.

The selection of an appropriate FITD product is critical to successful execution of the approach. An ideal candidate satisfies a number of criteria:

- It must mitigate customer risk, that is, be inexpensive enough to be purchased without hesitation by the customer.
- The fit between product functionality and customer requirements must be exceedingly close.
- Product quality should be impeccable and chance of failure nil.

Figure 10.3 Foot-in-the-Door Approach

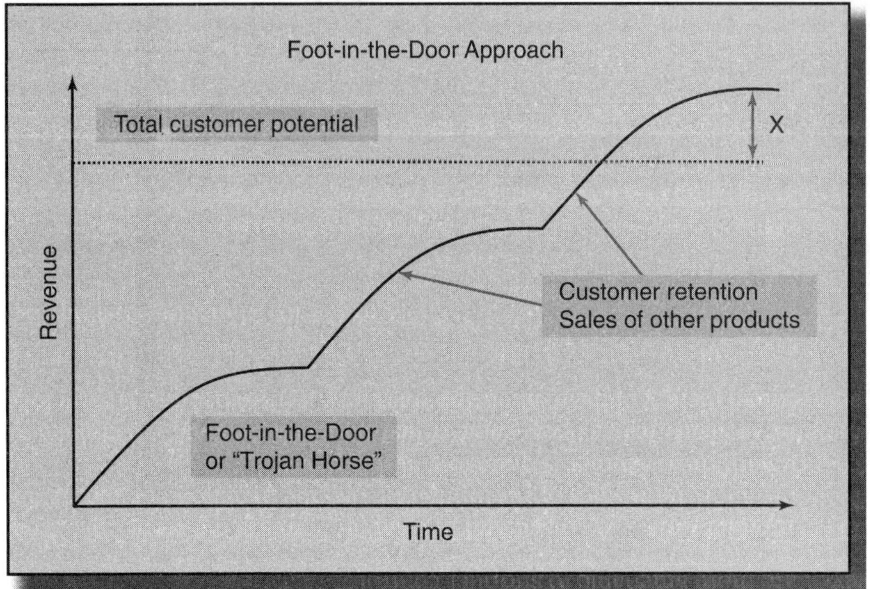

A highly visible customer problem must be solved in a unique way to enable the supplier not only to build credibility but also to forestall competitive entry at a later date. To choose, for example, a high-quality FITD product that solves a minor customer "pain" risks squandering excellent performance for want of an opportunity to truly impress the customer.

Because a positive experience with an FITD product should leave a customer anxious to do more business with the supplier, a progression path for future sales in the relationship should be clearly laid out. There needs to be a clear link between the FITD product and other products subsequently sold by the supplier. This is the concept of modularity that enables the building of complex products from smaller subsystems that can be designed independently yet function together as a whole. Baldwin and Clark provide the design rules that enable the development of modular products and therefore serve as the basis for designing an FITD product.[6] (The increase in customer potential signified by gap X in Figure 10.3 represents a customer's willingness to use the supplier as a source for products and services that would not have been considered at the start of the relationship.)

A similar approach was successfully used by Siebel Systems, a supplier of salesforce automation products.[7] Having established a foothold in a customer account, it would offer call center (service automation) products. When the e-commerce wave swept the business world, Siebel expanded its product suite to enable its customers to become e-businesses. The firm then added other products and created a new suite of products that enabled customers to manage their "demand chains." Siebel is a classic example of how eventual sales might far exceed initially perceived customer potential.

An example of how the FITD approach can be used as a competitive weapon to break into a competitor's customer base is provided by an international insurance

Figure 10.4 Customer Acquisition and Retention Using the FITD Approach

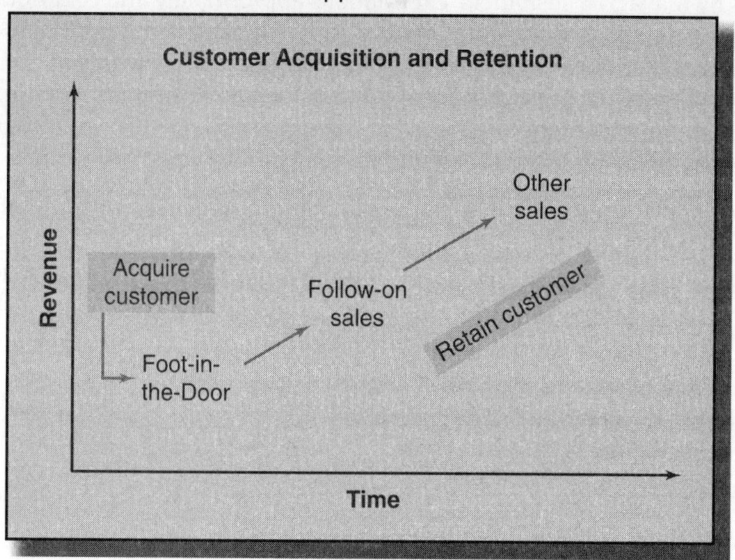

player that was trying to break into a new country market with a suite of risk management products. Encountering enormous resistance from prospects unwilling to switch entirely from their current suppliers when it tried to sell its entire product suite, the firm adopted an FITD approach, picking a product that historically had a high claim rate but not very high claim value. Customers were more willing to try just this product, and competitors, interestingly, were not unduly concerned with losing a small part of their business to a new entrant (it was rare for customers to buy their entire bundles from the same suppliers anyway) that they believed was destined to fail. Customers get to judge the quality of insurance service only when they claim damages; when a large number of customers did make claims and the supplier offered excellent and timely service, it not only gained a foothold but soon established credibility as a quality service provider. When contracts came up for renewal, large numbers of customers were willing to switch to the new supplier on the basis of favorable experience with the FITD product.

Figure 10.4 depicts relationship management using the FITD approach to design appropriate products, to *acquire* customers, and to support follow-on sales opportunities aimed at *retaining* them.

A classic problem with the FITD strategy is that absent the ability to manage customers' business strategies, a supplier's vision of a relationship trajectory is rendered meaningless. Other things that can go potentially wrong with the FITD approach, however, are more amenable to supplier control.

- ***FITD product fails.*** As discussed in Chapter 8, this is the worst-case scenario. Not only short-term sales opportunity but also the likelihood of getting another chance with the customer is quite low at this point.
- ***Supplier is identified as being good at just the FITD product.*** Without a reasonable mutual picture of the relationship trajectory, a customer might resist follow-on

sales and slot the supplier as a source for just the FITD product. Suppliers can counter this by managing customers' expectations appropriately and continuously communicating to them a vision evolutionary path of the relationship.

- ***Competitors get customers to switch by giving away the FITD product.*** Unless the FITD product generates substantial value and customers recognize that value, competitors might be able to convince them to purchase follow-on products by giving away the FITD product.

Whereas managers can deal with some of the things that can go wrong with the FITD, there are instances in which it is the wrong approach to begin with. In these situations, the supplier might prefer using an All-at-Once Approach. This approach is particularly useful in managing large customers that can complicate the selling process through a combination of temporal changes in:

- the customer's purchase decision making and buying units
- the nature of the products and services offered
- the selling skills required

Hewlett-Packard's Computer Systems Organization (HP-CSO), given the breadth of products and services it sold, broke its sales to enterprise customers into *downstream*, *midstream*, and *upstream* opportunities. Its account management organization was premised on the notion that HP, having traditionally enjoyed a price/performance advantage as a computer hardware supplier, would enter an account through downstream opportunities in the capacity of a product supplier.[8]

HP then would migrate up to IT infrastructure and enterprise-wide solutions by demonstrating industry-specific knowledge and delivering strong pre- and post-sales installation resources—the *mid-stream* business. Next, HP would leverage its position to work with the customer and help them in a broad spectrum of infrastructure projects to reduce customer costs and deliver significantly higher customer value. At this point HP effectively became a strategic partner to a customer (the *upstream* business). An example of such a strategy would be HP first supplying PCs to a large automaker, selling networks and information systems as a value-added supplier, and eventually working as a strategic partner with the customer helping it Web-enable its next-generation vehicles (Figure 10.5 depicts the resulting migration strategy).

HP's aspirations to build all three revenue streams with its enterprise customers were impeded by its migration strategy. Functional walls within customer accounts, its brand equity as a trusted hardware supplier, and the purchasing community's desire to control supplier pricing seemed to be keeping HP from evolving from a hardware supplier to a value-added supplier. Even if the account team was to scale these barriers, the IT community's desire to control supplier relationships and executive-level reluctance to include HP as an advisor effectively prevented further migration. Moreover, it was common for the customer senior management teams responsible for building and managing strategic alliances with important suppliers to stonewall efforts by HP personnel.

HP belatedly discovered that critical success factors and customer management competencies changed as one moved from managing downstream to managing upstream businesses. To survive in the downstream business, it was important to continuously improve operational efficiency in order to overcome ever-increasing

Figure 10.5 HP's Migration Strategy

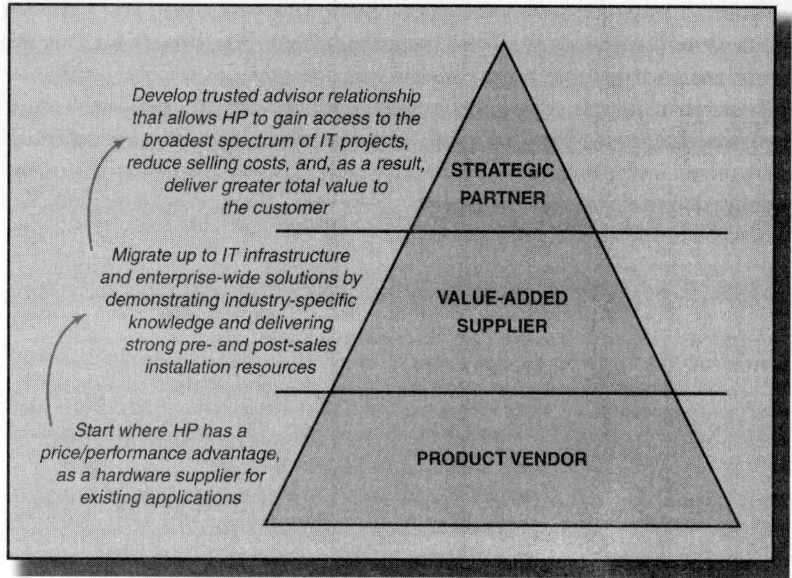

customer service requirements and continuous price discount pressures. In the midstream business, the focus shifted from efficiency to selection, suggesting that HP should perhaps not try to pursue every business opportunity. Here, HP had to be able to prioritize opportunities and choose projects on the basis of their potential and alignment with its competencies. Upstream business opportunities hinged on HP's ability to sell concepts and instill confidence among senior executives that it could deliver on its promises.

HP subsequently abandoned its migration strategy and adopted a model based on an *opportunity portfolio* management. The company resolved to service customer accounts at multiple levels from the outset using an approach tailored to the dynamics of the different types of sales opportunities. The new *"all-at-once"* approach forced HP to streamline processes for servicing downstream business, institutionalize midstream opportunity selection, identify a narrow band of upstream sales opportunities for proactive selling, and install a new set of measures for evaluating its customer management efforts. HP also had to change the sales organization and establish for each of the three business streams a team headed by a sales rep who reported to a client relationship manager with responsibility for managing the customer account. The change in strategy was validated when HP was able to significantly increase its share of large enterprise customers' total purchases.

Pursuing Continuity

Irrespective of the path chosen to grow a relationship, business market managers must address several ongoing behavioral issues to foster continuity in customer relationships and retain customers. These issues include honest and open communication, trust and commitment, coordination, and conflict resolution.[9]

Promote Honest and Open Communication

Communication is "the formal and informal sharing of meaningful and timely information between firms."[10] Business market managers from progressive firms make it a point to meet with partner firm managers periodically in formal and informal settings to discuss market conditions. By doing so over many years, customer and supplier managers often develop personal relationships and become comfortable sharing critical information. In Box 10.3, we discuss how Infosys uses this approach to sustain relationships with Cisco.

BOX 10.3

Infosys Sustains Relationships with Cisco

In 1999, Infosys had a small team of five members working for a company called Selsius, in the telecom industry, to develop an administrative tool for the customer firm's product, a voice-based communication solution (referred to as "voice solution" in the following paragraphs) that the customer firm marketed to its customers. The relationship of Infosys with Selsius continued even after the latter was acquired by Cisco.

Cisco rechristened the solution it acquired from Selsius as an enterprise-wide voice solution called Cisco CallManager. Cisco aggressively enhanced the product and increased its presence in the enterprise voice market. Today, Cisco is the market leader in the enterprise voice solution space. Cisco Unified Communication Manager is the central product around which the entire solution is designed.

As CallManager evolved into Communication Manager in Cisco, Infosys's relationship with Cisco also strengthened. This was largely attributable to both companies promoting honest and open communication with each other. Infosys engineers began working alongside those of Cisco's in various aspects of product development. Today, Infosys engineers are involved in all aspects of development, such as architecture; new features; sustenance, functional, regression, and performance testing; customer support; and developer support. In Cisco's IP Communication Business Unit (IPCBU), a large number of engineers from Infosys work alongside Cisco's team to drive growth.

The Cisco-Infosys Offshore Development Center (CIODC), set up in 1999, has since grown from strength to strength. It now has several hundred Infosys engineers working on various Cisco projects. Apart from IPCBU, CIODC works with other Cisco business units and technology groups. CIODC also works with Cisco for internal application development and maintenance.

The relationship that began years ago between Infosys and Cisco continues to grow stronger year after year. Although Infosys has thus made significant inroads into Cisco and become a solution provider of choice, Infosys has to continually innovate and create new avenues of customer value to continue to retain its preferred vendor status with the customer.

Contributed by Ramesh Shanbhag, Participant, PGSEM Program, Indian Institute of Management Bangalore. *Sources:* "Cisco Systems to Acquire Selsius Systems, Inc. for $145 Million," 14 October 1998, *http://newsroom.cisco.com/dlls/fspnisapi6d14.html;* "Technical Services Introduction, Cisco," *http://www.cisco.com/en/US/products/svcs/ps3034/ps2827/serv_category_home.html; http://www.infosys.com;* "VTech Selects Cisco and Intel RFID Solution for Supply Chain Pilot," press release, 28 April 2006, *http://newsroom.cisco.com/dlls/global/asiapac/news/2006/pr_04-28.html.*

Bridging is the establishment of multiple levels of communications between firms, across functions, management levels, and business strands. Perhaps the most common entails the creation of cross-functional and interfirm teams. By giving the teams a variety of projects to work on and encouraging members to meet with regularity, business market managers give them a common point of interaction and set of mutual tasks. Often, these group activities go beyond the workday to include social activities, such as attending sporting events or participating in golf or tennis outings.

Bridging enables both the supplier and customer firms to minimize the detrimental effects of the untimely departure of a key employee. Often, such an individual possesses unique skills and personal relationships that are crucial; thus, his or her loss might jeopardize the partnership. Professors Bendapudi and Leone recommend three steps that managers can take to ensure continuity in such situations. First, they advocate rotating staffs and using teams so that partners don't become attached to just one employee. Second, they argue that firms should develop other steady performers to work alongside essential personnel. Third, they urge firms to provide early notifications of personnel departures and to publicize transition plans to avoid catching the partner by surprise.[11]

Build Trust and Commitment

At the core of all successful working relationships are two essential behavioral characteristics: trust and commitment.[12] **Trust** in a working relationship is "the firm's belief that another company will perform actions that will result in positive outcomes for the firm, as well as not take unexpected actions that would result in negative outcomes for the firm. The strength of this belief may lead the firm to make a trusting response or action, whereby the firm commits itself to possible loss, depending upon the subsequent actions of the other company."[13] Professor Kumar argues that all firms build trust in three ways. First, a firm must demonstrate that it is dependable—it is reliable and honors its word. Second, it should strive to act in the partner firm's best interests. Third, the firm must cultivate a reputation for fairness.[14]

Leading firms demonstrate dependability over time. By starting on a small scale, perhaps through pilot projects, and then gradually increasing the scope of the alliance over exchange episodes, a firm shows that it can fulfill larger and larger promises. Moreover, as the two firms work together, managers gain a better understanding of their counterparts' goals, thought processes, corporate culture, and methods of operation. Rather than allow customer managers to draw conclusions about the firm's trustworthiness solely on intuition, some firms periodically verify relationship accomplishments. For example, in Box 10.4, we discuss how Tata Consultancy Services audits the value it delivers and reports those findings to customer firms. Through productive dealings with many companies over time, a supplier firm accumulates a track record and marketplace reputation for fairness.[15]

In doing business across borders, customer and supplier managers sometimes find it difficult to build trust, in part, because of their cultural differences. This difficulty is eased considerably when a customer firm and a supplier firm can have a collaborative relationship that extends across a number of country markets and cultures. Offering the capability of having a trustworthy relationship that extends across many country markets actually can be a distinctive supplier advantage, as the Cushman & Wakefield advertisement in Figure 10.6 conveys.[16]

BOX 10.4

Tata Consultancy Services Documents the Value it Adds to Customer Firms

Tata Consultancy Services (TCS), part of the well-known Tata Group, is India's largest IT services provider. With revenues of about INR 27,600 crores (2009) and employee headcount of about 1,50,000, it is one of the top 10 IT service providers in the world. It is headquartered in Mumbai but has an extensive worldwide network of sales and delivery offices.

In the recent past, the company has been reorganized into smaller businesses within the larger company, each focused on serving a single domain such as banking, insurance, retail, etc. The idea is to bring significant domain expertise to the clients, working with them to create more value and enabling them to be more successful in their respective businesses. Consequently, the company has launched several programs to orient its predominantly technical workforce to their respective assigned domains, so as to create a strong team of business consultants who deeply understand both the domain and the technology.

As a part of their focus to create and deliver superior customer value, some business units have begun to carefully track the value that Tata Consultancy Services creates for its clients. This entails auditing the value it delivers to customer firms and reporting these findings to them. This has required a considerable shift in orientation among client-facing TCSers, who are now counseled to not just focus on intricacies of technology, but to equally assess the value that TCS adds to the client during its engagement with the customer. This transformation is expected to yield considerable dividends in terms of increased share of customer wallet and better profitability margins, as TCS seeks to obtain an equitable share of the customer value delivered.

Commitment, on the other hand, "captures the perceived continuity or growth in the relationship between two firms."[17] It entails a "desire to develop a stable relationship, a willingness to make short-term sacrifices to maintain the relationship, and a confidence in the stability of the relationship."[18] Business market managers further relationship commitment through unilateral pledges and guarantees. A pledge involves actions one firm takes that demonstrate good faith and bind it to the relationship. Pledges signal that the firm will not behave opportunistically in the relationship. To make a pledge, a firm typically invests nonredeployable assets, which are those resources and capabilities that it cannot divert to another relationship.[19]

Through a **guarantee**, one firm promises through a legally binding contract or warranty to absorb the risk and costs associated with unfulfilled promises made to a partner firm. Guarantees mitigate the risks and expenses of a partner in the unlikely event that a relational promise is not kept. For example, Okuma America Corporation offers a 24-hour shipment guarantee to its customers. According to this arrangement, Okuma promises that if a customer orders machine-tool repair parts and they are not shipped within 24 hours, the customer receives the parts for free.

Companies increasingly back guarantees with a service recovery system. A **service recovery system** entails the resources, procedures, and authority that empower and enable front-line personnel to resolve customer problems or compensate customers for unexpected lapses in service. Psychological methods of service

Figure 10.6 Cushman & Wakefield Offers a Trustworthy Relationship

Source: Advertisement courtesy of Cushman & Wakefield.

recovery typically include an apology and an explanation of what went wrong. The supplier firm designs them to diffuse anger and restore the customer's favorable perception of the supplier. Tangible methods encompass monetary compensation for damages or inconvenience, immediate delivery of correct products or services ordered, and the resolution of customer problems. The supplier designs tangible service recovery to restore the customer's sense of equity in the business transaction.

Shrewd business market managers monitor every service recovery event to better understand and bolster the weak links in their firm's service delivery processes.[20]

Implement Coordination Mechanisms

By **coordination**, we mean the customer firm's and supplier firm's synchronization of activities, resources, and capabilities to accomplish a collective set of tasks. All working relationships require some degree of coordination. In some relationships, coordination tends to be mechanistic; that is, it is highly formalized and programmed and is implemented through rules, policy statements, and rigid hierarchical control. As relationships become more collaborative, coordination becomes more organic. Organic coordination originates at the grassroots level of organizations, entails extensive information exchange, and is flexible, cooperative, and innovative in nature. As a result, business market managers create distinct coordination mechanisms as a function of the types of working relationship their firms seek and governance systems employed.[21]

In the most transactional working relationships, *the market* provides a high level of coordination between firms without the benefit of managerial intervention. The mechanism that achieves synchronization is **market-clearing price**, which balances supply and demand for a given offering. In this situation, a business market manager achieves coordination by allowing the price of the market offering to float to the market-clearing level. Although this approach runs counter to many managers' desire to exert control, in a number of industries—agricultural products, petroleum, and fasteners, among others—coordination is left largely to the market.[22]

When one partner firm is significantly less dependent upon that relationship than the other firm, that partner firm is likely to rely on power. By **power** we mean the ability of one firm to get its partner to undertake activities that the partner firm would not do on its own. Many managers believe that gaining and using power is the best way to achieve coordination. The use of power has serious drawbacks, though. Most firms dislike being "told what to do" and aggressively seek to "get even." Thus, managers should be prudent and sparing in their reliance on power. Scholars have identified six strategies for gaining and using power: information exchange, recommendations, promises, threats, legalistic pleas, and requests.[23]

A key question that often arises relative to power is: How can the weaker firm ensure that its more powerful partner will treat it fairly? The answer is through dependence-balancing operations, which are courses of action that the weaker firm pursues to equalize the importance of the relationship to both firms. For example, the weaker firm might make greater investments in the relationship until the resources both firms have committed are roughly the same. Alternatively, the weaker firm might seek out other partners. By doing so, the firm would reduce its dependence on the relationship. In a related move, the weaker firm might try to change nonredeployable assets into redeployable assets by finding new uses for them.[24]

In the most collaborative relationships, coordination based on cooperation becomes essential. **Cooperation** entails similar or complementary actions firms take in interdependent relationships to achieve mutual outcomes or singular outcomes with expected reciprocation over time. To encourage cooperation, business market managers promote shared norms concerning how to work together, how to jointly create value, and how to share benefits. They demonstrate to partner firms that cooperation is rewarded. Perhaps most important, business market managers build mutual trust and commitment.[25]

Anticipate and Resolve Conflicts

Business market managers understand that every working relationship will eventually experience some sort of conflict. They know that it is just another part of doing business. By **conflict**, we mean "the overall level of disagreement in the working partnership. As such, conflict is determined by the frequency, intensity, and duration of disagreements."[26] Rather than glossing over or covering up disagreements, successful managers anticipate disputes and put into place mechanisms for immediately resolving them. By doing so, they avoid **pathological conflict** that serves to destroy, injure, or poison a relationship. Instead, they transform it into **functional conflict**. These productive discussions clear the air by ameliorating harmful tensions or ill will and result in policy changes and procedures that add value or reduce costs within the partnership.[27]

Business market managers must gain an understanding of the underlying causes of conflict and determine when and how each are likely to manifest themselves in their industry. In general, managers trace disagreements to three primary sources. Goal incompatibility captures the fact that the mission, goals, and objectives of partner firms are disparate. At times, these differences create situations in which one partner can achieve its goals only at the expense of the other firm. The lack of agreement over responsibilities within the working relationship is domain "dissensus." Perhaps the most recurring disputes over domain relate to functions that each partner should perform, how partners should accomplish tasks, and the timing of efforts. Differing perceptions of reality similarly lead to disagreements. For example, differing perceptions of market trends, competitive threats, and emerging technologies often lead to conflicts between partners.[28]

With an understanding of potential sources of disagreements, business market managers create appropriate conflict resolution mechanisms. As we previously discussed, one way to prevent conflicts from escalating to major crises is to implement a service recovery system. A closely related and highly effective alternative is to train boundary-spanning personnel—individuals who are in contact with the partner firm on a regular basis—to be sensitive to inherent trouble spots. These persons should learn to identify emerging problems and to try to resolve them informally and immediately before they escalate into relationship-threatening crises. Alternately, the partners can designate individuals within their respective firms to resolve conflicts.

For intractable disputes, business market managers turn to mediation or arbitration. **Mediation** is the process in which a third party is brought in to help resolve a dispute by either refocusing discussion on key issues or suggesting viable solutions. In general, their role is to promote clear understanding of each firm's position and to encourage the open discussion of issues. Under **arbitration**, the firms legally agree to have a third party settle the disagreement. The decision of the third party, often a professional arbitrator, is final and legally binding. For these extreme conflict resolution mechanisms to function properly, firms need to agree ahead of time what types of concerns will trigger either mediation or arbitration and who can be brought in as an acceptable mediator or arbitrator.[29]

Delivering Superior Value with Relationship-Specific Offerings

With the account development approach and timeline in mind, business market managers then need to construct and then implement relationship-specific offerings. Managers draw on the techniques of managing market offerings that we presented in Chapter 5. We add to that discussion in this section by describing a strategy for constructing relationship-specific offerings. Next, we describe how firms organize to deliver and sell relationship-specific offerings. Then, we suggest ways for business market managers to solve common relationship-offering implementation problems.

Construct Relationship-Specific Market Offerings

Business market managers configure a market offering to match the type of relationship pursued with a particular customer firm. In Chapter 3, we mentioned that the nature of the offering tends to expand from a single product or service in the case of a purely transactional relationship to a solution or bundle of products and services in a collaborative relationship to a partnership in a strategic alliance.[30] As a start in constructing the collaborative and transactional relationship offerings, the supplier firm does market research to determine the extent and intensity of collaborative and transactional efforts practiced in the industry. In other words, managers gain an understanding of the present industry bandwidth. At the same time, the supplier firm performs benchmark studies of other industries in an attempt to learn about collaborative and transactional practices that it might adopt or adapt into its current offerings. The supplier firm's strategy is then to extend the present industry bandwidth in both the collaborative as well as the transactional direction. By becoming more collaborative and more transactional in this manner, a supplier firm tries to gain a competitive advantage over other suppliers by better meeting customer requirements and preferences in both collaborative-emphasis and transaction-emphasis segments.[31] We refer to this strategy as **flaring out from the industry bandwidth**.

Managers modify the firm's market offering through flaring out by unbundling or flaring out with augmentation. To **flare out by unbundling**, business market managers either eliminate certain standard elements from the market offering entirely or transform them into options. In essence, the manager has moved the firm's market offering from *b* to *a* in Figure 10.7.

To **flare out with augmentation**, managers draw on the practices of more collaborative industries and add new programs and systems that collaborative accounts will value to the standard offering, or as options. Significantly, the supplier may not offer a number of these new programs and systems to transactional customers, even as options. In essence, business market managers move their firm's collaborative market offering from *c* to *d* in Figure 10.7.

As an example of augmentation, consider how Penske Logistics (PL) flared out to create a collaborative offering in a market populated with transactional relationships. As part of its service to General Motors (GM), PL hired operations researchers to build a model of GM's physical distribution requirements. Based on this model, PL designed a program to help GM schedule shipping routes, select car models for

Figure 10.7 Flaring Out from the Industry Bandwidth

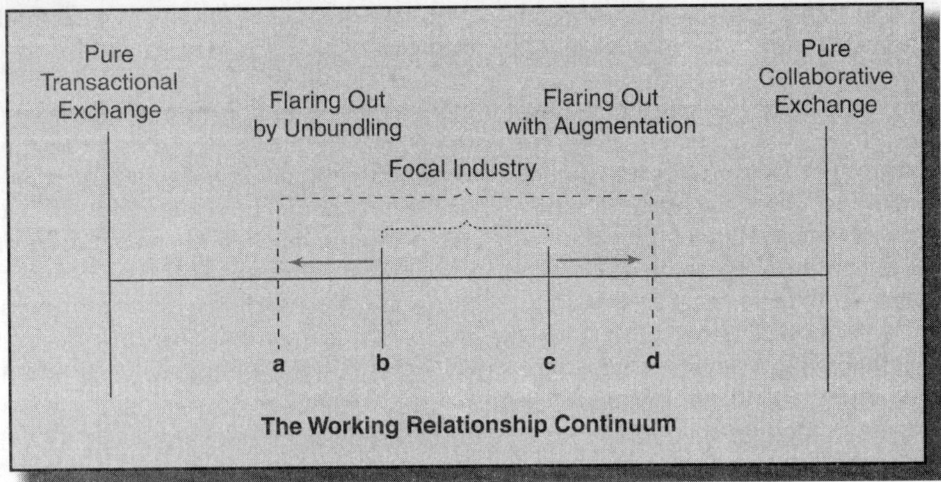

Source: Adapted from James C. Anderson and James A. Narus, "Partnering as a Focused Market Strategy," *California Management Review* (Spring 1991): 95–113.

shipping, and determine the optimal sequence for off-loading cars at GM dealers to minimize potential damage and delivery time. The computer model is highly interfaced with GM's in-house computer systems and can be utilized to troubleshoot emergency problems. Although PL has only a 30-day contract with GM, that contract has been in effect continuously for over 60 years. PL remains a major supplier of trucking services to GM.

Price Relationship-Specific Offerings

The relationship-specific pricing strategy and tactics reflect the underlying relationship strategy. For transactional relationships, business market managers lower the price for each service that is unbundled, but lower it less than the cost of presently performing the service, thereby improving the supplier's profit margin. The supplier firm markets its optional programs and services such as delivery, installation, training, maintenance, and technical service, in menu fashion, on an incremental price basis. A further feature of the pricing strategy for the transactional offering should be that the sum of the price increments for the entire set of unbundled services should be greater than any price premium granted for the collaborative offering. This pricing should reflect the economies of scope and scale that accrue from being a full-service supplier to a customer. Note that this pricing is market oriented in that it allows customer firms to choose the market offering and relationship that they perceive provides the greatest value.

The pricing strategy for collaborative market offerings takes an opposite tack. Because the only collaborative efforts undertaken are those that add value to or reduce the total cost of the exchange between firms, the supplier should seek a price premium in return for the collaborative offering. As an alternative, the supplier firm may seek a greater share of the customer's business, particularly when most potential cost savings occur in the customer firm's operation. In collaborative relationships there is another wrinkle that business marketers need to manage creatively. Contrary to what might be expected, firms often reduce margins on specialty products to make money on commodity products. Such behavior can be consequent to an industry's competitive dynamics. For example, in the elevator industry, it is common for major elevator manufacturers to sell their elevators (the specialty product that creates value for customers) at cost to lock in service and maintenance contracts (the commodity products) at high margins. The same holds for aircraft jet engine manufacturers; the industry's three major players literally give away engines to make money on maintenance contracts and in the spare parts business. These strategies risk the entry of service-oriented firms able to erode the margins in service contracts, as is the case in the elevator business.

A mechanism for modifying the pricing of relationship offerings is **defeaturing**, a tactic we introduced in Chapter 3. For transactional customers that represent significant business, a supplier may defeature its offering and share the cost savings, at least in part, as lower price. Another tactic is to selectively inquire about the transactional customer's willingness to relax its stated specifications in return for a lower price.

In collaborative relationships, the customer and supplier firms work together to gain a deeper understanding of the customer's requirements and preferences. Collaboration allows the supplier to more fully use its expertise to propose modifications in the customer's specifications that will enable it to lower its price. At times, the supplier may even be able to redesign its offerings to provide greater functionality at the same price. Thus, defeaturing is a way for the supplier to modify and adapt its offerings so its prices are more in line with what transactional or collaborative customers are seeking. In each case, the supplier may retain a portion of the cost savings as incremental profit and pass on the remainder to the customer as incentive to change.

Organize to Deliver Relationship-Specific Offerings

When a supplier firm decides to sustain a portfolio of diverse working relationships, it often establishes multiple sales forces. In Chapter 7, we described these alternative sales forces. Each of these sales forces provides a different level of service to targeted customer accounts.

Motorola's Semiconductor Products Sector provides an excellent example of how firms organize around relationships. The division has three field sales forces plus an inside sales force. Motorola's Strategic Market Sales Force is composed of teams of technical sales engineers, applications engineers, quality engineers, and service personnel, among others, that are assigned to strategic partnership accounts. It is the responsibility of these sales teams to deliver the technical and manufacturing know-how needed to make the partnerships successful.

Members of Motorola's Geographic Sales Force act individually, calling on the thousands of customers that buy Motorola products. They perform traditional selling tasks, such as making periodic customer visits, giving presentations, solving problems, and taking orders. Motorola's Distributor Sales Force represents Motorola to the trade. Member tasks include encouraging distributors to stock and sell Motorola products, coaching distributor sales personnel on merchandising techniques, and working with distributors to maintain sound working relationships with the smallest of Motorola customers. Finally, Motorola's Inside Sales Force makes outgoing telemarketing calls and takes incoming orders from transactional customers via the telephone and fax machines.

In Box 10.5, we illustrate the client management approach used by Cognizant Technology Solutions to implement a focused share-building strategy among major corporate accounts.

BOX 10.5
Client Management Approach at Cognizant Technology Solutions

Cognizant Technology Solutions (CTS) has been one of the most successful IT service providers of the last decade and a half. The company provides software solutions and services in various industry verticals such as @Banking & Financial Services, Telecommunication, Health Care, Hospitality, Media, Entertainment, Life Sciences, and Retail and Manufacturing.

The goal of CTS is "Making our customers' businesses stronger by empowering them to be more responsive to their customers and to the competitive environment." CTS is a pioneer of the fourth-generation offshore outsourcing business model that goes far beyond the typical on-site-offshore model. It does so by demonstrating deep knowledge of the customer's domain, leveraging its technological competence, providing state-of-the-art tools to manage technology deployment, and providing professional program management, thereby delivering superior solutions to the customer firm's problems.

The Two-in-a-Box model is a proprietary delivery methodology adopted by CTS, wherein CTS embeds professionals with proven domain expertise into the client organization to drive the IT strategy and ensure business alignment. Since the strategy of CTS has offshore outsourcing as one of its components, this model has both on-site and offshore aspects.

Onsite, CTS puts in place a strong relationship management team with a proven track record of industry/domain expertise at the client's location. This team includes a team leader, who is called the "client partner." He/she absorbs the client's culture, operational processes, and the environment in general. The client partner works very closely with the senior members of the customer's IT management team and nurtures deep relationships with them. Most importantly, the client partner is empowered to take executive decisions that can help CTS to obtain further business from the client.

The offshore team has a global delivery manager responsible for the delivery of offshore IT services. The client partner works very closely with the delivery manager so that the IT services are delivered as per the customer's requirements. The client partner and the delivery manager are two vital links in the relationship. They ensure that the offshore team is just a virtual extension of the customer's IT team.

This model is scalable depending upon the size and complexity of the project. On multi-project engagements, the client partner typically interacts with multiple client managers and CTS delivery managers.

However, this relationship model alone is not enough. The company backs this model with a tremendous focus on project planning, quality, process adherence, and consistent delivery. There is a lot of responsibility on the people who function as the client partners

(*continued*)

BOX 10.5
Continued

and the delivery managers. Consequently, it is not surprising that the company puts heavy emphasis on proper selection of the client partners and delivery managers.

CTS believes that partnering is integral to IT-outsourcing success. Hence, the Two-in-a-Box model is based on the premise of collaborative relationships in which CTS is a partner to its customer especially in the latter's IT strategy. The client partner's primary responsibility is to ensure that collaboration actually takes place. He/she is focused not only on delivery but also on operational flexibility and process improvements. Through this partnering with the client, CTS gets an intimate view of the client organization, enabling it to add value to the customer.

The Two-in-a-Box strategy enables CTS and its customer to operate as a single delivery center, with the deliverables being the primary focus. CTS makes a strong commitment towards its customer-facing resources for delivering a superior customer experience. This approach is a major factor for high customer satisfaction scores and strong customer retention rates. This has enabled CTS to differentiate itself from competition and sustain its impressive growth.

Contributed by Nikhil D. Kashyap, Participant, PGSEM Program, Indian Institute of Management Bangalore. *Sources:* Prashanth Rai, "Indian Outsourcing Industry Boom Continues," 29 January 2007, *http://www.cio-weblog.com/50226711/indian_outsourcing_industry_boom_continues.php;* Annual Reports, Cognizant, *http://investors.cognizant.com/index.php?s=52;* Cognizant Technology Solutions, *http://www.cognizant.com/ html/content/microsoft/techfddvsts.asp.*

In Box 10.6, we discuss how Tejas Networks has developed and implemented a strategy for growth through progressively broadening collaborative relationships with important customers in India.

BOX 10.6
Tejas Networks' Relationship Growth Strategy

Founded in the year 2000, Tejas started as a company to provide sales, marketing, and customer support for Sycamore in India. At that time, Sycamore was one of the "hot" telecom-networking equipment companies, providing high-end optical switches to manage high-speed and high-volume traffic in telecommunications networks.

Tata Power was one of the first customers of Sycamore Networks and wanted to become a telecommunications carrier in Mumbai. It had the architecture and equipment for a high-capacity telecom backbone and needed equipment that carried the smaller and slower streams of data into the fast backbone.

However, neither Sycamore nor other telecom-networking players had the equipment that could service Tata Power's needs. The challenging demands of Tata Power presented an opportunity for Tejas to build net-

BOX 10.6
Continued

working equipment specifically for the Indian market. Tejas decided that it would no longer be just the arm of Sycamore networks. This bold move was also motivated by the fact that India was fast becoming one of the largest markets for telecom equipment in the world. Tejas started to build cost-effective equipment that would support both voice and data services and that would provide speeds between two Mbps and 155 Mbps.

Tejas developed the TJ100 class of versatile, carrier-class optical access products. It enabled telecom carriers to augment their traditional voice-based networks with the new data-dominated networks in a cost-effective manner. The close partnership with Tata Power enabled Tejas to not only sell TJ100 equipment but also provide a network design and planning tool as well as installation and integration services for the broadband and access network of Tata Power. The successful implementation of the project stands as an example of "consultative selling," whereby Tejas worked with the customer to find solutions to customer problems. The project gave Tejas tremendous credibility that allowed it to approach other customers such as network service providers, utility companies, and large enterprises.

Utility companies already had infrastructure stretching across the country, which could be leveraged for building an optical fiber backbone. Tejas approached these companies for the creation of telecom infrastructure along utility lines. Tejas partnered with RailTel (part of the Indian Railways) to build an end-to-end solution to build a nationwide network along railway lines. This network consisted of over 35,000 kilometers of optical fiber and linked over 7,000 stations within the country. Tejas also partnered with Indian Oil Corporation to build optical fiber infrastructure along pipelines.

Large enterprises faced major challenges of network inflexibility and transmission issues due to the use of routers. The TJ100 MCl launched by Tejas in 2003 solved these problems by offering a single box that could accept an Ethernet connection and provide flexible bandwidth up to 100 Mbps. This equipment obviated the need for customers to use a router. Tejas also demonstrated the benefits of its offering to its customers' customers, who were typically large enterprises. This resulted in these large enterprises insisting that their telecom service provider purchase only Tejas equipment. In this manner, Tejas succeeded in the optical networking equipment market in India, gaining a large proportion of customer's share of business, by building relationships with the customer and delivering superior value.

Contributed by K. Shriram, Participant, PGP Program, Indian Institute of Management Bangalore.

Focused Share Building

The Tejas Networks approach is also a classic example of focused share building. The company avoids pursuing large-sales-revenue but marginally profitable business in favor of becoming a **focused single-source provider** of a customer's purchase requirements in that it attempts to attain 100% of a customer's business in targeted offering categories.

Pursue Single-Sourcing and Multiple Single-Sourcing

If a supplier continues to increase its share of a customer's business, it will ultimately end up in a single-sourcing arrangement. Given the traditional resistance of customer firms to single-sourcing, supplier firms must convince customer managers that such an arrangement will provide significant benefits and reduce risk. A longstanding concern of customers is that without competition, single-source suppliers will become complacent, causing product and service quality to decline. One way that Penske Logistics mitigates this fear is through a 30-day cancellation clause in their automobile shipping agreements. As we mentioned earlier in this chapter, although they have such an agreement with General Motors, their collaborative relationship has remained vibrant for over 60 years. Another way to demonstrate unflagging interest in the relationship is to increase service levels periodically.

Multiple single-sourcing is a concept that enables customers and suppliers to reap the benefits of single-source arrangements while minimizing the potential drawbacks. Under a multiple single-sourcing arrangement, each plant in a customer's manufacturing network is single-sourced, yet the customer maintains at least two suppliers across the network. For example, a customer with 10 manufacturing plants would have one single-source supplier at six of its plants and another single-source supplier at the other four plants, with each supplier serving as the backup to the other. As part of the arrangement, the customer might require each supplier to share process or product improvements with the other. The customer could then keep track of the improvements each supplier contributed and use that as a criterion for awarding future business.

Progressive suppliers often follow a two-step process for multiple single-sourcing: They first work with customers to persuade them of the value of being single-sourced at each location, regardless of which supplier is chosen. They then persuade those customers that selecting them as the single-source will deliver added value. We recount in Box 10.7 how Tata Motors as a customer firm practices multiple single sourcing.

Building New Organizational Capabilities

To gain a greater share of targeted customers' business, a supplier may decide to add expertise or a capability that it knows those customers would value. The supplier could then leverage that expertise or capability to provide a better solution to each of those customers—at a lower cost than any of them could replicate for themselves—in exchange for an incremental share of those customers' business.

For example, KLM Cargo, a unit of KLM Royal Dutch Airlines, has transformed its strategy from merely providing space on its airplanes to providing end-to-end supply-management solutions. When viewed simply as a space provider, KLM Cargo was in danger of being relegated to the low-margin, commodity portion of point-to-point air cargo transportation while complementary service providers controlled the whole transaction and captured the more profitable portions of it. To reposition itself, KLM's Special Cargo (SC) business unit studied the requirements and preferences of selected customers and improvements in value and cost that could be achieved with a reconfigured end-to-end solution. Significantly, the customers it studied were not the intermediaries, such as freight forwarders and consolidators, to whom it was selling airplane cargo-container space, but the importers and large retailers that initiated the transactions and received perishable goods. KLM SC

BOX 10.7

Tata Motors Practices Multiple Single-Sourcing

A penchant to keep costs under control motivated Tata Motors, India's largest automobile company, to revamp its outsourcing policy for the various categories of cars it manufactured. A conscious decision was taken in 2006 to maintain a lean vendor base by shifting from the existing multiple-vendor model for each outsourced component/raw material that goes into making a car to a single-vendor model. The company's exhaustive list of over 1,400 vendors was reduced to less than 700, with further reductions to come. The new vendor policy allowed Tata Motors to outsource 80% of its auto components, up from 60%, thereby substantially bringing down the material cost of its cars. It also allowed the company to consider implementing multiple single-sourcing, that is, to develop a single vendor for a particular product or product category, at each of its plants, wherever appropriate.

For the manufacture of the Tata Indica (a small car), Tata Motors maintained just 200 suppliers. This reduction in vendor base enabled Tata Motors to have a deep engagement with each chosen vendor. Simultaneously, it enhanced the commitment level of the vendor and leveraged the consequential learning curve that the vendor would experience while dealing with Tata Motors.

A similar approach was implemented when Tata Motors launched its paradigm-shifting Tata Nano. An ambitious and visionary car, the Tata Nano has changed the way the auto industry across the world thinks of automobiles, being the world's least expensive car. While small numbers of these cars have already been released into the market, the car is slated to hit the Indian roads in large numbers by 2012. The fuel-efficient, rear-engine small car, at a starting price of about $2,000 (INR 100,000), will be manufactured near Ahmedabad in Gujarat, India. While Tata Motors started the Nano project with 600 suppliers, the list was eventually trimmed down to 100, with about 75% of the components being single-sourced.

Tata Motors has been following this policy of multiple single-sourcing with its suppliers across all categories of cars manufactured in its various plants. This has helped the company reap the value of being single-sourced at each location, thereby reducing the material cost of its vehicles. Close to half of the 100 vendors for the Nano project will set up their facilities at a vendor park near the manufacturing plant. Tata Motors has entered into a long-term volume contract with these suppliers, thus cementing long-term relationships with them, while ensuring that the vendors continue innovating and driving down production costs even further.

"Tata Motors to Outsource Components," *http://www.indiacar.net/news/n38156.htm;* "Tata Nano Is A Unique Case Study Of OEM-Supplier Partnership," *http://www.supplierbusiness.com/news_endpoint.asp?id=5662.*

learned what problems these customers were experiencing, what percentage of spoilage was typical, and what price premium customers would be willing to pay for fresher products.

Under its *Fresh Partners* initiatives, KLM SC began to offer dedicated handling service that ensures an unbroken cool chain from producer to the point-of-delivery. The company now offers three levels of this cool handling service: fresh regular, fresh cool, and fresh super cool. Each service guarantees the maintenance of a specific temperature throughout transport, from truck, to warehouse, to plane, to warehouse, to truck, to the point-of-delivery. KLM SC ensures cool transport of orchids, for example, from producer locations in Thailand to the world's largest flower market in Alsmeer, the Netherlands, and then on to the point-of-delivery in other countries. Customers such as U.S. Florimex, the largest flower trader in the world, are willing to pay the price premium for this cool transport service because *its* customers are willing to pay more for a fresher product and *it* gains more of *their* business. KLM SC also provides cool transport of salmon that are farm-raised in the fiords of Norway to destinations in Tokyo, Osaka, Sapporo, Hong Kong, and Beijing within 48 hours.

Through these Fresh Partners initiatives, KLM SC has become the single-source provider to its import-export customer for orchids and gained as large a share of the salmon producer's business as its capacity can handle. The former space provider repositioned itself as a supply management provider of end-to-end solutions, provided itself with a more profitable service offering, and gained a greater share of selected customers' business through strategically building the scope of its market.

Adopt New Profit Models

In tandem with efforts to broaden working relationships and offerings to select customer accounts, business market managers strive to increase their yield on customer business by altering their firms' profit models. We discussed some of these new profit models in the context of marketing channels in Chapter 7. In transactional relationships, supplier firms focus on product sales and turnover and generate profits via full-cost pricing. As relationships become more collaborative and suppliers provide solutions, they often shift to variable-cost pricing and service fees to gain incremental revenues and profits. When they engage in the most collaborative of relationships or strategic alliances, business market managers turn to more unconventional and imaginative methods of garnering income such as licensing, syndication, and franchising agreements, agency and brokerage fees, referral fees, fees for service, percent of joint customer revenue, and joint promotional fees, among many others. One intriguing profit model is the risk-sharing, gain-sharing agreement.[32]

As we stressed at the beginning of this chapter, a supplier firm and customer firm engage in collaborative relationships and strategic alliances not because of altruism, but because of mutual self-interest. By mutual self-interest, we mean that both firms are motivated to work closely together because each firm reaps significant tangible and intangible benefits from doing so. **Risk-sharing, gain-sharing agreements** are mechanisms that partner firms can use to better align their self-interests. In these arrangements, a supplier assists its customers in becoming more profitable and exposes itself to potential or actual losses in accomplishing this. Common examples of risk-sharing agreements include warranties, guarantees, and joint investments. Gain-sharing agreements are another mechanism for aligning customer and supplier interests and refer to arrangements where a supplier assists its customers in becoming more profitable and shares in the extent to which it accomplishes this goal. Increasingly, the two are combined into risk-sharing, gain-sharing arrangements.[33]

Under risk-sharing, gain-sharing arrangements, the customer and supplier work together with the intent of improving the customer's performance. In so doing, the supplier not only receives a prespecified portion of any success, it exposes itself to potential losses, should the cost savings it promised the customer not be realized. Allegiance Healthcare, a hospital supply company of Cardinal Health, provides an instructive example in its collaboration with a hospital system located in the Southwestern United States. Spurred on by a request for assistance from this hospital system, Allegiance dispatched a multidisciplinary team to gather data on-site over an eight-week period to identify all possible ways for the hospital system to reduce costs through improved resource management, process efficiencies, and distribution logistics.

Working with clinicians and managers at the hospital system, the team found areas where the greatest cost savings were possible, such as rational consumption of supplies, materials management, laundry and linen, and sterile processing. For each area, the team quantified the range of savings that could be achieved, based on the commitment of the customer to embrace the changes. Senior management of the hospital system and Allegiance reached an agreement and planned to tackle these cost savings opportunities together. To implement the agreement, a steering committee composed of senior hospital managers and Allegiance account managers was formed to oversee the change efforts.

Under their five-year, risk-sharing, gain-sharing arrangement, Allegiance guaranteed cost savings of about $6 million per year, with a total, five-year guarantee of $28 million, taking into account the first-year implementation ramp-up. In return, Allegiance received 20% sales growth from the hospital system and 35% growth in Allegiance-manufactured products, which were demonstrated best value for their applications. These robust growth rates can be contrasted with the 3% sales growth, in general, in the health-care supplies market.

Document the Profitability of Greater Share

Gaining a greater share of a customer's business does a supplier little good when that incremental business comes at the expense of reduced profitability. Best-practice suppliers have the discipline to accurately assess their total cost to serve each customer, including the costs of providing supplementary services, programs, and systems. Furthermore, they formally document how a greater share of a customer's business translated into greater profits. Profitability may come from lowered costs, a higher price paid by the customer, or a more profitable mix of business with a customer. In turn, progressive firms use the knowledge gained to target customer firms for closer relationships and to tailor relationship-specific offerings during the upcoming year. In Box 10.8, we provide an illustration of how Indian Premier League grows its business, while simultaneously being hugely profitable.

Now that we have discussed the various aspects in the process of delivering superior value with relationship-specific offerings in individual customer relationships, we move the discussion to how suppliers can use these various approaches within a single framework to manage a portfolio of customer relationships at any single point in time and design appropriate customer migration strategies that optimize customer value and enhance customer profitability over time.

BOX 10.8
Indian Premier League Grows its Business Profitably

When it comes to growing business and making money, BCCI, Board of Control for Cricket in India, does much better than others. On 14 January 2008, it sold broadcasting rights to a new domestic competition, the Indian Premier League (IPL), for INR 4600 crores. On 24 January 2008, the BCCI sold eight 10-year franchises of IPL teams for a total of almost INR 1,256 crores.

Cricket is a religion in India and BCCI is the governing body. BCCI has the sole authority to select players, umpires, and officials to participate in international events. Without its recognition, no competitive cricket involving BCCI-contracted Indian players can be hosted in or outside the country. It has the highest revenue among all the cricket boards in the world.

In the past decade, Twenty20 cricket has emerged as a more explosive form of the sport and of late has been gathering support of most cricket lovers. As a result, BCCI started IPL, its own Twenty20 league, to generate higher revenues from TV rights, media rights, merchandise, ground signage rights, and league sponsorships.

IPL was the brainchild of BCCI's Vice President Lalit Modi. He wanted to use the Twenty20 format to provide a platform for cricket players who would otherwise go unrecognized. Eventually, the idea became a commercialization extravaganza. IPL became a cricket tournament among various city teams of India, where young players would get the chance to show their cricketing talent.

The question was, who would maintain these teams? BCCI itself lacked sufficient revenue to do so. Instead, Modi invited some of the world's richest people living in India to own and maintain each team. Why would they shell out their money on Twenty20, which is relatively new, and use some players who are not popular? This led to the development of the idea of "league teams" holding famous international-level cricketers with star power that the franchises could leverage to generate sponsorship revenue.

There was no turning back for Modi. He had a dream run from the day his idea developed into a market offering. This offering reached bigger proportions with television rights' revenues. Before the IPL format was even tested, a television consortium led by Sony bought the broadcasting rights for 10 years at INR 4,692 crores of which INR 496.8 crores was earmarked for marketing. It was a wise investment. Advertisement revenues spiraled—10-second TV slots during games could cost about INR 1 lakh.

The main customers of IPL are the team/franchise owners, who form the base segment and without whom the entire IPL offering brings no profits to BCCI, broadcasters from different media channels, which also provide significant revenues to BCCI, and finally merchandise companies, and league sponsors.

Though IPL directly targets individual cricket lovers for the entertainment quotient it provides, fans do not directly generate revenue for BCCI. Instead, stakeholders such as franchise owners, broadcast companies, merchandise companies, and league sponsors are direct sources of revenue. BCCI has formed strategic partnerships with each of these customer segments to maximize the value creation. IPL has been successful in rapidly growing its business, while being hugely profitable.

As a result of IPL's success, cricket boards of many other countries are trying to

BOX 10.8
Continued

imitate this format. BCCI's advantage is the huge demand for cricket in India, which makes it difficult for others to emulate. IPL has transformed BCCI into a cash-rich gorilla in the international cricket community, giving BCCI enormous clout in the world cricket landscape.

Commercialization of the sport and acquiring the right partners has been the key to IPL's success. Team buyouts may be an old story in the United States and Europe, but it is still a nascent phenomenon in India. It will mean reach and support for local-level sports teams in the future.

Contributed by K. M. V. Sasidhar, Participant, PGP Program, Indian Institute of Management Bangalore.

Managing a Portfolio of Customers

Throughout this book, we have articulated a vision of business market management that is data driven. Such data come from a variety of sources including the market, customers, accounting, and operations. So, it is appropriate that we begin this section by examining comprehensive data-driven systems and procedures that suppliers can use to understand their customer portfolio. These systems are popularly known as **customer relationship management (CRM)** systems.

CRM "is the bundling of customer strategy and processes, supported by relevant software, for the purpose of improving customer loyalty and, eventually, corporate profitability."[34] Consultants Rigby, Reichheld, and Schefter further argue that the imperatives of CRM are "acquiring the right customer, crafting the right value proposition, instituting the best processes, motivating employees, and learning to retain customers."[35] Endorsing the recommendation of pundits that a company should chart out its overall customer strategies, reformulate its business processes, and identify its information requirements before designing the system and acquiring software, we have deliberately addressed these issues in previous sections of the book before tackling CRM in earnest. And, we agree that the focus of CRM should be on systems and procedures rather than on technology and software. In fact, we find that many of the most productive CRM systems in use today are decidedly "low tech," relying upon a combination of manual procedures, telephone and fax machines, and rudimentary information technology networks.

In this section, we explore CRM. We begin by discussing an approach to measuring cost-to-serve customers and customer loyalty. Then, we discuss an approach using cost-to-serve customers and customer loyalty to monitor and evaluate customer relationships. Next, we discuss how suppliers can use this approach to migrate customer relationships by reassigning customer management effort based on restated objectives.

Measuring Cost-to-Serve Customers and Customer Loyalty

At the heart of a CRM system are databases and metrics for monitoring and evaluating the status of working relationships with individual customer accounts. In Chapter 8, we discussed the market and customer databases that are part of CRM systems. To improve decision-making capabilities, business market managers must also incorporate financial data on each account.

Sound CRM systems track cost-to-serve, transaction prices, and the contribution to profitability of each customer firm. Managers use this information to assess the results of their relationship-building efforts and take corrective actions such as reassigning accounts to different relational categories or redesigning relationship-specific offerings. Furthermore, as we discussed in Chapter 8, managers can build a profile of desirable prospective customer firms for use in future targeting decisions. Next we discuss an approach that can be used to design a portfolio of relationships strategies.

To understand the benefits a supplier derives from any customer relationship, one needs to go beyond just looking at a customer's commitment to consistently rebuy or repatronize a preferred product or service.[36] In fact, loyal customers in business markets commonly display a number of favorable behaviors that have direct and indirect impact on customer profitability, including the following:

Greater propensity to repurchase. A favorable orientation and the fact that acquisition costs have already been incurred ensure future revenues from and lower cost-to-serve loyal customers. Loyal customers are also likely to buy other products and services from the supplier as well. They actively seek opportunities to expand the scope of the relationships with their preferred suppliers.

Word-of-mouth effect. Loyal customers are more likely to engage in positive word-of-mouth promotion. Convincing other prospects to do business with the focal supplier generates additional revenues and lower the supplier's sales and marketing costs.

Resistance to competitors' blandishments. Because loyal customers are less likely to search for alternatives, competitors will have to offer significant incentives to induce switching. In fact, loyal customers are less likely to switch even in the presence of superior alternatives because of the reasoned expectation that the current supplier will strive to improve.

Pay a price premium. Loyal customers are sometimes willing to pay higher prices for greater value provided by a focal supplier's products. Moreover, modest price differences are often insufficient to offset a customer's uncertainties about an untried competitor's quality and service. Such behavior increases focal suppliers' revenues and reduces their costs.

Collaborate with supplier to improve performance and develop new products. Loyal customers are likely to provide feedback about areas needing improvement and to complain to suppliers rather than to other customers and prospects about poor performance, believing that constructive feedback will help suppliers not only improve current products and services, but also develop new products and solutions.

Invest in a relationship. It is common for business customers to invest in a supplier relationship. In addition to creating exit barriers to switching, customer investments also reduce a supplier's costs and enhance the benefits created. As a result, customer investments are usually a major inflection point in the evolution of customer relationships in business markets.

Each of the foregoing behaviors is a source of increased revenues or reduced costs, or both. Quantifying and then linking these loyal customer behaviors to a supplier's customer management effort would enable the supplier to calculate the returns on their efforts and, in turn, to make decisions on how much to invest in each customer relationship over time.

In business markets, we have found that loyalty behaviors are interdependent and submit to hierarchical ordering, that is, customers display different behaviors in an order defined by their underlying loyalty level. Customers therefore display the different favorable behaviors in a preset sequence as their loyalty levels increase over time. This is the basic principle of the Loyalty Ladder (see Figure 10.8).[37]

The rungs in Figure 10.8 represent different loyalty behaviors, the spacing between the rungs underlying loyalty levels. As customers become more loyal they move up the loyalty ladder. Although the loyalty behaviors associated with each rung are different across industries, they are constant across customers within an industry. Suppliers need to create an appropriate loyalty ladder for their customer base rather than use a generic one or a ladder for another industry.

Figure 10.8 The Loyalty Ladder

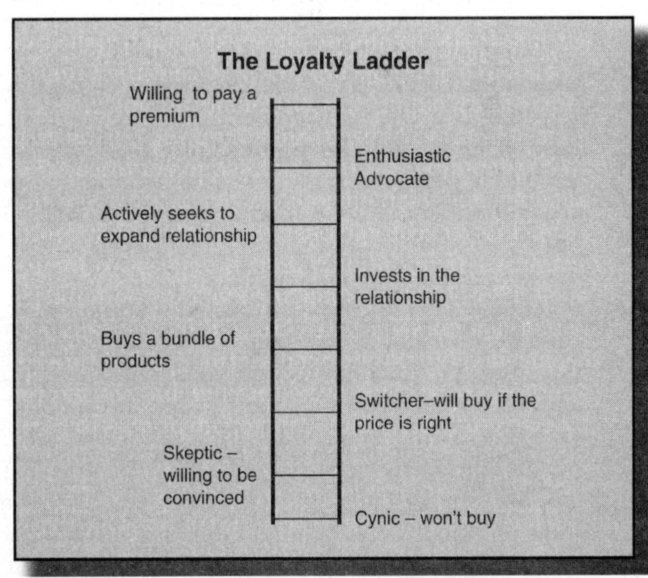

Figure 10.9 The Loyalty–Customer Management Effort (Cost-to-Serve) Framework

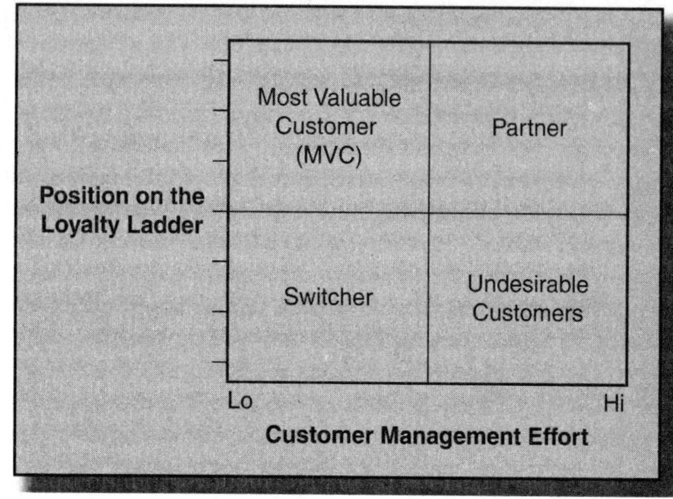

Using the Loyalty Ladder to Manage Customer Relationships

Mapping the current location of each customer on the loyalty ladder against the supplier's cost-to-serve creates the four types of customers as shown in Figure 10.9.[38]

As discussed earlier, transactional customers are customers that force a supplier to strip away all valued-added services and sell them just the basic, unbundled product offering. Because this reduces the supplier's cost-to-serve, the customer expects lower prices. These customers view the supplier's product as a commodity and are likely to switch suppliers if they are unable to get lower prices. In mature business markets, a large number of high-purchase-volume customers tend to be *switchers*. They do not have preference for any specific supplier. Yet, these customers can be very important for suppliers because they demand large volumes.

Suppliers are well advised to forgo trying to educate such customers about their value-added services and play the commodity game. The primary focus in these relationships is in the management of costs. Suppliers can also benefit from pushing these customers into long-term contracts in return for lower prices. The assurance of demand is very important in business markets, especially those with high fixed cost structures. Alternatively, migrating these customers to new products and technologies by decommoditizing the relationship is another viable opportunity (see the Wesco example that follows later).

Undesirable customers are created when suppliers mismanage switchers. In fact, a standard joke among sales reps is to call their large, unprofitable customers "strategic accounts" to convince management that current losses are an investment to achieve better returns in the future, an outcome that is usually never realized. Suppliers, owing to a combination of factors, are often willing to accept extremely low margins from large customers. In industries with a high fixed cost component, a supplier's biggest customers (in terms of volume) are often firmly ensconced in the undesirable customer quadrant because of customer threats and the need to keep the customer at any cost to fill production capacity that has prompted the supplier to gradually expand the level of services offered free just to keep the customer. As a result, these relationships suffer from low prices and *scope creep* that adversely affect customer profitability.

It is also common for a firm's *showcase accounts* to be in the undesirable customer quadrant. In most markets having a marquee customer in the portfolio enhances a supplier's reputation with other customers; these customers are "showcased" to attract additional customers. Because showcase customers typically leverage their position in a manner similar to large-volume customers, suppliers should develop systems to quantify the "showcase" effect. If, after accounting for the benefits, a customer continues to be in the undesirable customer quadrant, the costs of maintaining the customer relationship are not being recovered through additional sales to other customers.

Finally, customer relationships that suppliers try to buy their way into also populate the undesirable customer quadrant. Bribing customers with low prices and high levels of service in the expectation that things can be changed in the long run is rarely successful. Yet it is one of the most common mistakes made by business marketers.

From the supplier's perspective, it makes sense to have customers in this quadrant only temporarily. Three choices might be superior to the status quo.

Strategic accounts might be migrated to the switcher quadrant following a dialogue that identifies supplier services and efforts that the customer neither requires nor values (these supplier actions are typically based on the misperception that they are required to keep the customer account). Suppliers will find cutting back on such scope creep to be a very fruitful avenue.

It is also possible for the supplier to rationalize its cost-to-serve the customer, as in the case of an applications software supplier that adopted the loyalty ladder approach. Previously, its sales reps had frequently demanded significant levels of service that were expensive to provide and price breaks to large-volume strategic accounts. Lacking information on customer loyalty measures and focusing only on revenues from these customers, management seldom questioned these investments. But, once the firm was able to locate each of its customers on the loyalty ladder, any request for additional investments or price discounts in a customer relationship had to be supported by detailed assessments of the short- and long-term impact on the customer's location. Tighter control over its customer management effort enabled the supplier to link this effort to favorable customer behavior and, in turn, to economic returns.

Alternatively, these customers might be migrated to the partner quadrant by first communicating the true value stack to them. Often, in cases in which suppliers have given away services that are truly appreciated, customers are willing to consider appropriate price increases. It is important to note that trying to get customers to pay for something that was previously offered for free is not an easy task. The best time to attempt such an approach is when the supplier is able to offer customers other sources of value-addition as well, as was done by an industrial marketing firm that created cross-functional teams to brainstorm ideas and approaches for reducing the firm's cost-to-serve and creating additional customer value. Getting all parts of the organization into customer-facing roles generated a flood of creative ideas from product redesign to product deliveries and after-sales service. The firm subsequently mandated this practice for all major accounts.

Finally, a supplier, at times, must be willing to let certain customers "walk." If a supplier is truly providing unique value and not getting paid for it, it must also be true that the customer is unlikely to be able to obtain this value free from anyone else and is likely to come back after having realized this. A new relationship can then be established on the supplier's terms. This approach requires discipline and resolve; it is not easy to walk away from a major customer relationship. A supplier of engineered parts and components found this out the hard way. One of its most important customers had migrated their purchases to Internet-based reverse auction systems. Desperate to keep the business, the supplier dropped prices significantly to win the auctions and keep customer's business. It was not long after that the supplier realized that although it now charged lower prices, it was forced to continue to offer high levels of service. Discussions with the customer to get paid for additional services didn't work either—the customer did not think much about the supplier's services. Unable to justify this approach, the supplier finally decided to walk away from such business. The customer then distributed their purchase volumes to other low-cost suppliers that had bid on their reverse auctions. Much to the customer's surprise, the new suppliers were not willing to provide the high level of service given the low prices. Belatedly the customer realized that they were not actually buying commodities and came back to the supplier willing to now pay for the supplier's services. Letting the customer walk paid off for the supplier.

Partners are customers that are expensive to serve, but the returns usually justify the effort. These customers typically want *turnkey solutions* from suppliers because they have consciously chosen not to develop in-house expertise or make investments that would reduce their need for the supplier's value-added services. They typically view the supplier as a value-adding partner and look for a long-term commitment. Customers in the partner quadrant also want the *latest and best products* from the supplier and are willing to pay a price premium. Although they might not be actively involved in codeveloping new products, customers in the partner quadrant are major drivers of product innovation.

If these partners are not managed right, the supplier can end up with unexpected problems. For example, in high-tech markets, customers in the partner quadrant rapidly move to the undesirable customer quadrant because suppliers do not come to terms with the rapid commoditization cycles that are characteristic of these industries and lack the discipline to manage the cost-to-serve appropriately, being forced to drop prices significantly to keep the customer account.

Such customers are difficult to manage in mature markets as well for an entirely different set of reasons. As business markets mature, it is common for the customer's purchasing unit to transition from being dominated by technical staff to being managed by its procurement personnel. This transition is when suppliers are most likely to fumble and make a mistake. The supplier needs to build a new value stack with the new power bases in the customer's buying unit. New purchasing unit members need to be educated on all the joint investments and learning that have reduced the customer's total cost of ownership and that would be lost if they were to switch suppliers seeking lower prices. Suppliers can also proactively manage the migration of these customers to the MVC quadrant.

Most valuable customers (MVCs) are as loyal as partners. In addition, they are significantly more inexpensive to serve than partners. This is as a result of the supplier becoming more efficient at serving these customers and reducing their cost-to-serve without decreasing the customer benefits. It is achieved through *joint investments and learning* as when (a) the customer has invested in systems, processes, or people, (b) the customer has assumed some of the functions traditionally provided by the supplier, (c) the supplier has learned to serve the customer more efficiently, or (d) some combination of these effects has occurred. The Internet and other interactive technologies are enabling customers to take over activities that cut down the supplier's cost-to-serve. For example, customers might prefer to customize products to their requirements on their own using tools provided by the supplier. Further downstream in the purchase cycle, order-cycle related activities such as checking on order and delivery status, billing, and payments are now being offered on company Web sites. Every time customers use these functions, they reduce the supplier's cost-to-serve.

MVCs are also *grateful customers* that value their relationship with the supplier and, being focused beyond a single transaction, are willing to pay a price premium that rewards the supplier for past efforts and the guarantee of continued service. What appears to be irrational customer behavior at the transaction level becomes highly rational under the lens of a long-term relationship.

Finally, MVCs are also *advocates* and *reference accounts* that are willing of their own volition to talk to other customers and supplier prospects. They are powerful sales tools that can supplement a supplier's own sales efforts.

In most business markets, MVCs account for less than 10% of a supplier's revenue base. Given their value, suppliers should be very careful in cultivating and retaining these customers. In the presence of new competitors or technologies, suppliers should move these customers back to the partner quadrant by increasing service levels and enhancing the benefit stack to make competing alternatives unattractive to MVCs.[39]

Executing Migration Strategies

Customers in most business markets do not show up in the shape or form desired by suppliers. It is through a series of planned investments and thoughtful actions that suppliers can move the customer to the appropriate location on the loyalty ladder versus cost-to-serve grid. To do so, a supplier needs to first:

- Identify the customer management activities required to support a relationship at each rung;
- Quantify the benefits that are associated with each rung of the ladder relative to those of adjacent rungs; and
- Calculate the costs incurred in moving a customer from one rung to another using a combination of historical data and account managers' experience.

It is important that appropriate care be taken in the measurement of costs and revenues at the individual customer level.[40]

Knowing a customer's current position on the loyalty ladder can facilitate a supplier's assessment of its relationship with that customer. A supplier that discovers, for example, that it is expending more effort than required to serve a customer at a particular rung needs to immediately analyze the situation to determine whether the problem is due to competitive effort at the customer account, ineffective account management by supplier personnel, or idiosyncratic customer factors. Such analysis can help suppliers identify and take remedial actions to resolve the problems in individual customer relationships.[41]

Using this approach, the supplier can also plan customer migration paths on the loyalty ladder. Two examples that are related to these ideas are discussed in Boxes 10.9 and 10.10. These cases document the discipline required to successfully manage business customers.

BOX 10.9
Hewlett Packard—Turning Switchers into MVC's

In 2004, Bank of India (BOI), a premier nationalized bank, faced intensifying competition from a host of private and foreign banks. The liberalization of the Indian banking industry had led to a boom in retail banking. Private sector banks had pioneered a number of services such as phone banking, debit cards, automatic teller machines (ATMs), etc., and integrated them into the mainstream. BOI decided to focus on launching innovative banking products and services. For this to be a success, it felt the need to engage with an IT firm that could act as its IT partner.

In 2004, banks were redefining their business models and shifting their focus to become customer centric. At the same time, they were more cost conscious. Any IT solution that would be adopted had to be robust, have excellent back-up and recovery performance, be cost-effective, have a simple licensing policy, and be flexible and scalable to meet the bank's future growth needs. Since there were many well-established providers of IT services for banks, such as Infosys, TCS, Wipro, IBM Global Services, Accenture, Hewlett Packard, etc., there was a general tendency among banks to treat these services as a commodity, resulting in orders being finalized based on the lowest price. Banks perceived the service providers as interchangeable.

BOI's techno-commercial committee took a different view. It decided to award the contract to Hewlett Packard (HP), based on its technical know-how and in-depth experience in providing solutions for the banking industry. HP entered India with India Software Operations (ISO) in early 1990s. Sensing the potential for banking solutions in India, HP decided to target this industry as one of its many focal markets.

Based on BOI's specific needs, HP used its well-defined Service Oriented Architecture (SOA) Application Lifecycle Management program throughout the contract, encompassing these steps: defining functional specs, software customization and integration, deployment, ongoing application customization, maintenance, and support.

HP crafted a solution with BOI representatives by working with other solution/channel partners. This was also done as a part of HP's strategy to offer collaborative solutions. HP worked with Infosys to customize and implement the latter's own Finacle Core Banking Solutions and e-banking solutions across the bank's branches. It partnered with Oracle to customize an enterprise data warehouse and Oracle Financial Services Applications (OFSA) modules for risk management, performance management, transfer pricing, campaign management, and an executive information system. It partnered with Newgen Software to develop new document imaging and workflow solutions. It also partnered with BOI to implement enterprise-wide Mail and Messaging (Microsoft) and HRMS (PeopleSoft) systems. HP was also entrusted with developing centralized phone banking and inbound call management solution, and integrating banking channels (phone, the Internet, ATM) with the core banking system. Lastly, HP provided a disaster recovery solution, which offered 24/7 reliability for mission critical services.

BOX 10.9
Continued

HP's solution was robust and scalable. It helped BOI keep pace with its growth for the next decade. BOI, rather than treating IT services as a commodity, became HP's loyal customer. HP in turn reciprocated by delivering superior value, resulting in BOI becoming one of its most valued customers (MVCs).

Contributed by Sujaikumar Jayarao, Participant, PGSEM Program, Indian Institute of Management Bangalore. *Sources:* "HP Annual Report FYI 2003–04," *www.hp.com/lnvestorRehltions;* "Bank Of India Invests in IT-Enabled Transformation – An HP Case Study," *http://hp.com/casestudies/4AA1-73 66ENW.Pdf;* "HP enables Bank Of India be business agile and customer centric," *http://h71028.www7.hp.com/enterprise/downloads/856 22.pdf; www.hp.com.*

In Box 10.10, the Infosys case highlights the pro-active approach of top management to ensure account profitability, even if it sometimes entails having to terminate the relationship with the customer.

As shown in the case studies, business market managers should not limit the evaluation of relationships to quantitative, activity-based costing data and transaction price

BOX 10.10
Infosys—Ensuring Account Profitability

Infosys Technologies, established in 1981, is one of India's leading IT software service providers. With annual revenues of over INR 8,400 crores and employee headcount of over 1,00,000, Infosys is today one of the most celebrated and well-reputed IT companies in the world.

However, in 1995, Infosys was forced to refuse unreasonable demands from one of its biggest customers—General Electric, which accounted for 25% of sales at Infosys at that time. General Electric asked for a reduction in billing rates, which Co-founder and then CEO Mr. N.R. Narayana Murthy found impossible to honor. Had Infosys agreed to the unreasonable demands, it would have incurred a significant loss in delivering to that client.

Disagreement over the fees compelled Infosys to walk out on its key customer, who at the time contributed to 8% of Infosys's profits. Murthy felt that if all the other Indian software vendors employed by GE at the time also refused the lower rate, GE would be left with no choice but to give its vendors a fair deal. Accordingly, he met with senior executives of various other software firms. Finally, however, Infosys was the only vendor to walk away from doing business with GE under the terms stipulated by GE.

Subsequently, Infosys decided that it would not allow one customer to command more than 10% of its business. The company expanded its customer base by inking deals with Xerox, Levi Strauss, Nynex, etc. Murthy, later, attributed his refusal of GE's unreasonable conditions to the courage and principles that Infosys deeply believed in.

"25 Facts About Infosys," *http://teck.in/25-facts-about-infosys.html;* "ICMR India," *http://www.icmrindia.org/Casestudies/catalogue/Business%20Strategy3/Infosys%20Technologies.htm;* Infosys Newsroom, *http://www.infosys.com/newsroom/features/infosys-25-years/Pages/narayana-murthy-speech.aspx.*

data. Given that the purpose of partnering is often learning, managers should consider qualitative measures, such as new product ideas contributed and amount of technology transferred. At times, these qualitative measures will be more revealing than those derived from accounting data.

Motorola's Semiconductor Sector provides an instructive example of relationship evaluation procedures. When Motorola began partnering in earnest, senior management devised a one-page Statement of Partnership Goals, which summarized what Motorola expected to achieve for both itself and key customers from the partnership process. We paraphrase the key objectives from this statement as follows:

- All partnership programs such as codesign or joint development will result in profits for both Motorola and its partner firm.
- Motorola's sales to the partner firm will be substantial or exhibit significant growth potential.
- Motorola should have a significant, if not exclusive, share of the partner's business.
- The partnership should contribute to the achievement of Motorola's technology roadmap goals.

Periodically, senior management compares outputs from each of the Semiconductor Sector's approximately 60 partnerships to the goals specified in the partnership statement. They consider such things as changes in sales and profits as well as the mix of complementary products sold to the partner firms. In order to gauge the benefits of the partnership to the customer firm, managers examine results of Motorola's annual customer satisfaction survey. The survey summarizes Motorola's performance from the perspective of partner firms' managers in such functional areas as manufacturing, engineering, purchasing, and R&D.

Following consultation with customer managers, Motorola downgrades partnerships that do not meet objectives. They accomplish this distancing in two ways. First, managers transfer the responsibility for a downgraded account from the Strategic Market or Segment Sales Force to the Geographic Sales Force. Second, Motorola disengages itself from partnership programs, such as joint product development. Conversely, Motorola upgrades promising geographic accounts to partnerships.

Next, we review emerging CRM applications such as resource allocation, synchronization of marketing efforts, and updating value delivered that managers can use to effectively and efficiently monitor and manage customer relationships over time.

Emerging CRM Applications

Conventional CRM applications focus on account targeting, sales force automation, offering configuration and pricing, and information exchange. Evolving CRM uses include allocating resources, synchronizing marketing efforts, and updating delivered value.

Allocating Resources for Customer Acquisition, Retention, and Growth

As we mentioned previously, Blattberg, Getz, and Thomas urge companies to allocate marketing resources to the distinct tasks of customer acquisition, retention, and growth in proportion to their profit potential. A sound CRM system containing customer-specific longitudinal measures of requirements and preferences, customer value, cost-to-serve, transaction prices, and customer contribution to profitability enables managers to allocate marketing resources accordingly. For example, if managers discover that their firm serves primarily transactional-emphasis accounts, they may conclude that the likelihood of account retention and growth is meager. In this case, they would devote most of their marketing budget to finding new accounts. Conversely, if they learn that the number of potential accounts is limited and the cost of acquiring new customers is prohibitive, they would direct resources to customer retention and growth activities.[43]

Synchronizing Marketing Efforts

As marketing organizations become more complex, customer portfolios become more varied, and channels become more modular, supplier firms need to do more to synchronize operations, marketing, and service activities. CRM provides a means for ensuring that all managers who "touch the customer" are working in unison. In Box 10.11, we provide an example of how DHL India synchronizes its sales and service efforts.

BOX 10.11

DHL India Synchronizes its Sales and Service Efforts

DHL India (DHL) is a global logistics service provider with a fleet of over 250 vehicles and service centers in over a dozen key cities across the country. The company's international network links more than 220 countries and territories worldwide. It offers a full range of customized solutions from express document shipping to supply chain management. DHL focuses on select industry verticals, providing specialized benefits.

Industry verticals that DHL serves include automotive, industrial, life sciences/healthcare, chemical, retail, consumer goods, fashion, technology, aerospace and industrial projects. Companies in India are increasingly concentrating on their core competencies, outsourcing important but peripheral areas of their businesses that were traditionally handled in-house. Accordingly, a number of firms have been looking at the express industry to handle logistics of raw material supply, warehousing, and distribution of products.

DHL expects healthy double-digit growth levels in India and regional acquisitions are being targeted. DHL plans expansion of its Indian operations to strengthen its position as the country's leading express provider. DHL has a clear edge over its competitors, which is attributable to its superior market sensing. DHL gains customer feedback primarily through regular customer satisfaction surveys. Opinions are regularly garnered from top industry participants across various verticals as part of its customer feedback surveys. Respondents are asked to rate each of their logistics service providers on various parameters. Additional questions are asked relating to brand awareness and services. DHL is typically rated as a top express delivery service provider.

DHL India focuses on select industry verticals, providing customers the benefit of working with a specialist who brings deep domain knowledge of the industry and not just a logistics provider. It aims to build partnerships and works closely with customers. Knowledge of its people coupled with cutting-edge solutions provides DHL with a real competitive advantage. DHL's product innovations and customized solutions have contributed to its leadership position.

Two dedicated terminals were opened in Indira Gandhi International Airport, New

(continued)

BOX 10.11
Continued

Delhi, giving a big fillip to express cargo movement. The two terminals are operated by DHL Worldwide Express and the Express Industry Council of India (EICI). It is the first time that the government and the private industry are cooperating in this sector in such a partnership. The terminals happen to be the first company-dedicated facility with on-site presence of Indian customs in an airport in India.

To enhance customer relationships, DHL Express has launched Fast Forward, a service that brings increased efficiency and delivers cost savings to importers and exporters. Fast Forward is designed to meet the requirements of customers in the automobile, electronics, heavy engineering, publishing, and textile industries. Fast Forward has been designed as a one-stop service that provides customers greater cost transparencies, savings, convenience, flexibility, security, and speed. The company has also designed an online cost comparison tool that customers can use to compare costs of their current shipping method and those of Fast Forward to assess the potential savings and other benefits of using Fast Forward.

DHL's working relationship with customer firms is a significant asset. Through partnerships with airlines, DHL leverages its limited resources to deliver superior customer value. Through joint efforts with customers to gather ideas and experience, it provides value-added services. Having scaled up its supply chain efficiency, DHL has moved from its earlier motto, "No one knows Asia Pacific as good as we do," to the new tagline, "All the Way."

Contributed by Anish Chandrasekaran, Participant, PGSEM Program, Indian Institute of Management Bangalore.

Updating Customer Value

To ensure the vitality of their working relationships, progressive firms periodically update the value of their relationship-specific market offerings. At times, business market managers draw on their firm's CRM system information to assist with this process. To do so adroitly, these managers constantly search for significant changes in customer requirements. When a critical trend emerges, they respond quickly. For example, they might add new services or product modifications that customers now need, while eliminating or unbundling offering elements that customers no longer value. Rather than reacting haphazardly each time customer requirements change, progressive firms devise procedures ahead of time for handling these eventualities.

Supplier managers must try to avoid complacency, an insidious relationship killer. They must continuously ask questions in a way that encourages customers to relate problems and shortcomings. The question, "What have we not done lately?" should be periodically addressed to each customer.[44] This question's wording is significant in two respects. First, it is phrased in a manner so as to encourage the voicing of problems, rather than simply soliciting a socially desirable response, such as "Fine." Second, the inclusion of "lately" recognizes the natural inertia that occurs in relationships and that leads to complacency. Most unhappy customers never complain.[45]

Up to this point in the chapter, we focused on managing dyadic relationships between a supplier and a customer firm. Yet to fully understand and capitalize on the nature of a dyadic relationship, business market managers must also consider the **business network** or interconnections among relevant people and organizations within which each dyadic relationship is embedded.

Sustaining Customer Relationships Through Connected Relationships

Given the increasingly interconnected nature of commerce, suppliers must learn and implement a set of business network management skills. In fact, we already discussed some of these skills as they relate to supply and channel networks in Chapters 3, 7, and 9. In this section, we turn our attention to two more capabilities: managing within a business network context and adding value through business networks.[46]

Managing within a Business Network Context

The pioneering work of the International Marketing & Purchasing Group (IMP) emphasizes the importance of gaining an in-depth understanding of the business network within which a firm operates. IMP scholars evaluate business networks in terms of actors, activities, and resources. **Actors** are individuals, organizations, and institutions connected through personal or business relationships. Business market managers need to identify key actors, assess the strength of their bonds, and map their interactions. **Activities** are the tasks that the actors perform that create value. Supplier managers should learn how activities are clustered within firms into sets, how activities between actors are linked, and how they are assembled into processes or patterns. Finally, **resources** are competencies and capabilities embedded in the network. Managers must catalog the resources of the network, evaluate links among them, and determine how they can use the constellation of network resources to create value.[47]

Knowledge of the business network enables managers to craft superior strategies and tactics. To sustain a working relationship with one customer, for example, the supplier firm may have to secure changes in other connected relationships. Alternatively, the supplier may have to coordinate the activities of several partners to maintain the integrity of value it provides to the customer. Scholars suggest a framework for crafting strategies based on describing, evaluating, and interpreting networks. Managers begin by describing the strategic situation the supplier firm faces and identifying the set of actors involved. Then, they create and evaluate an interdependence matrix that specifies the pattern of linkages among the actors. Next, managers interpret the portfolio of interdependencies assessing the resources and activities each network actor contributes. Finally, managers craft a network strategy for resolving the strategic situation. The resulting network strategy will pivot on intensifying, preparing, controlling, or neglecting working relationships with each actor in order to maximize the value created.[48]

To underscore the importance of managing the business network context, we present the Bharti Airtel case study in Box 10.12.

BOX 10.12
Bharti Airtel Uses Connected Relations to Solve a Vexing Problem

Enterprise Communication Services as an industry stands for delivering an entire suite of communication services across data, voice, and managed services to large corporate clients. The services provided include the Internet, MPLS-VPN, domestic and international private-leased circuits, satellite services (VSAT), audio and video conferencing, data centre services, managed network services, EPBX and Centrex; contact centre solutions & toll free services, mobile enterprise solutions, etc. Some services such as conferencing are commoditized, while others such as data and IP solutions are highly customer centric. Bharti Airtel is a major player in all segments of Enterprise Communication Services.

A typical example of enterprise communication is the solution Bharti Airtel developed for Bajaj Allianz, a life insurance company, which is a joint venture between Bajaj Auto and Alliance AG of Germany. Bajaj Allianz has over 240 offices, employs more than 25,000 professionals and has several distribution channels. The challenge for Bajaj Allianz was to keep all its offices and branches connected at all times to share information seamlessly. Bharti Airtel offered MPLS and Internet-based connectivity to this extensive network, designed to guarantee 99.99% uptime. This enabled Bajaj Allianz to issue insurance policies from its branches rather than the central office, giving it a huge strategic advantage.

Airtel is able to constantly come up with innovative customer solutions such as the one for Bajaj Allianz described above, through an extensive network of partners, to jointly create superior customer value. This approach allows Airtel to stay focused in its core business. Yet, given the nature of the telecom business, which entails high technology that is rapidly changing, Airtel's business can only succeed if all other building blocks are strongly in place. These include broadband connectivity, telecommunication hardware and software, IT infrastructure, etc. Rather than build and maintain all these building blocks by itself, Airtel chose the partnering route to create its market offerings, as the following examples demonstrate.

Airtel has partnered with Alcatel/ Lucent, wherein the latter manages Bharti's entire pan-Indian broadband and telephone services network and also helps Airtel to migrate to next-generation networks. This move helped Airtel transform itself into an essentially marketing company to acquire and retain customers, leveraging the Airtel brand. Moreover, through this partnership, Airtel got experts in the industry to manage its network. This helped it to rapidly launch new products and services, leveraging its access to the latest technological solution capabilities that were provided by Alcatel/ Lucent.

Airtel formed non-exclusive partnerships with Google and Research in Motion (RIM) to provide value-added services to its customers. Airtel entered into partnership with Google in 2007 to offer customized content and associated Web-based services powered by Google free of cost to Airtel customers. The Airtel portal contains several of Google's services: Google Search, Gmail, Google Talk, Google Docs and spreadsheets, NetXpert for troubleshooting, Web SMS, security services, gaming, and music download services, etc. Likewise, Airtel partnered with Research in Motion (RIM), the company behind the Blackberry, to provide RIM's famous push-mail-based services to Indian customers.

BOX 10.12
Continued

Airtel then decided to partner with IBM, wherein IBM managed its entire IT infrastructure. The move greatly enhanced Airtel's future flexibility and growth potential, allowing it to stay focused on its core competencies: to implement and deliver new services rapidly and thus grow its customer base. Accordingly, Airtel entered into a 10-year agreement with IBM to transform its processes and manage its IT setup, primarily to enhance the experience of its customers. This enabled Airtel to add 1.5 million new customers every month.

Finally, Airtel entered into a partnership with leading telecom equipment manufacturer Ericsson to rapidly expand and upgrade its telecom network. The deal was expected to enable Airtel to rapidly expand its footprint in the country and increase its network capacity. In the intensely competitive telecom industry, rollout speed is vital for telecom service providers like Airtel. By partnering with Ericsson, Airtel has ensured that it can undertake massive, rapid expansion of its customer base, including in rural areas, without compromising the quality of its customers' experience.

By working closely with various leading global partners, Airtel has succeeded in leveraging world-class expertise available with its partners to create a winning telecom business. It has enabled Airtel to remain extremely focused on its core business, resulting in Airtel emerging as the leader in the Indian telecom industry. This approach has also ensured that Airtel will continue to have state-of-the-art telecom networks and equipment to deliver innovative products and services to its customers in the future.

Contributed by Alok Shukla, Participant, PGSEM Program, Indian Institute of Management Bangalore.

Adding Value Through Business Networks

Research suggests that in some cases the total value of a solution is a function not only of a supplier's offering but also of the compatibility, accessibility, and quality of the networks within which it is embedded. These networks include the user network, the complements network, and the producer network. For example, in the case of high-technology products, the greater the installed base for an offering, the broader the variety of complementary products such as compatible software modules, and the more producers utilizing common standards, the greater is the value of an offering. As evidence, researchers cite studies demonstrating that although purchasing managers rate Unix operating systems as technically superior to Windows NT®, they are overwhelmingly more likely to acquire Windows NT for their companies because of the strength of Microsoft's user, complements, and producer networks. They recommend that business market managers make a concerted effort to strengthen these business networks. By cultivating potent networks, a supplier firm, even if it produces comparable products, may be able to prosper in a market.[49]

LOOKING AHEAD—A FINAL THOUGHT ON MANAGING CUSTOMERS

Working relationships with customer firms are a significant asset of any supplier's business. However, it is important for the supplier to recognize that each customer relationship has an impact on the supplier's resources in the short-term and capabilities in the long-term. This, in turn, affects the supplier's ability to serve opportunities and customers in the future. This brings us to one of our sayings, "Whom we serve affects what we are, and what we are affects whom we can serve."

To cultivate and sustain disparate types of working customer relationships while recognizing the impact of these actions in the future of the business, business market managers must devise a coherent strategic approach that involves three important steps. First, they need to have a plan on how to grow each customer relationship over time and how to address several ongoing behavioral issues, including communication, trust and commitment, coordination, and conflict resolution in each case. Second, they need to construct and implement appropriate relationship-specific offerings at every stage in each customer relationship irrespective of relationship type. Third, they need to use a customer portfolio approach that (a) optimizes customer value in each individual customer relationship and adopts the basic premise that not all customers want the same working relationship—or value it the same and (b) enables the managers to recognize the impact of their various decisions on their firms' capacities and capabilities over time.

Done right, this systematic approach will enable supplier firms to constantly revisit their targeting and selection decisions and make the necessary adjustments when and as required to deliver superior customer value and to get a fair return in exchange. As discussed in the earlier chapters, all these efforts must be done in conjunction with effective environmental scanning that permits the business market managers to speculate on business changes that might significantly affect the nature of their business.

SUMMARY

In this chapter, we examined those activities associated with managing individual customer relationships over time and managing a portfolio of customer relationships simultaneously at a given point in time. We began by defining managing customers as the process of differentiating different customer types, delivering appropriate offerings that fulfill the respective requirements and preferences of the portfolio of customers in a superior way, and getting a fair return in exchange. The foundations of this process are the concepts of a relationship continuum and industry bandwidths, and a strategic approach we refer to as "partnering as a focused market strategy." That approach is based on the fundamental marketing concepts of segmentation, targeting, and positioning. Among its key premises is the belief that close, collaborative relationships are not for every firm. Instead, business market managers strive to cultivate a portfolio of working relationships.

Because different customers in a supplier's relationship portfolio have different requirements, business market managers need to deliver value in the form of relationship-specific offerings. As customer firms become more collaborative, managers will craft more elaborate market offerings. Conversely, as customer firms become more transactional, the supplier firm will sell the most basic offering with few options. Flaring out from the industry bandwidth is a strategy that business marketers can use to configure such imaginative relationship-specific offerings.

Although most managers readily grasp the concept of partnering, they have a much harder time understanding how to retain a portfolio of profitable customer relationships. We discussed the FITD and all-at-once approaches that managers can use to grow their share of profitable customer business. We also highlighted innovative business arrangements as single-sourcing, multiple single-sourcing, facilities management, and outsourcing to enhance customer value, and provided guidance on how a supplier firm can get the customer comfortable with these innovative ideas while ensuring an equitable distribution of the value they create through new profit models such as risk-sharing, gain-sharing agreements. Collaborative risk-sharing, gain-sharing agreements refer to arrangements in which a customer and supplier work together to improve the customer's performance, and in which, in doing so, the supplier exposes itself to potential losses, yet also receives a prespecified portion of any success.

We also explored the behavioral issues that managers must be prepared to address when working together with customer firms, including promoting open and honest communications, building trust and commitment, selecting coordination mechanisms, and resolving conflicts. By handling each behavioral issue in a superior way over time, business market managers make it advantageous for customers to engage in subsequent exchange episodes and to begin new business strands.

CRM is a comprehensive set of systems and procedures that firms use to differentially and profitably relate to customer firms. Market databases and activity-based costing systems provide the backbone for CRM. We discussed how managers can use such CRM systems to measure cost-to-serve customers and customer loyalty, and, in turn, use these metrics to monitor and evaluate customer portfolios: a process that might result in a redesign of specific customer account strategy when necessary through better allocation of scarce marketing resources, synchronized operations, marketing, and service efforts, while enhancing the value of relationship-specific market offerings. We concluded this chapter arguing that a supplier can potentially keep customer relationships vibrant by using business networks.

ENDNOTES

1. (New York: Free Press, 2001): 121.
2. (Spring 1991): 95-113.
3. Barbara B. Jackson, *Winning & Keeping Industrial Customers* (Lexington, MA: Lexington Books, 1985).
4. (June 1984): 265-288.
5. This discussion is based on the article, James C. Anderson and James A. Narus, "Selectively Pursuing More of Your Customer's Business," *MIT Sloan Management Review* (Spring 2003): 40–49.
6. Carliss Y. Baldwin and Kim B. Clark, *Design Rules: The Power of Modularity, Vol. I,* (Boston, MA: The MIT Press, 2000).
7. Siebel Systems Inc. was acquired by Oracle Corporation on Jan 31, 2006. See http://www.oracle.com/corporate/press/2006_jan/sieb_cl.html
8. Das Narayandas and Robert C. Dudley, "Hewlett-Packard—Computer Systems Organization: Selling to Enterprise Customers," *Harvard Business School Case 500-064* (Boston, MA: Harvard Business School, 2000).
9. F. Robert Dwyer, Paul H. Schurr, and Sejo Oh, "Developing Buyer-Seller Relationships," *Journal of Marketing* (April 1987): 11–27.
10. James C. Anderson and James A. Narus, "A Model of Distributor Firm and Manufacturer Firm Working Partnerships," *Journal of Marketing* (January 1990): 44.

11. Neeli Bendapudi and Robert P. Leone, "Managing Business-to-Business Customer Relationships Following Key Contact Employee Turnover in a Supplier Firm," *Journal of Marketing* (April 2002): 83–101; and Neeli Bendapudi and Robert P. Leone, "How to Lose Your Star Performer Without Losing Customers, Too," *Harvard Business Review* (November 2001): 104–112.
12. Robert M. Morgan and Shelby D. Hunt, "The Commitment-Trust Theory of Relationship Marketing," *Journal of Marketing* (July 1994): 20–38.
13. James C. Anderson and James A. Narus, "Toward a Better Understanding of Distribution Channel Working Relationships," in *Industrial Marketing: A German-American Perspective*, ed. K. Backhaus and D. Wilson (Berlin: Springer-Verlag, 1986): 326 and Denise M. Rousseau, Sim B. Sitkin, Ronald S. Burt, and Colin Camerer, "Not So Different After All: A Cross-Discipline View of Trust," *Academy of Management Review* (July 1998): 393–404.
14. Nirmalya Kumar, "The Power of Trust in Manufacturer-Retailer Relationships," *Harvard Business Review* (November–December 1996): 92–106.
15. Patricia M. Doney and Joseph P. Cannon, "An Examination of the Nature of Trust in Buyer-Seller Relationships," *Journal of Marketing* (April 1997): 35–51; Sungmin Ryu, Soonhong Min, and Nobuhide Zushi, "The Moderating Role of Trust in Manufacturer-Supplier Relationships," *Journal of Business and Industrial Marketing* 23 (2008): 48–58.
16. Patricia M. Doney, James M. Barry, Russell Abratt, "Trust Determinants and Outcomes in Global B2B Services," *European Journal of Marketing* 41 (2007): 1096–1116.
17. James C. Anderson, Håkan Håkansson, and Jan Johanson, "Dyadic Business Relationships Within a Business Network Context," *Journal of Marketing* (October 1994): 10.
18. Erin Anderson and Barton Weitz, "The Use of Pledges to Build and Sustain Commitment in Distribution Channels," *Journal of Marketing Research* (February 1992): 19.
19. Gregory T. Gundlach, Ravi S. Achrol, and John T. Mentzer, "The Structure of Commitment in Exchange," *Journal of Marketing* (January 1995): 78–92; and Anderson and Weitz, "The Use of Pledges," 18–34.
20. Christopher W. L. Hart, James L. Heskett, and W. Earl Sasser, Jr., "The Profitable Art of Service Recovery," *Harvard Business Review* (July–August 1990): 148–156; Anna S. Mattila and David Cranage, "The Impact of Choice on Fairness in the Context of Service Recovery," *Journal of Services Marketing* 19 (2005): 271–280.
21. Jakki Mohr and John R. Nevin, "Communication Strategies in Marketing Channels: A Theoretical Perspective," *Journal of Marketing* (October 1990): 36–51; Ferdinand Jaspers and Jan van den Ende, "The Organizational Form of Vertical Relationships: Dimensions of Integration," *Industrial Marketing Management* 35 (2006): 819–828; and Heide, "Interorganizational Governance in Marketing Channels."
22. Paul Milgrom and John Roberts, *Economics, Organization, and Management* (Upper Saddle River, NJ: Prentice Hall, 1995).
23. Anne T. Coughlan, Erin Anderson, Louis W. Stern, and Adel I. El-Ansary, *Marketing Channels*, 6th ed. (Upper Saddle River, NJ: Prentice Hall, 2001); Gary L. Frazier, "Interorganizational Exchange Behavior in Marketing Channels: A Broadened Perspective," *Journal of Marketing* (Fall 1983): 68–78; Gary L. Frazier and John O. Summers, "Interfirm Influence Strategies and Their Application Within Distribution Channels," *Journal of Marketing* (Summer 1984): 43–55; and Gary L. Frazier and Jagdish N. Sheth, "An Attitude-Behavior Framework for Distribution Channel Management," *Journal of Marketing* (Summer 1984): 43–55.
24. Jan B. Heide and George John, "The Role of Dependence Balancing in Safeguarding Transaction-Specific Assets in Conventional Channels," *Journal of Marketing* (May 1988): 20–35.
25. Das Narayandas and V. Kasturi Rangan, "Building and Sustaining Buyer-Seller Relationships in Mature Industrial

Markets," *Journal of Marketing* 68 (2004): 63–77.

26. Anderson and Narus, "A Model," 44.
27. Coughlan, Anderson, Stern, and El-Ansari, *Marketing Channels.*
28. Larry J. Rosenberg and Louis W. Stern, "Toward the Analysis of Conflict in Distribution Channels: A Descriptive Model," *Journal of Marketing* (October 1970): 40–46; Alberto Sa Vinhas and Erin Anderson, "How Potential Conflict Drives Channel Structure (Direct and Indirect) Channels," *Journal of Marketing Research* 42 (2005): 507–515.
29. Roy J. Lewicki and Joseph A. Litterer, *Negotiation* (Burr Ridge, IL: Irwin, 1985).
30. Neil Rackham and John DeVincentis, *Rethinking the Sales Force* (New York: McGraw-Hill, 1999).
31. Paul H. Andersen, "A Foot in the Door: Relationship Marketing Efforts Towards Transaction-Oriented Customers," *Journal of Market-Focused Management* 5 (2002): 91–108.
32. Sandy D. Jap, "Pie Sharing in Complex Collaboration Contexts," *Journal of Marketing Research* (February 2001): 86–99.
33. James B. L. Thomson and James C. Anderson, "Pursuing Risk-Sharing, Gain-Sharing Arrangements," *Marketing Management* (Summer 2000): 40–47.
34. Darrell K. Rigby, Frederick F. Reichheld, and Phil Schefter, "Avoid the Four Perils of CRM," *Harvard Business Review* (February 2002): 102.
35. Rigby, Reichheld, and Schefter, "Avoid the Four Perils of CRM," 106.
36. Das Narayandas, "Measuring and Managing the Benefits of Customer Retention: An Empirical Investigation," *Journal of Service Research* 1–2 (1998): 108–127.
37. Das Narayandas, "Measuring and Managing."
38. This section is based on the article, Das Narayandas, "Building Loyalty in Business Markets," *Harvard Business Review* 83 (September 2005): 131–139.
39. Along similar lines, examining cumulative profitability of a firm's customer accounts over an extended period of time, Professors Kaplan and Narayanan advise managers to create a "whale curve" of their portfolio by plotting cumulative profitability (i.e., percent of total firm profits) against specific customer accounts. In their research, they discovered that for the typical firm, the most profitable 20% of accounts generate between 150% and 300% of the firm's profits. The firm breaks even on the next 70% of customers and loses money on the rest. They recommend that suppliers strengthen relationships with the most profitable 20% of accounts, reduce cost-to-serve or increase prices paid by the middle group, and consider not serving the bottom 10% of customers. Robert S. Kaplan and V. G. Narayanan, "Measuring and Managing Customer Profitability," *Journal of Cost Management* (September–October 2001): 5–15; and Robert S. Kaplan, *Using ABC to Manage Customer Mix and Relationships* (Boston, MA: Harvard Business School Press, 1997).
40. In their research on customer loyalty, Professors Reinartz and Kumar have provided controversial findings that challenge major assumptions about the profitability of long-term relationships. For example, they contend that in certain industries the most loyal customers may not be the most profitable, because they expect and in fact pay lower prices because of their continued loyalty. Often, it is one-time transactional customers who pay the highest prices and are the most profitable. For the purpose of analyses, Reinartz and Kumar suggest creating a different 2×2 matrix by plotting cumulative profitability (i.e., high or low) against length of relationship (i.e., short-term or long-term customer) and then assigning each customer firm to one of four cells. They define "true friends" as highly profitable, long-term customers and advise suppliers to delight them with extraordinary levels of service. "Butterflies," on the other hand, are highly profitable short-term customers, and Reinartz and Kumar suggest that supplier firms actively seek them out and provide them with satisfying

transactions. They advise suppliers to pay little heed to "strangers," which are low-profit, short-term customers. Finally, they recommend either cross-selling or up-selling or reducing the cost-to-serve for "barnacles" or low-profit, long-term customers. It should be noted that the criticisms of these findings arise from the authors' substitution of measures of tenure for loyalty in their statistical analyses and their failure to examine customer profitability over a sufficiently long period of time. Werner J. Reinartz and V. Kumar, "The Impact of Customer Relationship Characteristics on Profitable Lifetime Duration," *Journal of Marketing* (January 2003); and Werner J. Reinartz and V. Kumar, "The Mismanagement of Customer Loyalty," *Harvard Business Review* (July 2002): 86–94.

41. Bowman, Douglas and Das Narayandas (2001), "Managing Customer-Initiated Contacts with Manufacturers: The Impact on Share of Category Requirements and Word-of-Mouth Behavior," *Journal of Marketing Research*, 38 (3), 281-297; Bowman, Douglas and Das Narayandas (2003), "Customer Profitability in Industrial Markets: Adapting and Extending the Service-Profit Chain," *Harvard Business School Working Paper # 02-031.*
42. Sundar Bharadwaj and Das Narayandas, "Why Do Supplier Firms Persist in Underperforming Customer Relationships?" *Harvard Business School Working Paper No. 02-032* (2003).
43. Blattberg, Getz, and Thomas, *Customer Equity*.
44. Theodore Levitt, "After the Sale Is Over," *Harvard Business Review* (September–October 1983): 87–93.
45. Reichheld and Sasser, "Zero Defections."
46. Judy K. Frels, Tasadduq Shervani, and Rajendra K. Srivastava, "The Integrated Networks Model: Explaining Resource Allocations in Network Markets," *Journal of Marketing* (January 2003): 29–45.
47. Håkan Håkansson and Ivan Snehota (eds.), *Developing Relationships in Business Networks* (London: Routledge, 1995); and David Ford, *Understanding Business Markets*, 2nd ed. (London: The Dryden Press, 1997).
48. Uta Jüttner and Lutz E. Schlange, "A Network Approach to Strategy," *International Journal of Research in Marketing*, 13 (1996): 479–494; Eng Teck-Yong, "Conceptualization of Strategy in Business Networks: An Assessment," *Journal of Marketing Channels* 13 (2005): 79–89.
49. Frels, Shervani, and Srivastava, "The Integrated Networks Model."

INDEX

C

D

E

F

G

H

I

J

K

L

M

N

O

P

T

U

V

W